최신 어휘 실전문제로 내신과 **수능 1등급** 굳히기

반석 수능
Vocabulary

반석 수능
Voca bulary

저 자 이재승
발행인 고본화
발 행 반석출판사
2013년 11월 1일 초판 1쇄 인쇄
2013년 11월 5일 초판 1쇄 발행
반석출판사 | **www.bansok.co.kr**
이메일 | **bansok@bansok.co.kr**

157-779 서울시 강서구 양천로 583번지 B동 904호
       (서울시 강서구 염창동 240-21 우림블루나인 비즈니스센터 B동 904호)
대표전화 02) 2093-3399 **팩 스** 02) 2093-3393
출 판 부 02) 2093-3395 **영업부** 02) 2093-3396
등록번호 제315-2008-000033호

ISBN 978-89-7172-720-1 (13740)

반석 수능

Voca bulary

Bansok

영어 공부를 시작한 지 얼마 되지 않았을 때, 선생님께서 다음과 같은 문장을 칠판에 적으시고는 해석을 해 보라고 하셨습니다.

The water in this well is good to drink.

많은 학생들이 문장 속의 well을 어떻게 해석해야 할지 몰라 당황해했습니다.

물론 여기서 well은 명사로서 '샘, 우물'이라는 뜻입니다. well을 '훌륭하게, 잘'이란 부사로 해석하는 데만 익숙했던 학생들은 '모르는 단어는 없는데 왜 해석이 안 될까?'하고 당황할 수밖에 없었습니다.

한 걸음 더 나아가서 well이 동사로 '솟아오르다, 분출하다'의 뜻으로도 쓰인다는 것도 알고 있어야 합니다.

Hot water welled up out of the ground. [본 교재 P. 118 well 참조]

이 책은 바로 이러한 다수의 뜻을 가지고 있는 영어 단어(다의어 多義語)들 중 가장 필수적이고 사용 빈도수가 높은 300개의 단어를 엄선하여 수록하였습니다. 이 책은 현재 사용되고 있는 모든 중, 고교 영어 교과서 내용과 1994학년도부터 2013학년도까지 출제된 대학입학수능시험문제를 분석하여 영어 실력향상에 꼭 필요한 시험빈출 다의어(多義語) 300개를 엄선하여 5단계의 반복학습과정을 통해 완전정복할 수 있도록 구성하였습니다.

다수의 뜻(Multiple Meanings)을 가진 단어 공부의 중요성에 대해서는 굳이 더 이상 언급을 하지 않겠습니다.

다음에 제시된 10개의 문장을 해석해 보세요. 해석이 제대로 되지 않는 학생들은 필히 이 책과 함께 단어 공부를 시작하시기 바랍니다.

01. Cinderella will go to the ball tonight. ... [P. 24 ball 참조]

02. Bacteria are minute organisms. ... [P. 312 minute 참조]

03. All save him attended the meeting. ... [P. 123 save 참조]

04. There is no means of helping her. ... [P. 322 mean 참조]

05. She is wearing a dress of novel design. ... [P. 115 novel 참조]

06. The hunters captured deer and wild game. ... [P. 249 game 참조]

07. My sister has been fasting all day. ... [P. 186 fast 참조]

08. They sell the goods by the score. ... [P. 187 score 참조]

09. He is always good company. ... [P. 271 company 참조]

10. The new president will form a new cabinet. ... [P. 206 cabinet 참조]

아무쪼록 이 책이 여러분들의 영어 공부에 많은 도움이 되기를 바라며 또 그렇게 되리라 확신합니다. 감사합니다.

2013년 10월
이재승

CONTENTS

본 교재만이 지닌 독특한 다의어 완전정복을 위한 5단계의 반복학습과정은 다음과 같습니다.

일자별[Day 01 ~ Day 30]로 학습할 수 있도록 구성되어 있어 1개월 집중 공략으로 다의어를 완전히 정복할 수 있으며 비교적 쉬운 단어가 앞부분에 배치되어 있어 편안한 마음으로 공부를 시작할 수 있습니다.

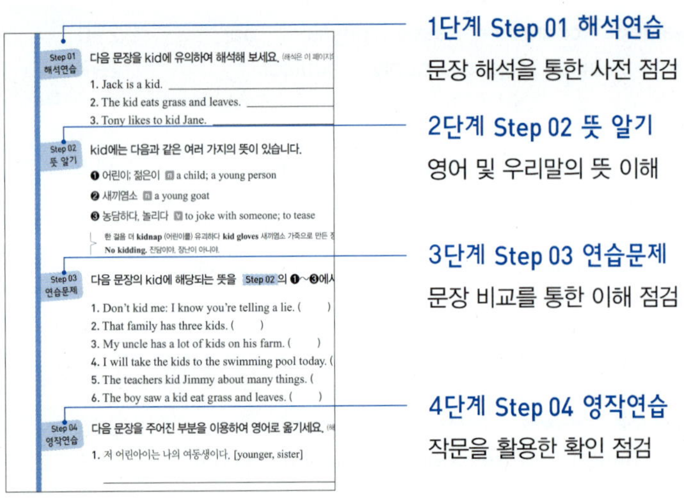

1단계 Step 01 해석연습
문장 해석을 통한 사전 점검

2단계 Step 02 뜻 알기
영어 및 우리말의 뜻 이해

3단계 Step 03 연습문제
문장 비교를 통한 이해 점검

4단계 Step 04 영작연습
작문을 활용한 확인 점검

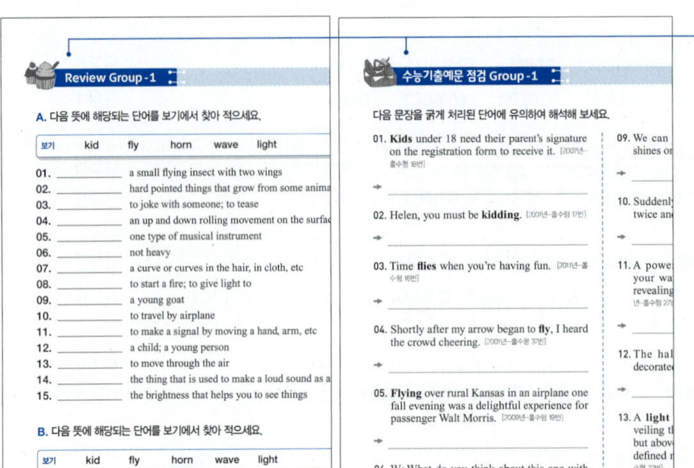

5단계 Review & 수능기출예문 점검
그룹별 단어 복습 및 해당 어휘가 포함된 수능기출예문 학습

다음에 제시된 10개의 문장을 해석해 보세요. 해석이 제대로 되지 않는 학생들은 필히 이 책과 함께 단어 공부를 시작하시기 바랍니다.

01. Cinderella will go to the ball tonight. ... [P. 24 ball 참조]

02. Bacteria are minute organisms. ... [P. 312 minute 참조]

03. All save him attended the meeting. ... [P. 123 save 참조]

04. There is no means of helping her. ... [P. 322 mean 참조]

05. She is wearing a dress of novel design. ... [P. 115 novel 참조]

06. The hunters captured deer and wild game. ... [P. 249 game 참조]

07. My sister has been fasting all day. ... [P. 186 fast 참조]

08. They sell the goods by the score. ... [P. 187 score 참조]

09. He is always good company. ... [P. 271 company 참조]

10. The new president will form a new cabinet. ... [P. 206 cabinet 참조]

아무쪼록 이 책이 여러분들의 영어 공부에 많은 도움이 되기를 바라며 또 그렇게 되리라 확신합니다. 감사합니다.

2013년 10월
이재승

CONTENTS

이 책을 공부하면, "일석오조(一石五鳥)"의 학습효과를 얻을 수 있습니다.

❶ 한 단어가 가지고 있는 다수의 뜻을 쉽게 이해하게 되며

❷ 영영사전 방식의 뜻풀이로 영영사전 활용에 익숙해지며

❸ 숙지한 단어를 이용한 작문연습을 통해 영작능력도 배양하며

❹ 관련된 파생단어, 숙어 및 동사변화 등의 공부를 통한 폭넓은 지식을 습득하고

❺ 수능기출예문 점검을 통한 실전문제에 대한 감각을 익히며 문제 해결능력이 극대화
  됩니다.

이 책이 내신, 수능, NEAT, TEPS, TOEIC 등 모든 영어 시험에 도움이 될 뿐 아니라
영어 실력향상의 필독서가 될 것이라 자부합니다.

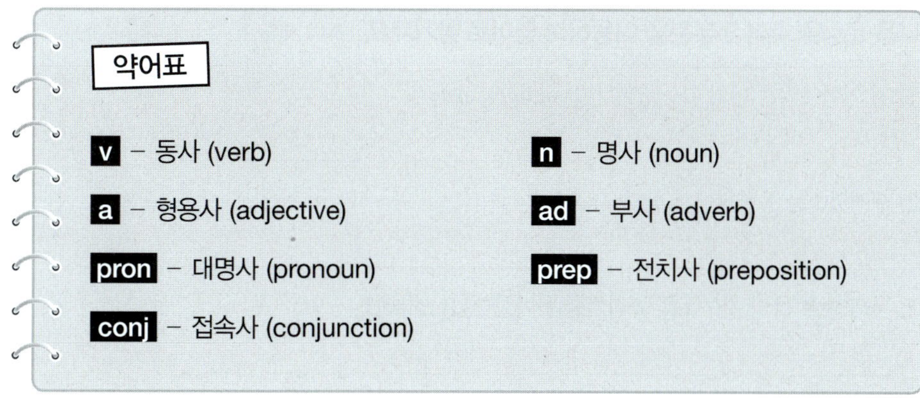

약어표

v – 동사 (verb)	**n** – 명사 (noun)
a – 형용사 (adjective)	**ad** – 부사 (adverb)
pron – 대명사 (pronoun)	**prep** – 전치사 (preposition)
conj – 접속사 (conjunction)	

A small rock holds back a great wave.
작은 바위가 산더미 같은 파도를 밀어 버린다.

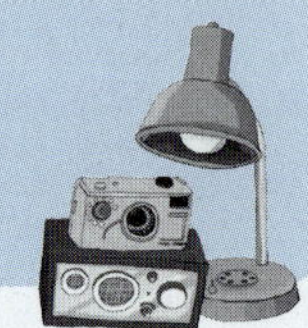

001 kid [kid]

Group 01

Step 01 해석연습

다음 문장을 kid에 유의하여 해석해 보세요. (해석은 이 페이지의 하단부에 있음)

1. Jack is a kid. ___________________________
2. The kid eats grass and leaves. ___________________________
3. Tony likes to kid Jane. ___________________________

Step 02 뜻 알기

kid에는 다음과 같은 여러 가지의 뜻이 있습니다.

❶ 어린이; 젊은이 n a child; a young person

❷ 새끼염소 n a young goat

❸ 농담하다, 놀리다 v to joke with someone; to tease

> 한 걸음 더 **kidnap** (어린이를) 유괴하다 **kid gloves** 새끼염소 가죽으로 만든 장갑 **make a kid of ~** ~을 어린애 취급하다
> **No kidding.** 진담이야, 장난이 아니야.

Step 03 연습문제

다음 문장의 kid에 해당되는 뜻을 Step 02 의 ❶～❸에서 고르세요. (해답은 431쪽)

1. Don't kid me: I know you're telling a lie. (   )
2. That family has three kids. (   )
3. My uncle has a lot of kids on his farm. (   )
4. I will take the kids to the swimming pool today. (   )
5. The teachers kid Jimmy about many things. (   )
6. The boy saw a kid eat grass and leaves. (   )

Step 04 영작연습

다음 문장을 주어진 부분을 이용하여 영어로 옮기세요. (해답은 431쪽)

1. 저 어린아이는 나의 여동생이다. [younger, sister]

____

2. 새끼염소는 동물원에서 산다. [zoo]

____

3. 나의 형은 나의 친구들을 놀리기를 좋아한다. [brother]

____

:: 1. Jack은 어린이다. 2. 새끼염소가 풀과 잎을 먹는다. 3. Tony는 Jane을 놀리는 것을 좋아한다.

002 fly [flai]

Step 01 해석연습

다음 문장을 fly에 유의하여 해석해 보세요. (해석은 이 페이지의 하단부에 있음)

1. A fly has big eyes. ___________________________
2. They will fly to London. ___________________________
3. The birds fly in the sky. ___________________________

Step 02 뜻 알기

fly에는 다음과 같은 여러 가지의 뜻이 있습니다.

❶ 파리, 날개 달린 곤충 **n** a small flying insect with two wings

❷ 비행기로 여행하다 **v** to travel by airplane

❸ 날다, 날아가다 **v** to move through the air

> 한 걸음 더 **fly** [flai] - **flew** [flu] - **flown** [floun]
> **The ship flew.** 배가 쏜살같이 달렸다. → 날아가듯 달리다, 빨리 지나가다, 퍼지다(=move or pass swiftly)
> **dragon fly** 잠자리 **butter fly** 나비

Step 03 연습문제

다음 문장의 fly에 해당되는 뜻을 **Step 02** 의 ❶~❸에서 고르세요. (해답은 431쪽)

1. The ball will fly to the other boy. (   )
2. David will fly to Los Angeles. (   )
3. There is a fly on the ceiling. (   )
4. He chased the fly out of the house. (   )
5. She was the first woman to fly the Atlantic. (   )
6. Birds fly north in the spring. (   )

Step 04 영작연습

다음 문장을 주어진 부분을 이용하여 영어로 옮기세요. (해답은 431쪽)

1. 파리 한 마리가 너의 코 위에 있다. [nose]

____

2. Jae-ho는 오늘 (비행기로) 시드니에 갈 것이다. [Sydney]

____

3. 새들은 겨울을 위해 남쪽으로 날아간다. [south, winter]

____

:: 1. 파리는 큰 눈을 가지고 있다. 2. 그들은 비행기로 런던에 갈 것이다. 3. 새들이 하늘을 난다.

 **003 horn** [hɔːrn]

Step 01
해석연습

다음 문장을 horn에 유의하여 해석해 보세요. (해석은 이 페이지의 하단부에 있음)

1. The horn is on the bicycle. ________________________________
2. Tom plays the horn in the band. ________________________________
3. The bull's horn is sharp. ________________________________

Step 02
뜻 알기

horn에는 다음과 같은 여러 가지의 뜻이 있습니다.

❶ 경적 [n] the thing that is used to make a loud sound as a signal or warning

❷ (관악기) 호른 [n] one type of musical instrument

❸ (소, 양, 염소 따위의) 뿔 [n] hard pointed things that grow from some animals' heads

> 한 걸음 더 **Save your horn.** (안내문) 경적금지
> **blow one's horn[trumpet]** 자기 자랑을 하다, 허풍을 떨다

Step 03
연습문제

다음 문장의 horn에 해당되는 뜻을 **Step 02** 의 ❶∼❸에서 고르세요. (해답은 431쪽)

1. The horn warned the little children. (   )
2. One horn fell off the ram's head. (   )
3. The driver blew his horn. (   )
4. An ox has two horns on its head. (   )
5. The French horn has a beautiful sound. (   )
6. They are blowing the horns in the orchestra. (   )

Step 04
영작연습

다음 문장을 주어진 부분을 이용하여 영어로 옮기세요. (해답은 431쪽)

1. 자동차 경적이 나를 놀라게 했다. [car, scare]

____

2. 나의 형은 저녁식사 후에 호른을 연주한다. [play, dinner]

____

3. 그 동물은 새 뿔이 자랄 것이다. [animal, grow]

____

:: 1. 자전거에는 경적이 있다. 2. Tom은 악단에서 호른을 연주한다. 3. 황소의 뿔은 날카롭다.

004 **wave** [weiv]

Step 01 해석연습

다음 문장을 wave에 유의하여 해석해 보세요. (해석은 이 페이지의 하단부에 있음)

1. The wave came onto the beach. ________________________

2. Her hair has a wave. ________________________

3. Judy is waving to her friend. ________________________

Step 02 뜻 알기

wave에는 다음과 같은 여러 가지의 뜻이 있습니다.

❶ 파도, 물결 n an up and down rolling movement on the surface of water

❷ (머리, 천 등의) 웨이브; 굴곡진 머리 n a curve or curves in the hair, in cloth, etc

❸ 손 따위를 흔들어 신호하다 v to make a signal by moving a hand, arm, etc

> 한 걸음 더 **Radio <u>waves</u> bring us news and music.** 라디오 전파는 우리에게 소식과 음악을 전달해 준다.
> → (전기, 빛, 소리 등의) 파동, 전파, 음파(=a wave-like movement of electric current, light, sound, etc)
> **The flags were <u>waving</u> gently in the breeze.** 깃발들이 산들바람에 나부끼고 있었다.
> → 물결치다, 나부끼다(=to move softly back and forth, up and down)
> **microwave** 극초단파 또는 전자레인지(=microwave oven) **electric wave** 전파 **seismic wave** 지진파
> **sound wave** 음파 **tidal wave** 해일

Step 03 연습문제

다음 문장의 wave에 해당되는 뜻을 **Step 02** 의 ❶∼❸에서 고르세요. (해답은 431쪽)

1. There is a wave in her hair. (   )

2. I will wave to my friends. (   )

3. The waves became very high. (   )

4. Judy will wave to her sister. (   )

5. He saw a boat tossing on the waves. (   )

6. She has a natural wave in her hair. (   )

Step 04 영작연습

다음 문장을 주어진 부분을 이용하여 영어로 옮기세요. (해답은 431쪽)

1. 수영선수들은 파도와 함께 움직였다. [swimmers, moved]

____

2. 내 머리는 아름다운 웨이브(굴곡)를 가지고 있다. [hair, beautiful]

____

3. 운전자들은 도로에서 서로 손을 흔들었다. [each other, street]

____

:: 1. 파도가 해변으로 왔다. 2. 그녀의 머리카락은 웨이브되어 있다. 3. Judy는 그녀의 친구에게 손을 흔들고 있다.

005 light [lait]

Step 01 해석연습

다음 문장을 light에 유의하여 해석해 보세요. (해석은 이 페이지의 하단부에 있음)

1. The light helps people to see. ________________________
2. Dad will light the fire. ________________________
3. A feather is very light. ________________________

Step 02 뜻 알기

light에는 다음과 같은 여러 가지의 뜻이 있습니다.

❶ 빛, 광선, 등불 **n** the brightness that helps you to see things

❷ 점화하다, (불을) 켜다 **v** to start a fire; to give light to

❸ 가벼운 **a** not heavy

> 한 걸음 더 **The lady is wearing a _light_ blue skirt.** 그 숙녀는 밝은 파란색 치마를 입고 있다.
> → 밝은, 즐거운, 어렵지 않은(=not dark; happy, cheerful; easy to do)
> **She regarded his conduct in a favorable _light_.** 그녀는 그의 행동을 호의적으로 생각했다.
> → 견해, 관점, 양상(= a way of understanding; aspect)
> **The bird _lighted_ on the branch.** 새가 나뭇가지에 내려앉았다.
> **He _lighted_ on a clue.** 그는 우연히 실마리를 발견했다.
> → (새가) 내려앉았다, (말, 차 등에서) 내리다, 우연히 만나다, 발견하다
> **lighter** 라이터, 점등기 **lighthouse** 등대 **traffic light** 교통신호등 **light industry** 경공업
> **light-year** 광년(빛이 1년 동안 가는 거리의 표시단위) **in the light of** ~에 비추어, ~을 고려하여

Step 03 연습문제

다음 문장의 light에 해당되는 뜻을 **Step 02** 의 ❶∼❸에서 고르세요. (해답은 431쪽)

1. My uncle will light his pipe. (　　　)
2. Her new overcoat is light but warm. (　　　)
3. The lamp makes light. (　　　)
4. A balloon is very light. (　　　)
5. A mirror reflects light. (　　　)
6. My brother likes to light candles on the cake. (　　　)

Step 04 영작연습

다음 문장을 주어진 부분을 이용하여 영어로 옮기세요. (해답은 431쪽)

1. 빛은 창문에 비친다. [shines, window]

____

2. Se-ri는 초에 불을 붙일 것이다. [candle]

____

3. 이 가방은 매우 가볍다. [bag]

____

∷ 1. 빛은 사람들이 보는 것을 돕는다. 2. 아빠는 불을 피우실 것이다. 3. 깃털은 매우 가볍다.

Review Group -1

해답은 431쪽

A. 다음 뜻에 해당되는 단어를 보기에서 찾아 적으세요.

보기	kid	fly	horn	wave	light

01. _____________ a small flying insect with two wings
02. _____________ hard pointed things that grow from some animals' heads
03. _____________ to joke with someone; to tease
04. _____________ an up and down rolling movement on the surface of water
05. _____________ one type of musical instrument
06. _____________ not heavy
07. _____________ a curve or curves in the hair, in cloth, etc
08. _____________ to start a fire; to give light to
09. _____________ a young goat
10. _____________ to travel by airplane
11. _____________ to make a signal by moving a hand, arm, etc
12. _____________ a child; a young person
13. _____________ to move through the air
14. _____________ the thing that is used to make a loud sound as a signal or warning
15. _____________ the brightness that helps you to see things

B. 다음 뜻에 해당되는 단어를 보기에서 찾아 적으세요.

보기	kid	fly	horn	wave	light

01. The ocean (   ) was tall yesterday.
02. The sun gives us (   ) and heat.
03. Mr. Brown honked the car (   ).
04. A (   ) is a young goat.
05. I will (   ) to New York next Sunday.
06. The animal's (   ) was broken.
07. The children like to (   ) at the moving train.
08. Dean will (   ) the fire in the fireplace.
09. He used to play the (   ) in an orchestra.
10. Don't (   ) me: I know you're telling a lie.
11. A (   ) is an insect with wings.
12. This box is as (   ) as a feather.
13. Chuck is a little (   ).
14. The girl has a natural (   ) in her hair.
15. The arrow will (   ) toward the target.

다음 문장을 굵게 처리된 단어에 유의하여 해석해 보세요.

01. **Kids** under 18 need their parent's signature on the registration form to receive it. [2007년-홀수형 18번]

→ _________________________

02. Helen, you must be **kidding**. [2001년-홀수형 17번]

→ _________________________

03. Time **flies** when you're having fun. [2011년-홀수형 16번]

→ _________________________

04. Shortly after my arrow began to **fly**, I heard the crowd cheering. [2001년-홀수형 37번]

→ _________________________

05. **Flying** over rural Kansas in an airplane one fall evening was a delightful experience for passenger Walt Morris. [2009년-홀수형 19번]

→ _________________________

06. W: What do you think about this one with a basket attached to the handlebars?
M: It's great, but do you have the same model with a **horn**? [2011년-홀수형 1번]

→ _________________________

07. These **waves** were rough and huge, and each wave was a horror to those in the boat. [1994년-2차 41번]

→ _________________________

08. Since his time, we have learned that light **waves** are characterized by different frequencies of vibration. [2008년-홀수형 41번]

→ _________________________

09. We can see an object only when a **light** shines on it. [1996년-홀수형 25번]

→ _________________________

10. Suddenly, the **lights** in the room dimmed twice and then went out. [2002년-홀수형 29번]

→ _________________________

11. A powerful flashlight will easily **light** your way and the creatures around you, revealing marine life in its true colors. [2008년-홀수형 27번]

→ _________________________

12. The hall was brilliantly **lighted**, and decorated with flowers. [1995년-홀수형 37번]

→ _________________________

13. A **light** mist lay along the earth, partly veiling the lower features of the landscape, but above it the taller trees showed in well-defined masses against a clear sky. [2006년-홀수형 32번]

→ _________________________

14. You feel **light** and happy as though you are sailing through life. [2005년-홀수형 22번]

→ _________________________

15. If you talk to somebody about your problem, you can come to see it in a different **light**. [1998년-홀수형 39번]

→ _________________________

006 **bat** [bæt]

Step 01 해석연습

다음 문장을 bat에 유의하여 해석해 보세요. (해석은 이 페이지의 하단부에 있음)

1. A bat flew into my room. ________________________
2. His bat is made of wood. ________________________
3. Mike will bat the ball into the air. ________________________

Step 02 뜻 알기

bat에는 다음과 같은 여러 가지의 뜻이 있습니다.

❶ 박쥐 ⓝ a mouse-like animal which flies, usually at night

❷ 배트, 방망이 ⓝ a heavy stick or club used to hit the ball in baseball, cricket, etc

❸ 방망이를 휘두르다; (공을) 치다 ⓥ to use a bat; to hit (a ball) with a bat

> 한 걸음 더 **The boy batted his eyes when dust got in them.** 소년은 먼지가 눈에 들어가자 눈을 깜박였다.
> → 눈을 깜박이다(=to open and close the eyelids quickly)
> **as blind as a bat** 잘 못 보는, 장님이나 다름없는

Step 03 연습문제

다음 문장의 bat에 해당되는 뜻을 Step 02 의 ❶~❸에서 고르세요. (해답은 431쪽)

1. He will bat first in the game. (　　)
2. The boy has a new bat and ball. (　　)
3. Bats fly at night. (　　)
4. He bats with his left hand. (　　)
5. Bats eat insects and fruit. (　　)
6. John hit the ball with a bat. (　　)

Step 04 영작연습

다음 문장을 주어진 부분을 이용하여 영어로 옮기세요. (해답은 431쪽)

1. 박쥐는 대개 밤에 먹이를 사냥한다. [usually, food]

____

2. 그는 방망이로 그 개를 때렸다. [beat, dog]

____

3. 그는 왼손으로 공을 쳤다. [with, hand]

____

:: 1. 박쥐 한 마리가 나의 방에 날아 들어왔다. 2. 그의 방망이는 나무로 만들어졌다. 3. Mike는 공을 공중으로 칠 것이다.

007 hand [hænd]

Step 01
해석연습

다음 문장을 hand에 유의하여 해석해 보세요. (해석은 이 페이지의 하단부에 있음)

1. Tony's hand was hurt. _______________________________
2. The clock hand was broken. _______________________________
3. Please hand me the book. _______________________________

Step 02
뜻 알기

hand에는 다음과 같은 여러 가지의 뜻이 있습니다.

❶ 손 **n** the part of the body at the end of the arm

❷ (시계 등의) 바늘 **n** a pointer on a clock, watch, etc

❸ 건네주다 **v** to pass, transfer

> 한 걸음 더 **Give me a hand with this box, please.** 이 상자 옮기는 것을 도와주세요. → 도움, 협력(=aid, assistance)
> **handout** 전단(=handbill) **handbook** 안내서 **handcuffs** 수갑 **handmade** 손으로 만든, 수제의
> **handshake** 악수 **upper hand** 우세, 우월 **at hand** 가까이에(=close) **at first hand** 직접, 직통으로
> **at second hand** ① 간접적으로 ② 중고로 **on the other hand** 다른 한편으로는, 반면에 **shake hands** 악수하다
> **hand in hand** 손을 마주잡고, 협조하여 **from hand to mouth** 하루 벌어 하루 먹는 **hand in** 제출하다
> **hand out** 나누어 주다 **hand over** 건네주다

Step 03
연습문제

다음 문장의 hand에 해당되는 뜻을 Step 02 의 ❶~❸에서 고르세요. (해답은 431쪽)

1. She moved her right hand. (   )
2. The hands of the clock pointed to four. (   )
3. The girl has a lily in her hand. (   )
4. He handed a book to his brother. (   )
5. Hand me the salt, please. (   )
6. At noon both hands of a clock are on 12. (   )

Step 04
영작연습

다음 문장을 주어진 부분을 이용하여 영어로 옮기세요. (해답은 431쪽)

1. 그는 왼손으로 글씨를 잘 쓴다. [writes, left]

____

2. 시계는 대개 시침과 분침을 가지고 있다. [hour, minute]

____

3. 나는 그녀에게 편지를 건네주었다. [letter]

____

:: 1. Tony의 손이 다쳤다. 2. 시계바늘이 부러졌다. 3. 나에게 책을 건네주렴.

18

008 watch [watʃ/ wɔtʃ]

Step 01 해석연습

다음 문장을 watch에 유의하여 해석해 보세요. (해석은 이 페이지의 하단부에 있음)

1. He wears a gold watch. _________________________
2. She is watching television now. _________________________
3. The night watch comes on duty soon. _________________________

Step 02 뜻 알기

watch에는 다음과 같은 여러 가지의 뜻이 있습니다.

❶ 손목시계, 회중시계 ⓝ a small clock that you wear on your wrist or carry in your pocket

❷ ∼을 보다, 지켜보다 ⓥ to look at, to observe

❸ 한 사람 또는 그룹으로 된 (야간) 경비원 ⓝ a person or a group of persons on guard

> 한 걸음 더 **Watch out! There is a car coming.** 조심해라! 차가 온다. → ∼을 조심하다, 경계하다(=be careful, look out)
> **Dogs watch over a flock of sheep.** 개들이 양떼를 지키고 있다. → ∼을 지키다, 감시하다(=to guard; keep a watchful eye on)
> **The National Weather Service issued a typhoon watch on July 16.** 기상청은 7월 16일 태풍주의보를 발령했다.
> → (기상청 발표의) 주의보, 경보(=warning, alert)
> **watchdog** 경비견 **watchman** 경비원 **watchmaker** 시계제조(수리)공 **wrist watch** 손목시계 **watch tower** 감시탑, 망루
> **watchful** 조심스러운, 경계하는

Step 03 연습문제

다음 문장의 watch에 해당되는 뜻을 **Step 02** 의 ❶∼❸에서 고르세요. (해답은 431쪽)

1. It is interesting to watch birds. (   )
2. They will be watch all night. (   )
3. She will watch the children playing. (   )
4. She has a new gold watch. (   )
5. He will be the night watch tomorrow. (   )
6. The watch is on his wrist. (   )

Step 04 영작연습

다음 문장을 주어진 부분을 이용하여 영어로 옮기세요. (해답은 431쪽)

1. 나는 늦었는지를 보기 위해 나의 시계를 보았다. [look at, late]

____

2. 엄마는 그녀의 아이들이 노는 것을 주의 깊게 보았다. [children, carefully]

____

3. 그는 오늘 밤 경비를 설 것이다. [will be, tonight]

____

∷ 1. 그는 금시계를 차고 있다. 2. 그녀는 지금 TV를 보고 있는 중이다. 3. 야간 경비원이 곧 근무를 할 것이다.

009 dish [diʃ]

Step 01
해석연습

다음 문장을 dish에 유의하여 해석해 보세요. (해석은 이 페이지의 하단부에 있음)

1. I helped my mother wash the dishes. _______________________

2. Curry and rice is her favorite dish. _______________________

Step 02
뜻 알기

dish에는 다음과 같은 여러 가지의 뜻이 있습니다.

❶ 접시 n a plate, bowl, etc used for serving food

❷ 음식, 요리 n food cooked or prepared in a particular way as a meal

> 한 걸음 더 **a meat dish** 고기 접시 **a vegetable dish** 야채 접시 **a cold dish** 차가운 요리
> **a dish of fish** 생선 한 접시 **three dishes of beans** 세 접시의 콩 **dish washer** 식기세척기
> **do[wash] the dishes** 설거지하다

Step 03
연습문제

다음 문장의 dish에 해당되는 뜻을 **Step 02** 의 ❶~❷에서 고르세요. (해답은 431쪽)

1. She cleared the table of dishes. (   )

2. What is your favorite dish? (   )

3. His favorite dish is steak and kidney pie. (   )

4. She bought a large shallow dish. (   )

Step 04
영작연습

다음 문장을 주어진 부분을 이용하여 영어로 옮기세요. (해답은 431쪽)

1. 그녀는 저녁 식탁에 접시들을 놓았다. [put, dinner]

____

2. 이 음식은 만드는 데 많은 시간이 걸리지 않는다. [take, make]

____

:: 1. 나는 어머니가 접시를 닦는 것을 도와드렸다. 2. 카레라이스는 그녀가 매우 좋아하는 음식이다.

010 ring [riŋ]

Step 01 해석연습

다음 문장을 ring에 유의하여 해석해 보세요. (해석은 이 페이지의 하단부에 있음)

1. Jane has a ring on her finger. _______________________
2. She drew a ring around the picture. _______________________
3. The teacher will ring the bell. _______________________
4. I will ring you (up) tonight. _______________________

Step 02 뜻 알기

ring에는 다음과 같은 여러 가지의 뜻이 있습니다.

❶ 반지 [n] a piece of jewellery that you wear on your finger

❷ 원, 고리, 테 모양의 둥근 것 [n] anything which is like a circle in shape

❸ (종, 벨 따위가) 울다, 울리다 [v] to (cause to) sound / 소리, 울림 [n] the sound made by a bell, etc

❹ ~에게 전화를 걸다 [v] to telephone (someone) / 전화하기 [n] a telephone call

> 한 걸음 더 **Students ringed around the teacher to listen to him.** 학생들은 경청하기 위해 선생님을 에워쌌다.
> → ~을 둘러싸다, 에워싸다(=to surround something; encircle)
> 이외에도 ring에는 나무의 나이테, 권투 경기장, 서커스 공연장이란 뜻도 있음

Step 03 연습문제

다음 문장의 ring에 해당되는 뜻을 **Step 02** 의 ❶~❹에서 고르세요. (해답은 431쪽)

1. If you ring the bell, a waiter will come to help you. (　　)
2. She wears a pretty ring. (　　)
3. Ring me up anytime. (　　)
4. The girl danced in a ring. (　　)
5. The bell began to ring. (　　)
6. I'll ring you again in an hour. (　　)
7. Steve's keys are on a ring. (　　)
8. The lady wears a diamond ring on her finger. (　　)

Step 04 영작연습

다음 문장을 주어진 부분을 이용하여 영어로 옮기세요. (해답은 431쪽)

1. Se-ri는 진주반지를 끼고 있다. [wears, pearl]

____

2. 도넛은 고리처럼 보인다. [looks like]

____

3. 현관에서 벨소리가 한 번 났다. [single, door]

____

4. 나는 어제 그녀에게 전화를 했는데 그녀는 없었다. [yesterday, but]

____

:: 1. Jane은 손가락에 반지를 끼고 있다. 2. 그녀는 그림 둘레에 둥근 모양을 그렸다. 3. 선생님은 종을 울리실 것이다.
4. 내가 오늘 밤 너에게 전화하겠다.

A. 다음 뜻에 해당되는 단어를 보기에서 찾아 적으세요.

| 보기 | bat | hand | watch | dish | ring |

01. ______________ a plate, bowl, etc used for serving food
02. ______________ to look at, to observe
03. ______________ anything which is like a circle in shape
04. ______________ food cooked or prepared in a particular way as a meal
05. ______________ a heavy stick or club used to hit the ball in baseball, cricket, etc
06. ______________ a small clock that you wear on your wrist or carry in your pocket
07. ______________ the part of the body at the end of the arm
08. ______________ a person or a group of persons on guard
09. ______________ a pointer on a clock, watch, etc
10. ______________ to telephone
11. ______________ a mouse-like animal which flies, usually at night
12. ______________ a piece of jewellery that you wear on your finger
13. ______________ to pass, transfer
14. ______________ to use a bat; to hit (a ball) with a bat
15. ______________ to (cause to) sound

B. 다음 뜻에 해당되는 단어를 보기에서 찾아 적으세요.

| 보기 | bat | hand | watch | dish | ring |

01. The long (   ) shows the minutes.
02. Tom will (   ) the baseball game on TV.
03. The player swung the (   ) at the ball.
04. She ate an onion (   ).
05. Could you (   ) me that bag, please?
06. I will be the (   ) from two o'clock to till six.
07. He will (   ) the ball high into the air.
08. She broke a shallow (   ) while washing.
09. I will (   ) you up tonight.
10. We have five fingers on each (   ).
11. She is always wearing a (   ) on her finger.
12. A (   ) is not a bird but an animal.
13. My (   ) keeps good time.
14. The church bell will (   ) at noon.
15. She made my favorite (   ) for dinner.

22

다음 문장을 굵게 처리된 단어에 유의하여 해석해 보세요.

01. A **bat** that fails to feed for two nights is likely to die. [2011년-홀수형 24번]

➡ ______________________________

02. I **handed** in my paper, leaving the question blank. [2003년-홀수형 40번]

➡ ______________________________

03. Certainly. I won't buy second-**hand** items again. [2009년-홀수형 16번]

➡ ______________________________

04. The little boy pulled his **hand** out of his pocket and studied a number of coins in it. [2008년-홀수형 30번]

➡ ______________________________

05. Design, on the other **hand**, is primarily concerned with problem solving, the function of a product. [2007년-홀수형 34번]

➡ ______________________________

06. If you can point out what is humorous or absurd about a situation and ease the tension by getting the other party to share your feeling, you will have the upper **hand**. [1998년-홀수형 28번]

➡ ______________________________

07. M: Do you want me to give you a **hand**?
W: No, that's alright. I'm about to get off the elevator. [2006년-홀수형 13번]

➡ ______________________________

08. When the door was opened, I said "Merry Christmas!" and **handed** some astonished child a beautifully wrapped gift. [2003년-홀수형 19번]

➡ ______________________________

09. Some speakers frequently look at their **watches** while giving their speeches. [2003년-홀수형 39번]

➡ ______________________________

10. "She called me up to protest that the tornado **watch** had kept her in her basement for five hours, and nothing happened," says Allen Pearson. [2001년-홀수형 44번]

➡ ______________________________

11. They **watch** and influence what governments do at home or abroad. [2000년-홀수형 35번]

➡ ______________________________

12. Many people think the secret is kimchi, a traditional Korean **dish** served with almost every meal. [2004년-홀수형 29번]

➡ ______________________________

13. There, placed neatly beside the empty **dish**, were fifteen pennies — my tip. [2008년-홀수형 30번]

➡ ______________________________

14. It had contained a gold **ring** with a small diamond that his grandmother had given to him. [2005년-홀수형 38번]

➡ ______________________________

15. A symphony orchestra can fill a whole building and make it **ring** with music. [2000년-홀수형 46번]

➡ ______________________________

16. Many years ago, psychologists performed an experiment in which they put a number of people in a room, alone except for a **ring** toss set. [2010년-홀수형 45번]

➡ ______________________________

17. W: But she keeps pushing me to the corner of the **ring**.
M: You can't let her keep you in the corner or you'll lose this fight. [2011년-홀수형 8번]

➡ ______________________________

011 ball [bɔːl]

Group 03

Step 01 해석연습

다음 문장을 ball에 유의하여 해석해 보세요. (해석은 이 페이지의 하단부에 있음)

1. The boy has a yellow ball. ________________________________
2. She made a sweater from balls of yarn. ________________________________
3. They danced at the ball. ________________________________

Step 02 뜻 알기

ball에는 다음과 같은 여러 가지의 뜻이 있습니다.

❶ 공, 볼 **n** a round object used in games

❷ 둥근 모양의 물체 **n** anything roughly round in shape

❸ 무도회 **n** a formal dance party

> 한 걸음 더 **ballpark** 야구장 **ballroom** 무도장 **ball-pointed pen** 볼펜 **snowball** 눈 뭉치
> **a knitting ball** 털실 **a fancy[masked] ball** 가장[가면] 무도회

Step 03 연습문제

다음 문장의 ball에 해당되는 뜻을 **Step 02** 의 ❶~❸에서 고르세요. (해답은 432쪽)

1. The boy has a big blue ball. (   )
2. She will dance at the ball. (   )
3. There is a ball of wool on the table. (   )
4. Cinderella will go to the ball tonight. (   )
5. The ball flew over the fence. (   )
6. The boy rolled the snow into a ball. (   )

Step 04 영작연습

다음 문장을 주어진 부분을 이용하여 영어로 옮기세요. (해답은 432쪽)

1. 축구선수가 공을 강하게 찼다. [kicked, strongly]

____

2. 그는 손수건을 둥글게 뭉쳤다. [made, handkerchief]

____

3. 수많은 사람들이 봄 무도회에 있었다. [a lot of, spring]

____

:: 1. 소년은 노란 공을 하나 가지고 있다. 2. 그녀는 (공 모양의) 뜨개실로 스웨터를 떴다. 3. 그들은 무도회에서 춤을 추었다.

 012 **space** [speis]

Step 01
해석연습

다음 문장을 space에 유의하여 해석해 보세요. (해석은 이 페이지의 하단부에 있음)

1. Tony's hope is space travel. ______________________________

2. There is no space in this room. ______________________________

3. These words have a space between them. ______________________________

Step 02
뜻 알기

space에는 다음과 같은 여러 가지의 뜻이 있습니다.

❶ 우주 ⓝ the area outside the earth's atmosphere where the stars and planets are

❷ 공간, 장소, 자리 ⓝ an empty or uncovered place; room

❸ 공백, 여백, 행간(行間) ⓝ an empty space between written or printed words, lines, etc.

> 한 걸음 더 **I spaced the cans neatly on the kitchen counter.** 나는 캔들을 부엌 조리대 위에 일정한 간격을 두고 정렬해 놓았다.
> → ~을 간격을 두고 배치하다(=arrange something at intervals)
> **a blank space** 여백 **space biology** 우주생물학 **spaceman** 우주인 **spaceship** 우주선 **spacecraft** 우주선
> **space shuttle** 우주왕복선 **space station** 우주정거장 **spacesuit** 우주복

Step 03
연습문제

다음 문장의 space에 해당되는 뜻을 **Step 02** 의 ❶～❸에서 고르세요. (해답은 별책 432쪽)

1. He left a space between words. (　　)

2. Mike enjoys looking out into space. (　　)

3. Fill in the blank spaces with the right words. (　　)

4. He couldn't find a space for my car. (　　)

5. We have entered the space age. (　　)

6. These books take up too much space on my desk. (　　)

Step 04
영작연습

다음 문장을 주어진 부분을 이용하여 영어로 옮기세요. (해답은 432쪽)

1. 우주를 통해 다른 행성으로 여행하는 것은 오늘날 많은 사람들의 흥미를 끈다. [travel, planets]

____

2. 우리에 갇힌 호랑이들은 충분한 공간을 갖지 못한다. [the caged tigers, enough]

____

3. 그녀는 줄과 줄 사이에 여백(행간)을 두었다. [between lines]

____

∷ 1. Tony의 소망은 우주여행이다. 2. 이 방에는 공간이 없다. 3. 이 단어들 사이에는 여백이 있다.

013 jack [dʒæk]

Step 01 해석연습

다음 문장을 jack에 유의하여 해석해 보세요. (해석은 이 페이지의 하단부에 있음)

1. He used a jack to change his truck's tire. _______________________

2. Judy has the jack of hearts. _______________________

3. He needs to buy an earphone jack. _______________________

Step 02 뜻 알기

jack에는 다음과 같은 여러 가지의 뜻이 있습니다.

❶ 잭(밀어 올리는 기계) **n** an instrument for lifting up a motor or other heavy weight
～을 잭으로 밀어 올리다 **v** to lift something with a jack

❷ (카드의) 잭 **n** a playing card with a picture of a young man

❸ 잭(플러그를 꽂아 전기를 접속시키는 장치) **n** an electric connection for a telephone or other electric machine

> 한 걸음 더 **All work and no play makes Jack a dull boy.** (공부만 하고 놀지 않으면 아이는 바보가 된다)
> → 흔한 남자 이름으로 John, James, Jacob의 애칭이기도 하며 일반적으로 남자(=man), 소년(=boy) 등을 나타내기도 함
> **Jack of all trades** 무엇이든, 만능꾼 **every man Jack; every Jack one** 누구나, 너나없이(=everyone)
> **Jack and Jill** 젊은 남녀

Step 03 연습문제

다음 문장의 jack에 해당되는 뜻을 **Step 02** 의 ❶～❸에서 고르세요. (해답은 432쪽)

1. She has a pair of jacks in her hand. (   )

2. He put the jack under the car. (   )

3. Connect this jack to that telephone. (   )

4. I carry a jack in my car in case I have a flat tire. (   )

5. I have a jack of diamonds in my hand. (   )

6. She bought a new earphone jack. (   )

Step 04 영작연습

다음 문장을 주어진 부분을 이용하여 영어로 옮기세요. (해답은 432쪽)

1. 그는 바람 빠진 타이어를 갈기 위해 잭으로 자동차를 들어올렸다. [change, flat tire]

____

2. 그녀는 카드 테이블에 잭(카드)을 내려놓았다. [put, card table]

____

3. 그는 두 개의 전기기구를 잭으로 연결했다. [electric machines]

____

:: 1. 그는 그의 트럭 타이어를 교환하기 위해 잭을 사용했다. 2. Judy는 하트 무늬의 잭(카드)를 가지고 있다. 3. 그는 이어폰 잭을 하나 사야 한다.

014 story [stɔ́ːri]

Step 01
해석연습

다음 문장을 story에 유의하여 해석해 보세요. (해석은 이 페이지의 하단부에 있음)

1. Grandmother told me the story of Cinderella. ________________________________

2. My house has two stories. ________________________________

Step 02
뜻 알기

story에는 다음과 같은 여러 가지의 뜻이 있습니다.

❶ 이야기, 설화, 소설 ⓝ anything told or written of an event, or series of event, real or imaginary

❷ (건물의) 층 (=storey [영국식 표현]) ⓝ a floor or level of a building

> 한 걸음 더 **a house of one story** 단층집 **a two-story house** 이층집
> **storybook** 이야기책 **storyteller** 이야기꾼 **the whole story** 일의 전말, 자초지종
> **to make a long story short** 간단히 말해, 대충 말한다면(=to make short of a long story)
> **The story goes that ~** ~라는 이야기이다. **a likely story** (구어) 그럴듯한[믿기지 않는] 이야기

Step 03
연습문제

다음 문장의 story에 해당되는 뜻을 **Step 02** 의 ❶~❷에서 고르세요. (해답은 432쪽)

1. I lived in a two-story house. (   )

2. He told me a very interesting story. (   )

3. My uncle told the story of his childhood in China. (   )

4. This is a building of thirty-five stories. (   )

Step 04
영작연습

다음 문장을 주어진 부분을 이용하여 영어로 옮기세요. (해답은 432쪽)

1. 나의 아저씨께서 나에게 한 충성스러운 개에 대한 이야기를 해 주셨다. [about, faithful]

____

2. 저것은 63층짜리 빌딩이다. [building]

____

⠿ 1. 할머니께서는 나에게 신데렐라 이야기를 해 주셨다. 2. 나의 집은 2층집이다.

 **015 band** [bænd]

다음 문장을 band에 유의하여 해석해 보세요. (해석은 이 페이지의 하단부에 있음)

1. The band played several marches. ________________________________

2. The band of robbers are very dangerous. ________________________________

3. She wore a band on her head. ________________________________

4. They banded together to resist the common enemy. ________________________________

band에는 다음과 같은 여러 가지의 뜻이 있습니다.

❶ 악단, 밴드 n a group of persons playing music together

❷ 그룹, 무리, 떼 n a group of people or animals

❸ 묶는 것, 끈, 띠 n a strip of material to put around something

❹ 단결하다 v to unite or gather together for a purpose

> 한 걸음 더 He **banded** the box before mailing it. 그는 우편으로 부치기 전에 상자를 묶었다. → 같이 묶다
> She wore a skirt with a **band** of red in it. 그녀는 빨간 줄무늬가 있는 치마를 입고 있었다. → 줄무늬(= a stripe)
> the medium wave **band** 중간 주파수대 → 라디오의 주파수대

다음 문장의 band에 해당되는 뜻을 Step 02 의 ❶~❹에서 고르세요. (해답은 432쪽)

1. The bottle has a band around the top. (　　)

2. The band played loudly. (　　)

3. The two parties will band together to form an alliance. (　　)

4. A band of thieves has been robbing the neighborhood. (　　)

5. The students banded together to oppose the new policy of the school. (　　)

6. There was a great musical band at the party. (　　)

7. He saw a band of wild dogs in the distance. (　　)

8. Bind this box with metal bands. (　　)

다음 문장을 주어진 부분을 이용하여 영어로 옮기세요. (해답은 432쪽)

1. In-ho는 우리 악단에서 드럼을 연주한다. [plays, drum]

____

2. 원숭이 떼들은 함께 모여 산다. [lives together]

____

3. 그녀는 상자 둘레를 고무줄로 묶었다. [tied, rubber]

____

4. 그들은 항의하기 위해 단결했다. [protest]

____

:: 1. 악단은 행진곡을 몇 곡 연주했다. 2. 강도 떼들은 매우 위험했다. 3. 그녀는 머리에 띠를 했다. 4. 그들은 공동의 적에 대항하기 위해 단결했다.

A. 다음 뜻에 해당되는 단어를 보기에서 찾아 적으세요.

보기	ball	space	jack	story	band

01. ______________ an empty space between written or printed words, lines, etc
02. ______________ anything told or written of an event, or series of event, real or imaginary
03. ______________ a strip of material to put around something
04. ______________ a round object used in games
05. ______________ a playing card with a picture of a young man
06. ______________ a group of persons playing music together
07. ______________ a floor or level of a building
08. ______________ a formal dance party
09. ______________ an electric connection for a telephone or other electric machine
10. ______________ to unite or gather together for a purpose
11. ______________ the area outside the earth's atmosphere where the stars and planets are
12. ______________ an instrument for lifting up a motor or other heavy weight
13. ______________ anything roughly round in shape
14. ______________ a group of people or animals
15. ______________ an empty or uncovered place; room

B. 다음 뜻에 해당되는 단어를 보기에서 찾아 적으세요.

보기	ball	space	jack	story	band

01. She is looking for a rubber (   ) to bind her hair.
02. The (   ), queen and king are the three face cards.
03. This sofa takes up too much (   ).
04. She lives in a two-(   ) house.
05. The boy can throw a (   ) fast and straight.
06. The workers will (   ) together to protest low wages.
07. Leave a wide (   ) between the lines.
08. The (   ) was written by Mark Twain.
09. She put on her best clothes to go to a (   ).
10. The (   ) will march through the street.
11. The (   ) lifted the front of the truck.
12. Someday we will travel in (   ).
13. There is a (   ) of wool on the table.
14. You had better check up the telephone (   ).
15. I saw a (   ) of goats in the field.

다음 문장을 굵게 처리된 단어에 유의하여 해석해 보세요.

01. The first true piece of sports equipment that man invented was the **ball**. [2008년–홀수형 19번]

→ ___________________________________

02. Comfortable living conditions include not only chemical and physical cleanliness, but also privacy, **space**, and quietness. [1994년–2차 46번]

→ ___________________________________

03. Huge amounts of **space** are given over to parking lots rather than to trees and birds. [2002년–홀수형 25번]

→ ___________________________________

04. Robots and astronauts use much of the same equipment in **space**. [2010년–홀수형 22번]

→ ___________________________________

05. With one technological change, cross-referencing became possible, while the physical **space** needed to house a collection of books was sharply reduced. [2008년–홀수형 25번]

→ ___________________________________

06. Scientists have sent people out into **space** and even to the moon. [1996년–홀수형 33번]

→ ___________________________________

07. M: The house next to the big tree is mine.
W: You mean the two-**story** house?
M: No, the one-**story** house.
W: I've got it. [2001년–홀수형 1번]

→ ___________________________________

08. The **story** starts in the world of Homer, where the stormy skies and the dark seas were ruled by the mythical gods. [2007년–홀수형 41번]

→ ___________________________________

09. Reading **stories** and poetry, for instance, can help us to understand and improve our own situations. [1999년–홀수형 41번]

→ ___________________________________

10. The smallmouth has a series of dark vertical **bands** along its sides. [2010년–홀수형 36번]

→ ___________________________________

11. **Bands** of blue-shirted farmers circle and lift and swing behind a drum and various wind instruments in the ancient Basque Riau-Riau dances. [2009년–홀수형 43번]

→ ___________________________________

12. And at night there is the beat of the big drums and the military **band** as the whole town dances in the great open square of the Plaza. [2009년–홀수형 43번]

→ ___________________________________

13. M: Wow, there are a lot of school clubs.
W: Hmm.... I'd like to join the school rock **band**. Let's sign up for it together. [2011년–홀수형 15번]

→ ___________________________________

016 punch [pʌntʃ]

Step 01 해석연습

다음 문장을 punch에 유의하여 해석해 보세요. (해석은 이 페이지의 하단부에 있음)

1. She put more ice in the punch. _______________________

2. He punched the robber on the head. _______________________

3. The guard punched my ticket. _______________________

Step 02 뜻 알기

punch에는 다음과 같은 여러 가지의 뜻이 있습니다.

❶ 펀치(포도주 따위에 물, 우유, 과즙, 향료 따위를 섞은 음료) n a drink made of wine or other liquor mixed with water, sugar, lemon, etc

❷ 주먹으로 치다 v to hit with the fist / 주먹으로 치기 n a blow with the fist

❸ (펀치로) ~에 구멍을 뚫다 v to make holes in something with a punch
구멍 뚫는 기구 n a tool or device for making holes in paper, leather, etc

> 한 걸음 더 **His speech was O.K. but it had no real punch.** 그의 연설은 좋았지만 생동감은 없었다.
> → 생동감, 활력(=liveliness, impact, vigor)
> **punch ball** 펀치 볼(권투 연습용으로 매달아 놓은 속을 채운 가죽 공) **punch bowl** 펀치 사발(펀치를 담아 내놓는 큰 그릇)
> **puncher** 구멍 뚫는 사람 또는 기구

Step 03 연습문제

다음 문장의 punch에 해당되는 뜻을 **Step 02** 의 ❶~❸에서 고르세요. (해답은 432쪽)

1. He punched me on the nose. (　　　)

2. She served green punch at the party. (　　　)

3. Mike must punch some papers. (　　　)

4. Judy made a fruit punch of orange and papaya juice. (　　　)

5. The ticket taker will punch your ticket. (　　　)

6. The boxer punched his opponent in the face. (　　　)

Step 04 영작연습

다음 문장을 주어진 부분을 이용하여 영어로 옮기세요. (해답은 432쪽)

1. 이 펀치는 딸기 같은 맛이 난다. [tastes, strawberries]

____

2. 그는 코에 강한 펀치를 맞았다. [strong, nose]

____

3. 그녀는 그녀의 기말 보고서에 구멍을 뚫기 위해 펀치를 사용했다. [holes, term paper]

____

1. 그녀는 펀치에 얼음을 더 넣었다. 2. 그는 강도의 머리를 주먹으로 때렸다. 3. 경비원이 나의 표에 구멍을 뚫었다.

017 **tail** [teil]

Step 01
해석연습

다음 문장을 tail에 유의하여 해석해 보세요. (해석은 이 페이지의 하단부에 있음)

1. This animal has a long tail. ________________________________

2. She was standing at the tail of the line. ________________________________

3. Every coin has a head and a tail. ________________________________

Step 02
뜻 알기

tail에는 다음과 같은 여러 가지의 뜻이 있습니다.

❶ (짐승, 새, 물고기 등의) 꼬리 Ⓝ the movable part at the end of the body of an animal, bird, or fish

❷ 꼬리 모양의 것; 후부, 말미, 끄트머리 Ⓝ something like a tail in its shape or position

❸ (대개 복수로 쓰여) 동전의 후면 Ⓝ (pl) the reverse side of a coin

> 한 걸음 더 **A strange man tailed me to the station.** 한 낯선 남자가 나를 정거장까지 미행했다.
> → tail에는 구어체로서 ~를 미행하다, ~의 뒤를 밟다(=follow someone closely and secretly)의 뜻도 있음
> **tail coat** 연미복(남자용 서양 예복) **tail light** (차의) 미등(뒤에 달린 등) **tail fin** (물고기의) 꼬리지느러미
> **tail away**(=tail off) 점점 사라지다, 점점 작아지다, 차츰 스러져 없어지다.

Step 03
연습문제

다음 문장의 tail에 해당되는 뜻을 **Step 02** 의 ❶~❸에서 고르세요. (해답은 433쪽)

1. My cat likes to chase his own tail. (   )

2. The words "five cents" are on the tail of a nickle. (   )

3. He was at the tail end of the race. (   )

4. I saw the tail of an airplane in the sky. (   )

5. The boy tossed the coin and it came down tails. (   )

6. A fish swims by moving its tail. (   )

Step 04
영작연습

다음 문장을 주어진 부분을 이용하여 영어로 옮기세요. (해답은 433쪽)

1. 개들은 만족스러울 때 꼬리를 흔든다. [wag, pleased]

____

2. 그는 모퉁이에서 사라지는 행렬의 꼬리를 보았다. [procession, disappearing]

____

3. 그 동전의 뒷면은 심하게 긁혀 있었다. [coin, scratched]

____

∷ 1. 이 동물은 긴 꼬리를 가지고 있다. 2. 그녀는 줄의 끄트머리에 서 있었다. 3. 모든 동전은 전면과 후면을 가지고 있다.

018 fire [faiər]

Step 01 해석연습

다음 문장을 fire에 유의하여 해석해 보세요. (해석은 이 페이지의 하단부에 있음)

1. The fire might burn our houses. _______________________
2. Police fired on the crowd. _______________________
3. The boss will fire the lazy worker. _______________________

Step 02 뜻 알기

fire에는 다음과 같은 여러 가지의 뜻이 있습니다.

❶ 불; 화염 **n** the process of burning, which produces heat and light; flame

❷ 발사하다, 발포하다 **v** to shoot a weapon[gun, cannon, missile, etc]

❸ 해고하다 **v** to make someone leave a job; to dismiss

> 한 걸음 더 **Her speeches were full of <u>fire</u>.** 그녀의 연설은 열정으로 가득 차 있다.
> → 열정, 불타는 정열, 활기(=passion, intensity, spirit)
> **fire alarm** 화재경보기 **fire brigade** 소방대, 소방서 **fire cracker** 폭죽, 딱총 **fire department** 소방서, 소방대
> **fire drill** 소방훈련, 화재대피훈련 **fire engine** 소방차 **fire extinguisher** 소화기(불 끄는 도구) **fire fighter** 소방관
> **fire house** 소방서 **fire hydrant** 소화전 **fire place** 벽난로 **fire proof** 내화의, 방화의, 불에 견디는
> **firework** 불꽃, 폭죽 **firefly** 개똥벌레, 반딧불이

Step 03 연습문제

다음 문장의 fire에 해당되는 뜻을 **Step 02** 의 ❶∼❸에서 고르세요. (해답은 433쪽)

1. The fire kept us warm. (   )
2. Those soldiers will fire their rifles. (   )
3. He will not fire a good worker. (   )
4. The airplane will fire at the ship. (   )
5. The boss wants to fire the worker. (   )
6. Several houses were destroyed in a fire. (   )

Step 04 영작연습

다음 문장을 주어진 부분을 이용하여 영어로 옮기세요. (해답은 433쪽)

1. 그 집은 불로 완전히 파괴되었다. [completely, destroyed]

____

2. 그 병사는 소총을 적에게 발사했다. [rifle, enemy]

____

3. 그녀는 최근의 일자리에서 지각 때문에 해고당했다. [last job, being late]

____

⁚⁚ 1. 그 불은 우리의 집들을 태울지도 모른다. 2. 경찰이 군중들에게 발포했다. 3. 사장은 그 게으른 일꾼을 해고할 것이다.

 **019 pretty** [príti]

Step 01
해석연습

다음 문장을 pretty에 유의하여 해석해 보세요. (해석은 이 페이지의 하단부에 있음)

1. What a pretty little garden it is! _______________________________

2. The man speaks French pretty well. _______________________________

Step 02
뜻 알기

pretty에는 다음과 같은 여러 가지의 뜻이 있습니다.

❶ 귀여운, 매력적인 　a　 charming, lovely, attractive

❷ 꽤, 상당히 　ad　 considerable in amount or extent; fairly

> 한 걸음 더 **Here's a <u>pretty</u> mess.** 난장판이군. 골치 아프게 됐군. → 말도 안 되는, 터무니없는(=awful; surprising)
> * a pretty state of affairs = a pretty kettle of fish 난장판, 뒤죽박죽, 혼란상태
> **That was a <u>pretty</u> sum of money.** 그것은 상당한 금액이었다. → (구어체) 상당한, 꽤 많은(=large)
> * make a pretty fortune 한 재산[상당한 재산] 벌다
> **pretty much** (구어체) 거의 **pretty soon** 곧

Step 03
연습문제

다음 문장의 pretty에 해당되는 뜻을 　Step 02　 의 ❶∼❷에서 고르세요. (해답은 433쪽)

1. He speaks Japanese pretty well. (　　)
2. She likes this pretty dress. (　　)
3. Jane has a pretty face. (　　)
4. He is pretty tall for a Korean. (　　)

Step 04
영작연습

다음 문장을 주어진 부분을 이용하여 영어로 옮기세요. (해답은 433쪽)

1. 장미는 5월에 매우 아름답다. [roses, May]

____

2. 공원은 나의 집에서 상당히 멀다. [park, far from]

____

:: 1. 얼마나 아름다운 작은 정원인가! 2. 그 남자는 불어를 상당히 잘한다.

 **020 part** [pɑːrt]

Step 01 해석연습

다음 문장을 part에 유의하여 해석해 보세요. (해석은 이 페이지의 하단부에 있음)

1. Please take part of my sandwich. ______________________________
2. The twins did not want to part. ______________________________
3. John wears a part on his right side. ______________________________
4. He played the part of Hamlet in the play. ______________________________

Step 02 뜻 알기

part에는 다음과 같은 여러 가지의 뜻이 있습니다.

❶ 부분, 일부 [n] a piece or portion of the whole

❷ 가르다, 헤어지다, 나누다 [v] to pull apart, separate, or divide

❸ (머리의) 가르마 [n] a line that separates the hair on a person's head

❹ 역할, 의무 [n] a role or duty to perform in some activity or event

> 한 걸음 더 **partial** 일부분의, 부분적인 **partially** 부분적으로 **parting** ① 헤어짐, 이별 ② (머리의) 가르마(=part)
> **part-time** 시간제의, 파트타임의 **for the most part** 대부분, 거의 **take part in ~** ~에 참여[참가]하다
> **in part** 부분적으로, 어느 정도

Step 03 연습문제

다음 문장의 part에 해당되는 뜻을 **Step 02** 의 ❶~❹에서 고르세요. (해답은 433쪽)

1. She divided the cake into three parts. (   )
2. The mother will part her fighting sons. (   )
3. She played the part of the queen. (   )
4. The boys parted at the school gate. (   )
5. Jae-ho usually wears a part on his left side. (   )
6. Jeff played a very important part in the work. (   )
7. Part of the house is used as an office. (   )
8. Joan wears her part on the right side of her head. (   )

Step 04 영작연습

다음 문장을 주어진 부분을 이용하여 영어로 옮기세요. (해답은 433쪽)

1. 그는 그의 삶의 초기 부분을 호주에서 보냈다. [spent, Australia]

____

2. 선생님은 싸우는 학생들을 떼어 놓을 것이다. [fighting students]

____

3. 그는 가르마를 타기 위해 빗을 사용했다. [used, comb]

____

4. 그녀는 영화에서 Juliet 역할을 할 것이다. [play, movie]

____

1. 내 샌드위치의 일부를 받으세요. 2. 쌍둥이들은 헤어지기를 원치 않았다. 3. John은 오른편으로 가르마를 탔다. 4. 그는 연극에서 햄릿 역할을 하였다.

A. 다음 뜻에 해당되는 단어를 보기에서 찾아 적으세요.

보기	punch	tail	fire	pretty	part

01. ______________ charming, lovely, attractive
02. ______________ a role or duty to perform in some activity or event
03. ______________ a drink made of wine or other liquor mixed with water, sugar, lemon, etc
04. ______________ to make someone leave a job; to dismiss
05. ______________ the movable part at the end of the body of an animal, bird, or fish
06. ______________ a blow with the fist
07. ______________ considerable in amount or extent; fairly
08. ______________ to shoot a weapon[gun, cannon, missile, etc]
09. ______________ a piece or portion of the whole
10. ______________ the reverse side of a coin
11. ______________ to pull apart, separate, or divide
12. ______________ something like a tail in its shape or position
13. ______________ a tool or device for making holes in paper, leather, etc
14. ______________ a line that separates the hair on a person's head
15. ______________ the process of burning, which produces heat and light; flame

B. 다음 빈칸에 가장 알맞은 단어를 보기에서 찾아 적으세요.

보기	punch	tail	fire	pretty	part

01. The ( ) of the coin said "Quarter Dollars."
02. I will ( ) holes in my term paper.
03. He will ( ) three bullets at the target.
04. She will ( ) the curtains to let in the sunlight.
05. Would you like to have a cup of ( )?
06. I was standing at the ( ) of the line.
07. Kangaroos live only in ( ) of the world.
08. What a ( ) doll this is!
09. Joan combed a new ( ) in her hair.
10. The ( ) might burn our house.
11. The boxers will ( ) each other.
12. It's ( ) cold outdoors today.
13. The dog began to wag his ( ).
14. The boss will ( ) all of the company's managers.
15. He was cast for the ( ) of Romeo.

다음 문장을 굵게 처리된 단어에 유의하여 해석해 보세요.

01. First, she told my parents about my amazing physical energy: "Lisa never tires of chasing and **punching** her classmates." [1997년–홀수형 43번]

→ _______________

02. Then instead of waiting in line in a pharmacy for your medicine, you go to a vending machine, **punch** in your ID number and get your medicine. [2006년–홀수형 6번]

→ _______________

03. For example, it is documented that if people are asked to bet on whether a coin toss is heads or **tails**, most bet larger amounts if the coin is yet to be tossed. [2012년–홀수형 26번]

→ _______________

04. "This can stem from many sources such as having an automobile crash, being **fired** from a job, falling suddenly ill, becoming involved in a legal suit, or losing a large sum of money. [1994년–1차 49–50번]

→ _______________

05. A **fire** chief, for example, needs to issue his orders with absolute clarity. [2010년–홀수형 38번]

→ _______________

06. Approaching Mr. Howard's, I at first thought that the house was on **fire**. [2003년–홀수형 32번]

→ _______________

07. We're sorry for the inconvenience, but there is a small **fire** in the snack bar. [1996년–홀수형 10번]

→ _______________

08. A child will often ask for approval openly. "Look at my painting! Isn't it **pretty**?" [2001년–홀수형 26번]

→ _______________

09. Well, the first part is **pretty** easy. But the second part is more difficult because it involves some rock-climbing. [2005년–홀수형 9번]

→ _______________

10. Most people realize only a small **part** of their potential. [2001년–홀수형 26번]

→ _______________

11. The next step is to put the different **parts** together with glue and nails. [2000년–홀수형 43번]

→ _______________

12. So she got the autograph, and the two **parted** good friends! [1998년–홀수형 30번]

→ _______________

13. Many things determine what foods people eat. Climate plays a **part**. So does soil. [1997년–홀수형 39번]

→ _______________

14. Asch assembled groups of twelve university students and announced that they were **taking part in** an experiment on visual perception. [2011년–홀수형 27번]

→ _______________

15. As we grew older, Mom made sure we did our **part** by keeping our rooms neat. [2004년–홀수형 30번]

→ _______________

DAY 03

Friendship is like wine — the older the better.
우정은 술과 같은 것 — 묵을수록 좋다.

021 kind [kaind]

Group
05

Step 01
해석연습

다음 문장을 kind에 유의하여 해석해 보세요. (해석은 이 페이지의 하단부에 있음)

1. Julie is very kind to everyone. _______________________________
2. What kind of sports do you like? _______________________________

Step 02
뜻 알기

kind에는 다음과 같은 여러 가지의 뜻이 있습니다.

❶ 친절한, 인정 많은 `a` having, showing thoughtfulness, sympathy or love for others; friendly; gentle

❷ 종류, 부류 `n` a sort or type of person or thing

> 한 걸음 더 **kindness** 친절함 **kindly** 친절하게 **a kind of** 일종의, ~와 같은(=a sort of)
> **all kinds of** 모든 종류의, 온갖

Step 03
연습문제

다음 문장의 kind에 해당되는 뜻을 **Step 02** 의 ❶~❷에서 고르세요. (해답은 433쪽)

1. I like all kinds of flowers. (   )
2. It is kind of you to invite me. (   )
3. What kind of house do you live in? (   )
4. Be specially kind to old people. (   )

Step 04
영작연습

다음 문장을 주어진 부분을 이용하여 영어로 옮기세요. (해답은 433쪽)

1. 그 의사는 자신의 환자들에게 항상 친절하다. [always, patients]

    ____

2. 그녀는 나의 것과 같은 종류의 시계를 가지고 있다. [same, mine]

    ____

1. Julie는 누구에게나 매우 친절하다. 2. 당신은 어떤 종류의 스포츠를 좋아합니까?

022 swing [swiŋ]

Step 01 해석연습

다음 문장을 swing에 유의하여 해석해 보세요. (해석은 이 페이지의 하단부에 있음)

1. The lamp is swinging gently in the wind. _______________________
2. Tony will swing the bat at the ball. _______________________
3. She sat on the swing at the playground. _______________________

Step 02 뜻 알기

swing에는 다음과 같은 여러 가지의 뜻이 있습니다.

❶ 흔들리다　**v** to move or sway in a curve from a fixed point

❷ (팔, 방망이 등을) 휘둘러 때리다　**v** to try to hit something with an extended, arching movement of the arm, a bat, etc
휘두르기, 흔들기, 진동　**n** an act of swinging

❸ 그네　**n** a seat for swinging, hung on ropes or chains from a supporting frame, etc

> 한 걸음 더 **swing** [swiŋ] - **swung** [swʌŋ] - **swung** [swʌŋ]
> **A big band played <u>swing music</u>.** 재즈밴드가 스윙음악을 연주했다.
> → 세련되고 흥취 있는 재즈음악(=a jazz music), 스윙음악리듬(=a strong dancing rhythm)
> **in full swing** 한창(진행 중)인, 한창 신이 나서

Step 03 연습문제

다음 문장의 swing에 해당되는 뜻을 **Step 02** 의 ❶～❸에서 고르세요. (해답은 433쪽)

1. Let's watch Tony swing his golf club. (　　)
2. The gate will swing in the wind. (　　)
3. Justine runs to the swing at recess. (　　)
4. His arms always swing as he walks. (　　)
5. A little girl is sitting on a swing. (　　)
6. Don't swing thc bat likc so. (　　)

Step 04 영작연습

다음 문장을 주어진 부분을 이용하여 영어로 옮기세요. (해답은 433쪽)

1. 저 문은 흔들릴 때마다 많은 소음이 난다. [door, noise]

____

2. 그 골프선수는 자신의 스윙(휘두르기)을 개선하고 싶어 한다. [golfer, improve]

____

3. Seri는 학교에서 그네 타는 것을 좋아했다. [ride, at school]

____

:: 1. 램프가 바람에 슬슬 움직이고 있다. 2. Tony는 공을 향해 방망이를 휘두를 것이다. 3. 그녀는 놀이터에서 그네에 앉아 있다.

023 **march** [mɑːrtʃ]

Step 01 해석연습 다음 문장을 march에 유의하여 해석해 보세요. (해석은 이 페이지의 하단부에 있음)

1. My sister's birthday in March. ________________________

2. The army marched into the town. ________________________

3. The band played a march. ________________________

Step 02 뜻 알기 march에는 다음과 같은 여러 가지의 뜻이 있습니다.

❶ (대문자로 사용) 3월　**n** the third month of the year

❷ 행진하다, 행군하다　**v** to walk with a regular step like soldiers
　행진　**n** the act of marching

❸ 행진곡　**n** a piece of music for marching to

> 한 걸음 더 the **march** of the time 시간의 흐름
> → 진행, 진전, 발전(=progress; advance)
> **a wedding march** 결혼행진곡　**a funeral march** 장송행진곡　**a forced march** 강행군　**a triumphal march** 개선행진곡

Step 03 연습문제 다음 문장의 march에 해당되는 뜻을 Step 02 의 ❶~❸에서 고르세요. (해답은 433쪽)

1. March comes before April. (　　)

2. The music of a march is very exciting. (　　)

3. We have a lot of windy days in March. (　　)

4. The Boy Scouts will march to their camp. (　　)

5. The band played marches that cheered everyone up. (　　)

6. They must march for ten miles. (　　)

Step 04 영작연습 다음 문장을 주어진 부분을 이용하여 영어로 옮기세요. (해답은 433쪽)

1. 어떤 꽃들은 3월에 핀다. [some, bloom]

____

2. 우리 학교 악대는 크리스마스 행렬에서 행진할 것이다. [band, parade]

____

3. 그는 트럼펫이 그 행진곡을 연주하는 것을 들었다. [trumpet, play]

____

:: 1. 나의 여동생의 생일은 3월이다. 2. 군대가 마을로 행진해 들어왔다. 3. 그 악단은 행진곡을 연주했다.

024 **block** [blak / blɔk]

Step 01 해석연습

다음 문장을 block에 유의하여 해석해 보세요. (해석은 이 페이지의 하단부에 있음)

1. Joe put a block in the yellow box. _______________________________

2. He walked two blocks to the bus stop. _______________________________

3. An old tree fell and blocked the road. _______________________________

Step 02 뜻 알기

block에는 다음과 같은 여러 가지의 뜻이 있습니다.

❶ (길을) 가로막다, 방해하다 **v** to make movement difficult or impossible; to obstruct; to oppose

❷ (나무, 돌 따위의) 덩어리; 장난감 블록 **n** a flat-sided mass of wood or stone etc; a children's toy consisting of wooden or plastic cubes

❸ (거리의) 1구획, 블록; 한 블록의 거리 **n** an area of buildings bounded by four streets; the length of one side of such an area

> 한 걸음 더 **An accident caused a <u>block</u> in traffic.** 사고가 교통에 방해가 되었다.
> → 방해물, 장애물(=obstruction, barrier)
> **blocking** ① 방해(저지)하는 것 ② (스포츠의) 가로막기(블로킹) **blockade** (교통, 통신 등의) 봉쇄, 차단 **blockage** 봉쇄, 장애물

Step 03 연습문제

다음 문장의 block에 해당되는 뜻을 **Step 02** 의 ❶~❸에서 고르세요. (해답은 433쪽)

1. The football players to try to block the ball. (   )
2. The block is made of wood. (   )
3. There are 20 houses on my block. (   )
4. The police must block the crowd from the President. (   )
5. Elijah lives two blocks from school. (   )
6. Your sister threw a block at me. (   )

Step 04 영작연습

다음 문장을 주어진 부분을 이용하여 영어로 옮기세요. (해답은 433쪽)

1. 그는 얼음 덩어리로 조각상을 깎았다. [carved, statue]

____

2. 여기서 그 가게까지는 5블록이다. [store, from here]

____

3. 그녀는 그의 선출을 막기 위해 온갖 노력을 다했다. [effort, election]

____

1. Joe는 블록 한 개를 노란 상자에 넣었다. 2. 그는 버스정거장까지 두 블록을 걸었다. 3. 오래된 나무 한 그루가 넘어져서 길을 가로막았다.

025 stand [stænd]

Step 01
해석연습

다음 문장을 stand에 유의하여 해석해 보세요. (해석은 이 페이지의 하단부에 있음)

1. The guard must stand for many hours. _______________________________

2. Eddie's hot dog stand is always busy. _______________________________

3. Please stand these desks in the corner. _______________________________

4. I can't stand his rudeness any longer. _______________________________

Step 02
뜻 알기

stand에는 다음과 같은 여러 가지의 뜻이 있습니다.

❶ 서다, 서 있다; 일어서다　ⓥ to be on one's feet; to rise to an upright position

❷ 가판대, 매점, 노점　ⓝ a small structure used for selling or showing things

❸ 세우다, ～을 세워 놓다　ⓥ to put in a particular position, especially upright

❹ 참고 견디다　ⓥ to endure or tolerate

> 한 걸음 더 **stand** [stænd] - **stood** [stud] - **stood** [stud]
> **The mayor took a <u>stand</u> for the building of a new museum.** 시장은 새 박물관을 지어야 한다는 입장을 취했다.
> → 태도, 입장, 견해, 의견(= an attitude, an opinion; a position supported with regard to something)
> 이외에도 받침대[～걸이, ～꽂이], (경기장, 체육관 등의) 관중석이란 뜻도 있음

Step 03
연습문제

다음 문장의 stand에 해당되는 뜻을 **Step 02** 의 ❶～❹에서 고르세요. (해답은 433쪽)

1. Can you stand the pain of a toothache? (　　　)

2. The crowd must stand during the song. (　　　)

3. A sandwich was a dollar at that stand. (　　　)

4. I don't like to stand in line. (　　　)

5. They will stand the flagpole in the dirt. (　　　)

6. He can't stand working in an office. (　　　)

7. I bought apples at the fruit stand. (　　　)

8. Don't stand this tin of petrol near the fire. (　　　)

Step 04
영작연습

다음 문장을 주어진 부분을 이용하여 영어로 옮기세요. (해답은 433쪽)

1. 악단(밴드)이 국가를 연주하면 모든 사람들은 일어설 것이다. [national anthem]

____

2. Joe는 어제 그의 매점에서 레모네이드 15잔을 팔았다. [sold, lemonade]

____

3. 그녀는 사다리를 벽에 기대어 세울 것이다. [ladder, wall]

____

4. 나는 이 더운 날씨를 더 이상 견딜 수가 없다. [weather, any longer]

____

∷ 1. 경비원은 몇 시간 동안 서 있어야 한다. 2. Eddie의 핫도그 매점은 항상 바쁘다. 3. 이 책상들을 구석에 세워 놓아 주세요.
　4. 나는 그의 무례함을 더 이상 참을 수 없다.

해답은 433쪽

Day 03

A. 다음 뜻에 해당되는 단어를 보기에서 찾아 적으세요.

보기   kind   swing   march   block   stand

01. ____________ to walk with a regular step like soldiers
02. ____________ to make movement difficult or impossible; to obstruct; to oppose
03. ____________ to endure or tolerate
04. ____________ to try to hit something with an extended, arching movement of the arm, a bat, etc
05. ____________ having, showing thoughtfulness, sympathy or love for others; friendly; gentle
06. ____________ a piece of music for marching to
07. ____________ a seat for swinging, hung on ropes or chains from a supporting frame, etc
08. ____________ an area of buildings bounded by four streets; the length of one side of such an area
09. ____________ to be on one's feet; to rise to an upright position
10. ____________ a sort or type of person or thing
11. ____________ to move or sway in a curve from a fixed point
12. ____________ a flat-sided mass of wood or stone etc; a children's toy consisting of wooden or plastic cubes
13. ____________ a small structure used for selling or showing things
14. ____________ the third month of the year
15. ____________ to put in a particular position, especially upright

B. 다음 빈칸에 가장 알맞은 단어를 보기에서 찾아 적으세요.

보기   kind   swing   march   block   stand

01. Please help me ( ) my bike up.
02. The soldiers will ( ) 90 miles in three days.
03. I walked a ( ) to the subway station.
04. The lamp hanging overhead will ( ) in the wind.
05. She can't ( ) the pressure of her job.
06. The ropes will ( ) people from entering the room.
07. We heard the band play the wedding ( ).
08. Bobbi threw a wooden ( ) at me.
09. A butterfly is a ( ) of insect.
10. The baseball player can ( ) the heavy bat easily.
11. Please ( ) straight, don't stoop.
12. She was ( ) enough to show me the way.
13. ( ) is the third month of the year.
14. Apples were 79 a pound at the ( )
15. Little Teddy likes the slide and the ( ) in the playground.

다음 문장을 굵게 처리된 단어에 유의하여 해석해 보세요.

01. M: Do you need a hand with that suitcase?
W: That's very **kind** of you, thanks. [1998년–홀수형 11번]

➡ ______________________________________

02. In general, parents feel a special **kind** of love for their own children that they do not feel for other children. [2001년–홀수형 35번]

➡ ______________________________________

03. When we arrived, my sister immediately ran off to the **swings**, and I recall being annoyed that my mother wasn't following her. [2009년–홀수형 46–48]

➡ ______________________________________

04. These symptoms are caused when you're exposed to motions such as **swinging**, turning, rocking, or up-and-down movements. [2010년–홀수형 3번]

➡ ______________________________________

05. I can also remember my emotions **swinging** from one extreme to another. [2002년–홀수형 40번]

➡ ______________________________________

06. He saw the male giraffes battling for mates by **swinging** their powerful necks, which were over six feet long and weighed more than 200 pounds. [2006년–홀수형 29번]

➡ ______________________________________

07. For a child, it could be placing with trembling fingers the last **block** on a tower she has built, higher than any she has built so far; for a sprinter, it could be trying to beat his own record; for a violinist, mastering an intricate musical passage. [2011년–홀수형 31번]

➡ ______________________________________

08. Michelangelo looked at a **block** of marble and saw a man. [2005년–홀수형 43번]

➡ ______________________________________

09. The people in dresses and suits **blocked** my view of the garden. [2003년–홀수형 32번]

➡ ______________________________________

10. You drive through a town and see a drunken man on the sidewalk. A few **blocks** further on you see another. [1998년–홀수형 54–55번]

➡ ______________________________________

11. Participants should bring comfortable clothes and shoes, insect spray, and sun **block** for the outdoor activities. [2009년–홀수형 12번]

➡ ______________________________________

12. Patience is clearly an important virtue, yet so many people **stand** in front of their microwaves thinking "Hurry up!" [2010년–홀수형 24번]

➡ ______________________________________

13. We would appreciate some guidance, since things will soon become too difficult to **stand**. [1999년–홀수형 47번]

➡ ______________________________________

14. But persons who are daring in taking a wholehearted **stand** for truth often achieve results that surpass their expectations. [2011년–홀수형 20번]

➡ ______________________________________

15. The doctor said playfully, "Shut your eyes and stick your tongue out of your mouth." Then he went away, leaving the man **standing** in the street with his tongue hanging out.... [1995년–홀수형 32번]

➡ ______________________________________

 **026 shop** [ʃɑp / ʃɔp]

Step 01
해석연습

다음 문장을 shop에 유의하여 해석해 보세요. (해석은 이 페이지의 하단부에 있음)

1. The Fairy chocolate shop closes at 7:00. ___________________________

2. My brother works at an automobile repair shop. ___________________________

3. The little girl likes to shop for candy. ___________________________

Step 02
뜻 알기

shop에는 다음과 같은 여러 가지의 뜻이 있습니다.

❶ 상점, 가게 🄝 a small store

❷ 일터, 직장; 공장, 제작소 🄝 a place of business; a place where things are made or repaired

❸ 물건을 사러 가다 🅅 to go to shops to buy things

> 한 걸음 더 **shop assistant** 점원 **shopkeeper** 가게 주인 **shopper** 손님, 물건 사는 사람 **shopping** 쇼핑, 물건 사기
> **shopwindow** 진열장(=show window) **go shopping** 장 보러 가다, 쇼핑 가다 **set up shop** 사업[일]을 시작하다

Step 03
연습문제

다음 문장의 shop에 해당되는 뜻을 Step 02 의 ❶~❸에서 고르세요. (해답은 434쪽)

1. There is a fruit shop near here. (   )

2. We shop for food every Wednesday. (   )

3. We build airplanes in our shop. (   )

4. They shop for food at the local supermarket. (   )

5. She bought some candies at that shop on the corner. (   )

6. Barbara works in an auto repair shop. (   )

Step 04
영작연습

다음 문장을 주어진 부분을 이용하여 영어로 옮기세요. (해답은 434쪽)

1. Mary는 모퉁이의 꽃가게에서 약간의 장미를 샀다. [some, corner]

____

2. 사업에서 은퇴하신 후 나의 아버지께서는 기계 공장에서 근무하셨다. [retiring, machine]

____

3. 그들은 매주 화요일마다 식료품을 사러 간다. [groceries, Tuesday]

____

∷ 1. Fairy 초콜릿가게는 7시에 닫는다. 2. 나의 형은 자동차 수리 공장에서 일한다. 3. 그 꼬마 소녀는 사탕 사러 가는 것을 좋아한다.

027 season [síːzn]

Step 01 해석연습

다음 문장을 season에 유의하여 해석해 보세요. (해석은 이 페이지의 하단부에 있음)

1. There are four seasons in a year. ________________________________

2. Strawberries are out of season now. ________________________________

3. Don't forget to season the stew. ________________________________

Step 02 뜻 알기

season에는 다음과 같은 여러 가지의 뜻이 있습니다.

❶ 계절 **n** one of the four main periods in a year; spring, summer, autumn, or winter

❷ (기후, 활동 따위로 특정 지어진) 시기, 철 **n** any period of time marked by something special

❸ 양념하다, ~에 맛을 내다 **v** to add spices or flavoring to food

> 한 걸음 더 **He seasoned himself to the heat.** 그는 더위에 익숙해졌다.
> **Her grandfather was a seasoned fisherman.** 그녀의 할아버지는 숙련된 어부였다.
> → 익숙해지게 하다, 단련시키다(=accustom)
> **the dry season** 건기 **the rainy season** 우기 **the strawberries season** 딸기철
> **the season of harvest** 추수철, 수확기 **seasoned** ① 조미한, 맛을 들인 ② 익숙한, 경험을 쌓은 **seasoning** 조미료, 양념
> **seasonable** 계절에 맞는 **season ticket** ① 1년 내내 입장할 수 있는 입장권 ② 정기승차권 **in season** 때맞춘, 제철인
> **out of season** 철 지난, 제철이 아닌 **at all seasons** 사철을 통해서

Step 03 연습문제

다음 문장의 season에 해당되는 뜻을 **Step 02** 의 ❶~❸에서 고르세요. (해답은 434쪽)

1. Summer is a hot, dry season. (   )

2. She will season the soup with salt. (   )

3. The baseball season begins in April in Korea. (   )

4. Watermelons are out of season now. (   )

5. He seasoned the meat with plenty of pepper. (   )

6. Spring is Michael's favorite season. (   )

Step 04 영작연습

다음 문장을 주어진 부분을 이용하여 영어로 옮기세요. (해답은 434쪽)

1. 가을은 여행하기에 가장 좋은 계절이다. [Autumn, travelling]

____

2. 한국에서 야구 시즌은 4월에 시작된다. [baseball, April]

____

3. 그녀는 수프를 후추로 양념하기를 좋아한다. [soup, pepper]

____

:: 1. 일 년에는 사계절이 있다. 2. 딸기는 지금 제철이 아니다. 3. 스튜(요리) 양념하는 것을 잊지 마라.

028 fan [fæn]

Step 01 해석연습

다음 문장을 fan에 유의하여 해석해 보세요. (해석은 이 페이지의 하단부에 있음)

1. He turned on the fan to keep cool. __________________________
2. The boy used the book to fan himself. __________________________
3. Jae-ho is a fan of the Los Angeles Dodgers. __________________________

Step 02 뜻 알기

fan에는 다음과 같은 여러 가지의 뜻이 있습니다.

❶ 부채, 선풍기, 바람을 일으키는 것 n an instrument to make a current of air

❷ 부채질하다, 바람을 일으키다 v to make air move around by waving a fan, piece of paper, etc

❸ 열광적인 지지자, 애호가, 팬 n an enthusiastic supporter; a fanatic

> 한 걸음 더 **a baseball fan** 야구팬 **an electric fan** 선풍기 **a folding fan** 접는 부채 **a fan letter** 팬레터
> **a ventilating fan** 환풍기 **fanatic** 열광적인 애호가, 광신자, 마니아 **fan a quarrel** 싸움을 부추기다
> **fan the flames** (아무의) 흥분[노여움]을 부추기다

Step 03 연습문제

다음 문장의 fan에 해당되는 뜻을 **Step 02** 의 ❶~❸에서 고르세요. (해답은 434쪽)

1. He fanned the flames in the fireplace. (   )
2. Our team has plenty of fans. (   )
3. This old fan still works well. (   )
4. The stadium was filled with football fans. (   )
5. The store sold the last electric fan today. (   )
6. Paul fanned himself with a road map. (   )

Step 04 영작연습

다음 문장을 주어진 부분을 이용하여 영어로 옮기세요. (해답은 434쪽)

1. 그녀는 시원하게 하려고 부채를 가지고 다니곤 했다. [carry, cool]

____

2. 그는 불이 확 타오를 때까지 부채질을 하였다. [fire, flames]

____

3. Nancy는 3년째 그 팀의 팬이다. [has been, for]

____

029 like [laik]

Step 01
해석연습

다음 문장을 like에 유의하여 해석해 보세요. (해석은 이 페이지의 하단부에 있음)

1. He likes tea better than coffee. ________________________

2. The boy climbs a tree like a monkey. ________________________

Step 02
뜻 알기

like에는 다음과 같은 여러 가지의 뜻이 있습니다.

❶ ～을 좋아하다; ～을 하고 싶다 **v** to be fond of; to be pleased with; to wish
좋아하는 것; 취미, 취향, 기호 **n** things that one likes; preference

❷ ～와 같은, ～처럼, ～와 마찬가지로 **prep** similar to or the same as
닮은, 비슷한 **a** similar, equal
닮은 사람, 닮은 것 **n** a person or thing that is like another

> 한 걸음 더 **likewise** ① 마찬가지로 ② 그 위에, 게다가 **likeness** ① 비슷함, 유사 ② 초상화, 사진, 닮은 것
> **liking** 좋아함, 기호 **likely** ～할 것 같은, 그럴듯한, 있음 직한 **feel like ~ing** ～하고 싶은 생각이 들다
> **would [should] like to + V** ～하고 싶다 **and the like** 그 밖의 같은 것, 기타 등등
> **look like** ① ～처럼 보이다 ② ～할 것 같다

Step 03
연습문제

다음 문장의 like에 해당되는 뜻을 **Step 02** 의 ❶～❷에서 고르세요. (해답은 434쪽)

1. Which of these colors do you like best? (　　　)

2. I can't play the guitar like you. (　　　)

3. He likes to swim in the river. (　　　)

4. The building looked like a church. (　　　)

Step 04
영작연습

다음 문장을 주어진 부분을 이용하여 영어로 옮기세요. (해답은 434쪽)

1. 우리 모두는 자신의 좋아하는 것과 싫어하는 것을 가지고 있다. [likes, dislikes]

____

2. 나의 형은 너의 것과 같은 차를 가지고 있다. [brother, yours]

____

∷ 1. 그는 커피보다 홍차를 더 좋아한다. 2. 그 소년은 원숭이처럼 나무를 오른다.

48

 030 sight [sait]

Step 01 해석연습

다음 문장을 sight에 유의하여 해석해 보세요. (해석은 이 페이지의 하단부에 있음)

1. As my sight is good, I don't need glasses. _______________________
2. He ran away at the sight of me. _______________________
3. The sunset was a wonderful sight. _______________________
4. Do what is right in your own sight. _______________________

Step 02 뜻 알기

sight에는 다음과 같은 여러 가지의 뜻이 있습니다.

❶ 시력, 시각 **n** the physical ability to see

❷ 봄; 보임, 보이는 모습 **n** the act of seeing; the state of seeing or being seen

❸ 경치, 장관; (복수) 명소 **n** something worth seeing; a spectacle; (pl) places worth seeing

❹ 의견, 판단, 견해 **n** an opinion; a judgement; a way of looking at something

> 한 걸음 더 **sightseeing** 관광, 구경 **sightseer** 관광객, 구경꾼 **near[short]sighted** 근시의
> **far[long]sighted** 원시의

Step 03 연습문제

다음 문장의 sight에 해당되는 뜻을 **Step 02** 의 ❶~❹에서 고르세요. (해답은 434쪽)

1. The plane was soon out of sight. (   )
2. He had lost his sight in a car accident. (   )
3. All men are equal in the sight of God. (   )
4. Her sight has become poor recently. (   )
5. She always does what is right in her own sight. (   )
6. We will see the sights of Paris tomorrow. (   )
7. At first sight the problem seemed insoluble. (   )
8. The sunrise is a wonderful sight. (   )

Step 04 영작연습

다음 문장을 주어진 부분을 이용하여 영어로 옮기세요. (해답은 434쪽)

1. 그는 전쟁에서 시력을 잃었다. [lost, war]

____

2. 그 소녀는 군중 속에서 엄마의 모습을 놓쳤다. [lost, crowd]

____

3. 그랜드 캐니언(The Grand Canyon)은 세계 명소 중의 하나이다. [one, of the world]

____

4. 나는 나의 판단으로 옳다고 여겨지는 것을 할 것이다. [do, right]

____

:: 1. 나는 시력이 좋기 때문에 안경이 필요 없다. 2. 그는 나를 보지마자 도망쳤다. 3. 일몰은 멋진 광경이었다.
4. 너의 판단으로 옳다고 여겨지는 것을 행하라.

A. 다음 뜻에 해당되는 단어를 보기에서 찾아 적으세요.

보기	shop	season	fan	like	sight

01. _____________ to be fond of; to be pleased with; to wish
02. _____________ any period of time marked by something special
03. _____________ a small store
04. _____________ the act of seeing; the state of seeing or being seen
05. _____________ to make air move around by waving a fan, piece of paper etc
06. _____________ one of the four main periods in a year; spring, summer, autumn, or winter
07. _____________ an opinion; a judgement; a way of looking at something
08. _____________ to go to shops to buy things
09. _____________ the physical ability to see
10. _____________ an enthusiastic supporter; a fanatic
11. _____________ an instrument to make a current of air
12. _____________ something worth seeing; a spectacle; (pl) places worth seeing
13. _____________ a place of business; a place where things are made or repaired
14. _____________ similar to or the same as
15. _____________ to add spices or flavoring to food

B. 다음 빈칸에 가장 알맞은 단어를 보기에서 찾아 적으세요.

보기	shop	season	fan	like	sight

01. I (   ) walking in the rain.
02. Please (   ) the spaghetti with a little pepper and garlic.
03. The sunrise is a wonderful (   ).
04. She opened a flower (   ) in her hometown.
05. Nancy is a big (   ) of Michael Jackson.
06. The lady has a beautiful (   ) in her hand.
07. As I have bad (   ), I need glasses.
08. Dave works at an auto repair (   ).
09. The girl sings (   ) a bird.
10. The Christmas (   ) is a happy time.
11. I lost (   ) of her in the crowd.
12. I like to (   ) my face with a notebook.
13. We need to (   ) for groceries.
14. Winter is a cold, snowy (   ).
15. He always does what is right in his own (   ).

다음 문장을 굵게 처리된 단어에 유의하여 해석해 보세요.

01. Despite the slow service, their **shop** is constantly packed with customers and their counter piled high with clothes. [2004년–홀수형 18번]

→ _______________________________

02. Also fix-it **shops** are getting rare. [1998년–홀수형 25번]

→ _______________________________

03. But truly improving ourselves or our lot is a superhuman task, so we do what we can instead: we **shop**, the economy grows, the world gets more complex, we feel more helpless and insecure, so we **shop** still more. [1995년–홀수형 48번]

→ _______________________________

04. Winter is just around the corner, and with it comes the flu **season**. [1997년–홀수형 12번]

→ _______________________________

05. Soon we will find out who is going to be named champion and who will have to train harder next **season**. [2002년–홀수형 47–48번]

→ _______________________________

06. When that filter mistakenly screens out something essential, then even **seasoned** masters can make mistakes. [2011년–홀수형 39번]

→ _______________________________

07. His mother asks Tony several times to wash it. But he insists that it's of no use to do so, because it's the rainy **season**. (it = Tony's family car) [1994년–2차 12–13번]

→ _______________________________

08. Overnight, **fans** slept outside the stadium to make certain they could get tickets. [2002년–홀수형 47–48번]

→ _______________________________

09. W: One last question. What do you do in your spare time?
M: Well, I'm busy replying to my **fans**. [1998년–홀수형 9번]

→ _______________________________

10. Falling in love is **like** being wrapped in a magical cloud. [2005년–홀수형 22번]

→ _______________________________

11. Some children, especially boys, **like** to have their own music players and may play these for very long periods of time. [2006년–홀수형 36번]

→ _______________________________

12. But isolation feels **like** being in a room with no way out. [2008년–홀수형 44번]

→ _______________________________

13. Just as we approached the exit after the game, I caught **sight** of Willie Mays. [2005년–홀수형 49–50번]

→ _______________________________

14. A friend of mine and his wife were in Hawaii, standing on a beach, watching a beautiful sunset–hardly able to believe how magnificent the **sight** was. [2010년–홀수형 49–50번]

→ _______________________________

15. Consequently, men are blind to their own faults but never lose **sight** of their neighbor's. [1997년–홀수형 36번]

→ _______________________________

To choose time is to save time.
시기를 잘 선택하는 것은 시간을 절약하는 일이다.

031 time [taim]

Step 01 해석연습

다음 문장을 time에 유의하여 해석해 보세요. (해석은 이 페이지의 하단부에 있음)

1. It is time to go to bed now. ___________________________
2. She has been to France three times. _______________________

Step 02 뜻 알기

time에는 다음과 같은 여러 가지의 뜻이 있습니다.

❶ 때, 시간, 시대 n the concept of past, present, and future, taken separately or as a whole

❷ ~번, ~회, ~배 n the state of being multiplied by a number

> 한 걸음 더 **timetable** 시간표, (행사 등의) 예정표 **time zone** (표준) 시간대 **timeless** 영원한 **timely** 때맞춘, 시기적절한
> **at times** 때때로, 이따금 **on time** 제시간에, 정각에 **behind the times** 시대에 뒤떨어진, 구식의
> **from time to time** 때때로, 이따금 **have a good time** 재미있게[즐겁게] 지내다

Step 03 연습문제

다음 문장의 time에 해당되는 뜻을 **Step 02** 의 ❶~❷에서 고르세요. (해답은 435쪽)

1. Time goes by so quickly these days. (   )
2. How many times have you been there? (   )
3. I'll be back in a short time. (   )
4. She goes swimming three times a week. (   )

Step 04 영작연습

다음 문장을 주어진 부분을 이용하여 영어로 옮기세요. (해답은 435쪽)

1. 우리는 허비할 시간이 없다. 서둘러야 한다. [lose, hurry up]

   ____

2. 이 상자는 저 상자보다 세 배나 크다. [box, as big as]

   ____

∷ 1. 이제 자야 할 시간이다. 2. 그녀는 프랑스에 세 번 다녀왔다.

032 **track** [træk]

Step 01 해석연습

다음 문장을 track에 유의하여 해석해 보세요. (해석은 이 페이지의 하단부에 있음)

1. Hunters will follow the lion's tracks. _______________________________

2. We have an oval track at our school. _______________________________

3. The track is made of heavy metal bars. _______________________________

Step 02 뜻 알기

track에는 다음과 같은 여러 가지의 뜻이 있습니다.

❶ 지나간 자국, 남겨진 자취, 흔적 **n** the mark left by something which has passed along
 ~를 추적하다, 뒤쫓다 **v** to follow the track of someone or something

❷ 트랙, 경주로 **n** a course for races

❸ 궤도, 선로, 철로 **n** metal rails on which trains or streetcars run

> 한 걸음 더 **The track leads through dense forest.** 그 오솔길은 울창한 숲으로 통한다.
> → 밟아서 생긴 길, 오솔길, 통로(=a narrow path)
> **a mountain track** 산중의 등산길 **a track meet** 육상경기대회 **the track of a storm** 폭풍의 진로
> **keep track of** ~을 따라가다 **lose track of** ~을 놓쳐버리다
> **off the track** ① (열차가) 탈선하여 ② (목표, 주제에서) 벗어나서 ③ 정도를 벗어나서
> **on the track** 정도를 따라, 주제를 벗어나지 않아

Step 03 연습문제

다음 문장의 track에 해당되는 뜻을 **Step 02** 의 ❶~❸에서 고르세요. (해답은 435쪽)

1. A train is coming down the track. (   )
2. The hunter found the tracks of a bear. (   )
3. Have you ever been to the race track? (   )
4. Be careful when you cross the railroad track. (   )
5. He ran on the Lincoln High School track. (   )
6. There were not any car tracks on the road. (   )

Step 04 영작연습

다음 문장을 주어진 부분을 이용하여 영어로 옮기세요. (해답은 435쪽)

1. 레이더(전파탐지기)는 비행기들의 움직임을 추적할 수 있다. [radar, movement]

____

2. 그는 경주로를 세 번 돌았다. [three times]

____

3. 두 대의 기차는 같은 선로를 달린다. [trains, run]

____

:: 1. 사냥꾼들은 사자의 발자국을 뒤쫓을 것이다. 2. 우리 학교는 타원형 트랙을 가지고 있다. 3. 철로는 무거운 긴 금속 덩어리들로 만들어진다.

 **033 hot** [hɑt / hɔt]

Step 01
해석연습

다음 문장을 hot에 유의하여 해석해 보세요. (해석은 이 페이지의 하단부에 있음)

1. You'd better have a cup of hot tea. _______________________________

2. Pepper and mustard are hot. _______________________________

3. It is a hot news item. _______________________________

Step 02
뜻 알기

hot에는 다음과 같은 여러 가지의 뜻이 있습니다.

❶ 더운, 뜨거운 ⓐ having a high temperature or great heat

❷ (음식이) 매운, (혀가) 얼얼한 ⓐ producing a burning sensation to the taste

❸ (뉴스 따위가) 새로운, 최신의 ⓐ (news, etc) new, fresh, recent

> 한 걸음 더 **hotheaded** 성급한, 흥분하기 쉬운(=hot tempered) **hot news** 최신 소식 **hot spring** 온천
> **hot pants** 짧은 바지, 핫팬츠

Step 03
연습문제

다음 문장의 hot에 해당되는 뜻을 **Step 02** **의 ❶~❸에서 고르세요.** (해답은 435쪽)

1. The weather is very hot today. (   )

2. The food is hot because I added much red peppers to it. (   )

3. It is too hot to play the game today. (   )

4. Long skirts are hot fashion this season. (   )

5. This curry is too hot for me. It's too spicy. (   )

6. Is there any hot news about your girl friend? (   )

Step 04
영작연습

다음 문장을 주어진 부분을 이용하여 영어로 옮기세요. (해답은 435쪽)

1. 여름은 일 년 중 가장 더운 계절이다. [season, year]

____

2. 칠레 고추는 매우 매운 맛이 난다. [chili peppers, taste]

____

3. 오늘 신문에는 새로운 소식이 많이 실려 있다. [today's newspaper]

____

:: 1. 뜨거운 차 한 잔을 마시는 것이 좋을 것이다. 2. 후추와 겨자는 맵다. 3. 이것은 최신 소식거리다.

034 pet [pet]

Step 01 해석연습

다음 문장을 pet에 유의하여 해석해 보세요. (해석은 이 페이지의 하단부에 있음)

1. Mike enjoys holding his pet. ________________________________
2. Mary is the teacher's pet. ________________________________
3. The cat's soft fur is fun to pet. ________________________________

Step 02 뜻 알기

pet에는 다음과 같은 여러 가지의 뜻이 있습니다.

❶ 애완동물 **n** a tame animal kept in the house and treated with care and affection

❷ 귀염둥이, 총애받는 것, 소중한 물건이나 사람 **n** a favorite; a darling

❸ 쓰다듬다, 귀여워하다 **v** to stroke or caress in a loving way; to fondle; to treat with affection

> 한 걸음 더 **Bill's pet word is "fantastic."** Bill이 좋아하는[즐겨 사용하는] 단어는 "fantastic"이다.
> → 좋아하는, 특기의(=favorite, special)
> **a pet shop** 애완동물가게 **pet name** 애칭

Step 03 연습문제

다음 문장의 pet에 해당되는 뜻을 Step 02 의 ❶～❸에서 고르세요. (해답은 435쪽)

1. Jane's pet sleeps on the floor. (   )
2. That little boy is the teacher's pet. (   )
3. A parrot can be a fun pet. (   )
4. She pats her dog on its back. (   )
5. The old lady sat by the fire petting her cat. (   )
6. Se-ri was the teacher's pet in her school days. (   )

Step 04 영작연습

다음 문장을 주어진 부분을 이용하여 영어로 옮기세요. (해답은 435쪽)

1. 그 노부인은 고양이를 애완동물로 키운다. [old lady, keeps]

____

2. 저 똑똑한 소녀는 그 선생님의 귀염둥이이다. [bright girl]

____

3. 그는 자신의 개의 등을 쓰다듬었다. [on its back]

____

:: 1. Mike는 그 자신의 애완동물을 안고 있는 것을 즐긴다. 2. Mary는 그 선생님의 귀염둥이이다. 3. 그 고양이의 부드러운 털은 쓰다듬기에 재미있다.

035 hard [hɑːrd]

Step 01 해석연습

다음 문장을 hard에 유의하여 해석해 보세요. (해석은 이 페이지의 하단부에 있음)

1. This desk is made of hard wood. ________________________
2. That's a hard question to answer. ________________________
3. He is a hard worker. ________________________
4. It rained hard last night. ________________________

Step 02 뜻 알기

hard에는 다음과 같은 여러 가지의 뜻이 있습니다.

❶ 단단한, 굳은 [a] firm and stiff; difficult to press down, break, or cut
   단단히 [ad] firmly; tightly

❷ (문제, 일 따위가) 힘이 드는, 어려운 [a] difficult to do or understand; requiring much effort

❸ 열심히 하는, 부지런한 [a] doing with energy; diligent
   열심히, 부지런히 [ad] with great energy, effort, or attention; earnestly; diligently

❹ 심하게, 세차게 [ad] with great force; heavily

▷ 한 걸음 더 **hardship** 고난, 역경 **hardworking** 근면한, 열심히 하는 **hard-and-fast** (규칙 따위가) 매우 엄격한, 명확한

Step 03 연습문제

다음 문장의 hard에 해당되는 뜻을 **Step 02** 의 ❶~❹에서 고르세요. (해답은 435쪽)

1. It is hard to say which is better. (   )
2. It blew hard last night. (   )
3. The surface of stone is hard and cold. (   )
4. It is raining hard outside. (   )
5. This desk is made of hard wood. (   )
6. The worker works very hard everyday. (   )
7. French is a hard language to learn. (   )
8. I studied hard to pass the college entrance examination. (   )

Step 04 영작연습

다음 문장을 주어진 부분을 이용하여 영어로 옮기세요. (해답은 435쪽)

1. 다이아몬드는 우리에게 알려진 가장 단단한 물질이다. [Diamond, substance]

   ____

2. 내가 이 강을 수영해 건너기는 어렵다. [swim across, river]

   ____

3. 그는 입학시험에 합격하기 위해서 열심히 공부했다. [pass, entrance examination]

   ____

4. 정말 어제 눈이 몹시 왔다. [indeed, yesterday]

   ____

:: 1. 이 책상은 단단한 나무로 만들어져 있다. 2. 그것은 대답하기 어려운 질문이다. 3. 그는 근면한 사람이다. 4. 어젯밤에 비가 세차게 내렸다.

해답은 435쪽

Day 04

A. 다음 뜻에 해당되는 단어를 보기에서 찾아 적으세요.

보기	time	track	hot	pet	hard

01. _____________ a tame animal kept in the house and treated with care and affection
02. _____________ a course for races
03. _____________ to stroke or caress in a loving way; to fondle; to treat with affection
04. _____________ having a high temperature or great heat
05. _____________ difficult to do or understand; requiring much effort
06. _____________ the concept of past, present, and future, taken separately or as a whole
07. _____________ with great force; heavily
08. _____________ (news, etc) new, fresh, recent
09. _____________ firm and stiff; difficult to press down, break, or cut
10. _____________ the state of being multiplied by a number
11. _____________ a favorite; a darling
12. _____________ metal rails on which trains or streetcars run
13. _____________ producing a burning sensation to the taste
14. _____________ with great energy, effort, or attention; earnestly; diligently
15. _____________ the mark left by something which has passed along

B. 다음 빈칸에 가장 알맞은 단어를 보기에서 찾아 적으세요.

보기	time	track	hot	pet	hard

01. She keeps a rabbit as a (   ).
02. We are anxious about the (   ) news from the front.
03. He found the (   ) of a wagon in the snow.
04. Red peppers taste very (   ).
05. At that (   ) he was away from home.
06. Sandra is the teacher's (   ).
07. He ran (   ) to win the race.
08. This coffee is too (   ) to drink.
09. It snowed (   ) last night.
10. He has three (   ) as many books as I have.
11. The train left the (   ) and was derailed.
12. The ground is too (   ) to dig.
13. We will have to run around the (   ) 10 times.
14. Christine likes to (   ) her parrot.
15. It is (   ) for an old man to change his way of living.

다음 문장을 굵게 처리된 단어에 유의하여 해석해 보세요.

01. There is plenty of **time** in life for people to follow other interests. [2006년–홀수형 46–48번]

➡ ____

02. Although you have heard an opera once, you can still hear it five or twenty **times** more. [2005년–홀수형 47–48번]

➡ ____

03. One gallon of diesel fuel will haul about four **times** as much by rail as by truck. [1997년–홀수형 40번]

➡ ____

04. In ancient **times**, as today, the basic type of shoes worn depended on the climate. [2007년–홀수형 40번]

➡ ____

05. But at school they learned, and very quickly, that children earn Nature Trail tickets for running the quarter-mile **track** during lunch recess. [2011년–홀수형 23번]

➡ ____

06. We became so interested in the mummies that we lost **track** of the time. [2002년–홀수형 29번]

➡ ____

07. A **hot** bath in water of 38℃ or 39℃ is best for relaxing muscles. [2001년–홀수형 34번]

➡ ____

08. There was a kind woman–by no means well off – who, in a **hot** Christmas rush, made a last attempt to catch up. [1998년–홀수형 19번]

➡ ____

09. Farmers don't like using chemicals to control weeds because such poisons can kill wild animals or even **pets**, like dogs. [2000년–홀수형 39번]

➡ ____

10. And some fears may extend only to one kind, as in the example of the child who wants to **pet** a lion at the zoo but wouldn't dream of petting the neighbor's dog. [2002년–홀수형 45번]

➡ ____

11. The early volunteers worked alone and did **hard** and unpleasant tasks. [1998년–홀수형 52–53번]

➡ ____

12. I have been working **hard** so that my family can enjoy an easy and convenient life. [2005년–홀수형 18번]

➡ ____

13. Recently, a severe disease hit Asian nations **hard**, causing several hundred deaths. [2004년–홀수형 29번]

➡ ____

14. Some of their artificial mothers were made of cold, **hard** wire while the others were made of warm, soft towel cloth. [2001년–홀수형 24번]

➡ ____

15. This hole helps the kite fly fast regardless of the wind speed by concentrating the wind on days when the wind is light, and letting it pass through when the wind is blowing **hard**. [2006년–홀수형 31번]

➡ ____

036 dull [dʌl]

Step 01 해석연습

다음 문장을 dull에 유의하여 해석해 보세요. (해석은 이 페이지의 하단부에 있음)

1. This knife is dull. I need a sharp one. _______________________

2. The clever students help the dull students. _______________________

3. That movie was very dull. _______________________

Step 02 뜻 알기

dull에는 다음과 같은 여러 가지의 뜻이 있습니다.

❶ (칼이) 무딘, 날카롭지 않은 ⓐ not sharp; blunt

❷ (머리가) 둔한, 우둔한, 모자라는 ⓐ slow to learn or understand; not intelligent

❸ 재미없는, 지루한 ⓐ not interesting or exciting; boring

> 한 걸음 더 **It was a dull day.** 흐린 날이었다. (우중충한 날이었다.)
> → 흐린, 산뜻하지 않은(=not bright or clear)
> **a dull pencil** 무딘 연필 **a dull light** 흐린 빛 **a dull sky** 흐린 하늘 **a dull color** 흐린 색깔
> **a dull sound** 둔탁한 소리 **a dull book** 재미없는 책

Step 03 연습문제

다음 문장의 dull에 해당되는 뜻을 Step 02 의 ❶~❸에서 고르세요. (해답은 435쪽)

1. Lisa was a dull student in her school days. (   )

2. That was a knife with a dull edge. (   )

3. The baseball game that I saw was dull. (   )

4. All I could find was a dull pencil. (   )

5. She is dull of apprehension. (   )

6. He had a dull time today. (   )

Step 04 영작연습

다음 문장을 주어진 부분을 이용하여 영어로 옮기세요. (해답은 435쪽)

1. 그 칼은 너무 무뎌서 아무 쓸모가 없다. [knife, too]

____

2. 그는 학교 다닐 때 우둔한 학생이었다. [in his school days]

____

3. 나는 오늘 영화를 한 편 보았는데 그것은 지루했다. [movie, today]

____

⠿ 1. 이 칼은 무디다. 날카로운 칼이 필요하다. 2. 똑똑한 학생들이 우둔한 학생들을 돕는다. 3. 그 영화는 매우 지루했다.

037 train [trein]

Step 01 해석연습

다음 문장을 train에 유의하여 해석해 보세요. (해석은 이 페이지의 하단부에 있음)

1. He got off the train at Suwon. ___________________________
2. There was a long train of cars on the road. ___________________________
3. They are training for Olympics. ___________________________

Step 02 뜻 알기

train에는 다음과 같은 여러 가지의 뜻이 있습니다.

❶ 열차, 기차 n a line of railroad cars

❷ (사람, 차 따위의 긴) 열, 줄 n a long line of moving people, animals, vehicles, etc

❸ 교육하다, 길들이다; 훈련하다 v to educate, instruct; to make obedient; to practice

> 한 걸음 더 **What an unlucky train of events!** 불행의 연속이구나!
> → (사건, 상황 따위의) 연속(=a series of connected events)
> **trainer** 훈련시키는 사람, 조련사 **training** 훈련, 연습 **a freight train** 화물열차 **a passenger train** 여객열차
> **an express train** 급행열차 **a through train** 직행열차 **by train** 열차로, 기차로 **in the train of** ～에 잇따라, ～의 결과로서

Step 03 연습문제

다음 문장의 train에 해당되는 뜻을 **Step 02** 의 ❶～❸에서 고르세요. (해답은 435쪽)

1. Travelling by train is very exciting. (   )
2. There was a long train of camels. (   )
3. Coaches train athletes for competition. (   )
4. We saw a long train of sightseers there. (   )
5. I will train my son to play the guitar. (   )
6. It is more comfortable to travel by train. (   )

Step 04 영작연습

다음 문장을 주어진 부분을 이용하여 영어로 옮기세요. (해답은 435쪽)

1. 기차로 여행하는 것이 보다 편리하다. [more convenient, travel]

____

2. 그들은 멀리서 낙타들의 긴 행렬을 보았다. [camels, in the distance]

____

3. 그는 자신의 개에게 토끼를 잡도록 훈련시켰다. [catch, rabbits]

____

∷ 1. 그는 수원에서 열차를 내렸다. 2. 길에는 차량들의 긴 줄이 있었다. 3. 그들은 올림픽을 위해 훈련 중이다.

038 **plant** [plænt / plɑːnt]

Step 01
해석연습

다음 문장을 plant에 유의하여 해석해 보세요. (해석은 이 페이지의 하단부에 있음)

1. Don't forget to water the plants. _______________________

2. He planted apple trees in the garden. _______________________

3. My uncle works for an automobile plant. _______________________

Step 02
뜻 알기

plant에는 다음과 같은 여러 가지의 뜻이 있습니다.

❶ 식물 **n** a living thing that grows in earth and has roots, stems and leaves

❷ (식물, 나무, 씨 등을) 심다 **v** to put plants, trees or seeds in the ground to grow

❸ 공장, 공장설비; 기계장치 **n** the building and equipment of a factory; industrial machinery

한 걸음 더 **Missionaries** <u>planted</u> **Christianity among the salvage.** 선교사들은 미개인들에게 기독교를 전파했다.
→ (학문, 사상 등을) 전파하다, 주입시키다(=introduce an idea, feelings, etc)
a water plant 수초, 수생식물 **a power plant** 발전소 **an automobile plant** 자동차공장 **a water-power plant** 수력발전소
a farming plant 농장 **plantation** 대규모 농장 **a chemical plant** 화학공장

Step 03
연습문제

다음 문장의 plant에 해당되는 뜻을 **Step 02** 의 ❶~❸에서 고르세요. (해답은 435쪽)

1. Humans and animals can't live without plants. (   )

2. We planted seeds in the field. (   )

3. There is a huge chemical plant in the factory. (   )

4. The farm has its own lighting plant. (   )

5. The park contains 3,000 different kinds of plants. (   )

6. He has planted vegetables in the garden. (   )

Step 04
영작연습

다음 문장을 주어진 부분을 이용하여 영어로 옮기세요. (해답은 435쪽)

1. 많은 식물들이 봄에 꽃을 피운다. [bloom, spring]

____

2. 그는 올 봄에 밀과 옥수수 작물을 심었다. [crops, wheat, corn]

____

3. 그들은 공장을 위한 새 설비에 투자할 예정이다. [invest, factory]

____

:: 1. 식물에 물을 주는 것을 잊지 마세요. 2. 그는 정원에 사과나무를 심었다. 3. 나의 삼촌은 자동차 공장에서 일을 하신다.

039 table [téibl]

Step 01
해석연습

다음 문장을 table에 유의하여 해석해 보세요. (해석은 이 페이지의 하단부에 있음)

1. There are some flowers on the table. _______________________________

2. That report has two tables showing the results of the examination.

____

Step 02
뜻 알기

table에는 다음과 같은 여러 가지의 뜻이 있습니다.

❶ 탁자, 테이블, 식탁 n a piece of furniture with a flat top and legs

❷ 표, 일람표, 목록 n a list; an orderly arrangement of facts, figures, information, etc

> 한 걸음 더 **table tennis** 탁구 **tablecloth** 식탁보 **a multiplication table** 곱셈구구표 **a table of contents** 책의 목차
> **table manners** 식사 예절 **timetable** 시간표, (행사 등의) 예정표 **at (the) table** 식사 중 **set[lay] the table** 식탁을 차리다

Step 03
연습문제

다음 문장의 table에 해당되는 뜻을 Step 02 의 ❶∼❷에서 고르세요. (해답은 435쪽)

1. The results of the experiments can be seen in table 3. (   )
2. She put some flowers on the table. (   )
3. Mary is cleaning the table now. (   )
4. He is looking at the table of contents of the book. (   )

Step 04
영작연습

다음 문장을 주어진 부분을 이용하여 영어로 옮기세요. (해답은 435쪽)

1. 어머니께서 저녁 식탁을 차리셨다. [set, dinner]

____

2. 이 책의 앞부분에 목차가 있다. [contents, at the front of]

____

:: 1. 테이블 위에 약간의 꽃이 있다. 2. 그 보고서에는 시험 성적을 보여 주는 두 개의 표가 있다.

040 square [skwɛər]

Step 01 해석연습

다음 문장을 square에 유의하여 해석해 보세요. (해석은 이 페이지의 하단부에 있음)

1. A square has four equal sides. _________________________

2. Many children are playing in the public square. _________________________

3. The square of 3 is 9. _________________________

4. It was a square game. _________________________

Step 02 뜻 알기

square에는 다음과 같은 여러 가지의 뜻이 있습니다.

❶ 정사각형; 정사각형 모양의 것 **n** a shape with four equal sides and four right angles; a piece of something in this shape
정사각형의 **a** having four equal sides and four right angles

❷ (도시의) 광장 **n** a broad open area in the middle of a town, with the buildings around it

❸ 제곱; 평방 **n** the result of multiplying a number by itself

❹ 공정한, 정직한 **a** fair or honest / 공정하게, 정직하게 **ad** fairly or honestly

▷ 한 걸음 더 **a square mirror** 네모진 거울 **a square deal** 공정한 거래, 공정한 처사 **fair and square** 공정하게, 정정당당하게

Step 03 연습문제

다음 문장의 square에 해당되는 뜻을 **Step 02** 의 ❶~❹에서 고르세요. (해답은 435쪽)

1. We were listening to the band playing in the square. (   )
2. I need a square piece of paper. (   )
3. The square of 4 is 16. (   )
4. There are several squares on the shirt. (   )
5. We played a square game yesterday. (   )
6. 9 is the square of 3. (   )
7. The public square was crowded with people. (   )
8. The two teams promised they would play square. (   )

Step 04 영작연습

다음 문장을 주어진 부분을 이용하여 영어로 옮기세요. (해답은 435쪽)

1. 이 상자의 옆면은 정사각형이다. [side, box]

____

2. 광장에 샌드위치 가게가 하나 있었다. [there, sandwich shop]

____

3. 36은 6의 제곱이다. [is, of]

____

4. 그것은 공정한 거래였다. [that, deal]

____

∷ 1. 정사각형은 4면이 똑같다. 2. 많은 아이들이 광장에서 놀고 있다. 3. 3의 제곱은 9이다. 4. 그것은 공정한 시합이었다.

A. 다음 뜻에 해당되는 단어를 보기에서 찾아 적으세요.

보기	dull	train	plant	table	square

01. ____________ a line of railroad cars
02. ____________ a living thing that grows in earth and has roots, stems and leaves
03. ____________ the building and equipment of a factory; industrial machinery
04. ____________ slow to learn or understand; not intelligent
05. ____________ a broad open area in the middle of a town, with the buildings around it
06. ____________ a list; an orderly arrangement of facts, figures, information, etc
07. ____________ a long line of moving people, animals, vehicles, etc
08. ____________ fair or honest; fairly or honestly
09. ____________ a piece of furniture with a flat top and legs
10. ____________ not sharp; blunt
11. ____________ a shape with four equal sides and four right angles; a piece of something in this shape
12. ____________ to educate, instruct; to make obedient; to practice
13. ____________ the result of multiplying a number by itself
14. ____________ not interesting or exciting; boring
15. ____________ to put plants, trees or seeds in the ground to grow

B. 다음 빈칸에 가장 알맞은 단어를 보기에서 찾아 적으세요.

보기	dull	train	plant	table	square

01. She will get off the (   ) at the next station.
02. My father worked in an automobile (   ).
03. There is a market in the (   ) every Wednesday.
04. That lecture was very (   ).
05. Put all the plates on the (   ).
06. I saw a (   ) of horses in the distance.
07. The girl has a tiny (   ) of mirror.
08. The knife is too (   ) to cut meat.
09. The (   ) of 5 is 25.
10. She waters the tomato (   ) every other day.
11. She is (   ); it takes her a long time to learn new things.
12. The boy wants to learn a multiplication (   ).
13. He will (   ) his dog to sit and stay.
14. If you ask him for the truth, he will be (   ) with you.
15. I will (   ) some trees in my garden.

다음 문장을 굵게 처리된 단어에 유의하여 해석해 보세요.

01. Forget **dull** lessons and the traditional methods of learning. [1994년–1차 48번]

➡ ________________________________

02. Through the **train** window, I could see crops ripening in the fields and trees turning red and yellow. [2003년–홀수형 26번]

➡ ________________________________

03. Have you considered taking night classes to **train** for another kind of job? [2002년–홀수형 28번]

➡ ________________________________

04. Researchers said that playing with a computer will not increase a preschooler's reading scores or **train** him or her in computer science. [1997년–홀수형 27번]

➡ ________________________________

05. The rainforests are full of **plants** and animals that need each other and help each other. [2004년–홀수형 34번]

➡ ________________________________

06. I know. They need to **plant** more trees on the street. [2008년–홀수형 15번]

➡ ________________________________

07. A small number of people have recognized the value of wild **plants** in Korea. [2004년–홀수형 35번]

➡ ________________________________

08. Page numbers became a possibility, as did indexes; **tables** of contents became workable references. [2008년–홀수형 25번]

➡ ________________________________

09. In the center of the room was a **table** with two old silver candlesticks and two glasses of red wine. [2005년–홀수형 38번]

➡ ________________________________

10. And we realize that our youngsters are ignorant of Latin, put Mussolini in the same category as Dostoevski, and cannot recite the Periodic **Table** by heart. [1998년–홀수형 32번]

➡ ________________________________

11. In India, for example, some coins have **square** sides. [1996년–홀수형 37번]

➡ ________________________________

12. Kathmandu sits almost in the middle of a basin, forming a **square** about 5km north-south and 5km east-west. [2005년–홀수형 20번]

➡ ________________________________

13. And at night there is the beat of the big drums and the military band as the whole town dances in the great open **square** of the Plaza. [2009년–홀수형 43번]

➡ ________________________________

14. M: Wow! They have a good selection. What kind of table should we get?
    W: I think a **square** one is better than a round one. [2010년–홀수형 1번]

➡ ________________________________

 **DAY 05**

Public before private and country before family.
개인보다는 공공을, 가정보다는 국가를 먼저 생각하라.

 NOTE

041 **country** [kʌ́ntri]

Group 09

Step 01 해석연습

다음 문장을 country에 유의하여 해석해 보세요. (해석은 이 페이지의 하단부에 있음)

1. We will fight for our country. ___________________________

2. I like to live in the country better than in the city. ___________________________

3. All the country is opposed to war. ___________________________

Step 02 뜻 알기

country에는 다음과 같은 여러 가지의 뜻이 있습니다.

❶ 나라; 국토; 조국 **n** a nation; the land occupied by a nation; the land of a person's birth or citizenship

❷ 시골, 전원, 교외 **n** a rural area outside cities and towns

❸ 국민 **n** the people of a nation

> 한 걸음 더 **This region is good <u>country</u> for sheep.** 이 지역은 양치기에 알맞은 지역이다.
> → (특정의) 지역, 지방, 땅(=area of land; a region; a district)
> **countryman** ① 시골사람 ② 동포, 동향인 **countryside** 시골, 전원, 지방 **a foreign country** 외국

Step 03 연습문제

다음 문장의 country에 해당되는 뜻을 **Step 02** 의 ❶~❸에서 고르세요. (해답은 436쪽)

1. There are many countries in the world. (   )

2. Does all the country want war? (   )

3. He has always wanted to live in the country. (   )

4. We drove to the country to relax. (   )

5. Many people came from foreign countries. (   )

6. The president has the strong support of the country. (   )

Step 04 영작연습

다음 문장을 주어진 부분을 이용하여 영어로 옮기세요. (해답은 436쪽)

1. 캐나다는 프랑스보다 큰 나라다. [larger, than]

____

2. 의사는 그녀에게 시골에서 몇 달 지내라고 충고했다. [advised, spend, several]

____

3. 새 대통령은 국민의 80퍼센트 이상의 지지를 받고 있다. [president, support]

____

⁚⁚ 1. 우리는 조국을 위해 싸울 것이다. 2. 나는 도시보다 시골에서 사는 것을 더 좋아한다. 3. 온 국민이 전쟁을 반대하고 있다.

042 **nail** [neil]

Step 01 해석연습

다음 문장을 nail에 유의하여 해석해 보세요. (해석은 이 페이지의 하단부에 있음)

1. The cat's nails are sharp. _______________________________________

2. I hammered a nail into the board. _______________________________

3. He will nail the picture on the wall. _______________________________

Step 02 뜻 알기

nail에는 다음과 같은 여러 가지의 뜻이 있습니다.

❶ 손톱, 발톱 **n** the hard smooth layer on the end of a finger or a toe

❷ 못 **n** a thin pointed piece of metal used to fasten pieces of wood, etc together

❸ ~을 못으로 박다, 고정시키다 **v** to fasten something else with a nail or nails

> 한 걸음 더 **nail clippers** 손톱깎이(=nail scissors) **nail file** 손톱 다듬는 줄 **hit the nail on the head** 바로 맞히다. 정곡을 찌르다 **tooth and nail** 필사적으로, 있는 힘을 다하여

Step 03 연습문제

다음 문장의 nail에 해당되는 뜻을 **Step 02** 의 ❶~❸에서 고르세요. (해답은 436쪽)

1. The carpenter is nailing something to the wall. (   )
2. Don't bite your nails. (   )
3. He needs some nails and a hammer. (   )
4. She wants to nail the picture to the wall. (   )
5. She caught her skirt on a nail. (   )
6. She scratched his face with her nail. (   )

Step 04 영작연습

다음 문장을 주어진 부분을 이용하여 영어로 옮기세요. (해답은 436쪽)

1. 그 꼬마 소년은 자신의 손톱을 깨무는 나쁜 버릇이 있었다. [habit, biting]

____

2. 그는 벽에 몇 개의 그림을 걸기 위해 망치와 몇 개의 못이 필요하다. [hammer, hang]

____

3. 그 군인은 게시문을 벽에 못을 박아 붙였다. [solder, notice]

____

∷ 1. 고양이의 발톱은 날카롭다. 2. 나는 판자에 못을 하나 박았다. 3. 그는 그 그림을 벽에 못 박을 것이다.

043 ask [æsk / ɑːsk]

Step 01
해석연습

다음 문장을 ask에 유의하여 해석해 보세요. (해석은 이 페이지의 하단부에 있음)

1. He asked me a question. _______________________

2. The teacher asked us to follow her example. _______________________

3. He asked her to dinner. _______________________

Step 02
뜻 알기

ask에는 다음과 같은 여러 가지의 뜻이 있습니다.

❶ 질문하다 Ⅴ to put a question; to inquire

❷ 부탁하다, 요청하다 Ⅴ to make a request for help, advice, information, etc; to beg

❸ 초대하다 Ⅴ to invite

▷ 한 걸음 더 **ask about** ~에 관하여 묻다 **ask after** 안부를 묻다 **ask for** ~를 요청하다

Step 03
연습문제

다음 문장의 ask에 해당되는 뜻을 Step 02 **의 ❶~❸에서 고르세요.** (해답은 436쪽)

1. He asked me where I came from? (   )

2. He asked her to his house for dinner. (   )

3. Please ask him when he will be back. (   )

4. She asked us not to make a noise. (   )

5. We asked her to the party. (   )

6. May I ask you a favor? (   )

Step 04
영작연습

다음 문장을 주어진 부분을 이용하여 영어로 옮기세요. (해답은 436쪽)

1. 나는 그에게 어디 있었는지를 물어보았다. [where, had been]

____

2. 도서관원은 우리들에게 도서관에서 떠들지 말라고 부탁했다. [librarian, noise]

____

3. 그녀는 자신의 생일파티에 몇 명의 친구를 초대할 예정이다. [several, party]

____

∷ 1. 그는 나에게 질문을 했다. 2. 선생님께서는 우리들에게 그녀를 본받으라고 요구하셨다. 3. 그는 그녀를 저녁식사에 초대했다.

044 left [left]

Step 01
해석연습

다음 문장을 left에 유의하여 해석해 보세요. (해석은 이 페이지의 하단부에 있음)

1. She left her hometown yesterday. _______________________

2. Raise your left hand. _______________________

Step 02
뜻 알기

left에는 다음과 같은 여러 가지의 뜻이 있습니다.

❶ 동사 leave의 과거 및 과거분사형 [v] the past tense and past participle of the verb "leave"

❷ 왼쪽의 [a] on or by the side of the body containing the heart
왼쪽으로 [ad] to or toward the left
왼쪽 [n] the left side, part, etc

> 한 걸음 더 **leave** [liːv] - **left** [left] - **left** [left]
> **left-handed** 왼손잡이의 **leftover** 나머지, 남은 것, 남은 음식

Step 03
연습문제

다음 문장의 left에 해당되는 뜻을 Step 02 의 ❶～❷에서 고르세요. (해답은 436쪽)

1. She left the room quietly. (   )
2. They drove on the left side of the road in Australia. (   )
3. She wears an engagement ring on her left hand. (   )
4. Somebody left an umbrella behind. (   )

Step 04
영작연습

다음 문장을 주어진 부분을 이용하여 영어로 옮기세요. (해답은 436쪽)

1. 나는 버스에 가방을 놓고 내렸다. [bag, bus]

____

2. 첫 번째 신호등에서 왼쪽으로 도시오. [turn, traffic light]

____

:: 1. 그녀는 어제 자신의 고향을 떠났다. 2. 왼손을 들어라.

045 die [dai]

Step 01
해석연습

다음 문장을 die에 유의하여 해석해 보세요. (해석은 이 페이지의 하단부에 있음)

1. My grandfather died in 1979. _______________________
2. She is dying for a cup of coffee. _______________________
3. The die is cast. _______________________
4. A die is used to make coins. _______________________

Step 02
뜻 알기

die에는 다음과 같은 여러 가지의 뜻이 있습니다.

❶ 죽다 **n** to stop living and become dead

❷ 몹시 하고 싶어 하다, 열망하다 **v** to have a strong desire (for something or to do something)

❸ 주사위 (주로 복수형으로 사용되며 복수형은 dice) **n** a small cube marked with figures from one to six, used in games of chance

❹ 주조용 틀, 형, 금형 **n** a metal block used to press or cut something into a particular shape

▷ 한 걸음 더 **dying** ① 죽어 가는 ② 몹시 ~하고 싶어 하는 **dead** 죽은 **death** 죽음

Step 03
연습문제

다음 문장의 die에 해당되는 뜻을 **Step 02** 의 ❶~❹에서 고르세요. (해답은 436쪽)

1. With one roll of the dice, he won $500. (   )
2. I used this die to make model cars. (   )
3. My grandmother died from a heart attack. (   )
4. I'm dying for a cup of coffee. (   )
5. Thomas Edison died in 1931. (   )
6. He lost his fortune at dice. (   )
7. This die was used to make coins. (   )
8. I'm dying to meet her again. (   )

Step 04
영작연습

다음 문장을 주어진 부분을 이용하여 영어로 옮기세요. (해답은 436쪽)

1. 많은 동물들이 눈 속에서 굶어 죽었다. [animals, starvation]

   ____

2. 그는 그녀의 비밀을 알고 싶어 안달이 났다. [know, secret]

   ____

3. 네가 주사위를 던질 차례다. [turn, throw]

   ____

4. 그들은 이 금형을 모형 열차를 만드는 데 사용할 것이다. [use, model trains]

   ____

:: 1. 나의 할아버지는 1979년에 돌아가셨다. 2. 그녀는 커피 한 잔을 마시고 싶어 죽을 지경이다. 3. 주사위는 던져졌다. 이미 운명은 결정되었다.
4. 금속 주형은 동전을 찍어 내는 데 사용된다.

A. 다음 뜻에 해당되는 단어를 보기에서 찾아 적으세요.

> **보기** country   nail   ask   left   die

01. ______________ to make a request for help, advice, information, etc; to beg
02. ______________ a rural area outside cities and towns
03. ______________ on or by the side the body containing the heart
04. ______________ a nation; the land occupied by a nation; the land of a person's birth or citizenship
05. ______________ to have a strong desire (for something or to do something)
06. ______________ to fasten something else with a nail or nails
07. ______________ a small cube marked with figures from one to six, used in games of chance
08. ______________ to invite
09. ______________ the hard smooth layer on the end of a finger or a toe
10. ______________ to stop living and become dead
11. ______________ the people of a nation
12. ______________ the past tense and past participle of the verb "leave"
13. ______________ a thin pointed piece of metal used to fasten pieces of wood, etc together
14. ______________ a metal block used to press or cut something into a particular shape
15. ______________ to put a question; to inquire

B. 다음 빈칸에 가장 알맞은 단어를 보기에서 찾아 적으세요.

> **보기** country   nail   ask   left   die (dice / dying)

01. She will (   ) you several questions.
02. He hammered a (   ) into the wall.
03. They used this (   ) to make model planes.
04. The dog bit my son in the (   ) leg.
05. The man will (   ) a notice on the door.
06. Brazil is a larger (   ) than Spain.
07. I would rather (   ) than surrender.
08. Please (   ) him to mail this letter tomorrow.
09. Tony (   ) school to help his father.
10. (   )-biting is a negative behavior.
11. I'm (   ) for a glass of beer.
12. The air is fresh in the (   ).
13. She throw the (   ) and moved her counter across the board.
14. He wishes to (   ) her to dinner.
15. All the (   ) wants peace.

해답은 436쪽

다음 문장을 굵게 처리된 단어에 유의하여 해석해 보세요.

01. The United States remains an underdeveloped **country** when it comes to language skills. [2006년–홀수형 25번]

➡ ______________________

02. A father took his son to the **country** to show him how poor people can be. [2003년–홀수형 37번]

➡ ______________________

03. Three times a month it brought the readers news about the **country** and the rest of the world. [2003년–홀수형 35번]

➡ ______________________

04. The next step is to put the different parts together with glue and **nails**. [2000년–홀수형 43번]

➡ ______________________

05. At the end of the round of introductions, the students were **asked** to write down the names of as many other students as they could remember. [2011년–홀수형 41번]

➡ ______________________

06. He showed them three line segments, and **asked** each one in turn which line was the longest. [2011년–홀수형 27번]

➡ ______________________

07. Then at the stage door the girl **asked** the violinist for his autograph. [1998년–홀수형 30번]

➡ ______________________

08. Many of the students threw papers on the floor or **left** them on the desks. [1995년–홀수형 43번]

➡ ______________________

09. To his **left** were seated the scholars who were to take part in the ceremony of the evening. [1995년–홀수형 37번]

➡ ______________________

10. W: I took a bus from Busan and I **left** my cell phone on the bus.
M: Okay. What time did your bus depart from Busan?
W: My bus **left** at four-twenty p.m.
[2011년–홀수형 4번]

➡ ______________________

11. One male musician suffered a stroke in his **left** brain, the area for speech. [1994년–2차 26번]

➡ ______________________

12. We do not, most of us, choose to **die**. But we do choose how we shall live. [1995년–홀수형 47번]

➡ ______________________

13. Ever since the coming of television, there has been a rumor that the novel is **dying**, if not already dead. [2005년–홀수형 30번]

➡ ______________________

14. Suddenly the engine **died**, and for mysterious reasons, the boat began to sink. [2007년–홀수형 46~48번]

➡ ______________________

046 pen [pen]

Step 01 해석연습

다음 문장을 pen에 유의하여 해석해 보세요. (해석은 이 페이지의 하단부에 있음)

1. He wrote the letter with a pen. _______________________________

2. The pigs live in a pen. _______________________________

Step 02 뜻 알기

pen에는 다음과 같은 여러 가지의 뜻이 있습니다.

❶ 펜 n an instrument used for writing in ink

❷ (가축용) 우리 n an enclosure used for keeping farm animals in

> 한 걸음 더 **I penned a few lines to my father today.** 오늘 부친께 짧은 편지를 썼다.
> → (펜으로) ~을 쓰다, (작품 등을) 저술하다(=to write)
> **a fountain pen** 만년필 **a ball-point pen** 볼펜 **a pen pal** 편지 친구, 펜팔 **pen name** 필명
> **a play pen for a baby** (우리 모양의 울로 둘러싸인) 유아용 놀이 울

Step 03 연습문제

다음 문장의 pen에 해당되는 뜻을 Step 02 의 ❶~❷에서 고르세요. (해답은 436쪽)

1. He will build a pen for his pigs. (   )

2. I forgot to bring a pen. Will you lend me one? (   )

3. The sheep live in a pen. (   )

4. She gave me a nice fountain pen. (   )

Step 04 영작연습

다음 문장을 주어진 부분을 이용하여 영어로 옮기세요. (해답은 436쪽)

1. 너의 이름과 주소를 펜과 잉크로 써라. [write, address]

____

2. 농부는 자신의 양을 위한 우리를 만들었다. [built, sheep]

____

1. 그는 편지를 펜으로 썼다. 2. 돼지들은 우리에 산다.

047 long [lɔːŋ / lɔŋ]

Step 01
해석연습

다음 문장을 long에 유의하여 해석해 보세요. (해석은 이 페이지의 하단부에 있음)

1. She has beautiful long hair. _______________________
2. How long have you lived in Seoul? _______________________
3. We long for peace and liberty. _______________________

Step 02
뜻 알기

long에는 다음과 같은 여러 가지의 뜻이 있습니다.

❶ (시간, 길이가) 긴; ~길이의　**a** great in distance or time from end to end; having a certain length

❷ 오랫동안　**ad** for a long time

❸ 열망하다, 간절히 바라다　**v** to wish very much; to desire earnestly

> 한 걸음 더 **longing** 열망, 갈망 **long-term** 장기간의, 지속적인 **length** 길이
> **long for** + (동)명사 = **long to** + V ~을[~하기를] 갈망하다 **as long as** ~하는 동안, ~하는 한
> **before long** 머지않아(=soon) **no longer** 더 이상 ~ 아니다(=not ~ any longer) **in the long run** 결국에는

Step 03
연습문제

다음 문장의 long에 해당되는 뜻을 **Step 02** 의 ❶~❸에서 고르세요. (해답은 437쪽)

1. She has really long hair. (　　)
2. We longed for her to say something. (　　)
3. I can't stay here long. (　　)
4. He longed to meet his mother. (　　)
5. Our happy days did not last long. (　　)
6. It's a long way from Hong Kong to Sydney. (　　)

Step 04
영작연습

다음 문장을 주어진 부분을 이용하여 영어로 옮기세요. (해답은 437쪽)

1. 그 테이블은 약 6피트 길이다. [about, feet]

____

2. 누구나 오래 살고 싶어 한다. [everybody, live]

____

3. 아이들은 여름방학을 몹시 기다리고 있다. [children, vacation]

____

:: 1. 그녀는 아름다운 긴 머리를 가지고 있다. 2. 당신은 얼마나 오랫동안 서울에서 사셨습니까? 3. 우리는 평화와 자유를 열망한다.

048 about [əbáut]

Step 01
해석연습

다음 문장을 about에 유의하여 해석해 보세요. (해석은 이 페이지의 하단부에 있음)

1. Jane told me about her family. _______________________________

2. The girl walked about the park. _______________________________

3. I will come back about three o'clock. _______________________________

Step 02
뜻 알기

about에는 다음과 같은 여러 가지의 뜻이 있습니다.

❶ ~에 관하여　[prep] concerning; regarding; in connection with

❷ ~의 여기저기; ~의 둘레에; ~의 근처에　[ad] [prep] here and there; (all) around; somewhere near

❸ 약, 거의, ~정도　[ad] [prep] near; nearly, almost

> 한 걸음 더 **He is <u>about</u> to leave the office.** 그는 사무실을 막 떠나려고 한다.
> → be about to의 형식으로 쓰여 '막 ~하려고 하다'(=be ready to)
> **about and about** 비슷비슷하여, 거의 같아

Step 03
연습문제

다음 문장의 about에 해당되는 뜻을 **Step 02** 의 ❶~❸에서 고르세요. (해답은 437쪽)

1. He worries about his health. (　　)

2. It's about three o'clock. (　　)

3. He likes watching movies about wild animals. (　　)

4. She walked about the park. (　　)

5. I looked about but I couldn't see anything. (　　)

6. I study about three hours every day. (　　)

Step 04
영작연습

다음 문장을 주어진 부분을 이용하여 영어로 옮기세요. (해답은 437쪽)

1. 그는 동물에 관한 책을 읽는 것을 좋아한다. [books, animals]

____

2. 정원 주위에 높은 담이 있다. [high wall, garden]

____

3. 약 30명 정도의 사람들이 회의에 참석했다. [people, attended]

____

:: 1. Jane은 나에게 자신의 가족에 대해 말했다. 2. 그 소녀는 공원을 여기저기 산책했다. 3. 나는 약 3시쯤 돌아올 것이다.

049 **stamp** [stæmp]

Step 01
해석연습

다음 문장을 stamp에 유의하여 해석해 보세요. (해석은 이 페이지의 하단부에 있음)

1. Jae-ho bought a stamp at the post office. _______________________

2. Mary always uses a date stamp when she files letters. _______________________

3. Donkeys stamped their feet on the ground. _______________________

Step 02
뜻 알기

stamp에는 다음과 같은 여러 가지의 뜻이 있습니다.

❶ 우표 n a piece of printed paper stuck on letters

❷ 도장 n a tool for pressing or printing a mark or pattern onto a surface
  도장을 찍다, 무늬를 찍다 v to print (or mark) on paper, cloth or other surface

❸ ~을 짓밟다, 발을 구르다 v to hit the ground with a foot

> 한 걸음 더 **stamp tax** 인지세 **revenue stamp** 수입 인지 → 인지(印紙)
> **He bears the stamp of genius.** 그는 천재의 특징[특질]을 지니고 있다. → 특징, 특질

Step 03
연습문제

다음 문장의 stamp에 해당되는 뜻을 **Step 02** 의 ❶~❸에서 고르세요. (해답은 437쪽)

1. He stamped his name on the envelop. (   )

2. The child stamps his foot when he is hungry. (   )

3. The lawyer stamped the paper to show it was legal. (   )

4. I need to buy some stamps at the post office. (   )

5. Carolyn likes to stamp her feet. (   )

6. The stamp is on a letter. (   )

Step 04
영작연습

다음 문장을 주어진 부분을 이용하여 영어로 옮기세요. (해답은 437쪽)

1. 우표 수집은 그의 취미다. [collecting, hobby]

____

2. 그녀는 계산서에 도장을 찍을 것이다. [will, bill]

____

3. Mi-ran은 발을 구르는 것을 좋아한다. [likes, feet]

____

:: 1. Jae-ho는 우체국에서 우표를 샀다. 2. Mary는 편지를 철해 둘 때 항상 날짜도장을 사용한다. 3. 당나귀들이 바닥에 그들의 발을 굴렀다.

76

050 case [keis]

Step 01 해석연습

다음 문장을 case에 유의하여 해석해 보세요. (해석은 이 페이지의 하단부에 있음)

1. I usually buy beer by the case. ________________________

2. In case of fire, press this button immediately. ________________________

3. The judge in this case seems to be fair. ________________________

4. "Him" is the object case of "He." ________________________

Step 02 뜻 알기

case에는 다음과 같은 여러 가지의 뜻이 있습니다.

❶ 상자, 용기, 케이스 [n] a protective cover for other things; box; container

❷ 사례, 경우, 상황 [n] an instance or example of the occurrence of something; a particular situation or set of circumstances

❸ 소송, 소송사건 [n] a matter for a law court to decide; a suit

❹ (문법) 격(格) [n] the form of a word showing its relationship with other words in a sentence

▷ 한 걸음 더 **a pencil case** 필통 **a packing case** 포장용 상자 **in case of** ~의 경우에 **just in case** 만일을 위해서

Step 03 연습문제

다음 문장의 case에 해당되는 뜻을 Step 02 의 ❶~❹에서 고르세요. (해답은 437쪽)

1. If you do so, you will make your case worse. (   )

2. I need a case for books. (   )

3. The first person has three cases, "I", "my" and "me." (   )

4. The case is still pending in court. (   )

5. She bought a case of canned beans. (   )

6. When will the case come before the Court? (   )

7. "Them" is the object case of "They." (   )

8. In case of fire, ring the alarm bell. (   )

Step 04 영작연습

다음 문장을 주어진 부분을 이용하여 영어로 옮기세요. (해답은 437쪽)

1. 그는 지난달 위스키 여섯 상자를 주문했다. [ordered, whiskey]

____

2. 나는 아프리카의 굶어 죽는 어린이들의 애처로운 상황을 들었다. [sad, starving]

____

3. 그는 소송에 패하고 손해를 배상해야 했다. [lost, damages]

____

4. "My"는 "I"의 소유격이다. [possessive, of]

____

:: 1. 나는 대개 맥주를 상자로 산다. 2. 화재의 경우 이 단추를 즉시 눌러라. 3. 이 소송의 판사는 공정해 보인다. 4. Him은 He의 목적격이다.

A. 다음 뜻에 해당되는 단어를 보기에서 찾아 적으세요.

| 보기 | pen | long | about | stamp | case |

01. ______________ to wish very much; to desire earnestly
02. ______________ an instrument used for writing in ink
03. ______________ for a long time
04. ______________ to hit the ground with a foot
05. ______________ the form of a word showing its relationship with other words in a sentence
06. ______________ concerning; regarding; in connection with
07. ______________ near; nearly, almost
08. ______________ a protective cover for other things; box; container
09. ______________ to print (or mark) on paper, cloth or other surface
10. ______________ great in distance or time from end to end; having a certain length
11. ______________ an instance or example of the occurrence of something; a particular situation or set of circumstances
12. ______________ a piece of printed paper stuck on letters
13. ______________ an enclosure used for keeping farm animals in
14. ______________ here and there; to and fro; (all) around; somewhere near
15. ______________ a matter for a law court to decide; a suit

B. 다음 빈칸에 가장 알맞은 단어를 보기에서 찾아 적으세요.

| 보기 | pen | long | about | stamp | case |

01. I need a (   ) to sign my check.
02. She is reading a book (   ) gardening.
03. This war is expected to last (   ).
04. I left my pencil (   ) in the classroom.
05. I put a (   ) on the letter.
06. This rule is only applicable to this (   ).
07. He will (   ) his seal on the papers.
08. She lives (   ) ten miles away.
09. They lost their (   ) in the High Court.
10. Monkeys (   ) their feet on the ground.
11. "Me" is the object (   ) of "I."
12. The highway is (   ) and straight.
13. He drove a herd of cows into the (   ).
14. I (   ) to see her again.
15. There is a fence (   ) the garden.

해답은 437쪽

다음 문장을 굵게 처리된 단어에 유의하여 해석해 보세요.

01. Richard Wagner found inspiration on this site in 1880, **penning** a part of Parsifal during a stay here. [2008년-홀수형 36번]

➡ ___________________________________

02. How **long** are you going to stay in this country? [2002년-홀수형 14번]

➡ ___________________________________

03. We seem to have created a society so harsh and complex that it makes us feel helpless and insecure and makes us **long** for improvement. [1995년-홀수형 48번]

➡ ___________________________________

04. There is a **long** back flap for the back of the neck, and ear flaps on both sides cover the ears. [2007년-홀수형 31번]

➡ ___________________________________

05. Suddenly, I saw a connection between those bumpy vegetables on our table and the quotation on the wall; I found a way to satisfy my **longing** for new friends. [2010년-홀수형 46-48번]

➡ ___________________________________

06. Chopsticks were developed **about** 5,000 years ago in China. [2002년-홀수형 32번]

➡ ___________________________________

07. They endure day after day, and just when they're **about** to make it, decide they can't take any more. [2006년-홀수형 21번]

➡ ___________________________________

08. Thanks to satellites, we can find out instantly **about** events that occur on the other side of the world. [2005년-홀수형 45-46번]

➡ ___________________________________

09. The back was divided to contain room enough for a message, an address, and a **stamp**. [2002년-홀수형 18번]

➡ ___________________________________

10. W: Give me ten **stamps** and two postcards, please.
M: That'll be seven fifty. [1999년-홀수형 12번]

➡ ___________________________________

11. Beneath the **stamped** imprint was a notation from the bank in ink. [1994년-1차 10번]

➡ ___________________________________

12. In that **case**, you must figure out what the sale price is. [2002년-홀수형 44번]

➡ ___________________________________

13. Rarer **cases** involve people selling paintings that were actually painted by famous painters. [2006년-홀수형 38번]

➡ ___________________________________

14. Just in **case**, I'll leave my phone number. It's 345-7575. Thank you. [2000년-홀수형 4번]

➡ ___________________________________

>>> DAY 06

Fear is stronger than arms.
공포는 무기보다 훨씬 강하다.

051 please [pliːz]

Step 01
해석연습

다음 문장을 please에 유의하여 해석해 보세요. (해석은 이 페이지의 하단부에 있음)

1. The news pleased her very much. ________________________

2. Take as much as you please. ________________________

3. Would you please open the window? ________________________

Step 02
뜻 알기

please에는 다음과 같은 여러 가지의 뜻이 있습니다.

❶ ~을 기쁘게 하다, 만족시키다　v to make someone happy or satisfied; to satisfy

❷ 좋아하다, ~을 바라다　v to want; to like; to desire

❸ 부디, 제발　ad a word added to an order or request in order to be polite

> 한 걸음 더 **pleasure** 기쁨, 즐거움 **pleased** 기쁜, 만족스러운 **pleasing** 즐거운, 기분 좋은
> **be pleased to** ~ 기꺼이 ~하다, ~하여 기쁘다 **be pleased with** ~에 만족하다, ~을 기뻐하다

Step 03
연습문제

다음 문장의 please에 해당되는 뜻을 　Step 02　의 ❶~❸에서 고르세요. (해답은 437쪽)

1. She will come here when she pleases. (　　)

2. I hope these flowers will please her. (　　)

3. Please sit down and take off your coat. (　　)

4. Will you please open the window? (　　)

5. We are very pleased to see you here. (　　)

6. You may go when you please. (　　)

Step 04
영작연습

다음 문장을 주어진 부분을 이용하여 영어로 옮기세요. (해답은 437쪽)

1. 모든 사람을 만족시키는 것은 어렵다. [difficult, everybody]

____

2. 나는 내가 좋을 대로 하겠다. [do, as]

____

3. 부디 그 편지 부칠 것을 잊지 말아 주십시오. [forget, mail]

____

:: 1. 그 소식은 그녀를 기쁘게 하였다. 2. 네가 원하는 만큼 가져가라. 3. 창문 좀 열어 주시겠습니까?

052 **grow** [grou]

Step 01
해석연습

다음 문장을 grow에 유의하여 해석해 보세요. (해석은 이 페이지의 하단부에 있음)

1. The girl will grow taller this year. ______________________________

2. The class will grow to 25 students. ______________________________

3. I will grow corn this summer. ______________________________

Step 02
뜻 알기

grow에는 다음과 같은 여러 가지의 뜻이 있습니다.

❶ 자라다, 성장하다　Ⅴ to live and become bigger; to mature

❷ (차츰) ~하게 되다, 커지다, 늘어나다　Ⅴ to increase in amount, quality, degree, etc

❸ 기르다, 재배하다　Ⅴ to plant and care for; to raise; to cultivate

> 한 걸음 더 **grow**[grou] - **grew**[gru:] - **grown**[groun]
> **grown-up** 성인(=adults) **growth** 성장, 성숙

Step 03
연습문제

다음 문장의 grow에 해당되는 뜻을 **Step 02** 의 ❶~❸에서 고르세요. (해답은 437쪽)

1. His business is growing by leaps and bounds. (　　)
2. I like to grow flowers. (　　)
3. The storm grew more and more severe. (　　)
4. He grows one inch every year. (　　)
5. Most Korean farmers grow rice. (　　)
6. Anything can grow in this fertile ground. (　　)

Step 04
영작연습

다음 문장을 주어진 부분을 이용하여 영어로 옮기세요. (해답은 437쪽)

1. 나는 매년 1인치 자란다. [inch, every year]

____

2. 그 작은 가게는 커져서 큰 회사가 되었다. [shop, firm]

____

3. Ye-ri는 정원에 장미를 기르는 것을 좋아한다. [roses, garden]

____

:: 1. 그 소녀는 올해에 크게 자랄 것이다. 2. 그 학급은 25명의 학생까지 늘어날 것이다. 3. 나는 올해에 옥수수를 재배할 것이다.

053 club [klʌb]

Step 01 해석연습 다음 문장을 club에 유의하여 해석해 보세요. (해석은 이 페이지의 하단부에 있음)

1. The policeman hit the robber with a club. _______________________________
2. Our club have a meeting every two months. _______________________________
3. I bought a new golf club. _______________________________

Step 02 뜻 알기 club에는 다음과 같은 여러 가지의 뜻이 있습니다.

❶ 곤봉, 경찰봉 n a heavy stick with one thick end

❷ (운동, 사교 따위의) 클럽, 동호회 n a special group of people who share a particular interest or enjoy similar activities

❸ (골프의) 클럽[골프채], (하키의) 스틱 n a stick for playing golf or hockey

한 걸음 더 **They _clubbed_ him with their rifles.** 그들은 그를 그들의 총으로 때렸다.
→ ~을 ~로 때리다
We _clubbed_ together to buy her a present. 우리는 그녀에게 선물을 사 주기 위해 돈을 분담했다.
→ 지출 따위를 분담하다, 서로 내놓다
club house 클럽회관, 클럽회원 집회소

Step 03 연습문제 다음 문장의 club에 해당되는 뜻을 Step 02 의 ❶~❸에서 고르세요. (해답은 437쪽)

1. Our club meets on Tuesday. (   )
2. The heavy club can hurt people. (   )
3. Tony hit the golf ball with his club. (   )
4. Don't beat the dog with a club. (   )
5. Mary belongs to a book club. (   )
6. He left his golf club in the lobby. (   )

Step 04 영작연습 다음 문장을 주어진 부분을 이용하여 영어로 옮기세요. (해답은 437쪽)

1. 곤봉은 나무로 만들어져 있다. [is made of]

____

2. 우리 동호회는 금요일에 만난다. [meets, Friday]

____

3. Jim은 나의 골프채로 골프공을 쳤다. [hit, golf ball]

____

:: 1. 경찰관이 강도를 곤봉으로 때렸다. 2. 우리 동호회는 두 달에 한 번씩 모임을 갖는다. 3. 나는 새 골프채를 샀다.

054 bank [bæŋk]

Step 01
해석연습

다음 문장을 bank에 유의하여 해석해 보세요. (해석은 이 페이지의 하단부에 있음)

1. The bank is open on Saturday. ___________________________
2. Young-ho banks his wages every week. ___________________________
3. Several fishermen sat on the bank. ___________________________

Step 02
뜻 알기

bank에는 다음과 같은 여러 가지의 뜻이 있습니다.

❶ 은행 **n** an office for receiving, lending, exchanging, and issuing money

❷ 은행에 예금하다 **v** to put money in a bank

❸ 강둑, 둑 **n** the land at the edge of a river, or lake

> 한 걸음 더 **bank account** 예금계좌 **bankbook** 예금통장, 은행통장 **a blood bank** 혈액은행
> **bankrupt** ⓐ 파산한 ⓝ 파산자 **bankruptcy** 파산(상태) * He has been declared bankruptcy. 그는 파산 선고를 받았다.

Step 03
연습문제

다음 문장의 bank에 해당되는 뜻을 Step 02 의 ❶~❸에서 고르세요. (해답은 437쪽)

1. Miss Evans works in a bank. (　　)
2. They took a walk along the bank. (　　)
3. I will bank some money today. (　　)
4. The river overflowed its banks. (　　)
5. His savings in the bank now count up to $50,000. (　　)
6. He wants to bank his check. (　　)

Step 04
영작연습

다음 문장을 주어진 부분을 이용하여 영어로 옮기세요. (해답은 437쪽)

1. 나는 오늘 은행에 가야 한다. [have to, today]

____

2. 그는 매달 100달러를 예금한다. [dollars, every month]

____

3. 그는 강둑을 따라 걸었다. [walked, river]

____

∷ 1.그 은행은 토요일에 연다. 2. 영호는 매주 그의 급료를 은행에 예금한다. 3. 몇 명의 낚시꾼들이 (강)둑에 앉아 있었다.

 **055 cup** [kʌp]

Step 01
해석연습

다음 문장을 cup에 유의하여 해석해 보세요. (해석은 이 페이지의 하단부에 있음)

1. The winner got a large silver cup. ____________________

2. She drank milk from a cup. ____________________

3. The recipe called for a cup of flour. ____________________

Step 02
뜻 알기

cup에는 다음과 같은 여러 가지의 뜻이 있습니다.

❶ 우승컵 ⓝ a large silver or gold vessel given to the winner

❷ 찻잔, 컵 ⓝ a small drinking vessel with a handle

❸ 한 컵 분량; 요리할 때의 계량단위 ⓝ the amount of liquid a cup can hold
(* 1 cup: 8 fluid ounces or 16 tablespoons)

> 한 걸음 더 **He cupped his hands to drink water from the stream.** 그는 개울에서 물을 떠 마시기 위해 손을 컵 모양으로 오므렸다. → 손바닥 등을 컵 모양으로 오므리다(=to form something in the shape of a cup)
> **an acorn cup** 도토리의 깍정이 → 컵 모양의 물건(=an object shaped liked a cup)
> **cupboard** 찬장 **cupful** 한 컵 분량 **a measuring cup** 계량컵 **a cup and saucer** 접시에 받친 찻잔
> **win the cup** 우승하다 **a flower cup** 꽃받침

Step 03
연습문제

다음 문장의 cup에 해당되는 뜻을 **Step 02** 의 ❶~❸에서 고르세요. (해답은 437쪽)

1. He won a big gold cup. (　　)

2. Add one cup of sugar to the batter. (　　)

3. Steve and Boyce will share a cup of soda pop. (　　)

4. Linda was given a first place cup. (　　)

5. She drank water from a cup. (　　)

6. Kris used one cup of flour. (　　)

Step 04
영작연습

다음 문장을 주어진 부분을 이용하여 영어로 옮기세요. (해답은 437쪽)

1. 클럽회장이 우승자에게 우승컵을 증정했다. [president, presented]

____

2. Steve는 언제나 녹색 잔으로 물을 마신다. [drinks, green]

____

3. 요리사는 요리하는 데 한 컵 분량의 설탕을 사용했다. [cook, sugar]

____

∷ 1. 우승자는 큰 은빛 우승컵을 받았다. 2. 그녀는 찻잔으로 우유를 마셨다. 3. 요리법에 밀가루 한 컵을 넣으라고 되어 있었다.

해답은 437쪽

A. 다음 뜻에 해당되는 단어를 보기에서 찾아 적으세요.

보기	please	grow	club	bank	cup

01. _____________ to increase in amount, quality, degree, etc
02. _____________ a small drinking vessel with a handle
03. _____________ to make someone happy or satisfied; to satisfy
04. _____________ an office for receiving, lending, exchanging, and issuing money
05. _____________ to plant and care for; to raise; to cultivate
06. _____________ the amount of liquid a cup can hold
07. _____________ a special group of people who share a particular interest or enjoy similar activities
08. _____________ a word added to an order or request in order to be polite
09. _____________ the land at the edge of a river, or lake
10. _____________ a heavy stck with one thick end
11. _____________ a large silver or gold vessel given to the winner
12. _____________ to live and become bigger; to mature
13. _____________ to put money in a bank
14. _____________ to want; to like; to desire
15. _____________ a stick for playing golf or hockey

B. 다음 빈칸에 가장 알맞은 단어를 보기에서 찾아 적으세요.

보기	please	grow	club	bank	cup

01. The number of Jane's friends will (   ) this year.
02. (   ) give my regards to your family.
03. The winner will be given a big gold (   ).
04. She took the (   ) from the golf bag.
05. You may do as you (   ).
06. She belongs to the local tennis (   ).
07. Sue will (   ) some money this afternoon.
08. This news will (   ) him very much.
09. He keeps his money in the (   ).
10. Linda always drinks from a green (   ).
11. Police officers usually carry (   ).
12. She likes to (   ) roses in her garden.
13. We sat on the river (   ).
14. The cook needs one (   ) of rice.
15. Carrots (   ) well in this soil.

다음 문장을 굵게 처리된 단어에 유의하여 해석해 보세요.

01. For more information, **please** call 432-7658. [2000년-홀수형 19번]

➡ ______________________________

02. However, it is not necessary for him to **please** everyone. If his facts are true, that is all that counts. [1997년-홀수형 21번]

➡ ______________________________

03. They were very **pleased** to see that it made a dark and dry line when it was rubbed over paper. [2001년-홀수형 21번]

➡ ______________________________

04. Moreover, these differences often cause local conflicts to **grow** into larger wars. [2002년-홀수형 46번]

➡ ______________________________

05. The rich soil could help farmers **grow** enough crops to feed the people in the cities. [2009년-홀수형 33번]

➡ ______________________________

06. As a child **grows**, fears may disappear. [2002년-홀수형 45번]

➡ ______________________________

07. But it can also happen that one's memories **grow** much sharper even after a long passage of time. [2008년-홀수형 22번]

➡ ______________________________

08. One more thing you need to do is to join a **club** devoted to mathematics. [2007년-홀수형 23번]

➡ ______________________________

09. Car **club** members were parading down the street. [1999년-홀수형 21번]

➡ ______________________________

10. A check was once returned to a millionaire from a **bank**. [1994년-1차 10번]

➡ ______________________________

11. While holding a fishing rod on the river **bank**, a little girl suddenly felt something and saw the fishing rod bowing like a question mark. [1999년-홀수형 22번]

➡ ______________________________

12. Soon she came back with the **cups** and saucers and put them down on a small side table. [2011년-홀수형 19번]

➡ ______________________________

13. Sometimes they find old boxes full of gold coins or silver **cups** or jewelry. [1999년-홀수형 20번]

➡ ______________________________

056 seal [siːl]

Step 01 해석연습

다음 문장을 seal에 유의하여 해석해 보세요. (해석은 이 페이지의 하단부에 있음)

1. He saw a seal sitting on a rock. _______________________________
2. The president put a seal on the paper. _______________________________
3. He licked and sealed the envelop. _______________________________

Step 02 뜻 알기

seal에는 다음과 같은 여러 가지의 뜻이 있습니다.

❶ 바다표범, 물개 n a large sea animal that eats fish

❷ 인장, 증표 n a mark that has a special design and shows the legal and official authority of a person or organization

❸ 봉인하다, 밀봉하다 v to close an envelop, pack etc by using something sticky

> 한 걸음 더 **break the seal** 개봉하다(=unseal) **seal off** 출입을 봉쇄하다 * The police sealed off the area where the murder happened. 경찰은 살인사건이 일어난 지역을 봉쇄했다.

Step 03 연습문제

다음 문장의 seal에 해당되는 뜻을 Step 02 의 ❶∼❸에서 고르세요. (해답은 438쪽)

1. The seal sits on a rock. (   )
2. She put a gold seal on the letter. (   )
3. Please seal the envelop and mail it. (   )
4. Seals are mammals which live on shore. (   )
5. He has a letter with the king's seal. (   )
6. I must seal the jar of jelly. (   )

Step 04 영작연습

다음 문장을 주어진 부분을 이용하여 영어로 옮기세요. (해답은 438쪽)

1. 그들은 많은 바다표범들이 바다에서 수영하고 있는 것을 보았다. [saw, swimming]

____

2. 우리는 왕의 인장이 있는 왕의 편지를 받았다. [received, king's]

____

3. 아직 편지를 밀봉하지 마라. [letter, yet]

____

:: 1. 그는 바다표범 한 마리가 바위에 앉아 있는 것을 보았다. 2. 회장이 서류에 인장을 붙였다. 3. 그는 침을 묻혀 편지를 봉했다.

Day 06

057 pick [pik]

Step 01
해석연습

다음 문장을 pick에 유의하여 해석해 보세요. (해석은 이 페이지의 하단부에 있음)

1. My uncle digs with a pick. ________________________________

2. The child will pick one book. ________________________________

3. She sat on the grass and picked some flowers. ________________________________

Step 02
뜻 알기

pick에는 다음과 같은 여러 가지의 뜻이 있습니다.

❶ 곡괭이, 후비는 도구 n a digging tool

❷ 고르다, 선택하다 v to choose or select

❸ (과일, 꽃, 채소 등을) 따다, 뜯다 v to pull off fruits or vegetables

> 한 걸음 더 **pickpocket** ⓝ 소매치기 ⓥ 소매치기하다
> **pick up** ① (차에) 태우다 * The bus picked us up on time. 버스는 정각에 우리를 태웠다.
> ② 집어 들다, 집어 올리다 * The boy picked a small stone. 그 소년은 작은 돌 하나를 집어 들었다.
> ③ 우연히 사다 (얻다, 배우다) * He picks up new languages easily. 그는 새로운 언어를 쉽게 배운다.

Step 03
연습문제

다음 문장의 pick에 해당되는 뜻을 **Step 02** 의 ❶~❸에서 고르세요. (해답은 438쪽)

1. Carolyn digs with a pick. (　　　)

2. The child will pick one toy. (　　　)

3. She is picking flowers in the garden. (　　　)

4. She asked me to pick a card. (　　　)

5. Julie will pick some apples today. (　　　)

6. The man put his pick and shovel over his shoulder. (　　　)

Step 04
영작연습

다음 문장을 주어진 부분을 이용하여 영어로 옮기세요. (해답은 438쪽)

1. 그는 곡괭이로 구멍을 만들었다. [made, hole]

____

2. 그녀는 밝은 핑크색 옷을 골랐다. [bright, dress]

____

3. 그는 사과나무에서 사과를 딸 것이다. [apples, from]

____

∷ 1. 나의 삼촌이 곡괭이로 (땅을) 파신다. 2. 어린이는 한 권의 책을 고를 것이다. 3. 그녀는 잔디에 앉아 약간의 꽃을 땄다.

058 **paper** [péipər]

Step 01
해석연습

다음 문장을 paper에 유의하여 해석해 보세요. (해석은 이 페이지의 하단부에 있음)

1. He has five pieces of paper. _______________________________

2. I read the paper every morning. _______________________________

3. She will paper the room. _______________________________

Step 02
뜻 알기

paper에는 다음과 같은 여러 가지의 뜻이 있습니다.

❶ 종이 n a thin material used for writing, printing, wrapping

❷ 신문 n a newspaper

❸ 도배하다, 종이를 바르다 v to cover with paper

> 한 걸음 더 **There were a lot of important papers in the safe.** 금고에는 많은 중요 서류가 있었다. → 서류, 문서
> **He wrote a paper on the teaching of Korean.** 그는 한국어 교수법에 관한 논문을 썼다. → 논문
> **wallpaper** 벽지 **paper money** 지폐 **paperback** 종이표지의 책 **paper knife** 봉투를 열 때 쓰는 칼

Step 03
연습문제

다음 문장의 paper에 해당되는 뜻을 **Step 02** 의 ❶∼❸에서 고르세요. (해답은 438쪽)

1. He reads the paper every morning. (   )

2. Paper can be made from wood. (   )

3. He will paper the whole kitchen. (   )

4. He has ten pieces of paper. (   )

5. Let me see today's paper. (   )

6. Beth will paper her bedroom. (   )

Step 04
영작연습

다음 문장을 주어진 부분을 이용하여 영어로 옮기세요. (해답은 438쪽)

1. 나는 종이 한 장에 편지를 썼다. [wrote, a piece of]

____

2. 당신은 오늘 신문을 읽었습니까? [read, today's]

____

3. Judy는 새 벽지로 그녀의 침실을 도배했다. [bedroom, wallpaper]

____

:: 1. 그는 5장의 종이를 가지고 있다. 2. 나는 매일 아침 신문을 읽는다. 3. 그녀는 방을 도배할 것이다.

059 date [deit]

Step 01 해석연습

다음 문장을 date에 유의하여 해석해 보세요. (해석은 이 페이지의 하단부에 있음)

1. What's the date today? ___________________________
2. He asked her for a date. ___________________________
3. I ate a date for lunch. ___________________________

Step 02 뜻 알기

date에는 다음과 같은 여러 가지의 뜻이 있습니다.

❶ (특정한) 날짜, 기일 ｎ a particular day, month, or year

❷ (특히 이성과의) 약속, 데이트 ｎ a social appointment, usually of a couple

❸ 대추야자의 열매 ｎ the fruit of a date palm tree

> 한 걸음 더 **The castle dates back to the 14th century.** 그 성의 건립연도는 14세기로 거슬러 올라간다.
> → (연대가 ~로) 거슬러 올라가다, (~시대에) 시작되다
> **date line** 날짜변경선(=International Date Line) **blind date** 상대를 모르는 남녀 간의 데이트
> **out of date** 시대에 뒤떨어진, 구식의(=old fashioned) **up to date** 지금까지(=to the present time)
> **up-to-date** 최신의, 최신식의

Step 03 연습문제

다음 문장의 date에 해당되는 뜻을 **Step 02** 의 ❶～❸에서 고르세요. (해답은 438쪽)

1. I will see the doctor on that date. (   )
2. She will eat a date for lunch. (   )
3. Today's date is June 23, 2009. (   )
4. They went skating for a date. (   )
5. Jane will go on a date with Mike. (   )
6. The date tastes sweet. (   )

Step 04 영작연습

다음 문장을 주어진 부분을 이용하여 영어로 옮기세요. (해답은 438쪽)

1. 그들이 결혼한 날은 1984년 9월 15일이었다. [marriage, September]

____

2. 그 남녀는 어젯밤에 데이트를 했다. [boy and girl]

____

3. 나는 대추야자를 몹시 먹고 싶다. [eat, eagerly]

____

∷ 1. 오늘이 며칠인가요? 2. 그는 그녀에게 데이트를 신청했다. 3. 나는 점심으로 대추야자 열매를 먹었다.

060 arm [ɑːrm]

Step 01
해석연습

다음 문장을 arm에 유의하여 해석해 보세요. (해석은 이 페이지의 하단부에 있음)

1. He has broken both his arms. _______________________
2. The chair's arms are made of wood. _______________________
3. The soldier uses arms in a war. _______________________

Step 02
뜻 알기

arm에는 다음과 같은 여러 가지의 뜻이 있습니다.

❶ 팔 **n** the part of the body between the shoulder and the hand

❷ 팔 모양의 것 **n** anything that is like an arm in shape or use

❸ 무기 **n** weapons used for fighting wars
무장시키다; 전쟁준비를 하다 **v** to provide weapons to someone; to prepare for war

> 한 걸음 더 **armful** 한 아름 **an armful of roses** 한 아름의 장미 **armchair** 안락의자 **armband** (팔에 차는) 완장
> **army** 군대 **armed** 무장한 **armament** (한 나라의) 군비, 군사적 무장 (=military forces of a nation)
> **disarm** 무장을 해제하다 **disarmament** 무장해제, 군비축소 **arm in arm** 팔짱을 끼고
> **with open arms** 두 팔을 벌리고; 충심으로 (환영하여); 기꺼이 **appeal to arms** 무력에 호소하다
> **armed to the teeth** (=armed at all points) 완전 무장하고; 빈틈없이 대비하고

Step 03
연습문제

다음 문장의 arm에 해당되는 뜻을 **Step 02** 의 ❶∼❸에서 고르세요. (해답은 438쪽)

1. The soldiers will shoot arms. (　　)
2. A chair has two arms. (　　)
3. Two cats sat on the chair's arms. (　　)
4. Judy has a puppy in her arms. (　　)
5. The soldiers have plenty of arms. (　　)
6. Arms are parts of the body. (　　)

Step 04
영작연습

다음 문장을 주어진 부분을 이용하여 영어로 옮기세요. (해답은 438쪽)

1. 그는 상자를 팔에 안고 운반했다. [carried, box]

____

2. 그녀는 소파의 팔걸이 부분에 앉았다. [sat, sofa]

____

3. 시민들은 적군에 대항하여 무장했다. [citizens, enemies]

____

⠿ 1. 그는 두 팔을 부러뜨렸다. 2. 그 의자의 팔걸이 부분은 나무로 만들어졌다. 3. 군인은 전쟁에서 무기를 사용한다.

A. 다음 뜻에 해당되는 단어를 보기에서 찾아 적으세요.

보기	seal	pick	paper	date	arm

01. _____________ anything that is like an arm in shape or use
02. _____________ a thin material used for writing, printing, wrapping
03. _____________ a mark that has a special design and shows the legal and official authority of a person or organization
04. _____________ weapons used for fighting wars
05. _____________ a digging tool
06. _____________ to cover with paper
07. _____________ to close an envelop, pack etc by using something sticky
08. _____________ the fruit of a date palm tree
09. _____________ to pull off fruits or vegetables
10. _____________ a particular day, month, or year
11. _____________ the part of the body between the shoulder and the hand
12. _____________ a large sea animal that eats fish
13. _____________ social appointment, usually of a couple
14. _____________ a newspaper
15. _____________ to choose or select

B. 다음 빈칸에 가장 알맞은 단어를 보기에서 찾아 적으세요.

보기	seal	pick	paper	date	arm(s)

01. The man digs with a (   ).
02. He put a gold (   ) on the paper.
03. Steve and Linda went on a (   ).
04. James wrote a letter on the blue (   ).
05. Howard will (   ) the leak in the car motor.
06. Have you read today's (   )?
07. The mother held her baby in her (   ).
08. He will (   ) tomatoes from the tomato plants.
09. The (   ) are loaded with bullets.
10. He will (   ) his bedroom with new wallpaper.
11. That (   ) is my birthday.
12. Mary will (   ) her favorite song.
13. The (   ) grows on a tree.
14. The brown (   ) eats fish.
15. He sat on the (   ) of the chair.

다음 문장을 굵게 처리된 단어에 유의하여 해석해 보세요.

01. Several countries like Norway and Denmark joined in the campaign to protect whales and **seals** in their national parks. [1996년–홀수형 36번]

➡ ______________________________

02. Customer: I have some film to be developed. Clerk: Okay. You can **pick** them up at 2:00. [1996년–홀수형 11번]

➡ ______________________________

03. They are not willing to risk the possible disappointment of **picking** the loser, so they give up the possible joy of picking the winner. [2009년–홀수형 34번]

➡ ______________________________

04. After the grapes are **picked**, either by hand or by machine, they are taken to the winery. [2006년–홀수형 22번]

➡ ______________________________

05. A clean sheet of **paper** is lying in front of you, and you have to fill it up. [2008년–홀수형 24번]

➡ ______________________________

06. W: Oh, hi. Did the book I ordered come in? M: That's why I'm calling. We've just received a message from the publishing company. There will be a delay on your order. W: Oh, no. I need it for a **paper** I'm writing. [2004년–홀수형 11번]

➡ ______________________________

07. The branches then go through a complex process to become strong and flexible **paper**. [2004년–홀수형 24번]

➡ ______________________________

08. Well, he has a job delivering **papers** in the morning and he said that I can get one, too. [2006년–홀수형 16번]

➡ ______________________________

09. I handed in my **paper**, leaving the question blank. [2003년–홀수형 40번]

➡ ______________________________

10. Before its target **date**, the end goal was achieved. [2000년–홀수형 32번]

➡ ______________________________

11. This action follows our letters of warning **dated** July 21 and August 17, 1992, concerning your carelessness in performing the work for which you were employed. [1995년–홀수형 44번]

➡ ______________________________

12. The textbook might enable you to increase your knowledge, and the **date** might mean an evening of merriment. [1994년–1차 47번]

➡ ______________________________

13. M: Well, the wallpaper and the curtains are quite out of **date**. W: I agree. It's time to make some changes. [2008년–홀수형 8번]

➡ ______________________________

14. It was so large that a grown man could not put his **arms** around it. [2009년–홀수형 38번]

➡ ______________________________

15. The idea of achieving security through an **arms** race is a false belief. [1999년–홀수형 43번]

➡ ______________________________

DAY 07

Fresh air impoverishes the doctor.
신선한 공기는 의사를 가난하게 한다.

061 change [tʃeindʒ]

Group 13

Step 01
해석연습

다음 문장을 change에 유의하여 해석해 보세요. (해석은 이 페이지의 하단부에 있음)

1. After work, I changed into my jeans. ________________________________

2. He paid with a dollar and got 5 cents change. ________________________

3. She has been ill – the change will do her good. ______________________

Step 02
뜻 알기

change에는 다음과 같은 여러 가지의 뜻이 있습니다.

❶ 변하다, 바꾸다, (옷을) 갈아입다 **v** to make or become different

❷ 거스름돈, 잔돈 **n** the money left over or given back from the amount given in payment

❸ 요양, 휴식 **n** a rest or holiday taken in another circumstances

> 한 걸음 더 **I have a pocket full of <u>change</u>.** 나는 주머니에 동전이 가득하다. → 동전(=coin)
> **Let's go out to a restaurant for a <u>change</u>.** 기분전환을 위해 레스토랑으로 외식 가자. → 기분전환
> **changeable** 변하기 쉬운 **changeability** 변하기 쉬운 성질, 가변성

Step 03
연습문제

다음 문장의 change에 해당되는 뜻을 **Step 02** 의 ❶〜❸에서 고르세요. (해답은 438쪽)

1. Some animals can change colors. (　　)
2. She went to Jeju-do land for a change. (　　)
3. I have some change in my pocket. (　　)
4. Connie will change clothes now. (　　)
5. Roy put the change in a box. (　　)
6. I will go to the country for a change. (　　)

Step 04
영작연습

다음 문장을 주어진 부분을 이용하여 영어로 옮기세요. (해답은 438쪽)

1. 그는 색깔을 빨강에서 노랑으로 바꾸었다. [red, yellow]

____

2. 나는 가게 주인이 나에게 거스름돈을 건네주기를 기다렸다. [shopkeeper, hand]

____

3. 그녀는 요양(휴식)을 위해 시골로 갔다. [country, for]

____

⠿ 1. 일이 끝난 후 나는 청바지로 갈아입었다. 2. 그는 1달러를 지불했고 거스름돈 5센트를 받았다. 3. 그녀는 아프다 – 요양이 좋을 것이다.

062 tablet [tǽblit]

Step 01
해석연습

다음 문장을 tablet에 유의하여 해석해 보세요. (해석은 이 페이지의 하단부에 있음)

1. Jane's tablet has 50 pages. ___________________________________

2. Take these tablets for your headache. ___________________________________

3. He found an old tablet in the sand. ___________________________________

Step 02
뜻 알기

tablet에는 다음과 같은 여러 가지의 뜻이 있습니다.

❶ (한 장씩 뜯어 쓰는) 편지 철, 공책 🄝 a number of sheets of writing paper fixed together at the end; a writing pad

❷ 알약, 정제 🄝 a small flat piece of medicine; a pill

❸ 석판, 명판, 패 🄝 a flat piece of stone or metal with words cut into it

> 한 걸음 더 **a memorial tablet** 기념패 **a sleeping tablet** 수면제
> *약의 종류 **pill** 알약(환약) **capsule** 캡슐 **ointment** 연고 **dose** (약) 일회분의 복용량

Day 07

Step 03
연습문제

다음 문장의 tablet에 해당되는 뜻을 **Step 02** 의 ❶〜❸에서 고르세요. (해답은 438쪽)

1. Ancient peoples wrote on tablets made of clay. (   )

2. Schoolchildren use tablets of writing paper. (   )

3. She put a tablet in her mouth. (   )

4. Tony's tablet had 70 pages. (   )

5. Take two tablets after each meal. (   )

6. They put up a marble tablet in memory of their teacher. (   )

Step 04
영작연습

다음 문장을 주어진 부분을 이용하여 영어로 옮기세요. (해답은 438쪽)

1. Tony는 (글씨를) 쓰기 위해 그의 공책을 학교에 가져갔다. [took, write on]

____

2. 의사는 그녀에게 매일 아침 알약 한 알씩을 복용하라고 말했다. [take, each morning]

____

3. 과학자는 오래된 목판에 쓰여 있는 글씨를 읽을 수 없었다. [scientist, wooden]

____

:: 1. Jane의 공책은 50페이지로 되어 있다. 2. 두통을 위해서 이 알약을 복용해라. 3. 그는 모래 속에서 오래된 패를 발견했다.

063 land [læ[nd]

Step 01 해석연습

다음 문장을 land에 유의하여 해석해 보세요. (해석은 이 페이지의 하단부에 있음)

1. He returned at last to his native land. ________________________

2. They will build a house on this land. ________________________

3. They will land at the airport. ________________________

Step 02 뜻 알기

land에는 다음과 같은 여러 가지의 뜻이 있습니다.

❶ 나라, 국가, 국민 n a country and its people

❷ 땅, 토지, 흙 n the ground or soil

❸ 착륙하다, 상륙하다 v to reach land

> 한 걸음 더 **landlord** 주인, 지주 **landlady** 여주인, 여자지주 **landfill** 매립지 **landslide** 산사태 **landowner** 토지소유자, 지주
> **landing** ① 착륙, 상륙 ② 부두 ③ 층계참[계단참] **landmark** ① 지상 참고물(경계표) ② 역사적 건물 ③ 획기적 사건
> **travel by land** 육로로 가다 **go[work] on the land** 농부가 되다

Step 03 연습문제

다음 문장의 land에 해당되는 뜻을 **Step 02** 의 ❶∼❸에서 고르세요. (해답은 438쪽)

1. Korea is my native land. (   )

2. The plane will land safely at the airport. (   )

3. The United States is a land of free people. (   )

4. That fly might land on the ground. (   )

5. Let's build a house on this land. (   )

6. Your land is great for growing vegetables. (   )

Step 04 영작연습

다음 문장을 주어진 부분을 이용하여 영어로 옮기세요. (해답은 438쪽)

1. 온 국민이 그 소식을 듣고 기뻐했다. [whole, rejoiced]

____

2. 이 지역의 토양은 꽃을 재배하기에 좋다. [area, growing]

____

3. 그는 용케 병원 지붕에 헬리콥터를 착륙시켰다. [managed to, helicopter]

____

∷ 1. 그는 마침내 그의 고국에 돌아왔다. 2. 그들은 이 땅 위에 집을 지을 것이다. 3. 그들은 공항에 착륙할 것이다.

064 gas [gæs]

Step 01 해석연습

다음 문장을 gas에 유의하여 해석해 보세요. (해석은 이 페이지의 하단부에 있음)

1. Air is a mixture of gases. _______________________________

2. Gas comes to our house in pipes. _______________________________

3. He put gas into the truck's tank. _______________________________

Step 02 뜻 알기

gas에는 다음과 같은 여러 가지의 뜻이 있습니다.

❶ 기체 **n** a substance like air

❷ (연료용) 가스 **n** any gas which is used for heating, cooking, etc

❸ 휘발유(gasoline의 줄임말) **n** gasoline

> 한 걸음 더 **gas mask** 방독면 **gas station** 주유소 **gaseous** 기체의, 가스의 **tear gas** 최루가스
> **gas range**(=gas stove) 요리용 가스레인지

Step 03 연습문제

다음 문장의 gas에 해당되는 뜻을 **Step 02** 의 ❶~❸에서 고르세요. (해답은 439쪽)

1. He put more gas in the car. (   )
2. We use gas when we cook. (   )
3. There are several kinds of gases in the air. (   )
4. Turn on the gas stove. (   )
5. Oxygen and Hydrogen are gases. (   )
6. His car might run out of the gas on the way. (   )

Step 04 영작연습

다음 문장을 주어진 부분을 이용하여 영어로 옮기세요. (해답은 439쪽)

1. 질소는 공기 중에 다량으로 존재하는 기체다. [Nitrogen, exists]

____

2. 그녀는 약간의 물을 끓이기 위해 가스레인지를 켰다. [turned on, boil]

____

3. 내 차가 고속도로에서 휘발유가 떨어졌다. [ran out of, highway]

____

1. 공기는 가스들의 혼합체이다. 2. 가스는 우리 집에 파이프[관]을 통해서 온다. 3. 그는 트럭의 연료통[탱크]에 휘발유를 넣었다.

Step 01
해석연습

다음 문장을 miss에 유의하여 해석해 보세요. (해석은 이 페이지의 하단부에 있음)

1. Miss Smith is our English teacher. ________________________________
2. We missed her in the crowd. ________________________________
3. I will miss you very much. ________________________________

Step 02
뜻 알기

miss에는 다음과 같은 여러 가지의 뜻이 있습니다.

❶ 양, 미스 **n** a polite title used before the name of a girl or an unmarried woman

❷ 놓치다, 빗맞히다 **v** to fail to hit, meet, see, catch, etc
   놓침, 못 맞힘, 못 찾음 **n** a failure to hit, meet, see, catch, etc

❸ ~이 없음을 아쉽게 생각하다, 그리워하다 **v** to feel a sense of loss

> 한 걸음 더 **She** __missed__ **her music lesson today.** 그녀는 오늘 음악 레슨을 빼먹었다.
> → 빼먹다, 불참하다, 생략하다(=to fail to go; neglect; omit)
> **missing** 찾지 못한, 행방불명의

Step 03
연습문제

다음 문장의 miss에 해당되는 뜻을 **Step 02** 의 ❶~❸에서 고르세요. (해답은 439쪽)

1. Miss White is our English teacher. (   )
2. I got up late and missed the bus. (   )
3. We'll miss you very much. (   )
4. Don't miss your opportunity. (   )
5. Our music teacher is Miss Evans. (   )
6. I miss my parents when they are away. (   )

Step 04
영작연습

다음 문장을 주어진 부분을 이용하여 영어로 옮기세요. (해답은 439쪽)

1. Jones 양이 다음 주 일요일에 우리를 보러 온다. [coming, next Sunday]

   ____

2. 그녀는 맞힌 것보다 못 맞힌 것이 더 많았다. [more ~ than, hits]

   ____

3. Tony가 떠났을 때 그녀는 정말로 그를 그리워했다. [went away, really]

   ____

:: 1. Smith 양은 우리의 영어선생님이시다. 2. 우리는 군중 속에서 그녀를 놓쳤다. 3. 나는 네가 몹시 그리울 것이다.

Review Group - 13

A. 다음 뜻에 해당되는 단어를 보기에서 찾아 적으세요.

> 보기   change   tablet   land   gas   miss

01. _____________ a substance like air
02. _____________ a flat piece of stone or metal with words cut into it
03. _____________ to feel a sense of loss
04. _____________ a number of sheets of writing paper fixed together at the end; a writing pad
05. _____________ a country and its people
06. _____________ a polite title used before the name of a girl or an unmarried woman
07. _____________ the money left over or given back from the amount given in payment
08. _____________ to reach land
09. _____________ gasoline
10. _____________ a rest or holiday taken in another circumstances
11. _____________ any gas which is used for heating, cooking, etc
12. _____________ a small flat piece of medicine; a pill
13. _____________ to make or become different
14. _____________ a failure to hit, meet, see, catch, etc
15. _____________ the ground or soil

B. 다음 빈칸에 가장 알맞은 단어를 보기에서 찾아 적으세요.

> 보기   change   tablet   land   gas   miss

01. Our stove uses natural (   ).
02. The helicopter will (   ) on the hospital roof.
03. The month will (   ) tomorrow.
04. The doctor told me to take one (   ) each morning.
05. (   ) is not a liquid or solid.
06. Korea is a (   ) of peace loving people.
07. Strange writing was on the stone (   ).
08. Hurry up, or you will (   ) the train.
09. He spent a month in the country for a (   ).
10. This (   ) is dry and sandy.
11. We will (   ) you when you leave.
12. Mrs. Evans has some (   ) in her purse.
13. Our history teacher is (   ) Green.
14. I bought a (   ) of lined paper.
15. My car uses too much (   ).

Day 07

해답은 439쪽

다음 문장을 굵게 처리된 단어에 유의하여 해석해 보세요.

01. Sunspots can **change** the weather, too, by increasing the amount of ozone. [1998–홀수형 46번]

→ ___________________________________

02. W: I'm glad this week is over. It was a long week.
M: Well, how about cycling to the lake tomorrow?
W: Sounds great. I really need a **change**.
[1999년–홀수형 13번]

→ ___________________________________

03. M: That sounds good. I'll take them. Do you have **change** for a $20.00 bill?
W: No problem. Here you go. [2005년–홀수형 7번]

→ ___________________________________

04. If we observe nature closely, however, we discover that there is a constant tension between **change** and balance. [2004년–홀수형 43번]

→ ___________________________________

05. After years of research and expensive experimentation, an independent laboratory with specialists in biotechnology has finally uncovered a naturally occurring substance that can be taken orally in **tablet** form. [1994년–1차 31번]

→ ___________________________________

06. And it awakens my imagination that I may walk on **land** that so few have ever visited before. [2002년–홀수형 20번]

→ ___________________________________

07. We awoke the next morning to a magical sunrise, which made me understand why Korea is often called "**Land** of the Morning Calm." [2001년–홀수형 18번]

→ ___________________________________

08. They're communicating with pilots and telling them which runways to use to take off or **land**. [2009년–홀수형 9번]

→ ___________________________________

09. We know that this **gas** causes a greenhouse effect. [2002년–홀수형 25번]

→ ___________________________________

10. There has been a fifty percent saving in the amount of natural **gas** and electricity used. [2001년–홀수형 42번]

→ ___________________________________

11. W: What's wrong?
M: I'm afraid we've run out of **gas**! I should have checked the **gas** gauge before leaving. [1997년–홀수형 14번]

→ ___________________________________

12. We **miss** you so much. We're looking forward to seeing you again. [1995년–홀수형 31번]

→ ___________________________________

13. If you **missed** this astronomical show, you're really out of luck. [2004년–홀수형 33번]

→ ___________________________________

14. She had this job for a year and never **missed** a day. [2001년–홀수형 49–50번]

→ ___________________________________

15. Yes. I got her application but her photo is **missing**. [1998년–홀수형 5번]

→ ___________________________________

066 grave [greiv]

Step 01
해석연습

다음 문장을 grave에 유의하여 해석해 보세요. (해석은 이 페이지의 하단부에 있음)

1. She is buried in a grave next to her husband's. ___________________

2. The condition of the patient is grave. ___________________

Step 02
뜻 알기

grave에는 다음과 같은 여러 가지의 뜻이 있습니다.

❶ 무덤 **n** the place in the ground where a dead body is buried

❷ 심각한, 진지한, 중대한 **a** serious and worrying; important

> 한 걸음 더 **graveyard** 묘지, 묘소 **gravestone** 묘비 **from the cradle to the grave** 요람에서 무덤까지, 일생 동안
> **as grave as a judge** (재판관처럼) 극히 엄숙한

Step 03
연습문제

다음 문장의 grave에 해당되는 뜻을 Step 02 **의 ❶~❷에서 고르세요.** (해답은 439쪽)

1. She laid flowers on the grave. (   )

2. He had a grave look on his face. (   )

3. The patient is very ill and in grave condition. (   )

4. He stands at the grave of a poet. (   )

Step 04
영작연습

다음 문장을 주어진 부분을 이용하여 영어로 옮기세요. (해답은 439쪽)

1. 그는 어떤 시인의 무덤에 꽃을 놓았다. [laid, poet]

____

2. 그녀는 취업 면접에서 중대한 실수를 했다. [mistake, job interview]

____

:: 1. 그녀는 남편 무덤 옆에 묻혀 있다. 2. 환자의 상태가 심상치 않다.

067 air [ɛər]

Step 01
해석연습

다음 문장을 air에 유의하여 해석해 보세요. (해석은 이 페이지의 하단부에 있음)

1. We need fresh air. ___________________________
2. Birds fly through the air. ___________________________
3. She came in with a sad air. ___________________________

Step 02
뜻 알기

air에는 다음과 같은 여러 가지의 뜻이 있습니다.

❶ 공기, 대기 **n** the mixture of gases that surrounds the earth and that we breathe

❷ 공중, 하늘 **n** the space above the earth; the sky

❸ 외관, 분위기, 태도 **n** an outward appearance; a style; a manner

> 한 걸음 더 **Don't _air_ your troubles too often.** 자네의 괴로움을 너무 떠벌리지 말게.
> → 말을 하다, 떠벌리다, 공표하다(=to speak about; display)
> **aircraft** 항공기 **air force** 공군 **airplane** 항공기 **airport** 공항 **air pollution** 대기 오염 **air mail** 항공우편
> **airline** ① 항공사 ② 항공로 **air-conditioner** 냉난방장치 **by air** 비행기로, 항공편으로(=by airplane)
> **on the air** 방송 중에, 방송되어(=to be broadcasting on the radio or television at the present)
> * My favorite program will be on the air in a few minutes. 내가 제일 좋아하는 프로가 몇 분 후에 방송된다.

Step 03
연습문제

다음 문장의 air에 해당되는 뜻을 **Step 02** 의 ❶~❸에서 고르세요. (해답은 439쪽)

1. I wish I could fly in the air. (   )
2. She has the air of a lady. (   )
3. He likes traveling by air. (   )
4. We cannot live without air. (   )
5. He came in with an air of triumph. (   )
6. The air in the countryside is cleaner than the air of the city. (   )

Step 04
영작연습

다음 문장을 주어진 부분을 이용하여 영어로 옮기세요. (해답은 439쪽)

1. 밖에 나가서 신선한 공기를 마시자. [go out, fresh]

____

2. 그 남자는 낙하산도 없이 하늘을 1,000미터나 낙하했다. [fell, parachute]

____

3. Mike는 어린 티가 난다. [has, child]

____

:: 1. 우리는 신선한 공기가 필요하다. 2. 새들은 하늘을 난다. 3. 그녀는 슬픈 태도로 들어왔다.

068 address n [ǽdres / ədrés] v [ədrés]

Step 01
해석연습

다음 문장을 address에 유의하여 해석해 보세요. (해석은 이 페이지의 하단부에 있음)

1. Write your name and address on the envelop. _______________________
2. She made a long and boring address. _______________________
3. A stranger addressed me in English. _______________________

Step 02
뜻 알기

address에는 다음과 같은 여러 가지의 뜻이 있습니다.

❶ 주소 n the specific location of a person, business, or institution

❷ 연설 n a speech or a talk (to an audience)

❸ 연설하다; 편지를 보내다; 주소를 쓰다 v to speak or write to

한 걸음 더 **The article does not <u>address</u> the real issues.** 그 기사는 진짜 문제점들에 대해서는 다루지 않고 있다.
→ (일, 문제 따위를 다루다, 대처하다, 검토하다(=to do or think about something about a particular problem or question)
* address에는 골프에서 골프채로 공의 목표를 정하다(=take an aim at a ball with a golf club)의 뜻도 있음
an opening address 개회사 **a closing address** 폐회사 **an address of welcome** 환영사
an inaugural address 취임사, 취임연설 **address book** 주소록 **give[make, deliver] an address** 연설(강연)을 하다

Step 03
연습문제

다음 문장의 address에 해당되는 뜻을 Step 02 의 ❶~❸에서 고르세요. (해답은 439쪽)

1. Here's my address and telephone number. (   )
2. This letter is addressed to you. (   )
3. Let me know if you change your address. (   )
4. She gave a long address to us. (   )
5. A stranger addressed me on the street. (   )
6. He will give an address to the nation on TV tonight. (   )

Step 04
영작연습

다음 문장을 주어진 부분을 이용하여 영어로 옮기세요. (해답은 439쪽)

1. 그녀는 아직도 같은 주소에 살고 있다. [still, same]

____

2. 그 작가는 청중에게 인상 깊은 연설을 하였다. [impressive, andience]

____

3. 그 편지들은 주소가 잘못 적혀 있었다. [letters, wrongly]

____

:: 1. 봉투에 당신의 이름과 주소를 써라. 2. 그녀는 길고 지루한 연설을 했다. 3. 한 낯선 사람이 나에게 영어로 말을 걸었다.

069 party [pάːrti]

Step 01
해석연습

다음 문장을 party에 유의하여 해석해 보세요. (해석은 이 페이지의 하단부에 있음)

1. I am going to have a dinner party tomorrow. ______________________________
2. How many are there in your party? ______________________________
3. The ruling party wants to raise taxes. ______________________________

Step 02
뜻 알기

party에는 다음과 같은 여러 가지의 뜻이 있습니다.

❶ 파티, 연회 **n** a social gathering of persons, by invitation, for pleasure

❷ 목적, 관심을 함께하는 사람들 **n** a group of people united for the same purpose or interest

❸ 정당 **n** a group of people who share the same political opinions, etc

> 한 걸음 더 **The two parties are having difficulty agreeing.** 두 당사자들은 의견의 일치를 보는 데 어려움을 겪고 있다.
> → (소송, 계약 등의) 당사자, 관계자(=one of the persons or sides in a legal agreement or dispute)
> **a search party** 수색대 **a rescue party** 구조대 **a party of tourists** 여행단 **a political party** 정당
> **the ruling party** 여당 **the opposition party** 야당 **a third party** 제3자 **an interested party** 이해관계자
> **a tea party** 다과회 **a luncheon party** 오찬회 **give[have, hold] a party** 파티를 열다

Step 03
연습문제

다음 문장의 party에 해당되는 뜻을 Step 02 의 ❶~❸에서 고르세요. (해답은 439쪽)

1. I invited her to the party. (   )
2. They formed a party of tourists. (   )
3. They will form a new political party. (   )
4. The search party went to look for the missing hikers. (   )
5. The party may lose its majority in the Assembly. (   )
6. We will have a party on New Year's Eve. (   )

Step 04
영작연습

다음 문장을 주어진 부분을 이용하여 영어로 옮기세요. (해답은 439쪽)

1. 우리는 떠나기 전에 송별회를 가질 것이다. [farewell, leave]

____

2. 그 코치는 연습을 위해 그의 팀을 두 편으로 나눴다. [divided, for exercise]

____

3. 정당 지도자들은 그들의 새 주택 정책을 토의하기 위해 만날 예정이다. [discuss, housing policy]

____

∷ 1. 나는 내일 만찬 파티를 열 예정이다. 2. 일행이 몇 분입니까? 3. 여당은 세금을 올리기를 원한다.

070 pop [pɑp / pɔp]

Step 01 해석연습

다음 문장을 pop에 유의하여 해석해 보세요. (해석은 이 페이지의 하단부에 있음)

1. This pop tastes good. _______________________________

2. My pop has a nice smile. _______________________________

3. My ballon has popped. _______________________________

4. They went to the pop concert last night. _______________________________

Step 02 뜻 알기

pop에는 다음과 같은 여러 가지의 뜻이 있습니다.

❶ 탄산수, 청량음료 ⓝ a sweet fizzy drink; a soft drink

❷ (비격식) 아빠, 아저씨 ⓝ a friendly term for one's father or an elderly man

❸ 느닷없이 열리다, 펑 하며 터지다 ⓥ to (cause to) open or burst abruptly with a loud noise
짧고 날카로운 펑 하는 소리 ⓝ a sharp, quick, explosive noise

❹ 대중적인 ⓐ popular / 대중음악 ⓝ popular music

▷ 한 걸음 더 **popgun** 장난감 총 **pop concert** 대중 음악회 **pop eyed** 퉁방울눈의; (놀라서) 눈이 휘둥그레진

Step 03 연습문제

다음 문장의 pop에 해당되는 뜻을 Step 02 의 ❶~❹에서 고르세요. (해답은 439쪽)

1. This pop tastes great. (   )

2. A sharp needle made the ballon pop. (   )

3. I like pop music. (   )

4. Pop said, "I can go skating now." (   )

5. There will be a big pop concert here tonight. (   )

6. Lisa's pop is always kind to us. (   )

7. Bubbles are in the pop. (   )

8. They tried to pop the soap bubbles. (   )

Step 04 영작연습

다음 문장을 주어진 부분을 이용하여 영어로 옮기세요. (해답은 439쪽)

1. 우리는 세 병의 탄산수를 샀다. [bought, bottles]

____

2. 나의 아빠는 지난달 직장에서 은퇴하셨다. [retired, work]

____

3. 종이봉지가 '펑' 하는 큰 소리와 함께 터졌다. [burst, loud]

____

4. 그녀는 대중음악 부르는 것을 좋아한다. [sing, song]

____

:: 1. 이 탄산수는 맛이 좋다. 2. 나의 아빠는 근사한 미소를 지니고 계신다. 3. 내 풍선이 갑자기 터졌다. 4. 그들은 어젯밤 팝 콘서트에 갔다.

해답은 439쪽

A. 다음 뜻에 해당되는 단어를 보기에서 찾아 적으세요.

보기	grave air address party pop

01. ______________ a friendly term for one's father or an elderly man
02. ______________ the specific location of a person, business, or institution
03. ______________ the space above the earth; the sky
04. ______________ the place in the ground where a dead body is buried
05. ______________ a group of people united for the same purpose or interest
06. ______________ the mixture of gases that surrounds the earth and that we breathe
07. ______________ a sweet fizzy drink; a soft drink
08. ______________ a group of people who share the same political opinions, etc
09. ______________ to speak or write to
10. ______________ popular; popular music
11. ______________ a social gathering of persons, by invitation, for pleasure
12. ______________ serious and worrying; important
13. ______________ a speech or a talk (to an audience)
14. ______________ to (cause to) open or burst abruptly with a loud noise
15. ______________ an outward appearance; a style; a manner

B. 다음 빈칸에 가장 알맞은 단어를 보기에서 찾아 적으세요.

보기	grave air address party pop

01. She looked (   ) when she told us the news.
02. The girl answered with a sad (   ).
03. Jane had a (   ) on her birthday.
04. I thought the stranger might (   ) me in English.
05. Birds are flying in the (   ).
06. He drank a bottle of (   ) for lunch.
07. The governor gave an (   ) on tax increase.
08. It's a beautiful mountain with clean (   ).
09. His body was buried in a (   ) on the hill.
10. He is a famous (   ) singer.
11. He wrote wrong (   ) on the envelope.
12. Sally's (   ) had a birthday yesterday.
13. The coach was rented by a (   ) of tourists.
14. Blow up your lunch sack and (   ) it.
15. The election was a complete victory for that political (   ).

다음 문장을 굵게 처리된 단어에 유의하여 해석해 보세요.

01. It is as a pupil and admirer that I stand at the **grave** of the greatest man who taught me in college. [1999년-홀수형 36번]

➡ ___________________________________

02. There is healing power in flowers — and in trees, fresh **air**, and sweet-smelling soil. [2008년-홀수형 33번]

➡ ___________________________________

03. No songs of birds were in the **air**, no pleasant scents, no moving lights and shadows from swift passing clouds. [1994년-2차 31번]

➡ ___________________________________

04. The **air** was alive with chatter and laughter, which became easier minute by minute. [2003년-홀수형 32번]

➡ ___________________________________

05. M: The drama will be on the **air** right before the evening news.
W: That's good, that's really good. [2002년-홀수형 2번]

➡ ___________________________________

06. There was a slow smiling **air** about her. [2006년-홀수형 33번]

➡ ___________________________________

07. When we arrived at the **address** I had given, I said goodbye, thanking him. [1999년-홀수형 46번]

➡ ___________________________________

08. Today the language policies in the United States **address** this problem primarily with efforts to teach "foreign" languages to monolingual Americans. [2006년-홀수형 25번]

➡ ___________________________________

09. These are among the basic questions that were **addressed** at the first world meeting on the environment, attended by more than 100 world leaders and 30,000 other scientists, newspeople, and citizens concerned. [2008년-홀수형 32번]

➡ ___________________________________

10. Imagine that you are in a meeting. Your **party** and the other **party** are sitting across a table. [2010년-홀수형 33번]

➡ ___________________________________

11. One day Sally, an American student, went to a **party** in England. [1997년-홀수형 29번]

➡ ___________________________________

12. Competition implies a set of rules that govern the conduct of the opposed **parties**. [1995년-홀수형 24번]

➡ ___________________________________

13. The ball curved cleanly into the basket, stiffly **popping** the chain-link net. [2009년-홀수형 46-48번]

➡ ___________________________________

14. W: Did you see the poster about the **pop** contest?
M: Yeah, I guess it's about time we began practicing. [2002년-홀수형 5번]

➡ ___________________________________

15. W: What kind of ads are you talking about, James?
M: **Pop**-up ads all over the Internet. They're really bothersome. [2011년-홀수형 7번]

➡ ___________________________________

DAY 08

Where there is a will, there is a way.
뜻이 있는 곳에 길이 있다.

071 chest [tʃest]

Group 15

Step 01
해석연습

다음 문장을 chest에 유의하여 해석해 보세요. (해석은 이 페이지의 하단부에 있음)

1. He hit me on the chest. _______________________________

2. The letters were kept in a wooden chest. _______________________________

Step 02
뜻 알기

chest에는 다음과 같은 여러 가지의 뜻이 있습니다.

❶ 가슴 **n** the front part of the body between the neck and the stomach

❷ 수납함, 보존함, 상자 **n** a large, strong wooden or metal box for storing things

> 한 걸음 더 **a jewelry chest** 보석함 **a medicine chest** 약상자 **a carpenter's chest** 목수의 연장통
> **a chest of drawers** (침실용) 옷장, (서랍 달린) 장롱 **a chest bed** (밑에) 서랍이 붙은 침대
> **get something off one's chest** (구어) (고민 따위를) 털어놓아 후련해지다
> **have something on one's chest** (구어) 마음에 걸리는 일이 있다

Step 03
연습문제

다음 문장의 chest에 해당되는 뜻을 **Step 02** 의 ❶∼❷에서 고르세요. (해답은 440쪽)

1. I had to go to hospital for a chest X-ray. (   )

2. There is some medicine in the medicine chest. (   )

3. He measures 38 inches round the chest. (   )

4. We keep the summer clothes in a chest. (   )

Step 04
영작연습

다음 문장을 주어진 부분을 이용하여 영어로 옮기세요. (해답은 440쪽)

1. 그녀는 가슴에 심한 통증을 느꼈다. [felt, severe pain]

____

2. 그녀는 겨울옷을 다락의 수납함에 보관한다. [keeps, clothes, attic]

____

:: 1. 그는 내 가슴을 쳤다. 2. 그 편지들은 나무상자에 보관되어 있었다.

 **072 title** [táitl]

Step 01 해석연습 · 다음 문장을 title에 유의하여 해석해 보세요. (해석은 이 페이지의 하단부에 있음)

1. The title of the novel is scary. ___________________________

2. He has the title of Doctor of Medical Dentistry. ___________________________

3. She has title to the land. ___________________________

Step 02 뜻 알기 · title에는 다음과 같은 여러 가지의 뜻이 있습니다.

❶ 제목 **n** the name of a book, play, painting, piece of music, etc

❷ 직함, 작위, 학위 **n** the name of a rank of nobility, academic degree, or office

❸ 소유권, 권리; 권리증서 **n** the legal right or ownership; the paper giving such right

> 한 걸음 더 **He titled his novel "Return to home."** 그는 자신의 소설에 "귀향"이라고 제목을 붙였다.
> → (책 따위에) 제목을 붙이다, ~에게 직함(칭호)을 주다(=to give a title something or someone)
> **The boxers will fight for the title tomorrow.** 권투선수들은 내일 타이틀매치를 치를 것이다.
> → (스포츠 등에서의) 선수권(=championship)
> **title deed** (부동산의) 권리증서, 토지권리증 **titleholder** ① (법률) 소유권자 ② (스포츠) 선수권 보유자
> **title role** 주제역(주인공 이름이 작품명인 극의 주인공) **title page** (책의) 속표지, 표제지(책이름, 저자명, 발행일 따위가 인쇄되어 있음)

Step 03 연습문제 · 다음 문장의 title에 해당되는 뜻을 **Step 02** 의 ❶~❸에서 고르세요. (해답은 440쪽)

1. He has the title of Lord Mayor. (   )

2. The title of the movie is funny. (   )

3. Elizabeth owns the title to a large apartment. (   )

4. He was granted the title of professor. (   )

5. You might know a book by only reading the title. (   )

6. He has the title to that villa. (   )

Step 04 영작연습 · 다음 문장을 주어진 부분을 이용하여 영어로 옮기세요. (해답은 440쪽)

1. 그 유명한 시의 제목은 "Annabel Lee"이다. [famous, poem]

____

2. 그의 공식 직함은 편집장이다. [official, editorial manager]

____

3. Sophia는 큰 별장에 대한 권리[증서]를 가지고 있다. [owns, villa]

____

∷ 1. 소설의 제목이 무시무시하다. 2. 그는 치과의학박사의 학위를 가지고 있다. 3. 그녀는 그 땅에 대한 소유권을 가지고 있다.

 **073 last** [læst / lɑːst]

Step 01
해석연습

다음 문장을 last에 유의하여 해석해 보세요. (해석은 이 페이지의 하단부에 있음)

1. December is the last month of the year. __________________________

2. Mary and I saw a movie last night. __________________________

3. How long will this fine weather last? __________________________

Step 02
뜻 알기

last에는 다음과 같은 여러 가지의 뜻이 있습니다.

❶ 마지막의 **a** coming after all others; final

❷ 최근의, 지난, 바로 전의 **a** most recent; coming immediately before the present

❸ 계속되다, 오래가다, 견디다 **v** to go on; to continue in time; to endure

> 한 걸음 더 **He is the last man to tell a lie.** 그는 결코 거짓말을 할 사람이 아니다.
> → 가장 ~할 것 같지 않은, 부적당한(=least likely, suitable, willing, etc)
> **last year** 작년 **last night** 지난밤, 어젯밤 **the last chance** 마지막 기회 **at last** 드디어, 마침내
> **to the last** 최후까지, 죽을 때까지 **for the last time** 마지막으로

Step 03
연습문제

다음 문장의 last에 해당되는 뜻을 **Step 02** 의 ❶~❸에서 고르세요. (해답은 440쪽)

1. The food will not last for a week. (　　　)
2. Today is the last day of the month. (　　　)
3. She has been sick for the last few days. (　　　)
4. Luckly I caught the last train. (　　　)
5. I visited my uncle last Saturday. (　　　)
6. Our meeting lasted until five. (　　　)

Step 04
영작연습

다음 문장을 주어진 부분을 이용하여 영어로 옮기세요. (해답은 440쪽)

1. 그는 10월 마지막 날에 런던을 향해 떠났다. [started for, October]

____

2. 나는 그를 지난번 회의 이후로 보지 못했다. [since, meeting]

____

3. 두 나라 사이의 좋은 관계는 오래 지속되지 못했다. [relationship, nations]

____

∷ 1. 12월은 한 해의 마지막 달이다. 2. Mary와 나는 지난밤 영화를 보았다. 3. 이 맑은 날씨는 언제까지 지속될 것인가?

074 leave [liːv]

Step 01
해석연습

다음 문장을 leave에 유의하여 해석해 보세요. (해석은 이 페이지의 하단부에 있음)

1. We are leaving for London next week. ________________________
2. He left his keys on the table. ________________________
3. She is at home on leave at the moment. ________________________

Step 02
뜻 알기

leave에는 다음과 같은 여러 가지의 뜻이 있습니다.

❶ ～을 떠나다, 출발하다 Ⓥ to go away or depart from (a certain place)

❷ 놓고 가다; (어떤 상태로) 남겨 두다; ～을 맡기다 Ⓥ to neglect or fail to take, bring or do something; to put in the care of; to entrust

❸ 허락, 허가; 휴가 Ⓝ permission; consent; permission to be absent from work or duty

> 한 걸음 더 **leave** [liːv] - **left** [left] - **left** [left]
> **maternity leave** 출산휴가 **sick leave** 병가 **paid leave** 유급휴가 **unpaid leave** 무급휴가
> **leave for** ～를 향해 떠나다, 출발하다 **leave ~ alone** ～을 그대로 내버려 두다 **on leave** 휴가로
> **without leave** 허가 없이, 무단으로 **leave out** 생략하다, 무시하다

Step 03
연습문제

다음 문장의 leave에 해당되는 뜻을 Step 02 의 ❶～❸에서 고르세요. (해답은 440쪽)

1. I usually leave at 7:00 to go to work. (   )
2. They left without my leave. (   )
3. Mr. Green will leave New York for Paris. (   )
4. She left her hat in the car. (   )
5. The soldier went on leave for two weeks. (   )
6. Someone left an umbrella behind. (   )

Step 04
영작연습

다음 문장을 주어진 부분을 이용하여 영어로 옮기세요. (해답은 440쪽)

1. 그는 대개 7시 30분에 학교를 향해 집을 나선다. [usually, leaves]

____

2. 당신은 그 일을 전문가에게 맡기는 것이 낫겠다. [had better, experts]

____

3. 너는 내 허락 없이는 아무것도 해서는 안 된다. [must not, without]

____

1. 우리는 다음 주에 런던으로 떠날 예정이다. 2. 그는 자신의 열쇠를 테이블에 놓고 갔다. 3. 그녀는 지금 휴가로 집에 있다.

111

075 present **a** **n** [préznt] **v** [prizént]

Step 01
해석연습

다음 문장을 present에 유의하여 해석해 보세요. (해석은 이 페이지의 하단부에 있음)

1. What is your present address? _______________________
2. Those present were all women. _______________________
3. He had many presents on his birthday. _______________________
4. She presented flowers to her teacher. _______________________

Step 02
뜻 알기

present에는 다음과 같은 여러 가지의 뜻이 있습니다.

❶ 현재의, 지금의 **a** at this time; now / 현재, 지금 **n** the present time

❷ (어떤 장소에) 참석한, 출석한; 있는, 존재하는 **a** being in a certain place; being or existing

❸ 선물 **n** a gift

❹ 증정하다, 소개하다; (보고서 따위를) 제출하다; (계획, 이론 따위를) 제안하다 **v** to give, especially formally or ceremonially; to introduce; to deliver; to offer

▷ 한 걸음 더 **presenter** 수여자, 제출자 **presentation** 증정, 공개, 공연, 상연 **at present** 현재, 지금은 **for the present** 당분간

Step 03
연습문제

다음 문장의 present에 해당되는 뜻을 **Step 02** 의 ❶~❹에서 고르세요. (해답은 440쪽)

1. She is satisfied with her present life. (   )
2. I have a present for you. (   )
3. We presented some flowers to the singer. (   )
4. We gave her a present. (   )
5. She presents her idea very briefly. (   )
6. All students were present in yesterday's class. (   )
7. How should we deal with the present situation? (   )
8. Oxygen is present in the air. (   )

Step 04
영작연습

다음 문장을 주어진 부분을 이용하여 영어로 옮기세요. (해답은 440쪽)

1. 현재의 상황은 매우 중요하다. [situation, critical]

____

2. 얼마나 많은 사람들이 오늘 아침 회의에 참석하였습니까? [people, this morning]

____

3. 그녀는 나에게 생일 선물로 아름다운 부채를 주었다. [fan, as]

____

4. 그는 그 문제에 대한 자신의 생각을 매우 분명하게 소개했다. [matter, clearly]

____

:: 1. 당신의 현재의 주소는 어디입니까? 2. 출석자는 전원 여성들이었다. 3. 그는 생일에 많은 선물을 받았다. 4. 그녀는 담임선생님께 꽃을 드렸다.

112

A. 다음 뜻에 해당되는 단어를 보기에서 찾아 적으세요.

> 보기   chest   title   last   leave   present

01. ______________ permission; consent; permission to be absent from work or duty
02. ______________ the name of a book, play, painting, piece of music, etc
03. ______________ to neglect or fail to take, bring or do something; to put in the care of; to entrust
04. ______________ to give, especially formally or ceremonially; to introduce; to deliver; to offer
05. ______________ the legal right or ownership; the paper giving such right
06. ______________ the front part of the body between the neck and the stomach
07. ______________ at this time; now
08. ______________ coming after all others; final
09. ______________ being in a certain place; being or existing
10. ______________ to go away or depart from (a certain place)
11. ______________ most recent; coming immediately before the present
12. ______________ a large, strong wooden or metal box for storing things
13. ______________ to go on; to continue in time; to endure
14. ______________ a gift
15. ______________ the name of a rank of nobility, academic degree, or office

B. 다음 빈칸에 가장 알맞은 단어를 보기에서 찾아 적으세요.

> 보기   chest   title   last   leave   present(s)

01. We went to the concert (   ) night.
02. The (   ) principal is very generous to his students.
03. Be careful not to (   ) your gloves in the car.
04. She has the (   ) of a city councilor.
05. Everyone must (   ) his passport to the customs officer.
06. She missed the (   ) bus home.
07. "The old man and sea" is the (   ) title of a famous book.
08. Julie took a (   ) of absence when she had her baby.
09. He will (   ) Seoul for Sydney soon.
10. This is your (   ) X-ray.
11. She owns the (   ) to a large villa.
12. Everybody was (   ) at the meeting.
13. She keeps her jewelry and other valuables in a (   ).
14. How long did the fight (   )?
15. He had many (   ) on his birthday.

다음 문장을 굵게 처리된 단어에 유의하여 해석해 보세요.

01. I'm looking for a book about traveling in South America. But I don't remember the **title**. [2012년–홀수형 9번]

→ __________________________________

02. I happened to do this when I was singing the **title** song from the film Annie. [1999년–홀수형 37번]

→ __________________________________

03. But only one winner will receive the **title** of Tea Master and a cash prize of 10,000 dollars. [2010년–홀수형 12번]

→ __________________________________

04. An uncut movie might **last** four or five hours. [2006년–홀수형 19번]

→ __________________________________

05. I felt ashamed for not having visited him for the **last** five years. [2003년–홀수형 26번]

→ __________________________________

06. Collecting the papers, the professor said the **last** question would count. [2003년–홀수형 40번]

→ __________________________________

07. What time is your flight supposed to **leave**? [1997년–홀수형 15번]

→ __________________________________

08. Mothers can **leave** their children here and go to work without worrying about them. [1995년–홀수형 17번]

→ __________________________________

09. Nowadays, we can enjoy athletic competition of every kind without **leaving** our homes. [2009년–홀수형 34]

→ __________________________________

10. In order to do so, they have to decide if they should add something to the painting or **leave** it as it is. [2005년–홀수형 31번]

→ __________________________________

11. Happiness is too seldom found in the **present**; it is remembered as a thing of the past or looked forward to as a part of the future. [2005년–홀수형 37번]

→ __________________________________

12. W: Ah, I have a good idea. My birthday is next week. Could you send some money to them as my **present**?
M: Wow, that's very thoughtful. [2008년–홀수형 7번]

→ __________________________________

13. These two possibilities are **presented** to us as options. [2002년–홀수형 34번]

→ __________________________________

14. When the students watched the film with an authority figure **present**, their faces showed only the slightest hints of reaction. [2008년–홀수형 31번]

→ __________________________________

15. This is considered necessary to **present** the best works of art to everyone free of charge. [2003년–홀수형 33번]

→ __________________________________

076 novel [návəl / nɔ́vəl]

Step 01 해석연습

다음 문장을 novel에 유의하여 해석해 보세요. (해석은 이 페이지의 하단부에 있음)

1. He wrote a novel about the Korean War. ___________________________________

2. Snow is a novel thing to people from hot countries. ___________________________

Step 02 뜻 알기

novel에는 다음과 같은 여러 가지의 뜻이 있습니다.

❶ 소설 **n** a long written story in which the characters and events are usually imaginary

❷ 새로운, 참신한, 진기한 **a** new and strange

> 한 걸음 더 **novelist** 소설가 **novelty** 새로움, 신기함, 진귀함, 신기한 것 **a history novel** 역사소설
> **a detective novel** 추리소설, 탐정소설

Step 03 연습문제

다음 문장의 novel에 해당되는 뜻을 Step 02 의 ❶～❷에서 고르세요. (해답은 440쪽)

1. He is writing a novel about the Korean War. (　　)

2. That man is full of novel ideas. (　　)

3. She is wearing a dress of novel design. (　　)

4. I read an Agatha Christie novel. (　　)

Step 04 영작연습

다음 문장을 주어진 부분을 이용하여 영어로 옮기세요. (해답은 440쪽)

1. 그녀의 새 소설은 젊은이들에게 널리 읽히고 있다. [widely, young people]

____

2. 그 일꾼은 그 문제에 대한 참신한 해결책을 생각해 냈다. [worker, solution]

____

:: 1. 그는 한국전쟁에 관한 소설을 썼다. 2. 눈은 더운 나라에서 온 사람들에게는 신기한 것이다.

077 **way** [wei]

Step 01 해석연습

다음 문장을 way에 유의하여 해석해 보세요. (해석은 이 페이지의 하단부에 있음)

1. Could you show me the way to the museum? _______________________
2. He does everything in his own way. _______________________
3. I am different from him in many ways. _______________________

Step 02 뜻 알기

way에는 다음과 같은 여러 가지의 뜻이 있습니다.

❶ 길, 도로, 방향 n a means used to go from one place to another; a path; a road; direction

❷ 방법, 방식, 수단 n a method of doing something; a manner; a style; a means

❸ 관점, 면, 사항 n an aspect or side of something; respect; point

> 한 걸음 더 **It is a long way to the school.** 학교까지는 먼 거리다. → 거리(=a distance)
> **all the way** 줄곧, 내내 **by the way** 그런데, 말이 나온 김에 **in the way** 방해가 되어 **on the way** 도중에(=on one's way)
> **in no way** 결코 ~아니다 **lose one's way** 길을 잃다 **make one's way** ① 나아가다, 가다 ② 출세하다

Step 03 연습문제

다음 문장의 way에 해당되는 뜻을 **Step 02** 의 ❶~❸에서 고르세요. (해답은 440쪽)

1. She lost her way in the crowd. (   )
2. This job is quite different in some ways. (   )
3. Her house is on the way from here to the park. (   )
4. I don't like the way he drives a car. (   )
5. Sophia is a clever woman in some ways. (   )
6. She showed me the way to use a video camera. (   )

Step 04 영작연습

다음 문장을 주어진 부분을 이용하여 영어로 옮기세요. (해답은 440쪽)

1. 우리는 숲 속에서 길을 잃었다. [lost, forest]

____

2. 당신은 이 야채들을 몇 가지 다양한 방법으로 요리할 수 있다. [vegetables, several]

____

3. 컴퓨터는 여러 가지 면에서 우리를 도울 수 있다. [computers, help]

____

:: 1. 박물관 가는 길을 가르쳐 주시겠습니까? 2. 그는 모든 것을 자기 방식대로 한다. 3. 나는 여러 면에서 그와는 다르다.

078 **will** [wil]

Step 01
해석연습

다음 문장을 will에 유의하여 해석해 보세요. (해석은 이 페이지의 하단부에 있음)

1. It will be fine tomorrow. _______________________

2. She has a strong will to succeed. _______________________

3. Have you made your will yet? _______________________

Step 02
뜻 알기

will에는 다음과 같은 여러 가지의 뜻이 있습니다.

❶ 미래를 나타내는 조동사 **v** (modal verb) used to form future tenses of other verbs

❷ 의지, 의도; 소망 **n** the mental power by which one controls one's thought, actions and decisions; a wish

❸ 유언, 유서 **n** a written statement showing what is to be done with one's belongings, body, etc after one's death

> 한 걸음 더 **The boy <u>willed</u> to be honest.** 그 소년은 정직해지려고 마음먹었다.
> → (본동사) ~하려 하다, 의도하다(=to determine; decide; wish), 이 경우 동사변화는 규칙임
> **will power** 의지력, 정신력 **free will** 자유의지 **willful** ① 고의로 ② 제멋대로의 **willing** 기꺼이 ~하는, 자발적인
> **at (one's) will** 마음대로, 임의로 **against one's will** 본의 아니게

Step 03
연습문제

다음 문장의 will에 해당되는 뜻을 **Step 02** 의 ❶~❸에서 고르세요. (해답은 440쪽)

1. Tony has a strong will to succeed. (   )

2. My father will be back tomorrow. (   )

3. She hasn't made her will yet. (   )

4. I will start early tomorrow morning. (   )

5. He did it against his will. (   )

6. He made a will leaving all his estate to his son. (   )

Step 04
영작연습

다음 문장을 주어진 부분을 이용하여 영어로 옮기세요. (해답은 440쪽)

1. 그는 내일 이맘때 뉴욕에 있을 것이다. [this time tomorrow]

____

2. 살려는 의지가 환자가 회복하는 것을 돕는다. [patient, recover]

____

3. 나의 어머니는 유언장에서 나에게 이 금반지를 남기셨다. [left, gold ring]

____

:: 1. 내일은 날씨가 좋을 것이다. 2. 그녀는 성공하겠다는 강한 의지를 가지고 있다. 3. 당신은 벌써 유언장을 작성하셨나요?

079 well [wel]

Step 01 해석연습 — 다음 문장을 well에 유의하여 해석해 보세요. (해석은 이 페이지의 하단부에 있음)

1. He speaks French very well. ___________________________
2. She lowered her bucket into the well. ___________________________
3. Oil welled up out of the ground. ___________________________

Step 02 뜻 알기 — well에는 다음과 같은 여러 가지의 뜻이 있습니다.

❶ 잘, 능숙하게, 훌륭하게 `ad` in a good, correct, successful way; skillfully, excellently

❷ 샘, 우물 `n` a deep hole in the ground from which people take water, oil, natural gas, etc

❸ 솟아오르다, 분출하다 `v` to come from; to spring

> 한 걸음 더 **He is a <u>well</u> of information.** 그는 지식의 샘이다; 소식통이다.
> → (지식 등의) 원천, 근원(=a source of much knowledge, etc)
> **It is <u>well</u> that you came.** 네가 와서 좋다.
> → 좋은, 바람직한, 건강한(=in a satisfactory state or condition; healthy)
> **an oil well** 유정(油井) **well-being** 복지, 안녕, 행복 **well-known** 잘 알려진, 유명한 **wellborn** 출생이 좋은, 집안이 좋은
> **well-bred** 교육을 잘 받고 자란, 예절 바른

Step 03 연습문제 — 다음 문장의 well에 해당되는 뜻을 Step 02 의 ❶∼❸에서 고르세요. (해답은 441쪽)

1. His business is going well. (   )
2. The maid lowered her bucket into the well. (   )
3. Does this cloth wash well? (   )
4. Tears welled up in her eyes. (   )
5. Hot water welled up out of the ground. (   )
6. They drew water from the well. (   )

Step 04 영작연습 — 다음 문장을 주어진 부분을 이용하여 영어로 옮기세요. (해답은 441쪽)

1. 그는 언제나 자신의 일을 몹시 잘해 왔다. [always, extremely]

____

2. 우리는 샘에서 펌프로 물을 퍼 올렸다. [pumped, water]

____

3. 그녀는 자신의 눈에서 눈물이 솟는 것을 느꼈다. [felt, tears]

____

:: 1. 그는 불어를 매우 잘 말한다. 2. 그녀는 양동이를 샘으로 내려보냈다. 3. 석유가 땅에서 솟아올랐다.

Step 01 해석연습

다음 문장을 fair에 유의하여 해석해 보세요. (해석은 이 페이지의 하단부에 있음)

1. You must be fair when you plat this game. ________________________________
2. The skies were fair today. ________________________________
3. She bought a doll at the church fair. ________________________________
4. His grades were just fair this semester. ________________________________

Step 02 뜻 알기

fair에는 다음과 같은 여러 가지의 뜻이 있습니다.

❶ 공정한, 바른, 편견 없는 a just, honest, right, not favoring one side

❷ (날씨가) 맑은, 갠 a (of the weather) fine, clear, not rainy or cloudy

❸ 박람회; (정기적으로 서는) 장; 바자회 n a large-scale exhibition of commercial and industrial goods; a market held periodically in a particular place, often with entertainment; a bazaar

❹ (성적, 일 따위가) 보통의, 평균의, 중간 정도의 a average, neither bad nor good

▷ 한 걸음 더 이외에도 fair에는 '금발이며 살결이 흰', '예쁜', '꽤 많은, 상당한' 이란 뜻도 있음

Step 03 연습문제

다음 문장의 fair에 해당되는 뜻을 Step 02 의 ❶∼❹에서 고르세요. (해답은 441쪽)

1. You must be fair or you can't play. (   )
2. She got a fair score in archery. (   )
3. Please be fair when you play this game. (   )
4. Organizers expect the fair to draw about 100,000 visitors. (   )
5. Fair weather is best for sailing. (   )
6. There is a famous book fair in New York every year. (   )
7. He is fair at mathematics. (   )
8. The weather was fair that day. (   )

Step 04 영작연습

다음 문장을 주어진 부분을 이용하여 영어로 옮기세요. (해답은 441쪽)

1. 그 판사의 판결은 양측 모두에게 공정했다. [decision, both sides]

____

2. 비가 온 뒤 맑은 날씨가 되었다. [weather, after]

____

3. 한국의 서울에서는 매년 유명한 음식 박람회가 열린다. [famous, every year]

____

4. 나는 철자법 시험에서 중간정도의 성적을 받았다. [grade, spelling test]

____

:: 1. 너는 이 경기를 할 때 공정해야 한다. 2. 오늘은 날씨가 맑았다. 3. 그녀는 교회 바자회에서 인형을 하나 샀다. 4. 그의 이번 학기 성적은 보통이었다.

Review Group-16

A. 다음 뜻에 해당되는 단어를 보기에서 찾아 적으세요.

보기	novel	way	will	well	fair

01. ______________ an aspect or side of something; respect; point
02. ______________ (modal verb) used to form future tenses of other verbs
03. ______________ (of the weather) fine, clear, not rainy or cloudy
04. ______________ a deep hole in the ground from which people take water, oil, etc
05. ______________ a long written story in which the characters and events are usually imaginary
06. ______________ a means used to go from one place to another; a path; a road; direction
07. ______________ the mental power by which one controls one's thought, actions and decisions
08. ______________ a market held periodically in a particular place, often with entertainment; a bazaar
09. ______________ a written statement showing what is to be done with one's belongings, body, etc after one's death
10. ______________ new and strange
11. ______________ just, honest, right, not favoring one side
12. ______________ in a good, correct, successful way; skillfully, excellently
13. ______________ a method of doing something; a manner; a style; a means
14. ______________ average, neither bad nor good
15. ______________ to come from; to spring

B. 다음 빈칸에 가장 알맞은 단어를 보기에서 찾아 적으세요.

보기	novel	way	will	well	fair

01. We lost our (   ) in the forest.
02. I (   ) be sixteen next month.
03. Yesterday was (   ) and warm.
04. I felt tears (   ) up in my eyes.
05. She is reading the writer's new (   ).
06. He is different from her in many (   ).
07. They pumped water from the (   ).
08. Was the movie poor, (   ), or very good?
09. He is a man of strong (   ).
10. Ice was a (   ) thing to them at that time.
11. This is the best (   ) to learn English.
12. You must be (   ) when you take a test.
13. Nobel prize was founded in 1900 according to his (   ).
14. Jae-ho can skate (   ).
15. I bought a toy at the church (   ).

다음 문장을 굵게 처리된 단어에 유의하여 해석해 보세요.

01. Ever since the coming of television, there has been a rumor that the **novel** is dying, if not already dead. [2005년-홀수형 30번]

→ ____

02. While this approach can work well for problems that are similar to those previously solved, it often fails, and fails miserably, when a new problem is particularly **novel**. [2011년-홀수형 39번]

→ ____

03. Walking is the easiest **way** to keep ourselves fit. [2008년-홀수형 15번]

→ ____

04. To one who must live in a world of darkness, the **way** ahead is as clear in the thickest fog as in the brightest sunshine. [1999년-홀수형 46번]

→ ____

05. Mars was so bright that even the lights of the city didn't get in the **way**. [2004년-홀수형 33번]

→ ____

06. Renaissance art was different from the art in the Middle Ages in many **ways**. [2005년-홀수형 27번]

→ ____

07. Each **will** influence the others, and each **will** be influenced by the others. [2000년-홀수형 36번]

→ ____

08. For example, a mole on one's nose means that he or she is strong-**willed** and trustworthy. [2005년-홀수형 42번]

→ ____

09. Successful people are **willing** to work hard, but within strict limits. [2000년-홀수형 40번]

→ ____

10. Aristotle's theory may be bad physics, but it describes reasonably **well** what we can see in the real world. [2006년-홀수형 45번]

→ ____

11. Next to the **well**, I found a gourd, the traditional Korean dipper. [2004년-홀수형 19번]

→ ____

12. On behalf of all the executives, we wish you **well** and hope you enjoy your well-earned retirement. [2005년-홀수형 25번]

→ ____

13. Later, Joan mentioned that she was looking for volunteers to work in a **fair** she was organizing. [2011년-홀수형 19번]

→ ____

14. The things we learned in kindergarten include "share everything," "play **fair**," and "say you're sorry when you hurt somebody." [1995년-홀수형 22번]

→ ____

15. Disharmony enters our relationships when we try to impose our values on others by wanting them to live by what we feel is "right," "**fair**," "good," "bad," and so on. [2006년-홀수형 34번]

→ ____

Day 08

DAY 09

The spoken words cannot be swallowed.
입 밖으로 나온 말은 되삼킬 수 없다.

081 swallow [swɑ́lou / swɔ́lou]

Group 17

Step 01 해석연습

다음 문장을 swallow에 유의하여 해석해 보세요. (해석은 이 페이지의 하단부에 있음)

1. A snake swallowed the frog in an instant. _______________________

2. A swallow is a small bird which likes eating insects. _______________________

Step 02 뜻 알기

swallow에는 다음과 같은 여러 가지의 뜻이 있습니다.

❶ ~을 삼키다 **v** to take (food, drink, etc) into the throat from the mouth
삼키기; 한 모금(의 양) **n** the act of swallowing; the amount swallowed at one time

❷ 제비 **n** a small insect eating bird with a divided tail, which comes to northern countries in the summer

> 한 걸음 더 **swallowtail** 제비꼬리 **swallow-tailed coat** 연미복 **swallow one's pride** 자존심을 버리다
> **swallow one's words** ① 말을 취소하다 ② 말을 웅얼거리다 **swallow the bait** 미끼를 삼키다; 덫에 걸리다
> **in one swallow** 한 입[모금]에 **take a swallow of** ~을 한 모금 마시다

Step 03 연습문제

다음 문장의 swallow에 해당되는 뜻을 Step 02 의 ❶~❷에서 고르세요. (해답은 441쪽)

1. Swallows will come soon. (   )
2. You must not swallow the chewing gum. (   )
3. She tried to swallow the pill. (   )
4. We saw some swallows flying in the sky. (   )

Step 04 영작연습

다음 문장을 주어진 부분을 이용하여 영어로 옮기세요. (해답은 441쪽)

1. 껌을 삼키지 않도록 주의해라. [careful, chewing gum]

____

2. 제비는 여름마다 우리나라에 온다. [country, every summer]

____

:: 1. 뱀이 개구리를 순식간에 삼켰다. 2. 제비는 벌레 잡아먹는 것을 좋아하는 작은 새다.

082 save [seiv]

Step 01
해석연습

다음 문장을 save에 유의하여 해석해 보세요. (해석은 이 페이지의 하단부에 있음)

1. Tom saved the child from the fire. _______________________
2. We saved enough money for the trip. _______________________
3. All save him attended the meeting. _______________________

Step 02
뜻 알기

save에는 다음과 같은 여러 가지의 뜻이 있습니다.

❶ 구하다, 지키다, 보호하다 v to make or keep safe from danger, harm, injury, etc

❷ (돈 등을) 저축하다, 모으다, 저장하다 v to store up (money, etc) for future use; to reserve
(시간, 돈, 힘 등을) 덜다, 줄이다, 절약하다 v to avoid losing or spending time, money, energy, etc

❸ ～을 제외하고, ～ 이외에는 prep except; but

> 한 걸음 더 **saving** ⓐ ① 구하는 ② 절약하는 ⓝ ① 구조, 구제 ② 절약; (복수로) 저금, 저축(액) ⓟ ～을 제외하고, ～ 이외는
> **savings account** 예금계정, 저축계좌 **the last save one** 끝에서 두 번째 **save for** ～을 제외하고는
> **save and except** ～ 이외에는, ～을 제외하면

Step 03
연습문제

다음 문장의 save에 해당되는 뜻을 **Step 02** 의 ❶～❸에서 고르세요. (해답은 441쪽)

1. He is saving some money to buy a computer for his son. (   )
2. All the guests have left save one. (   )
3. One should save for a rainy day. (   )
4. The dog saved his owner's life. (   )
5. All save him had were pleased with the news. (   )
6. The man saved a little boy from the river. (   )

Step 04
영작연습

다음 문장을 주어진 부분을 이용하여 영어로 옮기세요. (해답은 441쪽)

1. 그는 친구를 익사하려는 것으로부터 구하려고 필사적으로 노력했다. [desperately, drowning]

____

2. 그 기계는 우리에게 많은 수고를 덜어 줄 것이다. [machine, trouble]

____

3. 그 소년은 한 문제를 제외하고는 모든 문제에 답했다. [answered, questions]

____

∷ 1. Tom은 불 속에서 어린아이를 구했다. 2. 우리는 여행을 가기 위한 충분한 돈을 저축했다. 3. 그를 제외하고 모든 사람이 회의에 참석했다.

083 reason [ríːzn]

Step 01 해석연습

다음 문장을 reason에 유의하여 해석해 보세요. (해석은 이 페이지의 하단부에 있음)

1. I want to know the reason for her absence. _______________________________

2. Man has reason: animals do not. _______________________________

3. They reasoned that he was guilty. _______________________________

Step 02 뜻 알기

reason에는 다음과 같은 여러 가지의 뜻이 있습니다.

❶ 이유 🅽 the cause or justification for something that has happened or that someone has done

❷ 이성, 판단력 🅽 the ability or power to think, understand and form judgement

❸ 논리적으로 생각하다, 판단하다, 추론하다 🅥 to think logically; draw conclusions from data; to infer

> 한 걸음 더 **There is <u>reason</u> in what she says.** 그녀의 말에는 일리가 있다.
> → 일리, 도리(=what is right or generally accepted)
> **reasoning** 추리, 추론, 이론 **reasonable** 도리에 맞는, 타당한, 합당한, 적절한 **by reason of** ~라는 이유로
> **in reason** 도리상, 합당한 **lose one's reason** 이성을 잃다, 미치다 **out of reason** 도리에 맞지 않는

Step 03 연습문제

다음 문장의 reason에 해당되는 뜻을 **Step 02** 의 ❶~❸에서 고르세요. (해답은 441쪽)

1. Give me your reasons for doing it. (   )

2. Reason distinguishes man from the animals. (   )

3. We reasoned that she was innocent. (   )

4. I have no reason to refuse his proposal. (   )

5. They reasoned that they were guilty. (   )

6. Only man has reason. (   )

Step 04 영작연습

다음 문장을 주어진 부분을 이용하여 영어로 옮기세요. (해답은 441쪽)

1. 우리는 그가 왜 그 제안을 거절했는지 이유를 모른다. [why, offer]

____

2. 그 젊은이는 그 소식을 듣고 이성을 잃었다. [young, lost]

____

3. 인간만이 사고하는 능력을 가지고 있다. [man, ability]

____

:: 1. 그녀가 결석한 이유를 알고 싶다. 2. 사람에게는 이성이 있고 짐승에게는 없다. 3. 그들은 그가 유죄라고 판단했다.

084 direct [dirékt / dairékt]

Step 01
해석연습

다음 문장을 direct에 유의하여 해석해 보세요. (해석은 이 페이지의 하단부에 있음)

1. A policeman is directing the traffic. ________________________

2. Draw a direct line here. ________________________

3. He has direct control over the business. ________________________

Step 02
뜻 알기

direct에는 다음과 같은 여러 가지의 뜻이 있습니다.

❶ 지시하다, 지도하다, 감독하다 [v] to guide, control, manage

❷ 곧바른, 일직선의 [a] straight, not curved or crooked

❸ 직접의, 직통의, 직행의 [a] without anything or anyone in between; immediate

한 걸음 더 **The train goes there <u>direct</u>.** 그 열차는 직접 그곳으로 간다.
→ 직접, 곧장(=straight, without interruptions)
directly 똑바로, 직접적으로 **direction** ① 방향, 방면 ② 지도, 감독 ③ 지시, 명령
director ① 지휘자, 감독 ② 이사, 중역 **indirect** 간접적인, 곧지 않은

Step 03
연습문제

다음 문장의 direct에 해당되는 뜻을 **Step 02** 의 ❶~❸에서 고르세요. (해답은 441쪽)

1. There is a direct train to Madrid. (　　)
2. He directed me to leave the room. (　　)
3. Our house is in a direct line with the school. (　　)
4. He will direct the building of the new bridge. (　　)
5. We will drive along a direct road. (　　)
6. She could get a direct flight to London. (　　)

Step 04
영작연습

다음 문장을 주어진 부분을 이용하여 영어로 옮기세요. (해답은 441쪽)

1. 대장은 자신의 부하들에게 공격하도록 명령했다. [captain, attack]

____

2. 그는 곧은길을 따라 운전했다. [drove, road]

____

3. 이곳에서 파리까지 가는 직행열차는 없다. [train, Paris]

____

:: 1. 경찰관이 교통을 지도하고 있습니다. 2. 여기에 직선을 그어라. 3. 그가 그 일에 직접적인 관리를 한다.

Day 09

085 drive [draiv]

Step 01 해석연습

다음 문장을 drive에 유의하여 해석해 보세요. (해석은 이 페이지의 하단부에 있음)

1. Mike is learning to drive a car. _______________________________

2. Edd needs to drive a nail into the door. _______________________________

3. She will drive me mad. _______________________________

4. He is a man with drive. _______________________________

Step 02 뜻 알기

drive에는 다음과 같은 여러 가지의 뜻이 있습니다.

❶ (차 따위를) 운전하다 v to control and steer a vehicle / 자동차여행 n a trip in a vehicle

❷ 때려 박다; 세게 치다 v to force a nail, screw, stake, etc into something; to hit with force

❸ (어떤 방향 또는 상태로) 몰고 가다 v to force in some direction or state[condition]

❹ 추진력, 활력 n the energy and enthusiasm

> 한 걸음 더 **drive** [draiv] - **drove** [drouv] - **driven** [drívən]
> **Hunger is a human drive.** 굶주림은 인간적 본능[욕구]이다. → 본능적 욕구(=an instinctive need)
> * 이외에도 drive에는 컴퓨터의 디스크 넣는 곳, 테니스나 골프에서의 강타라는 뜻도 있음

Step 03 연습문제

다음 문장의 drive에 해당되는 뜻을 Step 02 의 ❶~❹에서 고르세요. (해답은 441쪽)

1. Bobbi needs to drive in one more nail. (   )

2. He seems to have the drive needed for the job. (   )

3. Paul likes to drive his red sport car. (   )

4. Cowboys on horseback will drive the cattle to the market. (   )

5. He is a man with initiative and drive. (   )

6. Hunger drives one to steal. (   )

7. Mike will drive a race car at the track. (   )

8. Jack will drive the ax into the tree. (   )

Step 04 영작연습

다음 문장을 주어진 부분을 이용하여 영어로 옮기세요. (해답은 441쪽)

1. 우리는 부산까지 장거리 자동차여행을 하기로 결정했다. [decided, Busan]

____

2. 그들은 그가 말뚝들을 땅바닥에 박는 것을 보았다. [posts, ground]

____

3. 이웃에서 나는 소음이 나를 미치게 한다. [noise, neighbors]

____

4. 나는 그녀가 추진력이 있는 여자라고 생각한다. [think, woman]

____

:: 1. Mike는 자동차 운전하는 것을 배우고 있다. 2. Edd는 못 하나를 문에 박을 필요가 있다. 3. 그녀는 나를 미치게 할 것이다.
　　4. 그는 추진력[활력]이 있는 사람이다.

A. 다음 뜻에 해당되는 단어를 보기에서 찾아 적으세요.

보기	swallow save reason direct drive

01. ______________ straight, not curved or crooked
02. ______________ to take (food, drink, etc) into the throat from the mouth
03. ______________ except; but
04. ______________ to guide, control, manage
05. ______________ to avoid losing or spending time, money, energy, etc
06. ______________ a small insect eating bird with a divided tail, which comes to northern countries in the summer
07. ______________ the cause or justification for something that has happened or that someone has done
08. ______________ to force a nail, screw, stake, etc into something; to hit with force
09. ______________ without anything or anyone in between; immediate
10. ______________ to think logically; draw conclusions from data; to infer
11. ______________ to control and steer a vehicle
12. ______________ to make or keep safe from danger, harm, injury, etc
13. ______________ the energy and enthusiasm
14. ______________ the ability or power to think, understand and form judgement
15. ______________ to force in some direction or state[condition]

B. 다음 빈칸에 가장 알맞은 단어를 보기에서 찾아 적으세요.

보기	swallow save reason direct drive

01. Mike will (   ) the pole into the grass.
02. He will (   ) the film.
03. He tried to (   ) the child from drowning.
04. A (   ) is associated with the beginning of summer.
05. She has lost her (   ) to hear the news.
06. All (   ) her attended the party.
07. The noise of the boys will (   ) me mad.
08. Man's ability to (   ) makes him different from the animals.
09. Pedro likes to (   ) his new truck.
10. We will (   ) a lot of time if we go by plane.
11. He drew a (   ) line on the paper.
12. She works very hard; she has a lot of (   ).
13. There is no (   ) train from here to Seoul.
14. What is the (   ) for this noise?
15. My throat was so painful that I could hardly (   ).

다음 문장을 굵게 처리된 단어에 유의하여 해석해 보세요.

01. Then, it seizes the unsuspecting prey with a lightning-fast snap of the jaws, and **swallows** the prey down head first. [2007년-홀수형 19번]

→ ______________________________

02. When I came back, I **swallowed** hard at what I saw. [2008년-홀수형 30번]

→ ______________________________

03. He who gets all he can honestly, and **saves** all he gets will certainly obtain his goal. [1994년-2차 21번]

→ ______________________________

04. Otherwise, we won't be able to **save** our children from pollution. [1997년-홀수형 17번]

→ ______________________________

05. The city is doing other things to **save** energy. [2001년-홀수형 42번]

→ ______________________________

06. I could **save** people the trouble of going into the store by making my produce accessible at the side of the road, and that would provide value, too. [2010년-홀수형 46-48번]

→ ______________________________

07. You scan your documents, and **save** them as computer files. [2007년-홀수형 10번]

→ ______________________________

08. One **reason** why I like the beach is its solitary atmosphere. [1995년-홀수형 19번]

→ ______________________________

09. I **reasoned** that since I was going to be a journalist, I'd need a very special notebook in which to write. [2012년-홀수형 46-48번]

→ ______________________________

10. Then, I met a man and asked him to **direct** me. [1999년-홀수형 46번]

→ ______________________________

11. The solvent comes into **direct** contact with them, carrying the caffeine with it. [2009년-홀수형 40번]

→ ______________________________

12. We are **directed**, nurtured, and sustained by others. [1997년-홀수형 24번]

→ ______________________________

13. When I learned how to **drive**, my father took me around our neighborhood to let me get a feel for the huge car we owned. [1998년-홀수형 48번]

→ ______________________________

14. Almost all railroads face serious problems that threaten to **drive** them out of business. [1997년-홀수형 40번]

→ ______________________________

15. If you **drive,** you are competent, responsible, and powerful – your own man. [1994년-2차 42번]

→ ______________________________

16. On the contrary, over forty years ago, controlled studies showed that fits of anger are more likely to intensify anger, and that tears can **drive** us still deeper into depression. [2009년-홀수형 32번]

→ ______________________________

086 **broke** [brouk]

Step 01 해석연습

다음 문장을 broke에 유의하여 해석해 보세요. (해석은 이 페이지의 하단부에 있음)

1. The plate broke into pieces. _______________________________
2. I'm broke till pay day. _______________________________

Step 02 뜻 알기

broke에는 다음과 같은 여러 가지의 뜻이 있습니다.

❶ 동사 break의 과거형 **v** the past tense of the verb "break"

❷ (비격식의) 무일푼의, 빈털터리의; 파산한 **a** (informal) having no money; bankrupt

> 한 걸음 더 **break** [breik] - **broke** [brouk] - **broken** [bróukən]
> **go broke** 무일푼이 되다, 파산하다

Step 03 연습문제

다음 문장의 broke에 해당되는 뜻을 **Step 02** 의 ❶～❷에서 고르세요. (해답은 442쪽)

1. The river broke its bank at last. (   )
2. A lot of small businesses went broke in the recession. (   )
3. She's broke till payday. (   )
4. He broke the world record for the marathon. (   )

Step 04 영작연습

다음 문장을 주어진 부분을 이용하여 영어로 옮기세요. (해답은 442쪽)

1. Jane은 빙판에 미끄러져 팔이 부러졌다. [slipped, ice]

____

2. 그 회사는 지난달에 파산했다. [company, last month]

____

:: 1. 접시가 산산조각이 났다. 2. 나는 급여일까지 빈털터리다.

087 wind (뜻) ❶ [wind] ❷❸ [waind]

Step 01
해석연습

다음 문장을 wind에 유의하여 해석해 보세요. (해석은 이 페이지의 하단부에 있음)

1. There is no strong wind today. _______________________________
2. I forgot to wind my watch. _______________________________
3. The road winds among the hills. _______________________________

Step 02
뜻 알기

wind에는 다음과 같은 여러 가지의 뜻이 있습니다.

❶ 바람; 인위적인 바람　**n** air in motion as the result of natural forces; air moved by a fan, etc

❷ ～을 감다, 감싸다, 조이다　**v** to wrap something around; to turn and tighten

❸ 구부러지다, (도로·강 따위가) 굽이치다, 구불구불 나아가다　**v** to go or move in a curving, spiral, or twisting manner

> 한 걸음 더 **wind** [waind] - **wound** [waund] - **wound** [waund] *뜻 ② ③에 해당됨
> **a gentle wind** 미풍, 산들바람 **a strong wind** 강풍 **a fair wind** 순풍 **a contrary wind** 역풍
> **windfall** ① 바람에 떨어진 과일 ② 뜻밖의 행운, 횡재 **windmill** 풍차 **winding** ⓝ ① 휨, 굴곡 ② 감기 ⓐ 굽은, 휜, 나선 모양의

Step 03
연습문제

다음 문장의 wind에 해당되는 뜻을 Step 02 의 ❶～❸에서 고르세요. (해답은 442쪽)

1. The wind was very strong last night. (　　)
2. I wind the clock once a week. (　　)
3. There is much wind today. (　　)
4. The road winds up the mountain. (　　)
5. She will wind a scarf around her neck. (　　)
6. The river winds through the woods. (　　)

Step 04
영작연습

다음 문장을 주어진 부분을 이용하여 영어로 옮기세요. (해답은 442쪽)

1. 배는 바람을 거스르며 나아갔다. [sailed, against]

____

2. 그녀는 자신의 팔로 아이를 감싸안았다. [arms, child]

____

3. 작은 길이 숲 속으로 구불구불 나 있다. [path, woods]

____

∷ 1. 오늘은 강한 바람이 없다. 2. 나는 시계의 태엽을 감는 것을 잊었다. 3. 도로가 언덕 사이로 구불구불 나 있다.

088 step [step]

Step 01 해석연습

다음 문장을 step에 유의하여 해석해 보세요. (해석은 이 페이지의 하단부에 있음)

1. The man was walking with slow steps. ________________________

2. The boy ran down the steps. ________________________

3. We should take steps to prevent it. ________________________

Step 02 뜻 알기

step에는 다음과 같은 여러 가지의 뜻이 있습니다.

❶ 걸음, 한 걸음, 스텝 **n** one movement of the foot in walking, running, dancing, etc
걷다, 걸음을 옮기다 **v** to make a step, or to walk

❷ 계단, 층계 **n** the place for the foot when going from one level to another

❸ 수단, 방법, 조치 **n** an act or a measure done for some purpose

한 걸음 더 **Every year we go up one <u>step</u> on the salary scale.** 우리는 매년 급여가 한 단계씩 올라간다.
→ 진보[발전]의 한 단계, 진척; 계급(=a stage in a progress or a position on a scale; rank)
stepladder 접사다리, 발판 사다리 **stepping-stone** ① 디딤돌, 징검다리 ② (출세 따위를 위한) 발판, 수단, 방법
step aside 옆으로 비키다, 양보하다 **step by step** 한 걸음 한 걸음, 조금씩, 착실히

Step 03 연습문제

다음 문장의 step에 해당되는 뜻을 **Step 02** 의 ❶~❸에서 고르세요. (해답은 442쪽)

1. We should take steps to help the homeless. (   )
2. My baby took his first step today. (   )
3. The boy waited on the church steps. (   )
4. I am too tired to walk a step farther. (   )
5. She put flowerpots on the front steps of the house. (   )
6. They took all possible steps to prevent it. (   )

Step 04 영작연습

다음 문장을 주어진 부분을 이용하여 영어로 옮기세요. (해답은 442쪽)

1. 그는 숙녀에게 길을 내주기 위해 옆으로 비켜섰다. [aside, give way to]

____

2. 그는 한 번에 세 개의 층계를 뛰어올랐다. [ran upstairs, at a time]

____

3. 그녀는 성공하기 위해 가능한 모든 수단을 다 취했다. [possible, succeed]

____

∷ 1. 그 남자는 천천히 걷고 있었다. 2. 그 소년은 계단을 달려 내려왔다. 3. 우리는 그것을 막기 위한 방법을 강구해야 한다.

089 bright [brait]

다음 문장을 bright에 유의하여 해석해 보세요. (해석은 이 페이지의 하단부에 있음)

1. The moon is bright tonight. _______________________________

2. A bright student learns quickly. _______________________________

3. Everybody was bright and cheerful at the party. _______________________________

bright에는 다음과 같은 여러 가지의 뜻이 있습니다.

❶ 빛나는, 밝은, 눈부신　ⓐ shining with plenty of light

❷ 영리한, 머리 좋은, 총명한　ⓐ quick at learning; intelligent; clever

❸ 쾌활한, 명랑한, 활기찬　ⓐ cheerful or full of life; lively

> 한 걸음 더 **a bright day** 화창한 날 **a bright boy** 영리한 소년 **a bright smile** 쾌활한 미소
> **(as) bright as a button[new pin]** 번쩍번쩍하는; (구어) 쾌활하고 똑똑한
> **look on[at] the bright side (of things)** (사물의) 밝은 면을 보다, 긍정적으로 생각하다

다음 문장의 bright에 해당되는 뜻을 Step 02 의 ❶~❸에서 고르세요. (해답은 442쪽)

1. The moon was bright last night. (　　　)

2. What a lovely and bright girl she is! (　　　)

3. Polished steel is bright. (　　　)

4. A bright boy learns quickly. (　　　)

5. Julie is a bright child — she should do well at school. (　　　)

6. She is really an outgoing, bright, and funny girl. (　　　)

다음 문장을 주어진 부분을 이용하여 영어로 옮기세요. (해답은 442쪽)

1. 해가 너무 밝아서 눈이 부셨다. [hurt, eyes]

____

2. Jae-ho는 반에서 가장 총명한 학생이다. [student, class]

____

3. 그의 목소리는 활기차고 즐겁게 들렸다. [sounded, cheerful]

____

⁛ 1. 오늘 밤 달이 밝다. 2. 머리 좋은 학생은 빨리 배운다. 3. 파티에 참석한 모든 사람들은 활기차고 즐거웠다.

090 set [set]

Step 01 해석연습

다음 문장을 set에 유의하여 해석해 보세요. (해석은 이 페이지의 하단부에 있음)

1. He bought a new set of tools. ________________________
2. She won the first set of the game. ________________________
3. She set a vase on the table. ________________________
4. The sun sets in the west. ________________________

Step 02 뜻 알기

set에는 다음과 같은 여러 가지의 뜻이 있습니다.

❶ 한 벌, 세트, 한 쌍 🅝 a group of things used or belonging together

❷ 테니스, 배구 등에서의 세트 🅝 one part of a game

❸ 놓다, 정하다; 조정하다; 준비시키다 🆅 to put or place; to decide; to adjust; to get something ready

❹ 해가 지다 🆅 to go below the horizon

> 한 걸음 더 **set** [set] - **set** [set] - **set** [set]
> **There was a very impressive <u>set</u> in the first act of the play.** 그 연극의 첫 번째 막에 매우 인상적인 무대장면이 있었다.
> → 연극, 영화 따위의 무대장면, 무대장치(=a place where a film or television programme is acted or filmed)

Step 03 연습문제

다음 문장의 set에 해당되는 뜻을 Step 02 의 ❶∼❹에서 고르세요. (해답은 442쪽)

1. The sun rises in the east and sets in the west. (   )
2. she bought a set of dishes. (   )
3. My mother set the table for the dinner party. (   )
4. We lost the first set and won the next two. (   )
5. I got a new pen and pencil set for my birthday. (   )
6. The sky turns red when the sun sets. (   )
7. We just set the picnic table. (   )
8. He won three sets of the game consecutively. (   )

Step 04 영작연습

다음 문장을 주어진 부분을 이용하여 영어로 옮기세요. (해답은 442쪽)

1. Tom은 자동차용 새 타이어 세트를 샀다. [bought, tools]

____

2. 그는 첫 번째 세트를 이겼으나 다음 두 세트는 졌다. [won, lost]

____

3. 그는 자명종이 6시에 울리도록 맞추어 놓았다. [alarm-clock]

____

4. 해가 질 땐 선선해진다. [cooler, when]

____

:: 1. 그는 공구 1세트를 샀다. 2. 그녀는 경기의 첫 번째 세트를 이겼다. 3. 그녀는 탁자 위에 꽃병을 하나 놓았다. 4. 태양은 서쪽으로 진다.

해답은 442쪽

A. 다음 뜻에 해당되는 단어를 보기에서 찾아 적으세요.

보기	broke wind step bright set

01. ______________ quick at learning; intelligent; clever
02. ______________ an act or a measure done for some purpose
03. ______________ air in motion as the result of natural forces; air moved by a fan, etc
04. ______________ the past tense of the verb "break"
05. ______________ the place for the foot when going from one level to another
06. ______________ to go below the horizon
07. ______________ to go or move in a curving, spiral, or twisting manner
08. ______________ a group of things used or belonging together
09. ______________ to put or place; to decide; to adjust; to get something ready
10. ______________ one movement of the foot in walking, running, dancing, etc
11. ______________ cheerful or full of life; lively
12. ______________ one part of a game
13. ______________ to wrap something around; to turn and tighten
14. ______________ shining with plenty of light
15. ______________ having no money; bankrupt

B. 다음 빈칸에 가장 알맞은 단어를 보기에서 찾아 적으세요.

보기	broke wind step bright set

01. Do you know who (   ) this window?
02. He used to sit on front (   ) with my brother.
03. She will (   ) the woolen thread into a ball.
04. Her voice sounded (   ) and gay.
05. We should take (   ) to preserve the nature.
06. Dave bought a new chess (   ).
07. The (   ) is blowing gently.
08. Try to look on the (   ) side of things.
09. If you move a (   ), I'll shoot!
10. The sun (   ) below the horizon.
11. A stream (   ) slowly through the meadows.
12. We lost the final (   ) of the game.
13. Our company went (   ) last month.
14. She is very (   ) and learns quickly.
15. Mom (   ) the table for dinner.

다음 문장을 굵게 처리된 단어에 유의하여 해석해 보세요.

01. True, but I'm nearly **broke**, and I won't get paid soon. [1996년-홀수형 16번]

→ __________________________________

02. My brother borrowed my notebook computer and he **broke** it! [1997년-홀수형 8번]

→ __________________________________

03. The shapes of Korean kites are based on scientific principleswhich enable them to make good use of the **wind**. [2006년-홀수형 31번]

→ __________________________________

04. At the same time her heart was thumping and she started at every sound, rushing out to the door and looking down the **winding** road, which was now dim with the shadows of evening. [1996년-홀수형 38번]

→ __________________________________

05. Bands of blue-shirted farmers circle and lift and swing behind a drum and various **wind instruments** in the ancient Basque Riau-Riau dances. [2009년-홀수형 43번]

→ __________________________________

06. Intent on one of the pictures, she took a **step** back and hit the small table, tipping it over. [2011년-홀수형 19번]

→ __________________________________

07. Within industries, companies are always trying to develop products that are one **step** better than those of other companies. [1999년-홀수형 42번]

→ __________________________________

08. It's about time that we took serious **steps**. [1997년-홀수형 17번]

→ __________________________________

09. She opened the door and **stepped** out into the backyard. [2009년-홀수형 30번]

→ __________________________________

10. You're one of the **brightest** people I know, so I'm sure you'll do just fine. [2004년-홀수형 41번]

→ __________________________________

11. The furniture is soft and comfortable, and the curtains are **bright** and cheerful. [1995년-홀수형 17번]

→ __________________________________

12. Look on the **bright** side of things. [1994년-1차 11–12번]

→ __________________________________

13. The sun is **setting**. [1998년-홀수형 37번]

→ __________________________________

14. Many years ago, psychologists performed an experiment in which they put a number of people in a room, alone except for a ring toss **set**. [2010년-홀수형 45번]

→ __________________________________

15. **Set** yourself realistic goals, and aim to achieve them one step at a time. [1996년-홀수형 47번]

→ __________________________________

16. People can **set** up a tent in the middle of the smell of wild flowers and trees. [2000년-홀수형 37번]

→ __________________________________

DAY 10

Do your best, and God will do the rest.
최선을 다해라, 그러면 신이 그 나머지를 하리라.

 091 **ruler** [rúːlər]

Step 01
해석연습

다음 문장을 ruler에 유의하여 해석해 보세요. (해석은 이 페이지의 하단부에 있음)

1. The king was a wise and generous ruler. ___________________________________

2. May I borrow your ruler? ___________________________________

Step 02
뜻 알기

ruler에는 다음과 같은 여러 가지의 뜻이 있습니다.

❶ 지배자, 통치자 **n** a person who rules or governs

❷ 자 **n** a flat narrow piece of plastic, metal, etc used in drawing straight lines or in measuring things

> 한 걸음 더 **rule** ⓥ ~을 통치하다, 지배하다 ⓝ ① 지배, 통치 ② 규칙, 규정; 습관, 관례 **rulership** 통치[지배]자의 지위; 통치권

Step 03
연습문제

다음 문장의 ruler에 해당되는 뜻을 Step 02 의 ❶~❷에서 고르세요. (해답은 442쪽)

1. He was a wise and honest ruler. (   )
2. Will you lend me your ruler? (   )
3. People revolted against their cruel ruler. (   )
4. She can draw straight line without a ruler. (   )

Step 04
영작연습

다음 문장을 주어진 부분을 이용하여 영어로 옮기세요. (해답은 442쪽)

1. 그 나라의 통치자는 온 국민으로부터 존경을 받고 있다. [admired, whole nation]

____

2. 그는 자가 없으면 직선을 그을 수가 없다. [draw, straight lines]

____

:: 1. 그 왕은 현명하고 관대한 통치자였다. 2. 자를 빌려 써도 되나요?

092 branch [bræntʃ /brɑntʃ]

Step 01
해석연습

다음 문장을 branch에 유의하여 해석해 보세요. (해석은 이 페이지의 하단부에 있음)

1. The farmer cut some branches off the tree. _______________________________

2. The bank has branches all over the country. _______________________________

3. Geometry is a branch of mathematics. _______________________________

Step 02
뜻 알기

branch에는 다음과 같은 여러 가지의 뜻이 있습니다.

❶ (나무의) 가지 n a part of a tree that grows outwards from the trunk

❷ 지사, 지부, 지점 n an office in a particular area that is part of a large company or institution

❸ 부문, 분야, 분파 n a division; a part of a large subject of study or knowledge

> 한 걸음 더 **a branch office** 지점 **a branch of a river** 강의 지류 **a branch of study** 한 학과
> **a branch line** (철도 등의) 지선, 분기선 **a local branch** 지방지점 **an overseas branch** 해외지점

Step 03
연습문제

다음 문장의 branch에 해당되는 뜻을 Step 02 의 ❶～❸에서 고르세요. (해답은 442쪽)

1. Monkeys hid among the branches. (　　)
2. Economics is a branch of science. (　　)
3. He is a branch manager of a cosmetic company. (　　)
4. The subject may be divided into three branches. (　　)
5. The bank has branches in all parts of the country. (　　)
6. He cut some branches off the oak tree. (　　)

Step 04
영작연습

다음 문장을 주어진 부분을 이용하여 영어로 옮기세요. (해답은 442쪽)

1. 원숭이 한 마리가 나무를 타고 올라가서 가지 사이에 숨었다. [climbed up, hid]

____

2. 우리 회사는 시드니에 지사를 두고 있다. [company, Sydney]

____

3. 영어는 게르만어족의 한 분파이다. [the Germanic family of languages]

____

:: 1. 그 농부는 약간의 나뭇가지를 잘라 냈다. 2. 그 은행은 전국에 걸쳐 지점을 가지고 있다. 3. 기하학은 수학의 한 분야이다.

093 **duty** [djúti]

Step 01
해석연습

다음 문장을 duty에 유의하여 해석해 보세요. (해석은 이 페이지의 하단부에 있음)

1. It is our duty to obey the law. _______________________________
2. I took over the new duties. _______________________________
3. The duty of tobacco has gone up recently. _______________________________

Step 02
뜻 알기

duty에는 다음과 같은 여러 가지의 뜻이 있습니다.

❶ 의무, 본분, 책임 **n** something that a person ought morally or legally to do; obligation

❷ 임무, 직무 **n** service that a person has to do as part of his job or because of his social position

❸ 세금, 관세 **n** a tax you pay on something you buy; tax on goods

> 한 걸음 더 **The student paid his <u>duty</u> to the teacher.** 그 학생은 선생님께 경의를 표했다.
> → 존경, 경의, 복종(=respect; obedience)
> **duty-free** 면세의 **duty-free shop** 면세점 **on duty** 당번인 **off duty** 비번인 **do one's duty** 의무를 다하다

Step 03
연습문제

다음 문장의 duty에 해당되는 뜻을 **Step 02** 의 ❶∼❸에서 고르세요. (해답은 442쪽)

1. Don't forget your duty to your parents. (   )
2. What are the duties of this position? (   )
3. I do my duty as a responsible citizen. (   )
4. What is the duty on tobacco? (   )
5. She was dismissed for neglecting her duties. (   )
6. Travellers usually buy some goods at duty-free shops. (   )

Step 04
영작연습

다음 문장을 주어진 부분을 이용하여 영어로 옮기세요. (해답은 442쪽)

1. 세금을 내는 것은 모든 시민의 의무이다. [every citizen, tax]

____

2. 우편집배원의 직무는 편지와 소포를 배달하는 것이다. [deliver, parcels]

____

3. 우리는 위스키를 국내로 들여올 때는 관세를 물어야 한다. [pay, whiskey]

____

:: 1. 법을 지키는 것은 우리의 의무다. 2. 나는 새로운 임무를 맡았다. 3. 담배에 대한 세금이 최근에 올랐다.

Step 01 해석연습

다음 문장을 view에 유의하여 해석해 보세요. (해석은 이 페이지의 하단부에 있음)

1. The ship soon went out of view. _______________________

2. The view from my window is very beautiful. _______________________

3. In my view, he is innocent. _______________________

4. He studies hard with a view to passing the examination. _______________________

Step 02 뜻 알기

view에는 다음과 같은 여러 가지의 뜻이 있습니다.

❶ 보기, 구경; 시야 n the act of seeing or inspecting; the field of vision

❷ 광경, 경치, 전망 n that which is seen; a scene

❸ 사물을 보는 방식, 의견 n the way of looking at a matter; a personal opinion

❹ 목적, 의도 n a purpose; an intention

한 걸음 더 Let's <u>view</u> the proposal from another angle. 다른 각도에서 그 제안을 살펴보자.
→ ~을 보다; 고려하다, ~라고 간주하다(=look at; consider, regard)
point of view 관점, 견해, 의견 **with a view to[of] ~ing** ~할 목적으로 **out of view** 보이지 않는 곳에서

Step 03 연습문제

다음 문장의 view에 해당되는 뜻을 Step 02 의 ❶~❹에서 고르세요. (해답은 443쪽)

1. The view from her window is very nice. (　　)

2. The island came into view to the southeast. (　　)

3. She renovated the villa with a view to selling it. (　　)

4. Tell me your view on that matter. (　　)

5. The rainbow suddenly came into view. (　　)

6. He gave us his views on that issue. (　　)

7. Jane studies hard with a view to entering the university. (　　)

8. His house commands an excellent view. (　　)

Step 04 영작연습

다음 문장을 주어진 부분을 이용하여 영어로 옮기세요. (해답은 443쪽)

1. 배 한 척이 서서히 수평선 위로 시야에 들어왔다. [gradually, horizon]

____

2. 우리 별장은 전망이 좋다. [villa, fine]

____

3. 그들은 그 문제에 대해 서로 다른 견해를 가지고 있다. [different, matter]

____

4. 그녀는 나를 볼 목적으로 나를 기다렸다. [waited, seeing]

____

∷ 1. 그 배는 곧 시야에서 사라졌다.　2. 내 창문에서 보는 경치는 매우 아름답다.　3. 내 견해로는 그는 결백하다.
4. 그는 시험에 합격할 목적으로 열심히 공부한다.

Day 10

095 lose [luːz]

Step 01
해석연습

다음 문장을 lose에 유의하여 해석해 보세요. (해석은 이 페이지의 하단부에 있음)

1. Be careful not to lose your way. _______________________

2. He always loses at cards. _______________________

3. Hurry up. There is no time to lose. _______________________

Step 02
뜻 알기

lose에는 다음과 같은 여러 가지의 뜻이 있습니다.

❶ ~을 잃어버리다, 분실하다; 상실하다 Ⅴ to become unable to find; to stop having

❷ (시합, 소송, 전쟁 따위에서) 지다, 패배하다 Ⅴ to fail to win a game, argument, lawsuit, war, etc

❸ (시간, 돈 등을) 낭비하다, 허비하다 Ⅴ to spend (time, money, opportunity, efforts) uselessly; to waste

> 한 걸음 더 **lose** [luːz] - **lost** [lɔ(ː)st] - **lost** [lɔ(ː)st]
> **My watch <u>loses</u> one minutes a day.** 내 시계는 하루에 1분 느려진다. → (시계가 ~만큼) 느려지다
> **The invalid is <u>losing</u>.** 환자는 쇠약해지고 있다. → 쇠퇴하다, 약해지다, 줄다
> **loss** 패배자, 손해, 손실, 상실 **loser** 패배자, 실패자, 손해 본 사람
> **lost** 잃어버린, 길 잃은; 허비한, 쓸모없게 된; 패배한 **lose sight of** ~을 시야에서 놓치다, ~을 못보다
> **lose oneself** ① (길을) 잃다 ② 몰두하다 **lose one's temper** 화를 내다

Step 03
연습문제

다음 문장의 lose에 해당되는 뜻을 **Step 02** 의 ❶~❸에서 고르세요. (해답은 443쪽)

1. When did you lose your camera? (   )

2. There is not a moment to lose. (   )

3. Do your best, or you will lose the game. (   )

4. She was unfortunate to lose her son in the war. (   )

5. He is likely to lose the lawsuit. (   )

6. We shall lose no time in beginning the project. (   )

Step 04
영작연습

다음 문장을 주어진 부분을 이용하여 영어로 옮기세요. (해답은 443쪽)

1. 표를 잃어버리면 우리는 영화를 볼 수 없다. [movie, tickets]

____

2. 아무래도 우리 팀이 오늘 밤 질 것 같다. [afraid, tonight]

____

3. 우리는 그녀가 도착하기를 기다리느라 많은 소중한 시간을 허비했다. [valuable, arrive]

____

:: 1. 길을 잃지 않도록 주의해라. 2. 그는 언제나 카드게임에서 진다. 3. 서둘러라. 지체할 시간이 없다.

A. 다음 뜻에 해당되는 단어를 보기에서 찾아 적으세요.

보기	ruler branch duty view lose

01. ______________ to spend (time, money, opportunity, efforts) uselessly; to waste
02. ______________ a flat narrow piece of plastic, metal, etc used in drawing straight lines or in measuring things
03. ______________ to become unable to find; to stop having
04. ______________ an office in a particular area that is part of a large company or institution
05. ______________ service that a person has to do as part of his job or because of his social position
06. ______________ the act of seeing or inspecting; the field of vision
07. ______________ a purpose; an intention
08. ______________ a part of a tree that grows outwards from the trunk
09. ______________ the way of looking at a matter; a personal opinion
10. ______________ to fail to win a game, argument, lawsuit, war, etc
11. ______________ a person who rules or governs
12. ______________ a division; a part of a large subject of study or knowledge
13. ______________ a tax you pay on something you buy; tax on goods
14. ______________ that which is seen; a scene
15. ______________ something that a person ought morally or legally to do; obligation

B. 다음 빈칸에 가장 알맞은 단어를 보기에서 찾아 적으세요.

보기	ruler branch duty view lose

01. The government decided to raise import (   ) on sugar.
02. The (   ) from the hill is wonderful.
03. David is on night (   ) all this week.
04. Be careful not to (   ) your ticket.
05. A bird is standing on a (   ) of a tree.
06. The man was the (   ) of the country.
07. I shall (   ) no time in doing it.
08. The president's car soon came into (   ).
09. There isn't a (   ) of the bank in this town.
10. She studies hard with a (   ) to gaining a scholarship.
11. It is your (   ) to obey the law.
12. We use a (   ) to draw straight lines.
13. Algebra is a (   ) of mathematics.
14. In my (   ), you are right.
15. I'm afraid Mike's team will (   ).

다음 문장을 굵게 처리된 단어에 유의하여 해석해 보세요.

01. As night fell, she could just perceive outside a huge tree swinging its **branches**.
[2009년-홀수형 30번]

➡

02. It has its headquarters in Chicago, and major **branches** in Washington, D.C., New York, and Los Angeles. [2009년-홀수형 36번]

➡

03. Peter doubts if he can do his **duties**, and tries to find the right person who can take them over. [2008년-홀수형 17번]

➡

04. One winter night I found myself **lost** in the fog and in a part of the city I didn't know.
[1999년-홀수형 46번]

➡

05. Consequently, men are blind to their own faults but never **lose** sight of their neighbor's. [1997년-홀수형 36번]

➡

06. Hotel guests can hope to experience breathtaking **views** of the deep blue sea from Palazzo Sasso. [2008년-홀수형 36번]

➡

07. Westerners came to admit that their **view** toward the distinctive behavior found in nativecultures was biased. [2008년-홀수형 45번]

➡

08. The people in dresses and suits blocked my **view** of the garden. [2003년-홀수형 32번]

➡

09. In this **view**, railroads are the form of transportation that has much to offer when the world is concerned about saving fuel.
[1997년-홀수형 40번]

➡

10. The body has been **viewed** as a "natural" phenomenon – a fixed, unchanging fact of nature. [2011년-홀수형 43번]

➡

11. Television **viewing** does not demand complex mental activities. [1997년-홀수형 30번]

➡

12. Lend your money and **lose** your friend. [1995년-홀수형 39번]

➡

13. Don't be one of them. Sure, your team might **lose**. [2009년-홀수형 34번]

➡

14. The most effective way to **lose** weight is to stay on a balanced diet. [1995년-홀수형 12번]

➡

096 stable [stéibl]

Step 01 해석연습

다음 문장을 stable에 유의하여 해석해 보세요. (해석은 이 페이지의 하단부에 있음)

1. There is a white horse in the stable. ________________________________

2. Be careful, that chair isn't stable. ________________________________

Step 02 뜻 알기

stable에는 다음과 같은 여러 가지의 뜻이 있습니다.

❶ 마구간 n a building where horses are kept

❷ 견고한, 안정된, 튼튼한 a firm; fixed; not likely to move or change

> 한 걸음 더 **stableman** 마구간지기, 마부 **stability** 안정, 착실, 견실 **a man of stable character** 착실한 사람
> **stable foundation** 견고한 토대 **stability** 안정, 고정; 안정성; 착실, 견실
> **stabilize** 안정시키다, 고정시키다 **stably** 안정되어, 고정되어

Step 03 연습문제

다음 문장의 stable에 해당되는 뜻을 Step 02 의 ❶～❷에서 고르세요. (해답은 443쪽)

1. The farmer fixed the stable. (   )

2. This is a stable table with four thick legs. (   )

3. He took his horse out of the stable. (   )

4. She is looking for a stable job. (   )

Step 04 영작연습

다음 문장을 주어진 부분을 이용하여 영어로 옮기세요. (해답은 443쪽)

1. 그 남자는 자신의 말을 막간에 몰아넣었다. [drove, horse]

____

2. 우리가 원하는 것은 안정된 정부다. [want, government]

____

1. 마구간에는 흰색 말이 한 마리 있다. 2. 조심해라. 그 의자는 불안정하다.

097 second [sékənd]

Step 01 해석연습

다음 문장을 second에 유의하여 해석해 보세요. (해석은 이 페이지의 하단부에 있음)

1. February is the second month of the year. _______________________
2. There are sixty seconds in a minute. _______________________
3. I'll be there in a second. _______________________

Step 02 뜻 알기

second에는 다음과 같은 여러 가지의 뜻이 있습니다.

❶ 두 번째의, 제2의 **a** next after or following the first in time, place, rank, quality, etc
제2위(두 번째)의 사람 또는 물건 **n** a person or thing next after the first

❷ 초(시간의 단위) **n** a unit for measuring time that is equal to 1/60 of a minute

❸ 매우 짧은 시간, 잠깐 **n** a very short time

> 한 걸음 더 **secondary** 제2의, 2차적인 **second hand** ① (시계의) 초침 ② 중고품, 고물 ③ 조수, 보조자
> **secondhand** ① (상품이) 중고의 ②간접의, 전해들은 **the second prize** 2등상 **goods of second quality[grade]** 2등품[2류품]
> **a second Solomon** 제2의 솔로몬(솔로몬 같은 현명한 사람) **second to none** 어느 것[누구]에도 뒤지지 않는
> **at second hand** 간접적으로 **every second day** 하루 걸러, 격일로(=every other day = every two days)

Step 03 연습문제

다음 문장의 second에 해당되는 뜻을 **Step 02** 의 ❶~❸에서 고르세요. (해답은 443쪽)

1. Sixty seconds make one minute. (　　)
2. The library is on the second floor. (　　)
3. I'll be there in a second. (　　)
4. The rocket will take off in 10 seconds. (　　)
5. Would you please wait a second? (　　)
6. Mike is the second tallest boy in his class. (　　)

Step 04 영작연습

다음 문장을 주어진 부분을 이용하여 영어로 옮기세요. (해답은 443쪽)

1. 당신은 이곳에 도착한 두 번째 사람이다. [arrive, here]

____

2. 5초 동안 숨을 멈춰라. [hold, breath]

____

3. 잠깐만 이곳에서 기다려라. [wait, a few]

____

∷ 1. 2월은 1년의 두 번째 달이다. 2. 1분은 60초이다. 3. 금방 그곳에 갈 것이다.

144

098 **rest** [rest]

Step 01
해석연습

다음 문장을 rest에 유의하여 해석해 보세요. (해석은 이 페이지의 하단부에 있음)

1. Let's have a rest around here. _______________________________

2. They rested (for) an hour after dinner. _______________________________

3. The rest of the students are absent. _______________________________

Step 02
뜻 알기

rest에는 다음과 같은 여러 가지의 뜻이 있습니다.

❶ 휴식, 휴양 n a period of time when you are not doing anything tiring and you can relax or sleep

❷ 쉬다, 휴식하다; 쉬게 하다 v to (allow to) stop working or doing an activity

❸ 나머지, 잔여, 여분 n what is left after everything else has been used, taken away, etc

> 한 걸음 더 **rest room** (극장, 백화점 등의) 화장실 **restful** 편안한, 안락한
> **restless** ① 쉬지 않는, 끊임없이 움직이는 ② 불안정한, 잠을 못 자는 **at rest** ① 잠들어, 휴식하여 ② 정지하여 ③ 안심하여
> **among the rest** 그 안에 끼어, 그중에서도, 특히

Step 03
연습문제

다음 문장의 rest에 해당되는 뜻을 **Step 02** 의 ❶~❸에서 고르세요. (해답은 443쪽)

1. What you need now is rest. (   )
2. My brother had some cake and I ate the rest. (   )
3. He rested (for) an hour after lunch. (   )
4. The rest of the guests are in the hall. (   )
5. We will take an hour's rest on the way. (   )
6. She stopped walking and rested her legs. (   )

Step 04
영작연습

다음 문장을 주어진 부분을 이용하여 영어로 옮기세요. (해답은 443쪽)

1. 너는 피곤한 것이 틀림없다. 휴식을 취하는 것이 좋겠다. [tired, had better]

____

2. 그는 독서를 잠시 중단하고 눈을 쉬게 했다. [reading, for a minute]

____

3. 원하는 것은 갖고 나머지는 버려라. [take, throw away]

____

:: 1. 이 근처에서 휴식을 취하자. 2. 그들은 저녁식사 후에 한 시간을 쉬었다. 3. 나머지 학생들은 결석이다.

 **099 but** [bʌt]

Step 01
해석연습

다음 문장을 but에 유의하여 해석해 보세요. (해석은 이 페이지의 하단부에 있음)

1. He is rich, but he is not happy. ___________________________
2. I go to school every day but Sunday. ___________________________
3. There is no one but knows it. ___________________________

Step 02
뜻 알기

but에는 다음과 같은 여러 가지의 뜻이 있습니다.

❶ 그러나, 하지만, 그렇지만　conj　in contrast; on the other hand; however

❷ ～을 제외하고; ～ 외에는　conj　prep　other than; except (for); save

❸ (관계대명사) (부정을 수반하는 말을 선행사로 하여) ～이 아닌; ～하지 않는
　pron　(relative pronoun) that[who] ～ not

> 한 걸음 더 **He is but a child.** 그는 그저 어린애에 불과하다. → 그저, 오직, 단지, 겨우(=only; merely)
> **all but** 거의(=nearly; almost) **but for** ～이 없다면[없었다면](=without) **anything but** 결코 ～이 아닌(=never; far from)
> **nothing but** 그저 ～일 뿐(=only)

Step 03
연습문제

다음 문장의 but에 해당되는 뜻을 **Step 02** 의 ❶～❸에서 고르세요. (해답은 443쪽)

1. There is no one but likes the movie. (　　)
2. This is not my book but my brother's. (　　)
3. Of those invited, all but Tony came to the party. (　　)
4. He is tall, but he is not strong. (　　)
5. We go to school every day but Sunday. (　　)
6. Nobody but has his faults. (　　)

Step 04
영작연습

다음 문장을 주어진 부분을 이용하여 영어로 옮기세요. (해답은 443쪽)

1. 너는 가도 좋다. 하지만 6시까지는 집에 돌아와 있어야 한다. [may, must]

____

2. Tony를 제외하고 아무도 그 사건이 일어나는 것을 보지 못했다. [accident, happen]

____

3. 예외 없는 규칙은 없다. [rule, exceptions]

____

∷ 1. 그는 부자이다. 그러나 행복하지는 않다. 2. 나는 일요일을 제외하곤 매일 학교에 간다. 3. 그것을 알지 못하는 사람은 없다.

146

100 master [mǽstər / mάːstər]

Step 01 해석연습

다음 문장을 master에 유의하여 해석해 보세요. (해석은 이 페이지의 하단부에 있음)

1. This dog likes his master. _______________________________

2. She is a master of piano. _______________________________

3. His master's degree is in literature. _______________________________

4. It is quite difficult to master English in a year. _______________________________

Step 02 뜻 알기

master에는 다음과 같은 여러 가지의 뜻이 있습니다.

❶ 주인, 소유주, 고용주 n a person who commands or controls; an owner; employer

❷ 달인, 대가, 숙련가 n a person who is very skilled in art, work, trade, etc

❸ 석사학위 n a degree given at a college or a university

❹ (기술, 기능 따위를) 습득하다, 숙달하다; 정복[극복]하다 v to become skillful in; to overcome

▷ 한 걸음 더 **masterpiece** 걸작, 명작 **master's degree** 석사학위 **master of ceremonies** 사회자, 진행자(MC)

Step 03 연습문제

다음 문장의 master에 해당되는 뜻을 Step 02 의 ❶~❹에서 고르세요. (해답은 443쪽)

1. She is a master of interior design. (   )
2. The dog ran to its master. (   )
3. Her master's degree is in French literature. (   )
4. Mr. Green is the master of the villa. (   )
5. You cannot master it in a day. (   )
6. He has a master's degree in engineering. (   )
7. He was a master of the short story. (   )
8. She made an effort to master typing. (   )

Step 04 영작연습

다음 문장을 주어진 부분을 이용하여 영어로 옮기세요. (해답은 443쪽)

1. Brown 씨는 그 집의 주인이다. [Mr. Brown, house]

____

2. 그는 탐정소설의 대가이다. [detective, story]

____

3. 그녀는 하버드에서 교육학 석사학위를 받았다. [degree, education]

____

4. 그는 마침내 자신의 고소공포증을 극복했다. [fear of heights]

____

:: 1. 이 개는 자신의 주인을 좋아한다. 2. 그녀는 피아노의 명연주자[대가]이다. 3. 그의 학위는 문학 석사이다.
4. 영어를 일 년 만에 습득하기는 매우 어렵다.

Day 10

147

A. 다음 뜻에 해당되는 단어를 보기에서 찾아 적으세요.

보기	stable　　second　　rest　　but　　master

01. _____________ a building where horses are kept
02. _____________ to (allow to) stop working or doing an activity
03. _____________ to become skillful in; to overcome
04. _____________ next after or following the first in time, place, rank, quality, etc
05. _____________ a period of time when you are not doing anything tiring and you can relax or sleep
06. _____________ in contrast; on the other hand; however
07. _____________ a person who is very skilled in art, work, trade, etc
08. _____________ what is left after everything else has been used, taken away, etc
09. _____________ firm; fixed; not likely to move or change
10. _____________ a very short time
11. _____________ a person who commands or controls; an owner; employer
12. _____________ other than; except (for); save
13. _____________ that[who] ~ not
14. _____________ a unit for measuring time that is equal to 1/60 of a minute
15. _____________ a degree given at a college or a university

B. 다음 빈칸에 가장 알맞은 단어를 보기에서 찾아 적으세요.

보기	stable　　second　　rest　　but　　master

01. The doctor advised me to take a (　　　　).
02. It's quite difficult to (　　　　) French in a month or two.
03. He'll be back in a (　　　　).
04. The world needs a (　　　　) peace.
05. She is pretty, (　　　　) he is ugly.
06. The (　　　　) of the money is still in my pocket.
07. Busan is the (　　　　) largest city in Korea.
08. A dog knows his own (　　　　).
09. We usually (　　　　) for an hour after dinner.
10. He received his (　　　　) of Arts degree in 2004.
11. There is no living creature (　　　　) dies.
12. This watch has a (　　　　) hand.
13. There are black horses in the (　　　　).
14. He is a real (　　　　) at painting.
15. No one (　　　　) George saw the accident happen.

다음 문장을 굵게 처리된 단어에 유의하여 해석해 보세요.

01. It rewards insects with a **stable** environment that enhances their ability to eat, mate, and prepare for flight. [2009년-홀수형-37번]

→ ______________________

02. But like all beings in the universe, we face a speed limit, the speed of light, which is about 300,000 kilometers per **second**. [2002년-홀수형 23번]

→ ______________________

03. In a **second** his brow relaxes, and his eyes brighten. [1997년-홀수형 42번]

→ ______________________

04. Certainly. I won't buy **second**-hand items again. [2009년-홀수형 16번]

→ ______________________

05. As for men, "sustainability" is the **second** most favored factor in choosing a job. [2008년-홀수형 35번]

→ ______________________

06. Ignorance of other languages and cultures handicaps the United States in dealing with the **rest** of the world. [2006년-홀수형 25번]

→ ______________________

07. Most scientists believe that by **resting** our bodies, we keep ourselves in good physical condition. [1996년-홀수형 18번]

→ ______________________

08. That accident made my friend spend the **rest** of his life in a wheelchair, and I learned a costly lesson. [2001년-홀수형 32번]

→ ______________________

09. Not only do the tides advance and retreat in their eternal rhythms but the level of the sea itself is never at **rest**. [1994년-1차 35번]

→ ______________________

10. If I were a genius, I would not mind being treated like one. **But** since I am not, I do. [2000년-홀수형 41번]

→ ______________________

11. No signs of life occurred near him **but** the sound of insects. [2002년-홀수형 39번]

→ ______________________

12. Electric bulbs transmit light **but** keep out the oxygen that would cause their hot filaments to burn up. [2008년-홀수형 18번]

→ ______________________

13. She listened with all her ears **but** could hear nothing **but** the night. [2009년-홀수형 30번]

→ ______________________

14. He has a **master**'s degree in engineering. He wants to have his own business some day. [1995년-홀수형 15번]

→ ______________________

15. The **master** sat throned in his great chair upon a raised platform, with the blackboard behind him. [1995년-홀수형 37번]

→ ______________________

16. Thus you are going to have to **master** these skills eventually anyway. So deal with them now. [1997년-홀수형 35번]

→ ______________________

DAY 11

From pure spring pure water flows.
윗물이 맑아야 아랫물이 맑다.

101 model [mádl / mɔ́dl]

Group 21

Step 01 해석연습

다음 문장을 model에 유의하여 해석해 보세요. (해석은 이 페이지의 하단부에 있음)

1. The model shows new clothes to people. ______________________________
2. She is a model of politeness. ______________________________
3. He enjoyed making airplane models. ______________________________

Step 02 뜻 알기

model에는 다음과 같은 여러 가지의 뜻이 있습니다.

❶ 화가 등의 모델 또는 패션모델 [n] a person who poses for artists or with products for sale

❷ 모범, 전형, 본보기 [n] a person or thing which is an excellent example

❸ 모형, 축소형, 원형 [n] a small copy of a building, vehicle, machine, etc

> 한 걸음 더 **The boy modeled a horse out of clay.** 그 소년은 점토로 말의 모형을 만들었다.
> → ~의 모형을 만들다(=to make a model)
> **She will model for Dave's painting.** 그녀는 Dave의 그림 모델을 할 것이다. → 모델로 일하다(=to work as a model)
> **My car is the latest model.** 내 차는 최신형이다. → 형, 양식(=a particular type or design of something)

Step 03 연습문제

다음 문장의 model에 해당되는 뜻을 Step 02 의 ❶~❸에서 고르세요. (해답은 444쪽)

1. The model wore a beautiful dress. (   )
2. She is a model of courtesy. (   )
3. She is a model for a painting. (   )
4. Make your father your model. (   )
5. He made a model of a house. (   )
6. This car is the latest model. (   )

Step 04 영작연습

다음 문장을 주어진 부분을 이용하여 영어로 옮기세요. (해답은 444쪽)

1. 그녀는 여러 달 동안 한 예술가의 모델로서 일해 왔다. [as, several]

____

2. 정치가로서 그는 청렴과 품위의 본보기이다. [integrity, decency]

____

3. Tony는 새 로켓의 모형을 만들었다. [made, rocket]

____

:: 1. 모델은 새 옷들을 사람들에게 보여 준다. 2. 그녀는 예의 바름의 모범이다. 3. 그는 비행기 모형 만들기를 즐겼다.

102 water [wɔ́ːtər / wátər]

Step 01 해석연습

다음 문장을 water에 유의하여 해석해 보세요. (해석은 이 페이지의 하단부에 있음)

1. I like to drink water. ________________________________

2. Their house is on the water. ________________________________

3. He watered the plants in the garden. ________________________________

Step 02 뜻 알기

water에는 다음과 같은 여러 가지의 뜻이 있습니다.

❶ 물 **n** a colorless liquid made of hydrogen and oxygen

❷ 강, 바다, 호수의 물 **n** a body of water, such as a river, lake, sea, etc

❸ ～에 물을 주다, 물을 먹이다 **v** to supply with water

> 한 걸음 더 **Her eyes watered in the smoke.** 그녀의 눈은 연기로 눈물이 가득 고였다.
> → 눈물이 가득 괴다(=fill with tears)
> **The smell made my mouth water.** 그 냄새를 맡고 나의 입에서 군침이 돌았다.
> → 분비액이 나오다(=to produce saliva)
> **watercolor** 수채화 **waterfront** 해안(강변)지역 **water polo** (운동경기) 수구 **waterfall** 폭포 **watermelon** 수박
> **waterproof** 방수의 **water supply** 상수도, 급수시설 **by water** 수로로, 배편으로

Step 03 연습문제

다음 문장의 water에 해당되는 뜻을 Step 02 의 ❶～❸에서 고르세요. (해답은 444쪽)

1. Please give me a glass of water. (　　　)

2. My father waters the plants every day. (　　　)

3. The boats are on the water. (　　　)

4. Water is changed into steam by heat. (　　　)

5. Let's go on the water this warm afternoon. (　　　)

6. Ann will water the animals. (　　　)

Step 04 영작연습

다음 문장을 주어진 부분을 이용하여 영어로 옮기세요. (해답은 444쪽)

1. 그는 두 잔의 물을 연달아 마셨다. [glasses, straightly]

____

2. 그녀는 매일 소들에게 물을 준다. [cows, every day]

____

3. 몇 개의 통나무들이 물 위에 떠다니고 있었다. [logs, floating]

____

:: 1. 나는 물을 마시고 싶다. 2. 그들의 집은 물 위에 있다. 3. 그는 정원에 있는 식물들에게 물을 주었다.

103 spring [spriŋ]

다음 문장을 spring에 유의하여 해석해 보세요. (해석은 이 페이지의 하단부에 있음)

1. Flowers grow in the spring. ______________________________
2. The spring has run dry. ______________________________
3. The spring on the gate was broken. ______________________________

spring에는 다음과 같은 여러 가지의 뜻이 있습니다.

❶ (계절) 봄 **n** the season between winter and summer

❷ 샘 **n** a natural well, fountain

❸ 용수철 **n** a coil or wire that returns to its first shape after being pulled or bent
(용수철처럼 갑자기 빨리) 튀다, 뛰어오르다, 도약하다 **v** to leap, jump, rise up suddenly

> 한 걸음 더 **spring** [spriŋ] - **sprang** [spræŋ] / **sprung** [sprʌŋ] - **sprung** [sprʌŋ]
> **the spring of mankind** 인류의 근원 → 근원(=a source or origin)
> **hot spring** 온천 **cold spring** 냉천 **springboard** 다이빙대, 체조의 도약판 **the spring of hope** 희망의 샘

다음 문장의 spring에 해당되는 뜻을 Step 02 **의 ❶~❸에서 고르세요.** (해답은 444쪽)

1. I prefer spring to autumn. (   )
2. A spring is ground water. (   )
3. The watch has a metal spring. (   )
4. Trees grows leaves in the spring. (   )
5. The child has a toy that works by a spring. (   )
6. There is a little spring by the hillside. (   )

다음 문장을 주어진 부분을 이용하여 영어로 옮기세요. (해답은 444쪽)

1. 봄은 희망의 계절이다. [season, hope]

____

2. 사슴이 샘물을 마셨다. [deer, drank]

____

3. 그는 그의 자리에서 벌떡 일어났다. [up, seat]

____

∷ 1. 꽃들이 봄에 자란다. 2. 샘이 말랐다. 3. 문에 달린 용수철이 부서졌다.

104 safe [seif]

Step 01 해석연습

다음 문장을 safe에 유의하여 해석해 보세요. (해석은 이 페이지의 하단부에 있음)

1. Are these toys safe for small children? _______________________

2. Paul was safe after his first jump. _______________________

3. The old safe was very heavy. _______________________

Step 02 뜻 알기

safe에는 다음과 같은 여러 가지의 뜻이 있습니다.

❶ 안전한, 위험이 없는 a free from danger; not dangerous

❷ 무사한, 탈 없는 a not hurt; unharmed

❸ 금고 n a strong metal box or chest with special locks where you keep money and valuable things

> 한 걸음 더 **The runner was safe.** 그 주자는 세이프되었다.
> → 야구에서 타자[주자]가 죽지 않고 산 것(=successful in reaching base)
> **a meat safe** 고기 냉장고 → 냉장고(찬장)(=an air-cooled cupboard for food)
> **safe and sound** 무사히, 탈 없이 **safely** 안전하게, 무사히 **safeguard** 보호수단, 안전장치 **safety** 안전, 무사
> **safe keeping** 보관, 보호 **safecracker** 금고털이범(=safebreaker)

Step 03 연습문제

다음 문장의 safe에 해당되는 뜻을 Step 02 의 ❶~❸에서 고르세요. (해답은 444쪽)

1. The birds were safe in their cage. (   )

2. John found a safe place to watch the sharks. (   )

3. The safe is a strong box. (   )

4. She found a safe street to walk at night. (   )

5. The lost girl was cold, but she was safe. (   )

6. The safe held 10,000 dollars. (   )

Step 04 영작연습

다음 문장을 주어진 부분을 이용하여 영어로 옮기세요. (해답은 444쪽)

1. 이 해변은 수영하기에 안전합니까? [beach, swimming]

____

2. 차가 충돌했으나 그녀는 무사했다. [crashed, but]

____

3. 벽의 그림 뒤에 숨겨진 작은 금고가 있었다. [hidden, behind]

____

:: 1. 이 장난감들은 작은 어린이들에게 안전합니까? 2. Paul은 그의 첫 번째 점프에서 무사했다. 3. 오래된 금고는 무거웠다.

105 top [tɑp / tɔp]

**Step 01
해석연습**

다음 문장을 top에 유의하여 해석해 보세요. (해석은 이 페이지의 하단부에 있음)

1. He reached the top of Mt. Everest. ___________________________
2. I lost the top of this paint can. ___________________________
3. Children play with toys. ___________________________

**Step 02
뜻 알기**

top에는 다음과 같은 여러 가지의 뜻이 있습니다.

❶ 정상; 최고, 절정 **n** the highest point or part; the highest rank or place; the highest degree or extent
최상의, 맨 위의, 수석의 **a** at the top, highest

❷ 뚜껑, 마개 **n** a lid, covering, cap

❸ 팽이 **n** a kind of toy that spins

> 한 걸음 더 **She bought a new skirt and <u>top</u>.** 그녀는 새 치마와 윗도리를 샀다.
> → 윗도리, 상의(=a shirt, a piece of clothing for the upper body)
> **We <u>topped</u> the mountain toward noon.** 우리는 정오 무렵에 산꼭대기에 도착했다. → ~의 정상에 오르다(=reach the top of ~)
> **She <u>topped</u> the cake with cream.** 그녀는 케이크를 크림으로 겉을 발랐다. → ~을 씌우다, 바르다, 덮다(=to cover on the top)
> **top secret** 일급비밀 **topping** (음식의) 위에 얹는 것 **from top to bottom[toe, tail]** 완전히

**Step 03
연습문제**

다음 문장의 top에 해당되는 뜻을 **Step 02** 의 ❶~❸에서 고르세요. (해답은 444쪽)

1. His name was at the top of the list. (   )
2. The top went around and around (   )
3. Put the top on the jar. (   )
4. I lost the top of this paint can. (   )
5. Lisa climbed to the top of the ladder. (   )
6. Can you spin the top? (   )

**Step 04
영작연습**

다음 문장을 주어진 부분을 이용하여 영어로 옮기세요. (해답은 444쪽)

1. 꼭대기 층에는 스카이라운지가 있다. [sky lounge, floor]

____

2. 그 병의 뚜껑은 금속으로 만들어져 있다. [jar, metal]

____

3. 그는 팽이를 마루 위에서 돌렸다. [spun, floor]

____

:: 1. 그는 에베레스트 산의 정상에 도달했다. 2. 나는 이 페인트 통의 뚜껑을 잃어버렸다. 3. 아이들은 팽이를 가지고 논다.

A. 다음 뜻에 해당되는 단어를 보기에서 찾아 적으세요.

보기	model water spring safe top

01. _____________ a natural well, fountain
02. _____________ a person who poses for artists or with products for sale
03. _____________ free from danger; not dangerous
04. _____________ to supply with water
05. _____________ a strong metal box or chest with special locks where you keep money and valuable things
06. _____________ a colorless liquid made of hydrogen and oxygen
07. _____________ a kind of toy that spins
08. _____________ the season between winter and summer
09. _____________ the highest point or part; the highest rank or place; the highest degree or extent
10. _____________ a small copy of a building, vehicle, machine, etc
11. _____________ not hurt; unharmed
12. _____________ a body of water, such as a river, lake, sea, etc
13. _____________ to leap, jump, rise up suddenly
14. _____________ a person or thing which is an excellent example
15. _____________ a lid, covering, cap

B. 다음 빈칸에 가장 알맞은 단어를 보기에서 찾아 적으세요.

보기	model(s) water spring safe top

01. No living things can live without (   ).
02. The fashion (   ) is thin as a stick.
03. Peter likes to hike on (   ) trails.
04. As (   ) comes, the birds move northward.
05. This is one of the latest (   ) of a Hyundai Car.
06. She lost the (   ) of the jar.
07. You need to (   ) the garden, it's very dry.
08. He is a (   ) of industry.
09. He was (   ) after his first jump.
10. A (   ) is inside that toy watch.
11. The goods came by (   ), not by air.
12. It's your turn to spin the (   ).
13. This hot (   ) contains many minerals.
14. The (   ) of the mountain was covered with snow.
15. He opened the door of the (   ) and saw the gold.

다음 문장을 굵게 처리된 단어에 유의하여 해석해 보세요.

01. But a manager's actions provide a clear **model** of exactly the kind of behavior required. [2010년-홀수형 39번]

➞ _______________________________________

02. W: One of my **models** came down with the flu. Could you help me find a replacement?
M: I can call one of my friends who works at a **modeling** agency. [2011년-홀수형 14번]

➞ _______________________________________

03. These are full-scale **models** of human beings. They weigh the same as humans, and their arms and legs perform the same motions. [2007년-홀수형 3번]

➞ _______________________________________

04. Bob's roommate Michael is crazy about mobile phones. He always has the newest **model** loaded with the latest features and services. [2006년-홀수형 17번]

➞ _______________________________________

05. An eighteenth-century scholar said, "**Water**, which is essential for life, costs nothing. On the other hand, diamonds, which are essential for nothing, cost a lot." [2002년-홀수형 27번]

➞ _______________________________________

06. According to your instruction, I **watered** the grass every day, before 10 a.m. or after 4p.m. [1994년-1차 40번]

➞ _______________________________________

07. Hanging at an angle in the **water**, the leaf fish is carried along by the currents until it comes near a smaller fish. [2007년-홀수형 19번]

➞ _______________________________________

08. That **spring**, I was taken to my first big-league game. [2005년-홀수형 49-50번]

➞ _______________________________________

09. The nearby Ocoee was among the most paddled rivers in the country and six major climbing sites **sprang** up within an hour's drive of city limits. [2010년-홀수형 37번]

➞ _______________________________________

10. They all reached the beach two hours later, exhausted but **safe**. [2007년-홀수형 46-48번]

➞ _______________________________________

11. Nations of the world must act together if we are to develop answers that will give a **safe** and healthy world to our children. [2008년-홀수형 32번]

➞ _______________________________________

12. It took about six hours to reach the **top**. [2001년-홀수형 18번]

➞ _______________________________________

13. The above chart shows the **top** five preferred factors for male and female job seekers aged 55 to 79 in 2006. [2008년-홀수형 35번]

➞ _______________________________________

14. This means their tender **tops** are easier to reach for the rabbit. [1999년-홀수형 40번]

➞ _______________________________________

15. **Top** male players play for an average of only four minutes per hour on grass, according to recent studies. [2006년-홀수형 49-50번]

➞ _______________________________________

106 **bag** [bæg]

Step 01 해석연습

다음 문장을 bag에 유의하여 해석해 보세요. (해석은 이 페이지의 하단부에 있음)

1. She bought a small bag of popcorn. ______________________________

2. Jane packed her bag for the trip. ______________________________

3. Do these pants bag? ______________________________

Step 02 뜻 알기

bag에는 다음과 같은 여러 가지의 뜻이 있습니다.

❶ 자루, 봉지, 부대 n a sack or case made of paper, cloth, leather, etc

❷ 여행가방 n a suitcase; a travelling bag

❸ 처지다, 부풀다, 축 늘어지다 v to sag; to swell outward; to hang loosely

> 한 걸음 더 **baggy** 헐렁한, 자루모양의, 축 늘어진 * She wears baggy trousers. 그녀는 헐렁한 바지를 입고 있다.
> **a paper bag** 종이봉지 **a rice bag** 쌀자루

Step 03 연습문제

다음 문장의 bag에 해당되는 뜻을 **Step 02** 의 ❶~❸에서 고르세요. (해답은 444쪽)

1. Lisa bought a small bag of popcorn. (   )
2. Jeff will pack his bag for the trip. (   )
3. The hot sun made her dress bag. (   )
4. Where is your lunch bag? (   )
5. Why do these trousers bag? (   )
6. The worker loaded the bag into the plane. (   )

Step 04 영작연습

다음 문장을 주어진 부분을 이용하여 영어로 옮기세요. (해답은 444쪽)

1. 그는 식료품을 종이봉지에 담아서 운반했다. [carried, groceries]

____

2. Tony는 자신의 옷과 타이를 여행 가방에 넣었다. [suit, tie]

____

3. 뜨거운 태양이 그의 옷을 축 늘어지게 만들었다. [hot, dress]

____

:: 1. 그녀는 작은 봉지의 팝콘을 샀다. 2. Jane은 자신의 여행 가방을 꾸렸다. 3. 이 바지는 축 늘어지는가?

Step 01
해석연습

다음 문장을 fine에 유의하여 해석해 보세요. (해석은 이 페이지의 하단부에 있음)

1. Emily has a fine brown hair. _______________________

2. What a fine day it is! _______________________

3. He paid a fine for parking illegally. _______________________

Step 02
뜻 알기

fine에는 다음과 같은 여러 가지의 뜻이 있습니다.

❶ 훌륭한, 좋은, 세련된 [a] very good, excellent

❷ 날씨가 좋은, 맑은 [a] (of weather) clear, bright, not raining

❸ 벌금, 과료 [n] sum of money (to be) paid as a penalty for breaking a law or rule
~에게 벌금을 과하다 [v] to make someone pay a fine

> 한 걸음 더 **Fine salt looks like sugar.** 고운 소금은 설탕처럼 보인다.
> → 가는, 미세한, 정교한(=very small, thin, delicate)
> **She has a fine ear for music.** 그녀는 음악을 듣는 예민한 귀를 가지고 있다.
> → 예민한, 날카로운, 감수성이 강한(=sharp, sensitive)
> **I feel fine today.** 나는 오늘 몸이 좋다. → 몸이 건강한, 좋은(=healthy, well)
> **a fine pen** 끝이 뾰족한 펜 **fine thread** 가는 실 **fine art** 미술품 **fine arts** (넓은 뜻의) 예술

Step 03
연습문제

다음 문장의 fine에 해당되는 뜻을 **Step 02** 의 ❶~❸에서 고르세요. (해답은 444쪽)

1. It was so fine yesterday that we went out for a walk. (   )

2. The store sells fine jewelry. (   )

3. The fine shall not exceed $500. (   )

4. There is a fine view from the window. (   )

5. It rained all morning, but it turned fine later. (   )

6. I have to pay the fine within two weeks. (   )

Step 04
영작연습

다음 문장을 주어진 부분을 이용하여 영어로 옮기세요. (해답은 444쪽)

1. 그녀는 옷에 있어서 세련된 취향을 가지고 있다. [taste, clothes]

____

2. 내일 날씨가 좋다면 우리는 소풍을 갈 것이다. [go on a picnic]

____

3. 그녀는 쓰레기 불법 투척으로 50달러의 벌금에 처해졌다. [dumping, garbage]

____

:: 1. Emily는 멋있는 갈색 머리를 가지고 있다. 2. 얼마나 좋은 날씨인가! 3. 그는 불법 주차로 벌금을 냈다.

108 saw [sɔː]

Step 01 해석연습

다음 문장을 saw에 유의하여 해석해 보세요. (해석은 이 페이지의 하단부에 있음)

1. He saw a good movie last night. _______________________________

2. This saw is rusty and dull. _______________________________

3. The carpenter must saw wood every day. _______________________________

Step 02 뜻 알기

saw에는 다음과 같은 여러 가지의 뜻이 있습니다.

❶ 동사 see의 과거형 Ⓥ the past tense of "see"

❷ 톱 Ⓝ a tool for cutting, having a toothed edge

❸ 톱질하다 Ⓥ to cut something with a saw

> 한 걸음 더 **Don't believe the old <u>saw</u> "a good medicine tastes bitter."** "좋은 약은 입에 쓰다"는 옛날 속담을 믿지 마세요.
> → 속담, 격언(=a proverb; a saying)
> **saw dust 톱밥 saw mill 제재소 saw a log in half[two]** 통나무를 톱질하여 반으로[둘로] 나누다

Step 03 연습문제

다음 문장의 saw에 해당되는 뜻을 Step 02 의 ❶〜❸에서 고르세요. (해답은 445쪽)

1. She saw the man steal the bag. (　　)

2. Alison will saw this long board. (　　)

3. He bought a new saw yesterday. (　　)

4. I sawed up the tree for firewood. (　　)

5. I saw my friend on TV. (　　)

6. My uncle is cutting wood with a saw. (　　)

Step 04 영작연습

다음 문장을 주어진 부분을 이용하여 영어로 옮기세요. (해답은 445쪽)

1. Jane은 그녀의 이웃들을 그 상점에서 보았다. [neighbors, store]

____

2. 그 남자는 나뭇가지를 자르기 위해 톱을 사용했다. [cut through, branch]

____

3. 그는 그 판자를 톱질해서 반으로 잘라야 했다. [board, in half]

____

:: 1. 그는 지난밤에 좋은 영화를 보았다. 2. 이 톱은 녹이 슬고 (날이) 무디다. 3. 목수는 매일 나무를 톱질해야 한다.

109 back [bæk]

Step 01 해석연습

다음 문장을 back에 유의하여 해석해 보세요. (해석은 이 페이지의 하단부에 있음)

1. She has a baby on her back. _______________________

2. There was a garden at the back of the house. _______________________

3. He went back down the trail. _______________________

Step 02 뜻 알기

back에는 다음과 같은 여러 가지의 뜻이 있습니다.

❶ (사람, 동물의) 등　n the hinder surface of the human body; the upper surface of an animal's body

❷ (사물의) 뒷부분, 뒤(쪽)　n the rear part of something; opposite the front
뒤(쪽)의　a of or at the back

❸ 뒤로, 뒤쪽으로; 본디 자리[상태]로, 되돌아가　ad at or to the rear; in or into an earlier, normal, true position, or condition

> 한 걸음 더 **She backed her car out of the garage.** 그녀는 차고에서 나오기 위해 차를 후진시켰다.
> → ~을 후진시키다(=to move backward)
> **The bill is backed by environmental lobbyists.** 그 법안은 환경 로비스트들의 지지를 받고 있다.
> → 지지하다, 후원하다(=to support or help)
> **backbone** 등뼈 **background** ① 배경 ② (사건 등의) 배후 ③ 출신, 학력 **backpack** 배낭 **backpacker** 배낭여행가
> **backup** 지원자, 후원자 **backyard** 뒤뜰 **backward** ① 뒤를 향한 ② 진보가 느린, 진보에 뒤떨어진
> **back up** ① 후원하다 ② (컴퓨터) 데이터 파일의 복사를 만들다 **backward and forward** 앞뒤로, 이리저리

Step 03 연습문제

다음 문장의 back에 해당되는 뜻을 　Step 02　의 ❶～❸에서 고르세요. (해답은 445쪽)

1. He will be back in a few days. (　　)

2. I have a sunburn on my back. (　　)

3. Put these books back where you found them! (　　)

4. A spider is crawling on your back. (　　)

5. There is enough room for your stuff in the back of the truck. (　　)

6. Sarah stood at the back of the fence. (　　)

Step 04 영작연습

다음 문장을 주어진 부분을 이용하여 영어로 옮기세요. (해답은 445쪽)

1. 그는 무거운 상자를 들다가 등을 다쳤다. [hurt, lifted]

____

2. 그녀는 뒷문을 통해서 레스토랑으로 들어왔다. [entered, restaurant]

____

3. 신사는 자신의 지팡이를 앞뒤로 흔들었다. [swung, forth]

____

:: 1. 그녀는 아이를 등에 업고 있다. 2. 집의 뒤편에 정원이 하나 있었다. 3. 그는 오솔길을 되돌아 내려갔다.

110 eye [ai]

Step 01 해석연습

다음 문장을 eye에 유의하여 해석해 보세요. (해석은 이 페이지의 하단부에 있음)

1. She has a pretty blue eyes. ________________________

2. Mother put white thread through the eye. ________________________

3. The cat eyed the mouse. ________________________

Step 02 뜻 알기

eye에는 다음과 같은 여러 가지의 뜻이 있습니다.

❶ 눈 n the part of the body with which one sees

❷ (바늘구멍, 감자의 싹 등) 눈 모양의 것 n an eye-like thing

❸ 주시하다, 관측하다 v to look at; to observe

> 한 걸음 더 **You are wrong in my <u>eyes</u>.** 내 견해로는 네가 틀렸다. → 의견, 견해(=opinion, point of view)
> **She has an <u>eye</u> for beauty.** 그녀는 미에 대한 안목이 있다. → 안목, 식별력(=the power of judgement)
> **an <u>eye</u> of a typhoon** 태풍의 눈 / **bull's <u>eye</u>** 과녁의 중심 → 중심(=something central)
> **an eye of a needle** 바늘 귀 **an eye of a potato** 감자의 눈[싹] **eyeball** 안구, 눈알 **eyebrow** 눈썹 **eyesight** 시력, 시각
> **eye-catching** 눈길을 끄는 **eye contact** 눈 맞춤, 시선의 마주침 **eyelid** 눈꺼풀 **an eye for an eye** 눈에는 눈, 보복
> **in the eyes of ~** ~의 관점에서 **keep an eye on** ① 감시하다 ② 보살펴 주다

Step 03 연습문제

다음 문장의 eye에 해당되는 뜻을 **Step 02** 의 ❶~❸에서 고르세요. (해답은 445쪽)

1. He seemed to eye me suspiciously. (   )

2. The soldier's eye was hurt. (   )

3. Julie put black thread through the eye. (   )

4. Johnny put drops in his eye. (   )

5. The eye on that needle is too small. (   )

6. A policeman eycd the man carefully. (   )

Step 04 영작연습

다음 문장을 주어진 부분을 이용하여 영어로 옮기세요. (해답은 445쪽)

1. 그는 한쪽 눈이 장님이다. [blind, one]

____

2. Lisa는 조그만 바늘구멍을 통해 실을 잡아당겼다. [thread, through]

____

3. 경비원은 그 남자를 주의 깊게 주시했다. [guard, carefully]

____

:: 1. 그녀는 아름다운 푸른색 눈을 가지고 있다. 2. 어머니께서는 흰 실을 바늘귀에 꿰셨다. 3. 고양이가 쥐를 주시했다.

A. 다음 뜻에 해당되는 단어를 보기에서 찾아 적으세요.

보기	bag fine saw back eye

01. _______________ a sack or case made of paper, cloth, leather, etc

02. _______________ the hinder surface of the human body; the upper surface of an animal's body

03. _______________ a tool for cutting, having a toothed edge

04. _______________ sum of money (to be) paid as a penalty for breaking a law or rule

05. _______________ the part of the body with which one sees

06. _______________ the past tense of "see"

07. _______________ the rear part of something; opposite the front

08. _______________ a suitcase; a travelling bag

09. _______________ very good, excellent

10. _______________ to cut something with a saw

11. _______________ in or into an earlier, normal, true position, or condition

12. _______________ an eye-like thing

13. _______________ clear, bright, not raining

14. _______________ to sag; to swell outward; to hang loosely

15. _______________ to look at; to observe

B. 다음 빈칸에 가장 알맞은 단어를 보기에서 찾아 적으세요.

보기	bag fine saw back eye

01. She couldn't see well because her (   ) was hurt.

02. Jane's school has a (   ) swimming pool.

03. I (   ) her on the street last night.

04. Birds fly (   ) to their nests.

05. Chris cut the board with a (   ).

06. The pilot carried his (   ) onto the airplane.

07. The baby monkey was on its mother's (   ).

08. Sam could not get the thick thread through the (   ).

09. What a (   ) day it is!

10. My eyes (   ) when I don't get enough sleep.

11. There is something stuck to the (   ) of your coat.

12. Can you (   ) the branch off the tree?

13. Sandra carried her groceries in a (   ).

14. Cowboys must (   ) the cattle carefully.

15. He has to pay a parking (   ).

다음 문장을 굵게 처리된 단어에 유의하여 해석해 보세요.

01. According to ancient lore, every man is born into the world with two **bags** suspended from his neck – one in front and one behind, and both are full of faults. [1997년-홀수형 36번]

➡ ______________________________

02. OK. I'll give you the money for the **fines** this time. But you have to clean the bathroom for the next week. [2009년-홀수형 14번]

➡ ______________________________

03. Don't worry. I'm sure he'll be **fine**. [1998년-홀수형 3번]

➡ ______________________________

04. He shaped his life, down to the smallest detail, like a **fine** work of art. [1999년-홀수형 36번]

➡ ______________________________

05. Suddenly, she **saw** her lost brother Amin! [2000번-홀수형 54–55번]

➡ ______________________________

06. Their use ranges from the drill in a dentist's office to **saws** for cutting rocks, and to glass cutters. [2007년-홀수형 30번]

➡ ______________________________

07. When others in the village **saw** their success, they did the same. [1999년-홀수형 35번]

➡ ______________________________

08. W: Are you **sawing** this board exactly as we planned?
M: Yes, you can trust me. I measured it twice. [2008년-홀수형 13번]

➡ ______________________________

09. I listened to their stories, and I **saw** universal truths in their simple lives. [2003년-홀수형 27번]

➡ ______________________________

10. Well, I always sit at the **back** of the classroom. [2001년-홀수형 14번]

➡ ______________________________

11. How can you make the person you are talking to on the phone feel special when you cannot pat their **back** or give them a little hug? [2010년-홀수형 44번]

➡ ______________________________

12. It didn't look safe enough but she didn't want to turn **back**. [2011년-홀수형 30번]

➡ ______________________________

13. What is important is to bring a painting **back** to an artist's original intent. [2005년-홀수형 31번]

➡ ______________________________

14. Large **eyes**, on the other hand, suggest suspicion or tension. [1994년-2차 25번]

➡ ______________________________

15. Some scientists have shown the practical power of looking at the world through "could-be" **eyes**. [2009년-홀수형 49–50번]

➡ ______________________________

Day 11

DAY 12

Always do what you know to be right.
언제나 옳다고 알고 있는 대로 행동하라.

111 firm [fə:rm]

Group 23

Step 01 해석연습

다음 문장을 firm에 유의하여 해석해 보세요. (해석은 이 페이지의 하단부에 있음)

1. His decision is firm and will not changed. ___________________________

2. He firmed the ground after planting trees. ___________________________

3. My father works for an electronics firm. ___________________________

Step 02 뜻 알기

firm에는 다음과 같은 여러 가지의 뜻이 있습니다.

❶ 견고한, 고정된, 안정된 **a** strong, solid, fixed, stable

❷ 단단하게 하다, 굳어지다, 안정되다 **v** to make strong, solid or stable; to become strong, solid or stable

❸ 회사, 상사 **n** a business company

> 한 걸음 더 **firmly** 단단히, 확고히 **firmness** 견고, 확고부동함 **a firm belief** 굳은 신념 **a firm muscle** 단단한 근육
> **a law firm** 법률회사 **an accounting firm** 회계회사 **firm up** 안정시키다 **as firm as a rock** 바위처럼 단단한, 요지부동의

Step 03 연습문제

다음 문장의 firm에 해당되는 뜻을 **Step 02** 의 ❶~❸에서 고르세요. (해답은 445쪽)

1. She has a firm belief. (   )

2. He works for a law firm. (   )

3. The farmer will firm the ground after planting. (   )

4. The government tries to firm up the prices of commodities. (   )

5. She belongs to an accounting firm. (   )

6. My muscles are firm from exercise. (   )

Step 04 영작연습

다음 문장을 주어진 부분을 이용하여 영어로 옮기세요. (해답은 445쪽)

1. 그 집은 견고한 기반 위에 세워졌다. [built, foundation]

____

2. 기름가격은 마침내 상승하기를 멈추고 안정되었다. [oil, stopped rising]

____

3. 그는 광고회사에 소속되어 있다. [belongs, advertising]

____

112 **tip** [tip]

Step 01
해석연습

다음 문장을 tip에 유의하여 해석해 보세요. (해석은 이 페이지의 하단부에 있음)

1. The tip of the pencil is sharp. ___________________________

2. I gave a tip to the kind porter. ___________________________

3. The boat tipped to one side. ___________________________

Step 02
뜻 알기

tip에는 다음과 같은 여러 가지의 뜻이 있습니다.

❶ 뾰족한 끝, 첨단 **n** the pointed or thin end of something

❷ 팁, 봉사료, 사례금 **n** a gift of money given to a waiter, porter, servant, etc for personal service

❸ 기울이다; 기울다 **v** to lean or tilt on one side or at one end

> 한 걸음 더 **He gave me some useful <u>tips</u> on gardening.** 그는 나에게 정원 가꾸는 것에 대한 약간의 유용한 정보를 주었다.
> → 정보, 귀띔, 조언(=a piece of useful information; a hint)
> **He <u>tipped</u> his hat to me.** 그는 모자를 살짝 들어 나에게 인사했다.
> → 인사하기 위해서 모자를 살짝 들어 올리다, 가볍게 치다(=to touch or strike lightly)
> **tiptoe** 발끝으로 걷다 **tiptop** 최고의, 절정의 **tip over** ~을 뒤집어엎다, 뒤집히다 **tip over a glass of water** 물 컵을 뒤엎다

Step 03
연습문제

다음 문장의 tip에 해당되는 뜻을 Step 02 의 ❶~❸에서 고르세요. (해답은 445쪽)

1. The tip of my pencil is dull. (   )

2. The tittle boy tried to tip over a chair. (   )

3. He gave a tip to the hardworking waiter. (   )

4. My sister might tip over the big plant. (   )

5. That bird sat on the tip of the flagpole. (   )

6. Bcn gave the barber a tip. (   )

Step 04
영작연습

다음 문장을 주어진 부분을 이용하여 영어로 옮기세요. (해답은 445쪽)

1. 그 노란 새는 깃대의 끝에 앉아 있었다. [yellow, flagpole]

____

2. 그녀는 부지런한 웨이터에게 후한 봉사료를 주었다. [hardwoking, generous]

____

3. 그는 양동이를 기울여 물을 쏟아 버렸다. [bucket, poured]

____

:: 1. 그 연필의 끝은 날카롭다. 2. 나는 친절한 짐꾼에게 봉사료를 주었다. 3. 보트가 한쪽으로 기울었다.

113 right [rait]

Step 01 해석연습

다음 문장을 right에 유의하여 해석해 보세요. (해석은 이 페이지의 하단부에 있음)

1. Raise your right hand. _______________________________

2. He gave the right answer to the question. _______________________________

3. You have no right to do that. _______________________________

Step 02 뜻 알기

right에는 다음과 같은 여러 가지의 뜻이 있습니다.

❶ 오른쪽의 a referring to the direction to the east when a person faces north

❷ 정확한, 올바른 a correct, true

❸ 권리 n a just claim; the proper authority

> 한 걸음 더 **They fought for the right.** 그들은 정의를 위해 싸웠다. → 정의(=justice, rue)
> **He went out right after dinner.** 그는 저녁식사 후 곧바로 나갔다. → 곧바로, 곧(=immediately)
> **right-handed** 오른손잡이의 **right angle** 직각 **righteous** 정당한, 당연한 **rightful** 합법적인
> **right now** 즉시, 바로 지금(=immediately) **right away** 즉시, 곧바로 **all right** 좋다

Step 03 연습문제

다음 문장의 right에 해당되는 뜻을 **Step 02** 의 ❶~❸에서 고르세요. (해답은 445쪽)

1. He raised his right hand. (   )
2. You are right, and he is wrong. (   )
3. There is a bakery on your right side. (   )
4. We must respect the rights of others. (   )
5. It isn't right to think so. (   )
6. I will fight for my right. (   )

Step 04 영작연습

다음 문장을 주어진 부분을 이용하여 영어로 옮기세요. (해답은 445쪽)

1. 그는 오른쪽 다리를 움직일 수 없었다. [move, leg]

____

2. 언제나 옳고 명예로운 일을 해라. [always, honorable]

____

3. 모든 사람은 행복을 추구할 권리가 있다. [everyone, pursue]

____

:: 1. 오른쪽 손을 들어라. 2. 그는 그 문제에 대한 정확한 답을 주었다. 3. 당신은 그렇게 할 권리가 없다.

114 needle [níːdl]

다음 문장을 needle에 유의하여 해석해 보세요. (해석은 이 페이지의 하단부에 있음)

1. Grandmother will thread the needle. ___________________________

2. The nurse put the needle in my arm. ___________________________

3. The needle is pointing southwest. ___________________________

needle에는 다음과 같은 여러 가지의 뜻이 있습니다.

❶ 바늘 🇳 a thin, sharp-pointed tool for sewing

❷ 바늘 모양의 것(뜨개바늘, 주사바늘, 축음기바늘 등) 🇳 any various instruments of a long narrow pointed shape

❸ (나침반 같은 계기 등의) 바늘, 지침 🇳 a thin moving pointer in a compass, etc

> 한 걸음 더 **A pine <u>needle</u> looks like a pin.** 솔잎은 핀처럼 보인다.
> → 침엽수의 잎, 바늘 잎(=a needle-shaped leaf of some trees)
> **She is always <u>needling</u> me about my big nose.** 그녀는 언제나 나의 큰 코에 대해 놀려댄다.
> → (구어체) 놀려대다, 괴롭히다(=to make fun of someone, to tease)
> **a knitting needle** 뜨개바늘 **needle work** 바느질, 자수 등 **a needle and thread** 실 꿴 바늘
> **needle match** 막상막하의 치열한 접전 **a needle's eye** 바늘 귀
> **look for[search for, find] a needle in a haystack** 건초더미 속에서 바늘을 찾다; 불가능한 일을 시도하다; 헛수고를 하다.

다음 문장의 needle에 해당되는 뜻을 **Step 02** 의 ❶~❸에서 고르세요. (해답은 445쪽)

1. The old lady tried to thread the needle. (   )

2. Medicine is inside the needle. (   )

3. The compass needle pointed to 180 degrees. (   )

4. I need to buy a phonograph needle. (   )

5. My mother is looking for a needle to sew her clothes. (   )

6. The magnetic needle points to the north. (   )

다음 문장을 주어진 부분을 이용하여 영어로 옮기세요. (해답은 445쪽)

1. 그녀는 그녀의 재봉틀에 새 바늘을 꿰었다. [put, sewing machine]

____

2. 아픈 어린이는 주사바늘을 두려워한다. [sick, afraid]

____

3. 나침반의 바늘은 당신에게 가야 할 방향을 보여 준다. [shows, direction]

____

∷ 1. 할머니는 바늘에 실을 꿸 것이다. 2. 간호사가 나의 팔에 주사바늘을 꽂았다. 3. 나침반의 바늘이 남서쪽을 가리키고 있다.

115 post [poust]

다음 문장을 post에 유의하여 해석해 보세요. (해석은 이 페이지의 하단부에 있음)

1. He tied his horse to the post. ________________________
2. She got a post as a receptionist. ________________________
3. Today's post has not come yet. ________________________

post에는 다음과 같은 여러 가지의 뜻이 있습니다.

❶ 기둥, 말뚝 🇳 a long piece of metal, wood, etc usually fixed upright in the ground; a pole

❷ 직장, 지위, 직책 🇳 a job; a position or appointment

❸ 우편제도; 우체국; 우편물 🇳 the official system of carrying and delivering letters, parcels, etc; a post office; a mail
편지나 카드 따위를 보내다, 우송하다 🇻 to send a letter, card, etc by post

> 한 걸음 더 **Don't <u>post</u> this wall. (=Post no bills.)** 벽보금지
> → (전단 따위를) 기둥, 벽 등에 붙이다, 게시하다(=to fix or put up a poster, etc on a wall, etc)
> **He is a <u>post</u>graduate student.** 그는 대학원생이다.
> → (접두사) ~후, 다음(=after, behind, following, later)
> **postbox** 우체통(=mailbox) **postcode** 우편번호(=postal code) * zip code 우편번호(미) **post card** 엽서
> **a telegraph post** 전신주 **a starting post** 출발점 **a winning post** 결승점 **by post** 우편으로

다음 문장의 post에 해당되는 뜻을 Step 02 의 ❶~❸에서 고르세요. (해답은 445쪽)

1. Please take this letter to the post. (   )
2. The car ran into a wooden post on the highway. (   )
3. He was given an important post. (   )
4. I will send you this book by post. (   )
5. She will be appointed to the post. (   )
6. I will support the leaning fence with a post. (   )

다음 문장을 주어진 부분을 이용하여 영어로 옮기세요. (해답은 445쪽)

1. 이 기둥들이 담장을 지탱한다. [hold up, fence]

____

2. 그는 총괄지배인의 지위가 부여되었다. [as, general manager]

____

3. 나는 친구에게 카드를 부쳤다. [card, friend]

____

:: 1. 그는 그의 말을 말뚝에 매었다. 2. 그녀는 접수계원으로서의 직책을 가지고 있었다. 3. 오늘의 우편물이 아직 안 왔다.

A. 다음 뜻에 해당되는 단어를 보기에서 찾아 적으세요.

보기	firm tip right needle post

01. _____________ a business company
02. _____________ a gift of money given to a waiter, porter, servant, etc for personal service
03. _____________ a long piece of metal, wood, etc usually fixed upright in the ground; a pole
04. _____________ a thin, sharp-pointed tool for sewing
05. _____________ strong, solid, fixed, stable
06. _____________ referring to the direction to the east when a person faces north
07. _____________ any various instruments of a long narrow pointed shape
08. _____________ the official system of carrying and delivering letters, parcels, etc; a mail
09. _____________ a thin moving pointer in a compass, etc
10. _____________ correct, true
11. _____________ the pointed or thin end of something
12. _____________ a job; a position or appointment
13. _____________ to lean or tilt on one side or at one end
14. _____________ to make strong, solid stable: to become strong, solid or stable
15. _____________ a just claim; the proper authority

B. 다음 빈칸에 가장 알맞은 단어를 보기에서 찾아 적으세요.

보기	firm tip right needle post

01. My brother works for this (   ).
02. She used a strong (   ) to sew her jacket.
03. Please send it to me by (   ).
04. If you (   ) the pot, tea will come out.
05. She couldn't move her (   ) leg.
06. He is hoping to (   ) up his muscles.
07. He gave the waitress a $2.00 (   ).
08. He has been offered the (   ) of ambassador to Canada.
09. The doctor's (   ) was 4 inches long.
10. Let me know the (   ) answer.
11. There was snow on the (   ) of the mountain.
12. I'll tie my horse to that (   ).
13. The magnetic (   ) of the compass began to move.
14. We have no (   ) to stop him.
15. His decision was as (   ) as a rock.

Day 12

다음 문장을 굵게 처리된 단어에 유의하여 해석해 보세요.

01. If your determination is **firm**, clear, and sincere, then you will be able to put that emotion and memory aside and find peace of mind. [2003년-홀수형-46번]

➜ ___________________________________

02. Since you started in the mail room in 1979, your contributions to this **firm** have been invaluable. [2005년-홀수형 25번]

➜ ___________________________________

03. There, placed neatly beside the empty dish, were fifteen pennies – my **tip**. [2008년-홀수형 30번]

➜ ___________________________________

04. One of the popular hand gestures is the "Hand Purse," in which the **tips** of all five fingers are brought together until they touch in a circle. [2003년-홀수형 31번]

➜ ___________________________________

05. Intent on one of the pictures, she took a step back and hit the small table, **tipping** it over. [2011년-홀수형 19번]

➜ ___________________________________

06. Thanks for the **tip**. I'll go see if I can use it. [2010년-홀수형 15번]

➜ ___________________________________

07. Having a mole over one's **right** eyebrow means he or she will be lucky with money and have a successful career. [2005년-홀수형 42번]

➜ ___________________________________

08. I know a beautiful barn where the corners are not at **right** angles. [2009년-홀수형 26번]

➜ ___________________________________

09. The purpose of the court system is to protect the **rights** of the people. [1996년-홀수형 17번]

➜ ___________________________________

10. All parents agree that children must learn the difference between **right** and wrong. [1999년-홀수형 26번]

➜ ___________________________________

11. As a result of the economy, there aren't many jobs available **right** now. [2002년-홀수형 28번]

➜ ___________________________________

12. We should, therefore, be ready to fight for the **right** to tell the truth whenever it is threatened. [2002년-홀수형 36번]

➜ ___________________________________

13. M: Can I borrow a **needle**?
W: Why? Do you want to sew something? [2004년-홀수형 13번]

➜ ___________________________________

14. It was one of those children' toys with a short wooden **post** held upright on the floor and a bunch of round rings. [2010년-홀수형 45번]

➜ ___________________________________

15. At that moment, his family picture **posted** on the inside of the aircar came into his eye. [2008년-홀수형 46–48번]

➜ ___________________________________

16. The **post**-cold war world is a very different place. [2002년-홀수형 46번]

➜ ___________________________________

17. She **posted** them the next morning, and gave a sigh of relief. [1998년-홀수형 19번]

➜ ___________________________________

18. Later in life, he was honored to serve a number of **posts** in the city government. [2013년-홀수형 33번]

➜ ___________________________________

116 general [dʒénərəl]

Step 01 해석연습

다음 문장을 general에 유의하여 해석해 보세요. (해석은 이 페이지의 하단부에 있음)

1. The general feeling toward her is not good. ___________________________

2. I will give you a general idea of the plan. ___________________________

3. A general commands an army. ___________________________

Step 02 뜻 알기

general에는 다음과 같은 여러 가지의 뜻이 있습니다.

❶ 전반적인, 전체의, 일반적인 [a] for all; of all; overall

❷ 대체적인, 개괄적인, 막연한 [a] not detailed; not specific

❸ 장군, 장성, 대장 [n] an officer of very high rank in the army

한 걸음 더 **a general description** 개괄적인 묘사 **a general election** 총선거 **a general hospital** 종합병원
a general opinion 여론 **a general manager** 총지배인 **a general meeting** 총회 **in general** 일반적으로(=generally)

Step 03 연습문제

다음 문장의 general에 해당되는 뜻을 **Step 02** 의 ❶~❸에서 고르세요. (해답은 446쪽)

1. The general opinion is that she is honest. (   )

2. The general lined up his troops. (   )

3. The general meeting is scheduled for October. (   )

4. He first made a general outline of the plan. (   )

5. My grandfather was a general during the Vietnam War. (   )

6. She gave me a general idea of the project. (   )

Step 04 영작연습

다음 문장을 주어진 부분을 이용하여 영어로 옮기세요. (해답은 446쪽)

1. 일반적인 견해는 그가 결백하다는 것이다. [opinion, innocent]

____

2. 그들은 우선 여름방학에 대한 개략적인 계획을 세웠다. [plan, vacation]

____

3. 그녀의 할아버지는 2차 세계대전 중에 유명한 장군이셨다. [during, World War Two]

____

:: 1. 그녀에 대한 전반적인 감정은 좋지 않다. 2. 너에게 그 계획의 대강을 말해 주겠다. 3. 장군은 군대를 지휘한다.

117 attend [əténd]

Step 01
해석연습

다음 문장을 attend에 유의하여 해석해 보세요. (해석은 이 페이지의 하단부에 있음)

1. He couldn't attend the class today. ___________________________

2. The tall waitress attended our table. ___________________________

3. Attend to your own business. ___________________________

Step 02
뜻 알기

attend에는 다음과 같은 여러 가지의 뜻이 있습니다.

❶ 참석하다, 출석하다 Ⅴ to go to or to be present at

❷ 돌보다, 시중들다 Ⅴ to look after; to serve or help

❸ 주의하다, 유의하다 Ⅴ to listen carefully or pay attention to

> 한 걸음 더 **attention** 주의, 유의, 돌봄 **attendance** 출석(자)
> **attendant** ⓝ ① 시중드는 사람 ② 출석자 ⓐ ① 수행하는, 시중드는 ② 수반하는, 부수적인 ③ 참석한, 출석한
> **attentive** 주의 깊은, 사려 깊은 **attend to** ~에 열중하다, ~에 주의하다 **attend on[upon]** ~의 시중을 들다, ~을 간호하다
> **pay[give, fix] attention to** ~에 주의하다, 유의하다

Step 03
연습문제

다음 문장의 attend에 해당되는 뜻을 **Step 02** 의 ❶~❸에서 고르세요. (해답은 446쪽)

1. The nurses attended on the sick kindly. (   )

2. A lot of people attended the funeral. (   )

3. Attend carefully to what the teacher is saying. (   )

4. Mike doesn't attend church very often. (   )

5. You must attend to money affairs. (   )

6. She attended on her sick mother with all her heart. (   )

Step 04
영작연습

다음 문장을 주어진 부분을 이용하여 영어로 옮기세요. (해답은 446쪽)

1. 그녀는 지난 주말 교회에서 거행된 결혼식에 참석했다. [wedding, last weekend]

____

2. 엄마는 자신의 아픈 아기를 밤낮으로 돌보았다. [sick, day and night]

____

3. 너는 선생님이 말씀하시는 것에 유의해야 한다. [must, saying]

____

∷ 1. 그는 오늘 수업에 참석하지 못했다. 2. 키 큰 여종업원이 우리 테이블을 시중들었다. 3. 당신 자신의 일이나 신경 써라.

118 hide [haid]

Step 01
해석연습

다음 문장을 hide에 유의하여 해석해 보세요. (해석은 이 페이지의 하단부에 있음)

1. Let's hide behind the wall. _______________________

2. Her boots are made of cowhide. _______________________

Step 02
뜻 알기

hide에는 다음과 같은 여러 가지의 뜻이 있습니다.

❶ ~을 숨기다; 숨다 **v** to put or keep (a person, thing, etc) in a place where it cannot be seen or easily found

❷ 짐승의 가죽 **n** the skin of an animal

> 한 걸음 더 **hide** [haid] - **hid** [hid] - **hid** [hid] / **hidden** [hídn]
> **hide and seek** 숨바꼭질 **hide oneself** 숨다 **have a thick hide** (구어) 낯가죽이 두껍다; 무신경하다
> **save one's hide** 벌[손실, 부상]을 면하다 **(in) hide and hair** 완전히, 아주 **hideaway** (구어) 숨는 곳; 은신[피난]처; 잠복 장소

Step 03
연습문제

다음 문장의 hide에 해당되는 뜻을 **Step 02** 의 ❶~❷에서 고르세요. (해답은 446쪽)

1. Hide yourself among the trees. (   )
2. He makes shoes out of animal's hide. (   )
3. She will hide the ring in a safe place. (   )
4. These are ox hide gloves. (   )

Step 04
영작연습

다음 문장을 주어진 부분을 이용하여 영어로 옮기세요. (해답은 446쪽)

1. 그 소년은 자신의 돈을 침대 밑에 숨긴다. [money, under]

____

2. 그들은 짐승의 가죽으로 장갑을 만든다. [gloves, animal's]

____

119 free [friː]

다음 문장을 free에 유의하여 해석해 보세요. (해석은 이 페이지의 하단부에 있음)

1. We live in a free country. ________________________________

2. Lincoln freed the slaves. ________________________________

3. Admission to the concert is free. ________________________________

free에는 다음과 같은 여러 가지의 뜻이 있습니다.

❶ 자유로운, 마음대로 할 수 있는 ⓐ not under any control; able to act or think as one pleases

❷ ~을 해방하다, 자유롭게 하다, 석방하다 ⓥ to make or set (someone or something) free; to release

❸ 공짜의, 무료의 ⓐ costing nothing; without payment

> 한 걸음 더 **Are you free tonight?** 오늘 밤 한가합니까?
> → 한가한, 일이 없는(=not busy, not working)
> **These goods are free of tax.** 이 상품들은 면세다.
> → ~이 없는, ~이 면제된(=without; exempt from)
> **freedom** 자유 **free-to-all** 참가자격 제한이 없는 대회 **freelance** 자유계약자(=freelancer) **freely** 자유롭게, 거리낌 없이
> **free trade** 자유무역 FTA (Free Trade Agreement) 자유무역협정 **be free from[of]** ~이 없는, 면제된
> **feel free to do** 마음대로[거리낌 없이] ~하다 **for free** 공짜로, 무료로(=for nothing) **get free** 놓아주다, 석방하다

다음 문장의 free에 해당되는 뜻을 Step 02 의 ❶~❸에서 고르세요. (해답은 446쪽)

1. We had a free and open discussion. (   )

2. He gave me a free ticket for the concert. (   )

3. You are free to think what you like. (   )

4. Lincoln freed the slaves from bondage. (   )

5. We were given a free lunch. (   )

6. She will free the bird out of the cage. (   )

다음 문장을 주어진 부분을 이용하여 영어로 옮기세요. (해답은 446쪽)

1. 그들은 정치에 관한 자유롭고 솔직한 토론을 했다. [discussion, politics]

____

2. 그는 토끼를 덫에서 풀어 주었다. [rabbit, trap]

____

3. 그들은 사람들에게 무료 탄산음료를 제공하고 있다. [serving, soft drinks]

____

∷ 1. 우리는 자유국가에서 산다. 2. 링컨은 노예들을 해방시켰다. 3. 그 콘서트의 입장은 무료이다.

120 mine [main]

Step 01
해석연습

다음 문장을 mine에 유의하여 해석해 보세요. (해석은 이 페이지의 하단부에 있음)

1. This book is mine, not yours. ___________________________

2. The mine is deep and dark. ___________________________

3. They will mine for gold. ___________________________

4. The roads are loaded with mines. ___________________________

Step 02
뜻 알기

mine에는 다음과 같은 여러 가지의 뜻이 있습니다.

❶ 나의 것 `pron` something which belongs to me

❷ 광산, 광갱(鑛坑) `n` a deep hole or tunnel made under the ground to find minerals

❸ 채굴[채광]하다 `v` to dig underground to take out minerals; to obtain minerals from mines

❹ 지뢰 `n` a hidden bomb or explosive device

> 한 걸음 더 **The road had been heavily _mined_.** 그 도로에는 지뢰가 많이 매설되었다. → 지뢰를 매설하다(=to lay mines)
> **miner** ① 광부 ② (군사) 지뢰부설공병 **mining** 광업 **coal mine** 탄광 **gold mine** 금광 **minefield** 지뢰밭

Step 03
연습문제

다음 문장의 mine에 해당되는 뜻을 Step 02 의 ❶～❹에서 고르세요. (해답은 446쪽)

1. The workers mine for coal all day. (   )
2. This book is yours, not mine. (   )
3. The enemy might lay mines on the road. (   )
4. Julie is an old friend of mine. (   )
5. The soldiers will remove mines from the field. (   )
6. We went into the old mine. (   )
7. They mine gold from deep under ground. (   )
8. The mine was cold and dark. (   )

Step 04
영작연습

다음 문장을 주어진 부분을 이용하여 영어로 옮기세요. (해답은 446쪽)

1. 이 펜들은 너의 것이냐 아니면 나의 것이냐? [yours, or]

____

2. 그는 석탄 광산에서 일을 한다. [works, coal]

____

3. 우리는 이 근처에서 많은 금을 캤다. [gold, diamonds]

____

4. 군인들이 길 위에 지뢰를 매설했다. [laid, road]

____

:: 1. 이 책은 너의 것이 아니라 나의 것이다. 2. 광산은 깊고 어둡다. 3. 그들은 금을 캐기 위해 땅을 팔 것이다. 4. 도로들은 지뢰가 묻혀 있다.

175

A. 다음 뜻에 해당되는 단어를 보기에서 찾아 적으세요.

보기	general	attend	hide	free	mine

01. ______________ to go to or to be present at
02. ______________ for all; of all; overall
03. ______________ a deep hole or tunnel made under the ground to find minerals
04. ______________ to listen carefully or pay attention to
05. ______________ to make or set (someone or something) free; to release
06. ______________ to dig underground to take out minerals
07. ______________ to put or keep (a person, thing, etc) in a place where it cannot be seen or easily found
08. ______________ not detailed; not specific
09. ______________ something which belongs to me
10. ______________ costing nothing; without payment
11. ______________ the skin of an animal
12. ______________ an officer of very high rank in the army
13. ______________ a hidden bomb or explosive device
14. ______________ not under any control; able to act or think as one pleases
15. ______________ to look after; to serve or help

B. 다음 빈칸에 가장 알맞은 단어를 보기에서 찾아 적으세요.

보기	general	attend	hide	free	mine(s)

01. Where did you (   ) your money?
02. The king will (   ) all the prisoners tomorrow.
03. My father works in the coal (   ).
04. I'll give you a (   ) idea of the project.
05. Unless you (   ) to your work, you won't succeed.
06. We want to live in a (   ) country.
07. I will (   ) the class tomorrow.
08. The tank was destroyed by a buried (   ).
09. The (   ) situation is favorable to us.
10. The tall waiter will (   ) your table.
11. Your watch is better than (   ).
12. The (   ) was in command of the army.
13. Our company has signed a contract to (   ) tin in Malaysia.
14. The soft drinks are (   ), but you have to pay for the beer.
15. They used polar bear (   ) as clothing.

다음 문장을 굵게 처리된 단어에 유의하여 해석해 보세요.

01. Further, television sets were priced beyond the means of a **general** public whose modest living standards, especially in the 1930s and 1940s, did not allow the acquisition of luxury goods. [2009년–홀수형 28번]

➡ ______________________________

02. In **general**, parents feel a special kind of love for their own children that they do not feel for other children. [2001년–홀수형 35번]

➡ ______________________________

03. At night she **attended** classes in composition and developed her writing skills. [2004년–홀수형 31번]

➡ ______________________________

04. They receive state grants for the university, and **attend** state-training programs if they lose their jobs. [1994번–1차 26번]

➡ ______________________________

05. One myth tells how a group of gods had a meeting to decide where to **hide** the "truth of the universe" from people. [2006년–홀수형 18번]

➡ ______________________________

06. It is brain power that can guarantee our economic success in the midst of the fierce competition of the current **free** world market. [1996년–홀수형 19번]

➡ ______________________________

07. Shouts of joy arose as the villagers saw their own children returning home after they were **freed** from the enemy. [1995년–홀수형 35번]

➡ ______________________________

08. For one thing, they say that the cost of **free** galleries is so high that visitors should pay admission. [2003년–홀수형 33번]

➡ ______________________________

09. W: Are you **free** this Saturday afternoon?
M: Yes. I have no plans. Why? [2002년–홀수형 10번]

➡ ______________________________

10. We owe it to a few writers of old times that the people in the Middle Ages could slowly **free** themselves from ignorance. [2006년–홀수형 23번]

➡ ______________________________

11. We are not always fortunate enough to enjoy a work environment **free** of noise pollution. [2006년–홀수형 43번]

➡ ______________________________

12. Suppose two friends of **mine** are sitting in my room. [2000년–홀수형 45번]

➡ ______________________________

13. The "cumbia" was created by African salves who were brought to the hot regions of the country to work in the gold **mines**. [1994년–2차 17번]

➡ ______________________________

14. I could also be called "buried gold" because of many valuable uses of **mine**. [1994년–1차 16번]

➡ ______________________________

Day 12

121 **bold** [bould]

Group **25**

Step 01 해석연습

다음 문장을 bold에 유의하여 해석해 보세요. (해석은 이 페이지의 하단부에 있음)

1. He was a very bold soldier. ________________________

2. The numbers in this book are in bold type. ________________________

Step 02 뜻 알기

bold에는 다음과 같은 여러 가지의 뜻이 있습니다.

❶ 대담한, 용감한 **a** not afraid of taking risks; fearless; brave; courageous

❷ 뚜렷한, 두드러진; (인쇄) 볼드체의 (선이 굵고 진한) **a** clear; striking and well-marked; (of type) thick and clear

> 한 걸음 더 **He is as <u>bold</u> as brass.** 그는 뻔뻔스럽다.
> → 뻔뻔스러운, 버릇없는(=without feelings of shame; immodest)
> **boldly** 대담하게 **boldness** 대담함 **(as) bold as a lion** 매우 용감한, 담이 큰 **(as) bold as brass** 철면피한, 뻔뻔스러운

Step 03 연습문제

다음 문장의 bold에 해당되는 뜻을 **Step 02** 의 ❶~❷에서 고르세요. (해답은 446쪽)

1. His letter was written in a bold sloping hand. (   )

2. He is a very bold boy. (   )

3. She wears a dress with bold stripes. (   )

4. My uncle was a bold soldier. (   )

Step 04 영작연습

다음 문장을 주어진 부분을 이용하여 영어로 옮기세요. (해답은 446쪽)

1. 그녀는 법정에서 대담한 진술을 했다. [statement, court]

____

2. 그 성의 뚜렷한 윤곽이 그들 앞에 나타났다. [outline, appeared]

____

:: 1. 그는 매우 용감한 군인이었다. 2. 이 책의 숫자는 선이 굵고 진한 체[볼드체]이다.

122 interest [íntərəst]

Step 01
해석연습

다음 문장을 interest에 유의하여 해석해 보세요. (해석은 이 페이지의 하단부에 있음)

1. I have no interest in sports. ______________________________

2. Which subject interests you most? ______________________________

3. The interest in the loan is 15% per year. ______________________________

Step 02
뜻 알기

interest에는 다음과 같은 여러 가지의 뜻이 있습니다.

❶ 흥미, 관심; 관심사 🄝 the feeling of wanting to know or to do; curiosity; an attraction

❷ 관심[흥미]을 갖게 하다 🅥 to cause or arouse the attention or curiosity of someone

❸ 이자 🄝 the money charged or paid for the use of money

> 한 걸음 더 **It is to your <u>interests</u> to do so.** 그렇게 하는 것이 너에게 이익이 될 것이다.
> → 이익(=advantage, benefit, profit)
> **He has sold all his <u>interests</u> in the company.** 그는 그 회사의 모든 주식을 팔아버렸다.
> → 주식, 이권(=a share in a company, business, etc)
> **interest rate** 이자율, 이율 **interest group** 이익단체 **the public interests** 공중의 이익, 공익
> **be interested in** 〜에 흥미를 가지다

Step 03
연습문제

다음 문장의 interest에 해당되는 뜻을 **Step 02** 의 ❶〜❸에서 고르세요. (해답은 446쪽)

1. He lent me the money at 5 percent interest. (   )

2. The story interests me very much. (   )

3. The investment brought in 15 percent interest. (   )

4. Julie watched the movie with great interests. (   )

5. Which subject interests you most? (   )

6. His interest in Australia began to grow. (   )

Step 04
영작연습

다음 문장을 주어진 부분을 이용하여 영어로 옮기세요. (해답은 446쪽)

1. 삶에 있어서 그녀의 두 가지 큰 관심사는 음악과 미술이다. [life, painting]

____

2. 정치적 논쟁은 더 이상 그녀의 관심을 끌지 못한다. [political, arguments]

____

3. 그는 대부금에 대해 7.5%의 이자를 내야만 한다. [pay, loan]

____

∷ 1. 나는 스포츠에 흥미가 없다. 2. 당신은 어느 과목에 가장 관심이 있습니까? 3. 그 대부금에 대한 이자는 연 15%이다.

123 **lay** [lei]

Step 01
해석연습

다음 문장을 lay에 유의하여 해석해 보세요. (해석은 이 페이지의 하단부에 있음)

1. He laid his hand on my shoulder. ________________________________
2. Birds and insects lay eggs. ________________________________
3. He lay down on the bed. ________________________________

Step 02
뜻 알기

lay에는 다음과 같은 여러 가지의 뜻이 있습니다.

❶ 놓다, 설치하다, 준비하다 Ⓥ to put down; to put in place; to put in order or arrange

❷ 알을 낳다 Ⓥ to produce eggs

❸ 동사 lie(눕다, ~에 있다)의 과거형 [lie – lay – lain] Ⓥ the past tense of "lie"

> 한 걸음 더 **I lay ten dollars that he will come.** 나는 그가 오는 쪽에 10달러를 걸겠다.
> → 내기에 걸다(=put down as a wager or stake; bet)
> **layer** ① 놓는[쌓는] 사람 ② 층, 지층 a bricklayer 벽돌공 **lay aside** 저축해 두다, 따로 떼어 놓다 **lay bricks** 벽돌을 쌓다
> **lay eggs** 알을 낳다 **lay out** ① 설계하다 ② 가지런히 늘어놓다

Step 03
연습문제

다음 문장의 lay에 해당되는 뜻을 **Step 02** 의 ❶~❸에서 고르세요. (해답은 446쪽)

1. This hen lays an egg every day. (   )
2. Lay the book on the table. (   )
3. The boy lay down on the grass. (   )
4. The hens don't lay in this cold weather. (   )
5. My grandmother lay on the sofa. (   )
6. She usually lays her keys under the mat. (   )

Step 04
영작연습

다음 문장을 주어진 부분을 이용하여 영어로 옮기세요. (해답은 447쪽)

1. 그녀는 대개 자신의 열쇠를 테이블 위에 놓는다. [usually, keys]

____

2. 이 암탉은 매주 3-4개의 알을 낳는다. [hen, each week]

____

3. 그 소년은 햇빛을 즐기면서 잔디에 누워 있었다. [enjoying, sunshine]

____

:: 1. 그는 그의 손을 나의 어깨에 놓았다. 2. 새와 곤충은 알을 낳는다. 3. 그는 침대에 누웠다.

124 **press** [pres]

Step 01
해석연습

다음 문장을 press에 유의하여 해석해 보세요. (해석은 이 페이지의 하단부에 있음)

1. She pressed the bell twice. _______________________
2. A press is a noisy machine. _______________________
3. The press had a story about a car crash. _______________________
4. Jane needs to press her wrinkled dress. _______________________

Step 02
뜻 알기

press에는 다음과 같은 여러 가지의 뜻이 있습니다.

❶ 누르다, 압착하다 **v** to push something with force; to compress; to squeeze

❷ 인쇄기 **n** a machine used for printing books, newspapers, magazines, etc

❸ 신문, 출판물; 언론기관종사자 **n** newspapers, magazines, and their reporters, journalists

❹ 다림질하다 **v** to iron

> 한 걸음 더 **He pressed me to stay for the night.** 그는 나에게 자고 가라고 졸랐다. → 조르다, 강요하다
> **printing press** 인쇄기 **press conference** 기자회견 **press release** 보도문, 보도자료 **a wine press** 포도주 압착기

Step 03
연습문제

다음 문장의 press에 해당되는 뜻을 Step 02 의 ❶~❹에서 고르세요. (해답은 447쪽)

1. The printing press is out of order. (   )
2. The baby likes to press the buttons on the phone. (   )
3. Kate read about the storm in the press. (   )
4. Tony will press his pants. (   )
5. She pressed her baby in her arms. (   )
6. Mike works for the press in his town. (   )
7. We need to feed paper into the press. (   )
8. The worker will press 100 jackets today. (   )

Step 04
영작연습

다음 문장을 주어진 부분을 이용하여 영어로 옮기세요. (해답은 447쪽)

1. 그는 전화기의 숫자 누름판을 눌렀다. [number buttons]

____

2. Jack은 그에게 고장 난 인쇄기를 고치라고 말했다. [fix, broken]

____

3. Sam은 신문에서 지진에 관한 것을 읽었다. [about, earthquake]

____

4. 그녀는 자신의 옷을 다림질하는 것을 좋아한다. [likes, clothes]

____

1. 그녀는 벨을 두 번 눌렀다. 2. 인쇄기는 소음이 많은 기계이다. 3. 신문에 자동차 충돌사고에 관한 이야기가 실렸다.
4. 그녀는 구겨진 옷을 다려야 한다.

125 bow (뜻) ❶ [bau] ❷❸ [bou]

Step 01 해석연습

다음 문장을 bow에 유의하여 해석해 보세요. (해석은 이 페이지의 하단부에 있음)

1. They bowed before the king. __________________________

2. The man shot arrows from a bow. __________________________

3. My brother always wears a bow tie. __________________________

Step 02 뜻 알기

bow에는 다음과 같은 여러 가지의 뜻이 있습니다.

❶ 머리를 숙이다, 허리를 굽히다, 절하다, 인사하다 🅥 to bend the head or body forward in order to greet or show respect, worship or obedience

❷ 활, 활 모양의 것 🅝 a piece of wood curved by a tight string, used for shooting arrows; anything shaped like this

❸ (끈, 리본 따위의) 나비매듭 🅝 a piece of knot, ribbon, etc tied into loops

> 한 걸음 더 **The little girl played the violin with a <u>bow</u>.** 그 작은 소녀는 활로 바이올린을 연주했다.
> → [bou] 현악기를 켜는 활(=a long thin stick with a tight string fastened along it, used to play a violin, etc)
> **He sat in the <u>bow</u> of the boat.** 그는 보트의 이물(앞머리)에 앉았다.
> → [bau] 배의 이물(앞머리) 또는 비행기의 기수(=the front part of a ship, boat or airship)
> **bow tie** 나비넥타이 **bow-legged** 안짱다리의, 다리가 밖으로 휜 **a bow and arrow** 활과 화살 **a violin bow** 바이올린 활

Step 03 연습문제

다음 문장의 bow에 해당되는 뜻을 **Step 02** 의 ❶~❸에서 고르세요. (해답은 447쪽)

1. She stood up to bow her teacher. (   )

2. My cousin wears a yellow bow tie. (   )

3. In Asia, people usually bow when they meet. (   )

4. He shot arrows with a bow. (   )

5. I received a little yellow box with a white bow. (   )

6. The man will hunt deer with bow and arrows. (   )

Step 04 영작연습

다음 문장을 주어진 부분을 이용하여 영어로 옮기세요. (해답은 447쪽)

1. 유럽에서는 사람들이 서로 만날 때 머리를 숙여 인사하지 않는다. [meet, each other]

____

2. 그는 활과 화살로 사슴을 사냥했다. [deer, arrows]

____

3. Mary는 머리에 핑크색 나비매듭 리본을 하고 있었다. [wore, ribbon]

____

∷ 1. 그들은 왕 앞에서 머리를 숙였다. 2. 그 남자는 활로 화살을 쏘았다. 3. 나의 동생은 항상 나비넥타이를 한다.

A. 다음 뜻에 해당되는 단어를 보기에서 찾아 적으세요.

보기	bold interest lay press bow

01. ______________ not afraid of taking risks; fearless; brave; courageous
02. ______________ to produce eggs
03. ______________ to bend the head or body forward in order to greet or show respect, worship or obedience
04. ______________ the money charged or paid for the use of money
05. ______________ to iron
06. ______________ a piece of wood curved by a tight string, used for shooting arrows
07. ______________ to push something with force; to compress; to squeeze
08. ______________ the feeling of wanting to know or to do; curiosity; an attraction
09. ______________ newspapers, magazines, and their reporters, journalists
10. ______________ clear; striking and well-marked; (of type) thick and clear
11. ______________ to cause or arouse the attention or curiosity of someone
12. ______________ a piece of knot, ribbon, etc tied into loops
13. ______________ to put down; to put in place; to put in order or arrange
14. ______________ a machine used for printing books, newspapers, magazines, etc
15. ______________ the past tense of "lie"

B. 다음 빈칸에 가장 알맞은 단어를 보기에서 찾아 적으세요.

보기	bold interest lay press bow

01. The (   ) boy challenged the giant.
02. They still hunt with (   ) and arrow.
03. Jack needs to fix the broken printing (   ).
04. He has no (   ) in art.
05. Please (   ) the packages on the kitchen table.
06. In case of fire, you need to (   ) this button immediately.
07. She had a (   ) of pink ribbon in her hair.
08. We saw the (   ) outline of the mountain.
09. This hen doesn't (   ) eggs any more.
10. Diane will (   ) her husband's trousers.
11. The rate of (   ) on this loan is 6 percent.
12. The man (   ) down on the grass to take a nap.
13. He always (   ) to my parents very politely.
14. He read about a plane crash in the (   ).
15. His story will (   ) the children very much.

Day 13

다음 문장을 굵게 처리된 단어에 유의하여 해석해 보세요.

01. People, therefore, have lost **interest** in modern arts and have turned to sports stars and other popular figures to find their role models. [2003년-홀수형 44번]

➡ _______________________________________

02. We must work to resolve conflicts in a spirit of reconciliation and always keep in mind the **interests** of others. [2010년-홀수형 32번]

➡ _______________________________________

03. Would you like to take advantage of our three-month or six-month installment plan? It's **interest**-free. [2011년-홀수형 5번]

➡ _______________________________________

04. For example, many Chinese students have become **interested** in Korean as they plan to work for Korean firms, which offer better opportunities and pay. [2005년-홀수형 28번]

➡ _______________________________________

05. One doll, found near Prati in Rome, was made of ivory and **lay** beside her owner who had died at the age of eighteen. [2009년–홀수형 23번]

➡ _______________________________________

06. Even though it may be annoying to have to **lay** a place at dinner or keep an extra seat in the family automobile for his "friend" who exists only in your child's imagination, it is probably well worthwhile. [2010년-홀수형 42번]

➡ _______________________________________

07. A light mist **lay** along the earth, partly veiling the lower features of the landscape, but above it the taller trees showed in well-defined masses against a clear sky. [2006년-홀수형 32번]

➡ _______________________________________

08. If you'd like to place an order, **press** "one" now. If you need product information, **press** "two" now. [1996년-홀수형 9번]

➡ _______________________________________

09. Few people are aware that 1883 is an important year in the history of the Korean **press**. [2003년-홀수형 35번]

➡ _______________________________________

10. The flat land now rolls away to the horizon with the sky **pressing** down like a dark blanket. [1998년-홀수형 37번]

➡ _______________________________________

11. While holding a fishing rod on the river bank, a little girl suddenly felt something and saw the fishing rod **bowing** like a question mark. [1999년-홀수형 22번]

➡ _______________________________________

126 **period** [píəriəd]

Step 01
해석연습

다음 문장을 period에 유의하여 해석해 보세요. (해석은 이 페이지의 하단부에 있음)

1. The heart beats by periods. _______________________________

2. The Jurassic period lasted for millions of years. _______________________________

3. Put a period after each sentence. _______________________________

Step 02
뜻 알기

period에는 다음과 같은 여러 가지의 뜻이 있습니다.

❶ (일정한) 기간, 동안, 주기 ⓝ a certain length or portion of time

❷ 시대, 시기 ⓝ a certain number of years in history, civilization, etc; an era

❸ 마침표, 종지부 ⓝ a punctuation mark of a dot ending a sentence; a full stop

> 한 걸음 더 **We have six periods on Monday.** 월요일엔 수업이 6시간 있다.
> → 학교의 수업시간, 경기의 전후반 따위의 구분(=a regular division of time in a school day or a game)
> **periodic** 주기적인, 정기적인 **periodical** ⓐ 주기적인, 정기적인 ⓝ 정기간행물 **periodically** 주기적으로, 정기적으로
> **the Socratic period** 소크라테스 시대 **the period of adolescence** 청년

Step 03
연습문제

다음 문장의 period에 해당되는 뜻을 Step 02 의 ❶~❸에서 고르세요. (해답은 447쪽)

1. We are studying the Goryeo period. (　　)

2. My heart beats by periods. (　　)

3. He stayed there for a short period. (　　)

4. The sentence ends with a period. (　　)

5. He studied the Joseon period at school. (　　)

6. Don't forget to put a period after each sentence. (　　)

Step 04
영작연습

다음 문장을 주어진 부분을 이용하여 영어로 옮기세요. (해답은 447쪽)

1. 그는 짧은 기간 동안 서울에 머물 것이다. [stay, short]

____

2. 우리는 프랑스혁명 시대를 공부할 것이다. [study, French Revolution]

____

3. 그의 문장은 끝에 마침표가 없다. [sentence, at the end]

____

:: 1. 심장은 주기적으로 뛴다. 2. 쥐라기는 수백만 년 동안 지속되었다. 3. 각 문장 끝에 마침표를 찍어라.

 **127 fast** [fæst / fɑːst]

Step 01 해석연습

다음 문장을 fast에 유의하여 해석해 보세요. (해석은 이 페이지의 하단부에 있음)

1. Tae Hwan is a very fast swimmer. _______________________________
2. The post is fast in the ground. _______________________________
3. He has just finished ten days' fast. _______________________________

Step 02 뜻 알기

fast에는 다음과 같은 여러 가지의 뜻이 있습니다.

❶ 빠른, 신속한 **a** quick; rapid / 빨리, 신속히 **ad** quickly; rapidly

❷ 단단한, 고정된 **a** firmly fixed; not easily moved
  단단히, 확고하게 **ad** firmly; tightly; fixedly

❸ 단식하다 **v** to go without food for a period of time, especially for religious or medical reasons
  단식하는 것 또는 단식하는 기간 **n** the act of fasting or the period of fasting

> 한 걸음 더 **fast food** 간이즉석식품, 패스트푸드 **fasten** 단단히 고정시키다, 붙들어 매다 **fast track** 출세 가도, 고속승진 코스
> **fasting** 단식 **breakfast** 아침식사 * 어원: 저녁식사 후 아침식사까지 긴 단식(fast)을 깬다(break)는 뜻
> **fastness** ① 요새, 보루, 성채 ② 빠름, 신속함 ③ 견고함, 고정 **thick and fast** 끊임없이, 줄기차게
> **be[fall] fast asleep** 깊이 잠들어 있다

Step 03 연습문제

다음 문장의 fast에 해당되는 뜻을 **Step 02** 의 ❶~❸에서 고르세요. (해답은 447쪽)

1. My watch is five minutes fast. (   )
2. Did you lock the door fast? (   )
3. "KTX" is a very fast train. (   )
4. My sister has been fasting all day. (   )
5. Bind it fast to the tree. (   )
6. Muslims fast during the festival of Ramadan. (   )

Step 04 영작연습

다음 문장을 주어진 부분을 이용하여 영어로 옮기세요. (해답은 447쪽)

1. 그가 너무 빨리 말을 하기 때문에 이해할 수가 없다. [understand, because]

____

2. 로프를 너의 허리 둘레에 단단히 묶어라. [tie, waist]

____

3. 그녀는 종종 살을 빼기 위해 하루 동안 단식을 한다. [lose, weight]

____

∷ 1. Tae Hwan은 매우 빠른 수영선수이다. 2. 그 기둥은 바닥에 단단히 고정되어 있다. 3. 그는 방금 10일 동안의 단식을 끝마쳤다.

128 score [skɔːr]

Step 01 해석연습

다음 문장을 score에 유의하여 해석해 보세요. (해석은 이 페이지의 하단부에 있음)

1. Our team scored two goals before halftime. _______________________
2. She scored the paper in the middle and cut it in half. _______________
3. They packed the books by the score. _______________________

Step 02 뜻 알기

score에는 다음과 같은 여러 가지의 뜻이 있습니다.

❶ 득점, 점수, 성적 **n** the record of points made in a game, competition, contest, test, etc
득점하다, 획득하다 **v** to gain points in a game, competition, contest, test, etc

❷ 새긴 금, 칼자국, 베인 상처 **n** a cut, scratch or line made on a surface
～에 칼자국을 내다, 표시를 하다, 선을 긋다 **v** to mark with cuts, scratches, lines, etc

❸ 20; 20명, 20개 **n** (number) twenty (persons or things)

> 한 걸음 더 **The orchestra members practiced in <u>score</u>.** 오케스트라 단원들은 총 악보(모음악보)를 보며 연습했다.
> → 악보, 총 악보(=a copy of a piece of music showing separate parts for different instruments or voices)
> **a piano score** 피아노의 악보 **scoreboard** 득점게시판 **by the score** 20개 단위로 **scores of** 많은

Step 03 연습문제

다음 문장의 score에 해당되는 뜻을 `Step 02` 의 ❶～❸에서 고르세요. (해답은 447쪽)

1. They sell the goods by the score. (   )
2. There were deep scores in the wood. (   )
3. Three score and ten is the age of man. (   )
4. The final score was 2-1. (   )
5. The man has the scores of the whip on his back. (   )
6. Jae-ho got a perfect score in math. (   )

Step 04 영작연습

다음 문장을 주어진 부분을 이용하여 영어로 옮기세요. (해답은 447쪽)

1. 그 소년은 과학시험에서 만점을 받았다. [perfect, science test]

____

2. 그는 나무의 깊게 베인 상처를 발견했다. [deep, in the wood]

____

3. 그 남자는 약 20년 전에 죽었다. [about, ago]

____

:: 1. 우리 팀은 전반전에 2골을 득점했다. 2. 그녀는 종이 가운데를 접어서 반으로 잘랐다. 3. 그들은 책을 20권씩 포장했다.

Day 13

129 stick [stik]

다음 문장을 stick에 유의하여 해석해 보세요. (해석은 이 페이지의 하단부에 있음)

1. He gathered dry sticks to make a fire. ________________________
2. A needle sticks in your shirt. ________________________
3. These labels don't stick very well. ________________________

stick에는 다음과 같은 여러 가지의 뜻이 있습니다.

❶ 잘라낸 나뭇가지, 막대 **n** a piece of wood cut or broken from a tree
　길고 가느다란 막대 모양의 물건 **n** a long thin piece of something shaped for a special purpose

❷ 꽂히다, 박히다 **v** (of a pointed thing) to be pushed into or through something
　(예리한 것으로) ～을 찌르다 **v** to push (a pointed thing) into or through someone or something

❸ 들러붙다, 고착하다, 접착하다 **v** to become attached or fastened; to adhere
　(풀 따위로) ～을 붙이다, 들러붙게 하다 **v** to fix or attach (something) with paste, glue, etc

> 한 걸음 더 **stick** [stik] - **stuck** [stʌk] - **stuck** [stʌk]
> **He always <u>sticks</u> his promise.** 그는 항상 약속을 어김없이 지킨다. → 고집하다, 끝까지 고수하다
> **a walking stick** 지팡이 **chop sticks** 젓가락 **sticky** 끈적끈적한 **stick to** ① ～에 집착하다, ～을 고수하다 ② ～에 충실하다
> **stick out** ① 튀어나오다, 내밀다 ② 끝까지 주장하다 ③ (일, 사실이) 분명하다

다음 문장의 stick에 해당되는 뜻을 Step 02 의 ❶～❸에서 고르세요. (해답은 447쪽)

1. My grandfather walks with a stick. (　　　)
2. Be careful not to stick your finger with a needle. (　　　)
3. Don't stick anything on the wall. (　　　)
4. Stop sticking your elbow into me. (　　　)
5. She will stick a stamp on the letter. (　　　)
6. The man hit the dog with a stick. (　　　)

다음 문장을 주어진 부분을 이용하여 영어로 옮기세요. (해답은 447쪽)

1. 나의 할아버지께서는 지팡이 없이는 걸으실 수가 없다. [walk, without]

____

2. 그녀는 생일케이크에 초를 꽂을 것이다. [candle, birthday cake]

____

3. 편지에 우표를 붙일 필요는 없습니다. [stamp, letter]

____

∷ 1. 그는 불을 피우려고 마른 나뭇가지를 모았다. 2. 바늘이 하나 너의 셔츠에 꽂혀 있다. 3. 이 라벨(꼬리표)들은 잘 붙지 않는다.

 **130 lie [lai]**

Step 01 해석연습

다음 문장을 lie에 유의하여 해석해 보세요. (해석은 이 페이지의 하단부에 있음)

1. She told a lie about her age. _______________________
2. Don't lie in the sun for too long. _______________________
3. Korea lies in the east of Asia. _______________________

Step 02 뜻 알기

lie에는 다음과 같은 여러 가지의 뜻이 있습니다.

❶ 거짓말하다 Ⓥ to say something which is not true, with the intention of deceiving
거짓말 Ⓝ a false statement made with the intention of deceiving

❷ 눕다 Ⓥ to be or put oneself in a flat or resting position

❸ ~에 있다, 위치하다, ~한 상태에 있다 Ⓥ to be situated; to be kept or remain in a certain state

> 한 걸음 더 **lie** [lai] - **lied** [laid] - **lied** [laid] 거짓말하다
> **lie** [lai] - **lay** [lei] - **lain** [lein] 눕다; ~에 있다, 위치하다
> **Happiness <u>lies</u> in contentment.** 행복은 만족에 달려 있다. → ~에 (달려) 있다(=be; exist)
> **liar** 거짓말쟁이 **lie detector** 거짓말탐지기 **a black lie** 악의적인 거짓말 **a white lie** 악의 없는 거짓말, 선의의 거짓말
> **tell a lie** 거짓말하다 **lie in the way** 방해가 되다, 길을 가로막고 있다 **let it[things] lie** 그대로 놓아두다, 방치하다

Step 03 연습문제

다음 문장의 lie에 해당되는 뜻을 **Step 02** 의 ❶~❸에서 고르세요. (해답은 447쪽)

1. I'm tired. I want to lie down. (   )
2. She lied me about it. (   )
3. They will lie in the sun all afternoon. (   )
4. This lake lies to the west of the city. (   )
5. Some people will lie to get out of trouble. (   )
6. The river lies near the town. (   )

Step 04 영작연습

다음 문장을 주어진 부분을 이용하여 영어로 옮기세요. (해답은 447쪽)

1. 그는 종종 곤란한 상황에서 빠져나가기 위해 거짓말을 한다. [get out of, trouble]

____

2. 소파에 누워서 휴식을 취해라. [sofa, rest]

____

3. 그 산은 도시의 서쪽에 있다. [west, city]

____

⠿ 1. 그녀는 나이를 속였다. 2. 태양 아래 너무 오래 누워 있지 마라. 3. 한국은 아시아의 동쪽에 위치한다.

Day 13

189

A. 다음 뜻에 해당되는 단어를 보기에서 찾아 적으세요.

보기	period fast score stick lie

01. ______________ a piece of wood cut or broken from a tree
02. ______________ a punctuation mark of a dot ending a sentence; a full stop
03. ______________ quick; rapid
04. ______________ to mark with cuts, scratches, lines, etc
05. ______________ a certain length or portion of time
06. ______________ a false statement made with the intention of deceiving
07. ______________ firmly; tightly; fixedly
08. ______________ twenty
09. ______________ to go without food for a period of time, especially for religious or medical reasons
10. ______________ to be situated; to be kept or remain in a certain state
11. ______________ a certain number of years in history, civilization, etc; an era
12. ______________ to push (a pointed thing) into or through someone or something
13. ______________ the record of points made in a game, competition, contest, test, etc
14. ______________ to be or put oneself in a flat or resting position
15. ______________ to become attached or fastened; to adhere

B. 다음 빈칸에 가장 알맞은 단어를 보기에서 찾아 적으세요.

보기	period fast score stick(s) lie(s)

01. You must not tell a (   ) under any circumstances.
02. We stayed in Seoul for a short (   ).
03. He is really a (   ) runner.
04. The (   ) in the tennis final was 6-3, 4-6, 7-5.
05. This stamp won't (   ) to the envelope.
06. The boy will (   ) down on the grass.
07. The Shilla (   ) lasted for a thousand years.
08. The golf balls are packed by the (   ).
09. He will (   ) a pin into the wall.
10. England (   ) in the western part of Europe.
11. Your sentence doesn't have a (   ) at the end.
12. The car was stuck (   ) in the mud.
13. I will (   ) the paper to fold easily.
14. We gathered (   ) to make a fire.
15. She has just finished seven days' (   ).

다음 문장을 굵게 처리된 단어에 유의하여 해석해 보세요.

01. Books can be renewed once for the original loan **period** unless they are on reserve. [2007년–홀수형 18번]

➡ ______________________________

02. In general, one's memories of any **period** necessarily weaken as one moves away from it. [2008년–홀수형 22번]

➡ ______________________________

03. A thirty-minute question-and-answer **period** will follow. [2000년–홀수형 19번]

➡ ______________________________

04. Driving too **fast** means putting other people in danger. [1998년–홀수형 17번]

➡ ______________________________

05. All this is part of expected ways of behaving in our social life, but it is not something that we can apply in formal institutions governed by hard-and-**fast** rules. [2008년–홀수형 42번]

➡ ______________________________

06. However, late evening walks can actually be bad for a good night's sleep, particularly if you're moving at a **fast** pace. Pleasant walking, and sweet dreams! [2000년 홀수형 8번]

➡ ______________________________

07. Researchers said that playing with a computer will not increase a preschooler's reading **scores** or train him or her in computer science. [1997년–홀수형 27번]

➡ ______________________________

08. Before sound recording, classical music was passed down through written **scores**, whereas early jazz mainly relied on live performance. [2007년–홀수형 27번]

➡ ______________________________

09. For instance, when two soccer teams play against one another, each team tries to **score** more points than the other. [1995년–홀수형 24번]

➡ ______________________________

10. People tend to **stick** to their first impressions, even if they are wrong. [2007년–홀수형 25번]

➡ ______________________________

11. The doctor said playfully, "Shut your eyes and **stick** your tongue out of your mouth." [1995년–홀수형 32번]

➡ ______________________________

12. They must have brought some **sticks** over here. [2006년–홀수형 15번]

➡ ______________________________

13. He is the Iceman, the intact mummy found **sticking** out of the ice by a German couple hiking in the Alps in 1991. [1997년–홀수형 41번]

➡ ______________________________

14. For instance, we can either tell the truth or tell a **lie**. [2002년–홀수형 34번]

➡ ______________________________

15. Their glory **lies** not in their achievements but in their sacrifices. [2007년–홀수형 33번]

➡ ______________________________

16. If you demand that children tell you the truth and then punish them because it is not very satisfying, you teach them to **lie** to you to protect themselves. [2009년–홀수형 25번]

➡ ______________________________

17. Now, as always, cities are desperate to create the impression that they **lie** at the center of something or other. [2010년–홀수형 40번]

➡ ______________________________

Day 13

DAY 14

So many races, so many customs.
세상에는 인종도 가지가지요, 풍습도 가지각색이다.

131 tie [tai]

Group 27

Step 01 해석연습 다음 문장을 tie에 유의하여 해석해 보세요. (해석은 이 페이지의 하단부에 있음)

1. He tied his shoelaces. _______________________________

2. He took off his jacket and his tie. _______________________________

3. The score for the game was a tie. _______________________________

Step 02 뜻 알기 tie에는 다음과 같은 여러 가지의 뜻이 있습니다.

❶ 묶다, (끈을) 매다, (매듭을) 짓다 ⓥ to fasten together, to bind

❷ 넥타이; (매는 데 쓰이는) 끈, 밧줄 ⓝ a necktie; a rope, cord, or string that is used to tie

❸ 동점이 되다, 비기다 ⓥ to score the same number of points (in a game, competition, etc)
동점; 무승부 ⓝ an equal score or result; a draw

> 한 걸음 더 **He still has close <u>ties</u> to his old neighborhood.** 그는 여전히 전에 살던 동네와 밀접한 인연을 맺고 있다.
> → 연줄, 인연(=a bond, link)
> **the ties of blood** 혈연관계 **political ties** 정치적 제휴(연줄)

Step 03 연습문제 다음 문장의 tie에 해당되는 뜻을 **Step 02** 의 ❶~❸에서 고르세요. (해답은 448쪽)

1. The baseball game was a tie. (   )

2. The fisherman will tie the rope to the dock. (   )

3. My uncle always wears a red tie. (   )

4. There was a tie for first place in the piano contest. (   )

5. Can you tie your shoes? (   )

6. He wore a green and blue tie. (   )

Step 04 영작연습 다음 문장을 주어진 부분을 이용하여 영어로 옮기세요. (해답은 448쪽)

1. 그는 그의 말을 나무에 묶었다. [horse, tree]

____

2. 우리는 그의 생일을 위해 새 넥타이를 하나 샀다. [bought, bithday]

____

3. 우리 팀은 그의 팀과 동점이 되었다. [Our, his]

____

:: 1. 그는 신발 끈을 묶었다. 2. 그는 재킷을 벗고 넥타이를 풀었다. 3. 그 게임의 스코어는 동점이었다.

192

132 **ground** [graund]

다음 문장을 ground에 유의하여 해석해 보세요. (해석은 이 페이지의 하단부에 있음)

1. The man was lying on the ground. ___________________________

2. On what grounds do you suspect her? ___________________________

3. They ground coffee beans every day. ___________________________

ground에는 다음과 같은 여러 가지의 뜻이 있습니다.

❶ 땅, 지면, 바닥 🇳 the surface of the earth

❷ (대개 복수로 쓰여) 원인, 근거, 기초 🇳 (usu. pl) cause; reason; foundation
　 ~에 근거[기초]를 두다 🇻 to base

❸ 동사 grind(갈다, 빻다)의 과거 및 과거분사형 🇻 the past tense and past participle of "grind"
　 * grind [graind] - ground [graund] - ground [graund]

> 한 걸음 더 **Let's find some common <u>ground</u> as a basis for agreement.** 합의의 기초로서 공통된 입장을 찾아봅시다.
> → 입장, 견해(=position, opinion)
> **groundless** 근거 없는 **ground coffee** 분말 커피 **a hunting ground** 사냥터 **a baseball ground** 야구장

다음 문장의 ground에 해당되는 뜻을 Step 02 의 ❶~❸에서 고르세요. (해답은 448쪽)

1. The ground is wet from the rain. (　　)

2. The boys ground coffee beans every day. (　　)

3. The boy will lie on the ground. (　　)

4. There are no grounds for anxiety. (　　)

5. He ground the knife carefully. (　　)

6. We have good grounds for believing it. (　　)

다음 문장을 주어진 부분을 이용하여 영어로 옮기세요. (해답은 448쪽)

1. 땅은 눈으로 덮여 있었다. [covered, snow]

____

2. 이 소설은 작가의 실제 경험을 근거로 하고 있다. [actual, experience]

____

3. 그는 밀을 가루로 만들었다. [wheat, flour]

____

:: 1. 그 남자는 바닥에 누워 있었다. 2. 무슨 근거로 당신은 그녀를 의심하는가? 3. 그들은 매일 커피 열매를 갈았다.

133 **race** [reis]

 다음 문장을 race에 유의하여 해석해 보세요. (해석은 이 페이지의 하단부에 있음)

1. She came first in the race. ___________________________
2. I will race you to that tree. ___________________________
3. The English are the white race. ___________________________

 race에는 다음과 같은 여러 가지의 뜻이 있습니다.

❶ 경주 **n** a competition to find who or which is the fastest in running, skating, swimming, etc

❷ 경주하다; 경주시키다 **v** to (cause someone or something) compete in a race
질주하다, 급히 달리다; 질주시키다 **v** to (make someone or something) move very quickly

❸ 인종, 민족 **n** any of the groupings of human beings according to the color of their skin and other physical features

> 한 걸음 더 **the human race** 인류 **the Korean race** 한민족 **the White race** 백인종 **the Yellow race** 황인종
> **a horse race** 경마 **an automobile race** 자동차경주

 다음 문장의 race에 해당되는 뜻을 **Step 02** 의 ❶∼❸에서 고르세요. (해답은 448쪽)

1. He exerted himself to win the race. (   )
2. My horse will race against five others. (   )
3. There are many different races of man in the world. (   )
4. I will race my dog against his. (   )
5. Let's have a race to the corner. (   )
6. We are members of the human race. (   )

 다음 문장을 주어진 부분을 이용하여 영어로 옮기세요. (해답은 448쪽)

1. 경주 후에 그는 완전히 지쳤다. [utterly, exhausted]

____

2. 그는 우산 때문에 집으로 급히 돌아가야 했다. [back home, umbrella]

____

3. Los Angeles에는 많은 인종들이 함께 산다. [live, together]

____

:: 1. 그녀는 경주에서 제일 먼저 들어왔다. 2. 저 나무까지 경주하자. 3. 영국인은 백색인종이다.

134 appear [əpíər]

Step 01
해석연습

다음 문장을 appear에 유의하여 해석해 보세요. (해석은 이 페이지의 하단부에 있음)

1. A strange ship appeared on the horizon. ________________________________

2. It appears that he is wrong. ________________________________

Step 02
뜻 알기

appear에는 다음과 같은 여러 가지의 뜻이 있습니다.

❶ 나타나다, 출현하다 **V** to come into view; to become visible

❷ ～처럼 보이다, ～처럼 생각되다, ～ 같다 **V** to seem; to look

> 한 걸음 더 **appearance** ① 출현, 나타남 ② 용모, 모습, 외관 **apparent** 눈에 보이는; 분명한, 명백한
> **apparently** 겉보기에는, 외견상; 분명하게, 명백하게 **disappear** 사라지다, 보이지 않게 되다.
> **appear in sight** 나타나다, 보이기 시작하다 **It appears (to me) that ~** (나에게는) ～인 것 같다; ～이 명백하게 되다.

Step 03
연습문제

다음 문장의 appear에 해당되는 뜻을 **Step 02** 의 ❶～❷에서 고르세요. (해답은 448쪽)

1. The moon will appear in the sky. (   )
2. He appears to have been rich. (   )
3. A pretty girl appeared on the stage. (   )
4. The plan appears to be a good one. (   )

Step 04
영작연습

다음 문장을 주어진 부분을 이용하여 영어로 옮기세요. (해답은 448쪽)

1. 갑자기 어떤 낯선 사람이 현관에 나타났다. [stranger, suddenly]

____

2. 그녀는 친구가 많은 것처럼 보인다. [have, a lot of]

____

:: 1. 낯선 배 한 척이 수평선에 나타났다. 2. 그가 틀린 것 같다.

135 charge [tʃɑːrdʒ]

Step 01
해석연습

다음 문장을 charge에 유의하여 해석해 보세요. (해석은 이 페이지의 하단부에 있음)

1. She charged two dollars for the telephone call. _______________________
2. How would you like to pay, cash or charge? _______________________
3. Soldiers charged at the enemy. _______________________
4. Please charge my car battery. _______________________

Step 02
뜻 알기

charge에는 다음과 같은 여러 가지의 뜻이 있습니다.

❶ (대금을) 청구하다 [v] to ask as the price for something
  요금, 값, 비용 [n] the amount of money you have to pay for goods or services; a price or fee

❷ 외상으로 사다 [v] to purchase on credit / 외상 [n] a purchase made on credit

❸ 돌진하다, 돌격하다 [v] to rush forward; to attack by moving quickly

❹ 충전하다; 장전하다; 채워 넣다 [v] to make filled with electricity; to load (a gun); to put into or fill

  한 걸음 더 He was <u>charged</u> with drunk driving. 그는 음주운전으로 고발당했다. → 비난(=blame), 고발(=accuse)
  Steve is in <u>charge</u> of the new project. Steve는 새로운 기획의 책임자이다. → 책임, 담당, 돌봄(=responsibility, control, care)

Step 03
연습문제

다음 문장의 charge에 해당되는 뜻을 **Step 02** 의 ❶～❹에서 고르세요. (해답은 448쪽)

1. The soldiers yelled, "Charge!" (   )
2. Do you want to pay cash or to charge this? (   )
3. The soldier charged his gun with bullets. (   )
4. How much do you charge for a room? (   )
5. Charge your glasses with wine. (   )
6. The restaurant charged me $50.00 for the wine. (   )
7. She charged the shoes on VISA. (   )
8. Those elephants might charge at us. (   )

Step 04
영작연습

다음 문장을 주어진 부분을 이용하여 영어로 옮기세요. (해답은 448쪽)

1. 음식 값은 15불이었다. [the food]

____

2. 나는 새 컴퓨터 한 대를 신용카드로 외상구매했다. [computer, credit card]

____

3. 큰 코뿔소가 우리 트럭을 공격할지 모른다. [rhinoceros, might]

____

4. 나는 나의 휴대폰의 배터리를 충전해야만 한다. [battery, cellular phone]

____

:: 1. 그녀는 전화요금으로 2달러를 청구했다. 2. 현금으로 지불하시겠습니까, 아니면 외상으로 하시겠습니까? 3. 군인들이 적군을 향해 돌격했다.
   4. 내 차의 배터리를 충전해 주세요.

196

A. 다음 뜻에 해당되는 단어를 보기에서 찾아 적으세요.

| 보기 | tie | ground | race | appear | charge |

01. _____________ the past tense and past participle of "grind"
02. _____________ to fasten together, to bind
03. _____________ the amount of money you have to pay for goods or services; a price or fee
04. _____________ cause; reason; foundation
05. _____________ a competition to find who or which is the fastest in running, skating, swimming, etc
06. _____________ a purchase made on credit
07. _____________ any of the groupings of human beings according to the color of their skin and other physical features
08. _____________ to rush forward; to attack by moving quickly
09. _____________ an equal score or result; a draw
10. _____________ to come into view; to become visible
11. _____________ to make filled with electricity; to load (a gun); to put into or fill
12. _____________ to (make someone or something) move very quickly
13. _____________ the surface of the earth
14. _____________ to seem; to look
15. _____________ a necktie; a rope, cord, or string that is used to tie

B. 다음 빈칸에 가장 알맞은 단어를 보기에서 찾아 적으세요.

| 보기 | tie | ground(s) | race | appear | charge |

01. The book will (   ) next week.
02. He dug a hole in the (   ).
03. The garage will (   ) your dead battery.
04. The game score was a (   ).
05. The (   ) for my car repair was $150.00.
06. He likes to (   ) along the road on his bike.
07. Do you have any (   ) for calling her a liar?
08. Will that be cash or (   ), sir?
09. The French are the white (   ).
10. Be careful! That bull might (   ) at you.
11. My sister just learned to (   ) her shoes.
12. Why does the boy (   ) so sad?
13. He came in third in the marathon (   ).
14. We gave Dad a new (   ) for his birthday.
15. The farmer (   ) wheat into flour.

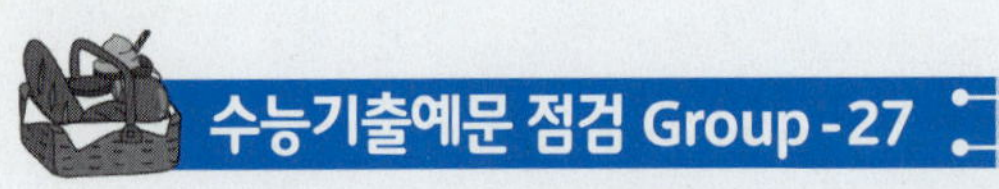

해답은 448쪽

다음 문장을 굵게 처리된 단어에 유의하여 해석해 보세요.

01. The sashes are **tied** under the chin to hold the hat tightly in place. [2007년-홀수형 31번]

➡ _______________________________________

02. He's in a grey suit with a checked **tie**. [2000년-홀수형 1번]

➡ _______________________________________

03. For me, happiness is closely **tied** to my family. I am happy if my wife and children live in harmony. [1994년-1차 44번]

➡ _______________________________________

04. A study of investment clubs showed that the worst-performing clubs were built on affective **ties** and were primarily social, while the best-performing clubs limited social connections and focused on making money. [2011년-홀수형 22번]

➡ _______________________________________

05. What's more, sometimes the weight of the snow causes some trees to bend to the **ground**. [1999년-홀수형 40번]

➡ _______________________________________

06. Some universities remain silent on the important issues of the day, justifying their silence on the **grounds** that universities are neutral and should not become involved. [1995년-홀수형 36번]

➡ _______________________________________

07. Coffee is one of the world's most popular beverages, and it is generally bought by consumers for home use in one of two forms: whole or **ground**. [2006년-홀수형 3번]

➡ _______________________________________

08. Social definitions of the body are **grounded** in social relations and influenced by those with the power to promote agreement about what should be considered "natural" when it comes to the body. [2011년-홀수형 43번]

➡ _______________________________________

09. I'm training hard to set a new world record in the 100 meter **race**. [1998년-홀수형 9번]

➡ _______________________________________

10. For instance, in warmer areas the sandal was, and still is, the most popular form of footwear, whereas the modern moccasin derives from the original shoes adopted in cold climates by **races** such as Eskimos and Siberians. [2007년-홀수형 40번]

➡ _______________________________________

11. The game in its present form first **appeared** in Scotland. [2001년-홀수형 43번]

➡ _______________________________________

12. Although an apple may **appear** red, its atoms are not themselves red. [2008년-홀수형 41번]

➡ _______________________________________

13. But when we feel we are in **charge** of our noisy environments, we may no longer suffer from anxiety and poor performance. [2006년-홀수형 43번]

➡ _______________________________________

14. We can deliver it in two hours for an extra **charge**. [2004년-홀수형 7번]

➡ _______________________________________

15. Thinking improves when parts of the mind are given other tasks, are **charged** with listening to music or following a line of trees. [2011년-홀수형 28번]

➡ _______________________________________

136 **bark** [baːrk]

Step 01
해석연습

다음 문장을 bark에 유의하여 해석해 보세요. (해석은 이 페이지의 하단부에 있음)

1. The dog barked at the stranger. ___________________________________

2. The bark of the tree is white and black. ___________________________________

Step 02
뜻 알기

bark에는 다음과 같은 여러 가지의 뜻이 있습니다.

❶ (개, 여우 등의) 짖는 소리 **n** the sharp, loud sound made by a dog, fox, etc
짖다 **v** to make sounds, as a dog does

❷ 나무껍질 **n** the outer covering of a tree
(나무껍질을) 벗기다; ～의 피부를 까다 **v** to take the bark off (a tree); to scrape the skin from

▷ 한 걸음 더 **the bark of a dog** 개 짖는 소리 **the bark of a gun** 요란한 총소리 **bark at** ～을 향해 짖다, 짖어대다

Step 03
연습문제

다음 문장의 bark에 해당되는 뜻을 **Step 02** 의 ❶～❷에서 고르세요. (해답은 448쪽)

1. The farmer stripped the bark off the tree. (   )

2. My dog always barks at the mailman. (   )

3. The bark of the tree is smooth. (   )

4. That dog barks from morning till night. (   )

Step 04
영작연습

다음 문장을 주어진 부분을 이용하여 영어로 옮기세요. (해답은 448쪽)

1. 그는 멀리서 개의 짖는 소리를 들었다. [in the distance]

____

2. 그는 계단에 넘어져서 피부가 까졌다. [fell down, skin]

____

:: 1. 개는 낯선 사람을 향해 짖었다. 2. 그 나무의 색깔은 흑백으로 얼룩얼룩하다.

137 close v [klouz] a [klous]

Step 01
해석연습

다음 문장을 close에 유의하여 해석해 보세요. (해석은 이 페이지의 하단부에 있음)

1. They close the store every Tuesday. ________________________

2. In Australia schools close in November. ________________________

3. Her birthday is close to mine. ________________________

Step 02
뜻 알기

close에는 다음과 같은 여러 가지의 뜻이 있습니다.

❶ 닫다, 덮다; 닫히다 v to make shut; to become shut

❷ 끝내다, 마감하다; 끝나다 v to finish; to come or bring to an end

❸ (거리, 시간적으로) 가까운, (관계가) 친한 a (of space, time) near; (in relationship) very friendly

> 한 걸음 더 **That was a <u>close</u> game.** 그것은 막상막하의 경기였다.
> → 대등한, 막상막하의(=nearly even or equal in ability, power, etc)
> **She stood <u>close</u> to her mother.** 그녀는 엄마 가까이 서 있었다.
> → 가까이(=near in time, place, etc)
> **a close friend** 친한 친구 **a close game** 막상막하의 경기 **closed** 닫힌, 폐쇄된 **closing** 폐쇄, 결산, 마감

Step 03
연습문제

다음 문장의 close에 해당되는 뜻을 Step 02 의 ❶~❸에서 고르세요. (해답은 448쪽)

1. She closed her eyes and tried to sleep. (   )

2. Her house is very close to the station. (   )

3. Would you mind if I close the window? (   )

4. Our office closes at five thirty. (   )

5. He wants to close his bank account. (   )

6. Paul is a close friend of mine. (   )

Step 04
영작연습

다음 문장을 주어진 부분을 이용하여 영어로 옮기세요. (해답은 448쪽)

1. 그는 눈을 감고 잠을 자려고 노력했다. [tried, sleep]

____

2. 그녀는 ABC 은행의 예금계좌를 해지할 예정이다. [bank account]

____

3. 나의 집은 공원에서 매우 가깝다. [house, park]

____

138 **bore** [bɔːr]

Step 01
해석연습

다음 문장을 bore에 유의하여 해석해 보세요. (해석은 이 페이지의 하단부에 있음)

1. He bored a hole in the wall. ________________________

2. This novel about the war bored me. ________________________

3. He bore the sorrow with tremendous courage. ________________________

Step 02
뜻 알기

bore에는 다음과 같은 여러 가지의 뜻이 있습니다.

❶ 구멍을 뚫다 Ⅴ to make a deep round hole in a hard surface

❷ ~을 지루하게 하다 Ⅴ to make someone feel tired and uninterested by being dull or tedious

❸ 동사 bear의 과거형 Ⅴ the past tense of "bear"
  * bear [bɛər] - bore [bɔːr] - born [bɔːrn] / borne [bɔːrn]

> 한 걸음 더 **boring** ① 구멍 뚫기, 천공 ② 지루한, 지겨운 **boredom** 권태, 지루함 **boring machine** 천공기, 구멍 뚫는 기계
> **a boring book** 지루한 책

Step 03
연습문제

다음 문장의 bore에 해당되는 뜻을 Step 02 의 ❶~❸에서 고르세요. (해답은 449쪽)

1. He bore the pain quietly. (   )
2. The documentary film bored us. (   )
3. They will bore a tunnel under the sea. (   )
4. She bores everyone with stories about her sons. (   )
5. He needs to bore a hole on the board. (   )
6. She bore a child last month. (   )

Step 04
영작연습

다음 문장을 주어진 부분을 이용하여 영어로 옮기세요. (해답은 449쪽)

1. 그들은 단단한 바위를 관통해서 터널을 뚫었다. [tunnel, solid]

   ____

2. 나의 삼촌은 자신의 학창시절 이야기로 우리를 지루하게 하신다. [stories, school days]

   ____

3. 이 나무는 작년에 많은 열매를 맺었다. [fruit, last year]

   ____

Day 14

:: 1. 그는 벽에 구멍을 하나 뚫었다. 2. 이 전쟁소설은 나에게 지루했다. 3. 그는 슬픔을 엄청난 용기로 견뎌 냈다.

139 check [tʃek]

Step 01
해석연습

다음 문장을 check에 유의하여 해석해 보세요. (해석은 이 페이지의 하단부에 있음)

1. Is it all right to pay check? ________________________________
2. The doctor will check Jane's eyes. ________________________________
3. He put a check at the top of the page. ________________________________
4. We have checked the enemy's advance. ________________________________

Step 02
뜻 알기

check에는 다음과 같은 여러 가지의 뜻이 있습니다.

❶ 수표 n a written order on a printed form to a bank to pay money

❷ 점검[확인, 대조]하다 v to examine in order to learn whether something is correct
점검, 확인, 대조 n an act of examining; examination

❸ (점검, 대조필 등의) 체크 표시 n a mark with a pen or pencil, usually (√); a tick

❹ 저지하다, 억제하다 v to hold back; to cause to go slow or stop

> 한 걸음 더 **His shirt was a black and white check.** 그의 셔츠는 흑백 체크무늬였다.
> → 바둑판[체크] 무늬(=a pattern of squares; a pattern of crossed lines forming squares)

Step 03
연습문제

다음 문장의 check에 해당되는 뜻을 **Step 02** 의 ❶~❹에서 고르세요. (해답은 449쪽)

1. He wrote a check for ten dollars. (   )
2. She started to say something, but checked herself. (   )
3. Check your answer with mine. (   )
4. She will put a check on the student's paper. (   )
5. David took his check to the bank. (   )
6. Put a check at the top of the page. (   )
7. He checked his horse with reins. (   )
8. The doctor will carefully check the X-ray film. (   )

Step 04
영작연습

다음 문장을 주어진 부분을 이용하여 영어로 옮기세요. (해답은 449쪽)

1. 매달 그녀는 청구서를 지불하기 위해 수표를 쓴다. [pay, bills]

____

2. 너는 우선 너의 데이터에 대한 점검을 하는 것이 좋겠다. [had better, data]

____

3. 선생님께서는 틀린 답 옆에 체크 표시를 하신다. [next to, wrong]

____

4. 모든 나라는 핵무기의 확산을 막아야 한다. [spread, nuclear weapons]

____

1. 수표로 지불해도 괜찮습니까? 2. 의사는 Jane의 눈을 검사할 것이다. 3. 그는 책의 페이지 상단에 체크 표시를 하였다.
4. 우리는 적군의 진격을 저지했다.

202

 **140 record** Ⓥ [rikɔ́:rd] Ⓝ [rékərd]

Step 01 해석연습

다음 문장을 record에 유의하여 해석해 보세요. (해석은 이 페이지의 하단부에 있음)

1. The nurse records his temperature every day. _______________________

2. She has a good school record. _______________________

3. I bought a record for my sister. _______________________

Step 02 뜻 알기

record에는 다음과 같은 여러 가지의 뜻이 있습니다.

❶ ~을 기록하다, 기록에 남기다 Ⓥ to set down in writing for reference
　녹음하다, 녹화하다 Ⓥ to store music, sound, television programs, etc on tape or disc

❷ 기록, 경력, 성적 Ⓝ a written account of events, facts, etc

❸ 음반, 레코드 Ⓝ a round flat piece of (usually black) plastic on which music, etc is recorded

> 한 걸음 더 **He holds the world <u>record</u> for the 200-meter dash.** 그는 200미터 달리기의 세계기록을 보유하고 있다.
> → (스포츠 따위의) 최고기록(=the best achievement, especially in sport)
> **The thermometer <u>records</u> 20℃.** 온도계는 섭씨 20도를 가리키고 있다.
> → (온도계 등이) ~을 나타내다(=show; indicate))
> **recorder** ① 기록자 ② 녹음기 **recording** 기록, 녹음 **record player** 레코드플레이어, 축음기 **school record** 학교 성적
> **break the record** 기록을 깨다 **hold the record** 기록을 보유하다 **off the record** 비공식의, 공표해서는 안 될

Step 03 연습문제

다음 문장의 record에 해당되는 뜻을 　Step 02 의 ❶~❸에서 고르세요. (해답은 449쪽)

1. This school has a good record of success in exams. (　　)

2. She records daily events in her diary. (　　)

3. My hobby is collecting music records. (　　)

4. I recorded the information into my notebook. (　　)

5. She kept a record of the day's events in her notebook. (　　)

6. He has a collection of Elvis Presley records from the 1950s. (　　)

Step 04 영작연습

다음 문장을 주어진 부분을 이용하여 영어로 옮기세요. (해답은 449쪽)

1. 나는 그 음악을 테이프에 녹음할 예정이다. [music, tape]

____

2. 그 남자는 전과(범죄기록)가 있다. [has, criminal]

____

3. 그녀는 음반에 많은 돈을 소비한다. [spends, a lot of]

____

:: 1. 간호사는 그의 체온을 매일 기록한다. 2. 그녀는 학교 성적이 좋다. 3. 나는 여동생을 위해 음반을 하나 샀다.

A. 다음 뜻에 해당되는 단어를 보기에서 찾아 적으세요.

> **보기**   bark   close   bore   check   record

01. ______________ to make a deep round hole in a hard surface
02. ______________ to make shut; to become shut
03. ______________ a mark with a pen or pencil, usually (√)
04. ______________ a round flat piece of (usually black) plastic on which music etc. is recorded
05. ______________ to make sounds, as a dog does
06. ______________ to hold back; to cause to go slow or stop
07. ______________ to store music, sound, television programs, etc on tape or disc
08. ______________ to make someone feel tired and uninterested by being dull or tedious
09. ______________ near; very friendly
10. ______________ the outer covering of a tree
11. ______________ a written order on a printed form to a bank to pay money
12. ______________ to finish; to come or bring to an end
13. ______________ the past tense of "bear"
14. ______________ to examine in order to learn whether something is correct
15. ______________ a written account of events, facts, etc

B. 다음 빈칸에 가장 알맞은 단어를 보기에서 찾아 적으세요.

> **보기**   bark   close   bore   check   record

01. She is going to (   ) tonight's concert.
02. That tree (   ) much fruit this year.
03. There is a bus stop (   ) to my house.
04. Is it all right to pay by (   )?
05. A mole (   ) its way under the ground.
06. I will (   ) my figures with yours.
07. He has a poor school (   ).
08. The dog will (   ) at the stranger.
09. He couldn't (   ) his anger.
10. We will (   ) our meeting at 5 P.M.
11. He bought a (   ) for his girl friend.
12. The (   ) of the tree is brown.
13. My teacher put a (   ) on my paper.
14. It's very cold. (   ) the door, please.
15. The teacher's lessons always (   ) us.

다음 문장을 굵게 처리된 단어에 유의하여 해석해 보세요.

01. Nowhere, indeed, was any sign or suggestion of life except the **barking** of a distant dog, which served to accentuate the solitary scene. [2006년–홀수형 32번]

→ _______________________________________

02. In spite of their **close** location to these countries, however, Korea has remained free of the deadly disease. [2004년–홀수형 29번]

→ _______________________________________

03. You will notice the same effect if you **close** your eyes, breathe calmly, and manage to relax the next time someone tickles you. [2008년–홀수형 40번]

→ _______________________________________

04. The **closing** event of the festival was highlighted by the appearance of all the prize winners. [2000년–홀수형 33번]

→ _______________________________________

05. Sumi, one of Vicky's **close** friends, has dropped by to say hello. [2004년–홀수형 42번]

→ _______________________________________

06. Due to serious smog caused by the recent forest fires, the Ministry of Education has announced that all schools will be **closed** until further notice. [1998년–홀수형 12번]

→ _______________________________________

07. But Jack wanted to stop reading the book because he found it very **boring**. [2001년–홀수형 40번]

→ _______________________________________

08. A person who feels bad with reasonable regularity will enjoy the occasional period of feeling good far more than somebody who feels good so often that he is **bored** by it. [1997년–홀수형 28번]

→ _______________________________________

09. Thank you for sending your **check** in payment of your July bill. [1994년–1차 25번]

→ _______________________________________

10. During a regular examination a doctor **checks** weight, vision and hearing problems, blood pressure, and so on. [2005년–홀수형 41번]

→ _______________________________________

11. M: Does your father wear glasses?
W: No, he doesn't. He's in a grey suit with a **checked** tie. [2000년–홀수형 1번]

→ _______________________________________

12. W: I want to **check** these two books out, please.
M: You can take this one out, but that one you can't. [2000년–홀수형 14번]

→ _______________________________________

13. My uncle runs a **record** shop and gives free guitar lessons. [2007년–홀수형 16번]

→ _______________________________________

14. If an explosion occurred on a star, scientists on the earth would **record** the time it happened. [1995–홀수형 23번]

→ _______________________________________

15. Whenever an Olympic swimmer sets a new world **record**, it inspires others to bring out the best within them and go beyond that achievement to set new records of human performance. [2011–홀수형 40번]

→ _______________________________________

16. W: Your personal **record** is very impressive, Mr. Jefferson. And you have a good letter from your boss, too.
M: Thank you, ma'am. [1999년–홀수형 9번]

→ _______________________________________

Day 14

 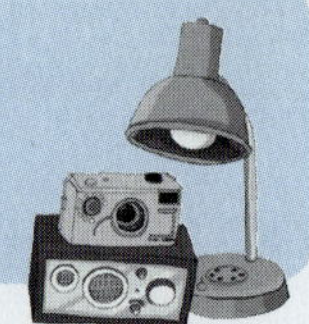

>>> DAY 15

No cross, no crown.
십자가가 없으면 왕관도 없다. (고난 없이 영광 없다.)

 **141 cabinet** [kǽbənit]

Group 29

Step 01
해석연습

다음 문장을 cabinet에 유의하여 해석해 보세요. (해석은 이 페이지의 하단부에 있음)

1. She has a large cabinet. ______________________
2. The new president will form a new cabinet. ______________________

Step 02
뜻 알기

cabinet에는 다음과 같은 여러 가지의 뜻이 있습니다.

❶ 보관용 장, 진열장, 캐비닛 n a piece of furniture with drawers or shelves for storing or displaying things

❷ 각료들, 내각 n a group of high level government officials who meet to make decisions or advise the leader of the government

> 한 걸음 더 **a medicine cabinet** 약장 **a kitchen cabinet** 찬장 **cabinet council** 각료[국무] 회의
> **a coalition cabinet** 연립내각 **the shadow cabinet** 재야내각

Step 03
연습문제

다음 문장의 cabinet에 해당되는 뜻을 **Step 02** 의 ❶~❷에서 고르세요. (해답은 449쪽)

1. There was an old cabinet in his office. (   )
2. She became a member of the Cabinet. (   )
3. He has a large cabinet. (   )
4. The Prime Minister has chosen a new cabinet. (   )

Step 04
영작연습

다음 문장을 주어진 부분을 이용하여 영어로 옮기세요. (해답은 449쪽)

1. 그 낡은 캐비닛은 도색할 필요가 있다. [needs, painted]

____

2. 마침내 그는 각료[장관]가 되었다. [at last, member]

____

:: 1. 그녀는 큰 캐비닛을 가지고 있다. 2. 새 대통령은 새 내각을 구성할 것이다.

142 lot [lɑt / lɔt]

다음 문장을 lot에 유의하여 해석해 보세요. (해석은 이 페이지의 하단부에 있음)

1. The committee will choose the chairman by lot. ________________________
2. There is an empty lot next to his house. ________________________
3. There were a lot of people at the party. ________________________

lot에는 다음과 같은 여러 가지의 뜻이 있습니다.

❶ 제비; 제비뽑기　ⓝ a thing used to decide something by chance; such a method for deciding

❷ (토지의) 한 구획, 대지, 부지　ⓝ a piece of land (used for building on or for another particular purpose)

❸ 많음, 다량　ⓝ a great amount or number (of)

> 한 걸음 더 **Her <u>lot</u> was not a happy one.** 그녀의 운명은 행복한 것이 아니었다.
> → 운명(=a person's fortune or fate)
> **a parking lot** 주차장 **a building lot** 부지, 대지 **lottery** 복권 **a lot of** 많은(=many 또는 much)
> **draw lots** 제비를 뽑아 결정하다

다음 문장의 lot에 해당되는 뜻을 Step 02 **의 ❶∼❸에서 고르세요.** (해답은 449쪽)

1. They will draw lots as to who should begin. (　　)
2. She knows a lot about gardening. (　　)
3. He said, "Thanks a lot." (　　)
4. I own a small lot next to my house. (　　)
5. We drew lots to decide who would remain. (　　)
6. There is an empty lot next to his house. (　　)

다음 문장을 주어진 부분을 이용하여 영어로 옮기세요. (해답은 449쪽)

1. 우리는 누가 제일 먼저 갈 것인지를 정하기 위해 제비를 뽑았다. [drew, go first]

____

2. 그들은 그 공터를 놀이터로 만들 것이다. [vacant, playground]

____

3. 그는 꽃들과 나비들에 대해 많이 알고 있다. [about, butterflies]

____

⁝ 1. 위원회는 추첨으로 위원장을 뽑을 것이다. 2. 그의 집 옆에 빈터가 있다. 3. 파티에는 많은 사람들이 있었다.

143 letter [létər]

 다음 문장을 letter에 유의하여 해석해 보세요. (해석은 이 페이지의 하단부에 있음)

1. I got a letter from her. _______________________________

2. A is the first letter of the Alphabet. _______________________________

3. Mr. Lee is a man of letters. _______________________________

 letter에는 다음과 같은 여러 가지의 뜻이 있습니다.

❶ 편지 **n** a written or printed message that is usually put in an envelop and sent by mail

❷ 글자, 문자 **n** a (written or printed) mark or sign representing a speech sound; a symbol of an alphabet

❸ (복수로 쓰여) 문학; 학문 **n** (pl) literature; learning

> 한 걸음 더 **a capital letter** 대문자 **a small letter** 소문자 **a letter of introduction** 소개장
> **a man of letters** 학자, 문인, 저술가 **to the letter** 글자 그대로, 엄밀히, 정확히

 다음 문장의 letter에 해당되는 뜻을 Step 02 **의 ❶～❸에서 고르세요.** (해답은 449쪽)

1. He grew up to be a man of letters. (　　　)

2. He sent a letter to his mother. (　　　)

3. "D" is a capital letter, "d" is a small letter. (　　　)

4. She got a long letter from him. (　　　)

5. The letter "R" follows the letter "Q". (　　　)

6. The professor is a man of letters. (　　　)

 다음 문장을 주어진 부분을 이용하여 영어로 옮기세요. (해답은 449쪽)

1. 그는 그의 부모님께 일주일에 한 번 편지를 쓴다. [once a week]

____

2. "N"이라는 글자는 "M" 다음에 온다. [follows]

____

3. 그는 자라서 문인이 되었다. [grew up, man]

____

:: 1. 나는 그녀로부터 편지를 한 통 받았다. 2. A는 알파벳의 첫 글자이다. 3. 이 선생님은 문인이시다.

144 circle [sə́ːrkl]

Step 01 해석연습

다음 문장을 circle에 유의하여 해석해 보세요. (해석은 이 페이지의 하단부에 있음)

1. The girls danced in a circle. _______________________

2. The moon circles the earth. _______________________

3. She is a newcomer to our circle. _______________________

Step 02 뜻 알기

circle에는 다음과 같은 여러 가지의 뜻이 있습니다.

❶ 원; 원형의 것 n a completely round shape; something in the form of a circle

❷ ~에 동그라미를 그리다, ~을 에워싸다 v to enclose something with a circle; to surround
~의 둘레를 돌다, 선회하다 v to move in a circle

❸ (동일한 이해집단의) ~집단, ~사회, 동아리 n a group of people with a shared interest

> 한 걸음 더 **Our teacher briefly explained the <u>circle</u> of the seasons.** 선생님은 사계절의 순환에 대해 간단히 설명하셨다.
> → 순환, 일주(=a series ending at the starting point)
> **business circles** 실업계, 사업계 **educational circles** 교육계 **social circles** 사교계 **the upper circles** 상류사회

Step 03 연습문제

다음 문장의 circle에 해당되는 뜻을 Step 02 의 ❶~❸에서 고르세요. (해답은 449쪽)

1. The children circled the christmas tree. (　　)

2. I hope to join your circle. (　　)

3. The girls stood round in a circle. (　　)

4. The helicopter will circle over the field before landing. (　　)

5. I will draw a circle on the blackboard. (　　)

6. He is a leading figure in economic circles. (　　)

Step 04 영작연습

다음 문장을 주어진 부분을 이용하여 영어로 옮기세요. (해답은 449쪽)

1. 그는 직경 5cm 크기의 원을 그렸다. [drew, diameter]

____

2. 네가 옳다고 생각하는 답에 동그라미를 쳐라. [answer, right]

____

3. 그런 생각들은 교육계에 큰 반향을 일으킬 것이다. [sensation, educational]

____

:: 1. 소녀들은 둥글게 춤을 추었다. 2. 달은 지구의 둘레를 돈다. 3. 그녀는 우리 동아리의 새내기(신참)이다.

145 **bound** [baund]

Step 01
해석연습

다음 문장을 bound에 유의하여 해석해 보세요. (해석은 이 페이지의 하단부에 있음)

1. The girl bound a ribbon round her head. _______________________

2. This rubber ball bounds well. _______________________

3. There are no bounds to her ambition. _______________________

4. The ship is bound for London. _______________________

Step 02
뜻 알기

bound에는 다음과 같은 여러 가지의 뜻이 있습니다.

❶ 동사 bind(묶다, 매다)의 과거 및 과거분사 ⓥ the past tense and past participle of "bind"

❷ 뛰다, 튀다, 도약하다 ⓥ to jump, spring, bounce; to move or run in jumping movements
  튀어 오름, 뜀, 도약 ⓝ jumping movement upward or forward

❸ ∼에 경계를 긋다, ∼을 제한하다 ⓥ to limit; to form the boundary of (a place)
  한도, 한계; 경계(선) ⓝ (usually in plural) a limit, a boundary, a limiting line

❹ (열차, 비행기 따위가) ∼행의 ⓐ going in a particular direction

▷ 한 걸음 더 **be bound for** ∼행의 **be bound to** ∼할 의무가 있는; 꼭 ∼할, ∼할 것이

Step 03
연습문제

다음 문장의 bound에 해당되는 뜻을 **Step 02** 의 ❶∼❹에서 고르세요. (해답은 449쪽)

1. His pet dog bounded to meet him. (   )
2. She bound a ribbon round her head. (   )
3. Our country is bounded on three sides by the sea. (   )
4. He bound the box with a rope. (   )
5. This plane is bound for London. (   )
6. The ball struck the wall and bounded back to me. (   )
7. I am bound for your home. (   )
8. Germany is bounded on the south by France. (   )

Step 04
영작연습

다음 문장을 주어진 부분을 이용하여 영어로 옮기세요. (해답은 449쪽)

1. 그들은 로프로 그녀의 팔과 다리를 묶었다. [arms, with rope]

   ____

2. 그 개는 한 번에 담을 뛰어넘었다. [jumped over, fence]

   ____

3. 이탈리아는 스위스와 북쪽에서 경계를 이루고 있다. [on the north, Switzerland]

   ____

4. 이 기차는 서울행이다. [train, Seoul]

   ____

:: 1. 소녀는 머리에 리본을 매었다. 2. 이 고무공은 잘 튄다. 3. 그녀의 야망에는 한계가 없다. 4. 이 배는 런던행이다.

A. 다음 뜻에 해당되는 단어를 보기에서 찾아 적으세요.

보기	cabinet lot letter(s) circle bound

01. _____________ a group of people with a shared interest
02. _____________ a written or printed message that is usually put in an envelop and sent by mail
03. _____________ a completely round shape; something in the form of a circle
04. _____________ a piece of land (used for building on or for another particular purpose)
05. _____________ a group of high level government officials who meet to make decisions or advise the leader of the government
06. _____________ a great amount or number (of)
07. _____________ the past tense and past participle of "bind"
08. _____________ literature; learning
09. _____________ to enclose something with a circle; to surround
10. _____________ a limit, a boundary, a limiting line
11. _____________ a mark or sign representing a speech sound; a symbol of an alphabet
12. _____________ going in a particular direction
13. _____________ a thing used to decide something by chance; such a method for deciding
14. _____________ a piece of furniture with drawers or shelves for storing or displaying things
15. _____________ jumping movement upward or forward

B. 다음 빈칸에 가장 알맞은 단어를 보기에서 찾아 적으세요.

보기	cabinet lot letter(s) circle bound(s)

01. They are new comers to our (   ).
02. There are three (   ) in the word "cat."
03. He caught the ball on the first (   ).
04. They chose their leader by (   ).
05. Draw a (   ) 10cm in diameter.
06. The new president formed a new (   ).
07. I have a (   ) to do today.
08. Mr. Kim is a man of (   ).
09. They (   ) the package with a rope.
10. The teacher will (   ) the correct answer.
11. We will turn that vacant (   ) into a playground.
12. The ship was (   ) for Africa.
13. I'm just going to post a (   ).
14. It is beyond the (   ) of human knowledge.
15. She keeps dishes and canned food in the (   ).

다음 문장을 굵게 처리된 단어에 유의하여 해석해 보세요.

01. Walking down the street, you may not even notice the trees, but, according to a new study, they do a **lot** more than give shade. [2007년-홀수형 24번]

➡ ______________________________

02. Huge amounts of space are given over to **parking lots** rather than to trees and birds. [2002년-홀수형 25번]

➡ ______________________________

03. But truly improving ourselves or our **lot** is a superhuman task, so we do what we can instead:we shop the economy grows, the world gets more complex, we feel more helpless and insecure, so we shop still more. [1995년-홀수형 48번]

➡ ______________________________

04. W: You have **lots** of bags. Let me help you.
M: Thanks a **lot**.
W: Come this way. My car's in the **parking lot**. [2000년-홀수형 2번]

➡ ______________________________

05. Unless you spend a reasonable amount of time together, talking on the phone, writing **letters**, and being together, friendship will go away. [1999년-홀수형 24번]

➡ ______________________________

06. They are made of numbers, **letters** of the alphabet, words, or simply pictures. [2001년-홀수형 3번]

➡ ______________________________

07. Next, make bigger **circles** with your forearms. [2006년-홀수형 41번]

➡ ______________________________

08. Bands of blue-shirted farmers **circle** and lift and swing behind a drum and various wind instruments in the ancient Basque Riau-Riau dances. [2009년-홀수형 43번]

➡ ______________________________

09. University students in several of my seminar classes sat in a **circle** and each student took turns telling the others his or her name. [2011년-홀수형 41번]

➡ ______________________________

10. It can be played with or without a net by defining the court and scoring against mistakes, such as dropping the tire in-court or throwing it out of **bounds** on the opponents' side. [2007년-홀수형 36번]

➡ ______________________________

11. You might think you're removing all the pesticide on the fruit when you wash it, but some chemicals are **bound** to remain on the surface of the peel. [2007년-홀수형 49~50번]

➡ ______________________________

12. An animal is **bound** to depend on other living creatures, ultimately plants, for its food supply; it must also depend upon the activities of plants for a continued oxygen supply for its respiration. [1994년-1차 21번]

➡ ______________________________

13. But in spite of this **boundless** outdoors potential, there remained the problem of Chattanooga proper, a post-industrial wasteland that made the city the kind of place you would visit but would never want to live in. [2010년-홀수형 37번]

➡ ______________________________

146 patient [péiʃənt]

Step 01 해석연습

다음 문장을 patient에 유의하여 해석해 보세요. (해석은 이 페이지의 하단부에 있음)

1. Be patient with children. _______________________________
2. Dr. Smith has many patients. _______________________________

Step 02 뜻 알기

patient에는 다음과 같은 여러 가지의 뜻이 있습니다.

❶ 인내심[참을성] 있는 ⓐ enduring pain, hardship, etc without becoming angry

❷ 환자 ⓝ a person (who is) receiving medical treatment from a doctor

▷ 한 걸음 더 **patience** 참을성, 인내심 **patiently** 참을성 있게, 끈기 있게

Step 03 연습문제

다음 문장의 patient에 해당되는 뜻을 Step 02 의 ❶〜❷에서 고르세요. (해답은 450쪽)

1. The hospital had too many patients. (   )
2. Her train wad late, but she was patient. (   )
3. Mr. Lee was a devoted, patient teacher. (   )
4. There are many patients waiting today. (   )

Step 04 영작연습

다음 문장을 주어진 부분을 이용하여 영어로 옮기세요. (해답은 450쪽)

1. 그녀는 인내심이 많은 사람이기 때문에 모든 사람들이 그녀를 좋아한다. [everyone, because]

____

2. 기름기 있는 음식은 그 환자에게 좋지 않다. [fatty, not good]

____

:: 1. 아이들을 인내심을 가지고 대해라. 2. Smith 선생님은 환자가 많다.

147 notice [nóutis]

Step 01
해석연습

다음 문장을 notice에 유의하여 해석해 보세요. (해석은 이 페이지의 하단부에 있음)

1. The notice on the wall says "No smoking." ____________________________

2. The maid left without notice. ____________________________

3. A sudden sound caught her notice. ____________________________

Step 02
뜻 알기

notice에는 다음과 같은 여러 가지의 뜻이 있습니다.

❶ 통지서, 공고문, 게시문 **n** a written or printed statement to announce something publicly

❷ 통고, 예고 **n** information or a warning about something that is going to happen
~에게 통지하다, 알리다 **v** to give notice to

❸ 주의, 주목 **n** attention; heed
~에 주의하다, 주목하다; ~을 알아차리다 **v** to pay attention to something or someone; to become aware of

> 한 걸음 더 **noticeable** 주목할 만한, 눈에 띄는, 두드러진 **notify** 통지하다, 알리다 **give notice to** ~에게 통보하다
> **take notice** 주의하다 **take notice of** ~을 알아차리다, 주의하다 **without notice** 예고 없이, 무단으로

Step 03
연습문제

다음 문장의 notice에 해당되는 뜻을 **Step 02** 의 ❶~❸에서 고르세요. (해답은 450쪽)

1. The notice says, "No swimming." (   )

2. Did you notice her hand shaking? (   )

3. He put a notice about the meeting. (   )

4. She gave notice to me that she'll be late. (   )

5. I noticed that she left early. (   )

6. He gave notice of his arrival in Korea. (   )

Step 04
영작연습

다음 문장을 주어진 부분을 이용하여 영어로 옮기세요. (해답은 450쪽)

1. 그는 통고문을 게시판에 붙였다. [stuck, board]

____

2. 그 요리사는 예고도 없이 해고되었다. [cook, fired]

____

3. 그때 그녀는 자신의 지갑이 없어진 것을 알았다. [purse, missing]

____

∷ 1. 벽에 붙은 공고문에는 '금연'이라고 쓰여 있었다. 2. 그 하녀는 통보도 없이 떠났다. 3. 갑작스러운 소리가 그녀의 주의를 끌었다.

Step 01
해석연습

다음 문장을 pole에 유의하여 해석해 보세요. (해석은 이 페이지의 하단부에 있음)

1. A long pole lies across the road. ________________________________

2. The North Pole is a cold and icy place. ________________________________

3. In physics, all magnets have two poles – the north pole and south pole.

____

Step 02
뜻 알기

pole에는 다음과 같은 여러 가지의 뜻이 있습니다.

❶ 장대, 기둥, 막대기　n　a long, slender piece of wood, metal, etc

❷ (지구, 천체의) 극; 극지　n　one of the two ends of the earth's axis

❸ (자석, 전지 등의) 극　n　each of the two terminal points of a magnet or battery

> 한 걸음 더 **I met a <u>Pole</u> on the street yesterday.** 나는 어제 길에서 폴란드 사람을 만났다.
> → 폴란드 사람(=a person of Polish origin)
> **a telegraph pole** 전신주 **a tent pole** 천막기둥 **a flag pole** 깃대 **pole vault** 장대높이뛰기
> **the North Pole** 북극 **the South Pole** 남극 **the positive pole** 양극 **the negative pole** 음극
> **polar** ① 북극[남극]의, 극지의 ② (전지, 자기의) 극의

Step 03
연습문제

다음 문장의 pole에 해당되는 뜻을　**Step 02** 의 ❶∼❸에서 고르세요. (해답은 450쪽)

1. They raised a flag up the pole. (　　)

2. The opposite poles of magnets will attract each other. (　　)

3. The airplane will fly over the North Pole. (　　)

4. The science teacher explained to us about the magnetic poles. (　　)

5. They went on an expedition to the South Pole. (　　)

6. We need several poles to support a tent. (　　)

Step 04
영작연습

다음 문장을 주어진 부분을 이용하여 영어로 옮기세요. (해답은 450쪽)

1. 그녀는 자신의 자전거를 기둥에 자물쇠로 채우고 있다. [locking, bike]

____

2. 그는 남극에 도착한 최초의 사람이었다. [first person, reached]

____

3. 자석의 반대 극들은 서로 끌어당긴다. [opposite, magnets, attract]

____

149 field [fiːld]

Step 01 해석연습

다음 문장을 field에 유의하여 해석해 보세요. (해석은 이 페이지의 하단부에 있음)

1. The field is filled with all sorts of flowers. ________________________
2. There is a baseball field near my school. ________________________
3. My brother is famous in the field of medicine. ________________________
4. This area is a well-known gold field. ________________________

Step 02 뜻 알기

field에는 다음과 같은 여러 가지의 뜻이 있습니다.

❶ (넓은) 들, 들판, 벌판 n an open land with few or no trees
   (구획된) 밭, 경작지 n an area of land on which a crop is grown

❷ 경기장, 광장 n an area of ground used for sports or another special purpose

❸ 분야, 범위, 영역 n an area of knowledge, interest, study, activity, etc

❹ (광물 등의) 매장지, 산지 n an area of land from which minerals, etc are obtained

> 한 걸음 더 **a corn field** 옥수수 밭 **a baseball field** 야구장 **an oil field** 유전 **a coal field** 석탄산지
> **field trip** 현장견학여행, 현지조사여행

Step 03 연습문제

다음 문장의 field에 해당되는 뜻을 **Step 02** 의 ❶~❹에서 고르세요. (해답은 450쪽)

1. My uncle is famous in the field of ancient history. (   )
2. Mountains, trees and fields are white with snow. (   )
3. The company owns 50 percent of the tungsten field. (   )
4. Dr. Hwang opened a new field in science. (   )
5. The boy is running across the soccer field. (   )
6. A river winds through the field. (   )
7. That area is a well-known coal field. (   )
8. There is a soccer field near my school. (   )

Step 04 영작연습

다음 문장을 주어진 부분을 이용하여 영어로 옮기세요. (해답은 450쪽)

1. 한 농부가 밭에 씨를 뿌리고 있다. [farmer, sowing]

____

2. 선수들이 축구경기장을 가로질러 달려가고 있다. [running across, soccer]

____

3. 그는 언제나 국제법 분야에 흥미를 가져 왔다. [interested, intermational law]

____

4. 그 회사는 이 유전의 지분을 15퍼센트 소유하고 있다. [owns, oil]

____

:: 1. 들엔 온갖 꽃들이 가득하다. 2. 나의 학교 근처에 야구장이 하나 있다. 3. 나의 형은 의학 분야에서 유명하다. 4. 이 지역은 유명한 금의 산지이다.

150 **cross** [krɔ(ː)s / krɑs]

Step 01 해석연습   다음 문장을 cross에 유의하여 해석해 보세요. (해석은 이 페이지의 하단부에 있음)

1. Put a cross next to the wrong answer. ___________________________

2. He crossed the street to catch the bus. ___________________________

3. The roads cross in the center of town. ___________________________

Step 02 뜻 알기   cross에는 다음과 같은 여러 가지의 뜻이 있습니다.

❶ 십자가, 십자가형 물체 또는 그림 **n** a symbol formed by two lines placed across each other; an object or picture in the shape of a cross used as a sign by Christian faith or for decoration

❷ ∼을 횡단하다, 가로지르다 **v** to go from one side to the other

❸ 교차시키다; 교차하다 **v** to place two things across each other; to go or be placed across each other

> 한 걸음 더 **I crossed her name off the list.** 나는 명부에서 그녀의 이름을 줄을 그어 지워버렸다.
> → 횡선을 긋다; 줄을 그어 지우다(=to draw a line or lines across)
> **His son's illness has been a very heavy cross to bear.** 그의 아들의 병은 참고 견디어야 할 매우 무거운 시련이었다.
> → 시련, 고난(=suffering; trial; burden of sorrow)
> **Why are you so cross with me?** 왜 나에게 그렇게 성을 내고 있니? → (구어체) 성난, 화가 난(=angry; bad tempered)
> **crossroad** 교차로, 네거리 **crosswalk** 건널목, 횡단보도 **the Red Cross** 적십자사 **cross one's fingers** 행운을 빌다

Step 03 연습문제   다음 문장의 cross에 해당되는 뜻을 **Step 02** 의 ❶∼❸에서 고르세요. (해답은 450쪽)

1. The teacher put a cross next to the wrong answer. (   )

2. The child crossed the road. (   )

3. He crossed his knife and fork. (   )

4. The girl wore a tiny gold cross around her neck. (   )

5. She sat down and crossed her legs. (   )

6. How are going to cross the river? (   )

Step 04 영작연습   다음 문장을 주어진 부분을 이용하여 영어로 옮기세요. (해답은 450쪽)

1. 그 소녀는 목에 작은 금 십자가를 착용하고 있었다. [wearing, tiny]

____

2. 거기서 길을 건너지 마라. 횡단보도를 이용해라. [street, crosswalk]

____

3. 그녀는 앉아서 다리를 꼬았다. [sat down, legs]

____

∷ 1. 틀린 답 옆에 X표를 해라. 2. 그는 버스를 타기 위해 길을 건넜다. 3. 길들은 마을 가운데서 교차한다.

A. 다음 뜻에 해당되는 단어를 보기에서 찾아 적으세요.

> 보기   patient   notice   pole   field   cross

01. ______________ an area of ground used for sports or another special purpose
02. ______________ information or a warning about something that is going to happen
03. ______________ one of the two ends of the earth's axis
04. ______________ a symbol formed by two lines placed across each other; an object or picture in the shape of a cross used as a sign by Christian faith or for decoration
05. ______________ an area of land on which a crop is grown
06. ______________ each of the two terminal points of a magnet or battery
07. ______________ to go from one side to the other
08. ______________ enduring pain, hardship, etc without becoming angry
09. ______________ attention; heed
10. ______________ an area of land from which minerals, etc. are obtained
11. ______________ to place two things across each other; to go or be placed across each other
12. ______________ a person (who is) receiving medical treatment from a doctor
13. ______________ an area of knowledge, interest, study, activity, etc
14. ______________ a written or printed statement to announce something publicly
15. ______________ a long, slender piece of wood, metal, etc

B. 다음 빈칸에 가장 알맞은 단어를 보기에서 찾아 적으세요.

> 보기   patient   notice   pole   field   cross

01. Be (   ) with your children.
02. The driver was fired without (   ).
03. Amundsen explored the South (   ).
04. The farmer is working in the (   ).
05. The news will attract our (   ).
06. The company owns 25 percent of the copper (   ).
07. He learned that all magnets have two (   ).
08. It is as large as a soccer (   ).
09. The (   ) is the symbol of Christianity.
10. He is an expert in the (   ) of computer engineering.
11. I will (   ) the river by boat.
12. A calm attitude is needed to care for the (   ).
13. Don't (   ) your legs.
14. The flag flies at the top of the (   ).
15. I will put a (   ) in the newspaper.

해답은 450쪽

다음 문장을 굵게 처리된 단어에 유의하여 해석해 보세요.

01. One of the most important shifts will be an increased recognition of **patient** individuality, a concept now largely ignored. [2010년-홀수형 25번]

➡ _______________________________

02. Remind yourself to be **patient** and wait. [2003년-홀수형 25번]

➡ _______________________________

03. The Ndembu people of Central Africa believe that illness is often the result of the anger of a relative, friend, of enemy towards the **patient**. [1998년-홀수형 38번]

➡ _______________________________

04. If you are like most people, you should **notice** something odd: Your friend will prefer the true print, but you will prefer the reverse image. [2010년-홀수형 26번]

➡ _______________________________

05. Students are not to go to school until further **notice**. [1998년-홀수형 12번]

➡ _______________________________

06. You'll **notice**, right away, how much the interactions with the people in your life will improve as a direct result of this simple act. [2003년-홀수형 25번]

➡ _______________________________

07. This wind, which has traveled from the North **Pole** toward which I am going, gives me a taste of the icy climate. [2002년-홀수형 20번]

➡ _______________________________

08. While design and styling are interrelated, they are completely distinct **fields**. [2007년-홀수형 34번]

➡ _______________________________

09. Not unlike many successful graduates in our long history, your children will go out into the world, and successfully participate in the **fields** of politics, economics, culture, and education. [2008년-홀수형 20번]

➡ _______________________________

10. Modern technology is addictive, so be sure to plan days away from its electromagnetic **fields**. [2008년-홀수형 49-50번]

➡ _______________________________

11. Through the train window, I could see crops ripening in the **fields** and trees turning red and yellow. [2003년-홀수형 26번]

➡ _______________________________

12. He introduced **field** hospitals, ambulance service, and first-aid treatment to the battlefield. [2007년-홀수형 35번]

➡ _______________________________

13. W: You **crossed** the street with the red light on.
M: Oh, I'm sorry. I didn't see the light. [2011년-홀수형 9번]

➡ _______________________________

14. He sat for a time in front of the fireplace, **cross**-legged, adding logs, and gazing at the warm fire. [2010년-홀수형 29번]

➡ _______________________________

15. He slips and slips, falls down, has trouble getting up, gets his skis **crossed**, tumbles again, and generally looks and feels like a fool. [2006년-홀수형 27번]

➡ _______________________________

DAY 16

By falling, we learn to go safely.
넘어짐으로써 안전하게 걷는 법을 배운다.

151 board [bɔːrd]

Group 31

Step 01
해석연습

다음 문장을 board에 유의하여 해석해 보세요. (해석은 이 페이지의 하단부에 있음)

1. The floor is made of boards. ______________________
2. The cost of room and board at college is usually high. ______________________
3. Sailors boarded their ship rapidly. ______________________

Step 02
뜻 알기

board에는 다음과 같은 여러 가지의 뜻이 있습니다.

❶ 널빤지, 판자, 평평한 판, 게시판 ⓝ a flat piece of wood or other material

❷ 식사 ⓝ food served; daily meals

❸ (배, 비행기 등에) 타다, 탑승하다 ⓥ to get on or into (a ship, train, plane, bus, etc)

> 한 걸음 더 **He boards at his aunt's.** 그는 아주머니 댁에서 하숙한다.
> → ~에 하숙하다, 기숙하다(=to live temporarily and take meals in someone else's house or school)
> **The school board appointed a new principal.** 학교 이사회는 새 교장을 임명하였다.
> → 위원회, 이사회, 정부기관의 부서(=a group of persons controlling a business or a government department)
> **a blackboard** 칠판 **boarding school** 기숙사제 학교 **boarding pass** (항공기의) 탑승권 **the board of directors** 이사회

Step 03
연습문제

다음 문장의 board에 해당되는 뜻을 **Step 02** 의 ❶~❸에서 고르세요. (해답은 451쪽)

1. The cost of room and board at that college is high. (   )
2. He put the list on the board. (   )
3. Flight KE 104 for London is now boarding at Gate 36. (   )
4. The carpenter fitted the boards together. (   )
5. The hotel porter has $150.00 a week and free board. (   )
6. Please board the aircraft now. (   )

Step 04
영작연습

다음 문장을 주어진 부분을 이용하여 영어로 옮기세요. (해답은 451쪽)

1. 그녀는 다이빙 보드에 서 있다. [standing, diving]

____

2. 그는 방값과 식대로 일주일에 150불을 지불한다. [pays, room]

____

3. 시드니행 항공기 CX 386편이 지금 14번 탑승구에서 탑승 중이다. [Flight, Gate]

____

∷ 1. 바닥은 널빤지로 되어 있다. 2. 대학의 숙식비는 대체로 비싸다. 3. 선원들은 자신들의 배에 신속히 올라탔다.

152 fall [fɔ:l]

Step 01 해석연습

다음 문장을 fall에 유의하여 해석해 보세요. (해석은 이 페이지의 하단부에 있음)

1. The baby might fall to the floor. _______________________

2. Fall is my favorite time of year. _______________________

3. He made the kite fall to the ground. _______________________

Step 02 뜻 알기

fall에는 다음과 같은 여러 가지의 뜻이 있습니다.

❶ 가을 [n] the season between summer and winter; autumn

❷ 넘어지다, 쓰러지다 [v] to move suddenly to the ground from a standing position; tumble

❸ 떨어지다, 낙하하다, 하락하다 [v] to come down from a higher place; to drop; to decline

> 한 걸음 더 **fall** [fɔ:l] - **fell** [fel] - **fallen** [fɔ:lən]
> the **fall** of rain[snow] for a year 1년간의 강우[강설]량 → 강우[강설]량(=the amount that falls)
> the **fall** of Roman Empire 로마제국의 멸망 → 몰락, 멸망(=downfall, ruin)
> **rainfall** 강우량 **snowfall** 강설량 **waterfall** 폭포 **Niagara Falls** 나이아가라 폭포 **fall back on[upon]** 의지하다
> **fall in love with** ~와 사랑에 빠지다 **fall behind** 뒤처지다 **fall short** 모자라다, 부족하다

Step 03 연습문제

다음 문장의 fall에 해당되는 뜻을 Step 02 의 ❶~❸에서 고르세요. (해답은 451쪽)

1. Football teams playing in the fall. (   )

2. He watched the water fall over the cliff. (   )

3. Leaves change their color in the fall. (   )

4. Leaves fall in autumn. (   )

5. Karen might fall and hurt herself. (   )

6. He fell on the stairs and broke his arm (   )

Step 04 영작연습

다음 문장을 주어진 부분을 이용하여 영어로 옮기세요. (해답은 451쪽)

1. 가을에 날씨는 선선해진다. [weather, cool]

____

2. 그녀는 넘어져서 머리를 마룻바닥에 부딪혔다. [hit, floor]

____

3. 겨울에 기온은 종종 영하로 내려진다. [temperature, below zero]

____

:: 1. 그 아기는 마룻바닥에 넘어질지도 모른다. 2. 가을은 1년 중 내가 가장 좋아하는 계절이다. 3. 그는 연을 땅바닥으로 떨어지게 했다.

153 note [nout]

Step 01
해석연습

다음 문장을 note에 유의하여 해석해 보세요. (해석은 이 페이지의 하단부에 있음)

1. Jane wrote a note to Tony. _______________________________
2. The musician played the wrong note. _______________________________
3. She noted that his hands were dirty. _______________________________

Step 02
뜻 알기

note에는 다음과 같은 여러 가지의 뜻이 있습니다.

❶ 짧은 편지, 메모, 필기 n a short written message
　～을 적어두다, 메모하다 v to write down

❷ (음악) 음, 음조, 음표 n a musical sound or tone

❸ 주목하다, 알아차리다 v to notice, to pay attention to / 주의, 주목 n notice, attention

> 한 걸음 더 **She received a ten-dollar <u>note</u>.** 그녀는 10달러짜리 지폐를 받았다.
> → 지폐 또는 어음(=a piece of paper used as money; bill)
> **He is a man of <u>note</u>.** 그는 저명인사다. → 저명, 명성, 중요성(=greatness, fame, importance)
> **bank note** 지폐 **notebook** 공책 **notable** 주목할 만한, 현저한, 중요한 **noted** 유명한, 저명한 **noteworthy** 주목할 만한
> **take note of** ～에 주목하다 **take notes**(=make notes) 적다, 필기하다

Step 03
연습문제

다음 문장의 note에 해당되는 뜻을 Step 02 의 ❶～❸에서 고르세요. (해답은 451쪽)

1. She sent me a note in the mail. (　　　)
2. The doctor will note how the patient looks. (　　　)
3. Will you play that note again? (　　　)
4. Mike will note how to get to the freeway. (　　　)
5. Barbara played the wrong note. (　　　)
6. Make a note before you forget. (　　　)

Step 04
영작연습

다음 문장을 주어진 부분을 이용하여 영어로 옮기세요. (해답은 451쪽)

1. 그녀는 그의 전화번호를 그녀의 일기장에 적어 놓았다. [telephone number, diary]

____

2. 그는 트럼펫으로 높은 음을 연주했다. [high, trumpet]

____

3. 그는 그녀의 행동의 변화를 알아차렸다. [change, behavior]

____

:: 1. Jane은 Tony에게 쪽지를 써 보냈다. 2. 그 음악가는 틀린 음을 연주했다. 3. 그녀는 그의 손이 지저분하다는 것을 알아차렸다.

154 pack [pæk]

Step 01
해석연습

다음 문장을 pack에 유의하여 해석해 보세요. (해석은 이 페이지의 하단부에 있음)

1. The climber carried a pack on his back. ______________________

2. She will pack for a trip to San Francisco. ______________________

3. The plumber packed the joint of the water pipe. ______________________

Step 02
뜻 알기

pack에는 다음과 같은 여러 가지의 뜻이 있습니다.

❶ 꾸러미, 다발, 배낭, 포장한 물건 **n** a set of things tied together to be carried

❷ 짐을 꾸리다, 포장하다 **v** to put things into cases, boxes, etc for taking somewhere or storing

❸ (증기, 물, 공기 따위가 새지 않도록) ～에 틈막이를 하다, 봉하다, 둘레를 채우다 **v** to cover, fill, or surround an object closely with a protective material

> 한 걸음 더 **A pack of hounds chased the deer.** 한 무리의 사냥개들이 사슴을 뒤쫓았다.
> → 동물의 한 떼, 무리 또는 (경멸적 표현으로) 사람의 패거리(= a group of animals or people)
> **People will pack the hall.** 사람들이 홀을 꽉 메울 것이다. → 사람이 꽉 들어차다(=crowd closely together)
> **Please shuffle the pack and deal.** 카드 패를 뒤섞고 분배하세요. → (카드의) 한 벌(=a set of playing cards))
> **a pack of thieves** 도둑 떼 **a pack of lies** 거짓말투성이 **a pack of matches** 성냥 한 통 **package** 꾸러미, 소포, 짐
> **packing** ① 포장, 짐 꾸리기 ② 포장재료[용품] **in packs** 떼 지어, 무리를 지어 **pack up** ① 짐을 꾸리다 ② 일을 그만두다

Step 03
연습문제

다음 문장의 pack에 해당되는 뜻을 Step 02 의 ❶～❸에서 고르세요. (해답은 451쪽)

1. The climber was carrying a 50 pound pack. (　　　)

2. Pack the sponge around the china cups. (　　　)

3. My father will pack for a trip. (　　　)

4. There was a glass packed in straw. (　　　)

5. Many things were in the pack. (　　　)

6. She will pack her clothes in this suitcasc. (　　　)

Step 04
영작연습

다음 문장을 주어진 부분을 이용하여 영어로 옮기세요. (해답은 451쪽)

1. 그는 가게에서 담배 한 갑을 샀다. [cigarette, store]

____

2. 그는 외국 여행을 위해 두 개의 여행 가방을 꾸렸다. [suitcases, overseas trip]

____

3. 깨어지지 않도록 꽃병 둘레를 신문지로 채워라. [newspaper, vase]

____

:: 1. 그 등산가는 등에 배낭을 메고 있었다. 2. 그녀는 샌프란시스코로 가는 여행을 위해 짐을 꾸릴 것이다. 3. 배관공은 송수관의 이음매를 패킹[틈막이]했다.

155 head [hed]

Step 01 해석연습

다음 문장을 head에 유의하여 해석해 보세요. (해석은 이 페이지의 하단부에 있음)

1. The ball hit him on the head. ___________________________
2. The president is the head of the country. ___________________________
3. The head of a hammer is made of metal. ___________________________

Step 02 뜻 알기

head에는 다음과 같은 여러 가지의 뜻이 있습니다.

❶ 머리 🅝 the part of the body above the neck

❷ 지도자, 우두머리 🅝 a leader, chief
이끌다, 책임지다; 선두에 서다 🆅 to lead or to be in charge of; to be first on (something)

❸ 머리(모양)의 부분; 상부 🅝 anything that is like a head in shape or position; the top part

> 한 걸음 더 **He has a good head for numbers.** 그는 셈하는 능력이 뛰어나다.
> → 능력(=ability)또는 지력(=intelligence)
> **They are heading for south.** 그들은 남쪽을 향해 나아가고 있었다. → (어떤 방향으로) 나아가다, 향하다
> **Which do you choose, heads or tails?** 어느 것을 고를 거니? 앞면, 아니면 뒷면? → (동전의) 앞면, 표면
> **headfirst** 곤두박질하여, 거꾸로 **dinner at $5.00 per head** 일인당 5달러짜리 식사 **lose one's head** 당황하다
> **make head or tail of** 알다, 이해하다 **headache** 두통 **headline** 제목 **headmaster** 교장 **headquarters** 본부, 사령부

Step 03 연습문제

다음 문장의 head에 해당되는 뜻을 **Step 02** 의 ❶~❸에서 고르세요. (해답은 451쪽)

1. The ball hit Cindy's head. (   )
2. Miss Jane is the head of finance committee. (   )
3. The head of a nail is flat. (   )
4. Gary has a large head. (   )
5. The principal is the head of our school. (   )
6. I will meet you at the head of the stairs. (   )

Step 04 영작연습

다음 문장을 주어진 부분을 이용하여 영어로 옮기세요. (해답은 451쪽)

1. 그녀는 머리를 돌리고 나를 말없이 쳐다보았다. [looked at, silently]

____

2. 그는 녹색에너지를 개발하는 기술자들의 팀을 이끌고 있다. [engineers, developing]

____

3. 그 소년은 줄의 맨 앞에 서 있다. [standing, line]

____

:: 1. 공이 그의 머리를 때렸다. 2. 대통령은 나라의 우두머리이다. 3. 망치의 머리 부분은 금속으로 되어 있다.

Review Group-31

해답은 451쪽

A. 다음 뜻에 해당되는 단어를 보기에서 찾아 적으세요.

보기	board fall note pack head

01. ______________ a leader, chief
02. ______________ a set of things tied together to be carried
03. ______________ a musical sound or tone
04. ______________ to cover, fill, or surround an object closely with a protective material
05. ______________ to come down from a higher place; to drop; to decline
06. ______________ to get on or into (a ship, train, plane, bus, etc)
07. ______________ anything that is like a head in shape or position; the top part; the front part
08. ______________ a flat piece of wood or other material
09. ______________ the season between summer and winter; autumn
10. ______________ to notice, to pay attention to
11. ______________ food served; daily meals
12. ______________ a short written message
13. ______________ to move suddenly to the ground from a standing position; tumble
14. ______________ to put things into cases, boxes, etc for taking somewhere or storing
15. ______________ the part of the body above the neck

B. 다음 빈칸에 가장 알맞은 단어를 보기에서 찾아 적으세요.

보기	board fall note pack head

01. He will saw this long (   ).
02. The horse had a hat on its (   ).
03. Helen wrote a (   ) to Frank.
04. The plumber will (   ) the leaking joint of the pipe.
05. Autumn and (   ) are the same time of year.
06. I played a high (   ) on my guitar.
07. Be careful not to (   ) on the stairs.
08. We will (   ) for a trip to Sydney.
09. We were standing at the (   ) of the line.
10. Please (   ) that the new due date is March 31.
11. Passengers are asked to (   ) half an hour before departure time.
12. Some food was in the (   ).
13. Are you the (   ) of this group?
14. The temperature will (   ) in the winter.
15. I pay $500 a month for room and (   ).

다음 문장을 굵게 처리된 단어에 유의하여 해석해 보세요.

01. Around them were lots of wooden barrels and **boards**. [2007년-홀수형 46~48번]

→ ______________________________

02. She's in an editorial **board** meeting at the moment. Can I help you? [2006년-홀수형 9번]

→ ______________________________

03. Expecting the graceful curves, woody heights, and reflected images along the river that I remembered from my childhood, I was thrilled as I **boarded** the boat. [2004-홀수형 27번]

→ ______________________________

04. W: Hey, Stuart. Take a look at the bulletin **board**.
M: Wow, there are a lot of school clubs. [2011년-홀수형 15번]

→ ______________________________

05. Outside, snow continued to **fall** quietly in the cones of light cast by the streetlights. [2010년-홀수형 29번]

→ ______________________________

06. Although there are numerous explanations for the **fall** of the Roman empire, the deeper cause lies in the declining fertility of its soil and the decrease in agricultural yields. [2012-홀수형 28번]

→ ______________________________

07. Flying over rural Kansas in an airplane one **fall** evening was a delightful experience for passenger Walt Morris. [2009년-홀수형 19번]

→ ______________________________

08. He slips and slips, **falls** down, has trouble getting up, gets his skis crossed, tumbles again, and generally looks and feels like a fool. [2006년-홀수형 27번]

→ ______________________________

09. After the **fall** of Napoleon, Larrey's medical reputation saved him, and he was named a member of the Academy of Medicine at its founding in 1820. [2007년-홀수형 35번]

→ ______________________________

10. **Note** the best price and the worst price and budget in between the two. [2009년-홀수형 20번]

→ ______________________________

11. When I hit the highest **note**, a large wine glass suddenly broke. [1999년-홀수형 37번]

→ ______________________________

12. I always included a **note** explaining my Christmas experience as a child. [2003년-홀수형 19번]

→ ______________________________

13. My belief is that all music has an expressive power, some more and some less, but that all music has a certain meaning behind the **notes**. [1998년-홀수형 35번]

→ ______________________________

14. The more meaning you can **pack** into a single word, the fewer words are needed to get the idea across. [2011년-홀수형 25번]

→ ______________________________

15. You are under the false impression that you do not have as many items to **pack** as you really do. [2009년-홀수형 22번]

→ ______________________________

16. W: Umm... Two pineapples, please. How much are these strawberries?
M: They're 10 dollars a **pack**. [2012년-홀수형 5번]

→ ______________________________

156 shade [ʃeid]

Group 32

Step 01 해석연습

다음 문장을 shade에 유의하여 해석해 보세요. (해석은 이 페이지의 하단부에 있음)

1. The trees give a pleasant shade to us. ______________________

2. He pulled down the shades of the windows. ______________________

3. She shaded her eyes with her hands. ______________________

Step 02 뜻 알기

shade에는 다음과 같은 여러 가지의 뜻이 있습니다.

❶ 그늘, 응달 **n** a slight darkness caused by the blocking of some light

❷ 차양, 블라인드, 전등의 갓 **n** something that shuts out light or brightness

❸ ~을 빛, 열 따위로부터 차단하다, 덮어 가리다 **v** to keep something from light or heat; to cover

> 한 걸음 더 **The patient is a <u>shade</u> better today.** 환자는 오늘 조금 상태가 좋다.
> → 극히 조금, 약간(=a slight amount or degree)
> **You'd better <u>shade</u> the background of that drawing.** 너는 그 그림의 배경을 어둡게 하는 것이 좋겠다.
> → 어둡게 하다(=to make darker)
> **all <u>shades</u> of blue** 여러 가지 색조의 청색 → 색조(=a degree of color)
> **light and shade** ① (그림의) 명암[밝고 어두움] ② (비유적) 천양지차, 현격한 차이 **shady** ① 그늘진 ② 수상쩍은, 의심스러운

Step 03 연습문제

다음 문장의 shade에 해당되는 뜻을 **Step 02** 의 ❶~❸에서 고르세요. (해답은 451쪽)

1. The temperature was 10℃ in the shade. (　　)

2. Gary needs to shade his eyes from the sun. (　　)

3. Pull down the shade at night. (　　)

4. The boy shaded his face with his hands. (　　)

5. He sat down in the shade of a tree. (　　)

6. He pulled down the shades of the windows. (　　)

Step 04 영작연습

다음 문장을 주어진 부분을 이용하여 영어로 옮기세요. (해답은 451쪽)

1. 아이들은 시원한 그늘에서 노는 것을 좋아한다. [play, cool]

____

2. 그녀는 침실용 새 블라인드를 샀다. [bought, bedroom]

____

3. 이 모자가 너를 뜨거운 태양으로부터 가려 줄 것이다. [hat, hot]

____

:: 1. 그 나무들은 우리들에게 시원한 그늘을 제공해 준다. 2. 그는 창문들의 블라인드를 잡아 내렸다. 3. 그녀는 손으로 자신의 눈을 가렸다.

157 roll [roul]

Step 01
해석연습

다음 문장을 roll에 유의하여 해석해 보세요. (해석은 이 페이지의 하단부에 있음)

1. Do you want to eat this roll? ________________________________
2. That pencil might roll off your desk. ________________________________
3. There are 30 students on the roll in our class. ________________________________

Step 02
뜻 알기

roll에는 다음과 같은 여러 가지의 뜻이 있습니다.

❶ 롤빵(둥글게 말아서 구운 빵) **n** a small round piece of bread

❷ 구르다, 회전하다; 굴리다 **v** to move along (or to cause something to move) by turning over and over
둥글게 만들다, 말다 **v** to make into a ball or tube shape

❸ 명부, 목록, 출석부 **n** a list of names of people in a group

> 한 걸음 더 **She bought two <u>rolls</u> of film for $10.00.** 그녀는 10달러를 주고 필름 두 통을 샀다.
> → 둥글게 말려진 것(=anything made into the shape of a pipe or cylinder by being rolled)
> **He heard the <u>roll</u> of drums from a distance.** 그는 멀리서 들려오는 북소리를 들었다.
> → (북, 천둥, 대포 등의) 울리는 소리(=a loud and echoing sound)
> **call a roll** 출석을 부르다 **roll up** ∼을 말다, 말아 올리다, 걷어 올리다 **unroll** (말린 것을) 풀다, 펴다

Step 03
연습문제

다음 문장의 roll에 해당되는 뜻을 **Step 02** 의 ❶∼❸에서 고르세요. (해답은 451쪽)

1. Do you want butter on that roll. (   )
2. Let's roll this rock down the hill. (   )
3. She ate a small roll for breakfast. (   )
4. Mr. Smith is calling the roll in his class. (   )
5. A square tire would not roll. (   )
6. Ms. Evans looked for Jim's name on the roll. (   )

Step 04
영작연습

다음 문장을 주어진 부분을 이용하여 영어로 옮기세요. (해답은 451쪽)

1. 그녀는 점심식사로 롤빵으로 만든 햄 샌드위치를 먹었다. [ham sandwich, lunch]

____

2. 그는 신문을 둥글게 말고 그 주위에 고무줄을 씌웠다. [rubber band, around]

____

3. 명부에 있는 모든 사람들이 회의에 참석했다. [everyone, meeting]

____

:: 1. 너는 이 롤빵 먹기를 원하느냐? 2. 저 연필은 굴러 떨어질지 모른다. 3. 우리 반 출석부에는 학생이 30명 있다.

228

158 sign [sain]

Step 01 해석연습

다음 문장을 sign에 유의하여 해석해 보세요. (해석은 이 페이지의 하단부에 있음)

1. The sign shows that the house is for sale. ________________________________
2. He made a sign to me to be quiet. ________________________________
3. He forgot to sign the check. ________________________________

Step 02 뜻 알기

sign에는 다음과 같은 여러 가지의 뜻이 있습니다.

❶ 간판, 표지판 **n** a board or poster with information on it

❷ 몸짓, 표시, 신호 **n** a gesture or signal used instead of words
   (몸짓 등으로) 알리다, 신호하다 **v** to show one's meaning with a gesture or signal

❸ 서명하다 **v** to write one's name on something

> 한 걸음 더 **There is no sign on life on Mars.** 화성에는 생명체가 있다는 흔적이 없다.
> → 흔적, 징후, 증거(=an indication or evidence of something coming or present; a trace; a proof)
> **The (+) is the sign for addition.** (+)는 덧셈부호이다.
> → 부호, 기호(=a mark used to mean something; a symbol)
> **a traffic sign** 교통표지 **signboard** 간판 **the minus sign** 뺄셈부호 **the plus sign** 덧셈부호 **the phonetic sign** 발음기호
> **neon sign** 네온사인 **sign up for** 참가하다, 가입[응모]하다 **signal** 신호 **signature** 서명

Step 03 연습문제

다음 문장의 sign에 해당되는 뜻을 **Step 02** 의 ❶~❸에서 고르세요. (해답은 451쪽)

1. Please give me a sign when you are finished. (　　　)
2. He taped a large green sign to the door. (　　　)
3. She refused to sign the paper. (　　　)
4. The policeman gave me a sign to stop. (　　　)
5. They are hanging a sign in the shop window. (　　　)
6. Mr. Smith must sign several important papers. (　　　)

Step 04 영작연습

다음 문장을 주어진 부분을 이용하여 영어로 옮기세요. (해답은 451쪽)

1. 벽에는 금연 표시판이 있었다. [no smoking, wall]

____

2. 그녀는 나에게 방을 나가라는 몸짓을 했다. [leave room]

____

3. 이곳에 너의 이름을 서명하는 것을 잊지 마라. [forget, name]

____

∷ 1. 그 간판은 그 집이 팔려고 내놓은 집인 것을 알려 주고 있다. 2. 그는 나에게 조용히 하라고 신호를 했다. 3. 그는 수표에 서명하는 것을 잊었다.

159 bit [bit]

Step 01 해석연습

다음 문장을 bit에 유의하여 해석해 보세요. (해석은 이 페이지의 하단부에 있음)

1. Tony has a bit of sand in his shoes. ___________________________________
2. Chris bit the red fruit. ___________________________________
3. The bit fits in the horse's mouth. ___________________________________

Step 02 뜻 알기

bit에는 다음과 같은 여러 가지의 뜻이 있습니다.

❶ 작은 조각, 소량, 조금, 약간 n a small piece; a small amount

❷ 동사 bite의 과거 및 과거분사형 v the past tense and past participle of the verb "bite"
   * bite[bait] - bit[bit] - bit[bit] / bitten[bítn]

❸ (말의) 재갈 n a metal bar that is put in the mouth of a horse and used for controlling
   its movement

> 한 걸음 더 **He lost one of the <u>bits</u> for his drill.** 그는 그의 드릴의 날 중에서 하나를 잃어버렸다.
> → 드릴의 날과 같은 연장의 날(=the cutting part of a tool)
> **Eight <u>bits</u> is equal to one byte.** 8비트는 1바이트와 같다. → 컴퓨터에서 정보량의 최소기본단위
> **a bit of chalk** 분필 한 토막 **a bit of cake** 케이크 한 조각 **a bit of advice** 충고 한 마디
> **bit by bit** 점점, 조금씩, 차츰(=little by little; gradually) **for a bit** 잠시 동안 **a bit of** 조금, 다소

Step 03 연습문제

다음 문장의 bit에 해당되는 뜻을 Step 02 의 ❶~❸에서 고르세요. (해답은 451쪽)

1. The glass broke into bits. (   )
2. That donkey bit my brother. (   )
3. Put the bit in the horse's mouth. (   )
4. Jeff cleaned the bit and other equipment. (   )
5. A bit of food fell on the floor. (   )
6. Annie's sister bit her finger. (   )

Step 04 영작연습

다음 문장을 주어진 부분을 이용하여 영어로 옮기세요. (해답은 451쪽)

1. 마룻바닥이 부서진 유리조각들로 덮여 있다. [covered, broken glass]

   ____

2. 개가 내 다리를 물었다. [dog, leg]

   ____

3. 재갈이 조랑말의 아픈 입을 다치게 했다. [pony's, sore]

   ____

⠿ 1. Tony는 신발에 약간의 모래를 가지고 있다. 2. Chris는 빨간 과일을 깨물었다. 3. 재갈은 말의 입에 잘 맞는다.

160 trunk [trʌŋk]

Step 01 해석연습

다음 문장을 trunk에 유의하여 해석해 보세요. (해석은 이 페이지의 하단부에 있음)

1. She keeps winter clothes in a trunk. ________________________

2. An elephant put out its trunk and picked up an apple. ________________

3. The trunk is the largest part of the tree. ________________________

Step 02 뜻 알기

trunk에는 다음과 같은 여러 가지의 뜻이 있습니다.

❶ 여행용 큰 가방[트렁크] n a large box or chest to hold or carry clothes or personal belongings

❷ 코끼리 코 n an elephant's long nose

❸ 나무줄기 n the main stem of a tree

> 한 걸음 더 **He is wearing only a pair of swimming trunks.** 그는 단지 수영팬츠만 입고 있다.
> → (남자의 경기, 수영용 따위의) 팬츠[반바지](=very short trousers worn by athletics, swimmers, etc)
> **Put your baggage in the trunk of my car.** 너의 짐을 나의 차 뒤의 짐칸에 넣어라.
> → 자동차 뒷부분의 짐 싣는 곳(=the part at the back of a car where you can put bags, tools, etc)
> **The man has a powerful trunk, but thin arms.** 그 남자는 강한 몸통을 가지고 있지만, 팔은 가늘다.
> → 몸통(=the central part of the body, without the head, arms, or legs)
> **trunk road** 간선도로(=main road)

Step 03 연습문제

다음 문장의 trunk에 해당되는 뜻을 **Step 02** 의 ❶∼❸에서 고르세요. (해답은 452쪽)

1. The elephant can pick up the food with its trunk. (　　)

2. The bark was falling off the trunk. (　　)

3. She keeps her blankets in her trunk. (　　)

4. That elephant has a long gray trunk. (　　)

5. He packed his trunk and sent it to Australia by ship. (　　)

6. Branches stick out of the trunk. (　　)

Step 04 영작연습

다음 문장을 주어진 부분을 이용하여 영어로 옮기세요. (해답은 452쪽)

1. 그는 차고에서 그의 할아버지의 오래된 여행용 큰 가방을 발견했다. [found, garage]

____

2. 코끼리는 코로 숨을 쉴 수 있다. [breathe, through]

____

3. 저 나무의 줄기는 두께가 3미터나 된다. [meters, thick]

____

:: 1. 그녀는 겨울옷들을 여행용 큰 가방에 보관한다. 2. 코끼리가 코를 뻗어 사과 하나를 집었다. 3. 나무줄기는 나무의 가장 큰 부분이다.

A. 다음 뜻에 해당되는 단어를 보기에서 찾아 적으세요.

보기	shade roll sign bit trunk

01. ______________ a board or poster with information on it
02. ______________ a small round piece of bread
03. ______________ an elephant's long nose
04. ______________ to keep something from light or heat; to cover
05. ______________ to write one's name on something
06. ______________ a metal bar that is put in the mouth of a horse and used for controlling its movement
07. ______________ to show one's meaning with a gesture or signal
08. ______________ a large box or chest to hold or carry clothes or personal belongings
09. ______________ something that shuts out light or brightness
10. ______________ the past tense and past participle of the verb "bite"
11. ______________ a list of names of people in a group
12. ______________ a slight darkness caused by the blocking of some light
13. ______________ a small piece; a small amount
14. ______________ the main stem of a tree
15. ______________ to make into a ball or tube shape

B. 다음 빈칸에 가장 알맞은 단어를 보기에서 찾아 적으세요.

보기	shade roll sign bit trunk

01. Diane wanted a ( ) with her lunch.
02. I bought a new ( ) for the living room.
03. The ( ) doesn't fit in the horse's mouth.
04. The ( ) outside the restaurant said, "Free French Fries."
05. It's too hot. Let's go sit in the ( ).
06. A ( ) is a big suitcase.
07. ( ) your name here, please.
08. Nancy ( ) her brother's hand.
09. The elephant has a long ( ) and big ears.
10. Michael will ( ) his face from the bright sun.
11. The child will ( ) the snow into a ball.
12. The ( ) of this tree is three meters thick.
13. Give me a little ( ) of that paint.
14. The teacher calls the ( ) every morning.
15. She will ( ) you to enter the house.

다음 문장을 굵게 처리된 단어에 유의하여 해석해 보세요.

01. Walking down the street, you may not even notice the trees, but, according to a new study, they do a lot more than give **shade**. [2007년–홀수형 24번]

➡ ________________________________

02. The stones on the river bank **rolled** under her feet, and she was being pulled into the river. [1999년–홀수형 22번]

➡ ________________________________

03. When people began to bind books with pages that could be turned rather than **unrolled** like papyrus, the process of locating information changed. [2008년–홀수형 25번]

➡ ________________________________

04. For many people, one of the classic **signs** of emotional eating is night eating. [2012년–홀수형 41번]

➡ ________________________________

05. W: Will you **sign** here, please?
M: Sure. Thanks for delivering it so quickly. [2001년–홀수형 2번]

➡ ________________________________

06. Ms. Davis, would you please come up to the stage to accept this as a small **sign** of our appreciation and say a few words? [2002년–홀수형 6번]

➡ ________________________________

07. There are no **signs** that the speed of development will slow down. [1995년–홀수형 46번]

➡ ________________________________

08. The state of Quebec, Canada, penalized individuals for speaking English and forbade English street **sings**. [1997년–홀수형 49번]

➡ ________________________________

09. There was no **sign** of a light anywhere. [2009년–홀수형 30번]

➡ ________________________________

10. M: Wow, there are a lot of school clubs.
W: Hmm.... I'd like to join the school rock band. Let's **sign** up for it together. [2011년–홀수형 15번]

➡ ________________________________

11. The girl looked in her purse and counted her money. She didn't have enough. She needed a price cut. "Could you come down a **bit**?" the girl asked. [2000년–홀수형 23번]

➡ ________________________________

12. The ants put **bits** of dead insects inside some of the tunnels, and then the ant plant uses them for food. [2004년–홀수형 34번]

➡ ________________________________

13. The **trunk** of a tree appears brown because brown is the only wavelength which is reflected. [1996년–홀수형 25번]

➡ ________________________________

DAY 17

A gentle word opens an iron gate.
부드러운 말씨는 철문을 연다.

 **161 age** [eidʒ]

Group 33

Step 01
해석연습

다음 문장을 age에 유의하여 해석해 보세요. (해석은 이 페이지의 하단부에 있음)

1. She looks young for her age. _______________________________

2. We are living in the computer age. _______________________________

3. His father aged rapidly. _______________________________

Step 02
뜻 알기

age에는 다음과 같은 여러 가지의 뜻이 있습니다.

❶ 나이 **n** the number of years someone has lived or something has existed

❷ (역사상의) 시대, 시기; 세대 **n** a period of time in history; a generation

❸ 나이를 먹다, 늙다; ~을 늙게 하다 **v** to grow old; to make someone old

> 한 걸음 더 **I haven't seen you for ages.** 오래간만입니다. → (구어체) 오랫동안(=a long time)
> **Three score and ten is the age of man.** 나이 70은 인간의 수명 → 수명(=the length of life)
> **Her eyes were dim with age.** 그녀의 눈은 노령으로 침침했다. → 노령(=old age)
> **aged** 늙은 **the aged** 노인들 **the Golden age** 황금시대 **the Stone age** 석기시대

Step 03
연습문제

다음 문장의 age에 해당되는 뜻을 **Step 02** 의 ❶~❸에서 고르세요. (해답은 452쪽)

1. His mother aged rapidly. (   )

2. She learned about the Stone Age in her history class. (   )

3. We are in the same age. (   )

4. The space age has already begun. (   )

5. My son is nine years of age. (   )

6. Henry's recent illness has aged him considerably. (   )

Step 04
영작연습

다음 문장을 주어진 부분을 이용하여 영어로 옮기세요. (해답은 452쪽)

1. 나의 형은 40살 나이 때 브라질에 가셨다. [brother, Brazil]

____

2. 우주 시대는 이미 시작되었다. [space, already]

____

3. 그녀는 내가 그녀를 마지막으로 본 이후로 많이 늙었다. [since, last]

____

⠿ 1. 그녀는 나이에 비해 젊어 보인다. 2. 우리는 컴퓨터 시대에 살고 있다. 3. 그의 아버지는 빨리 늙었다.

162 angle [ǽŋgl]

Step 01 해석연습

다음 문장을 angle에 유의하여 해석해 보세요. (해석은 이 페이지의 하단부에 있음)

1. These two lines meet at right angles. ________________________

2. What's your angle on this issue? ________________________

3. He angles in the summer as his hobby. ________________________

Step 02 뜻 알기

angle에는 다음과 같은 여러 가지의 뜻이 있습니다.

❶ 각, 각도 **n** the space between two straight lines or surfaces that meet

❷ 관점, 견해 **n** a point of view

❸ 낚시질하다 **v** to catch fish with a hook and line

> 한 걸음 더 **There were some plants in the angle of the wall.** 담 모퉁이에 약간의 식물이 있었다. → 모퉁이(=a corner)
> **The situation presents a new angle.** 상황은 새로운 국면을 보이고 있다.
> → (사물의) 양상, 국면(=an aspect of an event or situation)
> **He angled the mirror to reflect light from the window.** 그는 창문으로 들어오는 빛을 반사시키기 위해 거울을 구부렸다.
> → ~을 어떤 각도로 움직이다, 구부리다(=move or bend something in an angle)
> **a right angle** 직각 **angular** 모난, 각을 이룬 **angler** 낚시꾼 **angling** 낚시질

Step 03 연습문제

다음 문장의 angle에 해당되는 뜻을 **Step 02** 의 ❶∼❸에서 고르세요. (해답은 452쪽)

1. Try looking at the affair from a different angle. (   )

2. Those two lines will cross at right angles. (   )

3. He likes to go angling in the spring. (   )

4. What angle are you writing the story from? (   )

5. Angling is fun when there is a good take. (   )

6. Acute angles are less than 90°. (   )

Step 04 영작연습

다음 문장을 주어진 부분을 이용하여 영어로 옮기세요. (해답은 452쪽)

1. 그 입방체(정육면체)를 이 각도에서 보아라. [look at, cube]

____

2. 우리는 그 사건을 다른 각도에서 볼 필요가 있다. [need to, affair]

____

3. 나의 삼촌은 강에서 송어 잡는 것을 잘한다. [is good at, trout]

____

:: 1. 이 두 직선은 직각으로 만난다. 2. 이 문제에 대한 당신의 견해는 무엇입니까? 3. 그는 취미로 여름에 낚시질을 한다.

163 own [oun]

Step 01
해석연습

다음 문장을 own에 유의하여 해석해 보세요. (해석은 이 페이지의 하단부에 있음)

1. I saw it with my own eyes. ______________________________
2. Who owns that beautiful villa? ______________________________
3. At last she owned her guilt. ______________________________

Step 02
뜻 알기

own에는 다음과 같은 여러 가지의 뜻이 있습니다.

❶ 자기 자신의; 고유한 ⓐ belong to oneself; peculiar to oneself
   자신의 것 ⓝ that which belongs to oneself

❷ 소유하다, ~을 가지고 있다 ⓥ to have as property; possess

❸ 인정하다, 고백[자백]하다 ⓥ to admit that something is true; to acknowledge; to confess

> 한 걸음 더 **owner** 소유자 **ownership** 소유권

Step 03
연습문제

다음 문장의 own에 해당되는 뜻을 **Step 02** 의 ❶~❸에서 고르세요. (해답은 452쪽)

1. This is my own house. (   )
2. He owned to having stolen the camera. (   )
3. This fruit has its own flavor. (   )
4. My uncle owns a large farm. (   )
5. She owned that I was in the right. (   )
6. He owns an old car. (   )

Step 04
영작연습

다음 문장을 주어진 부분을 이용하여 영어로 옮기세요. (해답은 452쪽)

1. 그는 그 책이 자기 것이라고 말했다. [book, his]

____

2. 나의 할아버지께서는 이 지역에 많은 땅을 갖고 계신다. [land, area]

____

3. 그는 자신이 열심히 일하지 않은 것을 인정하고 있다. [working, hand]

____

:: 1. 나는 그것을 내 눈으로 보았다. 2. 누가 저 아름다운 별장을 소유하고 있느냐? 3. 마침내 그녀는 자신의 잘못을 인정했다.

236

 **164 iron** [áiərn]

Step 01 해석연습

다음 문장을 iron에 유의하여 해석해 보세요. (해석은 이 페이지의 하단부에 있음)

1. The gate is made of iron. _______________________________

2. She has to buy a new electric iron. _______________________________

3. I helped my mother iron clothes. _______________________________

Step 02 뜻 알기

iron에는 다음과 같은 여러 가지의 뜻이 있습니다.

❶ 철, 쇠 **n** a common hard metal that is used to make steel / 철의, 철제의 **a** of or made of iron

❷ 다리미 **n** a flat-bottomed instrument that is heated up and used for smoothing clothes, etc

❸ 다리미질하다 **v** to smooth with an iron

> 한 걸음 더 **You'd better eat more spinach to get more iron.** 너는 철분을 좀 더 섭취하기 위해 시금치를 많이 먹는 것이 좋겠다.
> → 철분(=metallic element which is found in very small quantities in food and blood)
> **The prisoners were put in irons.** 죄수들은 사슬에 매어 있었다.
> → (복수형으로 쓰여) 쇠사슬, 족쇄, 수갑(=chains, shackles)
> **He picked up the iron to hit the ball.** 그는 공을 치기 위해 아이언 채를 집어들었다.
> → 쇠머리 골프채(=a golf club with a metal head)
> **an iron bar** 철봉 **an iron will** 굳은 의지 **an iron horse** 기관차 **an electric iron** 전기다리미 **the Iron Age** 철기 시대

Step 03 연습문제

다음 문장의 iron에 해당되는 뜻을 Step 02 의 ❶~❸에서 고르세요. (해답은 452쪽)

1. Kate will iron her wrinkled slacks. (　　　)

2. The ground is as hard as iron. (　　　)

3. My mother uses an iron to press my shirts. (　　　)

4. This dress needs to be ironed. (　　　)

5. She bought a new electric iron. (　　　)

6. The fence is made of iron. (　　　)

Step 04 영작연습

다음 문장을 주어진 부분을 이용하여 영어로 옮기세요. (해답은 452쪽)

1. 그 저택의 앞에는 커다란 철제 대문이 있었다. [huge, mansion]

____

2. 그는 다리미로 그의 옷에 태워서 구멍을 내었다. [burnt a hole. dress]

____

3. 그녀는 그녀의 구겨진 바지를 다림질하였다. [wrinkled trousers]

____

∷ 1. 그 문은 철로 만들어져 있다. 2. 그녀는 새 전기다리미를 사야 한다. 3. 나는 엄마가 옷들을 다림질하시는 것을 도와드렸다.

165 catch [kætʃ]

Step 01
해석연습

다음 문장을 catch에 유의하여 해석해 보세요. (해석은 이 페이지의 하단부에 있음)

1. Can you catch that ball? ___________________________________

2. The kite might catch in a tree. ___________________________________

3. The fisherman made a good catch. ___________________________________

Step 02
뜻 알기

catch에는 다음과 같은 여러 가지의 뜻이 있습니다.

❶ 잡다, 붙들다 **v** to stop and hold something which is moving; to capture
   잡기, 붙들기 **n** the act of catching

❷ 걸리다, 끼다 **v** to become fixed or prevented from moving; to be entangled on or in something

❸ 포획량, 잡힌 것 **n** something that is caught; the total amount of something caught

> 한 걸음 더 **catch** [kætʃ] - **caught** [kɔːt] - **caught** [kɔːt]
> **I cannot catch what you say.** 나는 당신이 말하는 것을 이해할 수가 없다. → 이해하다(=to understand; hear)
> **He caught her a blow on the cheek.** 그는 그녀의 뺨을 한 대 갈겼다. → 때리다(=to strike suddenly; hit)
> **She catches a cold every winter.** 그녀는 매년 겨울 감기에 걸린다.
> → 병에 걸리다, 감염되다(=to become infected with a disease or illness)
> **The advertisement catches his eye.** 그 광고가 그의 주의를 끈다.
> → 주의를 끌다(=to attract someone's attention)

Step 03
연습문제

다음 문장의 catch에 해당되는 뜻을 **Step 02** 의 ❶∼❸에서 고르세요. (해답은 452쪽)

1. The dog catches the ball in its mouth. (   )

2. Be careful not to catch your coat in the car door. (   )

3. The policeman tried to catch the thief. (   )

4. The fisherman's catch was large. (   )

5. Your shoe might catch on this loose carpet. (   )

6. Fishermen are reporting good catches. (   )

Step 04
영작연습

다음 문장을 주어진 부분을 이용하여 영어로 옮기세요. (해답은 452쪽)

1. 그는 내가 던진 빠른 볼을 잡았다. 그것은 멋진 캐치(잡기)였다. [fast, threw]

   ____

2. 가끔 불운한 바다표범들이 우리의 그물에 걸린다. [unlucky seals, net]

   ____

3. 그 호수에서 그가 잡은 양은 적었다. [lake, small]

   ____

∷ 1. 너는 저 공을 잡을 수 있느냐? 2. 연이 나무에 걸릴지 모른다. 3. 그 어부는 고기를 많이 잡았다.

238

A. 다음 뜻에 해당되는 단어를 보기에서 찾아 적으세요.

보기	age angle own iron catch

01. ______________ the number of years someone has lived or something has existed
02. ______________ a common hard metal that is used to make steel
03. ______________ the space between two straight lines or surfaces that meet
04. ______________ to stop and hold something which is moving; to capture
05. ______________ to have as property; possess
06. ______________ a flat-bottomed instrument that is heated up and used for smoothing clothes, etc
07. ______________ to admit that something is true; to acknowledge; to confess
08. ______________ to become fixed or prevented from moving; to be entangled on or in something
09. ______________ a period of time in history; a generation
10. ______________ to catch fish with a hook and line
11. ______________ something that is caught; the total amount of something caught
12. ______________ to grow old; to make someone old
13. ______________ to smooth with an iron
14. ______________ belong to oneself; peculiar to oneself
15. ______________ a point of view

B. 다음 빈칸에 가장 알맞은 단어를 보기에서 찾아 적으세요.

보기	age angle own iron catch

01. As my hobby, I (   ) in the summer.
02. Fred can (   ) a fast ball.
03. That was her (   ) decision.
04. A hot (   ) makes clothes smooth.
05. This figure has an (   ) of 45°.
06. She went to school at the (   ) of six.
07. This region is rich in (   ) and coal.
08. This villa is mine; I (   ) it.
09. It is not easy to keep pace with this cyber (   ).
10. His (   ) at the lake was large.
11. He will (   ) his faults.
12. Could (   ) my trousers for me?
13. The kite strings might (   ) on the wires.
14. Worry and illness (   ) a man.
15. Let's view this problem from a different (   ).

다음 문장을 굵게 처리된 단어에 유의하여 해석해 보세요.

01. If we want to describe our society in terms of **age**, we may come up with four **age** groups – childhood, adolescence, maturity, and old **age**. [2008년–홀수형 42번]

➡ __________________________

02. If done regularly and over a long period of time, exercise can help prevent osteoporosis, a gradual process of bone loss that occurs naturally as people **age**. [1995년–홀수형 40번]

➡ __________________________

03. The claim that we have recently entered the information **age** is misleading. [2005년–홀수형 45–46번]

➡ __________________________

04. I wondered for **ages** at these amazing steel birds. [2001년–홀수형 23번]

➡ __________________________

05. Kids **aged** 7 through 12 often fear real situations that may happen to them, such as injuries or accidents. [2002년–홀수형 45번]

➡ __________________________

06. Renaissance art was different from the art in the Middle **Ages** in many ways. [2005년–홀수형 27번]

➡ __________________________

07. I try to stay away from houses or barns that have unusual **angles** of the roof, or objects that look incorrect in size, perspective, or design. [2009년–홀수형 26번]

➡ __________________________

08. Hanging at an **angle** in the water, the leaf fish is carried along by the currents until it comes near a smaller fish. [2007년–홀수형 19번]

➡ __________________________

09. In jazz, on the contrary, the performers often improvise their **own** melodies. [2007년–홀수형 27번]

➡ __________________________

10. Ordinary consumers can **own** a copy of the highly valued originals. [2009년–홀수형 24번]

➡ __________________________

11. We feel their loves and losses, their joys and sorrows, hopes and fears, somewhat as if they were our **own**. [2002년–홀수형 37번]

➡ __________________________

12. Strike while the **iron** is hot. [1999년–홀수형 18번]

➡ __________________________

13. Some clever fishermen in the village bought bigger and better equipped boats, and began to **catch** all the fish they could find. [1999년–홀수형 35번]

➡ __________________________

14. But right after that, I have to **catch** the train to see my grandpa. [1999년–홀수형 15번]

➡ __________________________

15. Here are some things you can do to prevent yourself from **catching** the flu. [1997년–홀수형 12번]

➡ __________________________

166 appointment [əpɔ́intmənt]

Step 01 해석연습

다음 문장을 appointment에 유의하여 해석해 보세요. (해석은 이 페이지의 하단부에 있음)

1. I have an appointment with him at noon. ________________________

2. His appointment as manager has caused a lot of friction. ________________________

Step 02 뜻 알기

appointment에는 다음과 같은 여러 가지의 뜻이 있습니다.

❶ 약속 🅝 an arrangement to meet someone

❷ 임명, 선정, 지정 🅝 the choosing of someone for a position or job

> 한 걸음 더 **All the <u>appointments</u> of the hotel were very luxurious.** 그 호텔의 모든 설비는 매우 호화스러웠다.
> → (복수로 쓰여) 설비, 장비, 가구(=equipment; furniture)
> **appoint** ① (시간, 장소 따위를) 정하다, 약속하다 ② ~을 임명하다, 지명하다
> **accept[decline] an appointment** 임명을 수락[사양]하다 **make[fix, arrange] an appointment** ~와 만날 약속을 하다

Step 03 연습문제

다음 문장의 appointment에 해당되는 뜻을 Step 02 의 ❶~❷에서 고르세요. (해답은 453쪽)

1. Susan's appointment as a new manager pleased us. (　　)

2. I have an appointment with her this evening. (　　)

3. His appointment as a professor was for one year only. (　　)

4. She has an appointment with her dentist at 2 p.m. (　　)

Step 04 영작연습

다음 문장을 주어진 부분을 이용하여 영어로 옮기세요. (해답은 453쪽)

1. 그녀는 2시에 진찰을 받기로 약속을 했다. [see the doctor]

____

2. 그가 조교로 임명되는 것은 확실하다. [teaching assistant, certain]

____

:: 1. 나는 그와 정오에 만날 약속이 있다. 2. 그가 지배인으로 임명된 것은 많은 불화를 일으켰다.

167 book [buk]

다음 문장을 book에 유의하여 해석해 보세요. (해석은 이 페이지의 하단부에 있음)

1. I am reading a book by Hemingway. ________________________________

2. She bought a book of bus tickets. ________________________________

3. I have booked two seats for the theater. ________________________________

book에는 다음과 같은 여러 가지의 뜻이 있습니다.

❶ 책, 서적, 저서 **n** a set of printed pages fastened together as a thing to be read

❷ 묶음 철 **n** a set of tickets, checks, etc bound together

❸ (좌석, 방 등을) 예약하다, 표를 사다 **v** to reserve or buy a seat, room, ticket, etc

> 한 걸음 더 **bookable** (좌석 따위가) 예약 할 수 있는 **bookcase** 책장 **booking** ① 예약 ② 장부 기입, 기재
> **booklet** 소책자, 팸플릿(=pamphlet) **bookkeeper** 장부계원, 경리사원 a **bankbook** 은행통장
> **bookmark** (책갈피에 끼우는) 서표, 북마크 **an address book** 주소록 **a notebook** 공책 **a phone book** 전화번호부

다음 문장의 book에 해당되는 뜻을 Step 02 의 ❶~❸에서 고르세요. (해답은 453쪽)

1. I will book two seats for Tuesday's concert. (   )

2. Open your books to page thirty. (   )

3. He booked a ticket for London. (   )

4. He sent me a check book. (   )

5. We read three books for our history class. (   )

6. I forgot to buy a book of bus tickets. (   )

다음 문장을 주어진 부분을 이용하여 영어로 옮기세요. (해답은 453쪽)

1. 그는 도서관에서 두 권의 책을 빌렸다. [borrowed, library]

____

2. 나는 은행으로부터 수표 철을 한 권 받았다. [received, bank]

____

3. 그녀는 토요일 콘서트의 네 좌석을 예약해 두었다. [Saturday's concert]

____

∷ 1. 나는 헤밍웨이 책을 읽고 있다. 2. 그녀는 한 묶음의 버스표를 샀다. 3. 나는 극장의 두 좌석을 예약해 두었다.

168 lead (뜻) ❶❷ [liːd] ❸ [led]

Step 01 해석연습

다음 문장을 lead에 유의하여 해석해 보세요. (해석은 이 페이지의 하단부에 있음)

1. A jazz band will lead the parade. ________________________________

2. Korea led Japan 1-0 by halftime. ________________________________

3. These pipes are made of lead. ________________________________

Step 02 뜻 알기

lead에는 다음과 같은 여러 가지의 뜻이 있습니다.

❶ 인도하다, 안내하다, 이끌다 [v] to guide or take someone to a place by going in front
선도, 지도, 안내 [n] the act of leading or conducting

❷ 선두에 서다, 앞서다 [v] to be first; to excel; to have the first place in (a game, race, competition, etc)
선두, (경기의) 리드; (극의) 주역 [n] the first place or position; a chief part in a play

❸ 납 [n] a soft, heavy, easily-melted gray metal

> 한 걸음 더 **lead** [liːd] - **led** [led] - **led** [led] * 뜻 ① ②에 해당
> **The lead of this pencil is soft.** 이 연필의 심은 부드럽다. → 연필의 심(=the central part of a pencil)
> **All dogs must be kept on a lead in the park.** 공원에서는 모든 개들은 끈에 매여 있어야 한다.
> → (개, 가축의) 끈, 끄는 줄(=a leather strap or chain for leading a dog, etc)
> **This road leads to the park.** 이 길은 공원으로 통한다.
> → (길 따위가) ~로 통하다(=to be a route to)
> **leader** 지도자, 인도자 **leadership** 지도(력), 통솔(력) **leaden** 납으로 된, 무거운 **as heavy as lead** 납처럼 무거운

Step 03 연습문제

다음 문장의 lead에 해당되는 뜻을 **Step 02** 의 ❶~❸에서 고르세요. (해답은 453쪽)

1. A dog leads the blind man. (   )

2. He led the race from start to finish. (   )

3. This metal is as heavy as lead. (   )

4. She will lead the brass band. (   )

5. Brazil led Spain 2-1. (   )

6. Are these pipes made of lead or steel? (   )

Step 04 영작연습

다음 문장을 주어진 부분을 이용하여 영어로 옮기세요. (해답은 453쪽)

1. 누가 이 장님을 그의 집으로 인도할 것이냐? [blind man, house]

____

2. 비로 게임이 중단되었을 때 우리 팀은 2점을 앞서고 있었다. [by two points]

____

3. 배관공은 관 연결 부위를 때우는 데 납을 사용했다. [seal, joints]

____

:: 1. 재즈 밴드가 행렬을 인도할 것이다. 2. 전반전까지 한국은 일본을 1-0으로 앞섰다. 3. 이 파이프들은 납으로 만들어졌다.

169 match [mætʃ]

Step 01 해석연습

다음 문장을 match에 유의하여 해석해 보세요. (해석은 이 페이지의 하단부에 있음)

1. He needs a match to light the candle. _______________________

2. We watched the tennis match on television. _______________________

3. His suit doesn't match the color of his tie. _______________________

Step 02 뜻 알기

match에는 다음과 같은 여러 가지의 뜻이 있습니다.

❶ 성냥 n a small wooden or paper stick, used to light a fire, cigarette, etc

❷ 시합, 경기 n an organized sports event between two teams or people; a contest or game

❸ 어울리다, 조화되다, 동등하다 v to be equal to or corresponding with; to go well together
서로 잘 어울리는 것[사람], 걸맞은 짝 n a thing or a person exactly like, or corresponding to, or combining well with another

> 한 걸음 더 **You are no <u>match</u> for me in swimming.** 너는 수영에서 나의 적수가 못 된다.
> → 호적수, 경쟁상대(=a person who is having equal power to another in a contest; a rival)
> **She <u>matched</u> her daughter with[to] the young man.** 그녀는 딸을 그 젊은이와 결혼시켰다.
> → ~를 결혼시키다(=to cause (someone) to be married), 결혼
> **matchbox** 성냥갑 **matching** 잘 어울리는, 조화되는 **matchless** 비길 데 없는, 무쌍의 **match maker** 결혼중매인

Step 03 연습문제

다음 문장의 match에 해당되는 뜻을 **Step 02** 의 ❶∼❸에서 고르세요. (해답은 453쪽)

1. The tie is a good match for your coat. (   )

2. There was a box of matches on the table. (   )

3. The man struck a match. (   )

4. The match ended in a tie. (   )

5. These trousers are an exact match for your jacket. (   )

6. Did you see the tennis match yesterday? (   )

Step 04 영작연습

다음 문장을 주어진 부분을 이용하여 영어로 옮기세요. (해답은 453쪽)

1. 그는 성냥을 켜서 묵은 서류들을 태웠다. [struck, burned]

____

2. 그 축구시합은 무승부로 끝났다. [ended, tie]

____

3. 그 모자는 네 옷에 완벽하게 어울리는 것이다. [perfect, coat]

____

:: 1. 그는 촛불을 붙이기 위해 성냥이 필요하다. 2. 우리는 TV로 테니스 경기를 보았다. 3. 그의 양복은 넥타이와 어울리지 않는다.

244

170 **bill** [bil]

Step 01 해석연습

다음 문장을 bill에 유의하여 해석해 보세요. (해석은 이 페이지의 하단부에 있음)

1. She has a twenty-dollar bill. ________________________________

2. The dry cleaning bill came to $23.50. ________________________________

3. A duck has a flat bill. ________________________________

4. Congress passed the anticrime bill. ________________________________

Step 02 뜻 알기

bill에는 다음과 같은 여러 가지의 뜻이 있습니다.

❶ 지폐 n a piece of paper money

❷ 청구서 n a list of things for which money should be paid / 청구서를 보내다 v to send a bill

❸ (새의) 부리 n a hard part of a bird's mouth; a beak

❹ 법안, 의안 n a new law or plan that legislators vote to accept or reject

▷ 한 걸음 더 이외에도 광고 전단(=poster), 어음(=a written or printed public note)이란 뜻도 있음

Step 03 연습문제

다음 문장의 bill에 해당되는 뜻을 Step 02 의 ❶~❹에서 고르세요. (해답은 453쪽)

1. A duck has an orange bill. (   )
2. Chris has a ten-dollar bill. (   )
3. There are some bills to pay. (   )
4. The new education bill will be passed. (   )
5. He paid his bill in cash. (   )
6. He gave me two twenty-dollar bills. (   )
7. The new bill passed the City Council. (   )
8. The bird picked the food up with his bill. (   )

Step 04 영작연습

다음 문장을 주어진 부분을 이용하여 영어로 옮기세요. (해답은 453쪽)

1. Peter는 거리에서 10달러짜리 지폐를 발견했다. [found, street]

____

2. 그 백화점은 고객들에게 매달 초에 청구서를 보낸다. [at the beginning of]

____

3. 저 새는 길고 노란 부리를 가지고 있다. [has, yellow]

____

4. 정부는 새로운 주택 법안을 제출할 것이다. [government, housing]

____

:: 1. 그녀는 20달러짜리 지폐를 가지고 있다. 2. 세탁요금청구서는 $23.50에 달했다. 3. 오리는 납작한 부리를 가지고 있다.
4. 국회는 범죄방지법안을 통과시켰다.

A. 다음 뜻에 해당되는 단어를 보기에서 찾아 적으세요.

> 보기   appointment   book   lead   match   bill

01. ______________ an arrangement to meet someone
02. ______________ a thing or a person exactly like, or corresponding to, or combining well with another
03. ______________ to guide or take someone to a place by going in front
04. ______________ a list of things for which money should be paid
05. ______________ a set of printed pages fastened together as a thing to be read
06. ______________ an organized sports event between two teams or people; a contest or game
07. ______________ to be first; to excel; to have the first place in (a game, race, competition, etc)
08. ______________ a new law or plan that legislators vote to accept or reject
09. ______________ to reserve or buy a seat, room, ticket, etc
10. ______________ a piece of paper money
11. ______________ the choosing of someone for a position or job
12. ______________ a soft, heavy, easily-melted gray metal
13. ______________ a hard part of a bird's mouth; a beak
14. ______________ a set of tickets, checks, etc bound together
15. ______________ a small wooden or paper stick, used to light a fire, cigarette, etc

B. 다음 빈칸에 가장 알맞은 단어를 보기에서 찾아 적으세요.

> 보기   appointment   book   lead(s)   match   bill

01. I would like to make an (   ) to see the doctor.
02. (   ) is a heavy soft grey metal.
03. He selected a hat to (   ) his suit.
04. That bird has a (   ) like a duck.
05. Andy likes to read a (   ).
06. Judy has a five-dollar (   ) in her pocket.
07. The servant will (   ) the visitors to their seats.
08. I will watch the tennis (   ) on television.
09. He will buy a (   ) of stamps.
10. A (   ) becomes a law when it passes the Parliament.
11. She (   ) her class in mathematics.
12. His (   ) as head of department was an unexpected thing.
13. He struck a (   ) and lit a candle.
14. I will (   ) a seat for the theater.
15. The (   ) for the repairs came to $930.00.

다음 문장을 굵게 처리된 단어에 유의하여 해석해 보세요.

01. They choose foods rich in fiber, such as bread and cereal for breakfast, and salads for lunch to prepare them for business **appointments**. [1996년–홀수형 44번]

➡ ___________________________

02. Well, I'm sorry. I have an **appointment** at that time. Why don't we meet at 4:00 on Thursday, instead? [1996년–홀수형 2번]

➡ ___________________________

03. **Books** can be renewed once for the original loan period unless they are on reserve. [2007년–홀수형 18번]

➡ ___________________________

04. SORRY-ALL TABLES FULLY **BOOKED** [1997년–홀수형 37번]

➡ ___________________________

05. Following your instincts could **lead** you to make impulsive decisions that you may regret later. [2006년–홀수형 37번]

➡ ___________________________

06. It did not feel like stone, clay, or dirt. They thought it was a type of **lead**, and so did others. [2001년–홀수형 21번]

➡ ___________________________

07. As the taxi gets near the destination, she sees some people walking along a beautiful trail **leading** up to the tower. [2011년–홀수형 17번]

➡ ___________________________

08. They said you're going to be cast for the **lead** role in that new drama. [2002년–홀수형 2번]

➡ ___________________________

09. The stranger who had **led** me so surely through the fog was blind. [1999년–홀수형 46번]

➡ ___________________________

10. But some individuals sit and watch a football game or tennis **match** without cheering for anyone or any team. [2009년–홀수형 34번]

➡ ___________________________

11. The amount of rice produced in 1990 **matched** the production in 1985. [2002년–홀수형 41번]

➡ ___________________________

12. Permanent home extensions traditionally built in brick or tiled to **match** your home. [1996년–홀수형 15번]

➡ ___________________________

13. When we think of money, we usually think of currency, or coins and **bills**. [1996년–홀수형 37번]

➡ ___________________________

14. Thank you for sending your check in payment of your July **bill**. [1994년–1차 25번]

➡ ___________________________

15. The company gives a price break to these buyers because they help cut the costs of selling, storing, shipping, and **billing**. [2001년–홀수형 31번]

➡ ___________________________

DAY 18

God gives all things to industry.
신은 근면한 사람에게 모든 것을 준다.

 **171 industry** [índəstri]

Group 35

Step 01 해석연습

다음 문장을 industry에 유의하여 해석해 보세요. (해석은 이 페이지의 하단부에 있음)

1. The computer industry of Korea has grown rapidly since 1985.

____

2. The teacher praised highly for his industry. _______________________________

Step 02 뜻 알기

industry에는 다음과 같은 여러 가지의 뜻이 있습니다.

❶ 산업, 공업 🅝 to make or become different

❷ 근면, 부지런함 🅝 hard work or effort; diligence

> 한 걸음 더 **industrial** 산업의, 공업의 **industrious** 근면한, 부지런한 **heavy industry** 중공업 **key industries** 기간산업
> **light industry** 경공업 **the chemical industry** 화학공업 **the tourist industry** 관광산업

Step 03 연습문제

다음 문장의 industry에 해당되는 뜻을 **Step 02** 의 ❶~❷에서 고르세요. (해답은 453쪽)

1. Agriculture is the first industry. (   )
2. Industry sometimes compensates for lack of ability. (   )
3. Los Angeles is the capital of the American film industry. (   )
4. She owed her success to both ability and industry. (   )

Step 04 영작연습

다음 문장을 주어진 부분을 이용하여 영어로 옮기세요. (해답은 453쪽)

1. 정부는 내년에 철강 산업에 보다 많은 돈을 투자할 것이다. [invest, steel]

____

2. Jane의 성공은 그녀의 근면과 검소함 때문이었다. [due to, thrift]

____

:: 1. 한국의 컴퓨터산업은 1985년부터 급속히 성장했다. 2. 선생님은 그의 부지런함을 몹시 칭찬했다.

172 game [geim]

Step 01
해석연습

다음 문장을 game에 유의하여 해석해 보세요. (해석은 이 페이지의 하단부에 있음)

1. They are watching a soccer game on TV. _______________________

2. We won three games out of five. _______________________

3. He is a big game hunter. _______________________

Step 02
뜻 알기

game에는 다음과 같은 여러 가지의 뜻이 있습니다.

❶ 놀이, 오락, 경기, 시합 ⓝ an activity or sport in which people compete with each other according to agreed rules

❷ (경기 중의 일부를 이루는) 한 승부, 한 판 ⓝ a match or part of a match

❸ (집합적) 사냥감, 사냥으로 잡은 것 ⓝ wild animals, birds, or fish that are hunted or caught

> 한 걸음 더 **a called game** 콜드게임, 중단경기 **a drawn game** 무승부 **fair game** 사냥이 허용된 사냥감
> **forbidden game** 사냥이 금지된 사냥감 **game keeper** 사냥터 관리인 **game preserve[reserve]** 사냥금지구역

Step 03
연습문제

다음 문장의 game에 해당되는 뜻을 Step 02 의 ❶～❸에서 고르세요. (해답은 453쪽)

1. He played computer games for hours. (   )

2. Federer leads, two games to one. (   )

3. Judy has never liked card games. (   )

4. He hunted the forbidden game illegally. (   )

5. She won four games in the second set. (   )

6. They are big game hunters. (   )

Step 04
영작연습

다음 문장을 주어진 부분을 이용하여 영어로 옮기세요. (해답은 453쪽)

1. 올림픽경기는 4년마다 개최된다. [every four years]

____

2. 그 테니스선수는 첫 번째 세트에서 4게임을 이겼다. [won, first set]

____

3. 사냥꾼들은 사슴과 야생사냥감을 포획했다. [captured, wild]

____

173 deliver [dilívər]

다음 문장을 deliver에 유의하여 해석해 보세요. (해석은 이 페이지의 하단부에 있음)

1. The boy delivers newspapers every morning. _______________________________

2. May god deliver us from all evil. _______________________________

3. The doctor delivered the twins safely. _______________________________

deliver에는 다음과 같은 여러 가지의 뜻이 있습니다.

❶ 배달하다, 전하다 Ⓥ to take goods, letters, etc to the place where they are addressed

❷ (위험, 죽음 따위에서) ~을 구해 내다, 자유롭게 하다 Ⓥ to help someone escape from something bad, danger, suffering, death, etc

❸ 분만시키다, 낳게 하다; 낳다 Ⓥ to help a woman give birth to a baby; to give birth to a baby

> 한 걸음 더 **He delivered a long speech.** 그는 긴 연설을 했다.
> → (연설, 강연 따위를) 하다, (의견을) 말하다(=to make a speech to a lot of people)
> **delivery** ① 배달, 전달 ② 분만, 출산 **deliverance** 구출, 구조, 해방

다음 문장의 deliver에 해당되는 뜻을 Step 02 **의 ❶~❸에서 고르세요.** (해답은 453쪽)

1. A mailman delivers letters and parcels. (   )

2. She was safely delivered of a baby girl. (   )

3. He has delivered us from danger. (   )

4. The doctor delivered the child. (   )

5. Do we have to pick it up, or will they deliver it? (   )

6. Deliver us from temptation. (   )

다음 문장을 주어진 부분을 이용하여 영어로 옮기세요. (해답은 453쪽)

1. 이 편지를 당신의 아버지께 전해 주시겠습니까? [Could you]

____

2. 우리는 적군으로부터 포로들을 구해 냈다. [prisoners, enemy]

____

3. 그녀는 오랜 진통 끝에 건강한 아들을 낳았다. [after a long labor]

____

∷ 1. 그 소년은 매일 아침 신문을 배달한다. 2. 신이여 우리를 모든 악에서 구원하소서. 3. 그 의사는 쌍둥이를 무사히 분만시켰다.

174 **still** [stil]

Step 01
해석연습

다음 문장을 still에 유의하여 해석해 보세요. (해석은 이 페이지의 하단부에 있음)

1. The night was very still. ________________________
2. It is still cold in March. ________________________
3. He is tall, but his brother is still taller. ________________________

Step 02
뜻 알기

still에는 다음과 같은 여러 가지의 뜻이 있습니다.

❶ 고요한, 조용한, 정지된 [a] without movement or sound; quiet; silent; calm

❷ 아직도, 지금도, 여전히 [ad] up to this or that time; now, as before; as yet

❸ (비교급 앞에서) 더욱더, 한층 더 [ad] (used with a comparative) even; in a greater degree

한 걸음 더 **He has his faults, <u>still</u> I love him.** 그는 결점이 있지만, 그럼에도 불구하고 나는 그를 사랑한다.
→ 그럼에도 불구하고 (=nevertheless; in spite of that)
She has a <u>still</u> of the movie. 그녀는 그 영화의 스틸사진 하나를 가지고 있다.
→ 영화의 스틸사진(=a photograph of a scene from a cinema film)
still life 정물화 **stillness** 고요, 정적, 정지됨, 평온 **still and all**(=all the same) 그럼에도 불구하고 **still more** 한층 더 ∼한

Step 03
연습문제

다음 문장의 still에 해당되는 뜻을 **Step 02** 의 ❶∼❸에서 고르세요. (해답은 453쪽)

1. Do you still play basketball? (　　　)
2. The days will grow still shorter. (　　　)
3. Please keep still while I brush your hair. (　　　)
4. He will still be here tomorrow. (　　　)
5. The town seems very still in the early morning. (　　　)
6. That would be still better. (　　　)

Step 04
영작연습

다음 문장을 주어진 부분을 이용하여 영어로 옮기세요. (해답은 454쪽)

1. 제발 내가 너의 신발 끈을 매는 동안 움직이지 말고 있어라. [while, tie]

____

2. 그녀는 아직도 그로부터의 편지를 희망하고 있다. [hoping, letter]

____

3. 오늘은 덥다. 그러나 내일은 한층 더 더울 것이다. [will be, hotter]

____

:: 1. 밤은 몹시 고요했다. 2. 3월인데도 여전히 춥다. 3. 그는 키가 큰데, 그의 형은 한층 더 크다.

175 point [pɔint]

Step 01 해석연습

다음 문장을 point에 유의하여 해석해 보세요. (해석은 이 페이지의 하단부에 있음)

1. Don't touch the point of this knife. _______________________________
2. He got 95 points on the quiz. _______________________________
3. The needle of a compass points to the north. _______________________________
4. What's your point in saying so? _______________________________

Step 02 뜻 알기

point에는 다음과 같은 여러 가지의 뜻이 있습니다.

❶ (막대기, 칼, 연필 등의) 뾰족한 끝 **n** a sharp end of a stick, pin, knife, needle, pencil, weapon, etc

❷ 점수; 눈금; 정도 **n** a score; a mark or grade; a degree of a thermometer; degree or limit

❸ 겨누다, 가리키다; ~을 지적하다 **v** to aim or direct (at, towards); to direct attention to

❹ 요점, 요지 **n** a main idea or purpose

> 한 걸음 더 **The two roads join at that <u>point</u>.** 두 길은 그 지점에서 합쳐진다. → 지점, 장소, 시점(=an exact place or position)
> **He knows my strong points and my weak <u>points</u>.** 그는 나의 강점과 약점을 알고 있다. → 특징, 특질

Step 03 연습문제

다음 문장의 point에 해당되는 뜻을 **Step 02** 의 ❶~❹에서 고르세요. (해답은 454쪽)

1. Look at the point of this sword. (　　　)
2. The temperature has gone up three point. (　　　)
3. The man pointed to the front door. (　　　)
4. Don't waste time and get to the point. (　　　)
5. The teacher pointed to a map on the wall. (　　　)
6. Be careful not to touch the point of this knife. (　　　)
7. I don't catch the point of your remarks. (　　　)
8. She has won by five points to three. (　　　)

Step 04 영작연습

다음 문장을 주어진 부분을 이용하여 영어로 옮기세요. (해답은 454쪽)

1. 그녀는 천에 바늘 끝을 꽂았다. [needle, cloth]

____

2. 우리 팀은 첫 번째 쿼터에서 15점을 득점했다. [scored, quarter]

____

3. 한 꼬마 아이가 장난감 권총을 그에게 겨누었다. [toy pistol]

____

4. 그녀는 그의 농담의 요점을 놓쳤다. [missed, joke]

____

⠿ 1. 이 칼 끝에 손 대지 마라. 2. 그는 퀴즈에서 95점을 받았다. 3. 나침반의 바늘은 북쪽을 가리킨다. 4. 그렇게 말하는 요지가 뭐냐?

Day 18

A. 다음 뜻에 해당되는 단어를 보기에서 찾아 적으세요.

보기	industry　game　deliver　still　point

01. ______________ the business of producing or making goods
02. ______________ an activity or sport in which people compete with each other according to agreed rules
03. ______________ to aim or direct (at, towards); to direct attention to
04. ______________ to help someone escape from something bad, danger, suffering, death, etc
05. ______________ even; in a greater degree
06. ______________ wild animals, birds, or fish that are hunted or caught
07. ______________ hard work or effort; diligence
08. ______________ to help a woman give birth to a baby; to give birth to a baby
09. ______________ without movement or sound; quiet; silent; calm
10. ______________ a score; a mark or grade; a degree of a thermometer; degree or limit
11. ______________ a match or part of a match
12. ______________ a main idea or purpose
13. ______________ up to this or that time; now, as before; as yet
14. ______________ a sharp end of a stick, pin, knife, needle, pencil, weapon, etc
15. ______________ to take goods, letters, etc to the place where they are addressed

B. 다음 빈칸에 가장 알맞은 단어를 보기에서 찾아 적으세요.

보기	industry　game(s)　deliver　still　point(s)

01. Please keep (　　　　) while I cut your hair.
02. We watched baseball (　　　　) on TV.
03. Our team scored two (　　　　) in the second quarter.
04. Postmen (　　　　) letters from door to door.
05. I told him not to (　　　　) his finger at me.
06. It is (　　　　) hot in October.
07. The man overcame his poverty through (　　　　) and thrift.
08. The hunter knows well the place rich in (　　　　).
09. I missed the (　　　　) of his statement.
10. The doctor will (　　　　) her of a baby.
11. Don't touch the (　　　　) of this needle.
12. He won two (　　　　) out of five.
13. The days will grow (　　　　) hotter.
14. We will (　　　　) him from the enemy.
15. The prospect of steel (　　　　) is not very hopeful.

다음 문장을 굵게 처리된 단어에 유의하여 해석해 보세요.

01. This plays an essential role in various scientific fields and in **industry**. [2008년-홀수형 18번]

→ ______________________________

02. In ancient Egypt, pitching stones was children's favorite **game**, but a badly thrown rock could hurt a child. [2008년-홀수형 19번]

→ ______________________________

03. The victims were mostly hunters and hikers who were mistaken for **game**. [2002년-홀수형 42번]

→ ______________________________

04. The **game** in its present form first appeared in Scotland. [2001년-홀수형 43번]

→ ______________________________

05. She got up at 5:30 every morning to **deliver** the newspapers to her customers. [2001년-홀수형 49-50번]

→ ______________________________

06. Peter will **deliver** a speech for the opening event and Sally will work as a stage assistant. [2008년-홀수형 17번]

→ ______________________________

07. These so-called non-governmental organizations **deliver** social services. [2000년-홀수형 35번]

→ ______________________________

08. I **still** believe old people deserve respect for their experience and wisdom. [1995년-홀수형 26번]

→ ______________________________

09. Tonight, however, people are unusually quiet and their flags strangely **still**. [2002년-홀수형 47-48번]

→ ______________________________

10. On the contrary, over forty years ago, controlled studies showed that fits of anger are more likely to intensify anger, and that tears can drive us **still** deeper into depression. [2009년-홀수형 32번]

→ ______________________________

11. The **point** is that the situation or the relationship between the people involved determines its meaning. [1994년-2차 15번]

→ ______________________________

12. For instance, when two soccer teams play against one another, each team tries to score more **points** than the other. [1995년-홀수형 24번]

→ ______________________________

13. Moreover, technology has advanced to the **point** that it is no longer necessary to kill whales for oil. [1994년-2차 27번]

→ ______________________________

14. Experts **point** out that this is a serious problem that could slow down the development of our economy. [2003년-홀수형 22번]

→ ______________________________

15. In Figure B, when the mirror temperature is at dew **point**, dew drops cover the surface of the mirror. [2010년-홀수형 30번]

→ ______________________________

16. At this **point** you realize you don't know who it is! [2005년-홀수형 36번]

→ ______________________________

176 anxious [ǽŋkʃəs]

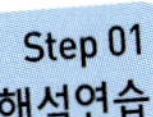

Step 01
해석연습

다음 문장을 anxious에 유의하여 해석해 보세요. (해석은 이 페이지의 하단부에 있음)

1. She is anxious about her mother's health. _______________________________

2. He is anxious for wealth and fame. _______________________________

Step 02
뜻 알기

anxious에는 다음과 같은 여러 가지의 뜻이 있습니다.

❶ ~을 걱정하여, 근심하여, 염려가 되는 ⓐ very worried about something that may happen or may have happened

❷ ~을 몹시 하고 싶어 하여 ⓐ wanting very much to do something or something to happen

> 한 걸음 더 **anxiety** ① 걱정, 불안 ② 열망, 갈망 **be anxious about** ~을 걱정하다 **be anxious for** ~을 갈망[열망]하다
> **be anxious to + V** ~을 몹시 하고 싶어 하다

Step 03
연습문제

다음 문장의 anxious에 해당되는 뜻을 **Step 02** 의 ❶~❷에서 고르세요. (해답은 454쪽)

1. I am very anxious about my son's health. (   )
2. He is anxious to meet her. (   )
3. Louis is anxious about travelling on his own. (   )
4. We are anxious for peace. (   )

Step 04
영작연습

다음 문장을 주어진 부분을 이용하여 영어로 옮기세요. (해답은 454쪽)

1. 그 남자는 항상 자신의 아들의 건강을 걱정했다. [always, health]

____

2. 그녀는 최종시험의 결과를 몹시 알고 싶어 한다. [result, final test]

____

:: 1. 그녀는 엄마의 건강을 걱정하고 있다. 2. 그는 재산과 명성을 열망한다.

177 order [ɔ́ːrdər]

Step 01
해석연습

다음 문장을 order에 유의하여 해석해 보세요. (해석은 이 페이지의 하단부에 있음)

1. The program shows the order of events for the show. _______________
2. Soldiers must obey orders. _______________
3. May I take your order now? _______________

Step 02
뜻 알기

order에는 다음과 같은 여러 가지의 뜻이 있습니다.

❶ 순서, 차례 n the way in which things are placed in relation to one another

❷ 명령, 지시 n a command given by someone in authority
명령하다 v to tell (someone) to do something (from a position of authority)

❸ 주문, 주문품 n a request for goods or services; goods to be supplied
주문하다 v to give an instruction to supply

> 한 걸음 더 **The machine is in good <u>order</u>.** 기계는 잘 작동되고 있다.
> → (정상적인) 상태, 컨디션(=state or condition)
> **He met the various people from all <u>orders</u> of society.** 그는 사회의 모든 계층 출신의 다양한 사람들을 만났다.
> → 계층, 계급(=a social rank, grade or class))
> **It is the work of the police to keep public <u>order</u>.** 경찰의 임무는 공공질서를 지키는 일이다.
> → (사회의) 질서, 치안(=a situation in which rules are obeyed and authority is respected)
> **the lower[higher] orders** 하층[상층]계급 **out of order** 고장 난, 규칙을 벗어난 **in order to** ∼을 위하여

Step 03
연습문제

다음 문장의 order에 해당되는 뜻을 **Step 02** 의 ❶∼❸에서 고르세요. (해답은 454쪽)

1. He gave orders that it should be done at once. (   )
2. They lined up in order of age. (   )
3. He will cancel the order for the magazine. (   )
4. Sally arranged the newspapers in order by their dates. (   )
5. A waiter will come over to take your order. (   )
6. We are under orders to search your house. (   )

Step 04
영작연습

다음 문장을 주어진 부분을 이용하여 영어로 옮기세요. (해답은 454쪽)

1. 우리들의 이름은 알파벳 순서로 정리되어 있었다. [arranged, alphabetical]

____

2. 그는 나에게 앉아서 침묵을 지키라고 명령했다. [keep silence]

____

3. 나는 미국에 약간의 신간 서적을 주문했다. [some, America]

____

:: 1. 프로그램은 쇼의 공연순서를 보여 준다. 2. 군인들은 명령에 복종해야 한다. 3. 주문하시겠습니까?

178 **sound** [saund]

Step 01 해석연습

다음 문장을 sound에 유의하여 해석해 보세요. (해석은 이 페이지의 하단부에 있음)

1. Sound travels slower than light. ___________________________

2. He came back safe and sound. ___________________________

3. The bell sounds at noon. ___________________________

Step 02 뜻 알기

sound에는 다음과 같은 여러 가지의 뜻이 있습니다.

❶ 소리, 음, 음향 **n** something that is heard or can be heard

❷ 건강한; 건전한; 정당한 **a** healthy; in good condition; reasonable

❸ 소리가 나다, 울리다; 소리 나게 하다 **v** to produce sound; to make something produce sound

> 한 걸음 더 **His story <u>sounds</u> like fiction.** 그의 이야기는 꾸며낸 것처럼 보인다.
> → ~하게 보이다, ~처럼 들리다(=to seem; appear)
> **She had a <u>sound</u> sleep last night.** 어젯밤 그녀는 푹 잘 잤다.
> → 충분한, 완전한, (잠이) 깊은(=full; thorough; (of sleep) deep)
> **He <u>sounded</u> the depth of the lake.** 그는 호수의 수심을 쟀다.
> → (바다, 호수, 연못 따위의) 수심을 재다(=to measure the depth of the sea, a lake, etc)
> **a sound sleep** 숙면, 깊은 잠 **a sound judgement** 올바른 판단 **safe and sound** 무사히

Step 03 연습문제

다음 문장의 sound에 해당되는 뜻을 **Step 02** 의 ❶~❸에서 고르세요. (해답은 454쪽)

1. He expressed a sound opinion. (　　)

2. Don't make a sound. (　　)

3. This key of the piano won't sound. (　　)

4. His method of business is very sound. (　　)

5. She heard a strange sound. (　　)

6. He tried to sound a trumpet. (　　)

Step 04 영작연습

다음 문장을 주어진 부분을 이용하여 영어로 옮기세요. (해답은 454쪽)

1. 우리는 옆방으로부터 이상한 소리를 들었다. [strange, next room]

____

2. 그는 노령에도 불구하고 여전히 몸과 마음이 건강하다. [still, in spite of]

____

3. 그녀는 때때로 다른 운전자들에게 주의를 주기 위해 경적을 울린다. [horn, warn]

____

:: 1. 소리는 빛보다 느리게 전달된다. 2. 그는 무사히 건강하게 돌아왔다. 3. 그 종은 정오에 울린다.

 **179 face** [feis]

Step 01
해석연습

다음 문장을 face에 유의하여 해석해 보세요. (해석은 이 페이지의 하단부에 있음)

1. The ball struck him on the face. _______________________

2. A dice has six faces. _______________________

3. Jane's house faces the sea. _______________________

Step 02
뜻 알기

face에는 다음과 같은 여러 가지의 뜻이 있습니다.

❶ 얼굴 n the front part of the head, from forehead to chin

❷ 표면, 정면, 면 n the surface of something, especially the front surface

❸ ~쪽을 향하다 v to have or turn the face to or in a certain direction; to be opposite to

한 걸음 더 **He decided finally to <u>face</u> his enemy.** 그는 마침내 자신의 적에 대항하기로 결심했다.
→ ~에 대항하다, 용기 있게 맞서다(=to meet confidently)
He will lose his <u>face</u> if he is defeated again. 그가 다시 패한다면 그는 체면을 잃을 것이다.
→ 체면(=respect; dignity)
facial ① 얼굴의 ② 표면상의 **a colorless face** 핏기 없는 얼굴 **the face of a building** 건물의 정면 **new face** 신인
in the face of ~에도 불구하고 **face to face** 마주보며, 얼굴을 맞대고 **lose one's face** 체면을 잃다
save one's face 체면을 세우다 **make a face** 얼굴을 찡그리다(=pull a face)

Step 03
연습문제

다음 문장의 face에 해당되는 뜻을 **Step 02** 의 ❶~❸에서 고르세요. (해답은 454쪽)

1. This watch has a silver face. (   )

2. Her house faces the sea. (   )

3. Judy has a lovely face. (   )

4. The hotel is facing the park. (   )

5. Don't forget to wash your face before breakfast. (   )

6. He was looking at the face of the building. (   )

Step 04
영작연습

다음 문장을 주어진 부분을 이용하여 영어로 옮기세요. (해답은 454쪽)

1. 저 숙녀는 매우 귀여운 얼굴을 가지고 있다. [lady, pretty]

____

2. 그는 그 산의 북쪽 면을 올랐다. [climbed, north]

____

3. 우리 교실의 창문들은 공원 쪽을 향하고 있다. [windows, park]

____

∷ 1. 공이 그의 얼굴을 때렸다. 2. 주사위는 6개의 면을 가지고 있다. 3. Jane의 집은 바다 쪽을 향해 있다.

180 **bear** [bɛər]

Step 01
해석연습

다음 문장을 bear에 유의하여 해석해 보세요. (해석은 이 페이지의 하단부에 있음)

1. We saw a bear at the zoo. _______________________

2. I cannot bear the cold weather. _______________________

3. This apple tree bears much fruit. _______________________

4. I had to bear a heavy trunk to the airport. _______________________

Step 02
뜻 알기

bear에는 다음과 같은 여러 가지의 뜻이 있습니다.

❶ 곰 **n** a large animal with thick fur, sharp teeth, and claws

❷ 참다, 견디다; 지탱하다 **v** to put up with or endure; to support, to sustain

❸ (아이를) 낳다, (꽃·열매를) 맺다, (이자를) 낳다 **v** to give birth to (someone); to produce; to yield

❹ 운반하다, 가지고 가다 **v** to carry, bring

> 한 걸음 더 **bear** [bɛər] - **bore** [bɔːr] - **born** [bɔːrn] / **borne** [bɔːrn]
> **I think that's excellent advice to <u>bear</u> in mind.** 나는 그것이 기억할 만한 훌륭한 충고라고 생각한다.
> → ~을 마음속에 기억하다, 지니다(=have; hold)
> **Who will <u>bear</u> the expense?** 누가 비용을 부담할 것인가? → 책임, 비용 등을 부담하다

Step 03
연습문제

다음 문장의 bear에 해당되는 뜻을 **Step 02** 의 ❶～❹에서 고르세요. (해답은 454쪽)

1. A big grey bear blocked our path. (　　　)
2. He had to bear a heavy box to the basement. (　　　)
3. The ice is too thin to bear your weight. (　　　)
4. Bears eat a lot during the spring and summer. (　　　)
5. She couldn't bear to see the scene. (　　　)
6. This tree bears no fruit. (　　　)
7. A messenger arrived, bearing a message from the king. (　　　)
8. She hoped to bear a daughter. (　　　)

Step 04
영작연습

다음 문장을 주어진 부분을 이용하여 영어로 옮기세요. (해답은 454쪽)

1. 갈색 곰 한 마리가 천천히 나에게 다가왔다. [brown, slowly]

____

2. 나는 이 의자가 나의 몸무게를 지탱해 낼지 의문이다. [doubt, weight]

____

3. 그는 가난한 집안에서 태어났다. [poor family]

____

4. 그는 아픈 친구를 방문할 때 항상 약간의 꽃을 가지고 간다. [visits, ill]

____

⠿ 1. 우리는 동물원에서 곰을 보았다. 2. 나는 추운 날씨를 견딜 수 없다. 3. 이 사과나무는 많은 열매를 맺는다.
4. 나는 무거운 여행용 큰 가방을 공항으로 가지고 가야했다.

A. 다음 뜻에 해당되는 단어를 보기에서 찾아 적으세요.

보기	anxious order sound face bear

01. _____________ something that is heard or can be heard
02. _____________ a request for goods or services; goods to be supplied
03. _____________ very worried about something that may happen or may have happened
04. _____________ to produce sound; to make something produce sound
05. _____________ to put up with or endure; to support, to sustain
06. _____________ the way in which things are placed in relation to one another
07. _____________ the front part of the head, from forehead to chin
08. _____________ to give birth to (someone); to produce; to yield
09. _____________ to have or turn the face to or in a certain direction; to be opposite to
10. _____________ to tell (someone) to do something (from a position of authority)
11. _____________ a large animal with thick fur, sharp teeth, and claws
12. _____________ to carry, bring
13. _____________ the surface of something, especially the front surface
14. _____________ wanting very much to do something or something to happen
15. _____________ healthy; in good condition; reasonable

B. 다음 빈칸에 가장 알맞은 단어를 보기에서 찾아 적으세요.

보기	anxious order sound face bear

01. The bell will (   ) at noon.
02. The general will (   ) his men to advance.
03. Wash your (   ) before breakfast.
04. The bell makes a big (   ).
05. After having three daughters, she hoped to (   ) a son.
06. The hunter will shoot the (   ).
07. We were (   ) about her safety.
08. I will (   ) a few books from Canada.
09. He will (   ) a gift to her on her birthday.
10. His advice is always very (   ).
11. She is (   ) to see her son.
12. Have you ever seen the (   ) of the moon?
13. She can't (   ) the hot weather.
14. The windows of my room (   ) south.
15. She called our names in alphabetical (   ).

다음 문장을 굵게 처리된 단어에 유의하여 해석해 보세요.

01. Because of new competition, we are **anxious** to get our products into the market as soon as possible. [2000년-홀수형 42번]

➡ ___________________________

02. She has become stressed and **anxious**. [2000년-홀수형 51–52번]

➡ ___________________________

03. The events of a story are usually told in the **order** in which they occur – usually, but not always. [1994년-2차 20번]

➡ ___________________________

04. There is also a quantity discount, which is offered to individuals who **order** large quantities of a product. [2001년-홀수형 31번]

➡ ___________________________

05. In 1457, he **ordered** his people not to play the game any more. [2001년-홀수형 43번]

➡ ___________________________

06. Take time out to do things you enjoy after work **in order to** reduce the stress you experience during your workday. [2002년-홀수형 28번]

➡ ___________________________

07. I'm trying to get into our apartment, but the new doorlock seems to be **out of order**. [2007년-홀수형 6번]

➡ ___________________________

08. No signs of life occurred near him but the **sound** of insects. [2002년-홀수형 39번]

➡ ___________________________

09. The way you **sound** makes up 35% of the first impression. [1998년-홀수형 23번]

➡ ___________________________

10. Do you have the courage which comes from the sincere conviction that you are a person of **sound** character, an honest, dependable, kind, and caring person? [1998년-홀수형 33번]

➡ ___________________________

11. You **sound** a little worried, but I think living in a foreign country can be more exciting than you might imagine. [2004년-홀수형 41번]

➡ ___________________________

12. It is not easy to show moral courage **in the face of** either indifference or opposition. [2011년-홀수형 20번]

➡ ___________________________

13. When we **face** problems or disagreements today, we have to arrive at solutions through dialog. [2010년-홀수형 32번]

➡ ___________________________

14. That is why the lines all over her **face** are so deep. [2003년-홀수형 28번]

➡ ___________________________

15. A United Nations report says that the number of polar **bears** is rapidly decreasing. [2007년-홀수형 12번]

➡ ___________________________

16. The strain is hard to **bear**. It grows harder as time passes. [1997년-홀수형 48번]

➡ ___________________________

Day 18

Better be alone than in bad company.
나쁜 교우관계보다는 혼자 있는 것이 더 낫다.

181 succeed [səksíːd]

Group 37

Step 01 해석연습

다음 문장을 succeed에 유의하여 해석해 보세요. (해석은 이 페이지의 하단부에 있음)

1. The boy has succeeded in solving the math problem. _______________________

2. She succeeded to her father's property. _______________________

Step 02 뜻 알기

succeed에는 다음과 같은 여러 가지의 뜻이 있습니다.

❶ 성공하다(~ in) Ⅴ to accomplish a task or reach a goal

❷ ~의 뒤를 잇다, 계승하다, 상속하다(~ to) Ⅴ to follow next in order and take the place of someone or something else

> 한 걸음 더 **successful** 성공한 **successive** 연속하는, 잇따르는, 상속의 **succeeding** 계속되는, 잇따르는 **success** 성공
> **succession** 계승, 상속 **successor** 후계자, 상속자, 후임자; 뒤를 잇는 것
> **succeed in** ~에 성공하다 **succeed to** ~을 계승하다, 이어받다

Step 03 연습문제

다음 문장의 succeed에 해당되는 뜻을 **Step 02** 의 ❶~❷에서 고르세요. (해답은 455쪽)

1. He succeeded to his father's estate. (   )

2. Thanks to your assistance, I succeeded in the attempt. (   )

3. The student succeeded in passing the entrance examination. (   )

4. Elizabeth succeeded Mary as Queen. (   )

Step 04 영작연습

다음 문장을 주어진 부분을 이용하여 영어로 옮기세요. (해답은 455쪽)

1. 우리는 극장에서 빈자리를 찾는 데 성공했다. [empty, theater]

____

2. 그는 머지않아 부친의 사업을 이어받을 것이다. [business, near future]

____

:: 1. 소년은 수학문제를 푸는 데 성공했다. 2. 그녀는 아버지의 재산을 상속했다.

182 suit [suːt / sjuːt]

Step 01
해석연습

다음 문장을 suit에 유의하여 해석해 보세요. (해석은 이 페이지의 하단부에 있음)

1. Mr. Brown is wearing a blue suit. ___________________________

2. I started my suit against the phone company. ___________________________

3. This hat suits me very well. ___________________________

Step 02
뜻 알기

suit에는 다음과 같은 여러 가지의 뜻이 있습니다.

❶ (한 벌의) 옷; (신사복, 여성복) 정장 한 벌(슈트) Ⅲ a set of clothes made of the same material including a jacket with trousers or a skirt

❷ 소송, 고소 Ⅲ a case brought to a law court by a private person or company

❸ 잘 맞다, 편리하다, 적합하다 Ⅴ to satisfy the needs of, or be convenient for; to be right for

> 한 걸음 더 **suitable** 적절한, 적당한, 잘 어울리는 **suitcase** (옷을 넣을 수 있는) 여행가방 **a suit of clothes** 한 벌의 옷
> **lawsuit** 소송 **a civil suit** 민사소송 **bring[file, enter, start] a suit against** ~을 상대로 소송을 제기하다
> **win[lose] a suit** 승소(패소)하다
> * sue [suː / sjuː]는 고소하다, 소송을 제기하다는 뜻의 동사임
> **suit oneself** 좋을 대로[마음대로] 하다

Step 03
연습문제

다음 문장의 suit에 해당되는 뜻을 **Step 02** 의 ❶~❸에서 고르세요. (해답은 455쪽)

1. A woman brought a suit against her husband. (   )

2. Short hair suits her very well. (   )

3. I will wear my best suit to the party. (   )

4. The suit is a civil battle. (   )

5. May I borrow your suit tonight? (   )

6. The seven o'clock train will suit us. (   )

Step 04
영작연습

다음 문장을 주어진 부분을 이용하여 영어로 옮기세요. (해답은 455쪽)

1. 그는 오늘 밤 자신의 가장 좋은 정장을 입을 것이다. [wear, tonight]

____

2. 그녀는 보험 회사를 상대로 한 소송에서 졌다. [lost, insurance company]

____

3. 이곳의 따뜻한 기후가 그녀의 건강에 적합하다. [warm climate, health]

____

:: 1. Brown 씨는 푸른 정장(양복)을 입고 있다. 2. 나는 전화 회사를 상대로 소송을 시작했다. 3. 이 모자가 나에게 아주 잘 어울린다.

183 court [kɔːrt]

다음 문장을 court에 유의하여 해석해 보세요. (해석은 이 페이지의 하단부에 있음)

1. Our house has a beautiful court. _______________________

2. Do you prefer grass courts or hard courts? _______________________

3. The accused is to appear before the court on Wednesday. _______________________

court에는 다음과 같은 여러 가지의 뜻이 있습니다.

❶ (담이나 건물에 둘러싸인) 안뜰, 공터 **n** a space partly or wholly enclosed by walls or buildings

❷ (테니스, 배구 등의) 경기장, 코트 **n** an area that has been specially made for playing games such as tennis on

❸ 법정, 법원 **n** a place where law-cases are held

> 한 걸음 더 **the court of King James** 제임스 왕의 궁전
> → 궁전, 왕궁(=the official place where a king or queen lives and works)
> **the queen and her court** 여왕과 그 조신들
> → 왕족, 조정신하(=the royal people and the people who work for them or advise them)
> **a tennis court** 테니스코트 **courtyard** (성, 호텔 등의) 안뜰 **courthouse** 법원 **courtier** 조정신하
> **go to court** ① 소송을 제기하다 ② 입궐하다 **out of court** 법정 밖에서, 당사자끼리 합의해서

다음 문장의 court에 해당되는 뜻을 Step 02 의 ❶~❸에서 고르세요. (해답은 455쪽)

1. Her house has a beautiful court. (   )

2. The courts do justice to the people. (   )

3. Two basketball courts are in the gymnasium. (   )

4. The case was settled out of court. (   )

5. This door leads to the court of my house. (   )

6. Do you prefer clay or grass courts? (   )

다음 문장을 주어진 부분을 이용하여 영어로 옮기세요. (해답은 455쪽)

1. 그녀의 집 안뜰에는 많은 아름다운 꽃들이 있다. [a lot of, flowers]

____

2. 우리 학교에는 여러 개의 테니스 코트가 있다. [has, several]

____

3. 그녀는 증인으로 법정에 출두할 것을 명령받았다. [summoned, witness]

____

:: 1. 우리 집은 아름다운 안뜰이 하나 있다. 2. 당신은 잔디코트를 선호합니까 혹은 하드코트를 선호합니까?
3. 피고인은 수요일에 법정에 출두할 예정이다.

184 mind [maind]

Step 01
해석연습

다음 문장을 mind에 유의하여 해석해 보세요. (해석은 이 페이지의 하단부에 있음)

1. He has a strong mind. _______________________________

2. Mind your own business. _______________________________

3. Would you mind opening the window? No, not at all. _______________________________

Step 02
뜻 알기

mind에는 다음과 같은 여러 가지의 뜻이 있습니다.

❶ 마음; 정신; 의견 **n** the power by which one thinks, feels, etc; opinion

❷ ~에 주의를 기울이다, 조심하다, 돌보다 **v** to attend to; to be careful of; to take care of

❸ 꺼려하다, 거북해하다, 반대하다 **v** to feel annoyed; to feel dislike; to feel objection to

> 한 걸음 더 **mindful** 주의 깊은, 경계하는 **mindless** 생각 없는, 어리석은 **mind and body** 심신; 마음과 몸
> **the public mind** 여론 **mind reading** 독심술, 독심 능력 **mind's eye** 마음의 눈, 상상력
> **make up one's mind** 결심하다(=decide) **keep[bear] in mind** 마음에 새겨 두다, 기억하고 있다(=remember)

Step 03
연습문제

다음 문장의 mind에 해당되는 뜻을 **Step 02** 의 ❶~❸에서 고르세요. (해답은 455쪽)

1. I will go there if you don't mind. (　　　)
2. His mind did not change his mind. (　　　)
3. Mind what I tell you. (　　　)
4. In my mind, she is honest. (　　　)
5. My sister minds the baby so I can go shopping. (　　　)
6. Would you mind shutting the door? (　　　)

Step 04
영작연습

다음 문장을 주어진 부분을 이용하여 영어로 옮기세요. (해답은 455쪽)

1. 그녀는 매우 늙었지만 정신은 아직도 맑다. [mind, clear]

____

2. 내가 표를 사는 동안 나의 가방을 돌봐 주시겠습니까? [while, ticket]

____

3. 그는 추운 날씨를 전혀 꺼려하지 않는다. [weather, at all]

____

∷ 1. 그는 강한 정신의 소유자이다. 2. 네 일이나 신경 써라. 3. 창문 좀 열어도 될까요? 네, 열어도 됩니다.

265

185 hold [hould]

Step 01 해석연습 다음 문장을 hold에 유의하여 해석해 보세요. (해석은 이 페이지의 하단부에 있음)

1. The little boy is holding his mother's hand. ________________________________
2. She holds shares in this company. ________________________________
3. We will hold the party in this hall. ________________________________
4. The rule still holds (good). ________________________________

Step 02 뜻 알기 hold에는 다음과 같은 여러 가지의 뜻이 있습니다.

❶ ~을 잡다, 쥐다, 껴안다 Ⅴ to have something in one's hand(s) or arms

❷ ~을 소유하다, 보유하다, 차지하다 Ⅴ to have and keep as one's own; to possess; to occupy

❸ (행사, 회의, 파티 등을) 개최하다, 열다 Ⅴ to arrange for an event, meeting, party, election, etc

❹ (법률 등이) 효력이 있다, 유효하다 Ⅴ to be effective; to be in force

> 한 걸음 더 **hold** [hould] - **held** [held] - **held** [held]
> **The room holds fifty persons.** 이 방은 50명을 수용할 수 있다. → (사람, 물건 등을) 수용할 수 있다
> **He holds that she told a lie.** 그는 그녀가 거짓말을 했다고 생각하고 있다.
> → (생각 따위)를 품다, 생각하다, 믿다, 주장하다(=to believe; affirm; maintain)
> **holder** ① 보유자 ② 받치는 물건 **hold good** 효력이 있다 **hold on** ① 계속하다 ② (전화를) 끊지 않고 기다리다

Step 03 연습문제 다음 문장의 hold에 해당되는 뜻을 **Step 02** 의 ❶~❹에서 고르세요. (해답은 455쪽)

1. The festival is usually held in October. (   )
2. She holds the position of company secretary. (   )
3. These rules hold under all circumstances. (   )
4. We hold a general election every four years. (   )
5. Mother asked me to hold her bag. (   )
6. He holds the world record for the marathon. (   )
7. The couple sat, holding hands under a tree. (   )
8. The contract still holds true. (   )

Step 04 영작연습 다음 문장을 주어진 부분을 이용하여 영어로 옮기세요. (해답은 455쪽)

1. 그 남자는 손에 칼을 쥐고 있었다. [knife, hand]

____

2. 그는 아직도 헤비급 타이틀을 갖고 있다. [heavy weight title]

____

3. 1988년 올림픽경기는 서울에서 개최되었다. [Olympic Games]

____

4. 그 규칙은 이 경우에 유효하지 않다. [rule, case]

____

:: 1. 그 어린 소년은 엄마의 손을 잡고 있다. 2. 그녀는 이 회사의 주식을 소유하고 있다. 3. 우리는 파티를 이 홀에서 열 것이다. 4. 그 규칙은 아직도 유효하다.

A. 다음 뜻에 해당되는 단어를 보기에서 찾아 적으세요.

> 보기   succeed   suit   court   mind   hold

01. ______________ the power by which one thinks, feels, etc; opinion
02. ______________ to follow next in order and take the place of someone or something else
03. ______________ a set of clothes made of the same material including a jacket with trousers or a skirt
04. ______________ to have and keep as one's own; to possess; to occupy
05. ______________ to feel annoyed; to feel dislike; to feel objection to
06. ______________ a case brought to a law court by a private person or company
07. ______________ a space partly or wholly enclosed by walls or buildings
08. ______________ to be effective; to be in force
09. ______________ to accomplish a task or reach a goal
10. ______________ to have something in one's hand(s) or arms
11. ______________ an area that has been specially made for playing games such as tennis on
12. ______________ to arrange for an event, meeting, party, election, etc
13. ______________ to satisfy the needs of, or be convenient for; to be right for
14. ______________ a place where law-cases are held
15. ______________ to attend to; to be careful of; to take care of

B. 다음 빈칸에 가장 알맞은 단어를 보기에서 찾아 적으세요.

> 보기   succeed   suit   court   mind   hold(s)

01. He is wearing a brown (   ).
02. Our offer will (   ) until next month.
03. The children used to play in the (   ) of his house.
04. I'm sure you'll (   ) if you work hard.
05. Would you (   ) my bags for a few minutes?
06. This necktie does not (   ) me.
07. He tried to (   ) me by the arm.
08. A volleyball (   ) is in the gymnasium.
09. They will (   ) the meeting in this hall.
10. Do you (   ) if I smoke?
11. He won his (   ) against the food company.
12. Who will (   ) to the throne?
13. The prisoner was brought to (   ) for trial.
14. He (   ) the copyright on the book.
15. I have no (   ) to go for a walk.

다음 문장을 굵게 처리된 단어에 유의하여 해석해 보세요.

01. When other people fail, you feel there's a better chance for you to **succeed**. [2011년–홀수형 40번]

➡ ____

02. Many of those who have **succeeded** in life owe this to the fact that their concentration is good. [2003년–홀수형 43번]

➡ ____

03. He's in a grey **suit** with a checked tie. [2000년–홀수형 1번]

➡ ____

04. Make a plan for a bookcase that **suits** your own library. [2000년–홀수형 43번]

➡ ____

05. M: Shall we take a break for a while?
W: Why not? **Suit yourself.** [1997년–홀수형 10번]

➡ ____

06. This can stem from many sources such as having an automobile crash, being fired from a job, falling suddenly ill, becoming involved in a legal **suit**, or losing a large sum of money. [1994년–1차 49–50번]

➡ ____

07. In other words, it is the responsibility of the **court** to prove that a person is guilty. [1996년–홀수형 17번]

➡ ____

08. Are you mad about the shouting from the tennis **courts**? [2001년–홀수형 4번]

➡ ____

09. Many of us do the same when we are speaking to someone and our **mind** is elsewhere. [2004년–홀수형 38번]

➡ ____

10. If I were a genius, I would not **mind** being treated like one. But since I am not, I do. [2000년–홀수형 41번]

➡ ____

11. I'd rather sit down, if you don't **mind**. [2003년–홀수형 15번]

➡ ____

12. There are a few things you should **keep in mind** when you travel in another country. [1999년–홀수형 6번]

➡ ____

13. **Hold** the chair tightly while I'm changing this bulb. [2008년–홀수형 13번]

➡ ____

14. They're **holding** a video contest to encourage citizens to ride bicycles. [2013년–홀수형 15번]

➡ ____

15. Remember that life is precious and you need to live in the present as well as **hold** on to your dreams for the future. [1996년–홀수형 47번]

➡ ____

16. The graduation ceremony will be **held** next Friday in Hutt High School's Assembly Hall. [2008년–홀수형 20번]

➡ ____

186 rare [rɛər]

Step 01 해석연습

다음 문장을 rare에 유의하여 해석해 보세요. (해석은 이 페이지의 하단부에 있음)

1. He has some rare books. _______________________

2. She likes her steak rare. _______________________

Step 02 뜻 알기

rare에는 다음과 같은 여러 가지의 뜻이 있습니다.

❶ 드문, 진귀한, 희박한 **a** scarce; not often found; unusual

❷ (고기가) 설익은, 살짝만 익힌 **a** (of meat) underdone; only slightly cooked

> 한 걸음 더 **a rare book** 희귀본 **a rare event** 드문 일 **the rare air** 희박한 공기 **rarely** 드물게, 좀처럼 ~하지 않는
> **in rare cases** 드물게(=on rare occasions)
> **rare and** ~ (구어) 대단히, 몹시 * I am rare and happy. 몹시 행복하다.

Step 03 연습문제

다음 문장의 rare에 해당되는 뜻을 **Step 02** 의 ❶~❷에서 고르세요. (해답은 455쪽)

1. I like my steak rare. (   )

2. He has a rare Roman coin. (   )

3. He is a man of rare talent. (   )

4. She doesn't like rare meat. (   )

Step 04 영작연습

다음 문장을 주어진 부분을 이용하여 영어로 옮기세요. (해답은 455쪽)

1. 그가 늦게 오는 것은 매우 드문 일이다. [arrive, late]

____

2. 나의 아저씨는 색깔이 여전히 붉은 설익은 고기를 좋아하신다. [meat, still]

____

:: 1. 그는 약간의 진귀한 책을 가지고 있다. 2. 그녀는 살짝만 익힌 고기를 좋아한다.

187 article [áːrtikl]

Step 01
해석연습

다음 문장을 article에 유의하여 해석해 보세요. (해석은 이 페이지의 하단부에 있음)

1. There is an interesting article in the newspaper. ______________________

2. She bought these articles at the same store. ______________________

3. Article 1 of the contract names the buyer and the seller of the villa.

____

Step 02
뜻 알기

article에는 다음과 같은 여러 가지의 뜻이 있습니다.

❶ (신문, 잡지의) 기사 ⓝ a piece of writing in a newspaper or magazine

❷ 물건, 물품 ⓝ a thing or an object

❸ (법률 또는 계약서의) 조항 ⓝ a part of a law or legal agreement

> 한 걸음 더 **The English definite article is "the."** 영어의 정관사는 the이다. → 영어문법의 "관사"
> **an editorial article** (신문의) 사설 **an article of furniture** 가구 1점
> **a definite article** 정관사 **an indefinite article** 부정관사
> **household articles** 가정용품(=domestic articles) **article by article** 조목조목, 축조적으로

Step 03
연습문제

다음 문장의 article에 해당되는 뜻을 **Step 02** 의 ❶~❸에서 고르세요. (해답은 455쪽)

1. These articles are superior in quality. (   )

2. She has written an article for a local newspaper. (   )

3. You need to read the contract article by article. (   )

4. That store sells articles of clothing. (   )

5. Look at the fifth article of the Constitution. (   )

6. He read an article on the magazine. (   )

Step 04
영작연습

다음 문장을 주어진 부분을 이용하여 영어로 옮기세요. (해답은 455쪽)

1. 그는 새로운 종류의 연료에 관한 잡지기사를 읽었다. [type, fuel]

____

2. 이 가게는 크리스마스 선물용품을 판다. [shop, presents]

____

3. 헌법의 제1조항은 종교의 자유를 보장하고 있다. [constitution, guarantees]

____

:: 1. 신문에 재미있는 기사가 있다. 2. 그녀는 이 물건들을 같은 가게에서 샀다. 3. 계약서의 제1조항은 전원주택의 구매자와 판매자의 이름을 명시하고 있다.

188 company [kʌ́mpəni]

Step 01 해석연습

다음 문장을 company에 유의하여 해석해 보세요. (해석은 이 페이지의 하단부에 있음)

1. I am working for a small publishing company. _______________________
2. He is always good company. _______________________
3. She is expecting company tonight. _______________________

Step 02 뜻 알기

company에는 다음과 같은 여러 가지의 뜻이 있습니다.

❶ 회사, 상사 n an organization that makes or sells goods or services in order to get money; a business form

❷ 친구, 동료; 교제 n persons with whom one spends one's time; friends; companionship

❸ 손님들, 초청객 n a number of guests

> 한 걸음 더 **He is a <u>company</u> commander in the army.** 그는 군대의 중대장이다.
> → 군대조직의 중대(=the part of an army commanded by a captain)
> **a publishing company** 출판사 **a trading company** 무역회사 **part company with** ~와 헤어지다
> **keep company with** ~와 친해지다

Step 03 연습문제

다음 문장의 company에 해당되는 뜻을 Step 02 의 ❶~❸에서 고르세요. (해답은 455쪽)

1. He runs a big publishing company. (   )
2. You should avoid bad company. (   )
3. We are having company for the weekend. (   )
4. The insurance company was set up in 1948. (   )
5. I am expecting company this evening. (   )
6. Don't keep company with bad friends. (   )

Step 04 영작연습

다음 문장을 주어진 부분을 이용하여 영어로 옮기세요. (해답은 455쪽)

1. 그녀는 화려한 완구를 만드는 회사를 소유하고 있다. [owns, fancy]

   ____

2. 당신은 그가 사귀는 사람을 보고 그 사람을 알 수 있을 것이다. [man, by, keeps]

   ____

3. 우리는 오늘 저녁식사에 손님들이 있다. [dinner, evening]

   ____

:: 1. 나는 조그마한 출판회사에서 근무하고 있다. 2. 그는 언제나 사귀기 좋은 친구다. 3. 그녀는 오늘 밤 손님이 있다.

189 draw [drɔː]

Step 01
해석연습

다음 문장을 draw에 유의하여 해석해 보세요. (해석은 이 페이지의 하단부에 있음)

1. Two horses were drawing a carriage. _______________________

2. Draw a circle with your pencil. _______________________

3. They drew 1-1 last night. _______________________

Step 02
뜻 알기

draw에는 다음과 같은 여러 가지의 뜻이 있습니다.

❶ ~을 끌다, 끌어당기다; ~을 꺼내다, 빼내다　[v] to pull or drag along; to take or pull out

❷ (연필, 펜 따위로) ~을 그리다　[v] to make a line, figure, etc with a pencil, pen, crayons, etc

❸ 시합을 비기게 하다; 비기다　[v] to end a game or match without either side winning
　비김, 무승부, 무승부의 경기　[n] a game that ends in a tie

> 한 걸음 더 **draw** [drɔː] - **drew** [druː] - **drawn** [drɔːn]
> **He picked the winning number on the first draw.** 그는 첫 번째 제비뽑기에서 우승숫자를 뽑았다.
> → 제비뽑기(=the act of choosing a winner in a lottery)
> **The music festival is likely to draw huge crowds.** 그 음악축제는 많은 군중을 끌 것 같다. → (주의, 사람 등을) 끌다
> **Winter is drawing near.** 겨울이 다가오고 있다. → 다가오다[가다]; 접근하다(=come near; approach)
> **drawing** ① 끎, 잡아당김 ② (연필, 펜, 분필, 숯 등에 의한) 그림 ③ 제비뽑기, 추첨 **drawback** 결점, 장애, 지장
> **draw back** 뒷걸음질치다; 철수하다; ~에서 손을 떼다 **draw lots** 제비를 뽑다 **draw near** 가까이 오다, 다가오다

Step 03
연습문제

다음 문장의 draw에 해당되는 뜻을 **Step 02** 의 ❶~❸에서 고르세요. (해답은 455쪽)

1. She drew the child toward her. (　　)

2. He was drawing a picture on the paper. (　　)

3. They drew (at) 3-3 last night. (　　)

4. The man drew a gun from his pocket. (　　)

5. Draw a straight line between A and B. (　　)

6. FC Seoul drew with Suwon Samsung yesterday. (　　)

Step 04
영작연습

다음 문장을 주어진 부분을 이용하여 영어로 옮기세요. (해답은 455쪽)

1. 불 주위로 의자를 끌어당기는 것이 좋을 것이다. [had better, around]

____

2. 그는 취미로 지도 그리기를 좋아한다. [map, hobby]

____

3. 그 게임은 무승부로 끝났다. [game, ended]

____

:: 1. 말 두 마리가 마차를 끌고 있었다. 2. 연필로 원을 그려라. 3. 그들은 어젯밤 1대 1로 비겼다.

190 major [méidʒər]

Step 01
해석연습

다음 문장을 major에 유의하여 해석해 보세요. (해석은 이 페이지의 하단부에 있음)

1. There are two major political parties in the United States. _________________

2. What's your major in college? _________________

3. He is a major in the Air Force. _________________

4. The music was a sonata in C major. _________________

Step 02
뜻 알기

major에는 다음과 같은 여러 가지의 뜻이 있습니다.

❶ 큰 쪽의, 대다수의, 주요한, 보다 상위의 **a** (contrasted with minor) greater or more important

❷ 전공, 전공과목 **n** the main subject that a student studies at college or university
전공하다 **v** to study a major subject at a college or university

❸ (군대 계급) 소령 **n** a military rank between a captain and a colonel

❹ 음악의 장조 **n** a key in music

> 한 걸음 더 이외에도 성년의, 성인의(=of full legal age)의 뜻이 있음

Step 03
연습문제

다음 문장의 major에 해당되는 뜻을 **Step 02** 의 ❶∼❹에서 고르세요. (해답은 456쪽)

1. He majored in journalism in college. (   )
2. The captain is beneath the major. (   )
3. We take major credit cards. No checks, please. (   )
4. What did you major in at the university? (   )
5. The music was a symphony in D major. (   )
6. The movie was a major success. (   )
7. The major returned the staff sergeant's salute. (   )
8. He will play a sonata in C sharp major. (   )

Step 04
영작연습

다음 문장을 주어진 부분을 이용하여 영어로 옮기세요. (해답은 456쪽)

1. 암의 주된 요인들 중의 하나는 흡연이다. [causes, cancer]

____

2. 그녀는 대학에서 경제학을 전공했다. [economics, university]

____

3. 나의 삼촌은 육군 소령이다. [uncle, army]

____

4. 그녀는 F장조 소나타를 연주했다. [played, sonata]

____

:: 1. 미국에는 두 개의 주요한 정당이 있다. 2. 당신의 대학에서의 전공은 무엇입니까? 3. 그는 공군 소령이다. 4. 그 음악은 C장조 소나타였다.

해답은 456쪽

A. 다음 뜻에 해당되는 단어를 보기에서 찾아 적으세요.

보기	rare　article　company　draw　major

01. ____________ a game that ends in a tie
02. ____________ to make a line, figure, etc with a pencil, pen, crayons, etc.
03. ____________ greater or more important
04. ____________ a thing or an object
05. ____________ an organization that makes or sells goods or services in order to get money; a business form
06. ____________ a military rank between a captain and a colonel
07. ____________ a number of guests
08. ____________ a part of a law or legal agreement
09. ____________ (of meat) underdone; only slightly cooked
10. ____________ a key in music
11. ____________ to pull or drag along; to take or pull out
12. ____________ scarce; not often found; unusual
13. ____________ the main subject that a student studies at college or university
14. ____________ a piece of writing in a newspaper or magazine
15. ____________ persons with whom one spends one's time; friends; companionship

B. 다음 빈칸에 가장 알맞은 단어를 보기에서 찾아 적으세요.

보기	rare　article　company　draw　major

01. He works for a small trading (　　　　).
02. My father likes (　　　　) meat.
03. Today's game ended in a (　　　　).
04. Drug addiction was the (　　　　) cause of her death.
05. I saw an interesting (　　　　) in the newspaper.
06. The music was a B sharp (　　　　).
07. We have (　　　　) for dinner tonight.
08. A (　　　　) is above a captain.
09. Read carefully every (　　　　) of the contract before signing.
10. Her (　　　　) is Spanish literature.
11. The air is (　　　　) on high mountains.
12. You may (　　　　) your chair around the fire.
13. I bought the (　　　　) at that store.
14. Try to keep (　　　　) with good people.
15. (　　　　) a line under your name.

다음 문장을 굵게 처리된 단어에 유의하여 해석해 보세요.

01. Any contact between humans and **rare** plants can be disastrous for the plants. [2008년–홀수형 37번]

➡ ______________________________

02. They found **rare** comfort in the simple songs that they sang aboard their ships. [2003년–홀수형 21번]

➡ ______________________________

03. Footwear has a history which goes back thousands of years, and it has long been an **article** of necessity. [2007년–홀수형 40번]

➡ ______________________________

04. It's an **article** about next year's fashion trends. [2006년–홀수형 12번]

➡ ______________________________

05. For the past 25 years you have been a valued and respected employee of this **company**. [2005년–홀수형 25번]

➡ ______________________________

06. I walked into a restaurant, and seated myself. My table companion rose. "Sir," said he, "do you wish to force your **company** on those who do not want you?" [1997년–홀수형 54–55번]

➡ ______________________________

07. One of the main principles I follow when I **draw** outside is not to select a subject that is too difficult or odd. [2009년–홀수형 26번]

➡ ______________________________

08. But as you **draw** nearer, the words on the sign turn out to be FOOD AHEAD. [2000년–홀수형 25번]

➡ ______________________________

09. In this way, they are given hints to better understand the play while the conclusion is left open so as to leave them to **draw** their own conclusions. [2010년–홀수형 28번]

➡ ______________________________

10. At length I found myself, as the evening shadows **drew** long, within view of the cheerless house. [2004년–홀수형 28번]

➡ ______________________________

11. One day he went to school with a sword. Seeing Timmy carry a sword, his startled teacher exclaimed, "A sword! Whatever do you need a sword in this painting class for?" "Well, you said," explained Timmy, "we would all learn how to **draw**." [1994년–1차 17번]

➡ ______________________________

12. Tony, have you thought about what your **major** will be in college? [1998년–홀수형 2번]

➡ ______________________________

13. They summarize the **major** world and national news stories. [2001년–홀수형 33번]

➡ ______________________________

14. Feelings and judgments of how others feel toward you play a **major** role in how you choose to solve your day-to-day problems. [2003년–홀수형 47–48번]

➡ ______________________________

Lean liberty is better than fat slavery.
여윈 자유인이 살찐 노예보다 낫다.

191 **share** [ʃɛər]

Group 39

Step 01 해석연습

다음 문장을 share에 유의하여 해석해 보세요. (해석은 이 페이지의 하단부에 있음)

1. I share a room with my brother. ___________________________
2. She paid her share of the total cost. ___________________________
3. He owns 500 shares in the bank. ___________________________

Step 02 뜻 알기

share에는 다음과 같은 여러 가지의 뜻이 있습니다.

❶ ~을 공유하다; ~을 나누다, 분배하다　Ⅴ to have or use something in common; to divide among a number of people

❷ 배당, 몫　ⓝ a part of something belonging to one individual

❸ 주식, 지분　ⓝ one of the equal proportions into which a company's capital stock is divided

▷ 한 걸음 더 **shareholder** 주주(=stockholder) **market share** 시장 점유율

Step 03 연습문제

다음 문장의 share에 해당되는 뜻을 Step 02 의 ❶~❸에서 고르세요. (해답은 456쪽)

1. Shares in the company declined nearly 10 percent today. (　　)
2. You can share the textbook with your friend. (　　)
3. Let me pay my share. (　　)
4. Robert had a share in the profit. (　　)
5. Mary shared her cake with her sister. (　　)
6. What are today's quotations for shares? (　　)

Step 04 영작연습

다음 문장을 주어진 부분을 이용하여 영어로 옮기세요. (해답은 456쪽)

1. 나의 부모님은 기쁨과 슬픔을 우리와 함께 나누신다. [joys, sorrows]

____

2. 그 어린 소년은 케이크의 자기 몫 이상을 먹었다. [more than, cake]

____

3. 그는 그 석유회사의 주식을 팔기로 결정했다. [decided, oil]

____

∷ 1. 나는 방을 동생과 함께 쓰고 있다. 2. 그녀는 전체 비용 중 자신의 몫을 냈다. 3. 그는 그 은행의 주식을 500주 소유하고 있다.

192 operation [àpəréiʃən / ɔ̀pəréiʃən]

Step 01 해석연습

다음 문장을 operation에 유의하여 해석해 보세요. (해석은 이 페이지의 하단부에 있음)

1. The operation of this machine is very easy. _______________________

2. She had an operation on her nose. _______________________

3. The general was in command of operations in the south. _______________________

Step 02 뜻 알기

operation에는 다음과 같은 여러 가지의 뜻이 있습니다.

❶ 작업, 조작, 운영 n an action; a way or process of working something

❷ 수술 n the act of surgically cutting a part of the body in order to cure disease

❸ 군사행동; (군사)작전 n a planned military or police action, especially one that involves a lot of people

> 한 걸음 더 **operate** ① 조작하다, 운전하다, 운영하다 ② 수술하다 ③ 군사작전을 펴다 **operator** 조작자, 운전기사, 전화교환원
> **operating room** 수술실 **the cost of operation** 운영비

Step 03 연습문제

다음 문장의 operation에 해당되는 뜻을 **Step 02** 의 ❶~❸에서 고르세요. (해답은 456쪽)

1. The liver operation is dangerous. (   )

2. I will explain the operation of this machine to you. (   )

3. The military operations were planned in covert. (   )

4. Operation of this system is automatic. (   )

5. He gained his sight after the operation. (   )

6. It was a perfect military operation. (   )

Step 04 영작연습

다음 문장을 주어진 부분을 이용하여 영어로 옮기세요. (해답은 456쪽)

1. 그는 나에게 카메라 조작법을 설명해 주었다. [explained, camera]

____

2. 나의 아저씨는 작년에 위 수술을 받았다. [stomach, last year]

____

3. 군사작전은 다음 주에 시작되는 것으로 예정되어 있다. [military, scheduled]

____

:: 1. 이 기계를 조작하는 것은 매우 쉽다. 2. 그녀는 코 수술을 받았다. 3. 그 장군은 남쪽지역의 작전을 수행 중이었다.

 **193 lean [liːn]**

다음 문장을 lean에 유의하여 해석해 보세요. (해석은 이 페이지의 하단부에 있음)

1. The tower leaned a little to the left. ________________________

2. The boy leaned his elbows on the table. ________________________

3. Most of the dancers at the stage were lean. ________________________

lean에는 다음과 같은 여러 가지의 뜻이 있습니다.

❶ 기울다, 구부러지다, 기울이다 **v** to slope or bend from an upright position

❷ 기대다, 의지하다 **v** to rest in a sloping position for support

❸ (사람, 동물이) 야윈, 마른 **a** (of a person or animal) thin

> 한 걸음 더 **You must not lean too much on [upon] others.** 너무 남에게 의존해서는 안 된다.
> → 의존하다, 의뢰하다(=depend on; rely on)
> **He ate lean meat with the fat cut off.** 그는 기름기를 떼어 내고 살코기를 먹었다.
> → (고기가) 기름기가 적은, 살코기의(=(of meat) having little or not fat)
> **Last year was a lean year.** 작년은 흉년이었다.
> → 수확이 적은, 모자라는(=not productive; poor in quality)
> **the Leaning Tower of Pisa** 피사의 사탑

다음 문장의 lean에 해당되는 뜻을 Step 02 의 ❶~❸에서 고르세요. (해답은 456쪽)

1. She has a lean body. (   )
2. The building leaned a little to the left. (   )
3. She leaned upon my arm. (   )
4. Professional dancers are usually thin. (   )
5. The boy often leans on his desk. (   )
6. We saw the Leaning Tower of Pisa. (   )

다음 문장을 주어진 부분을 이용하여 영어로 옮기세요. (해답은 456쪽)

1. 나는 그가 말하는 것을 들으려고 몸을 앞으로 기울였다. [forward, hear]

____

2. 그는 사다리를 벽에 세웠다. [ladder, against]

____

3. 그 소녀는 야위고 창백해 보였다. [looked, pale]

____

:: 1. 그 탑은 약간 왼쪽으로 기울었다. 2. 그 소년은 팔꿈치를 테이블에 기댔다. 3. 무대 위의 무용수들의 대부분은 말랐다.

194 **since** [sins]

Step 01
해석연습

다음 문장을 since에 유의하여 해석해 보세요. (해석은 이 페이지의 하단부에 있음)

1. I have known him since he was a child. _________________________________

2. Since you feel tired, you should take a rest. _________________________________

Step 02
뜻 알기

since에는 다음과 같은 여러 가지의 뜻이 있습니다.

❶ ～한 때부터 (지금까지), ～한 이래 **conj** from the time when ~ till now
　～때부터 (지금까지), ～이래 **prep** from the time of

❷ ～이므로, ～인 까닭에 **conj** because; seeing that

▷ 한 걸음 더 **since then** 그때 이래, 그때부터

Step 03
연습문제

다음 문장의 since에 해당되는 뜻을 **Step 02** **의 ❶～❷에서 고르세요.** (해답은 456쪽)

1. I haven't seen her since last Friday. (　　　)
2. Since you are going, I will go, too. (　　　)
3. It has been raining since last night. (　　　)
4. The gas company turned your heat off since you didn't pay your bill. (　　　)

Step 04
영작연습

다음 문장을 주어진 부분을 이용하여 영어로 옮기세요. (해답은 456쪽)

1. 그녀는 지난 금요일부터 아무것도 먹지 않았다. [anything, last Friday]

____

2. 돈이 없기 때문에 우리는 그것을 살 수 없다. [money, buy]

____

:: 1. 나는 그를 어릴 때부터 계속 알고 있다. 2. 너는 피곤하니까 쉬어야 한다.

 **195 heart** [hɑːrt]

Step 01 해석연습

다음 문장을 heart에 유의하여 해석해 보세요. (해석은 이 페이지의 하단부에 있음)

1. When a man's heart stops beating, he dies. _________________________

2. He is a man with a kind heart. _________________________

3. Her necklace is shaped like a heart. _________________________

4. She lives in the heart of the city. _________________________

Step 02 뜻 알기

heart에는 다음과 같은 여러 가지의 뜻이 있습니다.

❶ 심장 ⓝ the organ which pumps blood through the body

❷ 마음, 감정, 인정 ⓝ the part of the body where one's feelings of love, conscience etc existed; mind

❸ 심장 모양의 것, 하트형 ⓝ something shaped like the human heart

❹ 중심부, 복판, 중앙 ⓝ the central part

> 한 걸음 더 **Let's get to the <u>heart</u> of the matter.** 문제의 핵심을 파악합시다. → 핵심, 요점(=essential part; core)
> **He was beginning to lose <u>heart</u>.** 그는 용기를 잃기 시작했다. → 용기, 열의(=courage; enthusiasm)
> **heart attack** 심장마비 **heartbeat** 심장의 고동, 심장박동 **learn by heart** 암기하다 **heart and soul** 전적으로, 열심히

Step 03 연습문제

다음 문장의 heart에 해당되는 뜻을 Step 02 의 ❶~❹에서 고르세요. (해답은 456쪽)

1. The girl has a kind heart. (   )
2. The building is in the heart of New York. (   )
3. His heart began to beat fast. (   )
4. She drew a big red heart. (   )
5. They bombed the heart of the city. (   )
6. He has a jack of hearts in his hand. (   )
7. Her heart was moved at the sight. (   )
8. She has a weak heart and must not exercise too hard. (   )

Step 04 영작연습

다음 문장을 주어진 부분을 이용하여 영어로 옮기세요. (해답은 456쪽)

1. 너무 많은 기름진 음식들을 먹는 것은 심장에 좋지 않다. [fatty food, bad]

____

2. 그녀는 자신이 틀렸다는 것을 마음속으로는 알고 있었다. [knew, wrong]

____

3. Jane은 나에게 하트가 그려진 발렌타인 카드를 보내왔다. [sent, Valentine card]

____

4. 그 공원은 도시의 중심부에 있다. [park, city]

____

⁘ 1. 사람의 심장이 뛰기를 멈추면 죽는다. 2. 그는 친절한 마음씨를 가진 사람이다. 3. 그녀의 목걸이는 하트형이다. 4. 그녀는 도시의 중심부에 산다.

A. 다음 뜻에 해당되는 단어를 보기에서 찾아 적으세요.

보기	share operation lean since heart

01. ______________ the part of the body where one's feelings of love, conscience etc existed; mind
02. ______________ a planned military or police action, especially one that involves a lot of people
03. ______________ to have or use something in common; to divide among a number of people
04. ______________ because; seeing that
05. ______________ the act of surgically cutting a part of the body in order to cure disease
06. ______________ to slope or bend from an upright position
07. ______________ the organ which pumps blood through the body
08. ______________ one of the equal proportions into which a company's capital stock is divided
09. ______________ (of a person or animal) thin
10. ______________ from the time when ~ till now
11. ______________ the central part
12. ______________ an action; a way or process of working something
13. ______________ to rest in a sloping position for support
14. ______________ something shaped like the human heart
15. ______________ a part of something belonging to one individual

B. 다음 빈칸에 가장 알맞은 단어를 보기에서 찾아 적으세요.

보기	share(s) operation lean since heart

01. Ten years have passed (　　　　) she died.
02. He broke his leg and had an (　　　　).
03. A (　　　　) is a symbol of love.
04. Don't (　　　　) your elbows on the table.
05. Her song warmed his (　　　　).
06. The coalition forces continue the (　　　　) in Iraq.
07. She looks (　　　　) and pale.
08. He will (　　　　) his room with his friend.
09. (　　　　) I have no money, I can't buy that car.
10. He lives in the (　　　　) of Seoul.
11. We each paid our (　　　　) of the bill.
12. Your (　　　　) beats all of the time.
13. The lamppost might (　　　　) across the road.
14. She has 3,000 (　　　　) in the steel company.
15. The (　　　　) of this machine is very simple.

다음 문장을 굵게 처리된 단어에 유의하여 해석해 보세요.

01. But now the tools of the digital age give us a way to easily get, **share**, and act on information in new ways. [2003년–홀수형 30번]

➡ ____

02. However, sometimes he can't pay his **share** of the rent on time because he has spent too much money on a new phone or on his phone bill. [2006년–홀수형 17번]

➡ ____

03. He formed his own on-line company: Daedonggang Group. Soon all the yangban nobles bought **shares**, and Kim son-dal became rich. [2000년–홀수형 53번]

➡ ____

04. Have you heard the saying: "A problem **shared** is a problem halved"? [1998년–홀수형 39번]

➡ ____

05. Industrial diamonds are crushed and powdered, and then used in many grinding and polishing **operations**. [2007년–홀수형 30번]

➡ ____

06. "**Operation** Tigher" was a campaign in 1972 for the survival of the tiger. [1996년–홀수형 36번]

➡ ____

07. One day, his boss offered Steve a new job supervising the company's whole warehouse **operation**. [1998년–홀수형 22번]

➡ ____

08. Today, many people are suffering because there isn't enough blood for medical **operations**. [2009년–홀수형 3번]

➡ ____

09. Don't **lean** back and announce, "I'm through," when others are not finished. [2003년–홀수형 41번]

➡ ____

10. Finally, he had no choice but to **lean** toward his partner and whisper out of the corner of his mouth, "Where are we?" [2002년–홀수형 22번]

➡ ____

11. **Since** we moved into this house, Jack and I have watched you grow from the little girl next door into a confident young woman. [2003년–홀수형 18번]

➡ ____

12. **Since** people generally like what they are good at, I propose that our children focus on areas in which they excel. [2006년–홀수형 46–48번]

➡ ____

13. The car door closed, and her **heart** beat faster as the footsteps passed the window. [2006번–홀수형 33번]

➡ ____

14. If the government doesn't support the performing arts, this country will lose much of the **heart** and soul of its people. [2003년–홀수형 34번]

➡ ____

196 tongue [tʌŋ]

Step 01
해석연습

다음 문장을 tongue에 유의하여 해석해 보세요. (해석은 이 페이지의 하단부에 있음)

1. The dog is hanging out its tongue. _______________________________

2. English is his mother tongue. _______________________________

Step 02
뜻 알기

tongue에는 다음과 같은 여러 가지의 뜻이 있습니다.

❶ 혀 n the soft, movable organ in the mouth used for tasting, eating and speaking

❷ 언어 n a language

한 걸음 더 **mother tongue** 모국어 (=native tongue) **foreign tongue** 외국어
tongue-tied ① 혀가 짧은, 혀짤배기의 ② (놀라거나 부끄러워서) 말을 못 하는, 말문이 막힌
hold one's tongue 하고 싶은 말을 참다; 잠자코 있다 **watch one's tongue** 말을 조심해서 하다
on the tip one's tongue 말이 혀끝에서 뱅뱅 돌며 생각이 안 나는

Step 03
연습문제

다음 문장의 tongue에 해당되는 뜻을 **Step 02** 의 ❶~❷에서 고르세요. (해답은 457쪽)

1. Don't put your tongue out at me. (   )

2. Spanish is her mother tongue. (   )

3. The doctor looked at her tongue. (   )

4. Jeff speaks in his own tongue when he is excited. (   )

Step 04
영작연습

다음 문장을 주어진 부분을 이용하여 영어로 옮기세요. (해답은 457쪽)

1. 의사는 그에게 혀를 내밀라고 했다. [asked, put out]

____

2. 그녀는 외국어로 말한다. [speaks, foreign]

____

:: 1. 그 개는 혀를 축 늘어뜨리고 있다. 2. 영어는 그의 모국어다.

197 tear (뜻) ❶❷ [tɛər] ❸ [tiər]

Step 01 해석연습

다음 문장을 tear에 유의하여 해석해 보세요. (해석은 이 페이지의 하단부에 있음)

1. This paper is very old and tears easily. ___________________________

2. He had a big tear in his shirt. ___________________________

3. The girl's eyes were filled with tears. ___________________________

Step 02 뜻 알기

tear에는 다음과 같은 여러 가지의 뜻이 있습니다.

❶ ~을 찢다, 째다; 찢어지다 **v** to break (paper, cloth, etc) by pulling it apart; to become torn

❷ 찢어진 곳, 째진 틈, 터진 자리 **n** a cut or hole made by tearing

❸ 눈물 **n** a drop of salty water coming from the eye

> 한 걸음 더 **tear** [tɛər] - **tore** [tɔːr] - **torn** [tɔːrn]
> **tear gas** 최루가스 **teardrop** 눈물방울 **tearful** 눈물어린, 눈물에 젖은, 슬픈 **burst into tears** 울음을 터뜨리다
> **shed tears** 눈물을 흘리다 **tear down** 부수다, 파괴하다 **tear into pieces** 갈기갈기 찢다

Step 03 연습문제

다음 문장의 tear에 해당되는 뜻을 **Step 02** 의 ❶~❸에서 고르세요. (해답은 457쪽)

1. This paper tears easily. (   )
2. Tears just rolled down her face. (   )
3. She had a tear in her skirt. (   )
4. They all laughed till tears came. (   )
5. He will tear the newspaper into pieces. (   )
6. I had a big tear in my dress. (   )

Step 04 영작연습

다음 문장을 주어진 부분을 이용하여 영어로 옮기세요. (해답은 457쪽)

1. 그 개는 나의 바지를 찢으려고 했다. [tried, trousers]

____

2. 나의 옷에 작은 째진 곳이 있었다. [small, dress]

____

3. 그녀는 그 슬픈 소식을 듣고 눈물을 흘렸다. [shed, sad]

____

:: 1. 이 종이는 오래되어서 잘 찢어진다. 2. 그의 셔츠는 크게 찢어져 있었다. 3. 그 소녀의 눈에는 눈물이 가득했다.

198 nature [néitʃər]

Step 01
해석연습

다음 문장을 nature에 유의하여 해석해 보세요. (해석은 이 페이지의 하단부에 있음)

1. Nature teaches us many lessons. ______________________________
2. Chemists study the nature of gases. ______________________________
3. Books of this nature do not interest her. ______________________________

Step 02
뜻 알기

nature에는 다음과 같은 여러 가지의 뜻이 있습니다.

❶ 자연; 자연계 🅝 everything in the physical world that is not controlled by humans, such as the sky, trees, plants, animals, rivers, mountains, etc

❷ (사람의) 본성, 성질; (사물의) 특질 🅝 the qualities which naturally belong to a person or thing

❸ 종류, 유형 🅝 a kind; a type; a sort

> 한 걸음 더 **animal nature** 동물성 **human nature** 인간성 **nature reserve** 자연보호구역
> **by nature** 본래, 본질상, 날 때부터, 선천적으로 **in the nature of** ~한 성질[성격]의, ~의 성질을 띤

Step 03
연습문제

다음 문장의 nature에 해당되는 뜻을 Step 02 의 ❶~❸에서 고르세요. (해답은 457쪽)

1. Cats and dogs have different natures. (　　)
2. Movies of this nature do not interest me. (　　)
3. Julie has a kind nature. (　　)
4. Nothing is more perfect than nature. (　　)
5. I cannot accept money of that nature. (　　)
6. The poet gets inspiration from nature. (　　)

Step 04
영작연습

다음 문장을 주어진 부분을 이용하여 영어로 옮기세요. (해답은 457쪽)

1. 지진은 자연의 파괴적인 힘을 보여 준다. [earthquakes, destructive]

____

2. 나의 아버지께서는 관대한 성품을 지니고 계신다. [has, generous]

____

3. 나는 그런 종류의 그림에 관심이 없다. [pictures, interest]

____

:: 1. 자연은 우리에게 많은 교훈을 가르쳐 준다. 2. 화학자들은 가스의 성질을 연구한다. 3. 그녀는 이런 종류의 책들에 관심이 없다.

199 associate [əsóuʃièit]

Step 01
해석연습

다음 문장을 associate에 유의하여 해석해 보세요. (해석은 이 페이지의 하단부에 있음)

1. We associate Egypt with the Pyramids. ________________________
2. Never associate with dishonest people. ________________________
3. She has been my associate for a long time. ________________________

Step 02
뜻 알기

associate에는 다음과 같은 여러 가지의 뜻이 있습니다.

❶ 연상하다, 관련지어 생각하다 v to connect (things) in the mind

❷ 교제하다; 제휴하다 v to join (with someone) in friendship or work; to cooperate

❸ 동료, 동업자, 제휴자 n a colleague or partner; a companion

> 한 걸음 더 **She is an <u>associate</u> professor in that university.** 그녀는 그 대학의 부교수이다.
> → 준(準)..., 부(副)... (=having a lower position or rank)
> **an associate professor** 부교수 **an associate member** 준회원 **association** ① 연상 ② 교제, 제휴 ③ 협회
> **in association with** ① ~와 협동[공동]으로 ② ~에 관련하여

Step 03
연습문제

다음 문장의 associate에 해당되는 뜻을 Step 02 의 ❶~❸에서 고르세요. (해답은 457쪽)

1. We associate Paris with the Eiffel Tower. (   )
2. He has been my associate for a long time. (   )
3. We associated him with us in the business. (   )
4. My associates and I work for the city government. (   )
5. He always associates the smell of cigar with his uncle. (   )
6. You must not associate with bad companions. (   )

Step 04
영작연습

다음 문장을 주어진 부분을 이용하여 영어로 옮기세요. (해답은 457쪽)

1. 많은 사람들은 전쟁 하면 죽음과 굶주림을 연상한다. [war, hunger]

____

2. 그녀는 교회에서 이웃들과 교제한다. [neighbors, church]

____

3. 나의 동료들과 나는 국립박물관에서 근무한다. [work, National Museum]

____

∷ 1. 우리는 이집트 하면 피라미드를 연상한다. 2. 부정직한 사람들과 사귀지 마라. 3. 그녀는 오래전부터 내 동료이다.

200 **count** [kaunt]

Step 01 해석연습

다음 문장을 count에 유의하여 해석해 보세요. (해석은 이 페이지의 하단부에 있음)

1. Don't forget to count your change. _______________________________

2. First impressions really do count. _______________________________

3. A count's wife is a countess. _______________________________

4. I count myself lucky. _______________________________

Step 02 뜻 알기

count에는 다음과 같은 여러 가지의 뜻이 있습니다.

❶ 수를 세다; 계산[합계]하다; ~을 세다 Ⅴ to say numbers in order; to add up; to calculate

❷ 중요하다; 가치가 있다 Ⅴ to be of importance; to be of value; to matter

❸ (유럽 귀족의 작위) 백작 ⋒ a European nobleman ranked above baron

❹ ~라고 생각하다, ~라고 간주하다 Ⅴ to consider; to think

> 한 걸음 더 **countess** 백작부인 **countable** 셀 수 있는 **count for much** 중요하다 **count for little[nothing]** 중요치 않다

Step 03 연습문제

다음 문장의 count에 해당되는 뜻을 Step 02 의 ❶~❹에서 고르세요. (해답은 457쪽)

1. Everything you do counts for much. (　　　)
2. The little girl can count from one to ten. (　　　)
3. I count him as one of my best friends. (　　　)
4. Having money counts because we can't do much without it. (　　　)
5. The count's daughter has a warm heart. (　　　)
6. She counts that he will come. (　　　)
7. I will count the tickets one by one. (　　　)
8. Dukes and counts were members of the aristocracy. (　　　)

Step 04 영작연습

다음 문장을 주어진 부분을 이용하여 영어로 옮기세요. (해답은 457쪽)

1. 그녀는 자신의 옷을 한 벌씩 셌다. [suits, one by one]

____

2. 요즘에는 정직이 무가치한 것처럼 보인다. [honesty, seem]

____

3. 그 백작은 넓은 성에서 살았다. [lived, castle]

____

4. 그는 그렇게 하는 것이 어리석다고 생각한다. [foolish, so]

____

∷ 1. 잔돈 세는 것을 잊지 마라. 2. 첫인상은 정말로 중요하다. 3. 백작의 아내는 백작부인이다. 4. 나는 내 자신이 운이 좋다고 생각한다.

A. 다음 뜻에 해당되는 단어를 보기에서 찾아 적으세요.

보기	tongue	tear	nature	associate	count

01. _____________ to connect (things) in the mind
02. _____________ to break (paper, cloth, etc) by pulling it apart; to become torn
03. _____________ the soft, movable organ in the mouth used for tasting, eating and speaking
04. _____________ a drop of salty water coming from the eye
05. _____________ to say numbers in order; to add up; to calculate
06. _____________ to join (with someone) in friendship or work; to cooperate
07. _____________ a European nobleman ranked above baron
08. _____________ a cut or hole made by tearing
09. _____________ everything in the physical world that is not controlled by humans, such as the sky, trees, plants, animals, rivers, mountains, etc
10. _____________ to consider; to think
11. _____________ a colleague or partner; a companion
12. _____________ the qualities which naturally belong to a person or thing
13. _____________ a language
14. _____________ a kind; a type; a sort
15. _____________ to be of importance; to be of value; to matter

B. 다음 빈칸에 가장 알맞은 단어를 보기에서 찾아 적으세요.

보기	tongue	tear(s)	nature	associate	count

01. She drank hot tea and burned her (   ).
02. We (   ) with our neighbors at church.
03. It is the (   ) of a dog to bark.
04. I (   ) Egypt with the Pyramids.
05. He has a (   ) in his shirt.
06. I don't collect stamps of that (   ).
07. The man speaks in a foreign (   ).
08. Be careful you don't (   ) your dress on that nail.
09. Try to (   ) to ten before you lose your temper.
10. Mr. Green has been my (   ) since 1985.
11. All of us shed (   ) when he left.
12. The (   ) owns a large estate here.
13. Her promises don't (   ) for much.
14. Hurricanes show the destructive power of (   ).
15. I (   ) myself happy.

다음 문장을 굵게 처리된 단어에 유의하여 해석해 보세요.

01. Then he went away, leaving the man standing in the street with his **tongue** hanging out.... [1995년-홀수형 32번]

→ ____

02. Instead of focusing on immigrants' disabilities in English, why not encourage them to maintain their abilities in their mother **tongues** while they learn English? [2006년-홀수형 25]

→ ____

03. I didn't want to cry, but **tears** started falling down my cheeks, and there was nothing I could do to stop them. [2005년-홀수형 49-50번]

→ ____

04. It's the **nature** of water to run downhill. [2002년-홀수형 27번]

→ ____

05. If we observe **nature** closely, however, we discover that there is a constant tension between change and balance. [2004년-홀수형 43번]

→ ____

06. Since the beginning of time, the mysterious **nature** of dreaming has led people to believe that dreams were messages from the other world. [2012년-홀수형 49-50번]

→ ____

07. Laughing reduces hormones **associated** with stress response. [2012년-홀수형 6번]

→ ____

08. Then she asked me to **count** alone and I did. [1994년-2차 32번]

→ ____

09. Clearly, modern societies are facing a major change into a new economic system where human resourcefulness **counts** far more than natural resources. [1996년-홀수형 19번]

→ ____

10. The day's lesson was on how to **count**. [1999년-홀수형 23번]

→ ____

11. However, it is not necessary for him to please everyone. If his facts are true, that is all that **counts**. [1997년-홀수형 21번]

→ ____

DAY 21

Character is long-standing habit.
성격은 오래 간직해 온 버릇이다.

201 engagement [ingéidʒmənt / en–]

Group 41

Step 01 해석연습

다음 문장을 engagement에 유의하여 해석해 보세요. (해석은 이 페이지의 하단부에 있음)

1. I have a dinner engagement with her. ______________________________

2. We will announce our engagement next week. ______________________________

3. The admiral tried to bring out an engagement. ______________________________

Step 02 뜻 알기

engagement에는 다음과 같은 여러 가지의 뜻이 있습니다.

❶ (회합 따위의) 약속 ⓝ an arrangement to meet someone or do something at a fixed time

❷ 약혼 ⓝ an agreement to marry

❸ (군사) 교전, 전투 ⓝ a battle between armies, navies, etc

> 한 걸음 더 **After six months' engagement** he quit the job. 6개월 종사한 후에 그는 그 일을 그만두었다.
> → 고용, 근무(=employment)

an engagement ring 약혼반지 **a land[naval] engagement** 육상(해상)전투 **make an engagement** 약혼하다, 약속하다

Step 03 연습문제

다음 문장의 engagement에 해당되는 뜻을 Step 02 의 ❶~❸에서 고르세요. (해답은 457쪽)

1. I have a lot of engagements for next week. (　　)

2. There was a naval engagement this morning. (　　)

3. Do you have any engagements this evening? (　　)

4. Andrew put an engagement ring on Diana's finger. (　　)

5. That action was a military engagement. (　　)

6. They will announce their engagement next week. (　　)

Step 04 영작연습

다음 문장을 주어진 부분을 이용하여 영어로 옮기세요. (해답은 457쪽)

1. 그는 다음 주에 많은 약속이 있다. [numerous, next week]

____

2. 그들의 약혼은 신문에 발표되었다. [announced, newspapers]

____

3. 우리 군은 어제 적과의 교전을 가졌다. [our army, enemy]

____

:: 1. 나는 그녀와 저녁 약속이 있다. 2. 우리는 우리의 약혼을 다음 주에 발표할 것이다. 3. 함대사령관(제독)은 교전을 일으키려고 시도했다.

202 character [kǽriktər]

Step 01 해석연습

다음 문장을 character에 유의하여 해석해 보세요. (해석은 이 페이지의 하단부에 있음)

1. He is a man of good character. ________________________

2. Jane is one of the characters in this book. ________________________

3. What do these Chinese characters stand for? ________________________

Step 02 뜻 알기

character에는 다음과 같은 여러 가지의 뜻이 있습니다.

❶ 성격, 특성, 성질 🄝 qualities that make any person or thing different from others

❷ (연극, 소설, 영화의) 인물, 배역 🄝 a person in a play, novel, or film

❸ 문자, 기호 🄝 a single letter or mark used in writing or printing

> 한 걸음 더 **He has gained the <u>character</u> of a miser.** 그는 구두쇠라는 평판을 얻었다.
> → 평판, 명성(=reputation)
> **the national character** 국민성 **musical characters** (음악의) 악보 **a Chinese character** 한자
> **a well-known character** 저명인사, 명사 **lose one's character** 명성을 잃다 **regain one's character** 명성을 회복하다

Step 03 연습문제

다음 문장의 character에 해당되는 뜻을 **Step 02** 의 ❶～❸에서 고르세요. (해답은 457쪽)

1. I can't write any Chinese characters. (　　)
2. Liquids are different from gases in character. (　　)
3. We can tell a man's character from his hand writing. (　　)
4. There are only two characters in this play. (　　)
5. "Love" is a word with four characters. (　　)
6. I don't like the main character in that play. (　　)

Step 04 영작연습

다음 문장을 주어진 부분을 이용하여 영어로 옮기세요. (해답은 457쪽)

1. 당신은 그의 완고한 성격을 고려해야 한다. [consider, obstionate]

____

2. 그는 그 영화에서 어린왕자 역할을 했다. [played, film]

____

3. 내 타자기의 문자 몇 개가 고장 났다. [typewriter, broken]

____

∷ 1. 그는 성격이 좋은 사람이다. 2. Jane은 이 책의 등장인물 중 하나이다. 3. 이 한자는 무슨 뜻이냐?

Step 01
해석연습

다음 문장을 issue에 유의하여 해석해 보세요. (해석은 이 페이지의 하단부에 있음)

1. We issue our school paper every month. _______________________________

2. Have you seen the latest issue of this magazine? _______________________

3. This is a main issue in this discussion. _______________________________

Step 02
뜻 알기

issue에는 다음과 같은 여러 가지의 뜻이 있습니다.

❶ 발행하다, 배포하다 **v** to give or provide in a formal or official way
발행, 배포 **n** the act of publishing or distributing

❷ (잡지, 신문의) 발행물, ~호 **n** a magazine or newspaper printed for a particular day, week, or month

❸ 논쟁점, 주제, 문제 **n** a point or subject of argument, discussion, etc

> 한 걸음 더 **Blood issues from a cut.** 벤 상처에서 피가 나온다.
> → 흘러나오다, 유출하다(=go or come out; flow out)
> **at issue** 논쟁 중 **political issue** 정치문제 **the issue of money** 화폐 발행 **the recent issue** (신문, 잡지 등의) 최신호
> **raise a new issue** 새로운 문제를 제기하다

Step 03
연습문제

다음 문장의 issue에 해당되는 뜻을 **Step 02** 의 ❶~❸에서 고르세요. (해답은 457쪽)

1. I'm looking for the recent issue of this magazine. (   )

2. We issue our school paper every two weeks. (   )

3. She raised a new issue during the discussion. (   )

4. This is the latest issue of Reader's Digest. (   )

5. The officer will issue you a new passport. (   )

6. Unemployment was the issue of today's discussion. (   )

Step 04
영작연습

다음 문장을 주어진 부분을 이용하여 영어로 옮기세요. (해답은 457쪽)

1. 우표 수집가들은 새 우표를 발행일에 사기를 원한다. [stamp collectors, day]

____

2. 일요일 자 신문에는 천연색 만화가 실려 있다. [has, comics on color]

____

3. 오늘 우리가 토론할 주제는 대기 오염이다. [discussing, air pollution]

____

:: 1. 우리는 학교 신문을 매월 발행한다. 2. 당신은 이 잡지의 최근 호를 본 적이 있습니까? 3. 이것이 이번 토론의 중요한 쟁점이다.

204 **physical** [fízikəl]

Step 01
해석연습

다음 문장을 physical에 유의하여 해석해 보세요. (해석은 이 페이지의 하단부에 있음)

1. I have to take a physical examination today. ___________________________
2. We belong to the physical world. ___________________________
3. It is a physical impossibility to be in two places at once. ___________________________

Step 02
뜻 알기

physical에는 다음과 같은 여러 가지의 뜻이 있습니다.

❶ 신체의, 육체의 ⓐ related to the body

❷ 물질의 ⓐ related to matter and material things

❸ 자연법칙의, 물리적인; 물리학의 ⓐ related to the laws of nature; related to physics

한 걸음 더 **physics** 물리학 **physical education** 체육 **physician** 내과의사 cf. surgeon 외과의사 **physicist** 물리학자
physical changes 물리적 변화 **physical science** 자연과학 **physical examination** 신체검사 **a physical beauty** 육체미
physically ① 육체적으로 ② 물질적으로 ③ 물리(학)적으로

Step 03
연습문제

다음 문장의 physical에 해당되는 뜻을 **Step 02** 의 ❶～❸에서 고르세요. (해답은 458쪽)

1. He overcame his physical handicap. (   )
2. To prove his murder we need physical evidence. (   )
3. It is a physical impossibility for a man to fly like a bird. (   )
4. His physical strength is fading away. (   )
5. You must take two courses in the physical science. (   )
6. The physical damage of the war is serious. (   )

Step 04
영작연습

다음 문장을 주어진 부분을 이용하여 영어로 옮기세요. (해답은 458쪽)

1. 달리기는 신체운동의 한 형태이다. [form, exercise]

____

2. 물질세계는 정신세계와 다르다. [different, spiritual]

____

3. 그는 대학에서 물리화학을 전공했다. [majored in, chemistry]

____

:: 1. 나는 오늘 신체검사를 받아야 한다. 2. 우리는 물질세계에 속해 있다. 3. 동시에 두 장소에 존재하는 것은 물리학적으로 불가능하다.

 **205 bar** [bɑːr]

다음 문장을 bar에 유의하여 해석해 보세요. (해석은 이 페이지의 하단부에 있음)

1. The child loves eating candy bars. ______________________________
2. He will visit his favorite bar tonight. ______________________________
3. Swimming is barred here. ______________________________

bar에는 다음과 같은 여러 가지의 뜻이 있습니다.

❶ 막대, 막대 모양의 것; 빗장 **n** a long-shaped piece of hard, stiff material

❷ 술집, 카운터, 식당 **n** a place or counter where alcoholic drinks or food are served

❸ ~을 금지하다, 막다 **v** not to allow; to prohibit; to prevent from doing something

> 한 걸음 더 **The prisoner at the <u>bar</u> looked extremely tired.** 피고석에 있는 죄수는 극도로 피곤해 보였다.
> → 법정 또는 피고석(=a law court or the place in a law court where a prisoner stands)
> **He went to the <u>bar</u>.** 그는 변호사가 되었다. → 변호사 단체(=the professional organization of lawyers)
> **His carelessness was a <u>bar</u> to his promotion.** 그의 부주의함이 승진의 장애물이었다. → 장애물(=obstacle)
> **He played a few <u>bars</u>.** 그는 몇 소절을 연주했다. → 음악의 소절(=a measured division in music)
> **an iron bar** 쇠막대 **a gold bar** 금괴 **bar code** 바코드(상품식별용 컴퓨터 판독기호) **the bar of a door** 문의 빗장
> **a snack bar** 스낵바(스탠드 형식의 간이식당) **bar chart** 막대그래프(=bar graph)

다음 문장의 bar에 해당되는 뜻을 **Step 02** 의 ❶~❸에서 고르세요. (해답은 458쪽)

1. Could you tell me where the bar is in this hotel? (　　　)
2. Whenever she comes here, she brings chocolate bars. (　　　)
3. Police will bar entrance to the building. (　　　)
4. The bank keeps bars of gold in its safe. (　　　)
5. Soldiers barred the road ahead. (　　　)
6. Is there a snack bar near here? (　　　)

다음 문장을 주어진 부분을 이용하여 영어로 옮기세요. (해답은 458쪽)

1. 곰은 우리의 빗장을 부수려고 애썼다. [tried, break, cage]

____

2. 그녀는 종종 퇴근 후에 술집에 들른다. [visits, after work]

____

3. 경비원이 그가 그 건물에 들어가는 것을 막았다. [security guard, entrance]

____

:: 1. 그 어린아이는 막대사탕 먹는 것을 좋아했다. 2. 그는 오늘 밤 자신의 단골 술집에 들를 것이다. 3. 이곳에서는 수영이 금지되어 있다.

A. 다음 뜻에 해당되는 단어를 보기에서 찾아 적으세요.

보기	engagement character issue physical bar

01. ______________ an arrangement to meet someone or do something at a fixed time
02. ______________ qualities that make any person or thing different from others
03. ______________ a magazine or newspaper printed for a particular day, week, or month
04. ______________ related to the laws of nature; related to physics
05. ______________ not to allow; to prohibit; to prevent from doing something
06. ______________ a person in a play, novel, or film
07. ______________ a point or subject of argument, discussion, etc
08. ______________ an agreement to marry
09. ______________ related to matter and material things
10. ______________ to give or provide in a formal or official way
11. ______________ a long-shaped piece of hard, stiff material
12. ______________ related to the body
13. ______________ a battle between armies, navies, etc
14. ______________ a single letter or mark used in writing or printing
15. ______________ a place or counter where alcoholic drinks or food are served

B. 다음 빈칸에 가장 알맞은 단어를 보기에서 찾아 적으세요.

보기	engagement character(s) issue physical bar(s)

01. My father was a man of good (   ).
02. Please (   ) me a new library card.
03. The tiger broke the (   ) of the cage.
04. There isn't enough (   ) evidence to prove him guilty.
05. There was an (   ) between two armies yesterday.
06. Jae-ho will act the leading (   ) in the play.
07. He visited his favorite (   ) last night.
08. There are (   ) limits to how fast we can travel.
09. That isn't a main (   ) in this discussion.
10. He has a lunch (   ) with her.
11. You'd better do more (   ) exercise.
12. Soldiers will (   ) the road to the city.
13. "Freedom" is a word with seven (   ).
14. He bought an (   ) ring for his fiancee.
15. This is the New Year's (   ) of this magazine.

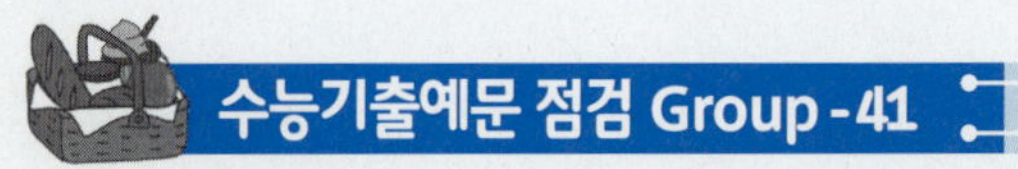

해답은 458쪽

다음 문장을 굵게 처리된 단어에 유의하여 해석해 보세요.

01. To awaken the active **engagement** of your whole body in drawing, try the following: Begin by drawing small circles in space with each of your fingers. [2006년–홀수형 41번]

→ _______________

02. At first, she wanted the role of Cinderella, the most important **character**. [2001년–홀수형 17번]

→ _______________

03. According to ancient superstitions, moles reveal a person's **character**. [2005년–홀수형 42번]

→ _______________

04. However, when we see the text, **characters**, and images on artifacts that serve other purposes, we generally interpret these marks as labels that do refer to their carriers. [2009년–홀수형 31번]

→ _______________

05. This time the bootmaker began to criticize the anatomy of one of the **characters**. [2011년–홀수형 36번]

→ _______________

06. Thus, the most important **issue** facing these countries is understanding the differences among cultures. [2002년–홀수형 46번]

→ _______________

07. In fact, police do **issue** permits to qualified hunters and advise hikers to wear bright, colorful clothing during hunting season. [2002년–홀수형 42번]

→ _______________

08. A fire chief, for example, needs to **issue** his orders with absolute clarity. [2010년–홀수형 38번]

→ _______________

09. The information from both check-ups and tests provides important insight into the patient's overall **physical** condition. [2005년–홀수형 41번]

→ _______________

10. With one technological change, cross-referencing became possible, while the **physical** space needed to house a collection of books was sharply reduced. [2008년–홀수형 25번]

→ _______________

11. In contrast, nonmaterial culture consists of human creations that are not **physical**. [1999년–홀수형 29번]

→ _______________

12. The left **bar** chart shows the costs of carrying them out, and the right bar chart shows the resulting savings during the same period. [2007년–홀수형 37번]

→ _______________

13. People brought drinks from the **bar** and gathered in groups. [2003년–홀수형 32번]

→ _______________

14. Children must be taught to perform good deeds for their own sake, not in order to receive stickers, stars, and candy **bars**. [2011년–홀수형 23번]

→ _______________

206 domestic [dəméstik]

Step 01 해석연습

다음 문장을 domestic에 유의하여 해석해 보세요. (해석은 이 페이지의 하단부에 있음)

1. Cooking and sewing are domestic tasks. _______________________________

2. This is a domestic airline. _______________________________

3. Cows, horses and sheep are domestic animals. _______________________________

Step 02 뜻 알기

domestic에는 다음과 같은 여러 가지의 뜻이 있습니다.

❶ 가정의, 가족의, 가사의　ⓐ related to the home, family or household affairs

❷ 국내의, 자국의　ⓐ related to national concerns; not foreign

❸ 길들여진, 집에서 기르는　ⓐ (of animals) not wild; tame and living with or used by people

> 한 걸음 더 **domestic affairs** 집안일, 가사 **domestic animals** 가축 **domestic airline** (항공기의) 국내선
> **domestic goods** 국산품 **domestic market** 국내시장 **domestic trade** 국내무역

Step 03 연습문제

다음 문장의 domestic에 해당되는 뜻을 Step 02 의 ❶~❸에서 고르세요. (해답은 458쪽)

1. Dogs and cats are domestic animals. (　　)

2. Her husband is good at domestic tasks. (　　)

3. Smoking is prohibited on all domestic flights. (　　)

4. A donkey is a domestic animal with long ears. (　　)

5. The couple has a happy domestic life. (　　)

6. The government has a plan to protect domestic market. (　　)

Step 04 영작연습

다음 문장을 주어진 부분을 이용하여 영어로 옮기세요. (해답은 458쪽)

1. 그녀는 꽤 많은 가정 문제를 가지고 있다.　[a lot of, troubles]

____

2. 이 잡지는 국내 소식보다 해외 소식을 더 많이 제공한다.　[provides, foreign news]

____

3. 그 농장에는 가축이 많다.　[animals, farm]

____

∷ 1. 요리와 바느질은 가정의 일이다. 2. 이 항공로는 국내선이다. 3. 소, 말, 양들은 집에서 기르는 동물이다.

207 **raise** [reiz]

Step 01 해석연습

다음 문장을 raise에 유의하여 해석해 보세요. (해석은 이 페이지의 하단부에 있음)

1. Raise your arm above your head. ________________________________

2. The farmer raises cows and pigs on the farm. ________________________________

3. We are raising money for a charity. ________________________________

Step 02 뜻 알기

raise에는 다음과 같은 여러 가지의 뜻이 있습니다.

❶ 들다, 들어 올리다; (가격, 양, 정도 등을) 올리다 Ⅴ to move or lift something to a higher position; to increase something in price, amount, degree, etc

❷ ~을 기르다, 재배하다, 키우다, 양육하다 Ⅴ to grow; to rear; to breed; to bring up

❸ (돈이나 사람 등을) 모으다, 뽑다, 편성하다 Ⅴ to collect or gather (money or people)

> 한 걸음 더 She always <u>raises</u> questions at the meeting. 그녀는 회의 때 항상 문제를 제기한다.
> → (문제 따위를) 제기하다, 일으키다(=to state a question, objection, etc; to cause)
> They will <u>raise</u> a tower. 그들은 탑을 세울 것이다. → 세우다, 건립하다(=build, construct)
> **raiser** 재배자, 사육자 **raise funds** 기금을 모으다 **raise armies** 군대를 모집하다, 모병하다 **raise a question** 문제를 제기하다
> **raise a family** 가족을 부양하다

Step 03 연습문제

다음 문장의 raise에 해당되는 뜻을 Step 02 의 ❶~❸에서 고르세요. (해답은 458쪽)

1. The girl raised her hand and waved. (   )
2. The parents raised him as a Catholic. (   )
3. We will raise money for a new scholarship. (   )
4. He raises horses on his ranch. (   )
5. The soldiers are raising their national flag. (   )
6. The king wanted to raise a vast army. (   )

Step 04 영작연습

다음 문장을 주어진 부분을 이용하여 영어로 옮기세요. (해답은 458쪽)

1. 정부는 현재 세금을 올릴 계획을 가지고 있지 않다. [taxes, at present]

____

2. 그녀는 바느질을 해서 세 아이를 키웠다. [children, sewing]

____

3. 우리 교회는 가난한 사람들을 돕기 위해 모금을 하기로 결정했다. [decided, the poor]

____

∷ 1. 팔을 머리 위로 올려라. 2. 그 농부는 농장에서 소와 돼지를 키운다. 3. 우리는 자선모금을 하고 있다.

208 figure [fígjər]

Step 01 해석연습

다음 문장을 figure에 유의하여 해석해 보세요. (해석은 이 페이지의 하단부에 있음)

1. He added up figures. _______________________________

2. Strange figures were painted on the wall. _______________________________

3. Mahatma Gandi was a famous historical figure. _______________________________

Step 02 뜻 알기

figure에는 다음과 같은 여러 가지의 뜻이 있습니다.

❶ 숫자 n a symbol representing a number

❷ 그림, 무늬, 도형, 도해 n a drawing; a design; a diagram to illustrate something

❸ (중요한) 인물, 명사 n an important person

> 한 걸음 더 **She is good at figures.** 그녀는 계산을 잘한다. → (복수로 쓰여) 계산, 셈(=calculation)
> **He bought the house at a high figure.** 그는 그 집을 높은 가격에 샀다. → 금액, 가격(=an amount of money, sum)
> **I figured she moved out.** 나는 그녀가 이사 갔다고 생각했다.
> → 생각하다, 상상하다(=to think, estimate, consider, imagine)
> **a man of figure** 명사, 지위가 있는 사람 **a man of figures** 계산을 잘하는 사람
> **figure out** ① 계산하다(=calculate) ② ~을 이해하다(=make out; understand)
> **cut[make] a fine figure** 두각을 나타내다 **be good[poor] at figures** 셈에 밝다[어둡다]

Step 03 연습문제

다음 문장의 figure에 해당되는 뜻을 **Step 02** 의 ❶~❸에서 고르세요. (해답은 458쪽)

1. The man is a mysterious figure. (   )

2. I found a six-figure telephone number. (   )

3. The boy can add up figures accurately. (   )

4. The statue has a fine figure. (   )

5. He is one of the greatest figures in history. (   )

6. The parts of a car are shown in figure 5. (   )

Step 04 영작연습

다음 문장을 주어진 부분을 이용하여 영어로 옮기세요. (해답은 458쪽)

1. 그 소년은 숫자를 정확하게 읽었다. [read, accurately]

____

2. 75쪽의 그림은 자동차 엔진이 어떻게 작동하는지를 보여 준다. [how, works]

____

3. 그는 당대의 가장 위대한 인물 중의 한 사람이었다. [greatest, of his age]

____

∷ 1. 그는 숫자들을 더했다. 2. 벽에는 이상한 그림들이 그려져 있었다. 3. 간디는 유명한 역사적 인물이었다.

209 apply [əplái]

Step 01 해석연습

다음 문장을 apply에 유의하여 해석해 보세요. (해석은 이 페이지의 하단부에 있음)

1. He applied a match to the candle. ___________________________________

2. He applied the theory to the case. ___________________________________

3. I will apply for a visa to travel abroad. ___________________________________

Step 02 뜻 알기

apply에는 다음과 같은 여러 가지의 뜻이 있습니다.

❶ (약 따위를) 바르다, 붙이다; (물건을) 대다 Ⓥ to put something on or against something else

❷ 적용하다, 응용하다 Ⓥ to use something such as a method, idea, or law in a particular situation, case, or process

❸ 지원하다, 신청하다 Ⓥ to make a formal request for something such as a job, place, visa, etc

> 한 걸음 더 **This rule does not <u>apply</u> to children.** 이 규칙은 어린이들에게는 해당되지 않는다.
> → 적합하다, 해당되다(=fit; concern; have a connection)
> **She <u>applied</u> herself to her research.** 그녀는 자신의 연구에 전념했다.
> → (재귀대명사와 함께 쓰여) ~에 전념하다(=to work hard with a lot of attention or energy)
> **applicable** 응용(적용)할 수 있는 **applicant** 지원자, 신청자 **application** ① 적용, 응용 ② 지원, 신청 ③ 붙임, 바름

Step 03 연습문제

다음 문장의 apply에 해당되는 뜻을 Step 02 의 ❶~❸에서 고르세요. (해답은 458쪽)

1. He applied what he had learned to the experience. (   )
2. You may apply in person or by letter. (   )
3. She applied a cream evenly over her skin. (   )
4. This rule cannot be applied in every case. (   )
5. He applied the medicine to the wound. (   )
6. I applied to three universities and was accepted by all of them. (   )

Step 04 영작연습

다음 문장을 주어진 부분을 이용하여 영어로 옮기세요. (해답은 458쪽)

1. 그녀는 상처에 붕대를 대었다. [bandage, wound]

____

2. 우리는 그가 발견한 것들을 이 실험에 응용할 수 있다. [findings, experiment]

____

3. 그는 그 대학교 입학을 지원할 것이다. [admisson, university]

____

∷ 1. 그는 초에 성냥불을 갖다 대었다. 2. 그는 그 경우에 그 이론을 적용했다. 3. 나는 해외여행 비자를 신청할 것이다.

210 subject [sʌ́bdʒikt]

Step 01 해석연습

다음 문장을 subject에 유의하여 해석해 보세요. (해석은 이 페이지의 하단부에 있음)

1. Her favorite subject at school was Mathematics. ______________________________

2. Let's change the subject of our conversation. ______________________________

3. What is the subject of this sentence? ______________________________

Step 02 뜻 알기

subject에는 다음과 같은 여러 가지의 뜻이 있습니다.

❶ 학과, 과목 ⓝ a course of study taught in a school, a college, etc

❷ (대화, 토론, 연구, 예술작품 등에서의) 주제, 문제, 대상(자), 피실험자 ⓝ something (to be) talked or written about or studied or treated in conversation, writing, study, painting, etc

❸ (문법) 주어 ⓝ (in grammar) the noun or pronoun governing a verb in a sentence

> 한 걸음 더 **We are loyal subjects of the Queen.** 우리는 (영국)여왕의 충실한 신하다.
> → (군주제하의) 국민, 신하(=someone who was born or live in a country that has a king or queen)
> **Ancient Rome subjected most of Europe to her rule.** 고대 로마는 유럽의 대부분을 자신의 지배하에 두었다.
> → ~을 종속(복종)시키다, 지배하에 두다(=to bring or get (a country, nation, people, etc) under control)
> * 이 경우 발음은 [səbdʒékt]
> **Everything is subject to the laws of nature.** 만물은 자연의 법칙에 지배를 받는다.
> → ~의 지배를 받는, 종속하는(=under the power of another)
> **an elective subject** 선택과목 **a required[compulsory] subject** 필수과목 **a hypnotic subject** 최면술의 실험대상자

Step 03 연습문제

다음 문장의 subject에 해당되는 뜻을 **Step 02** 의 ❶~❸에서 고르세요. (해답은 458쪽)

1. What subject does he teach? (   )

2. Don't try to change the subject of our debate. (   )

3. The word "I" is the subject in the sentence "I like English." (   )

4. She is good at all subjects, especially at biology. (   )

5. He sometimes drops the subject when he writes a sentence. (   )

6. What's the subject of the seminar? (   )

Step 04 영작연습

다음 문장을 주어진 부분을 이용하여 영어로 옮기세요. (해답은 458쪽)

1. 그는 모든 과목 중에서 영어를 가장 좋아한다. [best, subjects]

____

2. 그녀의 연구 주제는 "10대들의 흡연"이다. [study, Teenage smoking]

____

3. 문장을 쓸 때에는 주어를 빠뜨리면 안 된다. [drop, sentence]

____

A. 다음 뜻에 해당되는 단어를 보기에서 찾아 적으세요.

보기	domestic raise figure apply subject

01. ______________ a drawing; a design; a diagram to illustrate something

02. ______________ not wild; tame and living with or used by people

03. ______________ a course of study taught in a school, a college, etc

04. ______________ to grow; to rear; to breed; to bring up

05. ______________ the noun or pronoun governing a verb in a sentence

06. ______________ related to national concerns; not foreign

07. ______________ to put something on or against something else

08. ______________ to move something to a higher position; to increase something in price, degree, etc

09. ______________ a symbol representing a number

10. ______________ something (to be) talked or written about or studied or treated in conversation, writing, study, painting, etc

11. ______________ to make a formal request for something such as a job, place, visa, etc

12. ______________ related to the home, family or household affairs

13. ______________ an important person

14. ______________ to use something such as a method, idea, or law in a particular situation, case, or process

15. ______________ to collect or gather (money or people)

B. 다음 빈칸에 가장 알맞은 단어를 보기에서 찾아 적으세요.

보기	domestic raise figure apply subject

01. She will ( ) to the company for the job.

02. ( ) your hand if you know the answer.

03. A microwave oven is one the most convenient ( ) appliances.

04. J. F. Kennedy is a famous historical ( ) .

05. The ( ) of his study is "Greenhouse effect."

06. He is going to ( ) wheat next year.

07. The government took measures to promote ( ) industry.

08. The ( ) on page 32 shows a geographical map of Chile.

09. My favorite ( ) at school was chemistry.

10. The nurse will ( ) a bandage to his wound.

11. There are lots of ( ) animals on his farm.

12. His score reached double ( ).

13. We can ( ) his findings in new development.

14. The word "He" is the ( ) in the sentence "He makes her happy."

15. We decided to ( ) funds to build a new building.

다음 문장을 굵게 처리된 단어에 유의하여 해석해 보세요.

01. The **domestic** oil, natural gas, or steel industry, for example, may require protection because of its importance to national defense. [1995년-홀수형 34번]

➡ ______________________

02. When the class was over, a student **raised** his hand and asked. [1994년-1차 32번]

➡ ______________________

03. But a few minutes later I **raised** the point again, with growing impatience. [1996년-홀수형 26번]

➡ ______________________

04. Every mother and father wants to **raise** a child with a strong moral character. [2007년-홀수형 39번]

➡ ______________________

05. Jim **raised** over one hundred million dollars to provide relief for the drought victims in Africa. [1995년-홀수형 30번]

➡ ______________________

06. By competing with others in sports, for example, we can **raise** our level of athletic performance. [1999년-홀수형 42번]

➡ ______________________

07. This **figure** was only $1 million less than what the movie Fishermen earned. [2001년-홀수형 19번]

➡ ______________________

08. If they have to spend time **figuring** out what the writer means, they'll get impatient. [1994년-1차 20번]

➡ ______________________

09. In that case, you must **figure** out what the sale price is. [2002년-홀수형 44번]

➡ ______________________

10. People, therefore, have lost interest in modern arts and have turned to sports stars and other popular **figures** to find their role models. [2003년-홀수형 44번]

➡ ______________________

11. **Figures** A and B demonstrate how dew point is measured by a dew point hygrometer. [2010년-홀수형 30번]

➡ ______________________

12. Sadly, however, we don't **apply** these rules to our family life, work or government when we become adults. [1995년-홀수형 22번]

➡ ______________________

13. We hope many of you will **apply** for this program. [2012년-홀수형 12번]

➡ ______________________

14. The only thing students should be required to do is to study a broad range of **subjects** throughout middle and high school. [2006년-홀수형 46~48번]

➡ ______________________

15. However, when **subjects** either could predict when the bursts of noise would occur or had the ability to terminate the noise with a "panic button," the negative effects disappeared. [2006년-홀수형 43번]

➡ ______________________

16. Special-interest magazines, on the other hand, deal mainly with one particular **subject**. [2001년-홀수형 33번]

➡ ______________________

Day 21

211 **volume** [váːljum / vɔ́ljuːm]

Group 43

Step 01 해석연습

다음 문장을 volume에 유의하여 해석해 보세요. (해석은 이 페이지의 하단부에 있음)

1. Our school library has over 100,000 volumes. ______________________

2. The volume of the storeroom is 90 cubic meters. ______________________

3. Please turn down the volume of the radio. ______________________

Step 02 뜻 알기

volume에는 다음과 같은 여러 가지의 뜻이 있습니다.

❶ 책, 서적, (연작, 전집 등의) 권 ⓝ a book, especially one of a set of books

❷ 양, 부피, 용적, 용량 ⓝ the amount of space occupied by a substance, liquid or gas

❸ 음량, 볼륨 ⓝ the amount of sound produced by a radio, television, etc

> 한 걸음 더 **the volume of production** 생산량 **volume two of the novel** 소설의 제2권
> **a three-volumed novel** 3권으로 된 소설(=a novel in three volumes) **in volume** 대량으로, 다량으로

Step 03 연습문제

다음 문장의 volume에 해당되는 뜻을 **Step 02** 의 ❶~❸에서 고르세요. (해답은 459쪽)

1. What is the volume of the petrol tank. (   )

2. This is a novel in three volumes. (   )

3. They need a gas tank with great volume. (   )

4. Could you turn the volume up the television? (   )

5. He has a dictionary in 3 volumes. (   )

6. How do you adjust the volume of this stereo? (   )

Step 04 영작연습

다음 문장을 주어진 부분을 이용하여 영어로 옮기세요. (해답은 459쪽)

1. 나는 10권으로 된 백과사전을 가지고 있다. [encyclopedia]

____

2. 그녀는 용량이 큰 냉장고를 사기를 원한다. [refrigerator, great]

____

3. 그 가수는 풍부한 성량을 가지고 있다. [singer voice]

____

:: 1. 우리학교 도서관은 10만 권 이상의 책을 가지고 있다. 2. 그 저장실의 용적은 90입방미터이다. 3. 라디오의 볼륨을 낮춰 주세요.

212 **state** [steit]

Step 01
해석연습

다음 문장을 state에 유의하여 해석해 보세요. (해석은 이 페이지의 하단부에 있음)

1. Please state your name, address and date of birth. ___________________________
2. Water exists in three states: solid, liquid, and gaseous. ___________________________
3. Israel is an independent state. ___________________________

Step 02
뜻 알기

state에는 다음과 같은 여러 가지의 뜻이 있습니다.

❶ 명확하게 말하다, 진술하다 ⓥ to say or announce clearly, carefully and definitely; to declare

❷ 상황, 형편, 사정 ⓝ the condition in which someone or something is at a particular time

❸ 나라, 국가 ⓝ a country considered as a political community; a nation
(미국, 호주 등의) 주(州) ⓝ a part of a country that has its own government and laws in addition to those of the country

> 한 걸음 더 **statement** ① 진술, 성명, 성명서 ② (상업) 계산서, 명세서, 사업보고서 **a joint statement** 공동성명
> **a state of affairs** 일의 사태, 형세, 상태 **a welfare state** 복지국가 **a state forest** 국유림
> **state of the art** ⓝ 최첨단 기술(수준) **state-of-the-art** ⓐ 최첨단의, 최신식의

Step 03
연습문제

다음 문장의 state에 해당되는 뜻을 **Step 02** 의 ❶~❸에서 고르세요. (해답은 459쪽)

1. The house was in a dirty state. (　　　)
2. Hawaii became the 50th state of the U.S.A in 1959. (　　　)
3. Mr. Brown will state the facts in detail. (　　　)
4. He represents the State of California in the Senate. (　　　)
5. My father is in a poor state of health. (　　　)
6. The witness stated that he had seen the accused. (　　　)

Step 04
영작연습

다음 문장을 주어진 부분을 이용하여 영어로 옮기세요. (해답은 459쪽)

1. 그는 그 계획에 대한 솔직한 의견을 말했다. [frank opinion]

____

2. 그의 사업형편은 나빠지고 있다. [getting worse]

____

3. 미합중국은 50개의 주로 구성되어 있다. [is made up of]

____

⁘ 1. 너의 이름, 주소와 생년월일을 말해라. 2. 물은 고체, 액체, 기체의 세 가지 형태로 존재한다. 3. 이스라엘은 독립국가다.

213 object   n [ábdʒikt, –dʒekt / ɔ́b–]   v [əbdʒékt]

Step 01 해석연습   다음 문장을 object에 유의하여 해석해 보세요. (해석은 이 페이지의 하단부에 있음)

1. Can you tell me the name of this object? ________________________
2. What is the object of your life? ________________________
3. I objected to her absurd suggestion. ________________________

Step 02 뜻 알기   object에는 다음과 같은 여러 가지의 뜻이 있습니다.

❶ 물체, 사물, 물건   n a thing that can be seen or touched; a material thing

❷ 목표, 목적   n an aim or intention; a goal, a purpose; an end

❸ 싫어하다, 반대하다, ~에 이의를 제기하다   v to feel or express dislike or disapproval; to protest

> 한 걸음 더 **He is an object of hatred.** 그는 증오의 대상이다.
> → 감정, 관심의 대상(=a person or thing to which people direct their feeling, thought, or action)
> **The word "her" is the object in the sentence "I like her."** I like her.의 문장에서 her이 목적어이다.
> → (문법) 목적어(=the focus of a verb's action)
> **an object of study** 연구의 목적 **an object of love** 사랑의 대상 **objection** 반대, 이의
> **object to + (동)명사** ~에 반대하다, 이의를 제기하다

Step 03 연습문제   다음 문장의 object에 해당되는 뜻을 **Step 02** 의 ❶~❸에서 고르세요. (해답은 459쪽)

1. This object is made of metal. (   )
2. The object of this research is to study green energy use. (   )
3. There are various objects on the table. (   )
4. He will object to her plan. (   )
5. She worked hard with the object of earning fame. (   )
6. We will go there if you don't object. (   )

Step 04 영작연습   다음 문장을 주어진 부분을 이용하여 영어로 옮기세요. (해답은 459쪽)

1. 그는 하늘에 있는 이상한 물체를 보았다. [strange, sky]

____

2. 그녀의 인생의 주된 목적은 유명해지는 것이었다. [main, famous]

____

3. 그는 자신이 어린애 취급받는 것을 싫어한다. [treated, like]

____

:: 1. 이 물건의 이름을 말해 줄 수 있겠니? 2. 당신의 삶의 목적은 무엇입니까? 3. 나는 그녀의 터무니없는 제안에 반대했다.

214 current [kə́:rənt / kʌ́rənt]

Step 01
해석연습

다음 문장을 current에 유의하여 해석해 보세요. (해석은 이 페이지의 하단부에 있음)

1. The current temperature is 25℃. _______________________________

2. There are many currents in the sea. _______________________________

3. The mass media can influence the current of thoughts. _______________________________

Step 02
뜻 알기

current에는 다음과 같은 여러 가지의 뜻이 있습니다.

❶ 현재의, 지금의, 최신의 **a** belonging to the present time; now passing

❷ (물, 공기, 전류 등의) 흐름; 해류, 기류 **n** a flow of something such as water, air, electricity, etc

❸ (사상, 말, 여론 따위의) 추세, 경향, 풍조 **n** a general tendency, course or movement (of events, opinions, thought, etc)

> 한 걸음 더 **currently** 현재는, 지금은 **an electric current** 전류 **an air current** 기류 **a tidal current** 조류, 해류
> **the current month** 이달 **current money** 유통통화 **current topics** 오늘의 화제, 시사문제

Step 03
연습문제

다음 문장의 current에 해당되는 뜻을 **Step 02** **의 ❶~❸에서 고르세요.** (해답은 459쪽)

1. The current situation is peaceful. (   )

2. Nothing disturbs the peaceful current of his life. (   )

3. There was a strong current in the river. (   )

4. The president wants to know the current of public opinion. (   )

5. What's the current price of this item? (   )

6. The current was very strong in the sea. (   )

Step 04
영작연습

다음 문장을 주어진 부분을 이용하여 영어로 옮기세요. (해답은 459쪽)

1. 나는 이 잡지의 최신호를 사고 싶습니다. [issue, magazine]

____

2. 이 계기는 전류를 측정하는 데 사용된다. [meter, measuring]

____

3. 그는 그 문제에 대한 여론의 동향을 알고 싶어 한다. [public opinion, matter]

____

∷ 1. 현재의 온도는 섭씨 25도이다. 2. 바다에는 많은 해류가 있다. 3. 매스미디어(대중매체)는 생각하는 풍조에 영향을 줄 수 있다.

215 odd [ɑd / ɔd]

다음 문장을 odd에 유의하여 해석해 보세요. (해석은 이 페이지의 하단부에 있음)

1. Judy is an odd girl because she likes snakes. _______________________________
2. She found an odd stocking in her drawer. _______________________________
3. 1, 3, 5 and 7 are odd numbers. _______________________________

odd에는 다음과 같은 여러 가지의 뜻이 있습니다.

❶ 이상한, 별난, 기묘한 ⓐ unusual, strange, queer, peculiar

❷ 외짝의, 짝이 안 맞는 ⓐ separated from its pair, set or series

❸ 홀수의 ⓐ (of numbers) not even; not able to be divided by two

> 한 걸음 더 **He makes a living by doing <u>odd</u> jobs, such as weeding gardens and fixing cars.** 그는 정원의 잡초를 뽑거나 차를 수리하는 것과 같은 부업으로 생계를 꾸려나간다. → 임시의, 짬짬이 하는(=not regular; occasional)
> **Three hundred-odd students attended the graduation ceremony.** 300여명의 학생들이 졸업식에 참석했다. → (수량을 나타내는 말 뒤에서) ~남짓의, ~여의; 여분의(=a little more than; with a little extra; left over)
> **this <u>odd</u> and that end** 이것저것 잡동사니; 잡다한 끄트러기 → 자투리, 여분의 것, 나머지
> **odd number** 홀수(↔ even number 짝수) **an odd player** 대기선수 **odd jobs** 짬짬이 하는 일; 여러 가지 잡일
> **an odd month** 큰달 **odd and even** 홀수 짝수 알아맞히기 놀이 **oddly** ① 묘하게, 이상하게 ② 여분으로, 짝이 맞지 않게 ③ 홀수로
> **oddity** 괴벽스러움, 기이함, 별남; 괴짜, 기인, 별난 물건 **at odd moments[times]** 여가에; 때때로, 가끔

다음 문장의 odd에 해당되는 뜻을 Step 02 **의 ❶~❸에서 고르세요.** (해답은 459쪽)

1. Eight is not an odd number. (   )
2. Why do you make friends with such odd people. (   )
3. I found an odd shoe in the box. (   )
4. It's very odd that his boss lives in such a small house. (   )
5. January, March, and May are odd months. (   )
6. There was an odd glove on the sofa. (   )

다음 문장을 주어진 부분을 이용하여 영어로 옮기세요. (해답은 459쪽)

1. 그녀는 매우 이상한 옷을 입고 있다. [wearing, clothes]

____

2. 외짝 양말을 모아 둔 상자 하나가 세탁실에 보관되어 있었다. [kept, laundry room]

____

3. 홀수 번호를 가진 집들은 거리의 왼쪽 편에 있다. [left side, street]

____

∷ 1. Judy는 별난 소녀다. 왜냐하면 뱀을 좋아하니까. 2. 그녀는 서랍에서 한 짝뿐인 긴 양말을 찾았다. 3. 1, 3, 5와 7은 홀수이다.

A. 다음 뜻에 해당되는 단어를 보기에서 찾아 적으세요.

보기	volume state object current odd

01. ______________ the condition in which someone or something is at a particular time
02. ______________ an aim or intention; a goal, a purpose; an end
03. ______________ unusual, strange, queer, peculiar
04. ______________ the amount of space occupied by a substance, liquid or gas
05. ______________ a flow of something such as water, air, electricity, etc
06. ______________ to say or announce clearly, carefully and definitely; to declare
07. ______________ a thing that can be seen or touched; a material thing
08. ______________ a country considered as a political community; a nation
09. ______________ a book, especially one of a set of books
10. ______________ separated from its pair, set or series
11. ______________ to feel or express dislike or disapproval; to protest; to oppose
12. ______________ a general tendency, course or movement (of events, opinions, thought, etc)
13. ______________ not even; not able to be divided by two
14. ______________ belonging to the present time; now passing
15. ______________ the amount of sound produced by a radio, television, etc

B. 다음 빈칸에 가장 알맞은 단어를 보기에서 찾아 적으세요.

보기	volume(s) state object current odd

01. He will (   ) his view on the matter.
02. The woman had an (   ) hat.
03. A grey (   ) passed by me in the blink of an eye.
04. The tank can contain a great (   ) of water.
05. His main (   ) in life was to become rich.
06. Turn up the (   ) of the radio.
07. The (   ) of the world economy is getting worse.
08. There is no swimming against the (   ) of the times.
09. One, three, and five are (   ) numbers.
10. He found an (   ) sock in his drawer.
11. The (   ) temperature is 15℃.
12. Do you (   ) to my smoking?
13. There are 10 (   ) in my encyclopedia.
14. That country is now an independent (   ).
15. The balloons flew with the strong air (   ).

다음 문장을 굵게 처리된 단어에 유의하여 해석해 보세요.

01. Environmental psychologists have long known about the harmful effects of unpredictable, high-**volume** noise. [2006년-홀수형 43번]

➡ _______________________________________

02. No lasting results can be achieved unless the individual convinces himself that loneliness is just a **state** of mind. [1994년-2차 48번]

➡ _______________________________________

03. They receive **state** grants for the university, and attend **state**-training programs if they lose their jobs. [1994년-1차 26번]

➡ _______________________________________

04. And "Can you **state** in so many words what the meaning is?" My answer to that would be, "No." [1998년-홀수형 35번]

➡ _______________________________________

05. The **state**-of-the-art, legendary recordings feature world-renowned artists and orchestras. [1998년-홀수형 31번]

➡ _______________________________________

06. The rules of breaststroke **stated** that both arms must be pulled together underwater and then recovered simultaneously back to the start of the pulling position to begin the next stroke. [2012년-홀수형 32번]

➡ _______________________________________

07. In the modern world, almost every country uses coins and paper money to exchange for other **objects** of value. [1996년-홀수형 37번]

➡ _______________________________________

08. The more contact a group has with another group, the more likely it is that **objects** or ideas will be exchanged. [2007년-홀수형 20번]

➡ _______________________________________

09. People may disturb or anger us, but the fact that not everyone **objects** to their behavior indicates that the problem is probably ours. [2006년-홀수형 34번]

➡ _______________________________________

10. They floated completely along the North Pacific **currents**, ending up back in Sitka. [2012년-홀수형 20번]

➡ _______________________________________

11. There is still much room for development, however, and I am afraid they are not yet appropriate for publishing in any of our **current** poetry journals. [2007년-홀수형 21번]

➡ _______________________________________

12. She liked the clean, luxuriant feeling as she swept down with the **current**. [2011년-홀수형 30번]

➡ _______________________________________

13. Aristotle developed an entire theory of physics that physicists today find **odd** and amusing. [2006년-홀수형 45번]

➡ _______________________________________

 216 **barometer** [bərámətər]

Step 01 해석연습

다음 문장을 barometer에 유의하여 해석해 보세요. (해석은 이 페이지의 하단부에 있음)

1. The barometer is falling. It is going to rain. _______________________________

2. The GNP of a country is the barometer of economy. _______________________________

Step 02 뜻 알기

barometer에는 다음과 같은 여러 가지의 뜻이 있습니다.

❶ 기압계 🄝 an instrument for measuring the pressure of air

❷ 척도, 지표 🄝 something that shows or gives an idea of changes that are happening

> 한 걸음 더 **a barometer of public opinion** 여론의 척도 **barometric[barometrical]** 기압계의, 기압의
> **barometry** 기압측정법

Step 03 연습문제

다음 문장의 barometer에 해당되는 뜻을 Step 02 의 ❶~❷에서 고르세요. (해답은 460쪽)

1. A barometer shows possible changes in the weather. (   )

2. Construction is a barometer of business conditions. (   )

3. We can measure the pressure of air by using a barometer. (   )

4. The education of a country is the barometer of culture. (   )

Step 04 영작연습

다음 문장을 주어진 부분을 이용하여 영어로 옮기세요. (해답은 460쪽)

1. 기압계는 날씨가 어떻게 변하는지를 보여 준다. [the weather, changes]

____

2. 체중은 건강의 지표라고 일컬어진다. [weight, called, health]

____

∷ 1. 기압계가 떨어지고 있다. 비가 올 것이다. 2. GNP(국민 총생산)는 그 나라 경제의 척도이다.

 **217 minute** (뜻) ❶❷ [mínit] ❸ [mainjúːt]

Step 01
해석연습

다음 문장을 minute에 유의하여 해석해 보세요. (해석은 이 페이지의 하단부에 있음)

1. An hour has sixty minutes. _______________________________

2. The secretary will keep the minutes of the meeting. _______________________________

3. Bacteria are minute organisms. _______________________________

Step 02
뜻 알기

minute에는 다음과 같은 여러 가지의 뜻이 있습니다.

❶ (시간) 분 🅝 one of the 60 parts into which an hour is divided; sixty seconds

❷ 회의록, 의사록 🅝 an official written record of what is said and decided at a meeting

❸ 아주 작은, 상세한, 정밀한, 세심한 🅐 very small; exact, precise; careful

> 한 걸음 더 **Wait a minute.** 잠깐만 기다려라. → 잠시, 잠깐(=a very short time)
> **minute hand** (시계의) 분침 **minuteness** 미세함, 세심함 **minutely** ① 1분마다의, 끊임없이 이어지는 ② 세세하게, 상세하게
> **by the minute** 시시각각으로(=minute by minute) **in a minute** 곧, 즉시, 당장(=in minutes)
> **to the minute** 정확히, 1분도 틀림없이(=on the minute) **up to the minute** 최신식의, 최신의(=up to date)

Step 03
연습문제

다음 문장의 minute에 해당되는 뜻을 **Step 02** 의 ❶~❸에서 고르세요. (해답은 460쪽)

1. She is a minute observer. (   )
2. She kept the minutes of the meeting. (   )
3. It's five minutes to ten. (   )
4. The diamonds in the ring were very minute. (   )
5. It takes me ten minutes to walk to work. (   )
6. Let me show the minutes of the previous conference. (   )

Step 04
영작연습

다음 문장을 주어진 부분을 이용하여 영어로 옮기세요. (해답은 460쪽)

1. 계란들을 3분 동안 삶아라. [boil, for]

____

2. 의장은 지난번 회의의 회의록을 읽었다. [chairman, last meeting]

____

3. 그는 나에게 그 기계에 대한 상세한 사용법을 알려 주었다. [gave, instructions]

____

∷ 1. 한 시간은 60분이다. 2. 서기가 회의록을 작성할 것이다. 3. 박테리아는 미세한 유기체이다.

218 **express** [iksprés]

Step 01 해석연습

다음 문장을 express에 유의하여 해석해 보세요. (해석은 이 페이지의 하단부에 있음)

1. A smile expressed his joy at the good news. _______________________

2. He took an express train for Chicago. _______________________

3. Please send these books by express. _______________________

Step 02 뜻 알기

express에는 다음과 같은 여러 가지의 뜻이 있습니다.

❶ ~을 표현하다, 나타내다 **v** to say or show (a meaning, thought, feeling, etc)

❷ 급행의, 논스톱의 **a** speedy; with few steps or non stop

❸ (열차, 버스 따위의) 급행; 급행운송; 속달, 특급우편 **n** an express train or bus; an express delivery; an express postal service

> 한 걸음 더 **He came here with the <u>express</u> purpose of seeing her.** 그는 이곳에 그녀를 보기 위한 분명한 의도를 가지고 왔다.
> → 명확한, 명시된(=clearly stated, definite)
> **expression** 표현, 특징 **expressive** 표현하는, 표현적인, 의미 있는 **an express train** 급행열차 **an express highway** 고속도로

Step 03 연습문제

다음 문장의 express에 해당되는 뜻을 **Step 02** 의 ❶~❸에서 고르세요. (해답은 460쪽)

1. I found it difficult to express my meaning. (   )

2. Go to the express bus terminal right now. (   )

3. We are going to travel by express. (   )

4. Drawings couldn't express everything. (   )

5. I want to send this package by express. (   )

6. There was an express train for Madrid. (   )

Step 04 영작연습

다음 문장을 주어진 부분을 이용하여 영어로 옮기세요. (해답은 460쪽)

1. 그녀는 아직도 영어로 자기 자신을 표현할 수 없다. [unable, in English]

____

2. 다행히 나는 용케 런던행 급행열차에 올라탈 수 있었다. [luckily, manage to]

____

3. 이 편지를 속달로 보내면 얼마나 걸릴까요? [how long, send]

____

∷ 1. 미소는 좋은 소식에 대한 그의 기쁨을 나타냈다. 2. 그는 시카고행 급행열차를 탔다. 3. 이 책들을 속달로 보내 주세요.

219 rear [riər]

Step 01
해석연습

다음 문장을 rear에 유의하여 해석해 보세요. (해석은 이 페이지의 하단부에 있음)

1. The garage is at the rear of the house. ___________________________

2. The man rears all types of birds. ___________________________

3. The snake reared its head. ___________________________

Step 02
뜻 알기

rear에는 다음과 같은 여러 가지의 뜻이 있습니다.

❶ 뒤, 후부, 후방 **n** the back part of something

❷ ~을 기르다, 키우다; 사육[재배]하다 **v** to make someone or something grow; to bring up

❸ ~을 들어 올리다, 세우다, 치솟게 하다 **v** to raise; to lift up

> 한 걸음 더 **a rear gate** 뒷문 **a rear rank** 후열 **a rear attack** 배후 공격 **at [in, on] the rear of** ~의 배후[뒤]에
> **rear one's family** 가족을 돌보다[부양하다]

Step 03
연습문제

다음 문장의 rear에 해당되는 뜻을 **Step 02** 의 ❶~❸에서 고르세요. (해답은 460쪽)

1. We sat in the rear of the church. (   )

2. My uncle is rearing cows and pigs in the country. (   )

3. The enemy attacked the army in the rear. (   )

4. The Eiffel tower rears its form near Paris. (   )

5. She has reared seven children. (   )

6. The horse reared itself up. (   )

Step 04
영작연습

다음 문장을 주어진 부분을 이용하여 영어로 옮기세요. (해답은 460쪽)

1. 교회 뒤에는 정원이 하나 있었다. [garden, church]

____

2. 그녀는 자신의 자녀교육에 매우 관심이 크다. [concerned about, children]

____

3. 산이 그 봉우리를 구름 위로 세우고 있다. [top, above the clouds]

____

∷ 1. 차고는 집의 뒤쪽에 있다. 2. 그 남자는 온갖 종류의 새를 기른다. 3. 뱀이 머리를 치켜들었다.

220 deal [diːl]

Step 01
해석연습

다음 문장을 deal에 유의하여 해석해 보세요. (해석은 이 페이지의 하단부에 있음)

1. The children made a deal to play baseball after school. ________________________

2. This business deals in toys. ________________________

3. He has a great deal of money. ________________________

4. It is your turn to deal. ________________________

Step 02
뜻 알기

deal에는 다음과 같은 여러 가지의 뜻이 있습니다.

❶ 협약, 교역, 거래 **n** an agreement, trade, transaction

❷ 다루다, 취급하다, 거래[매매]하다 **v** to treat, to manage, to do business

❸ (특정한 문구와 함께 쓰여) 양, 액; 많음 **n** a quantity, an amount

❹ (카드놀이에서) 패를 돌리다 **v** to distribute cards

> 한 걸음 더 **deal** [diːl] - **dealt** [delt] - **dealt** [delt]
> **You paid only $20 for this? Wow, what a <u>deal</u>!** 이게 겨우 20달러라고? 와, 정말 잘 샀구나! → (구어체) 싸고 좋게 산 것
> **The prime minister promised a new <u>deal</u> for farmers.** 수상은 농민들을 위한 새 정책을 약속했다. → 정책

Step 03
연습문제

다음 문장의 deal에 해당되는 뜻을 **Step 02** 의 ❶∼❹에서 고르세요. (해답은 460쪽)

1. I spent a good deal of money on books. (   )

2. They made a deal to play basketball at recess. (   )

3. This paper deals with educational problems. (   )

4. In casino, the dealers deal the cards. (   )

5. The two teams did a deal and Joo Young was traded. (   )

6. Francis taught Judy how to deal cards. (   )

7. This shop deals in women's clothing. (   )

8. She has caused me a good deal of trouble. (   )

Step 04
영작연습

다음 문장을 주어진 부분을 이용하여 영어로 옮기세요. (해답은 460쪽)

1. 우리는 그 건물을 구입하는 계약을 했다. [made, buy]

____

2. 이 논문은 영어교수법에 관한 것을 다루고 있다. [paper, method, teaching]

____

3. Judy는 새 차에 많은 양의 돈을 소비했다. [spent, on, car]

____

4. 그 남자는 각 사람들에게 6장씩의 카드를 돌릴 것이다. [cards, each player]

____

∷ 1. 어린이들은 방과 후에 야구를 하기로 약속을 했다. 2. 이 업체는 장난감을 판매한다. 3. 그는 많은 양의 돈을 가지고 있다. 4. 네가 카드를 돌릴 차례다.

A. 다음 뜻에 해당되는 단어를 보기에서 찾아 적으세요.

> **보기** barometer   minute(s)   express   rear   deal

01. ______________ to make someone or something grow; to bring up
02. ______________ speedy; with few steps or non stop
03. ______________ to treat, to manage, to do business
04. ______________ one of the 60 parts into which an hour is divided; sixty seconds
05. ______________ an instrument for measuring the pressure of air
06. ______________ to say or show (a meaning, thought, feeling, etc)
07. ______________ an agreement, trade, transaction
08. ______________ an official written record of what is said and decided at a meeting
09. ______________ the back part of something
10. ______________ something that shows or gives an idea of changes that are happening
11. ______________ an express train or bus; an express delivery; an express postal service
12. ______________ to distribute cards
13. ______________ to raise; to lift up
14. ______________ a quantity, an amount
15. ______________ very small; exact, precise; careful

B. 다음 빈칸에 가장 알맞은 단어를 보기에서 찾아 적으세요.

> **보기** barometer   minute(s)   express   rear(s)   deal(s)

01. He has never been afraid to (   ) his opinion.
02. Both people were happy with the business (   ).
03. There are sixty (   ) in an hour.
04. A (   ) is used to measure the pressure of the atmosphere.
05. The (   ) train to Paris runs every half hour.
06. The kitchen is in the (   ) of the house.
07. She had to spend a great (   ) of money on medicines.
08. Crime rate is a (   ) of social conditions.
09. The parcel was sent by (   ).
10. Peter will (   ) the cards at tonight's game.
11. Mrs. Green (   ) all types of birds as a hobby.
12. The chairman will read the (   ) of the last meeting.
13. The snake will (   ) its head.
14. Bacteria are so (   ) that we can't see them without a microscope.
15. This book (   ) with the history of Japan.

다음 문장을 굵게 처리된 단어에 유의하여 해석해 보세요.

01. Fifteen **minutes** in warm water before going to bed helps those who suffer from sleeplessness. [2001년–홀수형 34번]

➡ _______________________________________

02. "It will be all right in a **minute**," she said in a low voice not to disturb the audience around. [1996년–홀수형 26번]

➡ _______________________________________

03. The air was alive with chatter and laughter, which became easier **minute** by **minute**. [2003년–홀수형 32번]

➡ _______________________________________

04. Yes. So, would you please ask her to send one to me by **express** mail? [1998년–홀수형 5번]

➡ _______________________________________

05. One key social competence is how well or poorly people **express** their own feelings. [2008년–홀수형 31번]

➡ _______________________________________

06. For decades, child-**rearing** advice from experts has encouraged the nighttime separation of baby from parent. [2010년–홀수형 21번]

➡ _______________________________________

07. Special-interest magazines, on the other hand, **deal** mainly with one particular subject. [2001년–홀수형 33번]

➡ _______________________________________

08. Science and technology have changed a great **deal** since the latter part of the nineteenth century. [1999년–홀수형 38번]

➡ _______________________________________

09. W: How much is it for a kid?
M: It depends. How old is she?
W: She's ten.
M: Then she'll get a 50% discount. So $3 for your child.
W: That's a good **deal**! [2002년–홀수형 3번]

➡ _______________________________________

Day 22

 **DAY 23**

A contented man is always rich.
만족하는 사람은 언제나 부자다.

 **221 content** ^(뜻) ❶ [kántent / kɔ́n-] ❷❸ [kəntént]

Step 01
해석연습

다음 문장을 content에 유의하여 해석해 보세요. (해석은 이 페이지의 하단부에 있음)

1. She drank the contents of the bottle. _______________________________

2. Nothing will ever content her. _______________________________

Step 02
뜻 알기

content에는 다음과 같은 여러 가지의 뜻이 있습니다.

❶ 내용, 내용물, 속에 든 것 **n** the things that are contained in a box, a room, a book, etc

❷ ~을 만족시키다, ~에게 만족을 주다 **v** to satisfy; to please
만족한, 기뻐하는 **a** happy and satisfied; pleased

> 한 걸음 더 **contented** 만족하고 있는 **contentment** 만족, 흐뭇함 **the contents of a book** 책의 내용
> **the table of contents** 목차 **the content of a speech** 연설의 취지 **be contented with** ~에 만족하다

Step 03
연습문제

다음 문장의 content에 해당되는 뜻을 **Step 02** 의 ❶~❷에서 고르세요. (해답은 460쪽)

1. The table of contents is at the beginning of the book. (   )

2. Be content with what you have now. (   )

3. She is content with her present job. (   )

4. The box had fallen over, and some of the contents had spilled out. (   )

Step 04
영작연습

다음 문장을 주어진 부분을 이용하여 영어로 옮기세요. (해답은 460쪽)

1. 세관 직원이 너의 짐의 내용물을 검사할 것이다. [customs official, baggage]

____

2. John은 현재의 자신의 생활에 만족하고 있다. [life, at present]

____

∷ 1. 그녀는 병에 든 것을 마셨다. 2. 아무것도 그녀를 만족시키지 못할 것이다.

222 move [muːv]

다음 문장을 move에 유의하여 해석해 보세요. (해석은 이 페이지의 하단부에 있음)

1. Don't move your head. _______________________

2. We are moving (house) next week. _______________________

3. The movie moved me deeply. _______________________

move에는 다음과 같은 여러 가지의 뜻이 있습니다.

❶ 움직이다, 이동하다; ~을 옮기다 Ⓥ to (cause to) change position; to transfer; to shift

❷ 이사하다, 이동하다 Ⓥ to change a house or office

❸ (남을) 감동시키다, (남의) 마음을 움직이다 Ⓥ to make someone feel strong feelings of pity, compassion, sympathy, etc

> 한 걸음 더 **He moved an amendment to the bill.** 그는 그 의안(법안)에 대한 수정안을 제안했다.
> → (회의, 법정 등에서) (동의를) 제안하다, 제출하다(=to officially make a proposal at a meeting)
> **a moving story** 감동적인 이야기 **moving** ① 움직이는 ② 감동시키는, 감동적인
> **movement** ① 움직임, 이동 ② 이사, 이주 ③ 동향, 흐름

다음 문장의 move에 해당되는 뜻을 **Step 02** 의 ❶~❸에서 고르세요. (해답은 460쪽)

1. Don't move – or I'll shoot. (   )

2. It was a moving sight. (   )

3. We moved into a new house last week. (   )

4. Will you move the table for me? (   )

5. They will move into a new office next week. (   )

6. I was deeply moved by the story. (   )

다음 문장을 주어진 부분을 이용하여 영어로 옮기세요. (해답은 460쪽)

1. 그는 자신의 책상을 창가 쪽으로 가까이 옮겼다. [nearer, window]

____

2. 우리는 어제 보다 큰 사무실로 이사했다. [bigger, office]

____

3. 그 가수는 청중을 깊이 감동시켜 울렸다. [audience, tears]

____

:: 1. 머리를 움직이지 마라. 2. 우리는 다음 주에 이사할 예정이다. 3. 그 영화는 나를 깊이 감동시켰다.

223 compose [kəmpóuz]

Step 01 해석연습

다음 문장을 compose에 유의하여 해석해 보세요. (해석은 이 페이지의 하단부에 있음)

1. Water is composed of hydrogen and oxygen. _______________________
2. The writer composed many short stories. _______________________
3. I tried to compose myself before the interview. _______________________

Step 02 뜻 알기

compose에는 다음과 같은 여러 가지의 뜻이 있습니다.

❶ (수동형으로) ~을 구성하다; ~의 일부를 이루다 Ⅴ to make something by putting its parts together; to make up; to constitute

❷ 시, 문장을 짓다; 음악을 작곡하다 Ⅴ to write a letter, poem, a piece of music, etc

❸ (마음을) 가라앉히다, 진정시키다 Ⅴ to make oneself calm

> 한 걸음 더 **composition** ① 구성 ② 작문, 작곡 ③ 혼합물, 합성물 **composer** 구성하는 사람, 제작자, 작곡가, 작가
> **composure** (마음의) 평정, 침착 **composed** (마음이) 가라앉은, 침착한, 평온한
> **composing** 진정시키는 *composing medicine 진정제 **be composed of** ~으로 구성되어 있다(= be made up of)

Step 03 연습문제

다음 문장의 compose에 해당되는 뜻을 **Step 02** 의 ❶~❸에서 고르세요. (해답은 460쪽)

1. Judy composes a piece of music every month. (   )
2. He composed himself to answer the letter. (   )
3. Our class is composed of 15 boys and 16 girls. (   )
4. He began to compose when he was seven years old. (   )
5. I needed a quiet place where I could compose my thoughts. (   )
6. What is this metal composed of? (   )

Step 04 영작연습

다음 문장을 주어진 부분을 이용하여 영어로 옮기세요. (해답은 460쪽)

1. 미합중국은 50개의 주로 이루어져 있다. [the United States, states]

____

2. 모차르트는 6살 때 작곡하는 것을 시작했다. [Mozart, when]

____

3. 그녀는 그 소식에 잠시 동안 마음을 가라앉힐 수가 없었다. [herself, for a while]

____

⠿ 1. 물은 산소와 수소로 구성되어 있다. 2. 그 작가는 많은 단편소설을 썼다. 3. 나는 인터뷰 전에 침착하려고 노력했다.

224 account [əkáunt]

Step 01 해석연습

다음 문장을 account에 유의하여 해석해 보세요. (해석은 이 페이지의 하단부에 있음)

1. He has an account with the Shinhan Bank. ______________________________

2. Don't always believe newspaper accounts of events. ______________________

3. Poor health accounts for his failure. ______________________________

Step 02 뜻 알기

account에는 다음과 같은 여러 가지의 뜻이 있습니다.

❶ 계정, 예금계좌 **n** an arrangement by which a person keeps his money in a bank

❷ (구체적이고 상세한) 설명(서), 보도, 이야기 **n** a written or spoken description which gives details of an event

❸ 설명하다; ∼의 이유를 밝히다 **v** to explain; to give a reason for

> 한 걸음 더 **The picnic was put off on account of rain.** 소풍이 비 때문에 연기되었다.
> → 이유, 근거, 동기(=a reason; causes and grounds)
> **Don't worry about what he said. It's of no account.** 그가 말한 것을 걱정하지 마라, 그것은 중요하지 않다.
> → 중요성, 가치(=importance; value)
> **She is quick at accounts.** 그녀는 계산이 빠르다. → 계산, 셈(=accounting, calculation)
> **bank account** 은행 예금계좌 **account for** 설명하다 **on account of** ∼ 때문에 **make much account of** ∼을 중시하다

Step 03 연습문제

다음 문장의 account에 해당되는 뜻을 **Step 02** 의 ❶∼❸에서 고르세요. (해답은 460쪽)

1. I have an account with the ABC Bank. (   )

2. She gave an account of her trip. (   )

3. How do you account for your absence yesterday? (   )

4. The boy gave his friend an account of the game. (   )

5. He has $5,000 in his account. (   )

6. That theory cannot account for this fact. (   )

Step 04 영작연습

다음 문장을 주어진 부분을 이용하여 영어로 옮기세요. (해답은 460쪽)

1. 그녀의 급여는 직접 그녀의 은행 계좌로 지급된다. [salary, directly]

____

2. 그 남자는 우리에게 자신의 모험에 대한 생생한 이야기를 해 주었다. [vivid, adventure]

____

3. 너는 네가 어제 결석한 이유를 설명해야만 한다. [have to, absence]

____

1. 그는 신한은행에 예금계좌를 갖고 있다. 2. 신문의 기사들을 언제나 믿지는 마라.
3. 건강치 못한 것이 실패의 원인이다. (좋지 않은 건강이 그의 실패 이유를 설명해 준다.)

225 mean [miːn]

Step 01 해석연습

다음 문장을 mean에 유의하여 해석해 보세요. (해석은 이 페이지의 하단부에 있음)

1. The red light means "stop." ___________________________

2. It is mean of you to cheat her. ___________________________

3. Three is the mean of series one to five. ___________________________

4. There is no means of helping her. ___________________________

Step 02 뜻 알기

mean에는 다음과 같은 여러 가지의 뜻이 있습니다.

❶ 의미하다; 의도하다 **v** to indicate, signify, express or show; to intend

❷ 비열한, 천한; 인색한; 질이 낮은 **a** morally low, base; not generous; poor quality, humble

❸ 중간의, 평균의 **a** occupying the middle position between two extremes; middle; average
중간 값, 중간, 중용 **n** the average amount, figure, or value

❹ (복수형으로 쓰여) 수단, 방법 **n** a method, way, or instrument in which something is done

> 한 걸음 더 **mean** [miːn] - **meant** [ment] - **meant** [ment]
> **My uncle is a man of considerable <u>means</u>.** 나의 아저씨는 상당한 재산의 소유자이다. → (복수형으로 쓰여) 재산, 재력

Step 03 연습문제

다음 문장의 mean에 해당되는 뜻을 **Step 02** 의 ❶～❹에서 고르세요. (해답은 460쪽)

1. All possible means have been tried. (   )
2. I didn't mean to interrupt your meal. (   )
3. The mean age of the students in our class is 22. (   )
4. She is mean about money. (   )
5. There is[are] no means of getting there. (   )
6. The mean annual temperature of the country is 18℃. (   )
7. The Latin word "amo" means "I love." (   )
8. It is mean of you to deceive him. (   )

Step 04 영작연습

다음 문장을 주어진 부분을 이용하여 영어로 옮기세요. (해답은 460쪽)

1. 그렇게 말하는 의도가 무엇이냐? [what, saying]

   ____

2. 그는 돈 문제에 다소 인색하다. [rather, money matter]

   ____

3. 5는 3과 7의 중간 숫자이다. [number, between]

   ____

4. 사상(생각)은 언어에 의해서 표현된다. [thoughts, expressed, words]

   ____

:: 1. 붉은 신호는 '정지'를 의미한다. 2. 그녀를 속이다니 너는 비열하다. 3. 3은 1에서 5까지 연속된 수의 중간 값이다. 4. 그녀를 도울 방법이 없다.

A. 다음 뜻에 해당되는 단어를 보기에서 찾아 적으세요.

> **보기**   content   move   compose   account   mean(s)

01. _____________ a written or spoken description which gives details of an event
02. _____________ morally low, base; not generous; poor quality, humble
03. _____________ to change a house or office
04. _____________ to write a letter, poem, a piece of music, etc
05. _____________ to satisfy; to please
06. _____________ to make someone feel strong feelings of pity, compassion, sympathy, etc
07. _____________ the average amount, figure, or value
08. _____________ the things that are contained in a box, a room, a book, etc
09. _____________ to (cause to) change position; to transfer; to shift
10. _____________ to make oneself calm
11. _____________ to indicate, signify, express or show; to intend
12. _____________ an arrangement by which a person keeps his money in a bank
13. _____________ a method, way, or instrument in which something is done
14. _____________ to explain; to give a reason for
15. _____________ to make something by putting its parts together; to make up; to constitute

B. 다음 빈칸에 가장 알맞은 단어를 보기에서 찾아 적으세요.

> **보기**   content(s)   move(s)   compose(d)   account(s)   mean(s)

01. My brother has a bank (   ).
02. Will it (   ) you if I allow you to go to the concert tomorrow?
03. Can you (   ) your car? It's blocking the road.
04. This sign (   ) that cars must stop.
05. He has to (   ) a letter to his lawyer.
06. Her illness (   ) for her absence.
07. A word is (   ) of several letters.
08. The (   ) of 5, 7 and 9 is 7.
09. He will (   ) from Sydney to Melbourne.
10. My uncle gave us a vivid (   ) of his trip.
11. I tried to (   ) myself before the interview.
12. Her singing always (   ) us.
13. The customs official examined the (   ) of my briefcase.
14. My uncle lives in a (   ) house.
15. There is no (   ) of learning what is happening.

다음 문장을 굵게 처리된 단어에 유의하여 해석해 보세요.

01. But he was not **content** with his own crops, and he stole crops from nearby farmers. [2001년-홀수형 25번]

➡ ______________________________________

02. For instance, goldfish bowls look stunning filled with flower heads or petals, magnifying their **contents**. [2009년-홀수형 42번]

➡ ______________________________________

03. I think I hurt my back helping my brother **move** yesterday. [2011년-홀수형 16번]

➡ ______________________________________

04. Poetry **moves** us to sympathize with the emotions of the poet himself or with those of the persons whom his imagination has created. [2002년-홀수형 37번]

➡ ______________________________________

05. Its mission is to **move** the nation and the world towards social, racial, and economic justice. [2009년-홀수형 36]

➡ ______________________________________

06. Above all, however, there can be hardly anyone who is not **moved** by some kind of music. [2008년-홀수형 28번]

➡ ______________________________________

07. Today's physicists say, "This is nonsense. A **moving** object continues to move unless some force is used to stop it." [2006년-홀수형 45번]

➡ ______________________________________

08. Upon closer analysis, "emerging" countries are not only vastly different from one another, they are also **composed** of numerous unique individuals and communities. [2006년-홀수형 26번]

➡ ______________________________________

09. In fact, people have been using birth order to **account** for personality factors such as an aggressive behavior or a passive temperament. [2009년-홀수형 21번]

➡ ______________________________________

10. Your check has been properly credited, and your **account** is now marked paid in full. [1994년-1차 25번]

➡ ______________________________________

11. Over the years he wrote a "diary," actually an occasional record in which he kept **accounts** of his commercial and family life. [2013년-홀수형 33번]

➡ ______________________________________

12. Having a mole over one's right eyebrow **means** he or she will be lucky with money and have a successful career. [2005년-홀수형 42번]

➡ ______________________________________

13. Work, too, is an effective **means** of working off anger and using overflowing energy. [2001년-홀수형 30번]

➡ ______________________________________

14. Further, television sets were priced beyond the **means** of a general public whose modest living standards, especially in the 1930s and 1940s, did not allow the acquisition of luxury goods. [2009년-홀수형 28번]

➡ ______________________________________

15. In recent years, however, biologists have been able to listen more carefully by **means** of these technologies and have realized that giraffes may talk, though not in a way that we can hear. [2004년-홀수형 47-48번]

➡ ______________________________________

226 constitution [kànstətjúːʃən / kɔ̀nstitjúːʃən]

Step 01 해석연습

다음 문장을 constitution에 유의하여 해석해 보세요. (해석은 이 페이지의 하단부에 있음)

1. The instructor explained the constitution of solar spectrum. ___________________
2. He has a good constitution. ___________________
3. The United States has a written constitution. ___________________

Step 02 뜻 알기

constitution에는 다음과 같은 여러 가지의 뜻이 있습니다.

❶ 구성, 구조, 본질 🄽 the way in which a thing is composed; nature

❷ 체질, 체격, 건강 🄽 the physical structure and condition of a human body

❸ 헌법 🄽 a systematic description of the fundamental laws and principles of government

> 한 걸음 더 **constitute** 구성하다, 조직하다 **a written constitution** 성문헌법
> **constitutional** ① 구성상의, 조직상의, 본질적인 ② 체질의, 체격의, 기질상의 ③ 몸[건강]에 좋은 ④ 헌법(상)의, 합헌의, 합법적인
> **by constitution** 타고난, 본질적으로 **suit[agree with] one's constitution** 체질[성미]에 맞다

Step 03 연습문제

다음 문장의 constitution에 해당되는 뜻을 **Step 02** 의 ❶~❸에서 고르세요. (해답은 461쪽)

1. My son has a good constitution. (   )
2. What's the constitution of the society? (   )
3. That's a violation of the Constitution. (   )
4. He wants to know the constitution of solar spectrum. (   )
5. He has a weak constitution and feels tired easily. (   )
6. Our country has a constitution giving rights to the people. (   )

Step 04 영작연습

다음 문장을 주어진 부분을 이용하여 영어로 옮기세요. (해답은 461쪽)

1. 선생님은 태양의 물리적 구조를 설명하셨다. [explained, physical]

____

2. 그녀는 튼튼한 체질을 가지고 있어 좀처럼 아프지 않다. [strong, seldom]

____

3. 한국의 헌법은 국민에게 특정한 권리가 있음을 보장하고 있다. [guarantees, rights]

____

∷ 1. 교사는 태양의 스펙트럼(분광현상)의 구조에 대해 설명했다. 2. 그는 좋은 체격을 가지고 있다. 3. 미국은 성문헌법을 가지고 있다.

227 complex **a** [kəmpléks / kámpleks] **n** [kámpleks]

Step 01 해석연습

다음 문장을 complex에 유의하여 해석해 보세요. (해석은 이 페이지의 하단부에 있음)

1. A car is a very complex machine. _______________________

2. They will build a vast new shopping complex in the town. _______________

3. She has a complex about her weight. _______________________

Step 02 뜻 알기

complex에는 다음과 같은 여러 가지의 뜻이 있습니다.

❶ 복합의, 복잡한 **a** composed of many parts; complicated or difficult

❷ 복합체, 합성물; 복합건물, 단지 **n** a complex whole; a group of buildings that are close together

❸ 강박관념, 강한 편견, 지나친 혐오[공포] **n** an abnormal mental state caused by experiences in one's past which affect one's behavior; obsessive concern or fear

> 한 걸음 더 **a housing complex** 주택단지 **a hospital complex** 종합병원 **a leisure complex** 종합레저센터
> **a petrochemical complex** 석유화학단지 **a woman complex** 여성공포증 **a height complex** 고소공포증
> **a inferiority complex** 열등감

Step 03 연습문제

다음 문장의 complex에 해당되는 뜻을 **Step 02** 의 ❶∼❸에서 고르세요. (해답은 461쪽)

1. We will visit the Ulsan industrial complex tomorrow. (   )

2. The process of making steel is complex. (   )

3. He seems to have a complex about being bald. (   )

4. My apartment complex contains 20 separate units. (   )

5. She suffers from an inferiority complex. (   )

6. This system has a very complex network. (   )

Step 04 영작연습

다음 문장을 주어진 부분을 이용하여 영어로 옮기세요. (해답은 461쪽)

1. 광합성은 매우 복잡한 과정이다. [photosynthesis, process]

____

2. 그 휴양단지는 골프코스, 수영장, 테니스코트, 도서관 등을 포함하고 있다. [leisure, includes]

____

3. 나의 아버지께서는 외국인에 대한 심한 편견을 가지고 있다. [against, foreigners]

____

:: 1. 차는 매우 복잡한 기계이다. 2. 그들은 마을에 큰 새로운 쇼핑단지를 지을 것이다. 3. 그녀는 자신의 몸무게에 대해 강박관념을 가지고 있다.

Step 01 해석연습

다음 문장을 file에 유의하여 해석해 보세요. (해석은 이 페이지의 하단부에 있음)

1. He read over the file on the murders carefully. ___________________________

2. The ducklings waked in single file. ___________________________

3. She files her nails every day. ___________________________

Step 02 뜻 알기

file에는 다음과 같은 여러 가지의 뜻이 있습니다.

❶ (정리된) 자료, 기록, 파일; 서류철, 목록 **n** information about a particular person or subject; a collection of information kept in a folder or on a computer
(서류 등을) 철하다, 정리하다 **v** to arrange (papers, etc) in order

❷ 열, 세로줄(↔ rank 가로줄) **n** a line of people or things one behind another
열을 지어 가다 **v** to walk in a line of people, one behind another

❸ 줄[공구] **n** a steel tool with a rough surface for smoothing or rubbing away wood, metal, etc
줄질하다, 다듬다 **v** to cut or rub something using a tool with a rough surface

> 한 걸음 더 **The woman filed a formal complaint against the department.** 그 여자는 그 부서를 정식으로 고소했다.
> → 고소, 서류 따위를 제출하다(=to officially record something such as a law case, official document, etc)

Step 03 연습문제

다음 문장의 file에 해당되는 뜻을 **Step 02** 의 ❶~❸에서 고르세요. (해답은 461쪽)

1. The students went down stairs in single file. (   )
2. Each book is filed alphabetically under the name of its author. (   )
3. He needs to file down the sharp edges. (   )
4. They will march in a file. (   )
5. The lady was filing her nails then. (   )
6. She flied the newspapers in order by date. (   )

Step 04 영작연습

다음 문장을 주어진 부분을 이용하여 영어로 옮기세요. (해답은 461쪽)

1. 이 편지들을 날짜순으로 철해 주세요. [order, date]

____

2. 군인들은 열을 지어 도로를 가로질러 갔다. [soldiers, across]

____

3. 그 직공은 날카로운 모서리를 갈아 내기 위해 줄을 사용했다. [rub off, edges]

____

:: 1. 그는 살인사건에 대한 자료를 주의 깊게 읽었다. 2. 새끼 오리들이 한 줄로 걸어갔다. 3. 그녀는 손톱을 매일 다듬는다.

229 **alternative** [ɔːltə́ːrnətiv]

Step 01
해석연습

다음 문장을 alternative에 유의하여 해석해 보세요. (해석은 이 페이지의 하단부에 있음)

1. The alternatives are death or submission. ___________________________

2. There is no alternative course. ___________________________

Step 02
뜻 알기

alternative에는 다음과 같은 여러 가지의 뜻이 있습니다.

❶ 양자택일의, 둘 중 하나의 **a** that which can be chosen between two things or possibilities
양자택일 **n** a choice between two things or possibilities

❷ 달리 취할, 대안의, 대신의 **a** that which can be used instead of something else
대안, 다른 방도 **n** another choice (means, way, etc)

> 한 걸음 더 **alternative energy** (태양력, 풍력 따위의) 대체에너지 **alternative punishment** (투옥 이외의) 대체형벌
> **alternative question** [문법] 선택의문문 **alternative school** 대안학교
> **alternative technology** 대체기술 (환경 친화적인 과학 기술) **alternatively** ① 양자택일로 ② 대신으로

Step 03
연습문제

다음 문장의 alternative에 해당되는 뜻을 **Step 02** 의 ❶~❷에서 고르세요. (해답은 461쪽)

1. We have the alternative of going or staying. (   )

2. There is no alternative but to sell the house. (   )

3. This is an alternative of that. (   )

4. The alternatives are surrender or fighting to the last. (   )

Step 04
영작연습

다음 문장을 주어진 부분을 이용하여 영어로 옮기세요. (해답은 461쪽)

1. 그는 소풍을 갈 것이냐 아니면 박물관을 방문할 것이냐의 양자택일의 안을 내놓았다.
[offered, picnic, museum]

____

2. 항복에 대신할 것은 죽음뿐이다. [surrender, death]

____

:: 1. 선택은 죽음이냐 항복이냐 둘 중의 하나이다. 2. 다른 수단(방도)은 없다.

230 **strike** [straik]

Step 01 해석연습

다음 문장을 strike에 유의하여 해석해 보세요. (해석은 이 페이지의 하단부에 있음)

1. He struck me on the head. ___________________________

2. Some snakes strike people. ___________________________

3. The workers are on strike. ___________________________

4. A good idea suddenly struck me. ___________________________

Step 02 뜻 알기

strike에는 다음과 같은 여러 가지의 뜻이 있습니다.

❶ 세게 치다, 때리다 Ⓥ to hit hard ❷ 공격하다 Ⓥ to attack

❸ 파업하다 Ⓥ to stop work as a protest / 파업 Ⓝ an act of striking

❹ (생각 따위가) 문득 떠오르다 Ⓥ to happen or appear suddenly

> 한 걸음 더 **At first sight I was <u>struck</u> by her beauty.** 나는 첫눈에 그녀의 아름다움에 매료되었다.
> → ~에게 감명을 주다, 인상 지우다(=to affect; influence; impress)
> **The baseball player might <u>strike</u> out.** 그 야구선수는 스트라이크 아웃을 당할지도 모른다. → (야구 또는 볼링의) 스트라이크
> **He <u>struck</u> a match and lit his cigar.** 그는 성냥을 그어 담배(여송연)에 불을 붙였다.
> → (성냥을) 긋다, (마찰하여) ~에 불(꽃)이 나게 하다(=to produce sparks or a flame by rubbing)

Step 03 연습문제

다음 문장의 strike에 해당되는 뜻을 **Step 02** 의 ❶～❹에서 고르세요. (해답은 461쪽)

1. The ball struck him in the eye. (   )
2. The laborers are on strike now. (   )
3. We will strike the enemy's fort with missiles. (   )
4. He seized a stick and tried to strike me. (   )
5. A happy thought struck her. (   )
6. The bus drivers' strike is expected to last long. (   )
7. A bright idea struck him as he was watching the movie. (   )
8. The hurt ram might strike the hiker. (   )

Step 04 영작연습

다음 문장을 주어진 부분을 이용하여 영어로 옮기세요. (해답은 461쪽)

1. 강사(연사)는 주먹으로 책상을 쳤다. [speaker, fist]

____

2. 성난 곰이 사냥꾼을 공격할지도 모른다. [angry, hunter]

____

3. 근로자들은 높은 임금을 위해 파업하기로 결심했다. [workers, higher wages]

____

4. 그는 신문을 읽다가 갑자기 좋은 생각이 떠올랐다. [idea, newspaper]

____

∷ 1. 그는 나의 머리를 때렸다. 2. 일부 뱀들은 사람들을 공격한다. 3. 근로자들은 파업 중이다. 4. 좋은 생각이 갑자기 떠올랐다.

A. 다음 뜻에 해당되는 단어를 보기에서 찾아 적으세요.

> 보기   constitution   complex   file   alternative   strike

01. ______________ a group of buildings that are close together
02. ______________ the physical structure and condition of a human body
03. ______________ that which can be chosen between two things or possibilities
04. ______________ to attack
05. ______________ a systematic description of the fundamental laws and principles of government
06. ______________ a collection of information kept in a folder or on a computer
07. ______________ another choice (means, way, etc)
08. ______________ to stop work as a protest
09. ______________ composed of many parts; complicated or difficult
10. ______________ a line of people or things one behind another
11. ______________ the way in which a thing is composed; nature
12. ______________ to hit hard
13. ______________ an abnormal mental state caused by experiences in one's past which affect one's behavior; obsessive concern or fear
14. ______________ a steel tool with a rough surface for smoothing or rubbing away wood, metal, etc
15. ______________ to happen or appear suddenly

B. 다음 빈칸에 가장 알맞은 단어를 보기에서 찾아 적으세요.

> 보기   constitution   complex   file(s)   alternative   strike

01. A black bear stood ready to (   ) the hunter.
02. She explained the physical (   ) of the moon.
03. This command means to delete (   ) from the directory.
04. The (   ) possibilities are surrender or fighting to the last.
05. She uses a (   ) to sharp her fingernails.
06. A bright idea might (   ) you unexpectedly.
07. He has a strong (   ) like iron.
08. The boy will (   ) the ball with the bat.
09. The children walked in single (   ).
10. They are building a vast new shopping (   ).
11. I don't like meat. Is there an (   ) on the menu?
12. She has a (   ) about her curly hair.
13. The workers will (   ) against bad working conditions.
14. Great Britain has an unwritten (   ).
15. An airplane is a very (   ) machine.

다음 문장을 굵게 처리된 단어에 유의하여 해석해 보세요.

01. Television viewing does not demand **complex** mental activities. [1997-홀수형 30번]

→ ______________________________

02. Global politics, as a result, has become more **complex**, involving countries from many civilizations. [2002년-홀수형 46번]

→ ______________________________

03. I know, but I couldn't open the **file** you sent. The password didn't work. [2010년-홀수형 2번]

→ ______________________________

04. For example, suppose that you have $ 25 to spend and have narrowed your **alternatives** to a textbook or a date. [1994년-1차 47번]

→ ______________________________

05. In contrast, students who were told that it was a dog's chewy toy did not find its **alternative** use. [2009년-홀수형 49-50번]

→ ______________________________

06. A stone can behave only in the way an outside force makes it behave. Unlike a stone, a person can start an action by himself or herself. The difference, then, is that a stone is not conscious of possibilities, whereas human beings are conscious that they face genuine **alternatives**. [2002년-홀수형 34번]

→ ______________________________

07. There are things which in a sense I remembered, but which did not **strike** me as strange or interesting until quite recently. [2008년-홀수형 22번]

→ ______________________________

08. This is a simple action which indicates agreement by **striking** one's palms together repeatedly. [2008년-홀수형 3번]

→ ______________________________

09. They often work for advertising agencies, where they create **striking** pictures and tasteful designs. [2000년-홀수형 20번]

→ ______________________________

10. **Strike** while the iron is hot. [1999년-홀수형 18번]

→ ______________________________

Day 23

231 decline [dikláin]

Group 47

Step 01 해석연습

다음 문장을 decline에 유의하여 해석해 보세요. (해석은 이 페이지의 하단부에 있음)

1. He declined my offer of help. ______________________________
2. The old man's health is in decline. ______________________________

Step 02 뜻 알기

decline에는 다음과 같은 여러 가지의 뜻이 있습니다.

❶ 거절하다, 사양하다 **v** to say "no" to (an invitation, etc); to refuse (something offered)

❷ 기울다; 감소하다, 쇠퇴하다 **v** to continue to become lower, smaller, weaker, worse, etc
떨어짐, 하락, 쇠퇴, 감소 **n** declining; gradual decrease to a lower level

> 한 걸음 더 **declination** ① 경사, 쇠약, 쇠퇴 ② (미국식) 정중한 거절 **declining** 기우는, 쇠퇴하는; 하락하는
> **a mental decline** 지능 감퇴 **a decline in prices** 물가의 하락 **fall[go] into a decline** 쇠퇴하다; 쇠약해지다 (특히 폐병에 걸리다)
> **on the decline** 기울어져, 쇠퇴하여; 내리막에

Step 03 연습문제

다음 문장의 decline에 해당되는 뜻을 **Step 02** 의 ❶~❷에서 고르세요. (해답은 462쪽)

1. I declined his offer of a life. (   )
2. There is a slight decline in prices this year. (   )
3. She declined his offer of financial help. (   )
4. There has been a gradual decline in the stock market. (   )

Step 04 영작연습

다음 문장을 주어진 부분을 이용하여 영어로 옮기세요. (해답은 462쪽)

1. 그녀는 만찬 초대를 정중히 거절했다. [politely, invitation]

____

2. 출생률이 몇 해 동안 계속 떨어지고 있다. [birth rate, some years]

____

∷ 1. 그는 도와주겠다는 나의 제의를 거절했다. 2. 그 노인의 건강이 쇠약해지고 있다.

232 range [reindʒ]

Step 01 해석연습

다음 문장을 range에 유의하여 해석해 보세요. (해석은 이 페이지의 하단부에 있음)

1. He has a wide range of knowledge. ________________________________

2. A range of mountains separates the two countries. ________________________________

3. He ranged the books on the shelf. ________________________________

Step 02 뜻 알기

range에는 다음과 같은 여러 가지의 뜻이 있습니다.

❶ 범위, 한계, 폭 **n** the extent or scope; area; a variety of things, ideas, or products

❷ 줄, 잇닿음; 산맥 **n** a row, line, or series; a chain of mountains

❸ 나란히 놓다, 정렬시키다 **v** to arrange (someone or something) in order or in a row or rows

> 한 걸음 더 **He lets his cattle graze on the range near his ranch.** 그는 가축들을 자신의 목장 주변의 방목 구역에서 풀을 뜯어 먹게 한다. → 방목장(=an open, large feeding area for cattle and sheep)
> **She is boiling the potatoes on the range.** 그녀는 레인지에 감자를 찌고 있다.
> → 조리용 레인지(=a stove for cooking)
> **There were 30 students whose ages ranged from 20 to 30.** 나이가 20살에서 30살에 걸쳐 있는 30명의 학생들이 있었다.
> → (범위, 활동 등이) ~에 걸치다, ~에 미치다, 분포되어 있다(=to stretch, extend, cover, be distributed)
> **a range of mountains** 산맥 **rangeland** 방목장, 방목지 **a gas range** 가스레인지 **within one's range** 자기 힘이 미치는
> **out of one's range** 자기 힘이 못 미치는 **at long[short] range** 원거리[근거리]에서

Step 03 연습문제

다음 문장의 range에 해당되는 뜻을 **Step 02** 의 ❶~❸에서 고르세요. (해답은 462쪽)

1. Several cars are available within this price range. (   )

2. A long range of mountains runs through the country. (   )

3. The lecturer spoke on a wide range of subject. (   )

4. She will range cups and plates on the shelves. (   )

5. The Rockies are a mountain range in North America. (   )

6. My father told me to range the albums on the shelf. (   )

Step 04 영작연습

다음 문장을 주어진 부분을 이용하여 영어로 옮기세요. (해답은 462쪽)

1. 그 소리는 인간이 들을 수 있는 한계 밖의 것이었다. [beyond, human hearing]

____

2. 그들은 멀리 있는 산맥을 보았다. [mountains, distance]

____

3. 그 장교는 자신의 병사들을 강둑을 따라 줄지어 배치했다. [his men, river bank]

____

:: 1. 그는 광범위한 지식을 가지고 있다. 2. 하나의 산맥이 두 나라를 분리시키고 있다. 3. 그는 책들을 책장에 가지런히 놓았다.

233 bond [band / bɔnd]

Step 01
해석연습

다음 문장을 bond에 유의하여 해석해 보세요. (해석은 이 페이지의 하단부에 있음)

1. Common tastes form a bond between the two men. ________________________
2. The prisoner will be freed from his bonds. ________________________
3. He put all his money into public bonds. ________________________

Step 02
뜻 알기

bond에는 다음과 같은 여러 가지의 뜻이 있습니다.

❶ (인간관계의) 유대, 결속 🄝 something that unites or joins people together

❷ 끈, 족쇄, 속박; 접착제 🄝 something used for tying or binding together

❸ 공채(증서), 회사채, 채권 🄝 an official document issued by a government or company
promising to pay back money, often with interest

> 한 걸음 더 **bondage** 노예의 신분, 속박, 굴레 **a bond of friendship** 우정의 유대 **national[government] bond** 국채(國債)
> **public bond** 공채(公債)

Step 03
연습문제

다음 문장의 bond에 해당되는 뜻을 **Step 02** 의 ❶∼❸에서 고르세요. (해답은 462쪽)

1. He felt a strong bond with his audience. (   )
2. She invested her money in stocks and bonds. (   )
3. The prisoner is in bonds. (   )
4. They released the man from his bonds. (   )
5. There is a bond of friendship between them. (   )
6. The government issued bonds to finance the new port construction. (   )

Step 04
영작연습

다음 문장을 주어진 부분을 이용하여 영어로 옮기세요. (해답은 462쪽)

1. 두 형제 사이에는 강한 유대감이 있다. [strong, between]

____

2. 그녀는 인습의 족쇄(속박)를 깨뜨리려고 시도했다. [break, convention]

____

3. 그 회사는 자금을 마련하기 위해 채권을 발행할 것이다. [sell, raise money]

____

:: 1. 공통된 취미는 사람들을 결속시켜 준다. 2. 그 죄수는 사슬(속박)에서 자유롭게 될 것이다. 3. 그는 자신의 돈 전부를 공채에 투자했다.

234 yield [ji:ld]

Step 01 해석연습

다음 문장을 yield에 유의하여 해석해 보세요. (해석은 이 페이지의 하단부에 있음)

1. The pear tree yields well this year. ________________________

2. The yields of the farm have decreased recently. ________________________

3. At last the enemy yielded to our soldiers. ________________________

Step 02 뜻 알기

yield에는 다음과 같은 여러 가지의 뜻이 있습니다.

❶ ~을 산출하다, 수확을 올리다, ~을 생기게 하다 **v** to produce; to bring forth

❷ 산출량, 생산액, 수확물, 이윤 **n** the amount yielded; result or profit

❸ 포기하다, 항복[굴복]하다, 양보하다 **v** to give up; to surrender; to give way

> 한 걸음 더 **the yield on bond** 채권의 수익률 **annual yield** 연간 산출량 **a large yield** 풍작
> **yielding** ① 다산의, 수확이 좋은 ② 고분고분한, 유연한, 잘 구부러지는 **yield to temptation** 유혹에 지다

Step 03 연습문제

다음 문장의 yield에 해당되는 뜻을 Step 02 의 ❶~❸에서 고르세요. (해답은 462쪽)

1. The investment yielded rich profits. (   )

2. They yielded the town to the enemy. (   )

3. The crop yield is higher than our expectation. (   )

4. The yields on my shares have increased this year. (   )

5. He will not yield an inch on that matter. (   )

6. This tree yields plenty of fruit. (   )

Step 04 영작연습

다음 문장을 주어진 부분을 이용하여 영어로 옮기세요. (해답은 462쪽)

1. 이 사업은 많은 이익을 낼 것이다. [business, profits]

____

2. 이 광산의 연간 산출량은 얼마입니까? [annual, mine]

____

3. 그는 그런 협박에 굴복할 그런 사람이 아니다. [man, such, threat]

____

Day 24

335

235 even [í:vən]

Step 01
해석연습

다음 문장을 even에 유의하여 해석해 보세요. (해석은 이 페이지의 하단부에 있음)

1. The ground was even, and the road was good. ________________________

2. 2, 4, 6, 8 and 10 are even numbers. ________________________

3. It is very cold here even in July. ________________________

4. Jennifer looks even better in real life. ________________________

Step 02
뜻 알기

even에는 다음과 같은 여러 가지의 뜻이 있습니다.

❶ 평평한, 규칙적인, 고른 a level, flat, smooth, regular

❷ 짝수의 a (of numbers) exactly divisible by two

❸ ~조차도, ~까지도 ad used to point out something unexpected in what one is saying

❹ (비교급 앞에 쓰여 비교급을 강조하여) 훨씬, 더욱, 더 한층 ad (with comparatives) still, yet

> 한 걸음 더 **Our scores are now <u>even</u>.** 우리의 점수는 이제 같다.
> → (점수, 등수 등이) 같은, 동일한, 비긴(=equal, tied, same)
> **even number** 짝수(↔ odd number 홀수) **even scores** 동점 **on even terms** 대등한 조건으로

Step 03
연습문제

다음 문장의 even에 해당되는 뜻을 Step 02 의 ❶~❹에서 고르세요. (해답은 462쪽)

1. Even the slightest noise disturbs him. (   )
2. Light travels even faster than sound. (   )
3. My sister has even teeth. (   )
4. The game can be played with any even number of players. (   )
5. It's hot here even in October. (   )
6. The two tables are of even height. (   )
7. Try to invite even number of guests if possible. (   )
8. My car is even more expensive than yours. (   )

Step 04
영작연습

다음 문장을 주어진 부분을 이용하여 영어로 옮기세요. (해답은 462쪽)

1. 당구대는 완벽하게 평평해야 한다. [billiard-table, perfectly]

____

2. 책의 왼쪽 페이지는 대개 짝수 번호를 가지고 있다. [usually, numbers]

____

3. 어린아이조차도 이 책을 이해할 수 있다. [child, understand]

____

4. 내 개가 너의 개보다 훨씬 더 크다. [bigger than]

____

∷ 1. 땅은 평탄하고 길은 좋았다. 2. 2, 4, 6, 8과 10은 짝수이다. 3. 이곳은 7월조차도 춥다. 4. 제니퍼는 실물이 훨씬 낫다.

A. 다음 뜻에 해당되는 단어를 보기에서 찾아 적으세요.

> **보기** decline range bond yield even

01. ______________ to give up; to surrender; to give way
02. ______________ the extent or scope; area; a variety of things, ideas, or products
03. ______________ exactly divisible by two
04. ______________ something used for tying or binding together
05. ______________ gradual decrease to a lower level
06. ______________ something that unites or joins people together
07. ______________ the amount yielded; result or profit
08. ______________ (with comparatives) still, yet
09. ______________ to arrange (someone or something) in order or in a row or rows
10. ______________ an official document issued by a government or company promising to pay back money, often with interest
11. ______________ level, flat, smooth, regular
12. ______________ a row, line, or series; a chain of mountains
13. ______________ used to point out something unexpected in what one is saying
14. ______________ to say "no" to (an invitation, etc); to refuse (something offered)
15. ______________ to produce; to bring forth

B. 다음 빈칸에 가장 알맞은 단어를 보기에서 찾아 적으세요.

> **보기** decline(s) range bond(s) yield(s) even

01. This table has an (   ) surface.
02. Stand up and (   ) your seat to the old.
03. I'm sorry I must (   ) your invitation.
04. There is a strong (   ) between the two sisters.
05. She is (   ) more beautiful than her sister.
06. Mr. Lee has a wide (   ) of knowledge.
07. The hill gently (   ) to a lake.
08. Companies sell (   ) to raise money.
09. What is the (   ) of this farm per acre?
10. Eight is an (   ) number.
11. A (   ) of high mountains stretches away like a wall.
12. The prisoners will be freed from their (   ).
13. (   ) a child can answer it.
14. The officer will (   ) his soldiers in order of size.
15. This land (   ) a good wheat crop.

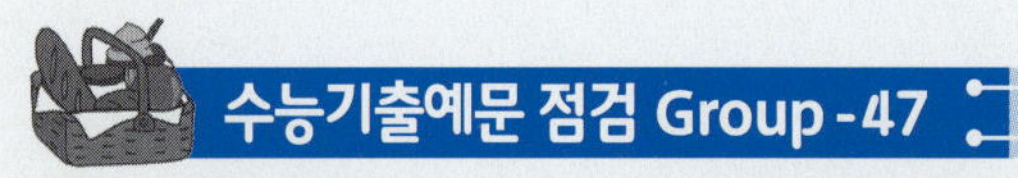

해답은 462쪽

다음 문장을 굵게 처리된 단어에 유의하여 해석해 보세요.

01. This year the numbers are expected to show a steeper **decline**. [1998년-홀수형 43번]

→ ______________________

02. There it was before me – smiling and inviting; it was difficult for anyone to **decline** that invitation. [2013년-홀수형 22번]

→ ______________________

03. The growth rate of total output **declined** from the 1960-1969 period to the 1980 1989 period. [2010년-홀수형 35번]

→ ______________________

04. They grow very slowly and **range** from 15 to 40 feet in height. [2011년-홀수형 37번]

→ ______________________

05. Infrasound is a low-pitched sound, whose frequency is far below the **range** of human ears. [2004년-홀수형 47-48번]

→ ______________________

06. Men's clothes will continue to vary only slightly and within a narrow **range** depending on where they work. [1994년-1차 37번]

→ ______________________

07. Afraid of the world that is portrayed on TV, people stay in their homes with close family and do not build **bonds** with their neighbors. [2012년-홀수형 43번]

→ ______________________

08. Every process of decaffeination, whether chemical-or water-based, starts with steaming the green beans to loosen the **bonds** of caffeine. [2009년-홀수형 40번]

→ ______________________

09. Greenery creates a natural gathering space for neighbors and, ultimately, stronger **bonds** in the community. [2007년-홀수형 24번]

→ ______________________

10. The cleared soil was rich in minerals and nutrients and provided substantial production **yields**. [2012년-홀수형 28번]

→ ______________________

11. One pig might have been worth five chickens in trade; a week's labor might have **yielded** one goat, and so on. [1998년-홀수형 45번]

→ ______________________

12. Today I'd like to talk about what you should do when driving. First, always observe the traffic signals. Second, do not speed. Finally, **yield** to other drivers. [1998년-홀수형 17번]

→ ______________________

13. Words can **yield** a variety of interpretations in terms of the kind of behaviors people think they mean. [2010년-홀수형 39번]

→ ______________________

14. First, farming will become **even** more efficient by using new types of technology. [1995년-홀수형 46번]

→ ______________________

15. People tend to stick to their first impressions, **even** if they are wrong. [2007년-홀수형 25번]

→ ______________________

16. But it can also happen that one's memories grow much sharper **even** after a long passage of time. [2008년-홀수형 22번]

→ ______________________

236 spell [spel]

Step 01 해석연습

다음 문장을 spell에 유의하여 해석해 보세요. (해석은 이 페이지의 하단부에 있음)

1. He spelled my name wrong. _______________________
2. The witch recited a spell and turned herself into a dove. _______________________
3. We had a spell of fine weather last week. _______________________

Step 02 뜻 알기

spell에는 다음과 같은 여러 가지의 뜻이 있습니다.

❶ (낱말의) 철자를 쓰다[말하다] **v** to write or say the letters of a word in correct order

❷ 주문, 마법 **n** words or actions that cause magic

❸ 한동안의 계속, 잠시 동안; (교대로 하는) 한 차례의 일 **n** a period of time or a particular kind of activity, weather, etc

> 한 걸음 더 **I was completely under the <u>spell</u> of her beauty.** 나는 완전히 그녀의 아름다움에 매료되었다.
> → 매력, 마력(=charm, fascination)
> **spelling** ① 철자법 ② (낱말의) 철자 **spellbound** ① 주문에 얽매인 ② 매혹된, 홀린

Step 03 연습문제

다음 문장의 spell에 해당되는 뜻을 **Step 02** 의 ❶~❸에서 고르세요. (해답은 462쪽)

1. How do you spell your name? (　　　)
2. I remember that foggy spell we had last week. (　　　)
3. The magician cast a spell on his daughter. (　　　)
4. Tell me how to spell the word. (　　　)
5. We will have a spell of hot weather this week. (　　　)
6. The prince was bounded by the old witch's spell. (　　　)

Step 04 영작연습

다음 문장을 주어진 부분을 이용하여 영어로 옮기세요. (해답은 462쪽)

1. 그 어린아이는 자신의 이름을 정확히 쓸 수 없었다. [child, correctly]

____

2. 그 마녀의 주문은 왕자를 개구리로 바꾸었다. [witch's, turn ~ into]

____

3. 시골에서 잠시 머문 후에 그는 집으로 돌아왔다. [after, brief, returned]

____

:: 1. 그는 내 이름의 철자를 틀리게 썼다. 2. 마녀는 주문을 외우고 비둘기로 변신했다. 3. 지난주는 한동안 계속되는 맑은 날씨였다.

237 column [kάləm /kɔ́ləm]

Step 01 해석연습 다음 문장을 column에 유의하여 해석해 보세요. (해석은 이 페이지의 하단부에 있음)

1. Those stone columns hold up the roof. _______________________________

2. She writes a weekly column about gardening. _______________________________

3. This book has two columns on every page. _______________________________

Step 02 뜻 알기 column에는 다음과 같은 여러 가지의 뜻이 있습니다.

❶ 기둥, 원주 **n** a tall, upright pillar used to support a building or as a decoration

❷ (신문 따위의) 난, 단, 특별 기고란 **n** a section in a newspaper, often written regularly by a particular person, on a particular subject

❸ 세로 열, 세로 행; 세로 단 **n** a vertical row; a vertical section of a page of print

> 한 걸음 더 **columnist** 칼럼리스트, 특별란 기고가 **the "wants" column** 구인[구직]란 **a column of water** 물기둥
> **a column of mercury** (온도계의) 수은주

Step 03 연습문제 다음 문장의 column에 해당되는 뜻을 **Step 02** 의 ❶～❸에서 고르세요. (해답은 462쪽)

1. The soldiers will parade a street in four columns. (   )
2. Huge columns support the cathedral roof. (   )
3. I read the sport column of the newspaper every day. (   )
4. The columns were made of white marble. (   )
5. Add the total of the right column to that of the left. (   )
6. He will write a daily column about finance from next week. (   )

Step 04 영작연습 다음 문장을 주어진 부분을 이용하여 영어로 옮기세요. (해답은 462쪽)

1. 그녀는 사원의 조각된 기둥들을 보고 감탄했다. [admired, carved, temple]

____

2. 그는 신문의 스포츠난을 읽는 것을 좋아한다. [sport, newspaper]

____

3. 나는 각각의 세로행에 있는 숫자들을 따로따로 더했다. [added up, separately]

____

∷ 1. 저 돌기둥들이 지붕을 떠받치고 있다. 2. 그녀는 매주 정원 가꾸기에 대한 칼럼을 쓴다. 3. 이 책은 각 페이지가 두 단으로 되어 있다.

238 observe [əbzə́ːrv]

Step 01
해석연습

다음 문장을 observe에 유의하여 해석해 보세요. (해석은 이 페이지의 하단부에 있음)

1. The boy observed the moon every night. ________________________

2. We should observe the rules of the game. ________________________

3. She observed nothing on the plan. ________________________

Step 02
뜻 알기

observe에는 다음과 같은 여러 가지의 뜻이 있습니다.

❶ ~을 보다, 알아차리다, 관찰하다, 관측하다 [v] to see and notice; to watch carefully

❷ (법, 규칙, 협정, 습관 등을) 지키다, 준수하다 [v] to obey, follow, or keep (law, rule, agreement, custom, etc)

❸ ~을 비평하다, (소견으로서) 말하다 [v] to say by way of comment; to remark

> 한 걸음 더 **observance** (법률, 규칙 따위의) 준수, 지킴 **observation** ① 관찰, 주목 ② 의견, 비평, 발언
> **observer** ① 관찰자, 감시자 ② (규칙 등의) 준수자 **observatory** 관측소, 천문대, 기상대

Step 03
연습문제

다음 문장의 observe에 해당되는 뜻을 **Step 02** 의 ❶~❸에서 고르세요. (해답은 462쪽)

1. Observe how the spider builds a web. (　　)

2. Do they observe Christmas Day in that country? (　　)

3. The policeman observed his behavior closely. (　　)

4. No one observed on that matter. (　　)

5. You should observe the school regulations. (　　)

6. The TV-news anchor observed on the President's speech. (　　)

Step 04
영작연습

다음 문장을 주어진 부분을 이용하여 영어로 옮기세요. (해답은 462쪽)

1. 나는 그녀가 몰래 방을 빠져나가는 것을 보았다. [steal, out of]

____

2. 이륙 혹은 착륙 중에는 안전규칙을 지켜 주십시오. [safety, take-off, landing]

____

3. 우리의 선생님은 우리 모두가 최종시험을 통과했다고 말씀하셨다. [passed, final exam]

____

:: 1. 그 소년은 밤마다 달을 관측했다. 2. 우리는 경기의 규칙을 지켜야 한다. 3. 그녀는 그 계획에 대해 한 마디의 의견도 말하지 않았다.

239 complimentary [kàmpləméntəri / kɔ̀m-]

Step 01 해석연습

다음 문장을 complimentary에 유의하여 해석해 보세요. (해석은 이 페이지의 하단부에 있음)

1. He made complimentary remarks to the restaurant owner about the good food.

____

2. She gave me two complimentary tickets to the play. _______________________________

Step 02 뜻 알기

complimentary에는 다음과 같은 여러 가지의 뜻이 있습니다.

❶ 칭찬의, 찬사의, 경의를 표하는 **a** expressing admiration, praise, respect, etc

❷ 무료의, 초대의 **a** given free, out of courtesy or kindness

> 한 걸음 더 **a complimentary remark** 찬사, 칭찬의 말 **a complimentary address** 축사 **a complimentary dinner** 초청만찬
> **a complimentary ticket** 무료초대권 **complimentary beverage** (기내의) 서비스[무료] 음료
> **compliment** ⓝ 찬사, (사교상의) 칭찬; 경의 ⓥ ① ~에게 찬사의 말을 하다, 칭찬하다 ② (남에게) 증정하다
> **complimentary copy** (책의) 증정본; 견본

Step 03 연습문제

다음 문장의 complimentary에 해당되는 뜻을 **Step 02** 의 ❶~❷에서 고르세요. (해답은 463쪽)

1. We've got two complimentary tickets for the concert. (   )
2. His writing has received many complimentary reviews from critics. (   )
3. Reply today to receive your complimentary copy. (   )
4. He was extremely complimentary about her work. (   )

Step 04 영작연습

다음 문장을 주어진 부분을 이용하여 영어로 옮기세요. (해답은 463쪽)

1. 나의 선생님은 나의 연구보고서에 대해 매우 칭찬하는 말씀을 하셨다. [remark, research paper]

____

2. 식당 주인은 그에게 와인 한 잔을 무료로 주었다. [owner, glass, wine]

____

⠿ 1. 그는 훌륭한 음식에 대하여 식당 주인에게 찬사를 건넸다. 2. 그녀는 나에게 연극초대권 두 장을 주었다.

240 capital [kǽpətl]

Step 01 해석연습

다음 문장을 capital에 유의하여 해석해 보세요. (해석은 이 페이지의 하단부에 있음)

1. London is the capital of England. ________________________________

2. This sentence begins with a capital "A." ________________________________

3. The company has a capital of $500,000. ________________________________

4. This is the capital point in our discussion. ________________________________

Step 02 뜻 알기

capital에는 다음과 같은 여러 가지의 뜻이 있습니다.

❶ 수도 **n** a city or town where the government of a country or state is located

❷ 대문자 **n** a letter of the alphabet written in its large form
대문자의, 대문자로 써진 **a** written or printed in its large form

❸ 자본(금), 자산 **n** money or property that is used in carrying on a business

❹ 주된, 주요한, 중요한 **a** main, chief, very important

> 한 걸음 더 **He made a <u>capital</u> speech.** 그는 멋진 연설을 했다. → 멋진, 훌륭한
> **Hollywood is the <u>capital</u> of the movie industry.** Hollywood는 영화산업의 중심지이다.
> → ~의 중심지(=a place that is a centre for an industry, business, or other activity)

Step 03 연습문제

다음 문장의 capital에 해당되는 뜻을 **Step 02** 의 ❶~❹에서 고르세요. (해답은 463쪽)

1. Each individual nation has its capital. (   )
2. Our company has a capital of $300,000. (   )
3. That was the capital point in the discussion. (   )
4. This map shows the region around the capital in detail. (   )
5. Don't forget to write your name in capitals. (   )
6. What's the capital products of this town? (   )
7. The name and address are written in capitals. (   )
8. Recently companies are having difficulty in raising capital. (   )

Step 04 영작연습

다음 문장을 주어진 부분을 이용하여 영어로 옮기세요. (해답은 463쪽)

1. 미국의 각 주는 수도를 가지고 있다. [each, state]

____

2. 너의 이름과 주소를 대문자로 써라. [write, address]

____

3. 당신은 새 사업을 시작하기 위해서 더 많은 자본금이 필요할 것이다. [start, business]

____

4. 우리는 지난주에 파리와 다른 주요한 도시들을 방문했다. [Paris, other, cities]

____

:: 1. 런던은 영국의 수도이다. 2. 이 문장은 대문자 "A"로 시작 된다. 3. 그 회사의 자본금은 50만 달러이다. 4. 이것이 우리 토론의 중요한 점이다.

Day 24

A. 다음 뜻에 해당되는 단어를 보기에서 찾아 적으세요.

> **보기**   spell   column   observe   complimentary   capital

01. ______________ to say by way of comment; to remark
02. ______________ words or actions that cause magic
03. ______________ a city or a town where the government of a country or state is placed
04. ______________ a tall, upright pillar used to support a building or as a decoration
05. ______________ to obey, follow, or keep
06. ______________ a letter of the alphabet written in its large form
07. ______________ a period of time or a particular kind of activity, weather, etc
08. ______________ a section in a newspaper, often written regularly by a particular person, on a particular subject
09. ______________ expressing admiration, praise, respect, etc
10. ______________ main, chief, very important
11. ______________ to write or say the letters of a word in correct order
12. ______________ given free, out of courtesy or kindness
13. ______________ to see and notice; to watch carefully
14. ______________ money or property that is used in carrying on a business
15. ______________ a vertical row; a vertical section of a page of print

B. 다음 빈칸에 가장 알맞은 단어를 보기에서 찾아 적으세요.

> **보기**   spell   column   observe   complimentary   capital

01. The company has 300 million won as (   ).
02. He added up a (   ) of figures.
03. I asked him to (   ) his name for me.
04. My teacher made some (   ) remarks about my work.
05. He will (   ) the height of the sun all day.
06. She writes a weekly (   ) about cooking.
07. Tomorrow we will visit Rome, the (   ) of Italy.
08. The witch's (   ) turned a prince into a little bear.
09. We should (   ) the traffic signal.
10. For a (   ) brochure, contact your travel agent.
11. We had a long (   ) of rainy weather.
12. They missed the (   ) point of the things.
13. We saw a graceful Ionic (   ) on the hill.
14. "It's a lovely day," the lady (   ).
15. A (   ) letter is used at the beginning of a sentence.

다음 문장을 굵게 처리된 단어에 유의하여 해석해 보세요.

01. He **observed** that in contests of this type, males with the longest, thickest necks usually won. [2006년–홀수형 29번]

➡ ________________________________

02. Today I'd like to talk about what you should do when driving. First, always **observe** the traffic signals. [1998년–홀수형 17번]

➡ ________________________________

03. Instead, the child acquires the heritage of his culture by **observing** and imitating adults in such activities as rituals, hunts, festivals, cultivation, and harvesting. [2011년–홀수형 45번]

➡ ________________________________

04. There is a difference between being an onlooker and being a true **observer** of art. [1998년–홀수형 49번]

➡ ________________________________

05. Upon receiving your last letter, I rushed to look up the word "flattering" in the dictionary. I was shocked to find out that it could imply something negative, which I certainly did not mean. I should have used some word like "**complimentary**" instead. [2010년–홀수형 20번]

➡ ________________________________

06. Some are concerned with the import or export of goods or services between one country and another. Others wish to move **capital** from one area to another. [2009년–홀수형 18번]

➡ ________________________________

07. It is now the **capital** of Nepal and, as such, the center of its government, economy, and culture. [2005년–홀수형 20번]

➡ ________________________________

08. Raising that kind of money is difficult for someone without a business record because the flow of venture **capital** has dried up. [1998년–홀수형 43번]

➡ ________________________________

Day 24

Credit is better than gold.
신용이 금보다 낫다.

241 appearance [əpíərəns]

Group 49

Step 01 해석연습

다음 문장을 appearance에 유의하여 해석해 보세요. (해석은 이 페이지의 하단부에 있음)

1. I was surprised at her sudden appearance. ___________________________________
2. Don't judge anyone by his appearance. ___________________________________
3. Appearances are against us. ___________________________________

Step 02 뜻 알기

appearance에는 다음과 같은 여러 가지의 뜻이 있습니다.

❶ 출현, 등장 **n** the act of coming into view or coming into a place

❷ 외모, 모양, 겉보기 **n** the way someone or something looks to other people

❸ (복수형으로 쓰여) 형세, 정세, 정황 **n** (pl) circumstances

> 한 걸음 더 **appear** ① 나타나다, 출현하다 ② ~처럼 보이다, ~같다 **apparent** ① 눈에 보이는, 명백한 ② 겉보기의, 외관상의, 피상적인
> **make an[one's] appearance** 나타나다, 얼굴을 내밀다

Step 03 연습문제

다음 문장의 appearance에 해당되는 뜻을 **Step 02** 의 ❶~❸에서 고르세요. (해답은 463쪽)

1. We are now under unfavorable appearances. (   )
2. He is gentle in appearance, but strong at heart. (   )
3. It was her first appearance on TV. (   )
4. The lady has such a nice appearance. (   )
5. At the appearance of the movie star, the crowd went mad. (   )
6. The man denied the crime against all appearances. (   )

Step 04 영작연습

다음 문장을 주어진 부분을 이용하여 영어로 옮기세요. (해답은 463쪽)

1. 그는 파티에 잠깐 모습을 보이고 떠났다. [made, brief]

____

2. 우리는 최근에 건물의 전체 모양을 바꾸었다. [whole, recently]

____

3. 형세가 갑자기 우리에게 유리한 쪽으로 바뀌었다. [suddenly, in our favor]

____

∷ 1. 나는 그녀의 갑작스러운 출현에 놀랐다. 2. 사람을 외모를 보고 판단하지 마라. 3. 형세가 우리에게 불리하다.

242 **credit** [krédit]

Step 01 해석연습

다음 문장을 credit에 유의하여 해석해 보세요. (해석은 이 페이지의 하단부에 있음)

1. He gave no credit to the rumor. ______________________

2. I bought this new suit on credit. ______________________

3. She took the course for three credits. ______________________

Step 02 뜻 알기

credit에는 다음과 같은 여러 가지의 뜻이 있습니다.

❶ 신용, 신뢰, 믿음　ⓝ trust; belief

❷ 외상, 신용거래　ⓝ an act of buying now and paying later

❸ 학점, 이수 단위, 이수 증명　ⓝ a unit of a course at a school, college, etc

> 한 걸음 더 **He is a <u>credit</u> to his school.** 그는 학교의 자랑거리이다.
> → 명예가 되는 것, 자랑거리(=a person or thing that adds honor)
> **The <u>credit</u> goes to him.** 그 공적은 그의 것이다. → 공적, 명예; 칭찬, 찬사(=honor; praise)
> **Our <u>credits</u> are greater than our debits.** 차변(借邊)보다 대변(貸邊)이 크다.
> → (부기) 대변(=an entry of money paid on account)
> **The check has been <u>credited</u> to your account.** 그 수표는 당신 계좌의 대변에 기입되었다.
> → (부기) 대변에 금액을 기입하다(=enter on the credit side of an account)
> **credit card** 신용카드 **credit rating** 신용등급 **on credit** 외상으로, 신용대출로 **No credit.** 외상사절

Step 03 연습문제

다음 문장의 credit에 해당되는 뜻을 **Step 02** 의 ❶～❸에서 고르세요. (해답은 463쪽)

1. They don't sell on credit at that store. (　　)

2. This story is gaining credit. (　　)

3. I need two more English credits to graduate. (　　)

4. My father gave no credit to my statement. (　　)

5. We accept all major credit cards. (　　)

6. The drama course gave her enough credits to finish her degree. (　　)

Step 04 영작연습

다음 문장을 주어진 부분을 이용하여 영어로 옮기세요. (해답은 463쪽)

1. 나는 그녀의 말을 믿을 수 없다. [give, statement]

____

2. 요즈음은 거의 모든 물건을 외상으로 살 수 있다. [nowadays, purchased]

____

3. 나는 이번 학기에 독일어에서 3학점을 땄다. [earned, German, semester]

____

∷ 1. 그는 그 소문을 전혀 믿지 않았다. 2. 나는 외상으로 이 새 정장을 샀다. 3. 그녀는 3학점짜리 과목을 이수했다.

243 utter [ʌ́tər]

Step 01
해석연습

다음 문장을 utter에 유의하여 해석해 보세요. (해석은 이 페이지의 하단부에 있음)

1. He is an utter stranger to me. ________________________________

2. She uttered a sigh of relief. ________________________________

Step 02
뜻 알기

utter에는 다음과 같은 여러 가지의 뜻이 있습니다.

❶ 완전한, 전적인, 철저한 **a** complete; total; absolute

❷ (말, 소리 등을) 입 밖에 내다; 말하다; 표현하다 **v** to make a sound with the mouth; to speak; to express

> 한 걸음 더 **an utter fool** 완전한 바보 **an utter stranger** 전혀 모르는 사람 **utter darkness** 칠흑 같은 어둠
> **utterly** 철저히, 완전히 **utterance** (말 따위를) 입 밖에 내기, 발언, 발음 **utter a sigh** 한숨을 쉬다
> **utter a cry of pain** 아파서 소리를 지르다

Step 03
연습문제

다음 문장의 utter에 해당되는 뜻을 **Step 02** 의 ❶~❷에서 고르세요. (해답은 463쪽)

1. What an utter waste of time! (   )

2. They gazed at her in utter amazement. (   )

3. He didn't utter a single word of encouragement. (   )

4. She uttered her own secret. (   )

Step 04
영작연습

다음 문장을 주어진 부분을 이용하여 영어로 옮기세요. (해답은 463쪽)

1. 그 새 연극은 완전한 성공작이었다. [play, success]

____

2. 그는 밤새도록 말 한마디 안 했다. [word, all night]

____

∷ 1. 그는 내가 생판 모르는 사람이다. 2. 그녀는 안도의 한숨을 쉬었다.

244 **cast** [kæst / kɑːst]

Step 01
해석연습

다음 문장을 cast에 유의하여 해석해 보세요. (해석은 이 페이지의 하단부에 있음)

1. There is a park within a stone's cast. ________________________________

2. He was cast for the part of Hamlet. ________________________________

3. The statue is cast in bronze. ________________________________

Step 02
뜻 알기

cast에는 다음과 같은 여러 가지의 뜻이 있습니다.

❶ ~을 던지다 [v] to throw / 던지기, 던짐 [n] the act of casting; a throw

❷ 배역하다, 배우에게 역을 배정하다 [v] to assign a part in a play, movie, etc
   배역, 출연진, 등장인물 [n] the act of actors or actresses in a play, movie, etc

❸ ~을 부어 만들다, 주조하다 [v] to form something by pouring (hot) liquid metal, plastic, etc
   into a mould
   주형, 거푸집; 거푸집에 부어 만든 것 [n] a mould; something formed by moulding

> 한 걸음 더 **cast** [kæst / kɑːst] - **cast** [kæst / kɑːst] - **cast** [kæst / kɑːst]
> **He** <u>cast</u> **his ballot in the election.** 그는 선거에서 투표를 했다. → 투표하다(=to give a vote)
> **The doctor put a** <u>cast</u> **on the soccer player's broken leg.** 의사가 축구선수의 부러진 다리에 깁스를 했다. → (의학) 깁스
> **A snake** <u>casts</u> **its skin in autumn.** 뱀은 가을이 되면 탈피한다. → (허물, 옷 따위를) 벗다(=to get rid of; to take off)
> **casting vote** 결정투표, 캐스팅보트 **castaway** 난파자, 표류자

Step 03
연습문제

다음 문장의 cast에 해당되는 뜻을 **Step 02** 의 ❶~❸에서 고르세요. (해답은 463쪽)

1. She was cast as the queen in the school play. (   )

2. The boy cast a stone at the dog. (   )

3. The worker will cast a bell in bronze. (   )

4. The director cast a famous actor in the leading role. (   )

5. A hurricane cast trees to the ground. (   )

6. Metal is melted before it is cast. (   )

Step 04
영작연습

다음 문장을 주어진 부분을 이용하여 영어로 옮기세요. (해답은 463쪽)

1. 어부가 그물을 물속에 던졌다. [fisherman, net]

____

2. 배우들의 리셉션은 공연이 끝난 뒤 열릴 것이다. [reception, performance]

____

3. 뜨거운 금속이 거푸집에 부어졌다. [metal, poured into]

____

:: 1. 가까운 곳에 공원이 있다. 2. 그는 햄릿의 역을 맡았다. 3. 그 상(像)은 청동으로 만든 것이다.

Step 01
해석연습

다음 문장을 term에 유의하여 해석해 보세요. (해석은 이 페이지의 하단부에 있음)

1. The first term begins in March in Korea. ___________________________

2. Myopia is a medical term for short-sightedness. ___________________________

3. He is on good terms with his friends. ___________________________

4. The terms of the agreement are not clear. ___________________________

Step 02
뜻 알기

term에는 다음과 같은 여러 가지의 뜻이 있습니다.

❶ 학기, 임기, 기간 **n** a fixed or limited period of time in schools, universities, businesses, etc

❷ 용어, 술어 **n** a word or expression that describes a special meaning or idea in science, art, etc

❸ (복수형으로 쓰여) 대인관계, 사이 **n** (pl) a relationship between people

❹ (복수형으로 쓰여) 조건, 조항 **n** (pl) the conditions of an agreement, contract or bargain

> 한 걸음 더 **She thinks of everything in <u>terms</u> of money.** 그녀는 모든 것을 돈의 관점에서 본다.
> → (복수형으로 쓰여) 관점, 견지, 견해(=standpoint; view)

Step 03
연습문제

다음 문장의 term에 해당되는 뜻을 Step 02 **의 ❶∼❹에서 고르세요.** (해답은 463쪽)

1. His grade went down this term. (   )
2. Those terms have been agreed. (   )
3. What is the scientific term for ozone? (   )
4. We are on friendly terms with each other. (   )
5. They agreed on the terms. (   )
6. The term derives from Greek. (   )
7. His term of office has expired. (   )
8. They are on good terms. (   )

Step 04
영작연습

다음 문장을 주어진 부분을 이용하여 영어로 옮기세요. (해답은 463쪽)

1. 그의 임기는 정확히 언제 시작되는가? [commence, exactly]

____

2. 이 책에는 많은 법률용어가 있다. [legal, book]

____

3. 그녀는 여러 해 동안 자신의 아버지와 사이가 좋지 않다. [bad, for years]

____

4. 그는 좋은 조건으로 고용되었다. [employed, favorable]

____

:: 1. 한국에서는 첫 학기가 3월에 시작된다. 2. Myopia는 근시(안)에 대한 의학용어이다. 3. 그는 친구들과 사이가 좋다. 4. 계약조건은 분명치가 않다.

A. 다음 뜻에 해당되는 단어를 보기에서 찾아 적으세요.

> **보기**   appearance(s)   credit   utter   cast   term(s)

01. ______________ a mould; something formed by moulding
02. ______________ the way someone or something looks to other people
03. ______________ a word or expression that describes a special meaning or idea in science, art, etc
04. ______________ to throw
05. ______________ an act of buying now and paying later
06. ______________ the act of coming into view or coming into a place
07. ______________ a fixed or limited period of time in schools, universities, jobs, businesses, etc
08. ______________ complete; total; absolute
09. ______________ a unit of a course at a school, college, etc
10. ______________ the conditions of an agreement, contract or bargain
11. ______________ circumstances
12. ______________ to make a sound with the mouth; to speak; to express
13. ______________ trust; belief
14. ______________ a relationship between people
15. ______________ to assign a part in a play, movie, etc

B. 다음 빈칸에 가장 알맞은 단어를 보기에서 찾아 적으세요.

> **보기**   appearance(s)   credit(s)   utter   cast   term(s)

01. His (   ) of office will expire next month.
02. She was (   ) for the part of Juliet.
03. The singer made her first (   ) on TV.
04. He will (   ) his view on the subject.
05. She bought the shoes on (   ).
06. The (   ) of the agreement are favorable to both sides.
07. Many anglers (   ) their lines in the river.
08. He took three (   ) in French this semester.
09. She used a lot of legal (   ) I don't know.
10. The whole room was in (   ) disorder.
11. His (   ) was tidy and neat.
12. The worker will pour bronze into a (   ).
13. She gave no (   ) to his statement.
14. They were on bad (   ) at first.
15. (   ) are in your favor.

다음 문장을 굵게 처리된 단어에 유의하여 해석해 보세요.

01. According to psychologists, your physical **appearance** makes up 55% of a first impression. [1998년-홀수형 23번]

➡ ___________________________________

02. The closing event of the festival was highlighted by the **appearance** of all the prize winners. [2000년-홀수형 33번]

➡ ___________________________________

03. Your check has been properly **credited**, and your account is now marked paid in full. [1994년-1차 25번]

➡ ___________________________________

04. W: This year must be really satisfying. Last year you finished in last place and this year you're competing for the championship.
M: It has been a great year, but our new owner deserves a lot of the **credit** for hiring a great coach. [2006년-홀수형 8번]

➡ ___________________________________

05. They said you're going to be **cast** for the lead role in that new drama. [2002년-홀수형 2번]

➡ ___________________________________

06. Our parents **cast** long shadows over our lives, and we become aware of their existence when we are infants. [2004년-홀수형 49-50번]

➡ ___________________________________

07. Paul Ekman uses the **term** "display rules" for the social agreement about which feelings can be properly shown when. [2008년-홀수형 31번]

➡ ___________________________________

08. In practical **terms**, it is more precise to define it as "rule by the majority, having respect for the rights of minority groups and individuals." [1995년-홀수형 16번]

➡ ___________________________________

09. The only **long-term** solution is to make life in the rural areas more attractive, which would encourage people to stay there. [1996년-홀수형 49-50번]

➡ ___________________________________

10. If we want to describe our society in **terms** of age, we may come up with four age groups – childhood, adolescence, maturity, and old age. [2008년-홀수형 42번]

➡ ___________________________________

246 critical [krítikəl]

Step 01 해석연습

다음 문장을 critical에 유의하여 해석해 보세요. (해석은 이 페이지의 하단부에 있음)

1. She has written several critical works on Hemingway. _______________
2. He looks on everything with a critical eye. _______________
3. The patient is in a critical condition. _______________

Step 02 뜻 알기

critical에는 다음과 같은 여러 가지의 뜻이 있습니다.

❶ 비평, 평론의, 비평적인 [a] judging and analysing; of the work of a critic

❷ 흠잡기 좋아하는, 혹평적인, 비판적인 [a] fault-finding; making severe judgements

❸ 위기의, 결정적인, 중대한 [a] of or at a crisis; crucial; very important; dangerous

> 한 걸음 더 **critic** 비평가, 평론가 **criticism** 비평, 평론, 비판 **critical essays** 평론 **a critical moment** 위기
> **a critical wound** 치명상 **a critical illness** 중병 **critical evidence** 결정적 증거 **critical problems** 결정적 문제
> **a critical disposition** 흠잡기 좋아하는 성질 **be in a critical condition** 위기[위험]에 처해 있는 **with a critical eye** 비판적으로

Step 03 연습문제

다음 문장의 critical에 해당되는 뜻을 Step 02 의 ❶~❸에서 고르세요. (해답은 464쪽)

1. I have written several critical works on Hemingway. (　　)
2. Don't look on everything with a critical eye. (　　)
3. He has critical eyes on art. (　　)
4. The patient's condition is critical. (　　)
5. He is very critical of his son's appearance. (　　)
6. The political situation has now reached a critical stage. (　　)

Step 04 영작연습

다음 문장을 주어진 부분을 이용하여 영어로 옮기세요. (해답은 464쪽)

1. 그 평론가는 미술에 대한 분석적인 의견[비평]을 잡지에 게재했다. [reviewer, comments]

____

2. 그는 언제나 자신의 딸의 헤어스타일에 매우 비판적이다. [always, hair style]

____

3. 부모의 돌봄은 아이의 사회화에 매우 중요하다. [parental attention, socialization]

____

:: 1. 그녀는 헤밍웨이에 대한 몇 편의 비평을 썼다. 2. 그는 모든 것을 비판적으로 본다. 3. 그 환자는 중태이다.

 ## 247 desert (뜻) ❶ [dézərt] ❷❸ [dizə́ːrt]

Step 01
해석연습

다음 문장을 desert에 유의하여 해석해 보세요. (해석은 이 페이지의 하단부에 있음)

1. The Sahara desert is in Africa. ______________________

2. She deserted her family and went abroad. ______________________

3. Your kindness is above his desert. ______________________

Step 02
뜻 알기

desert에는 다음과 같은 여러 가지의 뜻이 있습니다.

❶ 사막, 황무지 🄝 a large area of barren land, waterless and treeless, often sand-covered

❷ (사람, 지위, 책무 따위를) 버리다, 돌보지 않다, 버리고 떠나다 🆅 to leave without help or support; to abandon; to go away from

❸ (대개 복수로 쓰여) 마땅히 받아야 할 상 또는 벌 🄝 (usu. pl) suitable reward or punishment

> 한 걸음 더 **deserted** ① 황량한, 사람이 살지 않는 ② 버림받은 **deserter** 탈영병, 도망자
> **desertion** ① 버림, 유기 ② 버려진 상태, 황폐함 ③ 탈영, 탈주 **the ship of the desert** 사막의 배[낙타]
> ※ **dessert** [dizə́ːrt] 후식, 디저트 **above one's deserts** 과분하게
> **get[obtain, meet with] one's deserts** 마땅히 받아야 할 보답[상벌]을 받다

Step 03
연습문제

다음 문장의 desert에 해당되는 뜻을 **Step 02** 의 ❶∼❸에서 고르세요. (해답은 464쪽)

1. He got lost in the desert and starved to death. (　　)
2. They will punish the thief according to his deserts. (　　)
3. He deserted his wife, so she divorced him. (　　)
4. The desert spreads (out) for miles and miles. (　　)
5. She stole and was put in jail; she got her just deserts. (　　)
6. He was deserted by his friends. (　　)

Step 04
영작연습

다음 문장을 주어진 부분을 이용하여 영어로 옮기세요. (해답은 464쪽)

1. 낙타는 사막에서 매우 유용하다. [camels, useful]

____

2. 도망치는 군인은 처벌받는다. [soldier, punished]

____

3. 그는 자신의 공적(마땅히 받아야 할 상)에 따라 포상받았다. [rewarded, according to]

____

∷ 1. 사하라 사막은 아프리카에 있다. 2. 그녀는 자신의 가족을 버리고 외국으로 가 버렸다. 3. 너의 친절함은 그에게 과분하다.

248 correspond [kɔ̀ːrəspánd / kàr–]

Step 01
해석연습

다음 문장을 correspond에 유의하여 해석해 보세요. (해석은 이 페이지의 하단부에 있음)

1. These goods do not correspond to the samples. ______________________________

2. A bird's wing corresponds to a human arm. ______________________________

3. She often corresponds with her friends in Canada. ______________________________

Step 02
뜻 알기

correspond에는 다음과 같은 여러 가지의 뜻이 있습니다.

❶ 일치하다, 부합하다, 어울리다 **V** to be in agreement; to match; to be in harmony

❷ (구조, 기능 따위가) ~와 같다, ~에 상당[해당]하다 **V** to be very similar or like; to be equal to

❸ 서신[편지]왕래를 하다 **V** to communicate by letters; to exchange letters

> 한 걸음 더 **correspondence** ① 일치, 부합, 조화 ② 해당, 대응 ③ 통신, 편지왕래
> **correspondent** ⓝ ① 통신자, 편지왕래자 ② 특파원, 통신원, 기자 ⓐ 관련된, 일치하는, 상응하는
> **corresponding** ① 대응하는, ~에 상당하는 ② 통신하는, 거래하는
> **correspond to** ① ~에 일치[부합]하다 ② ~에 해당[상당]하다 **correspond with** ~와 서신 교환을 하다

Step 03
연습문제

다음 문장의 correspond에 해당되는 뜻을 **Step 02** 의 ❶~❸에서 고르세요. (해답은 464쪽)

1. The American Congress corresponds to the British Parliament. (　　)
2. The copy does not correspond with the original. (　　)
3. Do they often correspond with each other? (　　)
4. The broad lines on the map correspond to roads. (　　)
5. The house exactly corresponds with our needs. (　　)
6. She wishes to correspond with him regularly. (　　)

Step 04
영작연습

다음 문장을 주어진 부분을 이용하여 영어로 옮기세요. (해답은 464쪽)

1. 그의 행동은 그의 말과 일치하지 않는다. [actions, words]

____

2. 자동차의 엔진은 인간의 심장에 해당된다. [engine, heart]

____

3. 나는 정기적으로 런던에 있는 친구와 서신왕래를 한다. [regularly, London]

____

:: 1. 이 상품은 견본과 일치하지 않는다. 2. 새의 날개는 사람의 팔에 해당된다. 3. 그녀는 종종 캐나다에 있는 그녀의 친구들과 서신을 주고받는다.

249 sentence [séntəns]

Step 01
해석연습

다음 문장을 sentence에 유의하여 해석해 보세요. (해석은 이 페이지의 하단부에 있음)

1. Put the following sentences into English. _______________________

2. Mike was given a two-year jail sentence. _______________________

Step 02
뜻 알기

sentence에는 다음과 같은 여러 가지의 뜻이 있습니다.

❶ 문장, 문(文) **n** a group of words forming a complete statement

❷ 선고, 판결 **n** a judgement given on a prisoner by a law court; punishment
~에게 판결을 내리다, 형을 선고하다 **v** to pronounce a judgement on or decide a punishment for a person

한 걸음 더 **simple sentence** 단문 **compound sentence** 중문 **complex sentence** 복문
be under sentence of ~의 선고[판결]를 받다 **serve the sentence** 복역하다 **be sentenced to death** 사형을 선고받다

Step 03
연습문제

다음 문장의 sentence에 해당되는 뜻을 **Step 02** 의 ❶~❷에서 고르세요. (해답은 464쪽)

1. She received a light sentence. (　　)

2. I do not understand what this sentence means. (　　)

3. His sentence was five years in prison. (　　)

4. She quoted a whole sentence. (　　)

Step 04
영작연습

다음 문장을 주어진 부분을 이용하여 영어로 옮기세요. (해답은 464쪽)

1. 문장의 맨 처음 말은 언제나 대문자로 시작한다. [first word, capital letter]

____

2. 그 살인범은 사형을 선고받았다. [murderer, death]

____

:: 1. 다음 문장을 영어로 옮기시오. 2. 마이크는 징역 2년형을 선고받았다.

356

250 scale [skeil]

Step 01 해석연습

다음 문장을 scale에 유의하여 해석해 보세요. (해석은 이 페이지의 하단부에 있음)

1. A herring's scales are silver in color. _______________________

2. He weighed the meat on the scales. _______________________

3. My music teacher had me play my scales several times a day. _______________________

4. He is doing business on a large scale. _______________________

Step 02 뜻 알기

scale에는 다음과 같은 여러 가지의 뜻이 있습니다.

❶ (물고기, 뱀 따위의) 비늘; 비늘 모양의 얇은 조각, 박편 ⓝ one of the small flat pieces of skin that cover the bodies of fish, snake, etc

❷ 저울 ⓝ an instrument for weighing things

❸ (음악에서의) 음계 ⓝ (music) a series of tones going up or down in pitch

❹ 규모, 정도 ⓝ a relative size, degree, extent, etc

▷ 한 걸음 더 이외에도 scale에는 눈금, 저울눈, 척도, 축척, 비율 (보일러 속 따위에 끼는) 물때, (이에 끼는) 치석이란 뜻도 있음

Step 03 연습문제

다음 문장의 scale에 해당되는 뜻을 Step 02 의 ❶~❹에서 고르세요. (해답은 464쪽)

1. He does business on a small scale. (   )
2. Fish have scales and gills. (   )
3. Two violinists were practicing their scales. (   )
4. The scale is used to weigh vegetables. (   )
5. Auto makers are large-scale manufacturers. (   )
6. The paint on the house fell in scales. (   )
7. She weighed five apples on the scales. (   )
8. It is noted for its wide range of scales and clear tones. (   )

Step 04 영작연습

다음 문장을 주어진 부분을 이용하여 영어로 옮기세요. (해답은 464쪽)

1. 그녀는 생선의 비늘을 긁어 내었다. [scraped, off, fish]

____

2. 그 직원은 저울에 소포의 무게를 달았다. [clerk, weighed, parcel]

____

3. 그 소녀는 피아노로 자신의 음계를 연습했다. [practiced, piano]

____

4. 그들은 사업의 규모를 줄이기로 결정했다. [reduce, business]

____

∷ 1. 청어의 비늘은 은빛이다. 2. 그는 저울에 고기의 무게를 달았다. 3. 나의 음악선생님은 하루에도 몇 번씩 나에게 음계연습을 시켰다. 4. 그는 대규모로 사업을 하고 있다.

Day 25

Review Group -50

A. 다음 뜻에 해당되는 단어를 보기에서 찾아 적으세요.

보기	critical	dessert	correspond	sentence	scale

01. _______________ a group of words forming a complete statement

02. _______________ fault-finding; making severe judgements

03. _______________ to be in agreement; to match; to be in harmony

04. _______________ one of the small flat pieces of skin that cover the bodies of fish, snake, etc

05. _______________ a large area of barren land, waterless and treeless, often sand-covered

06. _______________ a series of tones going up or down in pitch

07. _______________ to leave without help or support; to abandon; to go away from

08. _______________ to be very similar or like; to be equal to

09. _______________ to pronounce a judgement on or decide a punishment for a person

10. _______________ suitable reward or punishment

11. _______________ a relative size, degree, extent, etc

12. _______________ judging and analysing; of the work of a critic

13. _______________ an instrument for weighing things

14. _______________ to communicate by letters; to exchange letters

15. _______________ of or at a crisis; crucial; very important; dangerous

B. 다음 빈칸에 가장 알맞은 단어를 보기에서 찾아 적으세요.

보기	critical	dessert	correspond(s)	sentence	scale(s)

01. There is scarcely any water in the (   ).

02. She will scrape the (   ) off the fish.

03. He can't even write a simple (   ).

04. A bird's wing (   ) to the arm and hand in humans.

05. He was shot for trying to (   ).

06. She tends to be (   ) of her children.

07. He engaged in business on a large (   ).

08. The judge will (   ) the thief to three years in prison.

09. He often (   ) with his friends in Australia.

10. She published her (   ) comments on art.

11. Christine is practicing her (   ) on the piano.

12. Her actions do not (   ) with her words.

13. His father is in a (   ) condition.

14. She will weigh the meat on the (   ).

15. Your kindness is above her (   ).

다음 문장을 굵게 처리된 단어에 유의하여 해석해 보세요.

01. Perhaps because you expected a different **critical** scrutiny in the two groups. [2012년–홀수형 29번]

➡ _______________________________________

02. Many people believe that it is **critical** to share similar, if not identical, beliefs and values with someone with whom they have a relationship. [2011년–홀수형 46–47번]

➡ _______________________________________

03. Then in a revised edition of Lives in 1568, complete with portraits of the artists, he combined biographical anecdotes with **critical** comment. [2012년–홀수형 38번]

➡ _______________________________________

04. Let's say you are driving across the **desert**. [2000년–홀수형 25번]

➡ _______________________________________

05. I scan the village, and there is no sign of movement. The whole village looks **deserted**. [1998년–홀수형 37번]

➡ _______________________________________

06. Thus, the European grade "good" **corresponds** to 20 of the American system, "fine" to 30, "very fine" to 40, "extremely fine" to 50, and "almost perfect" to 60. [2008년–홀수형 23번]

➡ _______________________________________

07. I hope that you no longer feel hurt or uncomfortable in any way as a result of our **correspondence**. [2010년–홀수형 20번]

➡ _______________________________________

08. You know it because you use your background knowledge of the policeman and Superman in order to understand these two **sentences**. [2004년–홀수형 36번]

➡ _______________________________________

09. The size of our world has not changed, but the **scale** of human activities has increased greatly. [1999년–홀수형 25번]

➡ _______________________________________

10. M: I'd like to send this parcel to Los Angeles.
    W: OK. Put it on the **scales**…. It weighs 10 pounds. How will you send this? [1994년–1차 4번]

➡ _______________________________________

11. These are full-**scale** models of human beings. They weigh the same as humans, and their arms and legs perform the same motions. [2007년–홀수형 3번]

➡ _______________________________________

Day 25

 **DAY 26**

Idleness is the parent of all vice.
태만은 모든 악덕의 근원.

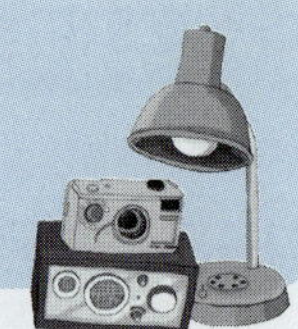

251 converse v [kənvə́ːrs] n [kɑ́nvəːrs] a [kənvə́ːrs / kɑ́nvəːrs]

Group 51

Step 01 해석연습

다음 문장을 converse에 유의하여 해석해 보세요. (해석은 이 페이지의 하단부에 있음)

1. She conversed about the picnic with her friends. ___________________________

2. He holds the converse opinion. ___________________________

Step 02 뜻 알기

converse에는 다음과 같은 여러 가지의 뜻이 있습니다.

❶ 대화하다, 환담하다, 이야기하다 v to talk informally; to chat

❷ 역(逆), 반대 n something that is opposite or contrary; the reverse
역(逆)의, 반대의 a opposite; contrary

> 한 걸음 더 **conversation** 대화, 대담 **conversely** 거꾸로, 반대로, 거꾸로 말하면
> **and converse** 그 반대도 역시 같다 * Lift your right leg three times and converse. (오른쪽 발을 세 번 들어 올리고 반대쪽도 역시 똑같이 하세요.)

Step 03 연습문제

다음 문장의 converse에 해당되는 뜻을 Step 02 의 ❶~❷에서 고르세요. (해답은 464쪽)

1. That is the converse of what most people would expect. (   )

2. She didn't converse outside of the family. (   )

3. We should reflect on the converse of that. (   )

4. While waiting at the bus stop, he conversed with an old lady about the weather. (   )

Step 04 영작연습

다음 문장을 주어진 부분을 이용하여 영어로 옮기세요. (해답은 464쪽)

1. 그는 Judy 옆에 앉아 그녀와 그 문제에 관하여 이야기를 나눴다. [next to, subject]

____

2. 나는 그녀가 방금 말한 것의 반대가 진실이라고 생각한다. [think, just, true]

____

:: 1. 그녀는 친구들과 소풍에 대하여 이야기를 나눴다. 2. 그는 반대 의견을 가지고 있다.

252 vice [vais]

Step 01 해석연습

다음 문장을 vice에 유의하여 해석해 보세요. (해석은 이 페이지의 하단부에 있음)

1. He has the vice of drunkenness. _______________________________

2. The carpenter held the piece of metal in a vice. _______________________________

3. She is the vice-chairman of that firm. _______________________________

Step 02 뜻 알기

vice에는 다음과 같은 여러 가지의 뜻이 있습니다.

❶ 악습, 죄, 비행, 악덕 ⓝ a bad habit or tendency; a sin or crime; evil conduct

❷ (관직 등의 명사에 붙어) 부(副), 차(次) ⓝ second in rank and acting as deputy for

❸ 바이스(공작물을 끼워 고정시키는 기계) [미국식 표현은 vise] ⓝ a tool for holding an object firmly, usually between two metal jaws

한 걸음 더 **virtue and vice** 미덕과 악덕 **have a vice of ~ing** ~하는 나쁜 버릇이 있다 **vice-chairman** 부의장, 부회장 **vice-president** 부통령, 부회장, 부사장 **as firm as a vice** 바이스처럼 단단한, 확고부동한

Step 03 연습문제

다음 문장의 vice에 해당되는 뜻을 Step 02 의 ❶~❸에서 고르세요. (해답은 464쪽)

1. He will put the piece of metal in the vice and cut it. (   )

2. That company has several vice presidents. (   )

3. There is a lot of vice in our big cities. (   )

4. You'd better use the vice to hold that metal firmly. (   )

5. Her father was the vice president of a national bank. (   )

6. Virtue leads to happiness and vice to misery. (   )

Step 04 영작연습

다음 문장을 주어진 부분을 이용하여 영어로 옮기세요. (해답은 464쪽)

1. 그는 끊임없이 거짓말을 하는 악습을 가지고 있다. [continual lying]

____

2. 그는 그 물건을 단단히 붙들기 위해 바이스를 사용했다. [hold, object, firmly]

____

3. Mike는 우리 팀의 부주장으로 선출되었다. [eleted, as, captain]

____

∷ 1. 그는 술에 취하는 악습이 있다. 2. 목수는 바이스로 금속조각을 고정시켰다. 3. 그녀는 그 회사의 부회장이다.

253 organ [ɔ́ːrgən]

Step 01 해석연습

다음 문장을 organ에 유의하여 해석해 보세요. (해석은 이 페이지의 하단부에 있음)

1. She is good at playing the organ. ___________________________________

2. A human body is made up of different organs. ___________________________________

3. He read the news from the organ of the government. ___________________________________

Step 02 뜻 알기

organ에는 다음과 같은 여러 가지의 뜻이 있습니다.

❶ 오르간　**n** a musical instrument similar to a piano played by touching keys and pressing pedals

❷ (생물의) 기관　**n** a part of an animal or plant that has a specific functions

❸ 정부 또는 정당의 기관지, (회사나 특정단체의) 사보, 신문　**n** a newspaper or magazine that publishes information, news etc for an organization

> 한 걸음 더 **Parliament is the chief <u>organ</u> of the government.** 국회는 정부의 주요한 기관이다.
> → 정부 등의 기관, 조직(=an organization)
> **organist** 오르간 연주자 **pipe organ** 파이프 오르간 **internal organs** 내장 **a sense organ** 감각기관
> **a reproductive organ** 생식기관 **organs of digestion** 소화기관 **organ transplant** 장기이식
> **the organs of government** 정부의 기관, 조직 **The organ of the government** 정부 기관지
> **a house organ** 사보, 업계통신(=a house journal)

Step 03 연습문제

다음 문장의 organ에 해당되는 뜻을 **Step 02** 의 ❶～❸에서 고르세요. (해답은 465쪽)

1. That church has a good pipe organ. (　　)

2. The eye ball is a very delicate organ. (　　)

3. There was an organ recital in Myungdong Cathedral. (　　)

4. This publication is the organ of the Democratic Party. (　　)

5. Smoking harms almost every organ of your body. (　　)

6. The library sends its house organ to employees and members every month. (　　)

Step 04 영작연습

다음 문장을 주어진 부분을 이용하여 영어로 옮기세요. (해답은 465쪽)

1. 파이프 오르간은 전자 오르간보다 비싸다. [more expensive, electric]

____

2. 심장은 가장 중요한 기관 중의 하나이다. [heart, important]

____

3. 그는 집권당의 기관지에서 읽은 기사를 믿지 않았다. [believe, ruling party]

____

:: 1. 그녀는 오르간 연주를 잘한다. 2. 사람의 몸은 다양한 기관으로 구성되어 있다. 3. 그는 정부에서 발간한 기관지를 읽었다.

254 page [peidʒ]

Step 01 해석연습 **다음 문장을 page에 유의하여 해석해 보세요.** (해석은 이 페이지의 하단부에 있음)

1. See page 23 for further details. _______________________________

2. She heard a page call her name in the hotel lobby. _______________________

3. Would you please page Mr. Campbell from Sydney? _______________________

Step 02 뜻 알기 **page에는 다음과 같은 여러 가지의 뜻이 있습니다.**

❶ 페이지, 면, 쪽 **n** one side of a leaf of paper in a book, periodicals, etc
  ～에 페이지를 매기다 **v** to number the pages of (a book, etc)

❷ (호텔 등의) 급사, 사환, 보이 **n** a boy servant usually in uniform, in a hotel, club, etc

❸ ～의 이름을 불러 찾게 하다 **v** to call someone's name out in a public place in order to find them

▷ 한 걸음 더 **a pageboy** 급사, 사동(=a page boy) **paging service** 무선 호출 서비스 **pager** 무선 호출기

Step 03 연습문제 **다음 문장의 page에 해당되는 뜻을 Step 02 의 ❶～❸에서 고르세요.** (해답은 465쪽)

1. She was paged repeatedly as the flight was boarding. (   )
2. There is a good picture on the next page. (   )
3. The pages at hotels usually wear uniforms. (   )
4. My brother is turning the pages of a sport magazine. (   )
5. Can I ask you to page Mr. John Brown? (   )
6. He got a part-time job as a page at the theater. (   )

Step 04 영작연습 **다음 문장을 주어진 부분을 이용하여 영어로 옮기세요.** (해답은 465쪽)

1. 첫 페이지 맨 위에 너의 이름을 써라. [top, first page]

____

2. Tony는 그 호텔에서 지난달부터 급사로 일하고 있다. [as, since]

____

3. 그녀는 공항에서 Smith 씨를 찾을 수가 없어서 그의 이름을 불러서 찾게 했다. [airport, so]

____

:: 1. 자세한 사항이 필요하면 23페이지를 보아라. 2. 그녀는 호텔 로비에서 급사가 자신의 이름을 부르는 것을 들었다.
3. 시드니에서 온 Campbell 씨를 호출해 주시겠습니까?

Day 26

255 school [skúːl]

Step 01
해석연습

다음 문장을 school에 유의하여 해석해 보세요. (해석은 이 페이지의 하단부에 있음)

1. Which school does your daughter go to? _______________________
2. I'll see him after school. _______________________
3. He belonged to the school of Positivism. _______________________
4. We saw a school of whales on the see. _______________________

Step 02
뜻 알기

school에는 다음과 같은 여러 가지의 뜻이 있습니다.

❶ 학교 n a place for teaching and learning

❷ 수업(시간); 학업 n time when teaching is given; lessons

❸ 파(派), 학파, 유파 n a group of thinkers or artists who have the same ideas etc

❹ (물고기, 고래 따위의) 떼 n a large group of fish swimming together

> 한 걸음 더 **He was well <u>schooled</u> in French.** 그는 프랑스어를 잘 교육받았다. → 가르치다, 교육하다(=to teach or train)
> **Mackerel are <u>schooling</u>.** 고등어가 떼를 지어 가고 있다. → (물고기 등이) 떼를 짓다(=to swim in large numbers)

Step 03
연습문제

다음 문장의 school에 해당되는 뜻을 **Step 02** 의 ❶~❹에서 고르세요. (해답은 465쪽)

1. We have no school today. (   )
2. A school of fish swim together. (   )
3. My father takes us to school every morning. (   )
4. The fishing-boats are searching for a large school of cuttlefish. (   )
5. He belonged to the Socratic school of philosophy. (   )
6. We are going to play baseball. (   )
7. There is an old church near the school. (   )
8. There are two schools of thought about the treatment of this new disease. (   )

Step 04
영작연습

다음 문장을 주어진 부분을 이용하여 영어로 옮기세요. (해답은 465쪽)

1. 나의 학교는 도서관과 박물관 사이에 있다. [between, and]

____

2. 수업은 매일 아침 8시 30분에 시작한다. [begins, at]

____

3. 돌고래 떼를 보는 것은 멋진 일이다. [wonderful, dolphins]

____

4. 그리스 철학자 제노(Zeno)가 스토아(the Stoic) 파를 설립했다. [philosopher, founded]

____

∷ 1. 너의 딸은 어느 학교에 다니니? 2. 나는 그녀를 수업 후에 볼 것이다. 3. 그는 실증주의 학파에 속했다. 4. 우리는 바다에서 고래 떼를 보았다.

해답은 465쪽

A. 다음 뜻에 해당되는 단어를 보기에서 찾아 적으세요.

보기   converse   vice   organ   page   school

01. _______________ a part of an animal or plant that has a specific functions
02. _______________ a large group of fish swimming together
03. _______________ to call someone's name out in a public place in order to find them
04. _______________ time when teaching is given; lessons
05. _______________ something that is opposite or contrary; the reverse
06. _______________ a bad habit or tendency; a sin or crime; evil conduct
07. _______________ a musical instrument similar to a piano played by touching keys and pressing pedals
08. _______________ a tool for holding an object firmly, usually between two metal jaws
09. _______________ a boy servant usually in uniform, in a hotel, club, etc
10. _______________ a place for teaching and learning
11. _______________ a newspaper or magazine that publishes information, news etc. for an organization
12. _______________ second in rank and acting as deputy for
13. _______________ one side of a leaf of paper in a book, periodicals, etc
14. _______________ a group of thinkers or artists who have the same ideas etc
15. _______________ to talk informally; to chat

B. 다음 빈칸에 가장 알맞은 단어를 보기에서 찾아 적으세요.

보기   converse   vice   organ   page   school

01. He has the (   ) of gluttony.
02. The tongue is the most important (   ) of speech.
03. Should I (   ) Jennifer and have her come here?
04. They are going to play basketball after (   ).
05. It is difficult to (   ) rationally with him.
06. He read the article from the (   ) of the Communist Party.
07. He belonged to the (   ) of Plato.
08. You will find a good picture on (   ) 57.
09. He gripped his stick like a (   ).
10. Our (   ) is opposite the post office.
11. He sent a (   ) to buy newspapers and pick up his mail.
12. "She is rich but not happy" is the (   ) of "She is happy but not rich."
13. A large (   ) of tuna swim together.
14. The girls were singing to the (   ).
15. She got a promotion to (   ) president last month.

Day 26

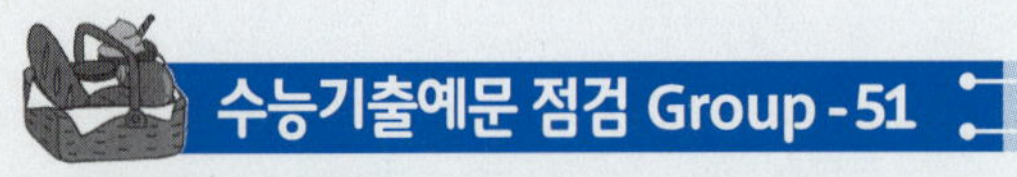

다음 문장을 굵게 처리된 단어에 유의하여 해석해 보세요.

01. She enjoyed playing the **organ** and writing poetry. [2003년–홀수형 27번]

➡ _______________________________________

02. When people began to bind books with **pages** that could be turned rather than unrolled like papyrus, the process of locating information changed. [2008년–홀수형 25번]

➡ _______________________________________

03. As a result, they are more likely to contribute to the improvement of the **school** and the learning of the students. [2004년–홀수형 45–46번]

➡ _______________________________________

04. In lakes, smallmouth often **school up**, which means that if you catch one, you can catch a bunch. [2010년–홀수형 36번]

➡ _______________________________________

05. **School** should be a time for students to develop their strengths because today's world requires specialists, not generalists. [2006년–홀수형 46–48번]

➡ _______________________________________

 **256 certain** [sə́:rtn]

**Step 01
해석연습** 다음 문장을 certain에 유의하여 해석해 보세요. (해석은 이 페이지의 하단부에 있음)

1. It is certain that the earth is round. ______________________________

2. A certain man came to see you this morning. ______________________________

**Step 02
뜻 알기** certain에는 다음과 같은 여러 가지의 뜻이 있습니다.

❶ 틀림없는, 확실한, 믿을 만한 ⓐ true; without doubt; sure; assured; reliable

❷ (알고는 있지만 확실히 말하고 싶지 않을 때 쓰임) 어떤, 어느 ⓐ known but not mentioned

> 한 걸음 더 **There is a <u>certain</u> charm about her.** 그녀에겐 다소의 매력이 있다.
> → 다소의, 어느 정도의, 약간의(=some; not much; slight)
> **certainly** 확실히, 꼭(=surely) **certainty** 확실성, 확신 **be certain of ~** (=be certain that ~) ~을 확신하고 있다
> **for certain** 확실히, 틀림없이

**Step 03
연습문제** 다음 문장의 certain에 해당되는 뜻을 **Step 02** 의 ❶~❷에서 고르세요. (해답은 465쪽)

1. There is a certain Mr. Brown on the phone for you. (   )

2. I'm certain she'll come soon. (   )

3. A certain person has been stealing books from the library. (   )

4. There is no certain cure for that disease. (   )

**Step 04
영작연습** 다음 문장을 주어진 부분을 이용하여 영어로 옮기세요. (해답은 465쪽)

1. Chris는 반드시 우리에게 가담할 것이다. [join]

____

2. 어떤 식물들은 이 지역에서 자라지 않는다. [grow, region]

____

⁛ 1. 지구가 둥글다는 것은 확실하다. 2. 어떤 남자가 오늘 아침에 너를 보러 왔다.

257 cell [sel]

Step 01 해석연습

다음 문장을 cell에 유의하여 해석해 보세요. (해석은 이 페이지의 하단부에 있음)

1. Our bodies are made up of many cells. _______________________
2. They kept him in a cell all night. _______________________
3. He bought two dry cells for his camera. _______________________

Step 02 뜻 알기

cell에는 다음과 같은 여러 가지의 뜻이 있습니다.

❶ 세포 ⓝ a very small unit of living things

❷ (교도소, 수도원 따위의) 작은 방, 독방 ⓝ a small room (especially in a prison or a monastery)

❸ (전기) 단일 구성의 전지(電池) ⓝ a piece of equipment for producing electricity

> 한 걸음 더 **Bees store honey in their cells.** 꿀벌은 벌집의 구멍에 꿀을 저장한다. → 벌집 따위의 구멍(=a very small hollow)
> **a Communist cell** 공산당 세포 / **a terrorist cell** 테러단 지부 → (정당, 비밀조직 따위의) 세포, 지부(=a small group of people who are working secretly as part of a larger political organization)
> **a dry cell** 건전지 **the cells of honey comb** 벌집구멍 **cancer cell** 암세포 **red blood cells** 적혈구 **stem cell** 줄기세포
> **the cells of the brain** 뇌세포 **cellular** ① 세포의 ② 구획식의, 이동전화의 **cellular phone** 휴대폰(=cell phone)

Step 03 연습문제

다음 문장의 cell에 해당되는 뜻을 Step 02 의 ❶~❸에서 고르세요. (해답은 465쪽)

1. Viruses do not have cell membranes. (   )
2. Tony needs some dry cells for his flashlights. (   )
3. The monk has only a small bed in his cell. (   )
4. The prisoner broke out of his cell and the building last night. (   )
5. Some cells change chemical energy into electrical energy. (   )
6. DNA exists in every cell of the body. (   )

Step 04 영작연습

다음 문장을 주어진 부분을 이용하여 영어로 옮기세요. (해답은 465쪽)

1. 그 세포는 여러 조각으로 분열될 것이다. [split up, pieces]

____

2. 그 죄수는 즉시 독방에 투옥되었다. [criminal, imprisoned]

____

3. 태양전지들은 햇빛을 받으면 곧 전기를 발생시킬 것이다. [sollar, generate]

____

:: 1. 우리의 몸은 많은 세포로 구성되어 있다. 2. 그들은 그를 밤새 독방에 가둬 두었다. 3. 그는 자신의 사진기에 사용할 건전지를 두 개 샀다.

258 channel [tʃǽnl]

Step 01 해석연습

다음 문장을 channel에 유의하여 해석해 보세요. (해석은 이 페이지의 하단부에 있음)

1. He watches the news on Channel 9 every evening. _______________________

2. The English Channel separates England from France. _______________________

3. His words opened up a channel to the solution of the issue. _______________________

Step 02 뜻 알기

channel에는 다음과 같은 여러 가지의 뜻이 있습니다.

❶ 채널, 주파수대 **n** (in radio, television, etc) a band of frequencies for sending or receiving signals

❷ 해협; 수로, 강바닥 **n** a narrow stretch of water joining two seas; a waterway; the bed of a river

❸ 경로; 루트; 수단 **n** the means by which something may travel; a route; a course

> 한 걸음 더 **the English Channel** 영국해협 **a irrigation channel** 관개수로 **channels of trade** 무역루트
> **distribution channel** 유통[판매]경로 **diplomatic channel** 외교경로[채널] **change the channel** [속어] 화제를 바꾸다

Step 03 연습문제

다음 문장의 channel에 해당되는 뜻을 **Step 02** 의 ❶~❸에서 고르세요. (해답은 465쪽)

1. The river is shallow at the sides. Keep to the channel. (   )

2. Channel 13 is showing a quiz program. (   )

3. The island can be seen across the channel on a clear day. (   )

4. She has secret channels of information. (   )

5. Which channel is the Oprah Winfrey Show shown? (   )

6. They already have a great distribution channel for the product. (   )

Step 04 영작연습

다음 문장을 주어진 부분을 이용하여 영어로 옮기세요. (해답은 465쪽)

1. 재미있는 다큐멘터리가 7번 채널에서 지금 막 시작하려고 한다. [documentary, start]

____

2. 우리는 영국해협을 건너 프랑스로 가기 위해서 비행기나 배를 타야 했다. [fly, sail]

____

3. 그는 그 정보를 공식적인 경로를 통해서 얻었다. [through, official]

____

:: 1. 그는 매일 저녁 채널 9에서 뉴스를 본다. 2. 영국해협은 영국과 프랑스를 갈라놓는다. 3. 그의 말이 그 문제 해결의 길을 열어 주었다.

259 beam [biːm]

다음 문장을 beam에 유의하여 해석해 보세요. (해석은 이 페이지의 하단부에 있음)

1. A worker is standing next to the steel beam. _______________________

2. Beams of light came from the car's headlights. _______________________

3. Look at the sun beaming overhead. _______________________

beam에는 다음과 같은 여러 가지의 뜻이 있습니다.

❶ 건물, 교각 등의 기둥, (대)들보 🄝 a long piece of wood or metal used to make buildings, bridges, etc

❷ 광선, 빛 🄝 a ray of light

❸ 빛, 광선을 발하다; 신호를 보내다, 방송하다 🅥 to shine; to send out (rays or radio waves, etc)

> 한 걸음 더 She **beamed** with delight. 그녀는 기뻐서 환하게 웃었다. → 환하게 미소 짓다(=to smile widely)
> **a beam of light** 한 줄기 빛 **the beams of smile** 환한 미소 **beam weapon** (레이저 총 따위의) 광선 무기
> **a program beamed to children** 어린이를 위한 방송 프로그램 **beaming** 밝게 빛나는, 환한

다음 문장의 beam에 해당되는 뜻을 Step 02 **의 ❶∼❸에서 고르세요.** (해답은 465쪽)

1. We saw the beams of searchlights scanning the sky. (   )
2. X-rays are beamed through the patient's body. (   )
3. You'd better use the high beams on country roads at night. (   )
4. This building needs more support beams. (   )
5. This program will be beamed to Europe. (   )
6. The carpenter is nailing down the beams together. (   )

다음 문장을 주어진 부분을 이용하여 영어로 옮기세요. (해답은 465쪽)

1. 이 강철 기둥들은 배를 만드는 데 사용될 것이다. [steel, ship]

____

2. 그는 등대로부터 비춰진 한 줄기 빛을 보았다. [radiated, lighthouse]

____

3. 이 새 송신기가 라디오 전파를 전국에 보낼 것이다. [transmitter, radio waves]

____

⠿ 1. 한 근로자가 강철 기둥 옆에 서 있다. 2. 자동차의 전조등에서 빛이 나오고 있었다. 3. 머리 위에 빛나는 태양을 보아라.

260 **cover** [kʌvər]

Step 01
해석연습

다음 문장을 cover에 유의하여 해석해 보세요. (해석은 이 페이지의 하단부에 있음)

1. She has an album in leather covers. _______________________________
2. The basket player covered his opponent well. _______________________________
3. His diaries cover almost thirty years. _______________________________
4. My salary fully covers all expenses. _______________________________

Step 02
뜻 알기

cover에는 다음과 같은 여러 가지의 뜻이 있습니다.

❶ 덮다, 씌우다 Ⓥ to put or spread something on or over something else
  가리개, 뚜껑, 표지 Ⓝ something that covers; a lid; binding of a book, magazine, etc

❷ (~을) 보호하다, 방어하다 Ⓥ to protect; to shelter / 보호(물), 피난처 Ⓝ protection; shelter

❸ (범위가) ~에 미치다[걸치다], 포함[망라]하다, ~을 다루다; 보도하다 Ⓥ to extend over; to
  comprise; to deal with; to report (for a newspaper, magazine, etc)

❹ (비용, 손실 따위를) 메우기에 충분하다, 감당하다 Ⓥ to be sufficient to meet (an expense, loss, etc)

Step 03
연습문제

다음 문장의 cover에 해당되는 뜻을 **Step 02** 의 ❶~❹에서 고르세요. (해답은 465쪽)

1. He was sent to Canada to cover the Winter Olympics. (   )
2. The floor is covered with a thick red carpet. (   )
3. He covered his girl friend from a madman's attack. (   )
4. This $300 will cover the cost of a new computer. (   )
5. Cover dish with foil and bake 30 minutes in preheated oven. (   )
6. Are you covered against fire and theft? (   )
7. How are you going to cover the cost? (   )
8. Her researches covered a wide field. (   )

Step 04
영작연습

다음 문장을 주어진 부분을 이용하여 영어로 옮기세요. (해답은 465쪽)

1. 그녀는 하얀 천으로 테이블을 덮을 것이다. [whith, cloth]

   ____

2. 사격이 시작되자 군인들은 신속하게 보호물로 달려갔다(피했다). [shooting, quickly]

   ____

3. A 교수의 강의는 주제를 철저히 다루지 못했다. [lecture, thoroughly]

   ____

4. 우리 회사가 모든 비용을 부담할 것이다. [company, expenses]

   ____

:: 1. 그녀는 가죽 표지의 앨범을 가지고 있다. 2. 농구선수가 상대선수를 잘 방어했다. 3. 그의 일기는 거의 30년에 걸친 것이다.
    4. 내 급여로 모든 지출을 충분히 감당할 수 있다.

Day 26

해답은 465쪽

A. 다음 뜻에 해당되는 단어를 보기에서 찾아 적으세요.

> 보기   certain   cell   channel   beam   cover

01. ______________ a small room
02. ______________ a narrow stretch of water joining two seas; a waterway; the bed of a river
03. ______________ to extend over; to comprise; to deal with; to report (for a newspaper, magazine, etc)
04. ______________ to shine; to send out (rays or radio waves, etc)
05. ______________ to put or spread something on or over something else
06. ______________ known but not mentioned
07. ______________ a very small unit of living things
08. ______________ a band of frequencies for sending or receiving signals
09. ______________ to be sufficient to meet (an expense, loss, etc)
10. ______________ a ray of light
11. ______________ true; without doubt; sure; assured; reliable
12. ______________ to protect; to shelter
13. ______________ a long stretch piece of wood or metal used to make buildings, bridges, etc
14. ______________ the means by which something may travel; a route; a course
15. ______________ a piece of equipment for producing electricity

B. 다음 빈칸에 가장 알맞은 단어를 보기에서 찾아 적으세요.

> 보기   certain   cell   channel(s)   beam(s)   cover(s)

01. They got the information through the proper (　　　).
02. Cancer begins as a single (　　　).
03. When the water boils, take the (　　　) from the pot.
04. This car operates on hydrogen fuel (　　　) power.
05. Steel (　　　) bear the weight of buildings.
06. This book does not fully (　　　) the subject.
07. This is boring. Let's switch to another (　　　).
08. It is (　　　) that two and two makes four.
09. The soldiers fought under the (　　　) of the artillery.
10. Radio stations will (　　　) their programs to listeners.
11. The captain will head the ship for the (　　　).
12. Will 150 dollars (　　　) your expenses for the journey?
13. A (　　　) person came to see you during your absence.
14. The police put the robber in a prison (　　　).
15. She saw a (　　　) from a flashlight.

다음 문장을 굵게 처리된 단어에 유의하여 해석해 보세요.

01. Why are some activities, such as eating and reproducing, common to all organisms, whereas other activities, such as nest-building, are limited to **certain** species? [2005년-홀수형 35번]

➡ ______________________________

02. Most important, they should take measures to be **certain** that company secrets remain protected. [2001년-홀수형 36번]

➡ ______________________________

03. In the case of human beings, the general shape and size of our body remains relatively constant while the **cells** within it are continually being replaced. [2004년-홀수형 43번]

➡ ______________________________

04. Likewise, when the fuel **cell** becomes the automotive engine of choice, the car companies focusing on increasing the efficiency of the internal combustion engine may find themselves left behind. [2011년-홀수형 33번]

➡ ______________________________

05. Tonight, the girl across from him was wearing it, **beaming**. [2005년-홀수형 38번]

➡ ______________________________

06. Seven satellites **beamed** the event to over one hundred countries. [1995년-홀수형 30번]

➡ ______________________________

07. Dozens of wildflowers of countless varieties **cover** the ground to both sides of the path. [2008년-홀수형 21번]

➡ ______________________________

08. M: How may I help you, ma'am?
W: I'm looking for a blanket to go with my mattress **covers**. [2007년-홀수형 1번]

➡ ______________________________

09. Before departure, you will be required to provide your tour leader with a copy of your insurance policy **covering** the period of travel. [2007년-홀수형 32번]

➡ ______________________________

10. Music **covers** the whole range of emotions: It can make us feel happy or sad, helpless or energetic, and some music is capable of overtaking the mind until it forgets all else. [2008년-홀수형 28번]

➡ ______________________________

11. If they don't, you will have to use your emergency fund to **cover** basic expenses such as food, transport, and accommodation, and there will be less money available for an unexpected situation that necessitates a sudden change of plan. [2009년-홀수형 20번]

➡ ______________________________

12. You indicate in your **cover letter** that you intend to follow a literary career. [2007년-홀수형 21번]

➡ ______________________________

Day 26

261 **drill** [dril]

Group 53

Step 01 해석연습 다음 문장을 drill에 유의하여 해석해 보세요. (해석은 이 페이지의 하단부에 있음)

1. The carpenter drilled holes in the wood. ___________________
2. Soldiers drill with their rifles everyday. ___________________

Step 02 뜻 알기 drill에는 다음과 같은 여러 가지의 뜻이 있습니다.

❶ 드릴, 송곳, 천공기 **n** a tool or machine for making holes
   송곳으로 구멍을 뚫다 **v** to make a hole with a drill

❷ 반복연습, 훈련 **n** thorough training by practical experiences, especially with much repetitions
   훈련시키다, 교육하다; 연습[훈련]하다 **v** to train or be trained by means of drills

> 한 걸음 더 drill에는 파종기[씨 뿌리는 기계](=a machine for planting seeds in rows)란 뜻도 있음
> **an electric drill** 전기드릴 **a pronunciation drill** 발음연습 **a fire drill** 소방훈련 **a civil defence drill** 민방위훈련
> **rifle drill** 소총(사용법) 훈련 **well-drilled** 잘 훈련받은

Step 03 연습문제 다음 문장의 drill에 해당되는 뜻을 **Step 02** 의 ❶∼❷에서 고르세요. (해답은 466쪽)

1. This drill won't bore well. (   )
2. School children do arithmetic drills. (   )
3. We are having a fire drill this afternoon. (   )
4. A drill was lying on top of some wood. (   )

Step 04 영작연습 다음 문장을 주어진 부분을 이용하여 영어로 옮기세요. (해답은 466쪽)

1. 그는 전기드릴로 나사못 구멍을 뚫었다. [holes for screws]

   ____

2. 선생님은 우리에게 매일같이 발음 연습을 시켰다. [pronunciation, every day]

   ____

∷ 1. 목수가 나무에 구멍을 뚫었다. 2. 군인들은 매일 소총을 가지고 훈련을 한다.

262 service [sə́:rvis]

Step 01 해석연습

다음 문장을 service에 유의하여 해석해 보세요. (해석은 이 페이지의 하단부에 있음)

1. The service in this restaurant is excellent. ___________________________
2. She attends a church service every Sunday. ___________________________
3. There is a good train service into the city. ___________________________

Step 02 뜻 알기

service에는 다음과 같은 여러 가지의 뜻이 있습니다.

❶ 봉사, 접대; 도움; 근무 🅝 the work or kindness done for a person or organization; help; the duty required in one's business

❷ (종교상의) 의식; 예식 🅝 a formal religious ceremony; worship

❸ 공공의 편의사업, 시설, 운행 🅝 a system or means for public use

한 걸음 더 **It's your service.** 네가 서브할 차례다.
→ (테니스, 배구 등에서의) 서브하기(=the act of serving a ball to begin the play)
public service 공공서비스, 공무 **telephone service** 전화사업 **water service** 급수사업(시설)
service station 주유소 **military service** 군복무, 병역 **a marriage service** 결혼식 **a funeral service** 장례식
serve ① 봉사하다, 제공하다, 대접하다 ② 근무하다, 복무하다 ③ (테니스 등에서의) 서브

Step 03 연습문제

다음 문장의 service에 해당되는 뜻을 Step 02 의 ❶~❸에서 고르세요. (해답은 466쪽)

1. I'm in the military service now. (   )
2. This temple has a service on Friday night. (   )
3. The new government will aim to improve public services. (   )
4. For refunds, please go to the customer service counter. (   )
5. The telephone service will be suspended until 6 p.m this evening. (   )
6. There will be a marriage service here this weekend. (   )

Step 04 영작연습

다음 문장을 주어진 부분을 이용하여 영어로 옮기세요. (해답은 466쪽)

1. 패스트푸드 식당은 서비스가 빠르기 때문에 인기가 있다. [popular, because, fast]

____

2. 오늘 아침 이 교회에서 장례식이 있었다. [funeral, this morning]

____

3. 여객선은 겨울철에 운행되지 않는다. [ferry, during, season]

____

∷ 1. 이 음식점의 서비스는 훌륭하다. 2. 그녀는 일요일마다 교회 예배에 참석한다. 3. 도시로 들어가는 열차운행시설이 좋다.

 ## 263 staff [stæf]

Step 01
해석연습

다음 문장을 staff에 유의하여 해석해 보세요. (해석은 이 페이지의 하단부에 있음)

1. My grandfather walks with the aid of a staff. _______________
2. She is on the staff of the elementary school. _______________

Step 02
뜻 알기

staff에는 다음과 같은 여러 가지의 뜻이 있습니다.

❶ 지팡이, 막대, 장대 🄝 a stick; a rod; a pole

❷ (집합적으로 쓰여) 직원, 부원, (군대의) 참모 🄝 (collectively) a group of persons working for an organization

> 한 걸음 더 **Bread is the <u>staff</u> of life.** (속담) 빵은 생명의 양식[생명의 지주]이다. → (비유적으로) 지주, 의지(=support)
> 이외에도 음악에서의 보표(譜表)(=the set of five lines that music is written on)란 뜻도 있음
> **a flag staff** 깃대 **the editorial staff** 편집부원 **the general and his staff** 장군과 그의 참모
> **the teaching staff of a college** 대학의 교수진 **the medical staff of a hospital** 병원의 의료진

Step 03
연습문제

다음 문장의 staff에 해당되는 뜻을 **Step 02** 의 ❶~❷에서 고르세요. (해답은 466쪽)

1. The cruel teacher hit the boy with his staff. (　　)
2. He will join the staff as an editor. (　　)
3. She entered the church slowly leaning on her staff. (　　)
4. My uncle served as a staff officer of the commander-in-chief. (　　)

Step 04
영작연습

다음 문장을 주어진 부분을 이용하여 영어로 옮기세요. (해답은 466쪽)

1. 그 남자는 기를 깃대에 말았다. [rolled, flag]

____

2. 그 호텔의 직원들은 매우 친절하고 예의 바르다. [friendly, courteous]

____

:: 1. 나의 할아버지는 지팡이의 도움으로 걸으신다. 2. 그녀는 그 초등학교의 직원이다.

264 regard [rigá:rd]

Step 01 해석연습

다음 문장을 regard에 유의하여 해석해 보세요. (해석은 이 페이지의 하단부에 있음)

1. We regarded her as a great artist. _______________________________
2. This matter does not regard me at all. _______________________________
3. He regards teachers and doctors. _______________________________
4. Give her my best regards. _______________________________

Step 02 뜻 알기

regard에는 다음과 같은 여러 가지의 뜻이 있습니다.

❶ 주의, 고려; 관심 [n] attention or consideration; concern
　～을 주시[주목]하다; ～을 ～하게 여기다 [v] to look at attentively; to watch; to consider

❷ 관계, 사항, 관련 [n] relation; point; reference / ～와 관계가 있다 [v] to concern; to relate to

❸ 존경, 존중 [n] respect; esteem / ～을 존경하다, 존중하다 [v] to respect

❹ (복수형태로 쓰여) 인사, 안부, 문안 [n] (pl) best[good] wishes; greetings

Step 03 연습문제

다음 문장의 regard에 해당되는 뜻을 Step 02 의 ❶～❹에서 고르세요. (해답은 466쪽)

1. We should show regard to our teachers. (　　　)
2. Mrs. Song sends her regards to you. (　　　)
3. She has no regard for his feelings. (　　　)
4. Would you give my regards to your mother? (　　　)
5. Her remarks have special regard to the matter. (　　　)
6. He is held in very high regard by his colleagues. (　　　)
7. In regard to your request, no decision has been made yet. (　　　)
8. He has no regard for destroying animals. (　　　)

Step 04 영작연습

다음 문장을 주어진 부분을 이용하여 영어로 옮기세요. (해답은 466쪽)

1. 우리는 안전규칙에 주의하여야 한다. [safety regulations]

____

2. 이 고지서는 너의 새 휴대폰의 대금지불에 관한 것이다. [bill, payment]

____

3. 그는 정치가로서 존경을 받고 있다. [as, statesman]

____

4. 당신의 부모님께 안부를 전해 주세요. [give, your parents]

____

:: 1. 우리는 그녀를 위대한 예술가로 생각했다. 2. 이 문제는 나와 전혀 관계가 없다. 3. 그는 교사들과 의사들을 존경한다. 4. 그녀에게 안부를 전해 주세요.

Day 27

265 run [rʌn]

Step 01 해석연습

다음 문장을 run에 유의하여 해석해 보세요. (해석은 이 페이지의 하단부에 있음)

1. I had to run to catch the school bus. ________________________________
2. The buses run every fifteen minutes. ________________________________
3. The river runs through the city. ________________________________
4. My uncle runs his own business. ________________________________

Step 02 뜻 알기

run에는 다음과 같은 여러 가지의 뜻이 있습니다.

❶ 달리다, 뛰다 🆅 (of a person or animal) to move with quick steps, faster than when in walking

❷ (기차, 버스 등이) 운행하다, 다니다 🆅 (of a train, a bus, a ship, etc) to travel regularly

❸ (물, 피, 강 따위가) 흐르다 🆅 (of water, etc) to flow

❹ (회사, 가게 따위를) 운영하다, 경영하다; 운행시키다 🆅 to manage; to cause to be in operation

> 한 걸음 더 **run** [rʌn] - **ran** [ræn] - **run** [rʌn]
> **Let's have a run.** 달리기하자. → 달리기, 뛰기, 경주, 경마(=the act of running; race)
> **The play had a long run of two years.** 그 연극은 2년간 장기공연을 했다. → 장기공연
> 이외에도 run에는 (동사) 불, 소문 따위가 급히 퍼지다, (명사) 야구, 크리켓의 득점; 작업, 작업시간, 생산량 등의 뜻도 있음

Step 03 연습문제

다음 문장의 run에 해당되는 뜻을 **Step 02** 의 ❶~❹에서 고르세요. (해답은 466쪽)

1. The buses don't run on Sundays. (   )
2. He runs a camera store in the city. (   )
3. The dog is running behind its mater. (   )
4. Blood is running from his wound. (   )
5. For a while, the theater was run by his son. (   )
6. The man suddenly started to run. (   )
7. They are running special buses to and from the fair. (   )
8. Big tears ran down his cheeks. (   )

Step 04 영작연습

다음 문장을 주어진 부분을 이용하여 영어로 옮기세요. (해답은 466쪽)

1. 그녀는 매일아침 학교 트랙 주위를 달린다. [around, school track]

____

2. 여객선은 목포와 제주 사이를 운행한다. [ferry, between]

____

3. 눈물이 Jane의 눈에서 흘러내렸다. [tears, from]

____

4. 그 식당은 한 일본계 미국인에 의해 운영되고 있다. [Japanese-American]

____

:: 1. 나는 학교 버스를 타기 위해 뛰어야 했다. 2. 버스는 15분마다 운행된다. 3. 그 강은 도시를 관통해 흐른다. 4. 나의 삼촌은 자영업을 하신다.

A. 다음 뜻에 해당되는 단어를 보기에서 찾아 적으세요.

> 보기　　drill　service　staff　regard　run

01. _____________ relation; point; reference
02. _____________ (of a person or animal) to move with quick steps, faster than when in walking
03. _____________ thorough training by practical experiences, especially with much repetitions
04. _____________ the work or kindness done for a person or organization; help; the duty required in one's business
05. _____________ to manage; to cause to be in operation
06. _____________ to look at attentively; to watch; to consider
07. _____________ a stick; a rod; a pole
08. _____________ (of a train, a bus, a ship, etc) to travel regularly
09. _____________ respect; esteem
10. _____________ a formal religious ceremony; worship
11. _____________ a group of persons working for an organization
12. _____________ best[good] wishes; greetings
13. _____________ (of water, etc) to flow
14. _____________ a tool or machine for making holes
15. _____________ a system or means for public use

B. 다음 빈칸에 가장 알맞은 단어를 보기에서 찾아 적으세요.

> 보기　　drill　service　staff　regard(s)　run(s)

01. That was a lovely Easter (　　　　), wasn't it?
02. Mountain streams (　　　　) to the ocean.
03. With (　　　　) to this matter, I have nothing further to say.
04. In December, the ferry is in (　　　　) only during the weekend.
05. There will be a civil defence (　　　　) this afternoon.
06. Do the subways (　　　　) all night?
07. An old man came along the road leaning on his (　　　　).
08. Jenny has very little (　　　　) for the feelings of others.
09. Please give my (　　　　) to your family.
10. We must (　　　　) to catch the last train.
11. The school has a large teaching (　　　　).
12. My uncle (　　　　) a bus company in the city.
13. The students no longer have high (　　　　) for the teacher.
14. He will (　　　　) a series of holes in the frame.
15. She didn't tip him for his poor (　　　　).

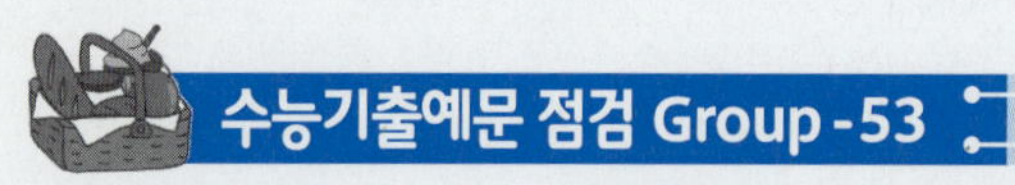

해답은 466쪽

다음 문장을 굵게 처리된 단어에 유의하여 해석해 보세요.

01. Their use ranges from the **drill** in a dentist's office to saws for cutting rocks, and to glass cutters. [2007년-홀수형 30번]

➡ ___________________________________

02. Because of this change, shop owners are changing store designs to make shopping and consumer **service** easier. [2004년-홀수형 44번]

➡ ___________________________________

03. Facilities in the rural areas, such as transport, health, and education **services**, should be improved to foster a more positive attitude to rural life. [1996년-홀수형 49–50번]

➡ ___________________________________

04. New or remodeled hospitals and nursing homes increasingly come equipped with healing gardens where patients and **staff** can get away from barren, indoor surroundings. [2008년-홀수형 33번]

➡ ___________________________________

05. For example, the Erie Canal, which took four years to build, was **regarded** as the height of efficiency in its day. [2011년-홀수형 33번]

➡ ___________________________________

06. Cultures sometimes vary tremendously in this **regard**. [2008년-홀수형 31번]

➡ ___________________________________

07. Min-ho: That's too bad. Take care of yourself, and give my best regards to your parents.
Susan: Thanks, I will. [1996년-홀수형 6번]

➡ ___________________________________

08. Dreams have been **regarded** as prophetic communications which, when properly decoded, would enable us to foretell the future. [2012년-홀수형 49–50번]

➡ ___________________________________

09. **Regarding** female children with asthma, the lowest percentage in urban areas was greater than the highest percentage in rural areas. [2011년-홀수형 38번]

➡ ___________________________________

10. People who **run** sports camps think of the children first. [2007년-홀수형 45번]

➡ ___________________________________

11. It's the nature of water to **run** downhill. [2002년-홀수형 27번]

➡ ___________________________________

12. Before he could reach the door, my mother and I **ran** out screaming. [2000년-홀수형 18번]

➡ ___________________________________

13. To my dismay, the other team scored three **runs**. [1996년-홀수형 34번]

➡ ___________________________________

14. Too many thoughts were **running** through my head. [2003년-홀수형 26번]

➡ ___________________________________

15. But Arthur was **running** out of money, because he had bought an expensive birthday gift for Jack. [1996년-홀수형 16번]

➡ ___________________________________

266 refrain [rifréin]

Step 01 해석연습

다음 문장을 refrain에 유의하여 해석해 보세요. (해석은 이 페이지의 하단부에 있음)

1. Please refrain from using the telephone for private purposes. ___________________
2. They sang the refrain of the song many times. ___________________

Step 02 뜻 알기

refrain에는 다음과 같은 여러 가지의 뜻이 있습니다.

❶ 삼가다, 억제하다 v to hold oneself back; not to do something that you want to do; to avoid

❷ 반복구, 후렴, 상투어[반복되는 말] n a phrase or verse repeated in a song or poem

> 한 걸음 더 **refrain oneself** 자제하다, 삼가다 **refrain from liquor** 술을 삼가다 **refrain from laughing** 웃음을 참다
> **refrain from greasy food** 기름기 많은 음식을 삼가다

Step 03 연습문제

다음 문장의 refrain에 해당되는 뜻을 Step 02 의 ❶∼❷에서 고르세요. (해답은 466쪽)

1. Students refrain from smoking in the classroom. (   )
2. This was a refrain I heard often. (   )
3. I could not refrain from laughing at his red nose. (   )
4. Each verse of the Psalm is followed by a refrain. (   )

Step 04 영작연습

다음 문장을 주어진 부분을 이용하여 영어로 옮기세요. (해답은 466쪽)

1. Jane은 생각한 것을 말하려다 참았다. [saying, what, thought]

____

2. 그 옛날 노래의 후렴은 결코 지루하지 않다. [old song, boring]

____

:: 1. 사적인 용도의 전화 사용을 삼가 주십시오. 2. 그들은 노래의 후렴을 반복해서 불렀다.

267 stalk [stɔːk]

Step 01
해석연습

다음 문장을 stalk에 유의하여 해석해 보세요. (해석은 이 페이지의 하단부에 있음)

1. My sister likes to eat celery stalks. ______________________________

2. The man stalked off without a word. ______________________________

3. The hunter is stalking a deer. ______________________________

Step 02
뜻 알기

stalk에는 다음과 같은 여러 가지의 뜻이 있습니다.

❶ (식물의) 줄기, 대 **n** non-woody part of a plant that supports leaves, flowers or fruits; stem 가늘고 곧바른 버팀대 **n** a thin upright object (like a stem)

❷ 당당하게 걷다, 활보하다 **v** to walk in a stiff, proud manner

❸ 살그머니 (사람 또는 짐승의) 뒤를 밟다, ～에 몰래 접근하다 **v** to follow or approach (a person or animal) secretly

> 한 걸음 더 **Disease and famine <u>stalked</u> (through) the country.** 질병과 기근이 나라를 휩쓸었다.
> → (질병, 재앙 따위가) ～에 퍼지다, ～을 휩쓸다(=to spread or move menacingly through a place)
> **stalker** ① 활보하는 사람 ② 스토커, 집요하게 남을 따라다니는 사람 ③ (몰래 접근하는) 사냥꾼
> **stalking** 스토킹, 남을 따라다니며 괴롭히기 **a deer stalker** 사슴사냥꾼

Step 03
연습문제

다음 문장의 stalk에 해당되는 뜻을 Step 02 의 ❶～❸에서 고르세요. (해답은 466쪽)

1. He is accused of stalking a woman. (　　)

2. If the stalk is damaged, the plant may die. (　　)

3. We saw a lion stalking a zebra. (　　)

4. Chris turned and stalked out of the room in disgust. (　　)

5. Remove and discard the tough central stalk. (　　)

6. I tried to tell him I was sorry, but he just stalked away. (　　)

Step 04
영작연습

다음 문장을 주어진 부분을 이용하여 영어로 옮기세요. (해답은 466쪽)

1. 그 식물의 줄기는 매우 억세다. [plant, tough]

____

2. 군인들이 어제 거리를 따라 활보했다. [along the street]

____

3. 그 여배우는 한 팬에게 2년 동안 스토킹을 당했다. [actress, fan]

____

:: 1. 나의 여동생은 샐러리 줄기 먹는 것을 좋아한다. 2. 그 남자는 한 마디도 하지 않고 성큼성큼 걸어가 버렸다.
3. 사냥꾼이 살그머니 사슴 한 마리의 뒤를 밟고 있다.

268 **code** [koud]

Step 01 해석연습

다음 문장을 code에 유의하여 해석해 보세요. (해석은 이 페이지의 하단부에 있음)

1. He is studying the Civil Procedure Code this semester. ______________________
2. We must observe the school code. ______________________
3. You must remember your access code for the computer. ______________________

Step 02 뜻 알기

code에는 다음과 같은 여러 가지의 뜻이 있습니다.

❶ 법, 법체계 **n** a set of laws arranged in an orderly manner

❷ 규칙, 관례, 규약 **n** a set of rules or principles that has been accepted by society or a group of people

❸ 신호(체계); 부호; 약호; 암호 **n** a set of signals showing numbers, letters, etc used in sending messages; a system of secret writing

> 한 걸음 더 **The spy coded a message.** 스파이는 메시지를 암호로 만들었다.
> → 기호[부호, 암호]로 만들다; 코드화하다(=to put (a message, etc) into a code; encode)
> **the civil code** 민법(전) **the criminal code** 형법(전) **the social code** 사회의 관례 **the moral code** 도덕율
> **the code of school** 학칙, 교칙 **the code of censor** 검열규정 **encode** 암호화하다 **decode** 암호문을 해독하다
> **zip code** (미) 우편번호 [=(영) post code]

Step 03 연습문제

다음 문장의 code에 해당되는 뜻을 Step 02 의 ❶~❸에서 고르세요. (해답은 467쪽)

1. There is a dress code for this party: no trainers or jeans. (   )
2. The legal system was reformed with the Code Napoleon. (   )
3. The bar codes on the products are read by lasers. (   )
4. The sport has a strict code of conduct. (   )
5. The signal will be converted into digital code automatically. (   )
6. Chapter 45 of the criminal code relates to drug offences. (   )

Step 04 영작연습

다음 문장을 주어진 부분을 이용하여 영어로 옮기세요. (해답은 467쪽)

1. 형법 3조 1항을 참조해라. [refer, Clause, Article]

____

2. 그 학교는 엄격한 복장규정이 있다. [strict, dress]

____

3. 거리명과 우편번호를 적어 주시겠습니까? [write down, street]

____

:: 1. 그는 이번 학기에 민사소송법을 공부하고 있다. 2. 우리는 교칙을 따라야 한다. 3. 컴퓨터의 접속 암호[패스워드]를 기억해야만 한다.

269 resort [rizɔ́ːrt]

Step 01
해석연습

다음 문장을 resort에 유의하여 해석해 보세요. (해석은 이 페이지의 하단부에 있음)

1. My family resorted to a hot spring. _______________________________

2. A small boat was the only resort left. _______________________________

3. We went to a resort in Jeju for our vacation. _______________________________

Step 02
뜻 알기

resort에는 다음과 같은 여러 가지의 뜻이 있습니다.

❶ 자주 가다; 잘 다니다 ⓥ to go often; to go in large numbers
  자주 다님; 자주 드나들기 ⓝ the act of resorting to a place

❷ 의지하다; 힘[도움]을 빌다; 호소하다 ⓥ to use something as a help or means
  의지하기; 수단; 의지가 되는 것 ⓝ turning to for help; means; a person or thing turned to for help

❸ 자주 가는 곳; 휴양지; 리조트 ⓝ a place where people often go for recreation or health

> 한 걸음 더 **He re-sorted out his books in the bookshelves.** 그는 서가의 책들을 재분류했다.
> → re-sort[riːsɔːrt]는 동사로서 재분류[재구분]하다(=re-classify)란 뜻으로도 쓰임
> **a summer resort** 피서지 **a resort hotel** 행락지 호텔 **as a last resort** 마지막 수단으로
> **without resort to** ~에 의지[호소]하지 않고 **resort to violence[force]** 폭력[힘]에 호소하다; 폭력[힘]을 쓰다

Step 03
연습문제

다음 문장의 resort에 해당되는 뜻을 **Step 02** 의 ❶~❸에서 고르세요. (해답은 467쪽)

1. My uncle runs a small resort hotel in Gangneung. (   )

2. She was known to resort to the cafe early morning. (   )

3. Nice is a favorite resort for the rich and famous. (   )

4. If other means fail, we shall resort to force. (   )

5. The police watched the bar to which the wanted man was known to resort. (   )

6. Sandra resorted to stealing when she had no more money. (   )

Step 04
영작연습

다음 문장을 주어진 부분을 이용하여 영어로 옮기세요. (해답은 467쪽)

1. 속초는 여름에 많은 관광객들이 잘 다니는 곳이다. [Sokcho, place, tourists]

____

2. 핵무기는 최후의 수단으로 사용되어야만 한다. [nuclear weapons, as, last]

____

3. 이곳은 겨울 휴양지로는 최적의 장소다. [optimal place]

____

:: 1. 나의 가족은 온천에 잘 다니곤 했다. 2. 작은 배 한 척이 남은 유일한 수단이었다. 3. 우리는 제주에 있는 휴양지로 휴가를 갔다.

270 due [dju:]

Step 01
해석연습

다음 문장을 due에 유의하여 해석해 보세요. (해석은 이 페이지의 하단부에 있음)

1. The report is due next week. _______________________

2. The train is due in Seoul at 9 p.m. _______________________

3. Half the money is due to her. _______________________

4. He was late to work due to the traffic congestion. _______________________

Step 02
뜻 알기

due에는 다음과 같은 여러 가지의 뜻이 있습니다.

❶ 지급기일이 된, 마감인 [a] (of a debt, bill, etc) required to be paid or submitted (at the stated time)

❷ ～하기로 되어 있는, ～할 예정인 [a] expected to happen or arrive at a particular time; scheduled

❸ ～에게 당연히 돌려져야 할, 당연한, 정당한 [a] that ought to be given; rightful; proper; suitable
당연히 돌려져야 할 것 [n] what is required as a right

❹ ～때문에, ～에 기인하는 [a] (due to) owing to; because of

▷ 한 걸음 더 **He paid the dues on the cargo.** 그는 화물세를 냈다. → 세금, 부과금, 회비(=charge, fee, tax)

Step 03
연습문제

다음 문장의 due에 해당되는 뜻을 **Step 02** 의 ❶～❹에서 고르세요. (해답은 467쪽)

1. Mr. Lee is due to speak this evening. (　　)
2. Our thanks are due to the doctor. (　　)
3. When is the budget report due? (　　)
4. The delay was due to the bad weather. (　　)
5. The payment will be due next month. (　　)
6. Our weekend plans were cancelled due to rain. (　　)
7. She is charged with driving without due care and attention. (　　)
8. Her baby is due in April. (　　)

Step 04
영작연습

다음 문장을 주어진 부분을 이용하여 영어로 옮기세요. (해답은 467쪽)

1. 이것들은 다음 주까지 내야 될 청구서들이다. [bills, next week]

____

2. 시드니에서 오는 비행기는 4시에 도착할 예정이다. [flight, Sydney]

____

3. 이번에는 가혹한 형벌이 그에게 가해져야 마땅하다. [severe punishment]

____

4. 그녀의 실패가 능력 부족에 기인한 것은 아니었다. [failure, lack, ability]

____

:: 1. 보고서는 다음 주까지 제출해야 한다. 2. 기차는 오후 9시 서울에 도착할 예정이다. 3. 돈의 절반은 그녀에게 주어야 한다.
4. 그는 교통체증 때문에 회사에 늦었다.

해답은 467쪽

A. 다음 뜻에 해당되는 단어를 보기에서 찾아 적으세요.

보기	refrain	stalk	code	resort	due

01. ______________ a set of laws arranged in an orderly manner
02. ______________ a place where people often go for recreation or health
03. ______________ owing to; because of
04. ______________ a phrase or verse repeated in a song or poem
05. ______________ expected to happen or arrive at a particular time; scheduled
06. ______________ a set of signals showing numbers, letters, etc used in sending messages; a system of secret writing
07. ______________ non-woody part of a plant that supports leaves, flowers or fruits
08. ______________ what is required as a right
09. ______________ a set of rules or principles that has been accepted by society or a group of people
10. ______________ to go often; to go in large numbers
11. ______________ required to be paid or submitted (at the stated time)
12. ______________ turning to for help; means; a person or thing turned to for help
13. ______________ to follow or approach (a person or animal) secretly
14. ______________ to hold oneself back; not to do something that you want to do; to avoid
15. ______________ to walk in a stiff, proud manner

B. 다음 빈칸에 가장 알맞은 단어를 보기에서 찾아 적으세요.

보기	refrain	stalk(ed)	code	resort	due

01. My family will go to a ski (　　　　) this weekend.
02. The accident was (　　　　) to his careless driving.
03. Naples is a place to which many tourists (　　　　) during summer season.
04. It comes under Article 5 of the Criminal (　　　　).
05. The man (　　　　) out of the room in disgust.
06. Please enter the country (　　　　) and telephone number that you are calling.
07. The final report is (　　　　) on July 6.
08. We found a hunter who (　　　　) deer in the woods.
09. Please (　　　　) from spitting in the public.
10. The plane is (　　　　) to arrive at 4:00.
11. If we can't fly to Denver, we can drive there as a last (　　　　).
12. She accepted the present as if it were her (　　　　).
13. Will you all join in singing the (　　　　), please?
14. The rabbit was eating a bean (　　　　).
15. Our school has a dress (　　　　) requiring boys to wear shirts and ties.

다음 문장을 굵게 처리된 단어에 유의하여 해석해 보세요.

01. He was relieved to hear the continued announcement: "They're at home over on that hill to the left, and they just sent me a Morse **code** message saying, 'Good night, Dad.'" [2009년–홀수형 19번]

→ _______________________________

02. Recently new building **codes** came into effect in our city. [2001년–홀수형 42번]

→ _______________________________

03. The third group is attracted by the **resort** with its colorful night life. [1994년–1차 36번]

→ _______________________________

04. Whenever he felt dissatisfied with a vague "conception of the brain," Poe said, " I **resort** forthwith to the pen, for the purpose of obtaining, through its aid, the necessary form, consequence and precision." [2013년–홀수형 46번]

→ _______________________________

05. He had been putting off doing his chemistry report which was **due** on Monday. [2010년–홀수형 19번]

→ _______________________________

06. A better place to store coffee is in a freezer, which has a much drier environment **due** to the very low temperatures. [2006년–홀수형 3번]

→ _______________________________

07. Unfortunately, however, these comforts will soon be unavailable if developments are continued without paying **due** attention to these needs. [1994년–2차 46번]

→ _______________________________

08. W: No problem. When do I have to return this book? I mean the **due date**.
M: It's two weeks from today.
[2000년–홀수형 14번]

→ _______________________________

Day 27

>>> DAY 28

A man apt to promise is apt to forget.
쉽게 약속을 하는 사람은 잊기도 잘한다.

271 coach [koutʃ]

Group 55

Step 01
해석연습

다음 문장을 coach에 유의하여 해석해 보세요. (해석은 이 페이지의 하단부에 있음)

1. He is a tennis coach of our school. ___________________________
2. The fairy changed a pumpkin into a beautiful coach. ___________________________

Step 02
뜻 알기

coach에는 다음과 같은 여러 가지의 뜻이 있습니다.

❶ (운동의) 코치, 지도원; 개인교사 **n** a trainer of sports teams, etc; a private teacher
지도하다, 코치하다 **v** to teach a person or team

❷ (열차의) 객차; 대형버스; 대형마차 **n** a railway carriage; a public motor bus; a large carriage pulled by horses

> 한 걸음 더 **Would you like first class or <u>coach</u>?** 1등석으로 하시겠습니까, 아니면 일반석으로 하시겠습니까?
> → 비행기나 기차의 일반석(=the cheapest type of seats on a plain or train)
> **private coach** (운동 따위의) 개인교사 **coach station** (장거리) 버스 정류소 **air coach** 운임이 싼 여객기
> **coach box** (마차의) 마부석 **coach-and-four** 말 네 필이 끄는 마차

Step 03
연습문제

다음 문장의 coach에 해당되는 뜻을 **Step 02** 의 ❶~❷에서 고르세요. (해답은 467쪽)

1. The coach will complain of the judge's partial ruling. (   )
2. The last two coaches of the train were derailed, causing many casualties. (   )
3. He is the coach of the Korean national baseball team. (   )
4. The coach was drawn by four brown horses. (   )

Step 04
영작연습

다음 문장을 주어진 부분을 이용하여 영어로 옮기세요. (해답은 467쪽)

1. 그는 여가시간에 볼링팀을 지도한다. [bowling, spare time]

____

2. 우리는 버스 여행으로 프랑스를 갔다. [France, tour]

____

:: 1. 그는 우리 학교의 테니스 코치다. 2. 요정은 호박을 아름다운 마차로 변하게 했다.

272 compact [kəmpǽkt / kámpækt]

Step 01
해석연습

다음 문장을 compact에 유의하여 해석해 보세요. (해석은 이 페이지의 하단부에 있음)

1. His new house was very compact. ________________________

2. She always carries her compact for make-up. ________________

3. He made an important compact last month. ________________

Step 02
뜻 알기

compact에는 다음과 같은 여러 가지의 뜻이 있습니다.

❶ 꽉 들어찬, 빽빽한, (차 따위가) 소형의, (문체가) 간결한 **a** closely packed together; neatly fitted; small and easy to carry; (of literary) condensed
～을 빽빽하게 하다, 꽉 채워 넣다 **v** to pack (things) tightly together; to condense

❷ 휴대용 분갑 **n** a small flat container with a mirror, containing face powder for a woman

❸ 계약, 협정, 맹약(盟約) **n** an agreement between two or more people, countries, etc

> 한 걸음 더 **compacted** 꽉 찬, 안정된 **a compact camera** (휴대용) 소형 카메라 **a compact car** 작고 경제적인 차
> **a compact disc** 콤팩트 디스크 (CD) **a three-nation compact** 삼국 협정 **in a compact mass** 밀집하여
> **make a compact** 합의하다, 계약을 맺다 **write compact sentences** 간결한 문장을 쓰다

Step 03
연습문제

다음 문장의 compact에 해당되는 뜻을 **Step 02** 의 ❶～❸에서 고르세요. (해답은 467쪽)

1. She took out a compact to fix her tear-stained face. (   )
2. The president's speech was short but compact. (   )
3. They made a compact not to discuss the matter further. (   )
4. The lady was looking for her compact in her handbag. (   )
5. The compact was concluded and signed in 1965. (   )
6. This new compact suitcase is easy to carry. (   )

Step 04
영작연습

다음 문장을 주어진 부분을 이용하여 영어로 옮기세요. (해답은 467쪽)

1. 나는 기름 값을 아끼기 위해 소형차를 구입할 것이다. [save money, gas]

____

2. Julie는 콤팩트를 꺼내서 화장을 고쳤다. [took out, fixed, makeup]

____

3. 한국과 프랑스 간에 협정이 이루어졌다. [reached, between]

____

:: 1. 그의 새 집은 매우 아담했다. 2. 그녀는 항상 화장을 위해 콤팩트를 가지고 다닌다. 3. 그는 지난달 중요한 계약을 맺었다.

273 room [ru(:)m]

Step 01
해석연습

다음 문장을 room에 유의하여 해석해 보세요. (해석은 이 페이지의 하단부에 있음)

1. The room was filled with smoke. ______________________________

2. This table takes up too much room. ______________________________

3. There is no room for doubt. ______________________________

Step 02
뜻 알기

room에는 다음과 같은 여러 가지의 뜻이 있습니다.

❶ 방, 실(室) [n] a part of a house or building enclosed by walls, floor and ceiling

❷ (사람, 물건 따위가 차지하는) 장소, 공간 [n] enough space for a particular purpose

❸ 여지, 여유, 기회, 가능성 [n] a need or possibility for something; chance; opportunity

> 한 걸음 더 **He rooms at Mr. Taylor's house.** 그는 Taylor 씨 집에 하숙하고 있다.
> **He is rooming with my friend Bob.** 그는 나의 친구 Bob와 방을 함께 쓰고 있다.
> → 기숙하다; 방을 함께 쓰다(=to lodge; to share a room with someone)
> **roommate** 동숙인, 한 방 쓰는 사람 **make room for** ~을 위해 자리를 비우다, 양보하다

Step 03
연습문제

다음 문장의 room에 해당되는 뜻을 **Step 02** 의 ❶~❸에서 고르세요. (해답은 467쪽)

1. There isn't enough room for a computer on your desk. (   )

2. The evidence left no room for doubt – Margie was guilty. (   )

3. The elevator was so full of people that there was no room to move. (   )

4. The conference room is upstairs on your left. (   )

5. There is still much room for compromise. (   )

6. It's bed time – you'd better go up to your room. (   )

Step 04
영작연습

다음 문장을 주어진 부분을 이용하여 영어로 옮기세요. (해답은 467쪽)

1. 거실은 깨끗하고 편안해 보인다. [neat, cozy]

____

2. 차에는 한 사람 더 탈 공간이 있다. [There is, for]

____

3. 그의 일에는 개선해야 할 여지가 좀 있다. [some, improvement, work]

____

:: 1. 그 방은 연기로 가득 차 있었다. 2. 이 테이블은 너무 많은 공간을 차지한다. 3. 의심할 여지가 없다.

274 hail [heil]

Step 01
해석연습

다음 문장을 hail에 유의하여 해석해 보세요. (해석은 이 페이지의 하단부에 있음)

1. It hailed last night for a few minutes. _________________________

2. They hailed him as hero. _________________________

3. He was trying to hail a cab. _________________________

Step 02
뜻 알기

hail에는 다음과 같은 여러 가지의 뜻이 있습니다.

❶ 싸락눈[우박]; 우박처럼 맹렬히 쏟아지는 것 **n** frozen rain drops falling from the sky
싸락눈[우박]이 내리다; 우박처럼 퍼붓다; ~을 빗발치듯 퍼붓다 **v** to come down in hail; to pour something in a shower like hail

❷ ~을 환호하여 맞이하다; 환영하다; ~에게 인사하다 **v** to give a welcoming cry to someone; to greet

❸ ~을 큰 소리로 부르다; 소리치다 **v** to shout; to call out so as to attract attention
소리침; 크게 부르는 소리 **n** a loud call

> 한 걸음 더 **hailstone** 싸락눈[우박]의 알갱이 **hailstorm** 마구 퍼붓는 우박; 싸락눈[우박]을 동반한 폭풍 **a hail of blows** 주먹세례
> **a hail of bullets** 우박처럼 쏟아지는 탄알 **a hail of questions** 빗발처럼 쏟아지는 질문 **hail a taxi** 택시를 부르다
> **within hail** 부르는 소리가 들리는 곳에(=within hailing distance) **hail from** (사람이) ~출신[태생]이다; (배가) ~항에서 오다

Step 03
연습문제

다음 문장의 hail에 해당되는 뜻을 **Step 02** 의 ❶~❸에서 고르세요. (해답은 467쪽)

1. Let's hail a taxi, shall we? (   )
2. The farmer's wheat crop suffered great damage from hail. (   )
3. She was hailed as the wonder girl of Korean golf. (   )
4. The captain didn't hail the passing ship. (   )
5. Cheerful voices hailed us as we appeared on the stage. (   )
6. The victim was hit by a hail of bullets. (   )

Step 04
영작연습

다음 문장을 주어진 부분을 이용하여 영어로 옮기세요. (해답은 467쪽)

1. 그가 집으로 운전해 갈 때 우박이 내렸다. [as, drove, home]

____

2. 군중들은 그녀를 피겨의 여왕이라고 부르며 환호했다. [crowd, as, Figure Queen]

____

3. 인도에 서서 그녀는 지나가는 택시를 큰 소리로 불렀다. [sidewalk, passing taxi]

____

:: 1. 지난밤 몇 분 동안 우박이 쏟아졌다. 2. 그들은 그를 영웅이라고 부르며 환호했다. 3. 그는 택시를 소리 쳐서 잡으려고 애쓰고 있었다.

Step 01
해석연습

다음 문장을 sense에 유의하여 해석해 보세요. (해석은 이 페이지의 하단부에 있음)

1. I sensed that she was lying. ___________________________

2. Dogs have a keen sense of smell. ___________________________

3. Mr. Hong is a gentleman in the true sense.

4. My father was a man of sense. ___________________________

Step 02
뜻 알기

sense에는 다음과 같은 여러 가지의 뜻이 있습니다.

❶ ~을 느끼다, 감지하다, 이해하다 Ⅴ to feel, become aware of, or realize; to understand

❷ 감각, 감각기능 ⓝ any of the five natural powers of sight, hearing, feeling, taste, and smell which give a person or an animal information about the outside world

❸ 뜻, 의미, 의도 ⓝ a meaning of a word, phrase, sentence, etc

❹ 분별력, 판단력, 사려 ⓝ the power to understand or judge; good judgment

한 걸음 더 **He has a good <u>sense</u> for business.** 그는 사업에 타고난 재능이 있다. → 타고난 지적감각, 재능
I fell and fainted, but soon came to my <u>senses</u>. 나는 쓰러져 정신을 잃었지만 곧 의식이 돌아왔다. → (정상적인) 의식, 정신

Step 03
연습문제

다음 문장의 sense에 해당되는 뜻을 Step 02 의 ❶~❹ 에서 고르세요. (해답은 467쪽)

1. He missed the sense of her statement. (   )

2. He sensed that there was someone in the room with him. (   )

3. The sense of the word is not clear. (   )

4. She has a poor sense of taste. (   )

5. I should have had more sense than to do that. (   )

6. I could sense the meaning of her words. (   )

7. Hearing is one of the five senses. (   )

8. You can rely on her – she has plenty of sense. (   )

Step 04
영작연습

다음 문장을 주어진 부분을 이용하여 영어로 옮기세요. (해답은 467쪽)

1. 말이 위험을 감지하고 갑자기 섰다. [danger, suddenly]

____

2. 나는 내 자신의 감각[오감]을 의심해 본 적이 없다. [doubted, own]

____

3. 나에게 그렇게 말하는 의도는 무엇이냐? [speaking, like that]

____

4. 네가 분별이 있다면 그렇게 행동하지 않을 것이다. [If, any, behave]

____

⠿ 1. 나는 그녀가 거짓말을 하고 있다는 것을 알아차렸다. 2. 개는 예민한 후각을 가지고 있다. 3. Hong 씨는 진정한 의미의 신사다.
4. 나의 아버지는 분별 있는 분이셨다.

Review Group-55

A. 다음 뜻에 해당되는 단어를 보기에서 찾아 적으세요.

> **보기**　　coach　　compact　　room　　hail　　sense

01. _______________ an agreement between two or more people, countries, etc
02. _______________ enough space for a particular purpose
03. _______________ a meaning of a word, phrase, sentence, etc
04. _______________ frozen rain drops falling from the sky
05. _______________ closely packed together; neatly fitted; small and easy to carry
06. _______________ a part of a house or building enclosed by walls, floor and ceiling
07. _______________ to feel, become aware of, or realize; to understand
08. _______________ to give a welcoming cry to someone; to greet
09. _______________ a small flat container with a mirror, containing face powder for a woman
10. _______________ a railway carriage; a public motor bus; a large carriage pulled by horses
11. _______________ the power to understand or judge; good judgment
12. _______________ a need or possibility for something; chance; opportunity
13. _______________ to shout; to call out so as to attract attention
14. _______________ any of the five natural powers of sight, hearing, feeling, taste, and smell which give a person or an animal information about the outside world
15. _______________ a trainer of sports teams, etc; a private teacher

B. 다음 빈칸에 가장 알맞은 단어를 보기에서 찾아 적으세요.

> **보기**　　coach　　compact　　room　　hail　　sense

01. The kitchen is (　　　　) but well equipped.
02. The Queen's (　　　　) was drawn by six white horses.
03. I can't make (　　　　) of what this author says.
04. We'll move the cabinet to make (　　　　) for the television.
05. The lady took out her (　　　　) to fix her makeup.
06. Her work isn't bad but there is still plenty of (　　　　) for improvement.
07. I could vaguely (　　　　) that danger was approaching.
08. We should (　　　　) them as heroes.
09. I'd like to book a (　　　　) at your hotel.
10. His actions are not in accordance with common (　　　　).
11. There was some (　　　　) during the rainstorm this morning.
12. My uncle smokes so many cigarettes that he has lost his (　　　　) of taste.
13. The (　　　　) will send some new players into the game tonight.
14. The management and trade union leaders signed a (　　　　) at last.
15. The hotel doorman will (　　　　) a cab for you.

다음 문장을 굵게 처리된 단어에 유의하여 해석해 보세요.

01. Unfortunately, some sports **coaches** in the camps occasionally become over-enthusiastic in their desire to help the children excel. [2007년-홀수형 45번]

➡ ______________________________

02. In Western Europe, steep gasoline taxes, investment policies favoring built-up areas over undeveloped greenfields, continuous investment in public transportation, and other policies have produced relatively **compact** cities. [2009년-홀수형 45번]

➡ ______________________________

03. But isolation feels like being in a **room** with no way out. [2008년-홀수형 44번]

➡ ______________________________

04. Making rope required **room** because rope had to be made in a straight line. [2001년-홀수형 29번]

➡ ______________________________

05. M: Come on! Get on. There's **room** for you.
W: No, the elevator is already too crowded.
[2006년-홀수형 13번]

➡ ______________________________

06. Perhaps the greatest thing about being a devoted operagoer is that there is so much **room** for growth. [2005년-홀수형 47–48번]

➡ ______________________________

07. **Common sense** aside, the most important asset in business is a **sense** of humor, an ability to laugh at yourself or the situation.
[1998년-홀수형 28번]

➡ ______________________________

08. When faced with things that are too big to **sense**, we comprehend them by adding knowledge to the experience. [2009년-홀수형 27번]

➡ ______________________________

09. Time itself remains unchanged in the **sense** that it carries on in the same way as it has for millions of years. [2004년-홀수형 26번]

➡ ______________________________

10. It is our parents who have given us our **sense** of right and wrong, our understanding of love, and our knowledge of who we are.
[2004년-홀수형 49–50번]

➡ ______________________________

11. In martial arts, this **sense** of looking freshly at something is known as "beginner's mind." [2011년-홀수형 39번]

➡ ______________________________

276 might [mait]

Step 01 해석연습

다음 문장을 might에 유의하여 해석해 보세요. (해석은 이 페이지의 하단부에 있음)

1. I said that she might go. ___________________________

2. He said, "Might is right." ___________________________

Step 02 뜻 알기

might에는 다음과 같은 여러 가지의 뜻이 있습니다.

❶ 조동사 may의 과거형 Ⅴ the past tense of auxiliary verb "may"

❷ 힘, 능력, 권력 ⓝ great strength; power

> 한 걸음 더 **mighty** 힘 있는, 강력한 **by might** 힘으로, 우격다짐으로 **with[by] all one's might** 전력을 다하여, 온 힘을 다하여 **with[by] might and main** 전력을 다하여, 힘껏

Step 03 연습문제

다음 문장의 might에 해당되는 뜻을 Step 02 의 ❶〜❷에서 고르세요. (해답은 468쪽)

1. The might of that athlete was impressive. (   )

2. He asked if he might open a window. (   )

3. The might of the enemy was too great for us. (   )

4. I'm afraid she might lose her way. (   )

Step 04 영작연습

다음 문장을 주어진 부분을 이용하여 영어로 옮기세요. (해답은 468쪽)

1. 그녀는 내일 올지도 모른다고 말했다. [that, come]

____

2. 그는 온 힘을 다하여 방망이를 휘둘렀다. [swung, bat]

____

:: 1. 나는 그녀에게 가도 좋다고 말했다. 2. 그는 "힘이 정의다."라고 말했다.

277 digest 🅥 [didʒést, dai–] 🅝 [dáidʒest]

Step 01
해석연습

다음 문장을 digest에 유의하여 해석해 보세요. (해석은 이 페이지의 하단부에 있음)

1. I can't digest milk well. _______________________
2. He struggled to digest the news. _______________________
3. Here is a monthly news digest. _______________________

Step 02
뜻 알기

digest에는 다음과 같은 여러 가지의 뜻이 있습니다.

❶ (음식을) 소화하다; (음식이) 소화되다 🅥 to change food into substances the body can use; to be digested

❷ (지식 따위를) 이해하다, 터득하다 🅥 to understand new information

❸ ～을 정리하다; 요약하다 🅥 to arrange; to reduce (a mass of facts, etc) to order
요약, 개요 🅝 a summary or outline of what is in a book, article, report, etc

> 한 걸음 더 **That conduct is more than I can digest.** 그 행동은 내가 더는 참을 수 없는 것이다.
> → ～을 참다, 견디다(=to put up with; to endure)
> **digestive** ⓐ 소화의, 소화를 촉진하는 ⓝ 소화촉진제 **digestion** ① 소화 ② 이해, 터득
> **digestible** ① 소화하기 쉬운 ② 이해하기 쉬운, 요약하기 쉬운

Step 03
연습문제

다음 문장의 digest에 해당되는 뜻을 **Step 02** 의 ❶～❸에서 고르세요. (해답은 468쪽)

1. Do you have a digest of today's news? (   )
2. Cheese is very difficult to digest. (   )
3. It took me some minutes to digest what she had said. (   )
4. Reader's Digest is a renowned monthly magazine. (   )
5. The food I ate for lunch isn't digesting very well. (   )
6. She paused, waiting for her son to digest the information. (   )

Step 04
영작연습

다음 문장을 주어진 부분을 이용하여 영어로 옮기세요. (해답은 468쪽)

1. 그녀는 위가 약해서 음식을 잘 소화하지 못한다. [weak stomach, so, food]

____

2. 이 책은 초등학생이 이해하기에는 너무 어렵다. [difficult, elementary school]

____

3. 그는 나에게 주간 뉴스 요약판을 주었다. [the week's news]

____

::: 1. 나는 우유를 잘 소화하지 못한다. 2. 그는 그 소식을 이해하려고 애썼다. 3. 여기에 월간 뉴스 요약판이 있습니다.

278 apt [æpt]

다음 문장을 apt에 유의하여 해석해 보세요. (해석은 이 페이지의 하단부에 있음)

1. The teacher made an apt remark. ________________________
2. He was a child apt to learn. ________________________
3. My brother is apt to catch cold. ________________________

apt에는 다음과 같은 여러 가지의 뜻이 있습니다.

❶ 적절한, 적당한 a suitable; appropriate; to the point

❷ 영리한; 이해가 빠른; 재주[솜씨]가 있는 a clever; quick to learn and understand; intelligent

❸ (to 부정사와 함께) ~하는 경향이 있는; ~하기 쉬운; ~할 것 같은 a (with to infinitive) having a natural tendency to do something; likely

> 한 걸음 더 **aptitude** ① 경향, 습성 ② 적합, 적성 ③ 소질, 재능 **an apt remark** 적절한 언급
> **be apt at** ~의 재주가 있다, 능란하다 **be apt for** ~에 적합하다 **be apt to (do)** ~하는 경향이 있다, ~하기 쉽다

다음 문장의 apt에 해당되는 뜻을 Step 02 의 ❶~❸에서 고르세요. (해답은 468쪽)

1. She is very apt at picking up a new subject. (   )
2. This is a quotation apt for the occasion. (   )
3. The table is apt to tilt over. (   )
4. My sister was apt at drawing portraits. (   )
5. The lecturer made apt remarks when answering questions. (   )
6. The rich are apt to despise the poor. (   )

다음 문장을 주어진 부분을 이용하여 영어로 옮기세요. (해답은 468쪽)

1. 그녀의 옷은 파티에 적합해 보인다. [dress, appears]

____

2. 그는 외국어에 재주가 있다. [foreign language]

____

3. 여름에는 음식물이 상하기 쉽다. [foods, go bad]

____

:: 1. 그 선생님은 적절한 평을 했다. 2. 그는 이해가 빠른 어린이였다. 3. 내 동생은 감기에 잘 걸린다.

279 withdraw [wiðdrɔ́: / wiθdrɔ́:]

Step 01
해석연습

다음 문장을 withdraw에 유의하여 해석해 보세요. (해석은 이 페이지의 하단부에 있음)

1. He withdrew a file from her briefcase. ___________________________
2. The boss withdrew his remarks, and apologized. ___________________________
3. He wants to withdraw some money from his savings account. ___________________________

Step 02
뜻 알기

withdraw에는 다음과 같은 여러 가지의 뜻이 있습니다.

❶ (손 따위를) 움츠리다; ~을 꺼내다; (군대 등을) 철수하다 Ⓥ to (cause to) move back or away; to pull back; to retreat

❷ (제안, 약속, 소송, 명령, 주장 등을) 철회하다, 취소하다 Ⓥ to take back something previously said

❸ (예금 등을) 인출하다, 꺼내다 Ⓥ to take money out of a bank account

> 한 걸음 더 **withdraw** [wiðdrɔ́:] - **withdrew** [wiðdrú:] - **withdrawn** [wiðdrɔ́:n]
> **withdrawal** ① 물러나기, 철수 ② 철회, 취소 ③ (예금 등의) 인출

Step 03
연습문제

다음 문장의 withdraw에 해당되는 뜻을 Step 02 의 ❶~❸에서 고르세요. (해답은 468쪽)

1. He withdrew all his savings and went abroad. (   )
2. The boy withdrew his head from the window. (   )
3. We argued her into withdrawing her complaint. (   )
4. They were ordered to withdraw from the headquarters. (   )
5. She was forced to withdraw the charges she'd made against him. (   )
6. Jane withdrew $100 from her bank account. (   )

Step 04
영작연습

다음 문장을 주어진 부분을 이용하여 영어로 옮기세요. (해답은 468쪽)

1. 그는 뜨거운 난로에서 재빨리 손을 뗐다. [quickly, stove]

____

2. 그녀는 우리 캠페인에 대한 지지를 철회할지도 모른다. [support, campaign]

____

3. 현금자동인출기(ATM)에서 얼마까지 인출할 수 있습니까? [How much, from]

____

:: 1. 그는 자신의 서류 가방에서 서류철 하나를 꺼냈다. 2. 사장은 자신의 말을 취소하고 사과했다.
3. 그는 자신의 예금계좌에서 약간의 돈을 인출하고 싶어 한다.

280 **spot** [spɑt / spɔt]

Step 01
해석연습

다음 문장을 spot에 유의하여 해석해 보세요. (해석은 이 페이지의 하단부에 있음)

1. There were a lot of spots of paint on the carpet. ___________________________

2. We found a nice spot to play baseball. ___________________________

3. The floor was spotted with paint. ___________________________

4. He spotted someone coming out of the building. ___________________________

Step 02
뜻 알기

spot에는 다음과 같은 여러 가지의 뜻이 있습니다.

❶ 얼룩, 반점, 여드름 🇳 a small mark different in color from what it is on; a dirty mark; a pimple

❷ (특정한) 장소, 지점; 현장 🇳 a particular place or area; a location

❸ ~에 반점을 찍다, ~을 얼룩지게 하다, ~을 더럽히다; 더럽혀지다 🇻 to make spots on something; to mark or stain; to become marked

❹ ~을 알아보다; 발견하다 🇻 to recognize; to pick out; to see (one person or thing out of many)

▷ 한 걸음 더 **His character is without a _spot_.** 그의 인격에는 한 점의 흠도 없다. → 결함, 흠(=a moral blemish; defect)

Step 03
연습문제

다음 문장의 spot에 해당되는 뜻을 Step 02 의 ❶~❹에서 고르세요. (해답은 468쪽)

1. The paint spotted his dress. (   )

2. Clean spots of mud on your boots. (   )

3. The bullet struck his head and he was killed on the spot. (   )

4. He spotted the wall with blue paint. (   )

5. No one spotted that the photo was a fake. (   )

6. This is the very spot where he was murdered. (   )

7. My sister was covered in spots when she had measles. (   )

8. We spotted them going through the back gate. (   )

Step 04
영작연습

다음 문장을 주어진 부분을 이용하여 영어로 옮기세요. (해답은 468쪽)

1. 그녀는 흰 점무늬가 있는 짙은 청색 치마를 입고 있었다. [wearing, dark blue]

____

2. 이 식물들은 양지바른 장소에서 가장 잘 자란다. [grow best, sunny]

____

3. 그 여학생은 손가락을 잉크로 더럽혔다. [fingers, ink]

____

4. 그녀는 마침내 군중 속에서 그를 찾아냈다. [finally, crowd]

____

‥ 1. 양탄자 위에는 많은 페인트 얼룩이 있었다. 2. 우리는 야구하기에 좋은 장소를 찾았다. 3. 마루는 페인트로 얼룩져 있었다.
4. 그는 누군가가 그 건물에서 나오는 것을 알아챘다.

A. 다음 뜻에 해당되는 단어를 보기에서 찾아 적으세요.

보기	might digest apt withdraw spot

01. _____________ clever; quick to learn and understand; intelligent
02. _____________ to change food into substances the body can use
03. _____________ to mark or stain; to become marked
04. _____________ the past tense of auxiliary verb "may"
05. _____________ a summary or outline of what is in a book, article, report, etc
06. _____________ to take back something previously said
07. _____________ suitable; appropriate; to the point
08. _____________ a small mark different in color from what it is on; a dirty mark; a pimple
09. _____________ to take money out of a bank account
10. _____________ having a natural tendency to do something; likely
11. _____________ great strength; power
12. _____________ a particular place or area; a location
13. _____________ to (cause to) move back or away; to pull back; to retreat
14. _____________ to recognize; to pick out; to see (one person or thing out of many)
15. _____________ to understand new information

B. 다음 빈칸에 가장 알맞은 단어를 보기에서 찾아 적으세요.

보기	might digest apt withdraw spot

01. He is a very ( ) student and learns quickly.
02. Here is a ( ) of today's news.
03. We found an ideal ( ) for a picnic.
04. The professor pointed up his remarks with ( ) illustrations.
05. Some foods ( ) more easily than others.
06. A gangster took her money by ( ).
07. White shirts ( ) easily.
08. Our troops were forced to ( ) from the city.
09. Mike is very tall, so he is easy to ( ) in a crowd.
10. You can ( ) money from the account at any time without penalty.
11. Young people are ( ) to be influenced by foreign culture.
12. The male bird has a yellow ( ) on its beak.
13. If she knew the fact, she ( ) be disappointed.
14. It took me some minutes to ( ) what she had said.
15. The buyer will ( ) his offer when the price becomes too high.

다음 문장을 굵게 처리된 단어에 유의하여 해석해 보세요.

01. If you walked into this place, you **might** easily think you are in a private house. [1995년–홀수형 17번]

→ ___________________________

02. All these things considered, it **might** be better to ask for the services of a moving company. [2009년–홀수형 22번]

→ ___________________________

03. Another reason for removing the peel before eating is that some fruits such as apples, pears, and grapes have a tough skin, which can be harder to chew and to **digest**. [2007년–홀수형 49–50번]

→ ___________________________

04. Anything that contributes to stress during mealtime can interfere with the **digestion** of food. [1994년–1차 38번]

→ ___________________________

05. W: I'd like to make a cash **withdrawal**.
M: No problem. How much would you like? [2011년–홀수형 13번]

→ ___________________________

06. Moles are dark **spots** on human skin. [2005년–홀수형 42번]

→ ___________________________

07. Amy, who is from Australia, is visiting Seoul for the first time. She has traveled to many tourist **spots** such as Gyeongbokgung and Namdaemun Market this week. [2011년–홀수형 17번]

→ ___________________________

08. But what appeared in the telescope looked more like large black **spots**. [1998년–홀수형 46번]

→ ___________________________

09. They are small cubes and each side has a different number of **spots** on it, ranging from one to six. [2005년–홀수형 3번]

→ ___________________________

Day 28

 **DAY 29**

Be great in act, as you have been in thought.
생각에 있어서 그러하듯, 행동에서 위대하라.

 **281 traffic** [trǽfik]

<table><tr><td>Step 01
해석연습</td><td>다음 문장을 traffic에 유의하여 해석해 보세요. (해석은 이 페이지의 하단부에 있음)</td></tr></table>

Group 57

1. He was injured in a traffic accident. ___________________________

2. They trafficked with the natives for ivory. ___________________________

<table><tr><td>Step 02
뜻 알기</td><td>traffic에는 다음과 같은 여러 가지의 뜻이 있습니다.</td></tr></table>

❶ (차, 사람 등의) 교통, 왕래, 통행; (왕래하는) 차량 🅝 the movement of people, cars, aircraft, ships, trains, etc from one place to another; the vehicles moving along a road or street

❷ 거래, 매매 🅝 trade; the act of buying and selling goods
거래[매매]하다, 부정한 거래를 하다 v to buy and sell goods; to deal in goods; to trade in illegally

> 한 걸음 더 **traffic** [trǽfik] - **trafficked** [trǽfikt] - **trafficked** [trǽfikt]
> **traffic jam** 교통 체증[마비] **traffic congestion** 교통 혼잡 **traffic light** 교통 신호등 **traffic sign** 교통 표지판
> **trafficker** (부정한) 무역상, 상인 **slave traffic** 노예 매매

<table><tr><td>Step 03
연습문제</td><td>다음 문장의 traffic에 해당되는 뜻을 Step 02 의 ❶～❷에서 고르세요. (해답은 468쪽)</td></tr></table>

1. We were stuck in a traffic jam for more than an hour. (   )
2. Steve was found guilty of trafficking in stolen goods. (   )
3. He was fined $50.00 for a violation of traffic regulations. (   )
4. They were trafficking in smuggled goods. (   )

<table><tr><td>Step 04
영작연습</td><td>다음 문장을 주어진 부분을 이용하여 영어로 옮기세요. (해답은 468쪽)</td></tr></table>

1. 그녀는 교통 정체로 지각했다. [because of, congestion]

____

2. 그 폭력단은 마약을 거래한다. [gang, drugs]

____

:: 1. 그는 교통사고로 부상당했다. 2. 그들은 원주민과 상아 거래를 했다.

282 relate [riléit]

Step 01
해석연습

다음 문장을 relate에 유의하여 해석해 보세요. (해석은 이 페이지의 하단부에 있음)

1. Strange to relate, they never met again. ______________________________

2. These two incidents are related each other. ______________________________

3. She and I are related by marriage. ______________________________

Step 02
뜻 알기

relate에는 다음과 같은 여러 가지의 뜻이 있습니다.

❶ ～에 대하여 말하다, 이야기하다 Ⓥ to tell (a story, etc) (to somebody)

❷ 관련시키다, 결부시키다 Ⓥ to show a connection between two or more things; to connect
～와 관련이 있다, 관계하다 Ⓥ to have a connection with

❸ (보통 수동형으로 쓰여) ～와 인척[친척, 혈연]관계이다 Ⓥ (usually in passive) to be
connected by birth or marriage

> 한 걸음 더 **Jessica finds it difficult to <u>relate</u> to her children.** 제시카는 자신의 아이들과 잘 지내기가 힘들다고 느낀다.
> **He doesn't <u>relate</u> well to his colleagues.** 그는 동료들과 사이가 좋지 않다.
> → ～와 잘 지내다(=to have a good relationship with others)
> **relation** ① 관계, 관련 ② (복수 형태로) 교제, 교우, 거래관계 **related** ① 관계[관련]있는, 서로 관련된 ② 친척의, 혈연관계가 있는
> **relative** ⓝ ① 친척, 인척 ② (문법) 관계사 ⓐ 상대적인, 비교상의

Step 03
연습문제

다음 문장의 relate에 해당되는 뜻을 **Step 02** 의 ❶～❸에서 고르세요. (해답은 468쪽)

1. The writer related his childhood experiences in the first chapter. (   )

2. I am related to her by marriage. (   )

3. This relates to something he mentioned earlier. (   )

4. This account relates to my grandfather. (   )

5. The explorer related many stories about his adventures. (   )

6. She is closely related to me. (   )

Step 04
영작연습

다음 문장을 주어진 부분을 이용하여 영어로 옮기세요. (해답은 468쪽)

1. 그녀는 자신에게 일어난 모든 것을 말했다. [all, happened]

____

2. 나는 이 법률이 당신의 경우와 관련이 없다고 생각합니다. [law, case]

____

3. 그들은 서로 친척 관계이다. [each other]

____

∷ 1. 이상한 말이지만 그들은 다시는 만나지 않았다. 2. 이 두 사건은 서로 관련되어 있다. 3. 그녀와 나는 인척관계이다.

283 sterile [stéril, –rail]

Step 01
해석연습

다음 문장을 sterile에 유의하여 해석해 보세요. (해석은 이 페이지의 하단부에 있음)

1. Her illness had made her sterile. ______________________________
2. Always use sterile needles. ______________________________
3. The professor gave a sterile lecture. ______________________________

Step 02
뜻 알기

sterile에는 다음과 같은 여러 가지의 뜻이 있습니다.

❶ 자식을[새끼를] 못 낳는,(토지가) 불모의, 흉작의 　a　unable to have babies; (of land) barren; unproductive

❷ 살균한, 무균의 　a　free from any living germs

❸ (사상, 독창성, 흥미 따위가) 없는, 빈약한, 무미건조한 　a　lacking new ideas or imagination

> 한 걸음 더 **That was a <u>sterile</u> negotiation.** 그것은 헛된 교섭이었다. → 효과가 없는, 헛된, 무익한(=useless, futile, vain)
> **a sterile cow** 새끼를 못 낳는 암소 **a sterile marriage** 자식이 없는 결혼(생활) **a sterile year** 흉년
> **a sterile bandage** 살균한 붕대 **sterile culture** 무균배양 **sterile hopes** 헛된 희망 **sterile negotiations** 헛된[소용없는] 교섭
> **a sterile lecture** 내용이 빈약한 강의 **sterilize** ① 살균하다 ② ~을 불임케 하다 **sterility** ① 불임 ② 불모 ③ 무미건조
> **sterilization** ① 살균소독 ② 불임케 함

Step 03
연습문제

다음 문장의 sterile에 해당되는 뜻을 　Step 02　의 ❶~❸에서 고르세요. (해답은 468쪽)

1. She felt creatively and emotionally sterile. (　　　)
2. The land in this region is too sterile to yield anything. (　　　)
3. Operations must be carried out in a sterile environment. (　　　)
4. Their relationship had become sterile over the years. (　　　)
5. Pack in sterile jars and seal immediately. (　　　)
6. Anna became sterile because of exposure to radiation. (　　　)

Step 04
영작연습

다음 문장을 주어진 부분을 이용하여 영어로 옮기세요. (해답은 468쪽)

1. 그 나무는 척박한 땅에서도 잘 자랐다. [grew, even, land]

____

2. 수술 칼은 항상 살균상태로 보관되어야 한다. [surgical knives, kept]

____

3. 그 방은 언제나 차고 단조롭게 느껴진다. [feels, cold]

____

∷ 1. 병 때문에 그녀는 아이를 낳을 수 없게 되었다. 2. 언제나 살균한 바늘을 사용해라. 3. 그 교수는 빈약한 내용의 강의를 했다.

404

284 degree [digríː]

다음 문장을 degree에 유의하여 해석해 보세요. (해석은 이 페이지의 하단부에 있음)

1. To what degree are you interested in astronomy? _______________________

2. A right angle has 90 degrees. _______________________

3. He received his degree from Cambridge. _______________________

degree에는 다음과 같은 여러 가지의 뜻이 있습니다.

❶ 정도, 범위; 단계 **n** an amount or extent; step or stage in a scale or process

❷ (온도, 각도 따위의) 도(度) **n** a unit for measuring temperature, angles, etc

❸ 대학 학위 **n** an academic title or certificate given by a university

> 한 걸음 더 **He was a man of high degree.** 그는 신분이 높은 사람이었다. → 지위, 신분, 계급(=position in society; rank)
> **the positive [comparative, superlative] degree** 원급 [비교급, 최상급]
> → (문법) 형용사 또는 부사의 비교를 나타내는 급(級)(=a grade of comparison of adjectives and adverbs)
> **a doctor's[master's, bachelor's] degree** 박사[석사, 학사] 학위 **a four-year degree course** 4년짜리 학위 과정
> **45 degrees** 45도 **degrees of latitude** 위도 **a man of high degree** 지체 높은 사람 **by degrees** 서서히, 점차
> **in a degree** 조금은, 어느 정도(= in some degree)

다음 문장의 degree에 해당되는 뜻을 Step 02 **의 ❶~❸에서 고르세요.** (해답은 468쪽)

1. My sister has a master's degree from Oxford. (   )

2. Their friendship grew into love by degrees. (   )

3. Bake about 30 minutes at 350 degrees. (   )

4. Where did you obtain your graduate degree? (   )

5. The temperature reads fifteen degrees of frost. (   )

6. The students show various degrees of skill in their uses of computers. (   )

다음 문장을 주어진 부분을 이용하여 영어로 옮기세요. (해답은 469쪽)

1. 그가 하는 일은 고도의 기술을 요한다. [job, demands, skill]

____

2. 물은 화씨 32도나 섭씨 0도에서 언다. [freezes, Fahrenheit, Celsius]

____

3. 그녀는 마침내 하버드 대학에서 박사 학위를 받았다. [took, Harvard]

____

Day 29

1. 당신은 어느 정도까지 천문학에 관심이 있느냐? 2. 직각은 90도이다. 3. 그는 캠브리지 대학에서 학위를 받았다.

285 act [ækt]

Step 01
해석연습

다음 문장을 act에 유의하여 해석해 보세요. (해석은 이 페이지의 하단부에 있음)

1. She will act the Queen in "Hamlet." _______________________________
2. The Gun Control Act was announced in 1968. _______________________________
3. The hero dies in Act 5, Scene 4. _______________________________
4. The pump is not acting well. _______________________________

Step 02
뜻 알기

act에는 다음과 같은 여러 가지의 뜻이 있습니다.

❶ 행동하다 (연극 등에서) 역을 맡아 하다 **v** to do something; to behave; to perform a role in a play
　 행동, 행위 **n** a deed; something done

❷ (종종 대문자로) 법령, 조례 **n** a law made by a legislative body

❸ (종종 대문자로) 연극, 오페라 따위의 막 **n** a section[part] of a play or drama

❹ (약 따위가) 효험이 있다; (기계 따위가) 작동하다 **v** to work; to function; to operate

> 한 걸음 더 **I'll act for you while you are away.** 안 계시는 동안 제가 대리를 맡아 보겠습니다.
> → ~의 대리[대행]을 하다(=to do the duties of another person for a time)

Step 03
연습문제

다음 문장의 act에 해당되는 뜻을 **Step 02** 의 ❶～❹에서 고르세요. (해답은 469쪽)

1. The brake will not act well. (　　)
2. To kick a dog is a cruel act. (　　)
3. Act 3 begins with a short dialogue between mother and daughter. (　　)
4. Attacking another nation is an act of war. (　　)
5. The president signed into law the Higher Education Act. (　　)
6. This medicine acts well to relieve pain. (　　)
7. "Romeo and Juliet" has five acts. (　　)
8. Five suspects are being held under the Prevention of Terrorism Act. (　　)

Step 04
영작연습

다음 문장을 주어진 부분을 이용하여 영어로 옮기세요. (해답은 469쪽)

1. 그녀는 나를 전에 전혀 본 적이 없었던 것처럼 행동을 했다. [as if, never, before]

____

2. 이 법은 공해방지법이라고 불린다. [Environmental Pollution Prevention]

____

3. 연극의 3막이 방금 시작되었다. [third, play, just]

____

4. 이 약은 심장에 효험이 있다. [medicine, heart]

____

⠿ 1. 그녀는 '햄릿'에서 왕비 역을 할 것이다. 2. 총기단속법은 1968년에 공포되었다. 3. 남자 주인공은 5막 4장에서 죽는다. 4. 펌프가 잘 작동하지 않는다.

A. 다음 뜻에 해당되는 단어를 보기에서 찾아 적으세요.

보기	traffic relate sterile degree act

01. ______________ unable to have babies; (of land) barren; unproductive
02. ______________ to have a connection with
03. ______________ the movement of people, cars, aircraft, ships, trains, etc from one place to another; the vehicles moving along a road or street
04. ______________ a section[part] of a play or drama
05. ______________ an academic title or certificate given by a university
06. ______________ a deed; something done
07. ______________ to be connected by birth or marriage
08. ______________ a unit for measuring temperature, angles, etc
09. ______________ a law made by a legislative body
10. ______________ free from any living germs
11. ______________ an amount or extent; step or stage in a scale or process
12. ______________ to tell (a story, etc) (to somebody)
13. ______________ to buy and sell goods; to deal in goods; to trade in illegally
14. ______________ to work; to function; to operate
15. ______________ lacking new ideas or imagination

B. 다음 빈칸에 가장 알맞은 단어를 보기에서 찾아 적으세요.

보기	traffic(s) relate(d) sterile degree act

01. A hospital's operating room is a (   ) area.
02. The corner of a square is a 90 (   ) angle.
03. In the (   ) of picking up the ball, the boy slipped and fell.
04. The soil in this region is too (   ) for farming.
05. The cat is distantly (   ) to the tiger.
06. The man (   ) with the natives for bear skins.
07. The company violated the Environmental Pollution Prevention (   ) at three plants.
08. I received a doctor's (   ) from Yale last year.
09. The growth of plants is closely (   ) to the weather.
10. There wasn't much (   ) on the roads yesterday.
11. Hamlet eventually kills the king in the fifth (   ).
12. I found my job as a bank teller to be very (   ).
13. My uncle would (   ) to us his childhood experiences.
14. The brakes wouldn't (   ) , so there was an accident.
15. Her work has reached a high (   ) of excellence.

Day 29

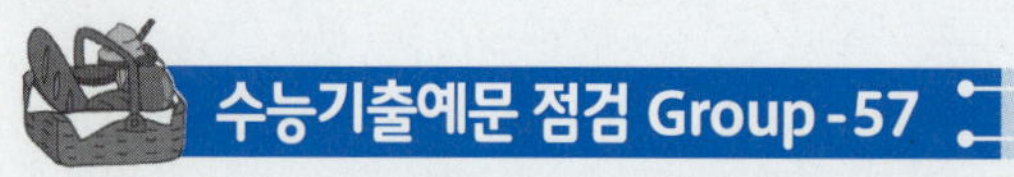

해답은 469쪽

다음 문장을 굵게 처리된 단어에 유의하여 해석해 보세요.

01. In conclusion, we cannot drive without **traffic** signals. [1998년–홀수형 17번]

➡ _______________________________________

02. You know where the mall is, and you choose the best route based on what you know about the distance, the number of stop lights, and the amount of **traffic**. [2003년–홀수형 47–48번]

➡ _______________________________________

03. Well, laughing isn't only **related** to emotional expressions. [2012년–홀수형 6번]

➡ _______________________________________

04. First of all, traditional classrooms are a place where students may **relate** to one another face to face. [2002년–홀수형 38번]

➡ _______________________________________

05. The problem **related** with wet ink could be avoided, and the need for something better was finally answered. [2001년–홀수형 21번]

➡ _______________________________________

06. The extent and rate of diffusion depend on the **degree** of social contact. [2007년–홀수형 20번]

➡ _______________________________________

07. He has a master's **degree** in engineering. He wants to have his own business some day. [1995년–홀수형 15번]

➡ _______________________________________

08. There are few people who do not react to music to some **degree**. [2008년–홀수형 28번]

➡ _______________________________________

09. M: But I had to finish it today. I don't have any other time.
W: But it must be almost 30 **degrees** out there.
M: It was hot, but at least now I'm all done. [2003년–홀수형 15번]

➡ _______________________________________

10. For example, we feel that a man in his thirties should **act** his age and not behave like an adolescent or an old man. [2008년–홀수형 42번]

➡ _______________________________________

11. "Oh, I know him," your friend replies. "He seems nice at first, but it's all an **act**." [2007년–홀수형 25번]

➡ _______________________________________

12. You'll notice, right away, how much the interactions with the people in your life will improve as a direct result of this simple **act**. [2003년–홀수형 25번]

➡ _______________________________________

13. But now the tools of the digital age give us a way to easily get, share, and **act** on information in new ways. [2003년–홀수형 30번]

➡ _______________________________________

286 **condemn** [kəndém]

Step 01
해석연습

다음 문장을 condemn에 유의하여 해석해 보세요. (해석은 이 페이지의 하단부에 있음)

1. Everyone condemned her foolish behavior. ________________________

2. He was condemned to death. ________________________

3. She was condemned to poverty. ________________________

Step 02
뜻 알기

condemn에는 다음과 같은 여러 가지의 뜻이 있습니다.

❶ ~을 비난하다, 책망하다 [v] to blame; to disapprove; to criticize as morally wrong or evil

❷ 형(刑)을 선고하다; ~을 유죄로 판결하다 [v] to sentence to a punishment; to declare (someone) to be guilty

❸ ~하게 운명 지우다; (수동형으로) ~할 운명이다 [v] to doom; (in passive) to be doomed to

▷ 한 걸음 더 **condemnation** ① 비난 ② 유죄 판결 **be condemned to death** 사형 선고를 받다

Step 03
연습문제

다음 문장의 condemn에 해당되는 뜻을 **Step 02** 의 ❶~❸에서 고르세요. (해답은 469쪽)

1. The judge condemned the murderer to life in prison. (   )
2. They were condemned to a life of hardship. (   )
3. The wife condemns her husband for drinking too much. (   )
4. He was condemned to be killed in the war. (   )
5. Condemn the offense, but pity the offender. (   )
6. He was condemned to hang for killing his wife and children. (   )

Step 04
영작연습

다음 문장을 주어진 부분을 이용하여 영어로 옮기세요. (해답은 469쪽)

1. 그는 반역자라고 비난받았다. [as, traitor]

____

2. 그 남자는 자동차를 훔친 죄로 유죄 판결을 받았다. [stealing, car]

____

3. 그는 고통의 생활을 보내도록 운명 지어졌다. [life, suffering]

____

:: 1. 모든 사람들이 그녀의 어리석은 행동을 비난했다. 2. 그는 사형을 선고받았다. 3. 그녀는 가난하게 살 운명이었다.

Step 01 해석연습

다음 문장을 stake에 유의하여 해석해 보세요. (해석은 이 페이지의 하단부에 있음)

1. A man chained his dog to a stake. ______________________________

2. She's going to stake $50 on that horse. ______________________________

Step 02 뜻 알기

stake에는 다음과 같은 여러 가지의 뜻이 있습니다.

❶ 말뚝, 막대기 **n** a strong stick or post sharpened at one end for driving into the ground
  ~을 말뚝에 (잡아) 매다, 말뚝으로 ~을 고정하다 **v** to fasten or strengthen something with stakes

❷ 내기에 건 돈[물건]; 위험부담; 내기 **n** money or something risked in betting; wager or betting
  ~을 내기에 걸다 **v** to risk money or something of value; to bet

> 한 걸음 더 **He has a 25% stake in the business.** 그는 그 사업에 25%의 지분[이해관계]을 가지고 있다.
> → 이해관계[재정적 관여](=a share or interest in property)
> **stake holder** 이해관계자 **at stake** 내기에 걸린, 성패가 달려 있는, 위태로운

Step 03 연습문제

다음 문장의 stake에 해당되는 뜻을 Step 02 의 ❶~❷에서 고르세요. (해답은 469쪽)

1. The man tied his horse to a stake. (   )
2. They often played cards for small stakes. (   )
3. The farmer beat a stake into the ground. (   )
4. A great deal of money was at stake. (   )

Step 04 영작연습

다음 문장을 주어진 부분을 이용하여 영어로 옮기세요. (해답은 469쪽)

1. 그는 자신의 정원에 있는 덩굴장미를 막대기로 받쳐 줄 것이다. [rose vines, garden]

____

2. Smith 씨는 그 사업에 온 재산을 걸었다. [fortune, business]

____

:: 1. 어떤 남자가 자신의 개를 말뚝에 사슬로 묶었다. 2. 그녀는 저 말에 50달러를 걸 예정이다.

 appropriate a [əpróupriət] v [əpróuprièit]

Step 01
해석연습

다음 문장을 appropriate에 유의하여 해석해 보세요. (해석은 이 페이지의 하단부에 있음)

1. Her dress is appropriate for the party. _________________________________

2. The minister appropriated public money for his own use. _________________________

Step 02
뜻 알기

appropriate에는 다음과 같은 여러 가지의 뜻이 있습니다.

❶ 적절한, 적당한, ~에 잘 어울리는; 특유의, 고유의 a suitable for a particular time, situation, or purpose; proper; peculiar

❷ (특별한 목적에) ~을 쓰다, 횡령[착복]하다; ~을 도용하다 v to use something for a special purpose; to take and use something as one's own; to steal

> 한 걸음 더 **appropriation** 사물화(私物化), 도용, 유용, 충당 **appropriateness** 타당성, 적절함
> **inappropriate** 부적절한, 적합하지 않는 **an appropriate response[measure, method]** 적절한 반응[조치, 방법]
> **appropriately** 적합하게, 적당하게 **be appropriate for[to]** ~에 어울리다

Step 03
연습문제

다음 문장의 appropriate에 해당되는 뜻을 Step 02 의 ❶~❷에서 고르세요. (해답은 469쪽)

1. Jeans are not appropriate for a formal party. (   )

2. The official is suspected of appropriating government funds. (   )

3. Mike is the most appropriate one for the task. (   )

4. $500,000 has been appropriated for the new school buildings. (   )

Step 04
영작연습

다음 문장을 주어진 부분을 이용하여 영어로 옮기세요. (해답은 469쪽)

1. 이 운동은 초보자에게 적합하지 않다. [exercise, beginners]

____

2. Nick은 클럽 기금을 횡령했다는 비난을 받고 있다. [accused, club funds]

____

:: 1. 그녀의 옷은 파티에 잘 어울린다. 2. 그 장관은 공금을 횡령했다.

289 spare [spεər]

Step 01
해석연습

다음 문장을 spare에 유의하여 해석해 보세요. (해석은 이 페이지의 하단부에 있음)

1. We have no spare room in our house. ___________________________
2. Don't spare your efforts. ___________________________
3. They spared the man out of mercy. ___________________________
4. Can you spare a few minutes for me? ___________________________

Step 02
뜻 알기

spare에는 다음과 같은 여러 가지의 뜻이 있습니다.

❶ 여분의; 예비의 **a** additional to what is usually needed; in reserve for use when needed; extra

❷ ～을 아끼다, 절약하다 **v** to use in small quantities, rarely or in an economical way

❸ ～의 목숨을 살려 주다; 해(害)를 가하지 않다 **v** to save someone from killing, punishing, etc

❹ 할애하다, 떼어 주다, ～을 나누어 주다 **v** to afford to give or share

> 한 걸음 더 They sell <u>spares</u> at that garage. 저 정비공장에서는 예비품을 판다. → 여분의 것, 예비품
> He is a tall, <u>spare</u> man. 그는 키가 큰 야윈 남자다. → 야윈, 마른, 빈약한, 적은(=thin, lean, poor, small)

Step 03
연습문제

다음 문장의 spare에 해당되는 뜻을 **Step 02** 의 ❶～❹에서 고르세요. (해답은 469쪽)

1. Could you spare me a few dollars? (   )
2. Julie's parents spared no expense on her wedding. (   )
3. She is studying music in her spare time. (   )
4. "Spare us!" they begged. (   )
5. I can spare a few liters of petrol for you. (   )
6. It's good to keep a spare key for just in case something happens. (   )
7. They killed the men but spared the children. (   )
8. He spared no pains to help her. (   )

Step 04
영작연습

다음 문장을 주어진 부분을 이용하여 영어로 옮기세요. (해답은 469쪽)

1. 당신은 여가시간을 어떻게 보내십니까? [how, spend]

____

2. 그녀는 자신의 아들을 즐겁게 해 주기 위해 수고를 아끼지 않았다. [no, pains, please]

____

3. 그는 가족을 살려 달라고 간청했다. [begged, family]

____

4. 우리에게 방을 하나 할애해 주실 수 있으십니까? [Could, room]

____

∷ 1. 우리 집에는 여분의 방이 없다. 2. 노력을 아끼지 마라. 3. 그들은 그 남자를 가엾게 여겨 살려 주었다. 4. 잠깐 시간을 내줄 수 있겠니?

290 project **v** [prədʒékt] **n** [prádʒekt, –dʒikt / prɔ́dʒ–]

Step 01 해석연습

다음 문장을 project에 유의하여 해석해 보세요. (해석은 이 페이지의 하단부에 있음)

1. Are you interested in volunteering for my project? ___________________________
2. The rocket will project the space vehicle into orbit. ___________________________
3. I will project the slides on the screen. ___________________________
4. A rock projects its top from the water. ___________________________

Step 02 뜻 알기

project에는 다음과 같은 여러 가지의 뜻이 있습니다.

❶ ~을 계획[기획]하다, 제안하다; 예측하다 **v** to make plans for; to propose; to predict
　계획, (대규모의) 사업, 프로젝트; 연구과제 **n** a plan or scheme; an undertaking; a specific task

❷ ~을 발사하다, 내던지다 **n** to throw something up or forward with great force

❸ (빛, 광선을) 투사(投射)하다; 영사하다 **v** to make (a beam of light or a shadow) fall on a surface

❹ ~을 돌출시키다, 톡 튀어나오게 하다; 돌출하다 **v** to make something stand out; to stand out

Step 03 연습문제

다음 문장의 project에 해당되는 뜻을 **Step 02** 의 ❶~❹에서 고르세요. (해답은 469쪽)

1. The breakwater projected far into the sea. (　　)
2. The New Dam project was cancelled in midstream. (　　)
3. Big guns can project shells for many miles. (　　)
4. A movie projector projects a motion picture onto a screen. (　　)
5. The entire project is to be finished by 2016. (　　)
6. A sharp rock projects from the sea. (　　)
7. Images are projected onto the retina of the eye. (　　)
8. They built up an apparatus to project missiles into space. (　　)

Step 04 영작연습

다음 문장을 주어진 부분을 이용하여 영어로 옮기세요. (해답은 469쪽)

1. 오바마 대통령의 방문이 11월로 계획되어 있다. [visit, President Obama]

____

2. 미사일은 우주로 발사되었다. [missile, space]

____

3. 오후에 구름이 초원에 그림자를 드리웠다. [clouds, shadows, grass]

____

4. 그의 집은 도로 위로 돌출되어 있는 발코니를 가지고 있다. [balcony, over, street]

____

∷ 1. 당신은 저의 계획에 지원해 볼 생각이 있습니까? 2. 로켓은 우주선을 궤도로 발사할 것이다. 3. 스크린에 슬라이드를 영사해 주겠다.
　 4. 바위 끝이 수면에 돌출해 있다.

A. 다음 뜻에 해당되는 단어를 보기에서 찾아 적으세요.

> **보기**   condemn   stake   appropriate   spare   project

01. _______________ a plan or scheme; an undertaking; a specific task
02. _______________ additional to what is usually needed; in reserve for use when needed; extra
03. _______________ suitable for a particular time, situation, or purpose; proper; peculiar
04. _______________ to make something stand [stick] out; to stand [stick] out
05. _______________ a strong stick or post sharpened at one end for driving into the ground
06. _______________ to afford to give or share
07. _______________ to sentence to a punishment; to declare (someone) to be guilty
08. _______________ money or something risked in betting
09. _______________ to save someone from killing, punishing, etc
10. _______________ to doom; (in passive) to be doomed to
11. _______________ to throw something up or forward with great force
12. _______________ to use something for a special purpose; to take and use something as one's own; to steal
13. _______________ to blame; to disapprove; to criticize as morally wrong or evil
14. _______________ to use in small quantities, rarely or in an economical way
15. _______________ to make (a beam of light or a shadow) fall on a surface

B. 다음 빈칸에 가장 알맞은 단어를 보기에서 찾아 적으세요.

> **보기**   condemn(s) / (ed)   stake(s)   appropriate   spare(d)   project(s)

01. Everyone (   ) her for being cruel to her children.
02. Could you (   ) the slides on the screen?
03. We are too busy to (   ) anyone to help you right now.
04. He will chain his dog to a (   ).
05. (   ) the rod and spoil the child.
06. They will (   ) a missile into space.
07. Her clothes are hardly (   ) for a job interview.
08. It's good to have a (   ) tire when driving long distance.
09. The balcony (   ) out beyond the wall of the house.
10. We often enjoyed playing cards for small (   ).
11. The college set up a (   ) to computerize the library system.
12. The government will (   ) $1 billion to the relief of the poor.
13. The judge will (   ) the criminal to life in prison.
14. The enemy soldier didn't shoot me; he (   ) me.
15. He was (   ) to a life of poverty.

다음 문장을 굵게 처리된 단어에 유의하여 해석해 보세요.

01. Everywhere in the world, the issue of how to manage urban growth poses the highest **stakes**, complex policy decisions, and strongly heated conflicts in the public area. [2009년–홀수형 45번]

➜ ___________________________

02. We need to constantly distinguish right from wrong, and to model **appropriate** behavior. [2007년–홀수형 39번]

➜ ___________________________

03. Your resolve to secure a sufficiency of food for yourself and your family will induce you to spend weary days in tilling the ground and tending livestock; but if Nature provided food and meat in abundance ready for the table, you would thank Nature for **sparing** you much labor and consider yourself so much the better off. [2011년–홀수형 26번]

➜ ___________________________

04. W: I'm sure you can. One last question. What do you do in your **spare** time?
M: Well, I'm busy replying to my fans. [1998년–홀수형 9번]

➜ ___________________________

05. Over the past decade, Chattanooga has made an incredible urban comeback: electric buses, organic markets, and a 120-million-dollar riverfront restoration **project** completed ast year. [2010년–홀수형 37번]

➜ ___________________________

06. When the time-lapse film is **projected** at the normal speed of twenty-four pictures per second, it is possible to see a bean sprout growing up out of the ground. [1994년–1차 41번] * time–lapse film 저속 촬영 필름

➜ ___________________________

07. W: How are your students' **projects** going? Are all of them done?
M: Well, one group is done, and the other four groups are still in progress. [2009년–홀수형 11번]

➜ ___________________________

DAY 30

Vision is the art of seeing the invisible.
비전은 보이지 않는 것을 보는 예술이다.

 **291 liable** [láiəbl]

Step 01
해석연습

다음 문장을 liable에 유의하여 해석해 보세요. (해석은 이 페이지의 하단부에 있음)

1. Glass is liable to break. _______________________
2. He is liable for damages. _______________________

Step 02
뜻 알기

liable에는 다음과 같은 여러 가지의 뜻이 있습니다.

❶ ~하기 쉬운, ~할 것 같은 **a** to be likely to do; to have a tendency to do

❷ 책임이 있는, 책임을 져야 할 **a** obliged to take the responsibility for something; to be responsible

> 한 걸음 더 **liability** ① 책임, 의무 ② ~하기 쉬움, ~한 경향이 있음 **be liable to** ~하기 쉽다; ~할 것 같다
> **be liable for** ~의 책임이 있다

Step 03
연습문제

다음 문장의 liable에 해당되는 뜻을 **Step 02** 의 ❶~❷에서 고르세요. (해답은 470쪽)

1. Offenders will be liable to a heavy fine. (   )
2. Watch the water – it's liable to boil over. (   )
3. All males between 18 and 40 are liable for military service. (   )
4. We are all liable to make mistakes when we are tired. (   )

Step 04
영작연습

다음 문장을 주어진 부분을 이용하여 영어로 옮기세요. (해답은 470쪽)

1. 아기들은 한층 더 감기에 걸리기 쉽다. [more, catch cold]

____

2. 그가 아내의 빚을 갚아야 할 것입니다. [pat, debts]

____

:: 1. 유리는 깨지기 쉽다. 2. 그에게 손해 배상의 책임이 있다.

292 speculate [spékjulèit]

Step 01 해석연습

다음 문장을 speculate에 유의하여 해석해 보세요. (해석은 이 페이지의 하단부에 있음)

1. He speculated about the meaning of life. ___________________________________
2. Edward likes to speculate in land. ___________________________________

Step 02 뜻 알기

speculate에는 다음과 같은 여러 가지의 뜻이 있습니다.

❶ 사색하다, 깊이 생각하다; 추측하다 **V** to consider a subject carefully; to guess about

❷ 투기하다; 투자하다 **V** to buy or sell goods, property, share, etc with the hope of profiting by a change in the price

> 한 걸음 더 **speculation** ① 사색, 추측 ② 투기, 투자 **speculative** ① 사색적인, 이론상의 ② 투기적인
> **speculate in shares[stocks]** 주식[증권]에 손을 대다 **speculate in land** 땅 투기를 하다

Step 03 연습문제

다음 문장의 speculate에 해당되는 뜻을 **Step 02** 의 ❶~❷에서 고르세요. (해답은 470쪽)

1. It is always hard to speculate about the future. (   )
2. My uncle had speculated in stocks and lost heavily. (   )
3. The philosopher speculated on the origin of the universe. (   )
4. George decided to speculate in oil shares. (   )

Step 04 영작연습

다음 문장을 주어진 부분을 이용하여 영어로 옮기세요. (해답은 470쪽)

1. 우리는 단지 그녀가 왜 그것을 했는지에 대해 추측할 따름이다. [only, about, why]

____

2. 그는 금에 투기해서 많은 이익을 얻었다. [gold, made, profit]

____

∷ 1. 그는 인생의 의미에 대해 사색했다. 2. Edward는 땅에 투기하는 것을 좋아한다.

Day 30

293 row (뜻) ❶❷ [rou] ❸ [rau]

Step 01 해석연습 **다음 문장을 row에 유의하여 해석해 보세요.** (해석은 이 페이지의 하단부에 있음)

1. They were sitting in the front row. ________________________
2. Shall I row you across the lake? ________________________
3. We had a terrible row recently. ________________________

Step 02 뜻 알기 **row에는 다음과 같은 여러 가지의 뜻이 있습니다.**

❶ 줄, 열(列) **n** a line of things or people placed side by side

❷ 배를 젓다; 배를 저어서 ~를 나르다 **v** to move a boat by using oars; to carry or take by rowing
   노젓기; 뱃놀이 **n** the act of using oars; a trip in a rowboat

❸ 말다툼; 소동, 소란 **n** a noisy and violent argument or quarrel; a continuous loud noise
   싸우다, 말다툼하다 **v** to quarrel noisily with

> 한 걸음 더 **rowboat** 노로 젓는 배, 보트 **rowing** 조정, 보트경주 **a street row** 거리에서의 난투, 소란
> **a row of trees** 한 줄로 늘어선 나무들 **go for a row** 보트 놀이하러 가다 **have a row with a person** 남과 말다툼하다
> **in a row** ① 일렬로 ② 잇따라, 연속적으로 **in the front row** 앞줄에

Step 03 연습문제 **다음 문장의 row에 해당되는 뜻을** **Step 02 의 ❶~❸에서 고르세요.** (해답은 470쪽)

1. We heard a row in the street. (   )
2. Our seats are on the seventh row. (   )
3. He will go for a row this afternoon. (   )
4. They had a row outside a barroom. (   )
5. Let's have a row on the lake. (   )
6. Our team won four times in a row. (   )

Step 04 영작연습 **다음 문장을 주어진 부분을 이용하여 영어로 옮기세요.** (해답은 470쪽)

1. 길을 따라 나무들이 한 줄로 서 있다. [trees, road]

____

2. 그는 오늘 아침 노를 저어 강을 건넜다. [across, river]

____

3. 그녀는 항상 이웃과 다툰다. [always, neighbors]

____

:: 1. 그들은 앞줄에 앉아 있었다. 2. 배를 저어 호수를 건너게 해 드릴까요? 3. 우리는 최근에 심한 말다툼을 했다.

294 vision [víʒən]

Step 01 해석연습

다음 문장을 vision에 유의하여 해석해 보세요. (해석은 이 페이지의 하단부에 있음)

1. The man was slowly losing his vision. ________________________

2. He was charmed with the beautiful vision. ________________________

3. My father was a man of broad vision. ________________________

4. God appeared to her in a vision. ________________________

Step 02 뜻 알기

vision에는 다음과 같은 여러 가지의 뜻이 있습니다.

❶ 시력, 시각 🅝 the ability to see or the sense of sight; eyesight

❷ 눈에 비치는 모습, 모양, 광경 🅝 something which can be seen; sight

❸ 선견지명, 통찰력 🅝 the ability to see or plan into the future; foresight

❹ 환영(幻影), 미래상, 이상형, 꿈 🅝 something seen in imagination or in a dream; an image of the future; hope

> 한 걸음 더 **broad vision** 고매한 식견 **poor vision** 약한 시력 **beyond our vision** 우리 눈에 안 보이는
> **a man of vision** 통찰력이 있는 사람

Step 03 연습문제

다음 문장의 vision에 해당되는 뜻을 **Step 02** 의 ❶∼❹에서 고르세요. (해답은 470쪽)

1. You must not laugh at the romantic visions of youth. (   )

2. There are leaders of vision in every industry. (   )

3. Cats have good night vision. (   )

4. What a glorious vision of the sunset! (   )

5. Have you ever had visions of great wealth and success? (   )

6. From there we were able to have a clear vision of the city. (   )

7. Her vision blurs when she wears her glasses. (   )

8. They needed a man of vision as their leader. (   )

Step 04 영작연습

다음 문장을 주어진 부분을 이용하여 영어로 옮기세요. (해답은 470쪽)

1. 그는 수술을 통해 시력을 잃을 수도 있다. [lose, surgery]

____

2. 해가 떠오르는 광경의 아름다음은 형언할 수 없다. [sunrise, beyond description]

____

3. 그는 선견지명이 없는 정치가였다. [states man, without]

____

4. 그는 전쟁이 없는 세상에 대한 환상을 갖고 있었다. [world, wars]

____

:: 1. 그 남자는 서서히 시력을 잃어 가고 있었다. 2. 그는 아름다운 광경에 넋을 잃었다. 3. 나의 아버지는 고매한 식견[통찰력]을 가지신 분이었다.
4. 신이 환영(幻影)이 되어 그녀에게 나타났다.

²⁹⁵ **stress** [stres]

Step 01 해석연습

다음 문장을 stress에 유의하여 해석해 보세요. (해석은 이 페이지의 하단부에 있음)

1. This metal object is subjected to great stress. _______________________________

2. She's under a lot of stress these days. _______________________________

3. The manager stressed the necessity of being punctual. _______________________________

4. Stress the second syllable of the word. _______________________________

Step 02 뜻 알기

stress에는 다음과 같은 여러 가지의 뜻이 있습니다.

❶ (물리적) 장력, 응력; 압력 ⓝ the physical force or pressure on an object; tension
~에 압력을 가하다 ⓥ to put pressure on something

❷ (정신적) 억압, 긴장, 스트레스 ⓝ the continuous feelings of worry or the state of anxiety

❸ 강조, 중요성 ⓝ emphasis; importance / ~을 강조하다 ⓥ to emphasize a statement, fact or idea

❹ 강세, 악센트 ⓝ accent given to a speech sound or to a music note
~에 강세를 두다, ~을 강하게 발음하다 ⓥ to give accent to (a syllable)

Step 03 연습문제

다음 문장의 stress에 해당되는 뜻을 Step 02 의 ❶~❹에서 고르세요. (해답은 470쪽)

1. The stress is on the first syllable in the word "orange." (   )

2. A heavy helmet increases the stress on my neck. (   )

3. His headaches may be caused by stress. (   )

4. The stress falls on the third syllable of this word. (   )

5. He stressed the need for cooperation. (   )

6. The increased flow will reduce stress on the dam. (   )

7. His wife stressed the idea that he should quit his job and relax. (   )

8. Stress at work caused her to quit. (   )

Step 04 영작연습

다음 문장을 주어진 부분을 이용하여 영어로 옮기세요. (해답은 470쪽)

1. 교량설계자들이 장력[압력]에 대해 아는 것은 필수적이다. [essential, designers]

____

2. 스트레스는 암 발생의 간접적인 원인이다. [indirect cause]

____

3. 우리 학교는 외국어 학습에 중점을 두었다. [study, foreign]

____

4. 단어 "hotel"은 둘째 음절에 강세가 있다. [word, syllable]

____

∷ 1. 이 금속 물체는 큰 압력을 받는다. 2. 그녀는 요즘 스트레스를 매우 많이 받고 있다. 3. 지배인은 시간을 엄수할 것을 강조했다.
4. 그 단어의 제2음절에 강세를 두어라.

420

A. 다음 뜻에 해당되는 단어를 보기에서 찾아 적으세요.

보기	liable speculate row vision stress

01. ______________ to emphasize a statement, fact or idea
02. ______________ something which can be seen; sight
03. ______________ to consider a subject carefully; to guess about
04. ______________ the ability to see or plan into the future; foresight
05. ______________ obliged to take the responsibility for something; to be responsible
06. ______________ the physical force or pressure on an object; tension
07. ______________ something seen in imagination or in a dream; an image of the future; hope
08. ______________ a noisy and violent argument or quarrel; a continuous loud noise
09. ______________ the continuous feelings of worry or the state of anxiety
10. ______________ to buy or sell goods, property, share, etc with the hope of profiting by a change in the price
11. ______________ a line of things or people placed side by side
12. ______________ to be likely to do; to have a tendency to do
13. ______________ the ability to see or the sense of sight; eyesight
14. ______________ to move a boat by using oars
15. ______________ accent given to a speech sound or to a music note

B. 다음 빈칸에 가장 알맞은 단어를 보기에서 찾아 적으세요.

보기	liable speculate row vision stress

01. The (   ) is on the second syllable in "cigar."
02. He likes to (   ) on the stock market.
03. If you work too hard, you'll build up (   ) and ruin your health.
04. With my new glasses my (   ) is perfect.
05. Ernest is so quiet; we can only (   ) about what he is thinking.
06. Airplane designers have to know about the (   ) exerted on an aircraft's wing.
07. We went for a (   ) on the river.
08. He was a well-informed man with broad (   ).
09. We are all (   ) to make mistakes occasionally.
10. He laid (   ) on the study of a foreign language.
11. The two women had a loud (   ) with lots of yelling.
12. An angel appeared to her in a (   ).
13. She was sitting in the front (   ) in the theater.
14. The lake, in the morning mist, was a wonderful (   ).
15. Is a man (   ) to pay his wife's debts in your country?

Day 30

다음 문장을 굵게 처리된 단어에 유의하여 해석해 보세요.

01. Introspective reflections which are **liable** to stall are helped along by the flow of the landscape. [2011년–홀수형 28번]

➡ ______________________________

02. Three **rows** of benches on each side and six **rows** in front of him were occupied by the respectable people of the town and by the parents of the pupils. [1995년–홀수형 37번]

➡ ______________________________

03. During a regular examination a doctor checks weight, **vision** and hearing problems, blood pressure, and so on. [2005년–홀수형 41번]

➡ ______________________________

04. World leaders should have the **vision** to protect our environment. [2008년–홀수형 32번]

➡ ______________________________

05. Then I had **visions** of mummies coming toward us with cold, dead hands. [2002년–홀수형 29번]

➡ ______________________________

06. I'm here to tell you about my **vision** of the future and to give you a chance to invest in a great new product. [2006년–홀수형 6번]

➡ ______________________________

07. Many difficulties and much **stress** today come from our thinking that there is not enough time. [2004년–홀수형 26번]

➡ ______________________________

08. Crowding **stresses** us. The more crowded we feel, the more **stressed** we get. Work **stresses** us, too. [1996년–홀수형 46번]

➡ ______________________________

296 remark [rimɑ́ːrk]

Step 01 해석연습

다음 문장을 remark에 유의하여 해석해 보세요. (해석은 이 페이지의 하단부에 있음)

1. "She's a pretty woman," he remarked. ___________________________

2. We remarked her sad face. ___________________________

Step 02 뜻 알기

remark에는 다음과 같은 여러 가지의 뜻이 있습니다.

❶ 말하다, 언급하다, 논평하다 ⓥ to comment; to say
말, 언급, 논평 ⓝ a comment; something said

❷ ~에 주의하다, 주목하다; ~을 알아차리다 ⓥ to notice; to see; to observe
주목, 관찰, 인지[알아차림] ⓝ notice; observation

> 한 걸음 더 **remarkable** 놀랄 만한, 주목할 만한 **remarkably** 두드러지게, 현저하게, 매우
> **a causal remark** 무심코[되는대로] 한 말 **a polite remark** 공손한 말
> **make a remark on[about]** ~에 관해 한마디 하다, 비평하다 **make remarks** 비평하다; 연설하다

Step 03 연습문제

다음 문장의 remark에 해당되는 뜻을 Step 02 의 ❶~❷에서 고르세요. (해답은 470쪽)

1. Did you remark the difference between the two? (   )

2. She remarked that she would be absent the next day. (   )

3. It would be rude to remark upon her appearance. (   )

4. He remarked the coldness as soon as he entered the room. (   )

Step 04 영작연습

다음 문장을 주어진 부분을 이용하여 영어로 옮기세요. (해답은 470쪽)

1. 그녀는 그의 말을 모욕으로 받아들였다. [took, insult]

____

2. 그 자동차 쇼에는 주목할 만한 가치가 있는 것이 아무것도 없었다. [worthy, Motor show]

____

:: 1. "그녀는 아름다운 여인이다"라고 그는 말했다. 2. 우리는 그녀의 슬픈 표정을 보았다.

297 submit [səbmít]

Step 01
해석연습

다음 문장을 submit에 유의하여 해석해 보세요. (해석은 이 페이지의 하단부에 있음)

1. Mike refused to submit to threats. _______________________

2. You have to submit the application by tomorrow. _______________________

Step 02
뜻 알기

submit에는 다음과 같은 여러 가지의 뜻이 있습니다.

❶ ~을 (~에) 복종[굴복]시키다; 복종[굴복]하다; 따르다, (일, 운명 따위를) 받아들이다 Ⓥ to put oneself under the control of another; to yield or surrender oneself to; to comply

❷ ~을 제출하다, 제기하다; 공손히 아뢰다 Ⓥ to give a plan, a piece of writing, etc to someone in authority for consideration, approval, etc; to suggest or say something

> 한 걸음 더 **submission** ① 복종, 순종 ② 제출, 제기 **submit oneself to ~** ~에 따르다, 복종하다; ~을 받다[감수하다]
> **submit to authority** 권위에 복종하다 **submit to one's fate** 운명을 달게 받다

Step 03
연습문제

다음 문장의 submit에 해당되는 뜻을 **Step 02** 의 ❶~❷에서 고르세요. (해답은 470쪽)

1. She submitted her claim for damages to the insurer. (   )
2. He will not submit to your bullying. (   )
3. He submitted his idea about a new city library to the mayor. (   )
4. You know more, so I submit to your decision. (   )

Step 04
영작연습

다음 문장을 주어진 부분을 이용하여 영어로 옮기세요. (해답은 470쪽)

1. 그는 모든 비난을 감수하기로 결심했다. [decided, criticism]

____

2. 나는 그가 유죄라는 확실한 증거는 없다고 생각합니다. [absolute proof, guilty]

____

:: 1. Mike는 협박에 굴복하기를 거부했다. 2. 신청서를 내일까지 제출해야 한다.

298 dispense [dispéns]

다음 문장을 dispense에 유의하여 해석해 보세요. (해석은 이 페이지의 하단부에 있음)

1. This vending machine dispenses hot coffee. ________________________________
2. The judicial system dispenses justice to the people. ________________________
3. My aunt was a dispensing chemist. ________________________________
4. We dispensed with all the formalities. ________________________________

dispense에는 다음과 같은 여러 가지의 뜻이 있습니다.

❶ ~을 나누어 주다, 분배하다 Ⅴ to distribute; to give out to each

❷ (법률, 법령 따위를) 시행하다, 실시하다 Ⅴ to carry out; to administer

❸ (처방에 의해 약을) 조제하다 Ⅴ to prepare medicines for giving out

❹ (dispense with의 형태로 쓰여) ~없이 지내다; 없애다; ~을 불필요하게 하다 Ⅴ to do without; to get rid of; to make something unnecessary

> 한 걸음 더 **dispenser** ① 분배자, 나누어 주는 사람 ② 약사, 약제사 ③ 자동판매기
> **dispense with** ~없이 지내다, ~을 불필요하게 하다, 없애다

다음 문장의 dispense에 해당되는 뜻을 `Step 02` 의 ❶~❹에서 고르세요. (해답은 470쪽)

1. Pharmacists have the legal authority to dispense drugs. (   )
2. Our courts exist to dispense justice. (   )
3. This machine dispenses a range of drinks and snacks. (   )
4. Your services can now be dispensed with. (   )
5. The local government dispenses free health care to the poor. (   )
6. Schools are not permitted to prescribe or dispense medicines. (   )
7. I find it very hard to dispense with green tea. (   )
8. Officials dispensed clothing to the sufferers. (   )

다음 문장을 주어진 부분을 이용하여 영어로 옮기세요. (해답은 470쪽)

1. 공무원들이 빈민들에게 식량과 의복을 나누어 주었다. [officials, food, clothing]

____

2. 우리 정부는 법을 공정히 시행한다. [law, justly]

____

3. 그 약들은 합법적인 방법으로 조제되었다. [drugs, lawful, manner]

____

4. 새 사무기기는 비서의 필요성을 없게 하였다. [office machine, need, secretary]

____

:: 1. 이 자판기는 뜨거운 커피가 나온다. 2. 사법제도는 국민들에게 정의를 실천한다. 3. 나의 고모는 약을 조제하는 약사였다.
4. 우리는 모든 형식적인 예절을 생략했다.

299 nut [nʌt]

Step 01 해석연습

다음 문장을 nut에 유의하여 해석해 보세요. (해석은 이 페이지의 하단부에 있음)

1. The nut is very hard to crack. _______________________
2. This tool is used to wring up the nut. _______________________
3. Stop behaving like a nut! _______________________
4. Daniel is a tough nut. _______________________

Step 02 뜻 알기

nut에는 다음과 같은 여러 가지의 뜻이 있습니다.

❶ 견과(호두, 밤 따위) **n** a dry fruit with a hard shell and seeds inside it

❷ 너트, 암나사 (↔ bolt) **n** a small piece of metal with a (threaded) hole for screwing on to a bolt

❸ (비격식) 미치광이, 괴짜; 바보, 멍청이 **n** a person who seems very odd or crazy; foolish person

❹ (비격식) 다루기 힘든 사람[문제] **n** a difficult problem or a person who is difficult to deal with

> 한 걸음 더 **She's a Yon-sama nut.** 그녀는 욘사마의 열광팬이다. → 어떤 일에 열중하는 사람, ~광(狂), 매니아
> **Come on, use your nut!** 자, 머리를 써라! → 머리(=the head or brain)

Step 03 연습문제

다음 문장의 nut에 해당되는 뜻을 **Step 02** 의 ❶∼❹에서 고르세요. (해답은 470쪽)

1. She is a kind of nut, but I like her. (   )
2. He was a hard nut to crack. (   )
3. The squirrels are storing nuts in their nest. (   )
4. Each bolt has a nut at each end. (   )
5. Alex is a very tough nut to crack. (   )
6. Come on! Don't talk like a nut! (   )
7. Add oatmeal and nuts and blend well. (   )
8. If it feels too tight, loosen the nut by the pliers. (   )

Step 04 영작연습

다음 문장을 주어진 부분을 이용하여 영어로 옮기세요. (해답은 470쪽)

1. 그녀는 호두 한 깡통을 사야 한다. [need, can]

____

2. 그는 플라이어(pliers)로 너트를 뽑으려 한다. [trying, unscrew, with]

____

3. 뭐하는 거야? 당신 미쳤어? [what, doing]

____

4. 그것은 내가 해결하기엔 어려운 문제다. [hard, to crack]

____

:: 1. 호두는 잘 깨지지 않는다. 2. 이 공구는 너트를 단단히 죄는 데 사용된다. 3. 정신 나간 사람처럼 행동하지 마라! 4. Daniel은 다루기 힘든 사람이다.

300 section [sékʃən]

다음 문장을 section에 유의하여 해석해 보세요. (해석은 이 페이지의 하단부에 있음)

1. She divided the orange into sections. ________________________________

2. This section of the road is still closed. ________________________________

3. Chapter Ⅳ has five sections. ________________________________

section에는 다음과 같은 여러 가지의 뜻이 있습니다.

❶ 잘라낸 부분, 조각 **n** a piece or part of something; one of the parts that can be fitted together

❷ 구역, (정당, 집단 등의) 당파; (회사, 관청 따위의) 부(部), 과(科), 반(班) **n** a district; a separate group; one of the parts of an organization, institution, department, etc

❸ (책, 법률, 규약 따위의) 절(節), 항(項); (신문 따위의) 난(欄) **n** a separate part of something that is written, such as a book, document, newspaper, etc

> 한 걸음 더 **This is a <u>section</u> of the stem of the flower.** 이것이 그 꽃줄기의 절단면이다.
> → 물건의 절단면, 입체의 단면도(=a picture or view of something seen as if cut straight through)
> **Parts of the town had been <u>sectioned</u> off.** 그 도시의 구역들은 분할되어 있었다.
> → ~을 분할하다, 구분하다(=to cut into sections)
> **an accounting section** 경리과 **a residental section** 주택지역 **a non-smoking section** 금연구역 **a cross section** 횡단면

다음 문장의 section에 해당되는 뜻을 Step 02 의 ❶~❸에서 고르세요. (해답은 470쪽)

1. That is in the final section of this chapter. (　　)

2. He divided the pie into four sections. (　　)

3. Where is the section dealing with customers complaints? (　　)

4. Check Article Ⅰ, Section 8, detailing the powers of Congress. (　　)

5. You need to fit together the sections of the bookcase. (　　)

6. Can I get a table in the non-smoking section? (　　)

다음 문장을 주어진 부분을 이용하여 영어로 옮기세요. (해답은 470쪽)

1. 낚싯대는 세 부분으로 이루어진다. [fishing rod]

____

2. Mike는 이번에 과장으로 승진되었다. [promoted, chief]

____

3. 그는 신문의 경제란을 읽었다. [financial, newspaper]

____

:: 1. 그녀는 오렌지를 조각내었다. 2. 도로의 이 구역이 여전히 폐쇄되어 있다. 3. 제4장은 5절로 되어 있다.

A. 다음 뜻에 해당되는 단어를 보기에서 찾아 적으세요.

보기	remark submit dispense nut section

01. ______________ to prepare medicines for giving out
02. ______________ a person who seems very odd or crazy; foolish person
03. ______________ to comment; to say
04. ______________ to do without; to get rid of; to make something unnecessary
05. ______________ a difficult problem or a person who is difficult to deal with
06. ______________ a district; one of the parts of an organization, institution, etc
07. ______________ to put oneself under the control of another; to yield or surrender oneself to
08. ______________ a small piece of metal with a (threaded) hole for screwing on to a bolt
09. ______________ a separate part of something that is written, such as a book, newspaper, etc
10. ______________ to distribute; to give out to each
11. ______________ to give a plan, a piece of writing, etc. to someone in authority for approval etc
12. ______________ to notice; to see; to observe
13. ______________ a dry fruit with a hard shell and seeds inside it
14. ______________ to carry out; to administer
15. ______________ a piece or part of something; one of the parts that can be fitted together

B. 다음 빈칸에 가장 알맞은 단어를 보기에서 찾아 적으세요.

보기	remark(s) submit dispense nut section

01. We have to (　　　　) the completed project by 10 June.
02. They've had to (　　　　) with a lot of luxuries since Fred lost his job.
03. Almond is an edible, flat, oval-shaped (　　　　).
04. We lived in the (　　　　) of town near the railroad station.
05. The Red Cross will (　　　　) medical supplies to the refugees.
06. She made a number of complimentary (　　　　) about the food.
07. Billy is a (　　　　). He believes in all kinds of nonsense.
08. The pharmacies (　　　　) medicines and offer a comprehensive advice service for medicine-related questions.
09. Did you (　　　　) the similarity between them?
10. It may be a tough (　　　　) to crack, but you can solve it.
11. Would you like a (　　　　) of this orange?
12. He uses a (　　　　) and bolt to fasten two things together.
13. We must (　　　　) ourselves to God's will.
14. We trust the Minister of Justice to (　　　　) justice.
15. He likes to read the sports (　　　　) of the newspaper.

다음 문장을 굵게 처리된 단어에 유의하여 해석해 보세요.

01. Albert Einstein **remarked**, "There is no chance that nuclear energy will ever be obtainable." [2005년–홀수형 40번]

➡ ______________________________

02. In other words, children and adults alike want to hear positive **remarks**. [2001년–홀수형 27번]

➡ ______________________________

03. I want to **submit** my new application tomorrow. [2006년–홀수형 14번]

➡ ______________________________

04. Now the reader could easily move backward in the text to find a previously read passage or browse between widely separated **sections** of the same work. [2008년–홀수형 25번]

➡ ______________________________

05. According to the study, violence and property crimes were nearly twice as high in sections of the buildings where vegetation was low, compared with the **sections** where vegetation was high. [2007년–홀수형 24번]

➡ ______________________________

06. W: Matthew, look at those old pots behind the glass.
M: You mean, over there in the **section** on ancient pottery? <in the museum>
[2007년–홀수형 9번]

➡ ______________________________

Day 30

DAY 01~30
정답 및 해설

Group-1

001 kid
Step 03 **1.** 3 **2.** 1 **3.** 2 **4.** 1 **5.** 3 **6.** 2
Step 04 **1.** That kid is my younger sister.
2. The kid lives at the zoo.
3. My brother likes to kid my friends.

002 fly
Step 03 **1.** 3 **2.** 2 **3.** 1 **4.** 1 **5.** 2 **6.** 3
Step 04 **1.** A fly is on your nose.
2. Jae-ho will fly to Sydney today.
3. Birds fly south for the winter.

003 horn
Step 03 **1.** 1 **2.** 3 **3.** 1 **4.** 3 **5.** 2 **6.** 2
Step 04 **1.** The car horn scared me.
2. My brother plays the horn after dinner.
3. The animal will grow a new horn.

004 wave
Step 03 **1.** 2 **2.** 3 **3.** 1 **4.** 3 **5.** 1 **6.** 2
Step 04 **1.** The swimmers moved with the wave.
2. My hair has a beautiful wave.
3. The drivers waved each other on the street.

005 light
Step 03 **1.** 2 **2.** 3 **3.** 1 **4.** 3 **5.** 1 **6.** 2
Step 04 **1.** The light shines in the window.
2. Se-ri will light the candle.
3. This bag is very light.

Review
A. 01. fly **02.** horn **03.** kid **04.** wave **05.** horn **06.** light
07. wave **08.** light **09.** kid **10.** fly **11.** wave **12.** kid
13. fly **14.** horn **15.** light
B. 01. wave **02.** light **03.** horn **04.** kid **05.** fly **06.** horn
07. wave **08.** light **09.** horn **10.** kid **11.** fly **12.** light
13. kid **14.** wave **15.** fly

수능기출예문 점검
01. 18세 이하의 아이들은 이것을 받기 위해서 등록 양식에 부모의 서명을 필요로 한다.
02. Helen, 너 지금 농담하고 있는 거지.
03. 즐거운 시간을 보낼 때는 시간이 빨리 지나가는 법이다.
04. 내 화살이 날아가기 시작하자마자, 나는 군중들이 환호성을 지르는 소리를 들었다.
05. 비행기 탑승객인 Walt Morris 씨에게, 어느 가을 저녁 비행기를 타고 한적한 Kansas 하늘 위를 나는 것은 유쾌한 경험이었습니다.
06. W: 핸들에 부착된 바구니가 있는 이것은 어때요?
M: 훌륭해요, 하지만 경적이 달려 있는 똑같은 모델이 있나요?
07. 이 파도는 난폭하고 거대했으며, 각각의 파도는 보트에 타고 있던 사람에게는 공포의 대상이었다.

08. 그가 살던 시대 이후로 우리는 빛의 파장이 다양한 진동의 주파수로 특징지어진다고 알아 왔다.
09. 우리는 빛이 비출 때만 어떤 물체를 볼 수 있다.
10. 갑자기 실내의 등이 두 번 희미해지더니 꺼져 버렸다.
11. 성능이 좋은 회중전등이 당신의 앞길과 주변의 생물을 쉽게 비추어 줄 것이고, 바닷속 모습을 진정한 색채 그대로 보여 줄 것이다.
12. 식장은 환하게 불이 켜져 있었으며 꽃으로 장식이 되어 있었다.
13. 가벼운 안개가 보다 낮은 곳에 있는 풍경의 지형을 부분적으로 감추면서 대지를 따라 깔려 있었지만, 그 위에는 보다 큰 나무들이 맑은 하늘을 배경으로 윤곽이 뚜렷한 무리를 이루어 드러나 있었다.
14. 당신은 삶이 순항하는 것처럼 즐겁고 행복하다고 느낀다.
15. 만약 당신이 자신의 문제에 관해 누군가에게 말한다면 당신은 그것을 다른 관점에서 보게 될 수 있다.

Group-2

006 bat
Step 03 **1.** 3 **2.** 2 **3.** 1 **4.** 2 **5.** 1 **6.** 3
Step 04 **1.** The bat usually hunts for food at night.
2. He beat the dog with a bat.
3. He batted the ball with his left hand.

007 hand
Step 03 **1.** 1 **2.** 3 **3.** 2 **4.** 3 **5.** 1 **6.** 2
Step 04 **1.** He writes well with his left hand.
2. Clocks usually have an hour hand and a minute hand.
3. I handed the letter to her.

008 watch
Step 03 **1.** 2 **2.** 3 **3.** 2 **4.** 1 **5.** 3 **6.** 1
Step 04 **1.** I looked at my watch to see if I was late.
2. The mother watched her children play carefully.
3. He will be the watch tonight.

009 dish
Step 03 **1.** 1 **2.** 2 **3.** 2 **4.** 1
Step 04 **1.** She put the dishes on the table for dinner.
2. This dish doesn't take much time to make.

010 ring
Step 03 **1.** 3 **2.** 1 **3.** 4 **4.** 2 **5.** 3 **6.** 4 **7.** 2 **8.** 1
Step 04 **1.** Se-ri wears a pearl ring.
2. A doughnut looks like a ring.
3. There was a single ring at the door.
4. I rang her yesterday but she wasn't in.

Review
A. 01. dish **02.** watch **03.** ring **04.** dish **05.** bat
06. watch **7.** hand **08.** watch **09.** ring **10.** ring
11. bat **12.** ring **13.** hand **14.** bat **15.** ring
B. 01. hand **02.** watch **03.** bat **04.** ring **05.** hand
06. watch **07.** bat **08.** dish **09.** ring **10.** hand
11. ring **12.** bat **13.** watch **14.** ring **15.** dish

01. 이틀 밤 동안 먹이를 먹지 못하는 박쥐는 죽을 가능성이 있다.

02. 나는 그 문제를 빈칸으로 남겨 둔 채 답안지를 제출했다.

03. 물론이지. 나는 중고 물건을 다시는 사지 않을 거야.

04. 그 어린 소년은 손을 주머니 밖으로 빼서 그 속의 많은 동전들을 자세히 살펴보았다.

05. 반면에, 디자인은 주로 문제 해결, 제품의 기능과 관련이 있다.

06. 만약 어떤 상황에 대해 우스꽝스럽거나 터무니없는 점을 지적하고 상대 방으로 하여금 당신의 감정을 공유하도록 함으로써 긴장을 완화할 수 있 다면, 당신은 유리한 위치에 서게 될 것이다.

07. M: 제가 도와드릴까요?
W: 아닙니다, 괜찮습니다. 승강기에서 내리려던 참이었습니다.

08. 그 문이 열렸을 때 나는 "메리 크리스마스!"라고 하면서 놀란 아이에게 아름답게 포장한 선물을 건네주었다.

09. 어떤 연사들은 연설 중에 종종 시계를 본다.

10. "그녀는 토네이도 경보가 그녀를 5시간 동안이나 지하실에 있게 하고 아 무 일도 일어나지 않았다는 것을 항의하기 위해 나에게 전화했지요."라 고 Allen Pearson이 말한다.

11. 그들은 정부가 국내에서 또는 해외에서 하는 일들을 지켜보고 영향력을 행사한다.

12. 많은 사람들은 그 비밀이 거의 모든 식사마다 나오는 전통 한국음식인 김치라고 생각한다.

13. 나에게 준 팁 15센트가 빈 접시 옆에 깨끗하게 놓여 있었다.

14. 그곳에는 그의 할머니가 주신 작은 다이아몬드가 박힌 금반지가 들어 있 었다.

15. 교향악단은 음악으로 빌딩 하나 전체를 다 채우고 울리도록 할 수 있다.

16. 여러 해 전 심리학자들이 한 가지 실험을 하였는데 그 실험에서 그들은 사람들을 고리 던지기 세트 외에는 아무것도 없는 방에 있게 하였다.

17. W: 하지만 그녀가 계속해서 나를 링(권투경기장)의 구석으로 밀어붙여요.
M: 그녀가 너를 구석에 가두지 못하게 해야 해. 그렇지 않으면 너는 이번 시합에서 질 거야.

>>> DAY 02

Group-3

011 ball

| Step 03 | **1.** 1 **2.** 3 **3.** 2 **4.** 3 **5.** 1 **6.** 2 |

Step 04
1. The football player kicked the ball strongly.
2. He made a handkerchief into a ball.
3. A lot of people were at the Spring Ball.

012 space

Step 03 **1.** 3 **2.** 1 **3.** 3 **4.** 2 **5.** 1 **6.** 2

Step 04
1. Travel through space to other planets interests many people today.
2. The caged tigers do not have enough space.
3. She left a space between lines.

013 jack

Step 03 **1.** 2 **2.** 1 **3.** 3 **4.** 1 **5.** 2 **6.** 3

Step 04
1. He jacked up the car to change the flat tire.
2. She put a jack on the card table.
3. He connected two electric machines with a jack.

014 story

Step 03 **1.** 2 **2.** 1 **3.** 1 **4.** 2

Step 04
1. My uncle told me a story about a faithful dog.
2. That is a 63-story building.

015 band

Step 03 **1.** 3 **2.** 1 **3.** 4 **4.** 2 **5.** 4 **6.** 1 **7.** 2 **8.** 3

Step 04
1. In-ho plays the drums in our band.
2. The band of monkeys lives together.
3. She tied a rubber band around the box.
4. They banded together to protest.

Review

A. 01. space **02.** story **03.** band **04.** ball **05.** jack
06. band **07.** story **08.** ball **09.** jack **10.** band
11. space **12.** jack **13.** ball **14.** band **15.** space

B. 01. band **02.** jack **03.** space **04.** story **05.** ball
06. band **07.** space **08.** story **09.** ball **10.** band
11. jack **12.** space **13.** ball **14.** jack **15.** band

01. 인간이 발명한 최초의 진정한 운동 장비 품목은 공이었다.

02. 안락한 생활 조건이란 화학적, 물리적인 청결뿐 아니라 사생활, 공간 그 리고 조용함을 포함한다.

03. 거대한 공간이 나무와 새를 위한 공간보다 주차장으로 쓰이고 있다.

04. 로봇과 우주 비행사는 우주 공간에서 거의 똑같은 장비를 사용한다.

05. 하나의 기술적 변화로 인해, 앞뒤 참조가 가능해졌고 동시에 전집을 소 장하기에 필요한 물리적 공간이 급격하게 줄어들었다.

06. 과학자들은 사람들을 우주와 심지어 달에까지 보냈다.

07. M: 큰 나무 옆에 있는 집이 우리 집이야. W: 이층 집 말이지? M: 아니, 일 층 집이야. W: 알았다.

08. 그 이야기는 Homer가 살았던 세상에서 시작되는데, 폭풍우 치는 하늘 과 검푸른 바다는 신화 속의 신들의 지배를 받았다.

09. 예를 들면, 소설이나 시를 읽는 것은 우리 자신의 상황을 이해하고 개선 하는 데 도움을 줄 수 있다.

10. 작은 입 배스는 그것의 옆면에 일련의 검은 수직의 띠를 가지고 있다.

11. 파란 셔츠를 입은 농부들로 이루어진 밴드는 고대의 Basque Riau-Riau 춤에 맞춰 북과 다양한 관악기 뒤에서 돌고 들고 흔든다.

12. 그리고 밤에는 넓은 공개된 광장에서 마을 사람 전부가 춤을 추면 큰 북 과 군악대의 소리가 울려 퍼진다.

13. M: 와, 학교 동아리가 많이 있구나.
W: 음… 나는 학교 록밴드에 가입하고 싶어. 거기에 함께 가입하자.

Group-4

016 punch

Step 03 **1.** 2 **2.** 1 **3.** 3 **4.** 1 **5.** 3 **6.** 2

Step 04
1. This punch tastes like strawberries.
2. He got a strong punch on the nose.
3. She used a punch to make three holes in her term paper.

017 tail

Step 03 　1. 1　2. 3　3. 2　4. 2　5. 3　6. 1
Step 04 　1. Dogs wag their tails when they are pleased.
　　　　2. He saw the tail of the procession disappearing round the corner.
　　　　3. The tail of the coin was badly scratched.

018 fire

Step 03 　1. 1　2. 2　3. 3　4. 2　5. 3　6. 1
Step 04 　1. The house was completely destroyed by fire.
　　　　2. The soldier fired his rifle at the enemy.
　　　　3. She was fired from her last job for being late.

019 pretty

Step 03 　1. 2　2. 1　3. 1　4. 2
Step 04 　1. The roses are very pretty in May.
　　　　2. The park is pretty far from my house.

020 part

Step 03 　1. 1　2. 2　3. 4　4. 2　5. 3　6. 4　7. 1　8. 3
Step 04 　1. He spent the early part of his life in Australia.
　　　　2. The teacher will part the fighting students.
　　　　3. He used a comb to make a part in his hair.
　　　　4. She will play the part of Juliet in the movie.

Review

A. 01. pretty　02. part　03. punch　04. fire　05. tail
　 06. punch　07. pretty　08. fire　09. part　10. tail
　 11. part　12. tail　13. punch　14. part　15. fire
B. 01. tail　02. punch　03. fire　04. part　05. punch
　 06. tail　07. part　08. pretty　09. part　10. fire
　 11. punch　12. pretty　13. tail　14. fire　15. part

수능기출예문 점검

01. 첫째로, 그녀는 나의 부모님께 놀라운 나의 체력에 대해서 말씀하셨다: "Lisa는 급우들을 쫓아가서 때리는 데 지치지 않습니다."
02. 그런데 약을 사기 위해 약국에서 줄을 서서 기다리는 대신에 자동판매기에 가셔서, 신분증 번호를 입력하시고, 여러분의 약을 받으십시오.
03. 예를 들어, 동전던지기에서 앞면이 나올 것인지 뒷면이 나올 것인지에 대해 내기를 걸도록 요청을 받으면 대부분의 사람들이 동전이 아직 던져지지 않았을 때 더 많은 금액을 거는 것으로 기록되어 있다.
04. 이것은 자동차 사고, 실직(해고당함), 갑자기 병이 들 경우, 법적 소송 사건에 말려들 경우나 많은 돈을 잃었을 때와 같은 여러 가지 많은 원인에 기인한다.
05. 예를 들어, 소방서장은 절대적으로 명료하게 그의 명령을 내릴 필요가 있다.
06. Howard 씨의 집에 가까워지자, 나는 그의 집에 불이 났다고 생각했다.
07. 불편을 드려 죄송하지만, 스낵바에 작은 화재가 발생했습니다.
08. 아이는 대놓고 인정해 달라고 요구하는 경향이 있다. "내 그림을 보세요. 예쁘지 않아요?"
09. 글쎄, 전반부는 꽤 쉬워. 그런데 후반부는 약간의 암벽 등반 부분이 있어서 좀 더 힘들어.
10. 대부분의 사람들은 자신의 잠재 능력의 작은 부분만을 인식한다.
11. 그 다음 단계로 접착제와 못으로 서로 다른 부속품을 조립하세요.

12. 그래서 그녀는 사인을 받았고, 그 두 사람은 좋은 친구로 헤어졌다.
13. 많은 것들이 우리가 어떤 음식을 먹느냐를 결정한다. 기후가 그런 역할을 하고 토양도 마찬가지이다.
14. Asch는 20명의 대학생들로 이루어진 집단들을 모아서, 그들이 시각적 지각에 관한 실험에 참여할 거라고 말했다.
15. 우리가 좀 더 나이가 들었을 때 엄마는 우리 방을 말끔하게 치워 우리가 맡은 일을 다했는지 확인했다.

>>> DAY 03

Group-5

021 kind

Step 03 　1. 2　2. 1　3. 2　4. 1
Step 04 　1. The doctor is always kind to his patients.
　　　　2. She has the same kind of watch as mine.

022 swing

Step 03 　1. 2　2. 1　3. 3　4. 1　5. 3　6. 2
Step 04 　1. That door makes much noise when it swings.
　　　　2. The golfer wants to improve his swing.
　　　　3. Seri loved to ride on the swing at school.

023 march

Step 03 　1. 1　2. 3　3. 1　4. 2　5. 3　6. 2
Step 04 　1. Some flowers bloom in March.
　　　　2. My school band will march in the Christmas parade.
　　　　3. He heard the trumpet play that march.

024 block

Step 03 　1. 1　2. 2　3. 3　4. 1　5. 3　6. 2
Step 04 　1. He carved a statue out of the block of ice.
　　　　2. It is five blocks to the store from here.
　　　　3. She made every effort to block his election.

025 stand

Step 03 　1. 4　2. 1　3. 2　4. 1　5. 3　6. 4　7. 2　8. 3
Step 04 　1. Everyone will stand up when the band plays the national anthem.
　　　　2. Joe sold fifteen cups of lemonade at his stand yesterday.
　　　　3. She will stand the ladder against the wall.
　　　　4. I can't stand this hot weather any longer.

Review

A. 01. march　02. block　03. stand　04. swing　05. kind
　 06. march　07. swing　08. block　09. stand　10. kind
　 11. swing　12. block　13. stand　14. March　15. stand
B. 01. stand　02. march　03. block　04. swing　05. stand
　 06. block　07. march　08. block　09. kind　10. swing
　 11. stand　12. kind　13. March　14. stand　15. swing

01. M : 그 가방 나르는 것을 도와드릴까요? W : 친절하시군요. 감사드립니다.

02. 일반적으로 부모님들은 그들이 다른 아이들에게서 느끼지 못하는 특별한 종류의 사랑을 자신의 아이들에게 느낀다.

03. 우리가 도착했을 때, 여동생은 즉시 그네로 뛰어가 버렸고, 나는 엄마가 여동생을 따라가지 않아서 짜증이 났던 것을 기억한다.

04. 이러한 증상은 흔들림이나, 회전, 요동, 상하로의 움직임 등과 같은 동작에 노출될 때 이러한 증상이 생긴다.

05. 나는 감정이 극에서 극으로 왔다 갔다 흔들렸던 기억도 난다.

06. 그는 짝을 얻기 위해서 그들의 강력한 목을 흔들면서 싸우고 있는 수컷 기린들을 보았는데, 그 목은 길이가 6피트 이상이고 무게는 200파운드 이상이나 나갔다.

07. 그것은 어린 아이에게는 자신이 지금까지 만든 그 어느 것보다 더 높은 탑 위에 떨리는 손가락으로 마지막 블록을 놓는 것일 수 있고, 단거리 선수에게는 자신의 기록을 깨려고 노력하는 것일 수 있으며, 바이올린 연주자에게 있어서는 복잡한 악절을 완벽하게 숙달하는 것일 수 있다.

08. Michelangelo는 대리석 덩어리를 보고 한 사람을 보았다.

09. 드레스와 정장 차림의 사람들의 모습이 정원을 바라보는 나의 시야를 가렸다.

10. 어떤 도시를 차를 몰고 나가면 보도에서 술에 취한 사람을 목격한다. 몇 블록 더 가면 술 취한 사람을 또 보게 된다.

11. 참가자들은 야외활동을 위한 편한 옷과 벌레약, 자외선 차단제를 지참해야 합니다.

12. 인내는 분명히 중요한 덕목이다. 하지만, 너무 많은 사람들이 "서둘레!"라는 생각을 하며 전자레인지 앞에 서 있다.

13. 머지않아 사태가 참기 어려울 지경에 이를 것이기 때문에 어떤 지도가 있으면 고맙겠습니다.

14. 그러나 대담하게 진리를 위한 진심 어린 입장을 취하는 사람들은 종종 그들의 기대를 넘어서는 결과를 성취한다.

15. 의사는 장난하는 투로 말했다. "눈을 감고 혀를 내미세요." 그런 다음 의사는 혀를 내밀고 있는 젊은이를 길거리에 세워 두고 사라졌다.

Group-6

026 shop

Step 03   **1.** 1   **2.** 3   **3.** 2   **4.** 3   **5.** 1   **6.** 2

Step 04   **1.** Mary bought some roses at the flower shop on the corner.
      2. After retiring from business, my father worked in a machine shop.
      3. They shop for groceries every Tuesday.

027 season

Step 03   **1.** 1   **2.** 3   **3.** 2   **4.** 2   **5.** 3   **6.** 1

Step 04   **1.** Autumn is the best season for travelling.
      2. In Korea the baseball season begins in April.
      3. She likes to season the soup with pepper.

028 fan

Step 03   **1.** 2   **2.** 3   **3.** 1   **4.** 3   **5.** 1   **6.** 2

Step 04   **1.** She used to carry a fan to keep herself cool.
      2. He fanned the fire until it burst into flames.
      3. Nancy has been a fan of the team for 3 years.

029 like

Step 03   **1.** 1   **2.** 2   **3.** 1   **4.** 2

Step 04   **1.** We all have our likes and dislikes.
      2. My brother has a car like yours.

030 sight

Step 03   **1.** 2   **2.** 1   **3.** 4   **4.** 1   **5.** 4   **6.** 3   **7.** 2   **8.** 1

Step 04   **1.** He had lost his sight in the war.
      2. The girl lost sight of her mother in the crowd.
      3. The Grand Canyon is one of the sights of the world.
      4. I will do what is right in my own sight.

Review

A. 01. like **02.** season **03.** shop **04.** sight **05.** fan **06.** season **07.** sight **08.** shop **09.** sight **10.** fan **11.** fan **12.** sight **13.** shop **14.** like **15.** season

B. 01. like **02.** season **03.** sight **04.** shop **05.** fan **06.** fan **07.** sight **08.** shop **09.** like **10.** season **11.** sight **12.** fan **13.** shop **14.** season **15.** sight

01. 서비스가 느림에도 불구하고, 그들의 가게는 끊임없이 손님이 꽉 차고 그들의 계산대는 옷들이 산적해 있다.

02. 또한 수리점도 점점 드물어져 가고 있다.

03. 그러나 올바르게 우리 자신이나 운명을 개선하기에는 초인적 일이므로 그 대신에 우리가 할 수 있는 일을 한다: 우리가 물건을 사고, 경제가 커지고, 세상이 보다 복잡해지고 우리는 더 무력하고 불안전하게 느낀다. 그래서 우리는 더더욱 많이 산다.

04. 겨울이 다가왔습니다. 그리고 겨울과 함께 감기의 계절도 왔습니다.

05. 곧 우리는 누가 챔피언이라고 불릴 것인지와 누가 다음 시즌에 더 열심히 훈련해야 할지를 알게 될 것이다.

06. 그 여과기가 실수로 필수적인 어떤 것을 잘못 걸러낼 때, 노련한 대가들도 실수를 저지를 수 있다.

07. 그의 어머니는 Tony에게 몇 번이나 세차하라고 말한다. 그러나 그는 장마철이기 때문에 그럴 필요가 없다고 고집한다.

08. 밤새도록 팬들은 티켓을 얻기 위해 공연장 밖에서 잠을 잤다.

09. W: 마지막 질문입니다. 여가시간에는 무엇을 하십니까?
     M: 팬들의 편지에 답장하느라 바쁩니다.

10. 사랑에 빠진다는 것은 마법의 구름에 사로잡히는 것과 같다.

11. 어떤 아이들은, 특히 남자 아이들은 그들 자신의 연주기기를 갖고 싶어하고, 아주 오랜 기간 동안 이것을 틀 수도 있다.

12. 하지만 고립 상태는 출구가 없는 방 안에 있는 것과 같다.

13. 경기가 끝나고 막 출구로 나왔을 때, 나는 Willie Mays를 보게 되었다.

14. 나의 한 친구가 아내와 함께 하와이에 가서 해변에 서서 아름다운 노을을 보고 있었는데 그 광경은 너무 장엄하여 믿을 수가 없을 정도였다.

15. 결과적으로, 인간은 자신의 잘못은 못 보지만 자기 이웃의 잘못은 반드시 본다.

>>> DAY 04

Group-7

031 time

Step 03 **1.** 1 **2.** 2 **3.** 1 **4.** 2

Step 04 **1.** We have no time to lose. We must hurry up.
2. This box is three times as big as that one.

032 track

Step 03 **1.** 3 **2.** 1 **3.** 2 **4.** 3 **5.** 2 **6.** 1

Step 04 **1.** Radar can track the movement of airplane.
2. He ran around the track three times.
3. The two trains run on the same track.

033 hot

Step 03 **1.** 1 **2.** 2 **3.** 1 **4.** 3 **5.** 2 **6.** 3

Step 04 **1.** Summer is the hottest season of the year.
2. Chili peppers taste very hot.
3. There's much hot news in today's newspaper.

034 pet

Step 03 **1.** 1 **2.** 2 **3.** 1 **4.** 3 **5.** 3 **6.** 2

Step 04 **1.** The old lady keeps a cat as a pet.
2. That bright girl is the teacher's pet.
3. He petted his dog on its back.

035 hard

Step 03 **1.** 2 **2.** 4 **3.** 1 **4.** 4 **5.** 1 **6.** 3 **7.** 2 **8.** 3

Step 04 **1.** Diamond is the hardest substance known to us.
2. It is hard for me to swim across this river.
3. He studied hard to pass the entrance examination.
4. Indeed it snowed hard yesterday.

Review

A. 01. pet **02.** track **03.** pet **04.** hot **05.** hard **06.** time
 07. hard **08.** hot **09.** hard **10.** time **11.** pet **12.** track
 13. hot **14.** hard **15.** track

B. 01. pet **02.** hot **03.** track **04.** hot **05.** time **06.** pet
 07. hard **08.** hot **09.** hard **10.** times **11.** track
 12. hard **13.** track **14.** pet **15.** hard

수능기출예문 점검

01. 사람들이 다른 관심 분야를 추구할 시간은 세상을 사는 동안 충분히 있다.
02. 오페라는 한 번 감상한 후에도, 여전히 다섯 번 또는 스무 번까지도 들을 수 있을 것이다.
03. 1갤런의 디젤 연료로 철도는 트럭보다 거의 4배 많이 운송한다.
04. 오늘날과 마찬가지로 고대 시대에 착용된 신발의 기본적 유형은 기후에 의해 결정되었다.
05. 그러나 학교에서 아이들은 점심 휴식시간 동안 4분의 1마일 트랙을 달려서 Nature Trail 티켓을 얻는 것을 매우 빨리 배웠다.
06. 우리는 미라에 너무 매료되어서 시간이 가는 줄을 몰랐다.
07. 38~39℃의 뜨거운 물에서의 목욕은 근육을 이완시키는 데 가장 좋다.
08. 크리스마스 열기 속에서 그 기분을 잡으려고 마지막으로 시도한, 결코 부유하지 않은 어떤 친절한 여자가 있었다.
09. 농부들은 화학약제가 야생동물이나 개와 같은 애완동물을 죽일 수 있기 때문에 잡초를 억제하기 위해 화학 약제를 사용하는 것을 좋아하지 않는다.
10. 옆집 강아지를 만져 볼 생각도 못했던 아이가 동물원에 있는 사자를 만지고 싶어 하는 예처럼 어떤 두려움은 한 가지 종류에서만 확장되는 경우도 있다.
11. 초기의 자원 봉사자들은 혼자서 힘들고 불쾌한 작업을 해냈다.
12. 나는 내 가족들이 편하고 안락한 삶을 즐길 수 있도록 하기 위해 열심히 일하고 있다.
13. 최근 혹독한 질병이 수백 명의 사상자를 내면서 아시아 국가들을 강타했다.
14. 가짜 엄마들의 일부는 차갑고 단단한 철사로 만들어져 있었고 한편 다른 것들은 따뜻하고 부드러운 타월 천으로 만들어져 있었다.
15. 이 구멍은 바람이 약할 때는 바람을 모으고, 바람이 강하게 불 때는 그것이 통과하도록 함으로써 바람의 속도에 상관없이 연을 빨리 날도록 도와준다.

Group-8

036 dull

Step 03 **1.** 2 **2.** 1 **3.** 3 **4.** 1 **5.** 2 **6.** 3

Step 04 **1.** The knife is too dull to be of any service.
2. He was a dull student in his school days.
3. I saw a movie today, but it was dull.

037 train

Step 03 **1.** 1 **2.** 2 **3.** 3 **4.** 2 **5.** 3 **6.** 1

Step 04 **1.** It is more convenient to travel by train.
2. He saw a long train of camels in the distance.
3. He trained his dog to catch rabbits.

038 plant

Step 03 **1.** 1 **2.** 2 **3.** 3 **4.** 3 **5.** 1 **6.** 2

Step 04 **1.** Many plants bloom in spring.
2. He planted crops of wheat and corn this spring.
3. They will invest in new plant for the factory.

039 table

Step 03 **1.** 2 **2.** 1 **3.** 1 **4.** 2

Step 04 **1.** My mother set the table for dinner.
2. There is a table of contents at the front of this book.

040 square

Step 03 **1.** 2 **2.** 1 **3.** 3 **4.** 1 **5.** 4 **6.** 3 **7.** 2 **8.** 4

Step 04 **1.** The side of this box is a square.
2. There was a sandwich shop in the square.
3. 36 is the square of 6.
4. That was a square deal.

Review

A. 01. train **02.** plant **03.** plant **04.** dull **05.** square
 06. table **07.** train **08.** square **09.** table **10.** dull
 11. square **12.** train **13.** square **14.** dull **15.** plant

B. 01. train **02.** plant **03.** square **04.** dull **05.** table
 06. train **07.** square **08.** dull **09.** square **10.** plant
 11. dull **12.** table **13.** train **14.** square **15.** plant

01. 지루한 강의와 전통적인 학습 방법은 잊으십시오.

02. 기차 창밖으로, 나는 들판에서 익어 가는 곡식과, 붉고 노랗게 단풍이 드는 나무를 볼 수 있었다.

03. 당신은 다른 종류의 직업을 위한 훈련으로 야간 수업에 참여해 보았는가?

04. 조사자들은 컴퓨터를 가지고 노는 것이 취학 전 아동의 읽기 능력을 증가시키지도 않을 것이며, 컴퓨터 과학에서 아이들을 훈련시키지도 않을 것이라고 말했다.

05. 열대 우림은 서로를 필요로 하며 서로 돕는 식물과 동물들로 가득하다.

06. 알고 있어. 거리에 나무를 더 심어야 해.

07. 소수의 사람들이 한국의 야생 식물들의 가치를 인식해 왔다.

08. 색인이 가능해진 것처럼 페이지 수를 매기는 것이 가능해졌다; 목차표도 참조할 수 있는 사항이 되었다.

09. 방 한가운데의 테이블 위에는 두 개의 낡은 은촛대와 붉은 와인이 담긴 두 개의 유리 잔이 놓여 있었다.

10. 또한 우리는 어린이들이 라틴어를 모르며, 무솔리니와 도스토예프스키를 같은 범주로 간주하며, 주기율표를 외우지 못한다는 것을 알고 있다.

11. 예를 들어, 인도에서는 어떤 동전은 정사각형이다.

12. 카트만두 시는 북남쪽으로 5Km와 동서쪽으로 5Km로 정사각형 모양으로 분지의 거의 정 가운데 위치한다.

13. 그리고 밤에는 넓은 공개된 광장에서 마을 사람 전부가 춤을 추면 큰 북과 군악대의 두드리는 소리가 울려 퍼진다.

14. M: 와! 선택할 수 있는 것들이 많이 있네. 어떤 형태의 식탁을 사야 할까?
W: 정사각형 모양의 것이 둥근 것보다 더 좋은 것 같은데.

>>> DAY 05

Group-9

041 country

Step 03　**1.** 1　**2.** 3　**3.** 2　**4.** 2　**5.** 1　**6.** 3

Step 04　**1.** Canada is a larger country than France.
2. The doctor advised her to spend several months in the country.
3. The new president has the support of over 80 percent of the country.

042 nail

Step 03　**1.** 3　**2.** 1　**3.** 2　**4.** 3　**5.** 2　**6.** 1

Step 04　**1.** The little boy had a bad habit of biting his nails.
2. He needs a hammer and some nails to hang some pictures on the wall.
3. The soldier nailed a notice on the wall.

043 ask

Step 03　**1.** 1　**2.** 3　**3.** 1　**4.** 2　**5.** 3　**6.** 2

Step 04　**1.** I asked him where he had been.
2. The librarian asked us not to make a noise in the library.
3. She is going to ask several friends to her birthday party.

044 left

Step 03　**1.** 1　**2.** 2　**3.** 2　**4.** 1

Step 04　**1.** I left my bag in the bus.
2. Turn left at the first traffic light.

045 die

Step 03　**1.** 3　**2.** 4　**3.** 1　**4.** 2　**5.** 1　**6.** 3　**7.** 4　**8.** 2

Step 04　**1.** Many animals died of starvation in the snow.
2. He is dying to know her secret.
3. It's your turn to throw the dice. (보통 두 개를 한 벌로 사용하므로 dice로 표시함)
4. They will use this die to make model trains.

Review

A. 01. ask　**02.** country　**03.** left　**04.** country　**05.** die
06. nail　**07.** die　**08.** ask　**09.** nail　**10.** die　**11.** country
12. left　**13.** nail　**14.** die　**15.** ask

B. 01. ask　**02.** nail　**03.** die　**04.** left　**05.** nail　**06.** country
07. die　**08.** ask　**09.** left　**10.** Nail　**11.** dying
12. country　**13.** dice　**14.** ask　**15.** country

01. 언어 기술 문제에 있어서는 미국은 여전히 저개발 국가이다.

02. 어떤 아버지가 가난한 사람들이 어떻게 사는지를 보여 주기 위해 자신의 아들을 시골로 데려갔다.

03. 한 달에 3번씩 이것은 독자들에게 국내와 국외 소식을 독자들에게 알려 주었다.

04. 다음 단계는 접착제와 못으로 서로 다른 부속품을 조립하는 것입니다.

05. 소개가 한 번 돌아간 후에 그 학생들은 그들이 기억할 수 있는 한 많은 다른 학생들의 이름을 적으라는 요청을 받았다.

06. 그는 그들에게 줄 세 조각을 보여 주고서 차례대로 각자에게 어느 줄이 가장 긴지를 물었다.

07. 그리고 무대로 통하는 문에서 그녀는 그 바이올리니스트에게 사인을 요청했다.

08. 많은 학생들이 종이를 마룻바닥 위에 버리거나 책상 위에 남겨 두었다.

09. 그의 왼쪽에는 저녁 기념식에 참가할 학자들이 앉아 있었다.

10. W: 저는 부산에서 버스를 탔는데 버스에 제 휴대전화를 두고 내렸어요.
M: 알겠습니다. 당신이 탄 버스가 부산에서 몇 시에 출발했나요?
W: 제가 탄 버스는 오후 4시 20분에 출발했습니다.

11. 한 남자 음악가가 언어영역인 좌뇌에 발작을 일으켰다.

12. 우리들 대부분은 선택해서 죽지는 않는다. 하지만 우리는 어떻게 살 것인가에 대해 선택을 한다.

13. 텔레비전이 도래한 이후로 소설이 이미 죽지는 않았다 하더라도 죽어 가고 있다는 소문이 있어 왔다.

14. 갑자기 엔진이 꺼지더니 알 수 없는 이유로 배가 가라앉기 시작했다.

Group-10

046 pen

Step 03　**1.** 2　**2.** 1　**3.** 2　**4.** 1

Step 04　**1.** Write your name and address in pen and ink.
2. The farmer built a pen for his sheep.

047 long
| Step 03 | **1.** 1 **2.** 3 **3.** 2 **4.** 3 **5.** 2 **6.** 1 |

Step 04 **1.** The table is about six feet long.

2. Everybody wants to live long.

3. The children are longing for summer vacation.

048 about

Step 03 **1.** 1 **2.** 3 **3.** 1 **4.** 2 **5.** 2 **6.** 3

Step 04 **1.** He likes reading books about animals.

2. There is a high wall about the garden.

3. About 30 people attended the meeting.

049 stamp

Step 03 **1.** 2 **2.** 3 **3.** 2 **4.** 1 **5.** 3 **6.** 1

Step 04 **1.** Collecting stamps[=Stamp-collecting] is his hobby.

2. She will stamp the bill.

3. Mi-ran likes to stamp her feet.

050 case

Step 03 **1.** 2 **2.** 1 **3.** 4 **4.** 3 **5.** 1 **6.** 3 **7.** 4 **8.** 2

Step 04 **1.** He ordered six cases of whiskey last month.

2. I heard the sad case of starving children in Africa.

3. He lost his case and had to pay damages.

4. "My" is the possessive case of "I."

Review

A. **01.** long **02.** pen **03.** long **04.** stamp **05.** case
06. about **07.** about **08.** case **09.** stamp **10.** long
11. case **12.** stamp **13.** pen **14.** about **15.** case

B. **01.** pen **02.** about **03.** long **04.** case **05.** stamp
06. case **07.** stamp **08.** about **09.** case **10.** stamp
11. case **12.** long **13.** pen **14.** long **15.** about

수능기출예문 점검

01. Richard Wagner는 여기에서 머무는 동안 Parsifal의 일부를 쓰면서 1880년에 이 장소에서 영감을 얻었다.

02. 이 나라에서 얼마나 오래 머무를 예정이니?

03. 우리가 너무 사회를 거칠고 어렵게 만들어서, 우리는 속수무책이고 위태롭게 느끼며 개선하기를 바라는 것 같다.

04. 목 뒷부분을 위한 긴 뒤 덮개가 있고, 양쪽의 귀 덮개는 귀를 덮어 준다.

05. 갑자기 나는 식탁 위의 울퉁불퉁한 채소들과 벽에 걸려 있던 글귀의 연관성을 깨달았다; 나는 새로운 친구들에 대한 나의 열망을 충족시킬 수 있는 방법을 찾아낸 것이다.

06. 젓가락은 대략 5,000년 전에 중국에서 개발되었다.

07. 그들은 매일 인내하다가 막 성공하려고 할 때 더 이상 참고 견딜 수 없다고 결정을 내린다.

08. 인공위성 덕택에 우리는 세계의 다른 쪽에서 일어나는 사건에 대해 즉각적으로 알 수 있다.

09. 그 뒷면은 메시지, 주소, 그리고 스탬프(도장)을 위한 충분한 공간을 포함하기 위해 나누어졌다.

10. W: 우표 10장과 엽서 2장 주세요. M: 7달러 50센트입니다.

11. 그 도장으로 찍힌 글자 아래에 은행 측에서 잉크로 쓴 글이 적혀 있었다.

12. 그러한 경우에 당신은 판매 가격이 얼마인지를 알아내야 한다.

13. 드문 경우이지만, 유명한 화가가 실제로 그린 그림을 파는 사람이 있다.

14. 만약을 위해서 제 전화번호를 남깁니다. 345-7575입니다. 감사합니다.

>>> DAY 06

Group-11

051 please

Step 03 **1.** 2 **2.** 1 **3.** 3 **4.** 3 **5.** 1 **6.** 2

Step 04 **1.** It is difficult to please everybody.

2. I will do as I please.

3. Please don't forget to mail the letter.

052 grow

Step 03 **1.** 2 **2.** 3 **3.** 2 **4.** 1 **5.** 3 **6.** 1

Step 04 **1.** I grow one inch every year.

2. The small shop grew into a large firm.

3. Ye-ri likes to grow roses in the garden.

053 club

Step 03 **1.** 2 **2.** 1 **3.** 3 **4.** 1 **5.** 2 **6.** 3

Step 04 **1.** The club is made of wood.

2. Our club meets on Friday.

3. Jim hit the golf ball with my club.

054 bank

Step 03 **1.** 1 **2.** 3 **3.** 2 **4.** 3 **5.** 1 **6.** 2

Step 04 **1.** I have to go to the bank today.

2. He banks 100 dollars every month.

3. He walked along the river bank.

055 cup

Step 03 **1.** 1 **2.** 3 **3.** 2 **4.** 1 **5.** 2 **6.** 3

Step 04 **1.** The president of the club presented the cup to the winner.

2. Steve always drinks water from a green cup.

3. The cook used one cup of sugar in cooking.

Review

A. **01.** grow **02.** cup **03.** please **04.** bank **05.** grow
06. cup **07.** club **08.** please **09.** bank **10.** club
11. cup **12.** grow **13.** bank **14.** please **15.** club

B. **01.** grow **02.** Please **03.** cup **04.** club **05.** please
06. club **07.** bank **08.** please **09.** bank **10.** cup
11. club **12.** grow **13.** bank **14.** cup **15.** grow

수능기출예문 점검

01. 더 많은 정보를 원하시면 (부디) 432-7658로 전화하십시오.

02. 그러나 그가 모든 사람을 만족시킬 필요는 없다. 그가 쓴 사실들이 진실이라면 그것이 가장 중요한 것이다.

03. 그들은 그것이 종이 위에 문질렀을 때 길고도 선명한 선을 만들어 낸다는 것을 알고 매우 기뻐하였다.

04. 더욱이 이런 차이점들은 종종 지역적 갈등을 보다 큰 전쟁으로 확산시킨다.

05. 비옥한 토양은 농부들이 도시 사람들이 먹기에 충분한 곡식을 기를 수 있게 해 주었다.

06. 아이들이 성장하면서 두려움도 사라질 것이다.

07. 그러나 사람의 기억력이 긴 시간이 경과한 후에도 훨씬 더 날카로워지는 일도 일어날 수 있다.

08. 해야 할 일이 하나 더 있다면 수학에 전념하는 클럽에 가입하는 것이다.

09. 자동차 클럽 회원들이 거리를 따라 행진하여 내려갔다.

10. 한번은 수표 한 장이 은행으로부터 백만장자에게 되돌아왔다.

11. 한 어린 소녀가 강둑에서 낚싯대를 쥐고 있을 때 갑자기 어떤 감각을 느꼈고 낚싯대가 물음표처럼 휘는 것을 보았다.

12. 곧 그녀가 컵과 받침접시를 가지고 들어와 그것을 작은 보조탁자에 놓았다.

13. 때때로 그들은 금화나 은잔이나 보석으로 가득 찬 낡은 상자를 발견하기도 한다.

Group-12

056 seal

Step 03　**1.** 1　**2.** 2　**3.** 3　**4.** 1　**5.** 2　**6.** 3

Step 04　**1.** They saw many seals swimming in the sea.

　　　2. We received a letter with the king's seal.

　　　3. Don't seal the letter yet.

057 pick

Step 03　**1.** 1　**2.** 2　**3.** 3　**4.** 2　**5.** 3　**6.** 1

Step 04　**1.** He made a hole with the pick.

　　　2. She picked a bright pink dress.

　　　3. He will pick apples from the apple trees.

058 paper

Step 03　**1.** 2　**2.** 1　**3.** 3　**4.** 1　**5.** 2　**6.** 3

Step 04　**1.** I wrote a letter on a piece of paper.

　　　2. Have you read today's paper?

　　　3. Judy papered her bedroom with new wallpaper.

059 date

Step 03　**1.** 1　**2.** 3　**3.** 1　**4.** 2　**5.** 2　**6.** 3

Step 04　**1.** The date of their marriage was September 15, 1984.

　　　2. The boy and girl went on a date last night.

　　　3. I like to eat dates eagerly.

060 arm

Step 03　**1.** 3　**2.** 2　**3.** 2　**4.** 1　**5.** 3　**6.** 1

Step 04　**1.** He carried a box in his arms.

　　　2. She sat on the arm of the sofa.

　　　3. The citizens armed themselves against their enemies.

Review

A. **01.** arm　**02.** paper　**03.** seal　**04.** arm　**05.** pick

　06. paper　**07.** seal　**08.** date　**09.** pick　**10.** date

　11. arm　**12.** seal　**13.** date　**14.** paper　**15.** pick

B. **01.** pick　**02.** seal　**03.** date　**04.** paper　**05.** seal

　06. paper　**07.** arms　**08.** pick　**09.** arms　**10.** paper

　11. date　**12.** pick　**13.** date　**14.** seal　**15.** arm

01. 노르웨이나 덴마크 같은 몇 나라는 자신의 국립공원 내의 고래와 바다표범을 보호하기 위한 캠페인에 참여했다.

02. 고객: 필름을 몇 장 현상하려고 합니다.

　　점원: 좋습니다. 2시에 찾으러 오시면 됩니다.

03. 그들은 패자를 골라 응원했을 때 올 수 있는 실망감을 견딜 생각이 없습니다. 그래서 승자를 응원했을 때의 즐거움도 포기합니다.

04. 포도는 손이나 기계로 따진 다음, 포도주 양조장으로 보내진다.

05. 깨끗한 종이 한 장이 당신 앞에 놓여 있고, 당신은 그것을 채워야만 한다.

06. W: 아, 안녕하세요. 제가 주문한 책이 도착했습니까?

　　M: 그것 때문에 전화드리는 겁니다. 방금 전에 출판사로부터 연락을 받았는데, 주문하신 책이 늦어질 것 같습니다.

　　W: 오, 저런. 제가 쓰고 있는 논문에 그 책이 필요한데.

07. 그다음, 나뭇가지는 질기고 유연한 종이가 되기 위한 복잡한 과정을 거친다.

08. 글쎄, 그 애가 아침에 신문배달을 하고 있는데 나도 해도 된다고 했어.

09. 나는 그 문제를 빈칸으로 남겨 둔 채 답안지를 제출했다.

10. 목표일[날짜] 전에 최종 목표가 달성되었다.

11. 이 조치는 당신이 고용된 일을 실행하는 데 있어 부주의한 점에 대한 1992년 7월 21일과 8월 17일자의 경고서한에 따르는 것이다.

12. 책으로 인해 지식을 증가시킬 수 있을 것이며, 데이트는 즐거운 저녁을 의미할 것이다.

13. M: 그런데 벽지와 커튼의 유행이 꽤 지났군요.

　　W: 그래요. 약간 변화를 줄 때예요.

14. 그것은 너무 커서 성인도 팔로 안을 수 없었다.

15. 군비(軍備) 경쟁을 통해 안전 보장을 확보한다는 생각은 잘못된 믿음이다.

>>> DAY 07

Group-13

061 change

Step 03　**1.** 1　**2.** 3　**3.** 2　**4.** 1　**5.** 2　**6.** 3

Step 04　**1.** He changed the color from red to yellow.

　　　2. I waited for the shopkeeper to hand me my change.

　　　3. She went to the country for a change.

062 tablet

Step 03　**1.** 3　**2.** 1　**3.** 2　**4.** 1　**5.** 2　**6.** 3

Step 04　**1.** Tony took his tablet to school to write on.

　　　2. The doctor told her to take one tablet each morning.

　　　3. The scientist could not read the words on the old wooden tablet.

063 land

Step 03　**1.** 1　**2.** 3　**3.** 1　**4.** 3　**5.** 2　**6.** 2

Step 04　**1.** The whole land rejoiced at the news.

　　　2. The land in this area is good for growing flowers.

　　　3. He managed to land the helicopter on the hospital roof.

064 gas

Step 03 **1.** 3 **2.** 2 **3.** 1 **4.** 2 **5.** 1 **6.** 3

Step 04 **1.** Nitrogen is a gas that exists in large quantities in the air.

2. She turned on the gas (range) to boil some water.

3. My car ran out of gas on the highway.

065 miss

Step 03 **1.** 1 **2.** 2 **3.** 3 **4.** 2 **5.** 1 **6.** 3

Step 04 **1.** Miss Jones is coming to see us next Sunday.

2. She made more misses than hits.

3. When Tony went away, she really missed him.

Review

A. 01. gas **02.** tablet **03.** miss **04.** tablet **05.** land
06. Miss **07.** change **08.** land **09.** gas **10.** change
11. gas **12.** tablet **13.** change **14.** miss **15.** land

B. 01. gas **02.** land **03.** change **04.** tablet **05.** gas
06. land **07.** tablet **08.** miss **09.** change **10.** land
11. miss **12.** change **13.** Miss **14.** tablet **15.** gas

수능기출예문 점검

01. 태양 흑점은 오존의 양을 증가시킴으로써 또한 날씨를 변화시킬 수 있다.

02. W: 이번 주가 끝나서 기쁘군. 긴 한 주였어.

　M: 내일 호수가로 자전거 타러 가는 거 어때?

　W: 좋지. 나는 정말 휴식(기분 전환)이 필요해.

03. M: 좋아요. 사겠습니다. 20달러짜리 지폐를 내면 잔돈은 있으신가요?

　W: 물론입니다. 여기 있습니다.

04. 그러나 우리가 자연을 면밀하게 관찰하면, 변화와 균형 사이에 끊임없는 긴장이 있음을 발견하게 된다.

05. 수년간의 연구와 비용이 많이 든 실험을 거친 후에 생물공학 전문가들이 몸담고 있는 독자적 연구소가 마침내 알약 형태로 입으로 복용할 수 있는 자연 발생적 물질을 발견하였다.

06. 그리고 그것은 전에 거의 아무도 찾은 적이 없을 땅을 걷게 될지 모른다는 상상력을 일깨운다.

07. 다음 날 아침에 일어나 일출을 보면서, 나는 왜 한국이 "조용한 아침의 나라"라고 불리는지 이해하게 되었다.

08. 그들은 파일럿들과 대화하고 그들에게 이륙 또는 착륙할 때 어느 활주로를 써야 하는지 말해 주고 있습니다.

09. 우리는 이 가스가 온실효과를 일으키고 있다는 것을 알고 있다.

10. 사용되는 천연가스와 전기의 양이 50% 절감되었다.

11. W: 무슨 일이예요?

　M: 휘발유가 다 떨어진 것 같아! 떠나기 전에 유량계를 점검했어야 했는데.

12. 너희가 몹시 보고 싶다. 너희를 다시 만나기를 고대한다.

13. 만일 이런 천문학적인 쇼를 놓쳤다면, 당신은 정말로 불운한 것이다.

14. 그녀는 일 년간 그 일을 했으며 하루도 빼먹지 않았다.

15. 예. 그녀의 지원서를 받았는데 사진이 빠졌어요.

066 grave

Step 03 **1.** 1 **2.** 2 **3.** 2 **4.** 1

Step 04 **1.** He laid flowers on the grave of a poet.

2. She made a grave mistake in her job interview.

067 air

Step 03 **1.** 2 **2.** 3 **3.** 2 **4.** 1 **5.** 3 **6.** 1

Step 04 **1.** Let's go out and have some fresh air.

2. The man fell 1,000 meters through the air without a parachute.

3. Mike has the air of a child.

068 address

Step 03 **1.** 1 **2.** 3 **3.** 1 **4.** 2 **5.** 3 **6.** 2

Step 04 **1.** She is still at the same address.

2. The writer gave an impressive address to the audience.

3. The letters were wrongly addressed.

069 party

Step 03 **1.** 1 **2.** 2 **3.** 3 **4.** 2 **5.** 3 **6.** 1

Step 04 **1.** We will have a farewell party before we leave.

2. The coach divided his team into two parties for exercise.

3. Party leaders will meet to discuss their new housing policy.

070 pop

Step 03 **1.** 1 **2.** 3 **3.** 4 **4.** 2 **5.** 4 **6.** 2 **7.** 1 **8.** 3

Step 04 **1.** We bought three bottles of pop.

2. My pop retired from work last month.

3. The paper bag burst with a loud pop.

4. She likes to sing a pop song.

Review

A. 01. pop **02.** address **03.** air **04.** grave **05.** party
06. air **07.** pop **08.** party **09.** address **10.** pop
11. party **12.** grave **13.** address **14.** pop **15.** air

B. 01. grave **02.** air **03.** party **04.** address **05.** air
06. pop **07.** address **08.** air **09.** grave **10.** pop
11. address **12.** pop **13.** party **14.** pop **15.** party

수능기출예문 점검

01. 대학에서 나를 가르치셨던 가장 훌륭한 분의 묘소에 서 있는 것은 제자이자 흠모하는 사람으로서이다.

02. 꽃 그리고 나무, 신선한 공기와 좋은 향이 나는 토양에는 치유력이 있다.

03. 하늘에는 새소리도 없었고, 어떤 향기도 없었으며, 빨리 지나가는 구름에서 나오는 움직이는 빛이나 그림자도 없었다.

04. 사람들의 말소리와 웃음소리로 분위기는 활기를 띠었으며, 시간이 흐를수록 분위기는 점점 편안해졌다.

05. M: 그 드라마가 저녁 뉴스 바로 전에 방송될 예정이다.

　W: 잘됐다. 정말 좋아.

06. 그녀의 주변에는 느리게 미소를 짓게 하는 분위기가 있었다.

07. 내가 제시한 주소에 도착했을 때 나는 작별 인사와 감사의 말을 그에게 했다.

08. 오늘날 미국의 언어 정책은 이 문제를 주로 1개 국어를 사용하는 미국인
들에게 외국어를 가르치려는 노력으로 다룬다.

09. 이것들은 100명 이상의 세계 지도자들과 30,000명의 다른 과학자들과
보도 관계자들, 그리고 관련 시민들이 참석한 환경에 대한 첫 번째 세계
회의에서 제기된(다뤄진) 기본적인 질문들 중에 있는 것들이었다.

10. 당신이 회의에 참석하고 있다고 상상해 보라. 당신 편과 상대방 편이 탁
자를 사이에 두고 마주앉아 있다.

11. 어느 날 미국 학생인 Sally가 영국에서 한 파티에 갔다.

12. 경쟁은 반대편의 행동을 다스리는 일련의 법칙을 뜻한다.

13. 공은 그물에 펑 하고 단단히 부딪히며 깔끔하게 골대에 구부러져 들어갔다.

14. W: 팝 콘테스트에 관한 포스터 봤니?
M: 그래. 우리가 연습을 시작할 때라고 생각해.

15. W: 어떤 종류의 광고에 대해 말하는 거니, James?
M: 인터넷 곳곳에 퍼져 있는 팝업 광고들 말이야. 그것들은 정말로 귀찮아.

>>> DAY 08

Group-15

071 chest

Step 03 **1.** 1 **2.** 2 **3.** 1 **4.** 2

Step 04 **1.** She felt a severe pain in her chest.
2. She keeps the winter clothes in a chest in the attic.

072 title

Step 03 **1.** 2 **2.** 1 **3.** 3 **4.** 2 **5.** 1 **6.** 3

Step 04 **1.** The title of that famous poem is "Annabel Lee."
2. His official title is editorial manager.
3. Sophia owns the title to a large villa.

073 last

Step 03 **1.** 3 **2.** 1 **3.** 2 **4.** 1 **5.** 2 **6.** 3

Step 04 **1.** He started for London on the last day of October.
2. I haven't seen him since the last meeting.
3. The good relationship between two nations didn't last long.

074 leave

Step 03 **1.** 1 **2.** 3 **3.** 1 **4.** 2 **5.** 3 **6.** 2

Step 04 **1.** He usually leaves home for school at seven thirty.
2. You'd better leave that job to the experts.
3. You must not do anything without my leave.

075 present

Step 03 **1.** 1 **2.** 3 **3.** 4 **4.** 3 **5.** 4 **6.** 2 **7.** 1 **8.** 2

Step 04 **1.** The present situation is very critical.
2. How many people were present at the meeting this morning?
3. She gave me a beautiful fan as a birthday present.
4. He presented his ideas on that matter very clearly.

Review

A. **01.** leave **02.** title **03.** leave **04.** present **05.** title
06. chest **07.** present **08.** last **09.** present **10.** leave
11. last **12.** chest **13.** last **14.** present **15.** title

B. **01.** last **02.** present **03.** leave **04.** title **05.** present
06. last **07.** title **08.** leave **09.** leave **10.** chest
11. title **12.** present **13.** chest **14.** last **15.** presents

수능기출예문 점검

01. 남아메리카 여행에 관한 책을 찾고 있는데요. 그런데 제목이 기억이 안
나요.

02. 저는 Annie라는 영화의 주제곡을 부르던 중에 우연히 이런 일을 경험하
였습니다.

03. 하지만 오직 한 명의 승자만이 차(茶)의 달인 칭호와 함께 현금 10,000
달러의 상을 받게 될 것입니다.

04. 삭제하지 않은 영화는 네 시간 내지 다섯 시간 동안 계속될 수 있다.

05. 지난 5년간 그를 방문하지 못한 것에 대해 나는 부끄러움을 느꼈다.

06. 답안지를 걷으면서 교수는 마지막 문제가 중요하다고 말했다.

07. 당신이 탈 비행기가 몇 시에 출발하기로 예정되어 있나요?

08. 어머니들은 아이들을 이곳에 남겨 두고 걱정 없이 일터로 나갈 수 있다.

09. 오늘날 우리는 집을 떠나지 않아도 모든 종류의 스포츠 경기를 즐길 수
있게 됐습니다.

10. 그렇게 하기 위해서 그들은 그 그림에 무엇을 더해야 할지 아니면 그대
로 두어야 할지를 결정해야 한다.

11. 행복은 현재에서는 거의 발견되지 않는다. 그것은 과거의 일로 기억되거
나 혹은 미래의 일로 기대된다.

12. W: 아, 좋은 생각이 있어요. 제 생일이 다음 주잖아요. 제 선물로 그들에
게 돈을 좀 보내 줄 수 있으세요? M: 와, 정말로 생각이 깊구나.

13. 이 두 가지 가능성은 우리에게 선택적인 것으로 제시되어 있다.

14. 권위 있는 인물이 참석한 상태에서 학생들이 영화를 봤을 때, 그들의 얼
굴은 단지 최소한의 반응의 기색만을 보였다.

15. 이것은 가장 훌륭한 예술 작품을 모든 사람에게 무료로 보여 주는 것이
필요하다고 간주한 것이다.

Group-16

076 novel

Step 03 **1.** 1 **2.** 2 **3.** 2 **4.** 1

Step 04 **1.** Her new novel is widely read among young people.
2. The worker thought of a novel solution to the problem.

077 way

Step 03 **1.** 1 **2.** 3 **3.** 1 **4.** 2 **5.** 3 **6.** 2

Step 04 **1.** We lost our way in the forest.
2. You can cook these vegetables in several diferent ways.
3. Computers can help us in many ways.

078 will

Step 03 **1.** 2 **2.** 1 **3.** 3 **4.** 1 **5.** 2 **6.** 3

Step 04 **1.** He will be in New York this time tomorrow.
2. The will to live helps a patient to recover.

3. My mother left me this gold ring in her will.

079 well
| Step 03 | **1.** 1 **2.** 2 **3.** 1 **4.** 3 **5.** 3 **6.** 2 |

Step 04 **1.** He has always done his job extremely well.

2. We pumped water from the well.

3. She felt tears well up in her eyes.

080 fair
Step 03 **1.** 1 **2.** 4 **3.** 1 **4.** 3 **5.** 2 **6.** 3 **7.** 4 **8.** 2

Step 04 **1.** The judge's decision was fair to both sides.

2. Fair weather came after the rain.

3. There is a famous food fair in Seoul, Korea, every year.

4. I got a fair grade on the spelling test.

Review

A. **01.** way **02.** will **03.** fair **04.** well **05.** novel **06.** way
  07. will **08.** fair **09.** will **10.** novel **11.** fair **12.** well
  13. way **14.** fair **15.** well

B. **01.** way **02.** will **03.** fair **04.** well **05.** novel **06.** ways
  07. well **08.** fair **09.** will **10.** novel **11.** way **12.** fair
  13. will **14.** well **15.** fair

수능기출예문 점검

01. 텔레비전이 도래한 이후로 소설이 이미 죽지는 않았다 하더라도 죽어가고 있다는 소문이 있어 왔다.

02. 이런 접근은 전에 해결했던 문제들과 유사한 문제들에 대해서는 효과가 있을 수 있는 반면에 새로운 문제가 아주 생소할 때에는 종종 실패하고, 비참히 실패하기도 한다.

03. 걷는 것이 건강을 유지하는 가장 수월한 방법이다.

04. 어둠의 세계에서 살아야 하는 사람에게는 앞에 있는 길이 가장 밝은 햇빛에서와 마찬가지로 가장 짙은 안개 속에서도 분명하다.

05. 화성이 아주 밝았기 때문에 도시의 불빛조차도 방해가 되지 못했다.

06. 르네상스 예술은 여러 가지 면에서 중세의 예술과 달랐다.

07. 각각의 개인들은 다른 사람들에게 영향을 줄 것이고 또한 다른 사람들로부터 영향을 받을 것이다.

08. 예를 들면, 코의 점은 그 사람이 의지가 강하고, 믿을 만하다는 것을 의미한다.

09. 성공한 사람들은 기꺼이 열심히 일하지만 엄격한 한도 내에서 일한다.

10. 아리스토텔레스의 이론은 형편없는 물리학일지 모르지만 그것은 우리가 실제 세계에서 볼 수 있는 것을 그럴듯하게 잘 설명한다.

11. 우물 옆에서 나는 한국의 전통적인 국자인 조롱박 한 개를 발견했다.

12. 모든 회사 중역들을 대신하여, 우리는 귀하의 건강을 빌며 열심히 일하신 결과인 은퇴에 축복을 기원합니다.

13. 나중에 Joan은 자신이 조직하고 있는 바자회에서 자원봉사자를 찾고 있다는 말을 했다.

14. 우리가 유치원에서 배운 것 중에는 "모든 것을 나누어서 하라", "공정하게 경기를 하라", "네가 누군가에게 속상하게 했을 때 '죄송합니다'라고 말하라" 등이 있다.

15. 우리가 "옳다", "공평하다", "좋다", "나쁘다"고 생각하는 것에 맞추어 다른 사람들이 살기를 바라면서 그들에게 우리의 가치를 강요하려고 할 때 부조화가 우리의 관계에 들어온다.

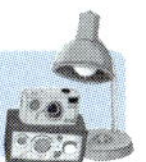

>>> DAY 09

Group-17

081 swallow
Step 03 **1.** 2 **2.** 1 **3.** 1 **4.** 2

Step 04 **1.** Be careful not to swallow the chewing gum.

2. Swallows come to our country every summer.

082 save
Step 03 **1.** 2 **2.** 3 **3.** 2 **4.** 1 **5.** 3 **6.** 1

Step 04 **1.** He desperately tried to save his friend from drowning.

2. That machine will save us a lot of trouble.

3. The boy answered all the questions save one.

083 reason
Step 03 **1.** 1 **2.** 2 **3.** 3 **4.** 1 **5.** 3 **6.** 2

Step 04 **1.** We don't know the reason why he didn't accept the offer.

2. The young man has lost his reason to hear the news.

3. Man alone has the ability to reason.

084 direct
Step 03 **1.** 3 **2.** 1 **3.** 2 **4.** 1 **5.** 2 **6.** 3

Step 04 **1.** The captain directed his men to attack.

2. He drove along a direct road.

3. There is no direct train from here to Paris.

085 drive
Step 03 **1.** 2 **2.** 4 **3.** 1 **4.** 3 **5.** 4 **6.** 3 **7.** 1 **8.** 2

Step 04 **1.** We decided to go for a long drive to Busan.

2. They watched him drive the posts into the ground.

3. The noise from the neighbors is driving me mad.

4. I think she is a woman with drive.

Review

A. **01.** direct **02.** swallow **03.** save **04.** direct **05.** save
  06. swallow **07.** reason **08.** drive **09.** direct
  10. reason **11.** drive **12.** save **13.** drive **14.** reason
  15. drive

B. **01.** drive **02.** direct **03.** save **04.** swallow **05.** reason
  06. save **07.** drive **08.** reason **09.** drive **10.** save
  11. direct **12.** drive **13.** direct **14.** reason **15.** swallow

수능기출예문 점검

01. 그다음, 그것은 번개같이 재빠르게 턱을 벌려 경계를 하고 있지 않던 먹이를 붙잡아 머리부터 먼저 삼킨다.

02. 내가 돌아왔을 때, 나는 내가 본 것에 대해 감정을 억누르기 어려웠다.

03. 모든 것을 정직하게 벌고, 그것을 모두 저축하는 사람은 분명히 목표를 달성할 것이다.

04. 그렇지 않으면 우리는 우리 자식들을 공해로부터 구할 수 없을 것입니다.

05. 시는 에너지를 절약하기 위해서 또 다른 일도 하고 있다.

06. 나는 도로변에서 사람들이 나의 농작물에 접근할 수 있게 함으로써 그들이 상점에 가야 하는 수고를 덜어 줄 수 있었고, 그렇게 하면 그들에게 가치도 제공하는 것이 되었을 것이다.

07. 네 문서들을 스캔한 다음, 그것들을 컴퓨터 파일로 저장하면 된다.

08. 내가 해변을 좋아하는 한 가지 이유는 외로운 분위기 때문이다.

09. 나는 언론인이 될 것이기 때문에, 글을 쓸 아주 특별한 공책이 필요할 것이라고 생각했다.

10. 그때 나는 한 남자를 만났고 그에게 길을 안내해 달라고 부탁했다.

11. 용매는 함께 카페인을 옮기면서 그것들과 직접 접촉을 한다.

12. 우리는 타인에 의해 지도받고, 양육되고, 부양된다.

13. 내가 운전하는 법을 배울 때, 나의 아버지는 우리가 가진 큰 승용차에 대한 감을 익힐 수 있도록 나를 이웃 동네로 데리고 다니셨다.

14. 거의 모든 철도가 운행이 중단될 지경에 이르게 하는 심각한 위험에 직면하고 있다.

15. 운전을 하면 유능하고 책임이 있고, 능력 있는, 즉 독립된 인간이다.

16. 반면에 40년도 전에 제어된 연구는 일시적 화는 오히려 화를 돋우고, 눈물은 우리를 더 우울하게 만들 수 있다는 것을 보여 줬습니다.

Group-18

086 broke

Step 03 1. 1 2. 2 3. 2 4. 1

Step 04 1. Jane slipped on the ice and broke her arm.
2. That company went broke last month.

087 wind

Step 03 1. 1 2. 2 3. 1 4. 3 5. 2 6. 3

Step 04 1. The ship sailed against the wind.
2. She wound her arms round the child.
3. A path winds through the woods.

088 step

Step 03 1. 3 2. 1 3. 2 4. 1 5. 2 6. 3

Step 04 1. He stepped aside to give way to the lady.
2. He ran upstairs three steps at a time.
3. She took all possible steps to succeed.

089 bright

Step 03 1. 1 2. 3 3. 1 4. 2 5. 2 6. 3

Step 04 1. The sun was so bright that it hurt my eyes.
2. Jae-ho is the brightest student in the class.
3. His voice sounded bright and cheerful.

090 set

Step 03 1. 4 2. 1 3. 3 4. 2 5. 1 6. 4 7. 3 8. 2

Step 04 1. Tom bought a new set of tools.
2. He won the first set and lost the next two.
3. He set the alarm-clock for[at] six.
4. It gets cooler when the sun sets.

Review

A. 01. bright 02. step 03. wind 04. broke 05. step
06. set 07. wind 08. set 09. set 10. step 11. bright
12. set 13. wind 14. bright 15. broke

B. 01. broke 02. steps 03. wind 04. bright 05. step
06. set 7. wind 08. bright 09. step 10. set 11. winds
12. set 13. broke 14. bright 15. set

수능기출예문 점검

01. 사실이지만 나는 돈이 없다. 그리고 월급을 곧 타지도 못한다.

02. 나의 형이 내 노트북 컴퓨터를 빌려가서는 고장 내 버렸다.

03. 한국 연들의 형태는 그것들이 바람을 잘 이용하게 해 주는 과학적인 원리에 기초를 두고 있다.

04. 동시에 그녀의 가슴은 두근거렸으며 모든 소리에 놀라서 급히 문으로 가 이제는 저녁의 그림자로 어둑해진 구불구불한 길을 내려다보았다.

05. 파란 셔츠의 농부 밴드는 드럼과 다양한 관악기 뒤에서 고대 바스크의 Riau–Riau 춤으로 돌고 들고 흔든다.

06. 그녀는 사진들 중 하나에 열중하면서 한 걸음 뒤로 물러나다가 작은 탁자에 부딪혔고 그것을 쓰러뜨렸다.

07. 산업 면에서 기업들은 다른 기업보다 한 단계 앞선 제품을 개발하기 위해 항상 노력한다.

08. 지금은 우리가 중대한 조처를 강구해야 할 때입니다.

09. 그녀는 문을 열고 뒤뜰로 걸어 나갔다.

10. 너는 내가 아는 가장 똑똑한 아이들 중 한 명이니까 네가 잘 해낼 것이라 확신해.

11. 가구는 부드럽고 안락하며 커튼은 밝으며 유쾌하다.

12. 긍정적인 면을 보도록 해라.

13. 해가 지고 있다.

14. 여러 해 전 심리학자들이 한 가지 실험을 하였는데 그 실험에서 그들은 사람들을 고리 던지기 세트 외에는 아무것도 없는 방에 있게 하였다.

15. 현실적인 목표를 세우고 한 번에 한 단계씩 달성하는 것을 목표로 삼아라.

16. 사람들은 야생화와 나무의 향기의 중간에 텐트를 칠 수 있다.

>>> DAY 10

Group-19

091 ruler

Step 03 1. 1 2. 2 3. 1 4. 2

Step 04 1. The ruler of the country is admired by the whole nation.
2. He can't draw straight lines without a ruler.

092 branch

Step 03 1. 1 2. 3 3. 2 4. 3 5. 2 6. 1

Step 04 1. A monkey climbed up the tree and hid among the branches.
2. Our company has a branch in Sydney.
3. English is a branch of the Germanic family of languages.

093 duty

Step 03 1. 1 2. 2 3. 1 4. 3 5. 2 6. 3

Step 04 1. It is the duty of every citizen to pay the tax.
2. The duty of a postman is to deliver letters and parcels.

3. We must pay duty when we bring whiskey into
the country.

094 view
`Step 03` **1.** 2 **2.** 1 **3.** 4 **4.** 3 **5.** 1 **6.** 3 **7.** 4 **8.** 2

`Step 04` **1.** A ship gradually came into view on the
horizon.
2. Our villa commands a fine view.
3. They have different views on the matter.
4. She waited me with a view to seeing me.

095 lose
`Step 03` **1.** 1 **2.** 3 **3.** 2 **4.** 1 **5.** 2 **6.** 3

`Step 04` **1.** We can not see the movie if we lose our
tickets.
2. I am afraid our team will lose tonight.
3. We lost a lot of valuable time waiting for her to
arrive.

Review
A. 01. lose **02.** ruler **03.** lose **04.** branch **05.** duty
06. view **07.** view **08.** branch **09.** view **10.** lose
11. ruler **12.** branch **13.** duty **14.** view **15.** duty

B. 01. duty **02.** view **03.** duty **04.** lose **05.** branch
06. ruler **07.** lose **08.** view **09.** branch **10.** view
11. duty **12.** ruler **13.** branch **14.** view **15.** lose

수능기출예문 점검
01. 밤이 오고 그녀는 바깥에 있는 큰 나무가 가지들을 흔드는 것을 알 수 있
었습니다.
02. 본부를 시카고에 두고, 주 지부는 워싱턴 DC, 뉴욕, 그리고 로스앤젤레
스에 두었습니다.
03. Peter는 임무를 수행할 수 있을까 하는 의구심이 들어서 그 일을 대신할
적임자를 찾아보려고 한다.
04. 어느 겨울밤에 나는 내가 알지 못하는 도시의 안개 긴 곳에서 길을 잃었다.
05. 결과적으로, 인간은 자신의 잘못은 못 보지만 자기 이웃의 잘못은 결코
못 보는 일이 없다.
06. 호텔의 손님들은 Palazzo Sasso로부터 깊고 푸른 바다의 숨막히는
경치를 경험할 희망을 가져도 좋다.
07. 서양인들은 원시적 문화에서 발견되는 구별되는 행동에 대한 그들의 관
점은 편견임을 인정하게 되었다.
08. 드레스와 정장 차림의 사람들의 모습이 정원을 바라보는 난의 시야를 가
렸다.
09. 이런 관점에서, 철도는 세계가 연료 절약을 걱정할 때에 많은 것을 제공
하는 운송 수단이다.
10. 신체는 자연의 고정되고 불변하는 사실, 즉 '자연의' 현상으로 여겨져 왔다.
11. TV 시청은 복잡한 정신 활동을 요구하지 않는다.
12. 친구와 돈 거래를 하면 친구를 잃는다.
13. 그들 중 하나가 되진 마세요. 당신의 팀이 질 수도 있습니다.
14. 체중을 줄이는 가장 효과적인 방법은 균형 잡힌 규정식을 하는 것이다.

096 stable
`Step 03` **1.** 1 **2.** 2 **3.** 1 **4.** 2

`Step 04` **1.** The man drove his horse into the stable.
2. What we want is a stable government.

097 second
`Step 03` **1.** 2 **2.** 1 **3.** 3 **4.** 2 **5.** 3 **6.** 1

`Step 04` **1.** You are the second to arrive here.
2. Hold your breath for a five seconds.
3. Just wait here for a few seconds.

098 rest
`Step 03` **1.** 1 **2.** 3 **3.** 2 **4.** 3 **5.** 1 **6.** 2

`Step 04` **1.** You must be tired. You'd better take a rest.
2. He stopped reading for a minute and rested
his eyes.
3. Take what you want and throw the rest away.

099 but
`Step 03` **1.** 3 **2.** 1 **3.** 2 **4.** 1 **5.** 2 **6.** 3

`Step 04` **1.** You may go, but you must be home by six
o'clock.
2. No one but Tony saw the accident happen.
3. There is no rule but has exceptions.

100 master
`Step 03` **1.** 2 **2.** 1 **3.** 3 **4.** 1 **5.** 4 **6.** 3 **7.** 2 **8.** 4

`Step 04` **1.** Mr. Brown is the master of the house.
2. He is a master of the detective story.
3. She got a master's degree in education from
Harvard.
4. He finally mastered his fear of heights.

Review
A. 01. stable **02.** rest **03.** master **04.** second **05.** rest
06. but **07.** master **08.** rest **09.** stable **10.** second
11. master **12.** but **13.** but **14.** second **15.** master

B. 01. rest **02.** master **03.** second **04.** stable **05.** but
06. rest **07.** second **08.** master **09.** rest **10.** Master
11. but **12.** second **13.** stable **14.** master **15.** but

수능기출예문 점검
01. 이것은 곤충들이 먹고, 짝짓기하고, 비행할 준비를 할 수 있는 능력을 향
상시켜 주는 안정된 환경을 보상해 준다.
02. 그러나 우주의 모든 존재들처럼, 우리는 속도의 한계, 즉 초당 30만 km
인 광속의 한계에 직면해 있다.
03. 잠시 후, 그의 얼굴에서 긴장이 풀리고 그의 눈이 밝아진다.
04. 물론이지. 나는 다시는 중고 물건을 사지 않겠다.
05. 남성에 관해서는, '안정성'이 직업 선택 시 두 번째로 선호되는 요소이다.
06. 다른 언어와 문화에 대한 무지는 세계의 다른 국가를 상대할 때 미국에
게 불리하게 작용한다.
07. 대부분의 과학자들은 우리의 신체를 쉬게 함으로써, 양호한 신체 상태를
유지한다고 믿는다.
08. 그 사고는 내 친구를 남은 일생을 휠체어에서 보내게 만들었고 나는 아

주 값비싼 교훈을 얻었다.

09. 그들의 영원한 리듬 속에서 조수는 밀려왔다 밀려갈 뿐만 아니라, 해수면 자체가 결코 안정적이지 않다.

10. 내가 천재라면 이처럼 대접받는 것에 전혀 신경 쓰지 않을 것이다. 그러나 내가 천재가 아니기 때문에 신경이 쓰인다.

11. 벌레 소리를 제외하고는 어떤 생명의 흔적도 없었다.

12. 전구는 빛을 전달하지만 뜨거운 필라멘트가 타 버리게 할 수도 있는 산소는 못 들어오게 한다.

13. 그녀는 귀를 기울여 들으려 하였지만 밤 이외에는 어떤 것도 들을 수 없었다.

14. 그는 공학석사 학위를 가지고 있다. 그는 언젠가 자기의 사업체를 갖고 싶어 한다.

15. 선생님은 칠판을 뒤에 두고 높은 교단 위의 큰 의자에 군주처럼 앉아 있었다.

16. 그러므로 여러분은 결국 어떻게 해서든지 이러한 기술들을 숙달시켜야 할 것입니다. 그러므로 지금 그러한 기술들을 다루어 보십시오.

>>> DAY 11

Group-21

101 model

Step 03 **1.** 1 **2.** 2 **3.** 1 **4.** 2 **5.** 3 **6.** 3

Step 04 **1.** She has worked as an artist's model for several months.
2. As a politician, he is a model of integrity and decency.
3. Tony made a model for a new rocket.

102 water

Step 03 **1.** 1 **2.** 3 **3.** 2 **4.** 1 **5.** 2 **6.** 3

Step 04 **1.** He drank two glasses of water straightly.
2. She waters the cows every day.
3. Several logs were floating on the water.

103 spring

Step 03 **1.** 1 **2.** 2 **3.** 3 **4.** 1 **5.** 3 **6.** 2

Step 04 **1.** Spring is the season of hope.
2. The deer drank from the spring.
3. He sprang up from his seat.

104 safe

Step 03 **1.** 2 **2.** 1 **3.** 3 **4.** 1 **5.** 2 **6.** 3

Step 04 **1.** Is this beach safe for swimming?
2. The car crashed but she was safe.
3. There was a small safe hidden behind the picture.

105 top

Step 03 **1.** 1 **2.** 3 **3.** 2 **4.** 2 **5.** 1 **6.** 3

Step 04 **1.** There is a sky lounge on the top floor.
2. The top of the jar is made of metal.
3. He spun his top on the floor.

Review

A. 01. spring **02.** model **03.** safe **04.** water **05.** safe
06. water **07.** top **08.** spring **09.** top **10.** model
11. safe **12.** water **13.** spring **14.** model **15.** top

B. 01. water **02.** model **03.** safe **04.** spring **05.** models
06. top **07.** water **08.** model **09.** safe **10.** spring
11. water **12.** top **13.** spring **14.** top **15.** safe

수능기출예문 점검

01. 그러나 관리자의 행동은 정확히 요구되는 행동의 종류를 분명하게 모범으로 보여 준다.

02. W: 모델 중의 한 명이 독감에 걸렸어요. 대신할 사람을 찾는 것을 도와줄 수 있나요?
M: 모델 에이전시에서 일하는 내 친구 중의 한 명에게 전화할 수 있어요.

03. 이것들은 인간의 실물 크기의 모형이다. 그것들은 인간과 동일한 무게가 나가고 팔과 다리는 인간과 동일한 동작을 한다.

04. Bob의 룸메이트인 Michael은 핸드폰에 푹 빠져 있다. 그는 늘 최신 기능과 서비스를 갖추고 있는 신형 모델을 가지고 있다.

05. 18세기의 한 학자가 "물은 살기 위해서는 필수적이지만 공짜이다. 반면에 다이아몬드는 어느 것에도 꼭 필요하지는 않지만 값이 비싸다."라고 말했다.

06. 당신이 일러 주신 대로 오전 10시 전이나 오후 4시 이후에 매일 잔디에 물을 주었습니다.

07. leaf fish는 물속에서 비스듬히 선 채로 물살을 따라 이동해 마침내 보다 작은 물고기 근처에까지 이르게 된다.

08. 그 해 봄, 나는 내 생애 처음으로 빅 리그 경기에 가게 되었다.

09. 근처에 있는 Ocoee는 그 지역에서 사람들이 가장 많이 노를 저었던 강들에 속했으며, 여섯 개의 주요 등반 장소가 도시 경계에서 차로 한 시간 이내의 거리에 생겨났다.

10. 두 시간 후, 그들은 모두 해변에 닿았고, 녹초가 되었지만 무사했다.

11. 세계의 국가들은 우리가 안전하고 건강한 세상을 우리의 아이들에게 주게 될 해답을 발전시키고자 한다면 함께 행동해야 한다.

12. 정상에 도착하는 데 약 여섯 시간이 걸렸다.

13. 위의 도표는 2006년 55세에서 79세 사이의 남성, 여성 구직자들이 가장 선호하는 다섯 개의 요소를 나타낸다.

14. 이것은 토끼가 나무의 부드러운 가지 끝에 쉽게 닿을 수 있다는 것을 의미한다.

15. 최근 연구에 따르면, 일류 남자 선수들의 플레이 상태의 시간은 잔디 코트에서 평균적으로 시간당 4분에 불과하다고 한다.

Group-22

106 bag

Step 03 **1.** 1 **2.** 2 **3.** 3 **4.** 1 **5.** 3 **6.** 2

Step 04 **1.** He carried his groceries in a paper bag.
2. Tony put his suit and tie into the bag.
3. The hot sun made his dress bag.

107 fine

Step 03 **1.** 2 **2.** 1 **3.** 3 **4.** 1 **5.** 2 **6.** 3

Step 04 **1.** She has fine taste in clothes.
2. If it is fine tomorrow, we will go on a picnic.
3. She was fined $50 for dumping garbage illegally.

108 saw

| Step 03 | **1.** 1 **2.** 3 **3.** 2 **4.** 3 **5.** 1 **6.** 2 |

Step 04 **1.** Jane saw her neighbors at the store.

2. The man used a saw to cut through the branch of the tree.

3. He had to saw the board in half.

109 back

Step 03 **1.** 3 **2.** 1 **3.** 3 **4.** 1 **5.** 2 **6.** 2

Step 04 **1.** He hurt his back when he lifted a heavy box.

2. She entered the restaurant by the back door.

3. The gentleman swung his stick back and forth.

110 eye

Step 03 **1.** 3 **2.** 1 **3.** 2 **4.** 1 **5.** 2 **6.** 3

Step 04 **1.** He is blind in one eye.

2. Lisa pulled the thread through the small eye.

3. The guard eyed the man carefully.

Review

A. 01. bag **02.** back **03.** saw **04.** fine **05.** eye **06.** saw **07.** back **08.** bag **09.** fine **10.** saw **11.** back **12.** eye **13.** fine **14.** bag **15.** eye

B. 01. eye **02.** fine **03.** saw **04.** back **05.** saw **06.** bag **07.** back **08.** eye **09.** fine **10.** bag **11.** back **12.** saw **13.** bag **14.** eye **15.** fine

수능기출예문 점검

01. 옛날 전설에 의하면, 모든 인간은 목에 두 개의 자루를 달고서 이 세상에 태어난다고 한다. 즉 하나는 목 앞에다, 하나는 목 뒤에다 달았는데, 이 두 개는 잘못으로 가득 차 있다고 한다.

02. 알았다. 그럼 이번엔 그 벌금을 내주도록 하마. 하지만 너는 다음 주까지 화장실 청소를 하도록 해라.

03. 걱정 마라. 그는 좋아질 거다.

04. 그는 가장 작은 세부 사항까지 훌륭한 예술 작품처럼 자신의 생애를 꾸몄다.

05. 갑자기 그녀는 잃어버린 오빠 Amin을 보았다!

06. 그것들의 사용 범위는 치과의 드릴부터 바위 절단용 톱과 유리 절단기까지 이른다.

07. 그 마을에 사는 다른 사람들도 그들의 성공을 보고 똑같이 했다.

08. W: 계획대로 정확하게 이 널빤지를 톱질하고 있는 건가요?
M: 그럼요, 날 믿어도 됩니다. 두 번이나 쟀어요.

09. 그들의 이야기를 귀 기울여 듣고서, 그들의 소박한 삶에서 보편적인 진리를 보았습니다.

10. 글쎄요, 저는 항상 교실의 뒷자리에 앉았거든요.

11. 당신이 전화로 이야기하는 사람의 등을 두드려 주거나 작은 포옹을 해 줄 수 없을 때 어떻게 그 사람이 특별하다고 느끼게 만들어 줄 수 있을까?

12. 그것은 충분히 안전해 보이지는 않았지만, 그녀는 돌아가고 싶지 않았다.

13. 중요한 것은 그림을 화가의 원래 의도대로 복원하는 일이다.

14. 반면에, 큰 눈은 의심이나 긴장을 암시한다.

15. 어떤 과학자들은 '그럴 수도 있다'는 관점으로 세상을 보는 것의 실질적인 힘을 보여 주었다.

Group-23

111 firm

Step 03 **1.** 1 **2.** 3 **3.** 2 **4.** 2 **5.** 3 **6.** 1

Step 04 **1.** That house is built on a firm foundation.

2. Oil price finally stopped rising and firmed up.

3. He belongs to an advertising firm.

112 tip

Step 03 **1.** 1 **2.** 3 **3.** 2 **4.** 3 **5.** 1 **6.** 2

Step 04 **1.** The yellow bird was sitting on the tip of the flagpole.

2. She gave the hardworking waiter a generous tip.

3. He tipped the bucket and poured water out of it.

113 right

Step 03 **1.** 1 **2.** 2 **3.** 1 **4.** 3 **5.** 2 **6.** 3

Step 04 **1.** He couldn't move his right leg.

2. Always do what is right and honorable.

3. Everyone has the right to pursue happiness.

114 needle

Step 03 **1.** 1 **2.** 2 **3.** 3 **4.** 2 **5.** 1 **6.** 3

Step 04 **1.** She put a new needle on her sewing machine.

2. The sick child is afraid of the needle.

3. The needle shows you the direction to go.

115 post

Step 03 **1.** 3 **2.** 1 **3.** 2 **4.** 3 **5.** 2 **6.** 1

Step 04 **1.** These posts hold up the fence.

2. He was given a post as general manager.

3. I posted a card to my friend.

Review

A. 01. firm **02.** tip **03.** post **04.** needle **05.** firm **06.** right **07.** needle **08.** post **09.** needle **10.** right **11.** tip **12.** post **13.** tip **14.** firm **15.** right

B. 01. firm **02.** needle **03.** post **04.** tip **05.** right **06.** firm **07.** tip **08.** post **09.** needle **10.** right **11.** tip **12.** post **13.** needle **14.** right **15.** firm

수능기출예문 점검

01. 만약 당신의 결심이 확고하고 분명하며 진실하다면 예전의 감정과 기억은 제쳐 두고 마음의 평화를 찾을 수 있을 것이다.

02. 귀하가 1979년에 우편실에서 (일을) 시작한 이후로, 이 회사에 대한 귀하의 공헌은 아주 소중한 것이었습니다.

03. 나에게 준 팁(봉사료) 15센트가 빈 접시 옆에 깨끗하게 놓여 있었다.

04. 유명한 손동작 중 하나는 모든 다섯 손가락의 끝이 원 모양으로 닿도록 같이 모아지는 'Hand Purse(손 주머니, 손 오므리기)'라는 것이다.

05. 그녀는 사진들 중 하나에 열중하면서 한 걸음 물러나다가 그 작은 탁자에 부딪혔고 그것을 쓰러뜨렸다.

06. 조언해 줘서 고마워요. 제가 그것을 사용할 수 있는지 가서 살펴볼게요.

07. 오른쪽 눈썹 위의 점은 그가 금전 운이 있을 것이고 성공적인 직업을 가

질 것임을 의미한다.

08. 나는 올바른 각도가 아닌 모서리를 가진 아름다운 헛간을 알고 있습니다.

09. 사법제도의 목적은 국민의 권리를 보호하는 것이다.

10. 모든 부모들은 아이들이 옳고 그름의 차이를 배워야 한다는 데 동의한다.

11. 경제 상황의 결과로 지금 당장 얻을 수 있는 일자리는 많지 않습니다.

12. 그러므로 진실을 말할 자유가 위협받는다면 언제라도 그 권리를 위해서 싸워야 한다.

13. M: 바늘 하나 빌릴 수 있나요? W: 왜요? 뭐가 꿰매시려고요?

14. 그것은 바닥에서 위로 똑바로 세워진 짧은 나무로 만든 기둥과 여러 개의 둥근 고리를 갖춘 아이들의 장난감 중 하나였다.

15. 그 순간 비행 차 내부에 붙어 있던 그의 가족사진이 그의 눈에 들어왔다.

16. 냉전 후 세계는 상당히 변했다.

17. 그녀는 다음 날 아침 그것들을 우편으로 부치고는 안도의 한숨을 내쉬었다.

18. 인생 후반에 그는 시 정부에서 다수의 직책을 맡는 영예를 얻었다.

Group-24

116 general

Step 03　**1.** 1　**2.** 3　**3.** 1　**4.** 2　**5.** 3　**6.** 2

Step 04　**1.** The general opinion is that he is innocent.
　　2. They first made a general plan for summer vacation.
　　3. Her grandfather was a famous general during World War Two.

117 attend

Step 03　**1.** 2　**2.** 1　**3.** 3　**4.** 1　**5.** 3　**6.** 2

Step 04　**1.** She attended the wedding at the church last weekend.
　　2. The mother attended on her sick baby day and night.
　　3. You must attend to what the teacher is saying.

118 hide

Step 03　**1.** 1　**2.** 2　**3.** 1　**4.** 2

Step 04　**1.** The boy hides his money under the bed.
　　2. They make gloves out of animal's hides.

119 free

Step 03　**1.** 1　**2.** 3　**3.** 1　**4.** 2　**5.** 3　**6.** 2

Step 04　**1.** They had a free and open discussion about politics.
　　2. He freed the rabbit from the trap.
　　3. They are serving free soft drinks to people.

120 mine

Step 03　**1.** 3　**2.** 1　**3.** 4　**4.** 1　**5.** 4　**6.** 2　**7.** 3　**8.** 2

Step 04　**1.** Are these pens yours or mine?
　　2. He works in the coal mines.
　　3. We mined a lot of gold and diamonds near here.
　　4. The soldiers laid mines on the road.

Review

A. 01. attend　**02.** general　**03.** mine　**04.** attend　**05.** free
　06. mine　**07.** hide　**08.** general　**09.** mine　**10.** free
　11. hide　**12.** general　**13.** mine　**14.** free　**15.** attend

B. 01. hide　**02.** free　**03.** mines　**04.** general　**05.** attend
　06. free　**07.** attend　**08.** mine　**09.** general　**10.** attend
　11. mine　**12.** general　**13.** mine　**14.** free　**15.** hide

수능기출예문 점검

01. 더욱이, 텔레비전 수상기는 수수한 생활수준으로 인해 특히 1930년대와 1940년대에 사치스러운 상품을 취득할 수 없었던 일반 대중의 수입을 넘어서서 가격이 매겨져 있었다.

02. 일반적으로, 부모들은 그들이 다른 아이들에게서 느끼지 못하는 특별한 종류의 사랑을 자신의 아이들에게 느낀다.

03. 밤에 그녀는 작문 수업에 참여하고 그녀의 작문 기술을 향상시켰다.

04. 그들은 대학에 다니기 위한 국가 보조금을 받으며, 실직하면 국가가 실시하는 훈련 프로그램에 참여한다.

05. 한 신화에 따르면 한 무리의 신들이 인간으로부터 '우주의 진리'를 어디에 감출 것인가 결정하기 위해 회의를 열었다.

06. 현재의 자유 세계 시장의 치열한 경쟁 속에서 우리의 경제 성장을 보장할 수 있는 것은 바로 지적인 힘이다.

07. 마을 사람들이 적으로부터 해방된 후 집으로 돌아오는 아이들 모습을 보았을 때 기쁨의 함성이 울렸다.

08. 한 가지로 그들은 무료 미술관에 들어가는 비용이 너무 많아서 관람객들은 입장료를 지불해야 한다고 말한다.

09. W: 이번 토요일 오후 한가하니? M: 그래. 아무 계획 없어. 왜?

10. 중세 사람들이 스스로를 무지로부터 서서히 해방시킬 수 있었던 것은 옛 시대의 몇몇 작가들의 덕분이다.

11. 우리는 늘 소음의 공해가 없는 근로 환경을 누릴 수 있을 만큼 운이 좋지는 않다.

12. 나의 친구 중 두 명이 내 방 안에 앉아 있다고 가정해 보자.

13. cumbia는 금광에서 일하기 위해 더운 지역으로 이송된 아프리카 노예에 의해 만들어졌다.

14. 나는 또한 내 자신의 여러 가지 가치 있는 유용성 때문에 '매장된 황금'이라고도 불리기도 한다.

>>> DAY 13

Group-25

121 bold

Step 03　**1.** 2　**2.** 1　**3.** 2　**4.** 1

Step 04　**1.** She made a bold statement in the court.
　　2. The bold outline of the castle appeared ahead of them.

122 interest

Step 03　**1.** 3　**2.** 2　**3.** 3　**4.** 1　**5.** 2　**6.** 1

Step 04　**1.** Her two great interests in life are music and painting.
　　2. Political arguments don't interest her any more.
　　3. He has to pay 7.5% interest on the loan.

123 lay

Step 03　**1.** 2　**2.** 1　**3.** 3　**4.** 2　**5.** 3　**6.** 1

Step 04　**1.** She usually lays her keys on the table.

　　2. This hen lays three or four eggs each week.

　　3. The boy lay on the grass enjoying the sunshine.

124 press

Step 03　**1.** 2　**2.** 1　**3.** 3　**4.** 4　**5.** 1　**6.** 3　**7.** 2　**8.** 4

Step 04　**1.** He pressed the number buttons on the telephone.

　　2. Jack told him to fix the broken printing press.

　　3. Sam read about the earthquake in the press.

　　4. She likes to press her clothes.

125 bow

Step 03　**1.** 1　**2.** 3　**3.** 1　**4.** 2　**5.** 3　**6.** 2

Step 04　**1.** People don't bow when they meet each other in Europe.

　　2. He hunted deer with bow and arrows.

　　3. Mary wore a bow of pink ribbon in her hair.

Review

A. 01. bold　**02.** lay　**03.** bow　**04.** interest　**05.** press
　06. bow　**07.** press　**08.** interest　**09.** press　**10.** bold
　11. interest　**12.** bow　**13.** lay　**14.** press　**15.** lay

B. 01. bold　**02.** bow　**03.** press　**04.** interest　**05.** lay
　06. press　**07.** bow　**08.** bold　**09.** lay　**10.** press
　11. interest　**12.** lay　**13.** bow　**14.** press　**15.** interest

수능기출예문 점검

01. 그러므로 사람들은 현대 예술에 흥미를 잃어버리고 자신의 역할 모델을 찾기 위해서 스포츠 스타나 다른 대중적인 인물들에게로 돌아섰다.

02. 우리는 화해의 정신으로 분쟁을 해결하기 위해 일해야 하고 항상 상대방의 이익을 염두에 두고 있어야 한다.

03. 우리의 3개월 또는 6개월 할부 판매를 이용하시겠습니까? 무이자입니다.

04. 예를 들면, 많은 중국 학생들은 더 좋은 기회와 급여를 주는 한국 회사에서 일하려고 계획함에 따라 한국어에 관심을 갖게 되었다.

05. 로마의 Prati에서 발견된 한 인형은 상아로 만들어져 있었고, 18세의 나이로 사망했던 주인 옆에 놓여 있었습니다.　＊ lie의 과거형

06. 비록 당신 아이의 상상 속에서만 존재하는 그의 '친구'를 위해 식사 때 자리를 하나 두어야 하거나 가족의 자동차에 여분의 좌석을 마련해 두어야 한다는 것이 짜증스러울지도 모르지만, 그것은 아마 상당히 가치 있는 일일 것이다.

07. 가벼운 안개가 보다 낮은 곳에 있는 풍경의 지형을 부분적으로 감추면서 대지를 따라 깔려 있었지만, 그 위에는 보다 큰 나무들이 맑은 하늘을 배경으로 윤곽이 뚜렷한 무리를 이루어 드러나 있었다.　＊ lie의 과거형

08. 주문하고 싶으시면 "1"번을 누르세요. 상품 정보가 필요하면 "2"번을 누르세요.

09. 한국 신문의 역사에서 1883년이 중요한 해라는 것을 아는 사람은 거의 없다.

10. 평지는 지금 지평선을 향해 밀려 가며 하늘은 어두운 담요처럼 짓누르고 있다.

11. 한 어린 소녀가 강둑에서 낚싯대를 쥐고 있을 때, 갑자기 무엇인가를 느꼈고 낚싯대가 물음표처럼 휘는 것을 보았다.

Group-26

126 period

Step 03　**1.** 2　**2.** 1　**3.** 1　**4.** 3　**5.** 2　**6.** 3

Step 04　**1.** He is going to stay in Seoul for a short period.

　　2. We will study the period of the French Revolution.

　　3. His sentence doesn't have a period at the end.

127 fast

Step 03　**1.** 1　**2.** 2　**3.** 1　**4.** 3　**5.** 2　**6.** 3

Step 04　**1.** I can't understand him because he speaks so fast.

　　2. Tie the rope fast around your waist.

　　3. She often fasts for a day to lose weight.

128 score

Step 03　**1.** 3　**2.** 2　**3.** 3　**4.** 1　**5.** 2　**6.** 1

Step 04　**1.** The boy got a perfect score on the science test.

　　2. He found the deep scores in the wood.

　　3. The man died about a score of years ago.

129 stick

Step 03　**1.** 1　**2.** 2　**3.** 3　**4.** 2　**5.** 3　**6.** 1

Step 04　**1.** My grandfather cannot walk without a stick.

　　2. She will stick candles in the birthday cake.

　　3. You don't need to stick a stamp on the letter.

130 lie

Step 03　**1.** 2　**2.** 1　**3.** 2　**4.** 3　**5.** 1　**6.** 3

Step 04　**1.** He often lies to get out of trouble.

　　2. Lie on the sofa and have a rest.

　　3. The mountain lies to the west of the city.

Review

A. 01. stick　**02.** period　**03.** fast　**04.** score　**05.** period
　06. lie　**07.** fast　**08.** score　**09.** fast　**10.** lie　**11.** period
　12. stick　**13.** square　**14.** lie　**15.** stick

B. 01. lie　**02.** period　**03.** fast　**04.** score　**05.** stick　**06.** lie
　07. period　**08.** score　**09.** stick　**10.** lies　**11.** period
　12. fast　**13.** score　**14.** sticks　**15.** fast

수능기출예문 점검

01. 책은 대출 예약이 되어 있지 않다면, 처음 빌려 주는 기간 동안 한 번 갱신할 수 있다.

02. 일반적으로 어떤 시기에 대한 사람의 기억력은 그것으로부터 멀어짐에 따라 필수적으로 약해진다.

03. 30분 정도의 질의 응답 시간이 이어질 것입니다.

04. 너무 빨리 운전하는 것은 다른 사람을 위험에 빠뜨리는 것입니다.

05. 이 모든 것은 우리의 사회생활에서 예상된 행동 방식의 일부이지만, 우리가 엄격한 규칙에 의해 지배되는 정식 제도에 의해 적용할 수 있는 것은 아니다.

06. 그러나 밤늦게 걸으면 좋은 수면에 해로울 수 있습니다. 특히 빠른 걸음으로 걸으면 그렇습니다.

07. 연구가들은 컴퓨터를 가지고 노는 것이 취학 전 아동의 독서 성적 증진이나 컴퓨터 과학 분야의 훈련에 도움이 되지 않는다고 말했다.

08. 소리로 녹음하기 전에, 고전 음악은 쓰인 악보를 통하여 전달이 된 반면에, 초기의 재즈는 주로 실제 공연에 의존했다.

09. 예를 들면, 두 개의 축구팀이 시합할 때 각 팀은 상대방 팀보다 더 많은 득점을 하려고 애쓴다.

10. 사람들은 그들의 첫인상이 잘못된 것일지라도 그것에 집착하는 경향이 있다.

11. 의사는 장난하는 투로 "두 눈을 감고 입 밖으로 혀를 내밀도록 하시오." 라고 말했다.

12. 그들이 여기다가 나뭇가지를 갖다 놓은 것임에 틀림없다.

13. 그는 얼음 인간으로, 1991년 알프스에서 도보 여행을 하던 독일인 부부가 발견한, 얼음 위로 삐쭉 올라온 손상되지 않은 미이라이다.

14. 예를 들면, 우리는 진실을 말하거나 거짓을 말할 수 있다.

15. 그들의 영광은 그들의 성취가 아니라, 그들의 희생에 있다.

16. 만일 아이들에게 사실을 말하라고 했으면서 그 내용이 만족스럽지 않아 아이들을 혼냈다면, 그것은 아이들에게 자신을 보호하기 위해서는 당신에게 거짓말을 하라고 가르친 꼴이 되고 맙니다.

17. 항상 그렇듯이 지금 도시는 무언가의 중심에 놓여 있다는 인상을 만들어 내기 위해 필사적이다.

>>> **DAY 14**

Group-27

131 tie

Step 03 **1.** 3 **2.** 1 **3.** 2 **4.** 3 **5.** 1 **6.** 2

Step 04 **1.** He tied his horse to a tree.
2. We bought a new tie for his birthday.
3. Our team tied with his.

132 ground

Step 03 **1.** 1 **2.** 3 **3.** 1 **4.** 2 **5.** 3 **6.** 2

Step 04 **1.** The ground was covered with snow.
2. This novel is grounded on the writer's actual experience.
3. He ground wheat into flour.

133 race

Step 03 **1.** 1 **2.** 2 **3.** 3 **4.** 2 **5.** 1 **6.** 3

Step 04 **1.** After the race, he was utterly exhausted.
2. He had to race back home for his umbrella.
3. Many races live together in Los Angeles.

134 appear

Step 03 **1.** 1 **2.** 2 **3.** 1 **4.** 2

Step 04 **1.** A stranger appeared at the door suddenly.
2. She appears to have a lot of friends.

135 charge

Step 03 **1.** 3 **2.** 2 **3.** 4 **4.** 1 **5.** 4 **6.** 1 **7.** 2 **8.** 3

Step 04 **1.** The charge for the food was $15.
2. I charged a new computer on my credit card.
3. The large rhinoceros might charge at our truck.
4. I need to charge the battery of my cellular phone.

Review

A. 01. ground **02.** tie **03.** charge **04.** ground **05.** race **06.** charge **07.** race **08.** charge **09.** tie **10.** appear **11.** charge **12.** race **13.** ground **14.** appear **15.** tie

B. 01. appear **02.** ground **03.** charge **04.** tie **05.** charge **06.** race **07.** grounds **08.** charge **09. race** **10.** charge **11.** tie **12.** appear **13.** race **14.** tie **15.** ground

수능기출예문 점검

01. 머리띠는 모자를 제자리에 고정시키기 위해 턱 아래로 묶는다.

02. 그는 체크무늬 넥타이에 회색 옷을 입고 있다.

03. 나에게 있어서 행복은 나의 가족과 밀접하게 관련되어 있다. 내 아내와 자식들이 조화롭게 살면 나는 행복하다.

04. 투자 클럽에 대한 한 연구는 최악의 성과를 내는 클럽이 정서적인 유대를 바탕으로 이루어졌고 주로 사교적이었던 반면, 최고의 성과를 내는 클럽은 사교적인 관계를 제한했고 돈을 버는 데만 주력했다는 것을 보여주었다.

05. 또한 때때로 쌓인 눈의 무게는 나무들을 땅으로 휘게 한다.

06. 어떤 대학들은 대학은 중립적이고 (현실에) 참여해서는 안 된다는 근거를 들어 자신들의 침묵을 정당화하면서 당대의 중요한 문제들에 대하여 침묵한다.

07. 커피는 세계적으로 가장 대중적인 음료 중의 하나이다. 일반적으로 소비자들은 집에서 사용하기 위해 두 가지 중의 한 가지 형태로, 즉 가공하지 않은 형태이거나 가루로 만든 형태로 커피를 산다.

08. 신체에 대한 사회적인 정의는 사회적인 관계에 토대를 두고 있으며, 신체에 관해서 무엇이 '자연적인' 것으로 여겨져야 하는지에 대해 동의를 이끌어 낼 수 있는 힘을 가진 사람들에 의해 영향을 받는다.

09. 100m 경주에서 세계신기록을 세우기 위해 열심히 훈련하고 있습니다.

10. 예를 들어, 따뜻한 지역에서는 샌들이 가장 인기 있는 신발의 형태였고 지금도 여전히 그런 반면, 오늘날의 moccasin이라는 신발은 에스키모와 시베리아인과 같은 종족들이 추운 기후에서 사용했던 신발을 원형으로 하여 파생된 것이다.

11. 현재 형태의 게임은 Scotland에서 처음 나타났다.

12. 사과는 빨갛게 보일지 모르지만 그것을 이루는 원자는 전혀 빨간색이 아니다.

13. 그러나 우리가 소음으로 가득 찬 환경을 관리하고 있다고 느끼면, 더 이상 불안과 형편없는 업무 수행으로 고통을 겪을 필요는 없을지도 모른다.

14. 추가 요금을 내시면 2시간 안에 배달할 수 있습니다.

15. 정신의 일부분에 다른 일들이 주어지거나, 그것이 음악을 듣거나 가로수를 따라 걷는 일로 가득 채워질 때 사고는 향상된다.

Group-28

136 bark

Step 03 **1.** 2 **2.** 1 **3.** 2 **4.** 1

Step 04 **1.** He heard the bark of a dog in the distance.
2. He fell down the steps and barked his skins.

137 close

Step 03 **1.** 1 **2.** 3 **3.** 1 **4.** 2 **5.** 2 **6.** 3

Step 04 **1.** He closed his eyes and tried to sleep.
2. She will close her bank account with ABC bank.

3. My house is very close to the park.

138 bore

Step 03 **1.** 3 **2.** 2 **3.** 1 **4.** 2 **5.** 1 **6.** 3

Step 04 **1.** They bored a tunnel through solid rock.

2. My uncle bores us with stories about his school days.

3. This tree bore much fruit last year.

139 check

Step 03 **1.** 1 **2.** 4 **3.** 2 **4.** 3 **5.** 1 **6.** 3 **7.** 2 **8.** 4

Step 04 **1.** Every month, she writes checks to pay her bills.

2. You'd better make a check on your data first.

3. The teacher puts a check next to the wrong answer.

4. Every nation has to check the spread of nuclear weapons.

140 record

Step 03 **1.** 2 **2.** 1 **3.** 3 **4.** 1 **5.** 2 **6.** 3

Step 04 **1.** I am going to record the music on tape.

2. The man has a criminal record.

3. She spends a lot of money on records.

Review

A. 01. bore **02.** close **03.** check **04.** record **05.** bark
  06. check **07.** record **08.** bore **09.** close **10.** bark
  11. check **12.** close **13.** bore **14.** check **15.** record

B. 01. record **02.** bore **03.** close **04.** check **05.** bores
  06. check **07.** record **08.** bark **09.** check **10.** close
  11. record **12.** bark **13.** check **14.** Close **15.** bore

수능기출예문 점검

01. 멀리 개 짖는 소리를 제외하고는 실제로 어느 곳에도 생명의 표시나 암시도 없었는데, 그 소리도 외로운 정경을 두드러지게 했다.

02. 그러나 그 나라들과 가까운 위치에도 불구하고 한국은 그 치명적인 질병에서 벗어난 상태에 있다.

03. 다음에 다른 사람이 당신을 간지럽게 할 때 눈을 감고 침착하게 숨을 쉬며 차분함을 유지하게 된다면 똑같은 효과를 보게 될 것이다.

04. 이 영화제의 마지막 행사(폐회식)는 수상자들 모두가 그 모습을 보임으로써 주목을 받았다.

05. Vicky의 가장 친한 친구들 중 한 명인 수미가 인사를 하기 위해 들렀다.

06. 최근의 산림 화재로 인한 스모그 때문에 교육부는 모든 학교가 더 이상의 지시가 있을 때까지 문을 닫을 것이라고 발표했습니다.

07. 그러나 Jack은 그것이 매우 지루하다는 것을 알았기 때문에 그 책을 읽는 것을 그만두고 싶었다.

08. 적당히 정기적으로 기분이 나빠지는 사람은 너무나 자주 기분이 좋아서 기분 좋은 상태에 지루해하는 사람보다 이따금씩 찾아오는 기분 좋은 시간을 훨씬 더 만끽할 수 있다.

09. 7월분 대금 청구서 지불을 위한 수표를 보내 주신 데 대해 감사드립니다.

10. 정기 검진을 하는 동안 의사는 체중, 시력, 청력 문제, 혈압 등을 점검한다.

11. M: 너의 아버지는 안경을 쓰셨니?

W: 아니. 체크무늬 넥타이에 회색 옷을 입으셨어.

12. W: 이 책 두 권을 대출하려고 합니다.

M: 이 책 한 권은 대출할 수 있지만 다른 책 한 권은 대출할 수 없어요.

13. 나의 삼촌이 레코드 가게를 운영하시는데, 공짜로 기타 레슨을 해 주셔.

14. 어느 별에서 폭발이 있다면, 지구상의 과학자들은 그것이 발생한 시간을 기록할 것이다.

15. 한 명의 올림픽 수영 선수가 세계신기록을 세울 때마다, 그것은 다른 사람들이 자신들 속에 있는 최고의 능력을 이끌어 내고, 인간 성과의 새로운 기록을 세운 그 업적을 뛰어넘도록 고취시킨다.

16. W: Jefferson 씨, 당신의 개인 기록은 매우 인상적이군요. 그리고 당신의 사장으로부터 훌륭한 추천서도 받았습니다.

M: 감사합니다. 부인

>>> DAY 15

Group-29

141 cabinet

Step 03 **1.** 1 **2.** 2 **3.** 1 **4.** 2

Step 04 **1.** The old cabinet needs to be painted.

2. At last he became a member of the Cabinet.

142 lot

Step 03 **1.** 1 **2.** 3 **3.** 3 **4.** 2 **5.** 1 **6.** 2

Step 04 **1.** We drew lots to see who would go first.

2. They will turn that vacant lot into a playground.

3. He knows a lot about flowers and butterflies.

143 letter

Step 03 **1.** 3 **2.** 1 **3.** 2 **4.** 1 **5.** 2 **6.** 3

Step 04 **1.** He writes a letter to my friends once a week.

2. The letter "N" follows the letter "M."

3. He grew up to be a man of letters.

144 circle

Step 03 **1.** 2 **2.** 3 **3.** 1 **4.** 2 **5.** 1 **6.** 3

Step 04 **1.** He drew a circle 5cm in diameter.

2. Circle the answer you think is right.

3. These ideas will create a sensation in educational circles.

145 bound

Step 03 **1.** 2 **2.** 1 **3.** 3 **4.** 1 **5.** 4 **6.** 2 **7.** 4 **8.** 3

Step 04 **1.** They bound her arms and legs with rope.

2. The dog jumped over the fence with one bound.

3. Italy is bounded on the north by Switzerland.

4. This train is bound for Seoul.

Review

A. 01. circle **02.** letter **03.** circle **04.** lot **05.** cabinet
  06. lot **07.** bound **08.** letters **09.** circle **10.** bound
  11. letter **12.** bound **13.** lot **14.** cabinet **15.** bound

B. 01. circle **02.** letters **03.** bound **04.** lot **05.** circle
  06. cabinet **07.** lot **08.** letters **09.** bound **10.** circle
  11. lot **12.** bound **13.** letter **14.** bounds **15.** cabinet

01. 거리를 따라 걸어갈 때 나무를 인식하지 못할 수도 있지만, 한 새로운 연구에 따르면, 나무는 그늘을 제공하는 것보다 더 많은 일을 한다.

02. 엄청나게 많은 공간이 나무와 새들에게 주어지는 것이 아니라, 주차장으로 사용된다.

03. 그러나 우리 자신이나 우리의 운명을 진정으로 개선하는 것은 초인적인 일이므로 그 대신에 우리가 할 수 있는 일을 한다. 즉, 우리는 쇼핑을 하고, 경제는 성장하고, 세상은 보다 복잡해지고, 우리는 더 무력하고 불안하게 느끼고, 그래서 우리는 더더욱 많이 소비한다.

04. W: 짐이 많군요. 도와 드릴게요. M: 대단히 감사합니다.
W: 이쪽으로 오시죠. 제 차는 주차장에 있습니다.

05. 전화를 하고, 편지를 쓰고, 같이 지내면서 적당한 만큼 시간을 함께 보내지 않으면 우정은 없어질 것이다.

06. 이것들은 숫자, 알파벳 글자, 단어 또는 단순히 그림들로 만들어져 있다.

07. 다음에 팔뚝을 가지고 좀 더 큰 원을 그려라.

08. 파란 셔츠의 농부 밴드는 드럼과 다양한 관악기 뒤에서 고대 바스크의 Riau-Riau춤을 추며 돌고 들고 흔든다.

09. 나의 몇몇 세미나 수업의 대학생들은 빙 둘러앉았고, 각각의 학생들은 돌아가며 자신들의 이름을 말했다.

10. 이것은 네트를 두거나 네트 없이 실시될 수 있는데, 코트의 경계를 정해서 타이어를 자기 코트에 떨어뜨리거나 그것을 상대방 코트의 경계를 벗어나게 던지는 것과 같은 실수에 대해 득점을 매긴다.

11. 여러분이 과일을 씻을 때 과일에 묻은 모든 농약을 제거하고 있다고 생각할지 모르겠지만, 몇몇 화학 성분은 틀림없이 껍질의 표면에 남게 된다.

12. 어떤 동물이든지 식량 공급을 위해 반드시, 궁극적으로는 식물이지만, 다른 생명체에 의존한다. 또한 동물은 호흡에 필요한 지속적인 산소 공급을 식물들의 활동에 의존한다.

13. 그러나 이 무한한 야외활동의 잠재력에도 불구하고, Chattanooga 본래의 문제점은 남아 있었는데, 그것은 그 도시가 산업화 후의 황폐한 지역으로, 그곳을 방문은 하지만 결코 살고 싶지는 않은 그러한 종류의 도시로 만든다는 것이었다.

Group-30

146 patient

Step 03　**1.** 2　**2.** 1　**3.** 1　**4.** 2

Step 04　**1.** Everyone likes her because she is a very patient woman.
2. Fatty food is not good for the patient.

147 notice

Step 03　**1.** 1　**2.** 3　**3.** 1　**4.** 2　**5.** 3　**6.** 2

Step 04　**1.** He stuck the notice on the board.
2. The cook was fired without notice.
3. Then she noticed that her purse was missing.

148 pole

Step 03　**1.** 1　**2.** 3　**3.** 2　**4.** 3　**5.** 2　**6.** 1

Step 04　**1.** She is locking her bike to the pole.
2. He was the first person to reach the North Pole.
3. The opposite poles of magnets attract each other.

149 field

Step 03　**1.** 3　**2.** 1　**3.** 4　**4.** 3　**5.** 2　**6.** 1　**7.** 4　**8.** 2

Step 04　**1.** A farmer is sowing in the field.
2. The players are running across the soccer field.
3. He has always been interested in the field of international law.
4. The company owns 15 percent of the oil field.

150 cross

Step 03　**1.** 1　**2.** 2　**3.** 3　**4.** 1　**5.** 3　**6.** 2

Step 04　**1.** The girl was wearing a tiny gold cross around her neck.
2. Don't cross the street there. Use the crosswalk.
3. She sat down and crossed her legs.

Review

A. 01. field　**02.** notice　**03.** pole　**04.** cross　**05.** field
06. pole　**7.** cross　**08.** patient　**09.** notice　**10.** field
11. cross　**12.** patient　**13.** field　**14.** notice　**15.** pole

B. 01. patient　**02.** notice　**03.** Pole　**04.** field　**05.** notice
06. field　**07.** poles　**08.** field　**09.** cross　**10.** field
11. cross　**12.** patient　**13.** cross　**14.** pole　**15.** notice

01. 가장 중요한 변화 중의 하나는, 현재 매우 무시당하고 있는 개념인 환자의 개인적 특성에 대한 인식의 증가가 될 것이다.

02. 스스로에게 인내심을 가지고 기다리는 것을 상기시켜라.

03. 중앙아프리카의 Ndembu족 사람들은 질병을 흔히 친척, 친구 또는 적의 환자를 향한 분노의 결과물이라고 믿는다.

04. 대부분의 사람들과 비슷하다면 당신은 이상한 점을 알아챌 것이다, 그것은 당신의 친구는 원래 모습을 담은 것을 더 좋아하겠지만 당신은 반대된 이미지를 더 좋아할 것이라는 점이다.

05. 학생들은 더 이상의 지시(통지)가 있을 때까지 학교에 가서는 안 됩니다.

06. 이 단순한 행동의 직접적인 결과로 당신 삶에서 사람들과의 상호 작용이 얼마나 많이 향상될 것인지 즉시 알아챌 수 있을 것이다.

07. 내가 가고자 하는 북극으로부터 불어오고 있는 이 바람은 추운 날씨를 맛보게 해 주었다.

08. 디자인과 스타일링이 서로 관련되어 있지만, 그것들은 완전히 별개의 영역이다.

09. 저희 학교의 긴 역사를 통해 배출된 많은 성공한 졸업생들과 마찬가지로, 귀하의 자녀들도 세상에 진출해 정치, 경제, 문화, 그리고 교육 분야에 성공적으로 참여하게 될 것입니다.

10. 현대 기술은 중독성이 있으므로 반드시 하루하루를 전자기장에서 멀리 떨어지도록 계획해라.

11. 기차 창문으로 나는 농작물이 들판에서 무르익고 나무들이 빨갛고 노랗게 변해 가는 것을 볼 수 있었다.

12. 그는 야전 병원, 구급차 서비스, 그리고 응급처치를 전장에 도입했다.

13. W: 빨간 신호등이 켜져 있는데 도로를 건너가셨습니다.
M: 오, 죄송합니다. 신호등을 보지 못했습니다.

14. 한동안 그는 다리를 꼬고 벽난로 앞에 앉아 땔감을 넣으면서 따뜻한 불을 쳐다보았다.

15. 그는 계속 미끄러지고, 넘어지고, 일어서는 데 어려움을 겪고, 스키를 엇갈리게 하고, 다시 넘어지며, 그리하여 대개는 바보가 된 것처럼 보이고 느끼게 된다.

>>> DAY 16

Group-31

151 board
Step 03 1. 2 2. 1 3. 3 4. 1 5. 2 6. 3
Step 04 1. She is standing on the diving board.
2. He pays $150 a week for room and board.
3. Flight CX 386 for Sydney is now boarding at Gate 14.

152 fall
Step 03 1. 1 2. 3 3. 1 4. 3 5. 2 6. 2
Step 04 1. The weather becomes cool in the fall.
2. She fell and hit her head on the floor.
3. In winter the temperature often falls below zero.

153 note
Step 03 1. 1 2. 3 3. 2 4. 3 5. 2 6. 1
Step 04 1. She noted down his telephone number in her diary.
2. He played a high note on his trumpet.
3. He took a note of the change in her behavior.
(= He noticed a change in her behavior.)

154 pack
Step 03 1. 1 2. 3 3. 2 4. 3 5. 1 6. 2
Step 04 1. He bought a pack of cigarette at the store.
2. He packed two suitcases for his overseas trip.
3. Pack the newspaper around the vase so that it doesn't break.

155 head
Step 03 1. 1 2. 2 3. 3 4. 1 5. 2 6. 3
Step 04 1. She turned her head and looked at me silently.
2. He heads a team of engineers developing green energy.
3. The boy was standing at the head of the line.

Review

A. 01. head 02. pack 03. note 04. pack 05. fall
06. board 07. head 08. board 09. fall 10. note
11. board 12. note 13. fall 14. pack 15. head

B. 01. board 02. head 03. note 04. pack 05. fall
06. note 07. fall 08. pack 09. head 10. note
11. board 12. pack 13. head 14. fall 15. board

수능기출예문 점검

01. 그들 주변에는 많은 나무통과 나무판이 널려 있었다.
02. 그분은 지금 편집 이사회에 참석 중이십니다. 도와 드릴까요?
03. 강을 따라서 내 어린 시절에 기억했던 멋진 강굽이와 수목이 우거진 산봉우리와 강물에 비친 경치들을 기대하면서, 나는 배에 오르며 전율했다.
04. W: 이봐, Stuart, 게시판을 봐라. M: 와, 학교 동아리가 많이 있구나.
05. 바깥에는 가로등이 내던지는 원뿔 모양의 불빛 속에서 눈이 조용히 계속 내리고 있었다.
06. 로마 제국의 멸망에 대한 수많은 설명들이 있지만, 더 깊은 원인은 토양의 비옥함이 줄어들고 농작물의 산출이 감소한 데 있다.
07. 비행기 탑승객인 Walt Morris 씨에게, 어느 가을 저녁 비행기를 타고 한적한 Kansas 하늘 위를 나는 것은 유쾌한 경험이었습니다.
08. 그는 계속 미끄러지고, 넘어지고, 일어서는 데 어려움을 겪고, 스키를 엇갈리게 하고, 다시 넘어지며, 그리하여 대개는 바보가 된 것처럼 보이고 느끼게 된다.
09. Napoleon의 몰락 후에, Larrey의 의학적 명성은 그를 구해 주었으며 그는 1820년 의학협회에 창단 회원으로 임명되었다.
10. 가장 적절한 가격과 최악의 가격을 기록하고 그 둘 사이에서 예산을 짜세요.
11. 가장 높은 음을 냈는데, 갑자기 큰 포도주 잔이 깨졌습니다.
12. 나는 어렸을 적 내 크리스마스 경험을 설명해 주는 쪽지를 항상 같이 넣었다.
13. 모든 음악은 표현력을 가지고 있고, 정도의 차이는 있지만 모든 음악은 음표의 이면에 어떤 의미를 지니고 있다는 것이 나의 믿음이다.
14. 한 단어에 더 많은 의미를 채워 넣을수록 그 생각이 전달되게 하기 위해서는 더 적은 단어가 필요하게 된다.
15. 당신은 실제 당신이 꾸려야 할 것만큼 많은 짐들을 가지고 있지 않다고 생각하는 잘못된 생각에 사로잡혀 있을 것이다.
16. W: 음... 파인애플 두 개 주시죠. 이 딸기들은 얼마죠?
M: 한 팩에 10달러입니다.

Group-32

156 shade
Step 03 1. 1 2. 3 3. 2 4. 3 5. 1 6. 2
Step 04 1. Children like to play in the cool shade.
2. She bought a new shade for the bedroom.
3. This hat will shade you from the hot sun.

157 roll
Step 03 1. 1 2. 2 3. 1 4. 3 5. 2 6. 3
Step 04 1. She had a ham sandwich on a roll for lunch.
2. He rolled the newspaper and put a rubber band around it.
3. Everyone on the roll was at the meeting.

158 sign
Step 03 1. 2 2. 1 3. 3 4. 2 5. 1 6. 3
Step 04 1. There is a no smoking sign on the wall.
2. She signed me to leave the room.
(= She made a sign to me to leave the room.)
3. Don't forget to sign your name here.

159 bit
Step 03 1. 1 2. 2 3. 3 4. 3 5. 1 6. 2
Step 04 1. The floor is covered with bits of broken glass.
2. The dog bit me in the leg.

3. The bit hurt the pony's sore mouth.

160 trunk

`Step 03` 1. 2 2. 3 3. 1 4. 2 5. 1 6. 3

`Step 04` 1. He found his grandfather's old trunk in the garage.
2. The elephant can breathe through its trunk.
3. The trunk of that tree is three meters thick.

Review

A. 01. sign 02. roll 03. trunk 04. shade 05. sign 06. bit
07. sign 08. trunk 09. shade 10. bit 11. roll
12. shade 13. bit 14. trunk 15. roll

B. 01. roll 02. shade 03. bit 04. sign 05. shade
06. trunk 07. Sign 08. bit 09. trunk 10. shade
11. roll 12. trunk 13. bit 14. roll 15. sign

수능기출예문 점검

01. 당신이 길을 걸어갈 때 나무를 인식하지 못할 수도 있지만, 새로운 연구에 따르면, 나무는 그늘을 제공하는 것보다 더 많은 역할을 한다.

02. 강둑에 있는 돌멩이들이 소녀의 발 밑으로 굴렀고, 그녀는 강물 속으로 끌려 들어가고 있었다.

03. 사람들이 파피루스처럼 펼쳐지는 것보다 넘겨질 수 있는 페이지를 가진 책을 제본하기 시작했을 때, 정보를 찾는 과정이 변했다.

04. 많은 사람들에게 있어서, 감정적인 식사의 고전적인 표시들 중 하나는 야식이다.

05. W: 여기 서명해 주시겠습니까? M: 예. 빨리 배달해 주셔서 감사합니다.

06. Davis 양, 이 무대로 나오셔서 우리의 감사의 작은 표시인 이 상을 받으시고 몇 마디 해 주시겠습니까?

07. 발달의 속도가 늦춰질 조짐(징후)은 없다.

08. 캐나다의 퀘벡 주에서는 영어를 사용하는 사람에게 벌을 주고 영어 도로 표시판을 금지했다.

09. 어디에도 빛의 흔적은 없었다.

10. M: 와, 학교 동아리가 많이 있구나.
W: 음… 나는 학교 록밴드에 가입하고 싶어. 거기에 함께 가입하자.

11. 소녀는 지갑을 들여다보고 돈을 셌다. 돈이 충분하지 않아, 값을 깎기를 원했다. "(값을) 조금 깎아 줄 수 있나요?"라고 소녀가 물었다.

12. 개미가 죽은 곤충들 부스러기를 굴 안에 넣어 주면 개미식물은 그것들을 양분으로 사용한다.

13. 나무의 줄기는 갈색이 반사되는 유일한 파장이기 때문에 갈색으로 보인다.

>>> **DAY 17**

`Group-33`

161 age

`Step 03` 1. 3 2. 2 3. 1 4. 2 5. 1 6. 3

`Step 04` 1. My brother went to Brazil at the age of forty.
2. The space age has already begun.
3. She has aged a lot since I last saw her.

162 angle

`Step 03` 1. 2 2. 1 3. 3 4. 2 5. 3 6. 1

`Step 04` 1. Take a look at the cube from this angle.
2. We need to look at the affair from a different angle.
3. My uncle is good at angling for trout in the river.

163 own

`Step 03` 1. 1 2. 3 3. 1 4. 2 5. 3 6. 2

`Step 04` 1. He said that the book was his own.
2. My grandfather owns a lot of land in this area.
3. He owns that he has not been working hard.

164 iron

`Step 03` 1. 3 2. 1 3. 2 4. 3 5. 2 6. 1

`Step 04` 1. There was a huge iron gate in front of the mansion.
2. He has burnt a hole in his dress with the iron.
3. She ironed her wrinkled trousers.

165 catch

`Step 03` 1. 1 2. 2 3. 1 4. 3 5. 2 6. 3

`Step 04` 1. He caught the fast ball that I threw. It was a nice catch.
2. Sometimes unlucky seals catch in our net.
3. His catch at the lake was small.

Review

A. 01. age 02. iron 03. angel 04. catch 05. own
06. iron 07. own 08. catch 09. age 10. angle
11. catch 12. age 13. iron 14. own 15. angle

B. 01. angle 02. catch 03. own 04. iron 05. angle
06. age 07. iron 08. own 09. age 10. catch
11. own 12. iron 13. catch 14. age 15. angle

수능기출예문 점검

01. 나이를 기준으로 사회 집단을 설명하고자 한다면 우리는 유년기, 청년기, 장년기, 노년기라는 4개의 연령 집단을 제시할 것이다.

02. 만일 규칙적으로 오랜 기간 동안 한다면 운동은 골다공증, 즉 사람들이 나이를 먹으면서 자연적으로 발생하는 뼈의 점진적인 손상 과정을 예방한다.

03. 우리가 최근에 정보의 시대로 들어섰다는 주장은 잘못된 것이다.

04. 저는 한동안 이 신기한 강철 새가 몹시 궁금했습니다.

05. 7~12세의 어린이들은 종종 부상이나 사고와 같이 그들에게 일어날지도 모르는 현실적인 상황들을 두려워한다.

06. 르네상스 예술은 여러 가지 면에서 중세의 예술과 달랐다.

07. 나는 이상한 지붕 각도 또는 크기나 원근감, 또는 디자인이 부정확해 보이는 물체가 있는 집이나 헛간은 피하려고 합니다.

08. 물속에서 비스듬히 선 채로 있으면서, 그것은 좀 더 작은 물고기 근처에까지 이르게 될 때까지 물살을 따라 이동한다.

09. 반면에, 재즈에서는 공연을 하는 사람들이 종종 자신들의 멜로디를 즉석에서 만든다.

10. 평범한 소비자들이 아주 귀중하게 여겨지는 원작들의 복사본을 소유할 수 있다.

11. 우리는 그들의 사랑과 상실, 기쁨과 슬픔, 희망과 공포를 어느 정도는 마치 우리 자신의 것인 듯이 느낀다.

12. 쇠는 달았을 때 쳐라. (기회를 놓치지 마라.)

13. 마을의 몇몇 영리한 사람들이 더 크고 더 좋은 장비가 있는 배를 구입해서 찾을 수 있는 물고기를 모두 잡기 시작했다.

14. 그러나 그 이후에는 기차를 타고 할아버지를 뵈러 가야 합니다.

15. 감기에 걸리지 않도록 하는 몇 가지 예방책이 여기 있습니다.

Group-34

166 appointment

Step 03   **1.** 2   **2.** 1   **3.** 2   **4.** 1

Step 04   **1.** She made an appointment to see the doctor at two o'clock.
  2. His appointment as a teaching assistant is certain.

167 book

Step 03   **1.** 3   **2.** 1   **3.** 3   **4.** 2   **5.** 1   **6.** 1

Step 04   **1.** He borrowed two books from the library.
  2. I received a check book from the bank.
  3. She has booked four seats for Saturday's concert.

168 lead

Step 03   **1.** 1   **2.** 2   **3.** 3   **4.** 1   **5.** 2   **6.** 3

Step 04   **1.** Who will lead this blind man to his house?
  2. Our team was leading by two points when rain stopped play.
  3. The plumber used lead to seal the joints in pipes.

169 match

Step 03   **1.** 3   **2.** 1   **3.** 1   **4.** 2   **5.** 3   **6.** 2

Step 04   **1.** He struck a match and burned the old paper.
  2. The soccer match ended in a tie.
  3. The hat is a perfect match for your coat.

170 bill

Step 03   **1.** 3   **2.** 1   **3.** 2   **4.** 4   **5.** 2   **6.** 1   **7.** 4   **8.** 3

Step 04   **1.** Peter found a ten-dollar bill in the street.
  2. The department store bills its customers at the beginning of every month.
  3. That bird has a long yellow bill.
  4. The government will introduce a new housing bill.

Review

A. 01. appointment   **02.** match   **03.** lead   **04.** bill   **05.** book
  06. match   **07.** lead   **08.** bill   **09.** book   **10.** bill
  11. appointment   **12.** lead   **13.** bill   **14.** book   **15.** match

B. 01. appointment   **02.** Lead   **03.** match   **04.** bill
  05. book   **06.** bill   **07.** lead   **08.** match   **09.** book
  10. bill   **11.** leads   **12.** appointment   **13.** match
  14. book   **15.** bill

수능기출예문 점검

01. 그들은 아침식사로는 섬유질이 풍부한 빵과 곡류와 같은 음식을 선택하며, 사업상의 약속을 준비하기 위해 점심으로는 샐러드를 선택한다.

02. 그런데, 미안합니다. 그 시간에는 약속이 있습니다. 대신에 목요일 4시에 만나면 어떨까요?

03. 책은 대출 예약이 되어 있지 않으면, 처음 빌려 주는 기간 동안 한 번 갱신할 수 있다.

04. 죄송합니다만, 모든 테이블이 예약이 되었습니다.

05. 여러분의 직감을 따르는 것은 여러분이 나중에 후회하게 될지도 모르는 충동적인 결정을 하게 할 수가 있다.

06. 그것은 돌, 진흙 또는 흙과는 느낌이 달랐다. 그들은 그것이 일종의 납이라고 생각했고, 다른 사람들 역시 그렇게 생각했다.

07. 택시가 목적지에 가까워지자, 그녀는 일부 사람들이 타워로 이어지는 아름다운 오솔길을 따라 걷고 있는 것을 본다.

08. 당신이 새 드라마에서 중요한 배역을 맡게 될 거라고 말했어.

09. 안개 속에서 그처럼 확실하게 나를 인도했던 낯선 사람은 장님이었다.

10. 그러나 몇몇 개인들은 어떤 선수나 팀도 응원하지 않으며 앉아서 축구경기나 테니스 시합을 관람한다.

11. 1990년도에 생산된 쌀의 양은 1985년도의 생산량과 일치한다.

12. 영구적인 가옥 증축은 당신 집에 어울리도록 전통 방식으로 벽돌이나 타일로 지어진다.

13. 우리가 돈에 관해 생각할 때, 대개 현금(통화), 즉 동전이나 지폐를 생각한다.

14. 7월분 대금 청구서 지불을 위한 수표를 보내주신 데 대해 감사합니다.

15. 상품 판매, 보관, 선적, 청구서 작성 등의 비용을 줄일 수 있기 때문에 이런 구매자들에게 회사는 가격 할인을 해 준다.

>>> **DAY 18**

Group-35

171 industry

Step 03   **1.** 1   **2.** 2   **3.** 1   **4.** 2

Step 04   **1.** The government will invest more money in the steel industry next year.
  2. Jane's success was due to her industry and thrift.

172 game

Step 03   **1.** 1   **2.** 2   **3.** 1   **4.** 3   **5.** 2   **6.** 3

Step 04   **1.** The Olympic Games are held every four years.
  2. The tennis player won four games in the first set.
  3. The hunters captured deer and wild game.

173 deliver

Step 03   **1.** 1   **2.** 3   **3.** 2   **4.** 3   **5.** 1   **6.** 2

Step 04   **1.** Could you deliver this letter to your father?
  2. We delivered the prisoners from the enemy.
  3. She delivered a healthy boy after a long labor.

174 still

Step 03   **1.** 2   **2.** 3   **3.** 1   **4.** 2   **5.** 1   **6.** 3

Step 04 1. Please keep still while I tie your shoes.
　　　2. She is still hoping for a letter from him.
　　　3. It is hot today, but it will be still hotter tomorrow.

175 point

Step 03 1. 1 2. 2 3. 3 4. 4 5. 3 6. 1 7. 4 8. 2

Step 04 1. She stuck the point of the needle through the cloth.
　　　2. Our team scored 15 points in the first quarter.
　　　3. A boy pointed a toy pistol at him.
　　　4. She missed the point of his joke.

Review

A. 01. industry 02. game 03. point 04. deliver 05. still
　06. game 07. industry 08. deliver 09. still 10. point
　11. game 12. point 13. still 14. point 15. deliver

B. 01. still 02. games 03. points 04. deliver 05. point
　06. still 07. industry 08. game 09. point 10. deliver
　11. point 12. games 13. still 14. deliver 15. industry

수능기출예문 점검

01. 이것은 다양한 과학적인 분야와 산업에서 중요한 역할을 한다.
02. 고대 이집트에서는 돌을 던지는 것이 아이들이 좋아하는 놀이였지만, 잘 못 던진 돌이 아이를 다치게 할 수 있었다.
03. 희생자들은 대부분 사냥꾼이거나 사냥감으로 오인된 등산객들이었다.
04. 현재 형태의 게임은 Scotland에서 처음 나타났다.
05. 그녀는 고객들에게 신문을 배달하기 위해 매일 아침 5시 30분에 일어났다.
06. Peter는 개막 행사에 연설을 할 것이고, Sally는 무대 보조원으로 일을 할 예정입니다.
07. 이러한 소위 비정부 기구들은 사회봉사활동을 한다.
08. 나는 아직도 나이 든 사람들은 그들의 경험과 지혜에 대해 존경을 받을 만하다고 믿는다.
09. 그러나 오늘 밤은 사람들이 평소와 달리 조용하고 또한 들고 있는 깃발들 역시 이상할 만큼 가만히 있다.
10. 오히려, 40년이 넘는 동안의 통제된 연구의 결과에 따르면, 분노의 폭발은 분노를 강화시킬 가능성이 더 많으며, 눈물은 우리를 훨씬 더 깊은 우울증으로 몰고 갈 수 있다고 한다.
11. 요점은 관련된 사람들 사이의 상황이나 관계가 그 의미를 결정한다는 점이다.
12. 예를 들면, 두 개의 축구팀이 시합할 때 각 팀은 상대방 팀보다 더 많은 골(점수)를 얻으려고 애쓴다.
13. 게다가, 과학 기술은 기름을 얻기 위해 고래를 죽일 필요가 없을 정도로 진보했다.
14. 전문가들은 이것이 우리 경제의 발전을 늦추는 심각한 문제라고 지적한다.
15. 거울 온도가 이슬점에 있는 그림 B에서는 이슬방울이 거울의 표면을 덮는다.
16. 이 시점에서 당신은 그 사람이 누구인지를 알지 못한다.

Group-36

176 anxious

Step 03 1. 1 2. 2 3. 1 4. 2

Step 04 1. The man was always anxious about his son's health.
　　　2. She is anxious to know the result of the final test.

177 order

Step 03 1. 2 2. 1 3. 3 4. 1 5. 3 6. 2

Step 04 1. Our names were arranged in alphabetical order.
　　　2. He ordered me to sit down and keep silence.
　　　3. I have ordered some new books from America.

178 sound

Step 03 1. 2 2. 1 3. 3 4. 2 5. 1 6. 3

Step 04 1. We heard a strange sound from the next room.
　　　2. He is still sound in mind and body in spite of his old age.
　　　3. She sometimes sounds the horn to warn other drivers.

179 face

Step 03 1. 2 2. 3 3. 1 4. 3 5. 1 6. 2

Step 04 1. That lady has such a pretty face.
　　　2. He climbed the north face of the mountain.
　　　3. The windows of our classroom face the park.

180 bear

Step 03 1. 1 2. 4 3. 2 4. 1 5. 2 6. 3 7. 4 8. 3

Step 04 1. A brown bear came close to me slowly.
　　　2. I doubt if this chair will bear my weight.
　　　3. He was born of a poor family.
　　　4. He always visits friends who are ill, bearing some flowers.

Review

A. 01. sound 02. order 03. anxious 04. sound 05. bear
　06. order 07. face 08. bear 09. face 10. order
　11. bear 12. bear 13. face 14. anxious 15. sound

B. 01. sound 02. order 03. face 04. sound 05. bear
　06. bear 07. anxious 08. order 09. bear 10. sound
　11. anxious 12. face 13. bear 14. face 15. order

수능기출예문 점검

01. 새로운 경쟁 때문에 우리는 가능한 한 빨리 우리의 제품을 시장에 내놓기를 갈망합니다.
02. 그녀는 점점 스트레스를 받았고 걱정에 휩싸였다.
03. 소설 속의 사건은 늘 그런 것은 아니지만, 대개 일어난 순서대로 기술된다.
04. 수량할인도 있는데, 그것은 대량의 물건을 주문하는 개인에게 제공된다.
05. 1457년, 그는 백성들에게 더 이상 골프를 하지 못하도록 명령을 내렸다.
06. 직장에서 일하는 동안 얻는 스트레스를 줄이기 위해서, 퇴근 후 당신이 즐기는 일에 시간을 할애하라.
07. 아파트에 들어가려고 하는데, 새 자물쇠가 고장 난 것 같아요.
08. 벌레 소리를 제외하고는 어떤 생명의 흔적도 없었다.
09. 여러분들이 말하는 방식은 첫인상의 35%를 차지한다.
10. 당신은 당신이 건전한 성격의 사람이며, 정직하고, 믿을 수 있고, 친절하

고, 사람들을 배려하는 사람이라는 진정한 신념에서 비롯된 용기를 가지고 있습니까?

11. 네가 약간 걱정하는 것같이 보이는데, 외국에서 사는 것은 생각하는 것 이상으로 더 재미있을 수 있어.

12. 무관심이나 반대에도 불구하고 도덕적 용기를 보여 주는 것은 쉽지 않다.

13. 오늘날 여러 문제나 의견불일치에 직면할 때 우리는 대화를 통해 해결점에 도달해야 한다.

14. 이것이 그녀 얼굴 전체에 있는 주름이 왜 그렇게 깊어졌는지를 말해 준다.

15. 유엔 발표에 따르면, 북극곰의 숫자가 급격히 감소하고 있다고 합니다.

16. 정신적인 긴장은 참기 어렵다. 시간이 지날수록 그것은 더 심해진다.

>>> DAY 19

Group-37

181 succeed

Step 03 **1.** 2 **2.** 1 **3.** 1 **4.** 2

Step 04 **1.** We succeeded in finding empty seats at the theater.
2. He will succeed to his father's business in the near future.

182 suit

Step 03 **1.** 2 **2.** 3 **3.** 1 **4.** 2 **5.** 1 **6.** 3

Step 04 **1.** He will wear his best suit tonight.
2. She lost her suit against the insurance company.
3. The warm climate here suits her health.

183 court

Step 03 **1.** 1 **2.** 3 **3.** 2 **4.** 3 **5.** 1 **6.** 2

Step 04 **1.** There are a lot of beautiful flowers in the court of her house.
2. Our school has several tennis courts.
3. She was summoned to appear in court as a witness.

184 mind

Step 03 **1.** 3 **2.** 1 **3.** 2 **4.** 1 **5.** 2 **6.** 3

Step 04 **1.** She is very old, but her mind is still clear.
2. Would you mind my bag while I buy my ticket?
3. He doesn't mind the cold weather at all.

185 hold

Step 03 **1.** 3 **2.** 2 **3.** 4 **4.** 3 **5.** 1 **6.** 2 **7.** 1 **8.** 4

Step 04 **1.** The man was holding a knife in his hand.
2. He still holds the heavy weight title.
3. The 1988 Olympic Games were held in Seoul.
4. The rule does not hold in this case.

Review

A. 01. mind **02.** succeed **03.** suit **04.** hold **05.** mind
06. suit **07.** court **08.** hold **09.** succeed **10.** hold
11. court **12.** hold **13.** suit **14.** court **15.** mind

B. 01. suit **02.** hold **03.** court **04.** succeed **05.** mind

06. suit **07.** hold **08.** court **09.** hold **10.** mind
11. suit **12.** succeed **13.** court **14.** holds **15.** mind

수능기출예문 점검

01. 다른 사람이 실패할 때, 당신은 당신이 성공할 더 좋은 기회가 있다고 생각한다.

02. 인생에서 성공한 사람 중 대다수가 자신의 성공을 집중력이 좋기 때문이라고 말하고 있다.

03. 그는 체크무늬 넥타이에 회색 정장을 입었다.

04. 자신의 서재에 맞는 책장을 설계하세요.

05. M: 잠깐 쉴까요? W: 왜 안 되겠어요? 마음대로 하세요.

06. 이것은 자동차 사고, 실직, 갑자기 찾아온 병마, 법적 소송 사건에 말려드는 경우 또는 많은 액수의 돈을 잃었을 때와 같은 여러 가지 원인에 기인한다.

07. 다시 말하자면, 유죄를 입증하는 것은 법정의 책임이라는 것이다.

08. 테니스 코트에서 나오는 고함 소리 때문에 화가 나셨나요?

09. 우리들 중 많은 이들이 타인과 대화를 나누며 마음은 다른 곳에 가 있을 때, 이와 같은 행동을 하게 된다.

10. 내가 천재라면 이처럼 대접받는 것에 전혀 신경 쓰지 않을 것이다.

11. 당신이 괜찮다면 앉겠어요.

12. 외국에서 여행을 할 때 명심해야 할 일이 몇 가지 있습니다.

13. 전구를 갈고 있는 동안 의자를 단단히 잡고 있어요.

14. 시민들에게 자전거 타기를 장려하기 위해서 비디오 콘테스트를 개최할 예정이래.

15. 인생은 귀중하며 미래에 대한 꿈을 간직하는 것뿐만 아니라 현재에 살 필요가 있다는 것을 기억해라.

16. 졸업식은 다음 주 금요일에 Hutt 고등학교 강당에서 열릴 것입니다.

Group-38

186 rare

Step 03 **1.** 2 **2.** 1 **3.** 1 **4.** 2

Step 04 **1.** It is very rare for him to arrive late.
2. My uncle likes rare meat that is still red.

187 article

Step 03 **1.** 2 **2.** 1 **3.** 3 **4.** 2 **5.** 3 **6.** 1

Step 04 **1.** He read a magazine article on a new type of fuel.
2. This shop sells articles for Christmas presents.
3. Article 1 of the constitution guarantees freedom of religion.

188 company

Step 03 **1.** 1 **2.** 2 **3.** 3 **4.** 1 **5.** 3 **6.** 2

Step 04 **1.** She owns a company that makes fancy toys.
2. You may know a man by the company he keeps.
3. We shall have company for dinner this evening.

189 draw

Step 03 **1.** 1 **2.** 2 **3.** 3 **4.** 1 **5.** 2 **6.** 3

Step 04 **1.** You'd better draw your chair around the fire.

2. He likes drawing a map as a hobby.

(= He likes to draw a map as a hobby.)

3. The game ended in a draw.

190 major

Step 03	**1.** 2 **2.** 3 **3.** 1 **4.** 2 **5.** 4 **6.** 1 **7.** 3 **8.** 4
Step 04	**1.** One of the major causes of cancer is smoking.
	2. She majored in economics at the university.
	3. My uncle is a major in the army.
	4. She played a sonata in F major.

Review

A. 01. draw **02.** draw **03.** major **04.** article **05.** company
06. major **07.** company **08.** article **09.** rare **10.** major
11. draw **12.** rare **13.** major **14.** article **15.** company
B. 01. company **02.** rare **03.** draw **04.** major **05.** article
06. major **07.** company **08.** major **09.** article
10. major **11.** rare **12.** draw **13.** article **14.** company
15. draw

수능기출예문 점검

01. 인간과 희귀 식물 간의 어떠한 접촉도 식물에게는 재난이 될 수 있다.

02. 그들이 배를 타는 동안 불렀던 간단한 노래에서 아주 작은 위안을 찾았다.

03. 신발은 그 역사가 수천 년 거슬러 올라가며, 오랫동안 필수적인 물건이 되어 왔다.

04. 이것은 내년 패션 유행에 관한 기사다.

05. 지난 25년 동안 귀하는 이 회사에서 높이 평가받고 존경받는 직원이었습니다.

06. 나는 한 식당에 들어가 자리에 앉았다. 내가 앉은 탁자의 손님이 일어났다. "선생, 당신은 원하지 않는 사람에게 당신과 함께 앉도록 강요하고 싶으신가요?"라고 말했다.

07. 바깥에서 그림을 그릴 때 내가 따르는 중요한 원칙들 중 하나는 너무 어렵거나 이상한 대상은 선택하지 않는 것이다.

08. 하지만 가까이 다가가자, 표지판의 글씨는 FOOD AHEAD(전방에 식당)임이 드러난다.

09. 이러한 방식으로 그들은 극을 더 잘 이해할 수 있도록 힌트를 부여받으면서, 결국 나름대로의 결론을 이끌어 낼 수 있도록 결론은 개방된 상태로 남겨지게 된다.

10. 마침내 저녁 그림자가 길게 드리워질 무렵 음침한 집이 시야에 들어오는 곳에 있는 나 자신을 발견했다.

11. 어느 날 그는 칼을 가지고 학교에 갔다. Timmy가 칼을 가지고 있는 것을 보고 놀란 선생님이 다음과 같이 말했다. "칼이라! 도대체 미술 시간에 칼이 왜 필요하지?" Timmy는 다음과 같이 설명했다. "우리는 모두 칼 뽑는 법을 배울 거라고 말씀하셨잖아요?"

12. Tony, 대학에서 무엇을 전공할까 생각해 보았습니까?

13. 그것들은 국내외의 주요한 뉴스 이야기를 요약해 준다.

14. 다른 사람이 자신에 대해 어떻게 생각하는지에 대한 느낌과 판단은 날마다 부딪치는 문제를 해결하는 방법을 선택할 때 중요한 역할을 한다.

>>> DAY 20

Group-39

191 share

Step 03	**1.** 3 **2.** 1 **3.** 2 **4.** 2 **5.** 1 **6.** 3
Step 04	**1.** My parents share joys and sorrows with us.
	2. The little boy ate more than his share of the cake.
	3. He decided to sell his shares in the oil company.

192 operation

Step 03	**1.** 2 **2.** 1 **3.** 3 **4.** 1 **5.** 2 **6.** 3
Step 04	**1.** He explained the operation of the camera to me.
	2. My uncle had an operation on his stomach last year.
	3. Military operations are scheduled to commence from next week.

193 lean

Step 03	**1.** 3 **2.** 1 **3.** 2 **4.** 3 **5.** 2 **6.** 1
Step 04	**1.** I leaned forward to hear what he said.
	2. He leaned the ladder against the wall.
	3. The girl looked lean and pale.

194 since

Step 03	**1.** 1 **2.** 2 **3.** 1 **4.** 2
Step 04	**1.** She hasn't eaten anything since last Friday.
	2. Since we have no money, we can't buy it.

195 heart

Step 03	**1.** 2 **2.** 4 **3.** 1 **4.** 3 **5.** 4 **6.** 3 **7.** 2 **8.** 1
Step 04	**1.** Eating too many fatty foods is bad for the heart.
	2. She knew in her heart that she was wrong.
	3. Jane sent me a Valentine card with a heart on it.
	4. The park is in the heart of the city.

Review

A. 01. heart **02.** operation **03.** share **04.** since
05. operation **06.** lean **07.** heart **08.** share **09.** lean
10. since **11.** heart **12.** operation **13.** lean **14.** heart
15. share
B. 01. since **02.** operation **03.** heart **04.** lean **05.** heart
06. operation **07.** lean **08.** share **09.** Since **10.** heart
11. share **12.** heart **13.** lean **14.** shares **15.** operation

수능기출예문 점검

01. 그러나 지금은 디지털 시대의 도구들이 우리에게 새로운 방식으로 손쉽게 정보를 모으고, 공유하고, 실행시키는 방법을 제공한다.

02. 그러나 그는 새로운 전화 구입과 전화요금에 너무 많은 돈을 썼기 때문에 방세 중 자신의 몫을 제때에 내지 못하는 경우도 종종 있다.

03. 그는 '대동강 그룹'이라는 온라인 회사를 직접 설립했다. 곧, 모든 양반 계급의 사람들이 이 회사의 주식을 샀고 김선달은 부자가 되었다.

04. "걱정은 나누면 반이 된다."란 격언을 들어 본 적이 있는가?

05. 산업용 다이아몬드는 으깨지고 가루가 되어 많은 연마, 광택 작업에 사용된다.

06. "호랑이 작전"은 1972년의 호랑이 생존을 위한 운동이었다.

07. 어느 날 사장이 회사 전체의 창고 운영을 감독하는 새로운 일자리를 제안했다.

08. 오늘날, 많은 사람들이 의과 수술을 위한 혈액이 충분치 못해 고통을 받고 있습니다.

09. 다른 사람의 식사가 끝나지 않았을 때, 뒤로 기대면서 "다 먹었다"고 말하지 마십시오.

10. 마침내, 그는 그의 파트너 쪽으로 몸을 기울여 입을 조그맣게 해서 "지금 어디니?"라고 속삭이지 않을 수가 없었다.

11. 우리가 이 집으로 이사 온 이후로 Jack과 나는 네가 옆집 어린 소녀에서 자신감 있는 젊은 여성으로 자라는 것을 지켜보았다.

12. 일반적으로 사람들은 자신이 잘하는 일을 좋아하기 때문에 나는 아이들에게 그들이 뛰어난 분야에 집중하라고 말한다.

13. 차 문이 닫혔고, 발자국 소리가 창문을 지나면서 그녀의 가슴은 더 빨리 뛰기 시작했다.

14. 만약 정부가 공연 예술을 지원하지 않는다면, 이 나라는 국민의 마음과 영혼의 많은 것을 잃게 될 것이다.

Group-40

196 tongue

Step 03 **1.** 1 **2.** 2 **3.** 1 **4.** 2

Step 04 **1.** The doctor asked him to put out his tongue.
2. She speaks in a foreign tongue.

197 tear

Step 03 **1.** 1 **2.** 3 **3.** 2 **4.** 3 **5.** 1 **6.** 2

Step 04 **1.** The dog tried to tear my trousers.
2. There was a small tear in my dress.
3. She shed tears to hear the sad news.

198 nature

Step 03 **1.** 2 **2.** 3 **3.** 2 **4.** 1 **5.** 3 **6.** 1

Step 04 **1.** Earthquakes show the destructive power of nature.
2. My father has a generous nature.
3. Pictures of that nature do not interest me.

199 associate

Step 03 **1.** 1 **2.** 3 **3.** 2 **4.** 3 **5.** 1 **6.** 2

Step 04 **1.** Many people associate war with death and hunger.
2. She associates with her neighbors at church.
3. My associates and I work for the National Museum.

200 count

Step 03 **1.** 2 **2.** 1 **3.** 4 **4.** 2 **5.** 3 **6.** 4 **7.** 1 **8.** 3

Step 04 **1.** She counted her suits one by one.
2. Honesty doesn't seem to count these days.
3. The count lived in a large castle.
4. He counts it foolish to do so.

Review

A. 01. associate **02.** tear **03.** tongue **04.** tear **05.** count **06.** associate **07.** count **08.** tear **09.** nature **10.** count **11.** associate **12.** nature **13.** tongue **14.** nature **15.** count

B. 01. tongue **02.** associate **03.** nature **04.** associate **05.** tear **06.** nature **07.** tongue **08.** tear **09.** count **10.** associate **11.** tears **12.** count **13.** count **14.** nature **15.** count

수능기출예문 점검

01. 그런 다음 의사는 젊은이가 혀를 내민 채 길거리에 서 있게 하고 사라졌다.

02. 이민자들이 영어를 하지 못하는 것에 초점을 맞추는 대신에 그들이 영어를 배우는 동안에 그들의 모국어에 대한 능력을 유지하도록 장려하는 것이 어떨까?

03. 나는 울고 싶지 않았지만, 눈물이 내 뺨 아래로 흘러내리기 시작했고, 어떤 것도 눈물을 그치게 할 수 없었다.

04. 아래로 흐르는 것이 물의 본성(본질)이다.

05. 그러나 우리가 자연을 면밀하게 관찰하면, 변화와 균형 사이에 끊임없는 긴장이 있음을 발견하게 된다.

06. 태초부터 사람들은 꿈의 불가사의한 성질 때문에, 꿈은 다른 세상으로부터의 메시지라고 믿었다.

07. 웃음은 스트레스 반응과 관련된 호르몬을 줄여 줍니다.

08. 그러고 나서 어머니가 나에게 혼자 세어 보라고 해서 나는 그렇게 했다.

09. 분명히 현대 사회는 인적 재능이 천연 자원보다 훨씬 중요한 새로운 경제 체계로의 중대한 변화에 직면하고 있다.

10. 그날의 수업은 수를 세는 법에 관한 것이었다.

11. 그러나 그가 모든 사람을 기쁘게 해 줄 필요는 없다. 그가 쓴 내용이 진실이라면, 그것이 가장 중요한 것이다.

>>> DAY 21

Group-41

201 engagement

Step 03 **1.** 1 **2.** 3 **3.** 1 **4.** 2 **5.** 3 **6.** 2

Step 04 **1.** He has numerous engagements for next week.
2. Their engagement was announced in the newspapers.
3. Our army had an engagement with the enemy yesterday.

202 character

Step 03 **1.** 3 **2.** 1 **3.** 1 **4.** 2 **5.** 3 **6.** 2

Step 04 **1.** You should consider his obstinate character.
2. He played the character of young prince in that film.
3. Some characters on my typewriter are broken.

203 issue

Step 03 **1.** 2 **2.** 1 **3.** 3 **4.** 2 **5.** 1 **6.** 3

Step 04 **1.** Stamp collectors want to buy new stamps on

the day of issue.

2. The Sunday issue of the newspaper has the comics in color.

3. The main issue we are discussing today is air pollution.

204 physical

Step 03 1. 1 2. 2 3. 3 4. 1 5. 3 6. 2

Step 04 1. Running is one form of physical exercise.

2. The physical world is different from the spiritual world.

3. He majored in physical chemistry at college.

205 bar

Step 03 1. 2 2. 1 3. 3 4. 1 5. 3 6. 2

Step 04 1. The bear tried to break the bars of the cage.

2. She often visits a bar after work.

3. A security guard barred his entrance to the building.

Review

A. 01. engagement 02. character 03. issue 04. physical
05. bar 06. character 07. issue 08. engagement
09. physical 10. issue 11. bar 12. physical
13. engagement 14. character 15. bar

B. 01. character 02. issue 03. bars 04. physical
05. engagement 06. character 07. bar 08. physical
09. issue 10. engagement 11. physical 12. bar
13. characters 14. engagement 15. issue

수능기출예문 점검

01. 그림을 그릴 때 몸 전체를 능동적으로 참여시키기 위해 다음과 같이 시도해 보라. 당신의 손가락을 가지고 공간에 작은 원을 그리며 시작하라.

02. 처음에 그녀는 가장 중요한 인물인 신데렐라 역을 원했다.

03. 고대의 미신에 따르면, 점은 사람의 성격을 나타낸다고 한다.

04. 그러나 우리가 다른 목적으로 제공되는 인공물에 담긴 본문, 글자, 그림을 볼 때 이 표시를 대개 전달 수단을 나타내는 꼬리표로 해석한다.

05. 이번에 구두장이는 인물들 중 한 사람의 해부학적 구조를 비판하기 시작했다.

06. 이러한 나라들이 직면하고 있는 가장 중요한 문제는 문화 간의 차이를 이해하는 것이다.

07. 사실, 경찰은 자격이 있는 사냥꾼들에게만 허가증을 발급하고, 등산객들에게는 사냥철에 밝고 화려한 색의 옷을 입으라고 충고한다.

08. 예를 들어, 소방서장은 절대적으로 명료하게 명령을 내릴 필요가 있다.

09. 검진과 테스트로 얻은 정보는 환자의 전체적인 신체 상태에 대한 중요한 통찰력을 제공한다.

10. 하나의 기술적 변화로 인해, 앞뒤 참조가 가능해졌고 동시에 전집을 소장하기 위해 필요한 물리적 공간이 급격하게 줄어들었다.

11. 대조적으로, 비물질적인 문화는 물질이 아닌 인간의 창조물로 구성되어 있다.

12. 왼쪽의 막대 도표는 그것을 실행하는 비용을 보여 주며 오른쪽 막대 도표는 같은 기간 동안 그 결과로 생긴 절약 비용을 보여 준다.

13. 사람들은 바에서 마실 것을 가져왔고 무리 지어 모였다.

14. 아이들은 스티커나, 별, 막대사탕을 받기 위해서가 아니라 오히려 스스로를 위해 좋은 행동을 하는 것을 배워야 한다.

Group-42

206 domestic

Step 03 1. 3 2. 1 3. 2 4. 3 5. 1 6. 2

Step 04 1. She has a lot of many domestic troubles.

2. This magazine provides more foreign news than domestic news.

3. There are many domestic animals on the farm.

207 raise

Step 03 1. 1 2. 2 3. 3 4. 2 5. 1 6. 3

Step 04 1. The government has no plans to raise taxes at present.

2. She raised her three children by sewing.

3. Our church decided to raise money to help the poor.

208 figure

Step 03 1. 3 2. 1 3. 1 4. 2 5. 3 6. 2

Step 04 1. The boy read the figures accurately.

2. The figure on page 75 shows how a car engine works.

3. He was one of the greatest figures of his age.

209 apply

Step 03 1. 2 2. 3 3. 1 4. 2 5. 1 6. 3

Step 04 1. She applied a bandage to her wound.

2. We can apply his findings to this experiment.

3. He will apply for admission to the university.

210 subject

Step 03 1. 1 2. 2 3. 3 4. 1 5. 3 6. 2

Step 04 1. He likes English best of all subjects.

2. The subject of her study is "Teenage smoking."

3. You should not drop the subject when you write a sentence.

Review

A. 01. figure 02. domestic 03. subject 04. raise
05. subject 06. domestic 07. apply 08. raise
09. figure 10. subject 11. apply 12. domestic
13. figure 14. apply 15. raise

B. 01. apply 02. Raise 03. domestic 04. figure
05. subject 06. raise 07. domestic 08. figure
09. subject 10. apply 11. domestic 12. figures
13. apply 14. subject 15. raise

수능기출예문 점검

01. 예를 들면, 자국의 석유, 천연가스, 혹은 철강 산업은 국가 방위에 중요하기 때문에 보호가 요구된다.

02. 강의가 끝났을 때 한 학생이 손을 들고 물었다.

03. 그러나 몇 분 후에 나는 심해지는 짜증에 그 점을 다시 제기했다.

04. 모든 부모들은 자녀를 도덕성을 잘 갖춘 아이로 양육하기를 바란다.

05. Jim은 아프리카의 가뭄 이재민을 위한 구호기금을 마련하기 위해 100만 달러 이상을 모금했다.

06. 예를 들어, 스포츠에서 다른 사람들과 경쟁을 함으로써 우리는 경기의 수준을 높일 수 있다.

07. 이 수치는 영화 Fishermen이 벌어들인 금액보다 불과 1백만 달러 적은 것이었다.

08. 만약 독자들이 작가가 의도하는 바를 이해하는 데 시간을 소비해야 한다면, 그들은 참을 수 없어 할 것이다.

09. 그러한 경우에 당신은 판매 가격이 얼마인지를 계산해야 한다.

10. 그러므로 사람들은 현대 예술에 흥미를 잃어버리고 자신의 역할 모델을 찾기 위해서 스포츠 스타나 다른 대중적인 인물들에게로 돌아섰다.

11. 그림 A와 B는 이슬점 습도계로 이슬점이 어떻게 측정되는지를 보여 준다.

12. 하지만 슬프게도 우리가 어른이 되었을 때 이 규칙들을 가족생활과 일이나 정부에 적용하지 않는다.

13. 여러분 중 많은 사람들이 이 프로그램에 지원하기를 바랍니다.

14. 학생들이 요구받아야 할 유일한 일은 중·고등학교 재학기간 동안 폭넓은 범위의 교과(학과)를 공부하는 것이다.

15. 그러나 피실험자들이 갑작스러운 소음이 발생할 것이라는 점을 예측할 수 있거나 소음을 "비상벨"로 중단시킬 수 있었을 때, 그러한 부정적인 효과는 사라졌다.

16. 반면에, 특정한 관심사에 관한 잡지들은 주로 한 가지 특정한 주제만을 다룬다

>>> DAY 22

Group-43

211 volume

Step 03 **1.** 2 **2.** 1 **3.** 2 **4.** 3 **5.** 1 **6.** 3

Step 04 **1.** I have an encyclopedia in 10 volumes.
2. She wants to buy a refrigerator with great volume.
3. The singer has a voice of great volume.

212 state

Step 03 **1.** 2 **2.** 3 **3.** 1 **4.** 3 **5.** 2 **6.** 1

Step 04 **1.** He stated his frank opinion on the plan.
2. The state of his business is getting worse.
3. The United States of America is made up of fifty states.

213 object

Step 03 **1.** 1 **2.** 2 **3.** 1 **4.** 3 **5.** 2 **6.** 3

Step 04 **1.** He saw a strange object in the sky.
2. Her main object in life was to become famous.
3. He objects to being treated like a child.

214 current

Step 03 **1.** 1 **2.** 3 **3.** 2 **4.** 3 **5.** 1 **6.** 2

Step 04 **1.** I want to buy the current issue of this magazine.
2. This meter is used in measuring electric current.

3. He wants to know the current of public opinion on the matter.

215 odd

Step 03 **1.** 3 **2.** 1 **3.** 2 **4.** 1 **5.** 3 **6.** 2

Step 04 **1.** She is wearing very odd clothes.
2. A box of odd socks was kept in the laundry room.
3. The houses with odd numbers are on the left side of the street.

Review

A. 01. state **02.** object **03.** odd **04.** volume **05.** current **06.** state **07.** object **08.** state **09.** volume **10.** odd **11.** object **12.** current **13.** odd **14.** current **15.** volume

B. 01. state **02.** odd **03.** object **04.** volume **05.** object **06.** volume **07.** state **08.** current **09.** odd **10.** odd **11.** current **12.** object **13.** volumes **14.** state **15.** current

수능기출예문 점검

01. 환경 심리학자들은 예측할 수 없는 큰 소리로 발생하는 소음의 해로운 영향을 오랫동안 알아 왔다.

02. 만약 개인이 스스로 고독이 단지 마음의 상태라는 것을 확신하지 않으면 어떤 지속적인 결과도 얻을 수 없다.

03. 그들은 대학에 다니기 위한 국가 보조금을 받으며, 실직하면 국가 시행 프로그램에 참여한다.

04. 그리고 "당신은 그렇게 많은 단어로 그 의미가 무엇인지 표현할 수 있는가?" 이 질문에 대한 나의 대답은 "아니오."일 것이다.

05. 최고 수준의 전설적인 녹음은 세계적으로 유명한 예술가들과 오케스트라를 특징으로 합니다.

06. 평영의 규칙은 두 팔이 물 밑에서 함께 당겨져야 하고, 그런 다음 동시에 다음번 팔젓기를 시작하기 위해서 당기는 자세의 출발로 돌아와야 한다고 진술했다.

07. 현대 세계에서 거의 모든 나라가 다른 가치 있는 물건과 교환하기 위한 수단으로 동전이나 지폐를 사용한다.

08. 어떤 집단이 다른 집단과 접촉을 더 많이 하면 할수록, 사물이나 사상이 교환될 가능성이 더 많다.

09. 사람들은 우리를 방해하거나 화나게 할 수도 있지만, 모든 사람이 그들의 행동에 반대하지는 않는다는 사실은 아마 문제가 우리에게 있을 수 있다는 것을 가리킨다.

10. 그것들은 완전히 북태평양 해류를 따라 떠다녔고, 결국에는 Sitka로 되돌아갔다.

11. 하지만, 여전히 발전의 여지가 많이 있으며, 현재 우리의 어떤 시 잡지에도 출판을 하기에는 아직 적절하지 않다고 생각합니다.

12. 그녀는 물의 흐름을 따라 쓸려 가면서 느껴지는 맑고 풍요로운 느낌이 좋았다.

13. 아리스토텔레스는 오늘날 물리학자들이 이상하고 재미있게 생각하는 하나의 총체적인 물리학 이론을 펼쳤다.

216 barometer

Step 03   **1.** 1   **2.** 2   **3.** 1   **4.** 2

Step 04   **1.** A barometer shows how the weather changes.
2. The weight of one's body is called a barometer of one's health.

217 minute

Step 03   **1.** 3   **2.** 2   **3.** 1   **4.** 3   **5.** 1   **6.** 2

Step 04   **1.** Boil the eggs for three minutes.
2. The chairman read the minutes of the last meeting.
3. He gave me minute instructions of the machine.

218 express

Step 03   **1.** 1   **2.** 2   **3.** 3   **4.** 1   **5.** 3   **6.** 2

Step 04   **1.** She is still unable to express herself in English.
2. Luckily I managed to get on the express train to London.
3. How long will it take if I send this letter by express?

219 rear

Step 03   **1.** 1   **2.** 2   **3.** 1   **4.** 3   **5.** 2   **6.** 3

Step 04   **1.** There was a garden at the rear of the church.
2. She is very concerned about rearing her children.
3. The mountain rears its top above the clouds.

220 deal

Step 03   **1.** 3   **2.** 1   **3.** 2   **4.** 4   **5.** 1   **6.** 4   **7.** 2   **8.** 3

Step 04   **1.** We have made a deal to buy the building.
2. This paper deals with methods of teaching English.
3. Judy spent a great deal of money on a new car.
4. The man will deal six cards to each player.

Review

A. 01. rear   **02.** express   **03.** deal   **04.** minute   **05.** barometer
06. express   **07.** deal   **08.** minutes   **09.** rear
10. barometer   **11.** express   **12.** deal   **13.** rear   **14.** deal
15. minute

B. 01. express   **02.** deal   **03.** minutes   **04.** barometer
05. express   **06.** rear   **07.** deal   **08.** barometer
09. express   **10.** deal   **11.** rears   **12.** minutes   **13.** rear
14. minute   **15.** deals

수능기출예문 점검

01. 불면증으로 고생하는 사람들은 잠자리에 들기 전에 따뜻한 물에서 15분 정도 있으면 큰 도움을 받을 수 있다.
02. 그녀는 주위의 관객을 방해하지 않으려고 "곧 괜찮아질 거예요."라고 낮은 목소리로 말했다.
03. 분위기는 얘기와 웃음소리로 활기찼고, 시간이 흐를수록 더 편안해졌다.
04. 네. 그러면 그녀에게 속달로 한 장 보내 달라고 해 주세요.
05. 한 가지 중요한 사교 능력은 사람들이 그들 자신의 감정을 얼마나 잘 표현하는가 혹은 못하는가 하는 것이다.

06. 수십 년 동안, 아이 양육에 대한 전문가들의 충고는 밤 시간에 아이를 부모로부터 분리하는 것을 장려해 왔다.
07. 반면에, 특정한 관심사에 관한 잡지들은 주로 한 가지 특정한 주제만을 다룬다.
08. 과학과 기술은 19세기 후반 이후 상당히 많이 변했다
09. W: 어린이는 얼마인가요? M: 나이에 따라 다릅니다. 몇 살이죠? W: 열 살인데요. M: 그러면 50% 할인이 됩니다. 그러니까 댁의 아이는 3달러가 됩니다. W: 그거 좋군요. [이익이 되는 거래, 싸고 좋게 산 것]

>>> DAY 23

221 content

Step 03   **1.** 1   **2.** 2   **3.** 2   **4.** 1

Step 04   **1.** A customs official will examine the contents of your baggage.
2. John is very content with his life at present.

222 move

Step 03   **1.** 1   **2.** 3   **3.** 2   **4.** 1   **5.** 2   **6.** 3

Step 04   **1.** He moved his desk nearer to the window.
2. We moved into a bigger office yesterday.
3. The singer moved the audience to tears.

223 compose

Step 03   **1.** 2   **2.** 3   **3.** 1   **4.** 2   **5.** 3   **6.** 1

Step 04   **1.** The United States is composed of fifty states.
2. Mozart began to compose when he was six years old.
3. She was not able to compose herself for a while at the news.

224 account

Step 03   **1.** 1   **2.** 2   **3.** 3   **4.** 2   **5.** 1   **6.** 3

Step 04   **1.** Her salary is paid directly into her bank account.
2. The man gave us a vivid account of his adventure.
3. You have to account for your absence yesterday.

225 mean

Step 03   **1.** 4   **2.** 1   **3.** 3   **4.** 2   **5.** 4   **6.** 3   **7.** 1   **8.** 2

Step 04   **1.** What do you mean by saying that?
2. He is rather mean over money matter.
3. 5 is the mean number between 3 and 7.
4. Thoughts are expressed by means of words.

Review

A. 01. account   **02.** mean   **03.** move   **04.** compose
05. content   **06.** move   **07.** mean   **08.** content
09. move   **10.** compose   **11.** mean   **12.** account
13. means   **14.** account   **15.** compose

B. 01. account **02.** content **03.** move **04.** means
05. compose **06.** accounts **07.** composed **08.** mean
09. move **10.** account **11.** compose **12.** moves
13. contents **14.** mean **15.** means

수능기출예문 점검

01. 그러나 그는 자신의 수확량에 만족하지 않았고, 이웃 농부의 곡식을 훔쳤다.

02. 예를 들어, 금붕어 어항은 내용물을 확대해 보여 주기 때문에, 꽃송이나 꽃잎으로 채워지면 멋져 보인다.

03. 어제 오빠가 이사하는 것을 돕다가 허리를 다친 것 같아.

04. 시는 우리를 감동시켜서 시인 자신의 감정이나 시인의 상상력에 의해 만들어진 사람들의 감정에 공감하도록 한다.

05. 이 단체의 소명은 국가와 세계를 사회적, 인종적, 경제적 정의로 이동시키는[이끄는] 것이다.

06. 그러나 무엇보다도, 어떤 종류의 음악에 의해 감동받지 않는 사람은 거의 있을 수가 없다.

07. 오늘날 물리학자들은 "그것은 터무니없는 생각이다. 움직이는 사물은 어떤 힘이 그것을 멈추기 위해 사용되지 않는 한 계속 움직인다."라고 말한다.

08. 좀 더 상세히 분석을 해 보면, "떠오르는" 국가들은 서로서로 아주 다를 뿐 아니라, 수많은 독특한 개인들과 공동체들로 구성되어 있다.

09. 사실, 사람들은 공격적 성향이나, 수동적 태도 따위의 성격 요인을 설명하는데 출생 순서를 사용해 왔습니다.

10. 보내 주신 수표는 정확히 입금되었으며, 귀하의 계좌는 지불 완납으로 표시되었습니다.

11. 그는 여러 해에 걸쳐 '일기'를 썼는데, 사실 그것은 가끔씩 쓴 기록으로, 상인으로서의 생활과 가족생활에 관한 이야기를 쓴 것이다.

12. 오른쪽 눈썹 위의 점은 그가 금전 운이 있을 것이고 성공적인 직업을 가질 것임을 의미한다.

13. 일 또한 화를 가라앉히고 넘쳐나는 에너지를 사용하는 데 효과적인 방법이다.

14. 더욱이, 텔레비전 수상기는 수수한 생활수준으로 인해 특히 1930년대와 1940년대에 사치스러운 상품을 취득할 수 없었던 일반 대중의 수입을 넘어서서 가격이 매겨져 있었다.

15. 그러나 최근 몇 년 동안, 생물학자들은 이러한 기술을 이용해서 더 주의 깊게 귀를 기울일 수 있었고, 비록 우리가 들을 수는 없지만 기린이 의사소통을 한다는 것을 알아냈다.

Group-46

226 constitution

`Step 03` **1.** 2 **2.** 1 **3.** 3 **4.** 1 **5.** 2 **6.** 3

`Step 04` **1.** The teacher explained the physical constitution of the sun.
   2. She has a strong constitution and is seldom sick.
   3. The Korean constitution guarantees that the people have certain rights.

227 complex

`Step 03` **1.** 2 **2.** 1 **3.** 3 **4.** 2 **5.** 3 **6.** 1

`Step 04` **1.** Photosynthesis is a highly complex process.
   2. The leisure complex includes a golf course, a swimming pool, tennis court, a library, etc.
   3. My father has a complex against foreigners.

228 file

`Step 03` **1.** 2 **2.** 1 **3.** 3 **4.** 2 **5.** 3 **6.** 1

`Step 04` **1.** Please file these letters in order by date.
   2. The soldiers filed across the road.
   3. The worker used a file to rub off the sharp edges.

229 alternative

`Step 03` **1.** 1 **2.** 2 **3.** 2 **4.** 1

`Step 04` **1.** He offered the alternative plans of having a picnic or visiting a museum.
   2. The alternative of surrender is death.

230 strike

`Step 03` **1.** 1 **2.** 3 **3.** 2 **4.** 1 **5.** 4 **6.** 3 **7.** 4 **8.** 2

`Step 04` **1.** The speaker struck the table with his fist.
   2. The angry bear may strike the hunter.
   3. The workers decided to strike for higher wages.
   4. A good idea struck him as he was reading the newspaper.

Review

A. 01. complex **02.** constitution **03.** alternative
04. strike **05.** constitution **06.** file **07.** alternative
8. strike **9.** complex **10.** file **11.** constitution
12. strike **13.** complex **14.** file **15.** strike

B. 01. strike **02.** constitution **03.** files **04.** alternative
05. file **06.** strike **07.** constitution **08.** strike **09.** file
10. complex **11.** alternative **12.** complex **13.** strike
14. constitution **15.** complex

수능기출예문 점검

01. 텔레비전 시청은 복잡한 정신 활동을 요구하지 않는다.

02. 이 결과, 국제 정치는 여러 문명권의 국가들과 관계를 맺게 되어 더욱 복잡해지고 있다.

03. 알아. 하지만 네가 보내준 파일[자료]을 열 수가 없었어. 암호가 먹히지를 않았어.

04. 예를 들어, 사용할 수 있는 돈 25달러를 가지고 있다고 가정하고, 당신의 선택을 교과서나 데이트로 좁혀 보자.

05. 반대로, 그것이 강아지의 씹는 장난감이라고 들은 학생들은 그것의 다른[대안의] 용도를 발견하지 못했다.

06. 돌은 다만 외부의 힘이 그것이 행동하도록 하는 대로 행할 수 있을 뿐이다. 돌과는 달리 사람은 혼자서 행동을 시작할 수 있다. 따라서 그 차이는 돌은 가능성에 대해 인식하지 못한다는 것이고, 반면에 인간은 진정한 양자택일의 문제에 직면해 있다는 것을 인식하고 있다는 것이다.

07. 어떤 의미에서 내가 기억했지만 아주 최근까지 나에게 이상하거나 흥미로운 것으로 다가오지 않았던[나의 머리에 떠오르지 않았던] 일들이 있다.

08. 이것은 두 손바닥을 서로 반복적으로 맞부딪침으로써 동의한다는 것을 나타내는 간단한 동작입니다.

09. 그들은 종종 광고 대행사에서도 일하는데, 그곳에서 그들은 인상적인 그림과 멋진 디자인을 만들어 낸다.

10. 쇠는 달았을 때 쳐라. (기회를 놓치지 마라.)

>>> DAY 24

231 decline

Step 03	**1.** 1 **2.** 2 **3.** 1 **4.** 2
Step 04	**1.** She politely declined the invitation to dinner.
	2. The birth rate has been declining for some years.

232 range

Step 03　**1.** 1　**2.** 2　**3.** 1　**4.** 3　**5.** 2　**6.** 3

Step 04　**1.** That sound was beyond the range of human hearing.

2. They saw a range of mountains in the distance.

3. The officer ranged his men along the river bank.

233 bond

Step 03　**1.** 1　**2.** 3　**3.** 2　**4.** 2　**5.** 1　**6.** 3

Step 04　**1.** There is a strong bond between the two brothers.

2. She tried to break the bonds of convention.

3. The company will sell bonds to raise money.

234 yield

Step 03　**1.** 1　**2.** 3　**3.** 2　**4.** 2　**5.** 3　**6.** 1

Step 04　**1.** This business will yield a lot of profits.

2. What's the annual yield of this mine?

3. He is not a man to yield to such a threat.

235 even

Step 03　**1.** 3　**2.** 4　**3.** 1　**4.** 2　**5.** 3　**6.** 1　**7.** 2　**8.** 4

Step 04　**1.** A billiard-table must be perfectly even.

2. The pages on the left side of a book usually have even numbers.

3. Even a child can understand this book.

4. My dog is even bigger than yours.

Review

A. 01. yield　**02.** range　**03.** even　**04.** bond　**05.** decline　**06.** bond　**07.** yield　**08.** even　**09.** range　**10.** bond　**11.** even　**12.** range　**13.** even　**14.** decline　**15.** yield

B. 01. even　**02.** yield　**03.** decline　**04.** bond　**05.** even　**06.** range　**07.** declines　**08.** bonds　**09.** yield　**10.** even　**11.** range　**12.** bonds　**13.** Even　**14.** range　**15.** yields

수능기출예문 점검

01. 금년에 그 숫자는 더 급격한 감소 추세를 보이리라 예상된다.

02. 거기에 그것이 (내게) 웃으며 (나를) 초대하는 것처럼 내 앞에 있었다. 그러니 누구라도 그런 초대를 거절하는 것은 어려웠다.

03. 총생산의 증가율은 1960～1969년 기간부터 1980～1989년 기간까지 감소했다.

04. 그것들은 매우 천천히 자라며 높이는 15～40피트 범위에 이른다.

05. 초저주파 음은 저음역의 소리로, 그 저주파는 인간의 가청 영역보다 훨씬 낮다.

06. 남성복은 앞으로 계속 일하는 장소에 따라 약간씩 그리고 좁은 범위 내에서 바뀔 것이다.

07. 텔레비전에서 묘사되는 세상을 두려워하여, 사람들은 가까운 가족들과 함께 그들의 가정에 머물면서 그들의 이웃들과 유대를 형성하지 않는다.

08. 카페인을 없애는 모든 과정은 화학약품이건 물로 하건 카페인과의 결합을 끊기 위해 녹색 콩에 증기를 쐬는 것부터 시작한다.

09. 푸른 나무들은 이웃 사람들이 자연스럽게 모일 수 있는 곳을 만들고, 궁극적으로 공동체 내에 보다 강한 유대를 만들어 낸다.

10. 개간된 토양은 미네랄과 영양분이 풍부하였고 상당한 (농작물) 산출량을 제공했다.

11. 돼지 한 마리는 교환에 있어 다섯 마리의 닭의 가치가 있었을 것이고, 일주일의 노동은 염소 한 마리의 이익을 만들었을 것이고 등등이다.

12. 오늘 나는 운전 중 행동요령에 대해 말씀드리고 싶습니다. 첫째, 항상 교통 신호를 지키십시오. 둘째, 과속하지 마십시오. 마지막으로, 다른 운전자에게 양보하십시오.

13. 말이란 행동이 의미한다고 사람들이 생각하는 행동의 종류의 관점에서는 다양한 해석을 낳을 수 있다.

14. 첫째, 농업은 새로운 종류의 기술을 사용함에 따라 훨씬 더 효율적이 될 것이다.

15. 사람들은 그들의 첫인상이 잘못된 것일지라도 그것에 집착하는 경향이 있다.

16. 그러나 사람의 기억력이 긴 시간이 경과한 후에(조차)도 훨씬 더 날카로워지는 일 또한 일어날 수 있다.

236 spell

Step 03　**1.** 1　**2.** 3　**3.** 2　**4.** 1　**5.** 3　**6.** 2

Step 04　**1.** The child couldn't spell his name correctly.

2. The witch's spell turned a prince into a frog.

3. After a brief spell in the country he returned home.

237 column

Step 03　**1.** 3　**2.** 1　**3.** 2　**4.** 1　**5.** 3　**6.** 2

Step 04　**1.** She admired at the carved columns in the temple.

2. He likes reading the sport column of the newspaper.

3. I added up the numbers in each column separately.

238 observe

Step 03　**1.** 1　**2.** 2　**3.** 1　**4.** 3　**5.** 2　**6.** 3

Step 04　**1.** I observed her steal out of the room.

2. Please observe the safety rules during take-off

or landing.

    3. Our teacher observed that we all passed the final exam.

239 complimentary

`Step 03` **1.** 2　**2.** 1　**3.** 2　**4.** 1

`Step 04` **1.** My teacher made some very complimentary remarks about my research paper.

2. The restaurant owner gave him a complimentary glass of wine.

240 capital

`Step 03` **1.** 1　**2.** 3　**3.** 4　**4.** 1　**5.** 2　**6.** 4　**7.** 2　**8.** 3

`Step 04` **1.** Each state of the United States has a capital.

2. Write your name and address in capitals.

3. You will need more capital to start a new business.

4. We visited Paris and other capital cities last week.

Review

A. 01. observe　**02.** spell　**03.** capital　**04.** column
    05. observe　**06.** capital　**07.** spell　**08.** column
    09. complimentary　**10.** capital　**11.** spell
    12. complimentary　**13.** observe　**14.** capital　**15.** column

B. 01. capital　**02.** column　**03.** spell　**04.** complimentary
    05. observe　**06.** column　**07.** capital　**08.** spell
    09. observe　**10.** complimentary　**11.** spell　**12.** capital
    13. column　**14.** observed　**15.** capital

수능기출예문 점검

01. 그는 이러한 형태의 경쟁에서 가장 길고 가장 두꺼운 목을 가진 수컷들이 보통 이긴다는 것을 관찰했다.

02. 오늘 나는 운전 중 행동요령에 대해 말씀드리고 싶습니다. 첫째, 항상 교통 신호를 지키십시오.

03. 대신에, 아이는 의식, 사냥, 축제, 경작, 그리고 추수와 같은 활동에서 어른들을 관찰하고 흉내 냄으로써 문화유산을 습득한다.

04. 예술품의 구경꾼이 되는 것과 진정한 관찰자가 되는 것에는 큰 차이가 있다.

05. 당신의 편지를 받자마자, 저는 서둘러 사전에서 flattering[아첨하는]이라는 단어를 찾았습니다. 저는 그것이 부정적인 것을 암시할 수도 있다는 것을 알게 되어 깜짝 놀랐는데, 이는 정말로 제가 의도한 바가 아니었습니다. 저는 complimentary[경의를 표하는]와 같은 단어를 대신 사용했었어야 했습니다.

06. 어떤 사람들은 한 국가와 다른 국가 사이의 상품이나 용역의 수입 또는 수출에 관여하고 있다. 다른 이들은 자본을 한 지역에서 다른 지역으로 이동시키기를 원한다.

07. 이곳은 지금 네팔의 수도이며 네팔의 정치, 경제, 문화의 중심지이다.

08. 그 정도 돈을 모으는 것은 벤처기업자본의 흐름이 고갈되었기 때문에 사업 경력이 없는 사람에게는 어렵다.

`Group-49`

241 appearance

`Step 03` **1.** 3　**2.** 2　**3.** 1　**4.** 2　**5.** 1　**6.** 3

`Step 04` **1.** He made a brief appearance at the party and then left.

2. We have changed the whole appearance of the building recently.

3. Appearances have suddenly turned in our favor.

242 credit

`Step 03` **1.** 2　**2.** 1　**3.** 3　**4.** 1　**5.** 2　**6.** 3

`Step 04` **1.** I can't give credit to her statement.

2. Nowadays almost everything can be purchased on credit.

3. I earned three credits in German this semester.

243 utter

`Step 03` **1.** 1　**2.** 1　**3.** 2　**4.** 2

`Step 04` **1.** That new play was an utter success.

2. He didn't utter a word all night.

244 cast

`Step 03` **1.** 2　**2.** 1　**3.** 3　**4.** 2　**5.** 1　**6.** 3

`Step 04` **1.** The fisherman cast his net into the water.

2. A cast reception will be held after the performance.

3. The hot metal was poured into a cast.

245 term

`Step 03` **1.** 1　**2.** 4　**3.** 2　**4.** 3　**5.** 4　**6.** 2　**7.** 1　**8.** 3

`Step 04` **1.** When does his term commence exactly?

2. There are many legal terms in this book.

3. She has been on bad terms with her father for years.

4. He was employed on favorable terms.

Review

A. 01. cast　**02.** appearance　**03.** term　**04.** cast　**05.** credit
    06. appearance　**07.** term　**08.** utter　**09.** credit
    10. terms　**11.** appearances　**12.** utter　**13.** credit
    14. terms　**15.** cast

B. 01. term　**02.** cast　**03.** appearance　**04.** utter　**05.** credit
    06. terms　**07.** cast　**08.** credits　**09.** terms　**10.** utter
    11. appearance　**12.** cast　**13.** credit　**14.** terms
    15. Appearances

수능기출예문 점검

01. 심리학자들에 따르면, 여러분의 신체적 외모는 첫인상의 55%를 차지한다고 한다.

02. 이 영화제의 마지막 행사는 수상자들 모두가 모습을 보임으로써 주목을 받았다.

03. 당신이 보내 주신 수표는 정확히 입금 처리[대변에 기재]되었으며, 귀하의 계좌는 지불 완납으로 표시되었습니다.

04. W: 틀림없이 금년은 정말로 만족스럽군요. 작년에는 꼴등으로 마무리했는데, 금년에는 결승전에 진출할 거잖아요.
M: 대단한 한 해였어요. 하지만 우리 팀의 새로운 소유주는 훌륭한 코치를 영입한 점에 대해 많은 칭찬을 받을 만해요.

05. 당신이 새 드라마에서 중요한 배역을 맡게 될 거라고 말하더군.

06. 부모들은 우리의 삶에 오랜 그림자를 드리우고 있으며, 우리는 유아기 때 부모의 존재를 인식하게 된다.

07. Paul Ekman은 어떤 감정이 언제 적절하게 표현될 수 있는지에 대한 사회적인 합의에 대해 '표현 규칙'이라는 용어를 사용한다.

08. 실질적 관점에서 그것을 소수의 집단과 개인의 권리를 존중하는 다수의 통치로 정의하는 것이 더 정확하다.

09. 유일한 장기적인 해결책은 농촌 지역의 생활을 더 매력적으로 만드는 것인데, 그 이유는 그것이 사람들을 농촌 지역에 머물도록 장려할 것이기 때문이다.

10. 나이를 기준으로[나이에 의하여] 사회 집단을 설명하고자 한다면 우리는 유년기, 청년기, 장년기, 노년기라는 4개의 연령 집단을 제시할 것이다.

Group-50

246 critical

| Step 03 | **1.** 1 **2.** 2 **3.** 1 **4.** 3 **5.** 2 **6.** 3 |

| Step 04 | **1.** The reviewer published his critical comments on art in the magazine. |
2. He is always very critical of his daughter's hair style.
3. Parental attention is very critical to the child's socialization.

247 desert

| Step 03 | **1.** 1 **2.** 3 **3.** 2 **4.** 1 **5.** 3 **6.** 2 |

| Step 04 | **1.** Camels are very useful in the desert. |
2. A soldier who deserts is punished.
3. He was rewarded according to his deserts.

248 correspond

| Step 03 | **1.** 2 **2.** 1 **3.** 3 **4.** 2 **5.** 1 **6.** 3 |

| Step 04 | **1.** His actions do not correspond with his words. |
2. The engine of a car corresponds to the heart of a man.
3. I correspond regularly with a friend in London.

249 sentence

| Step 03 | **1.** 2 **2.** 1 **3.** 2 **4.** 1 |

| Step 04 | **1.** The first word in a sentence always begins with a capital letter. |
2. The murderer was sentenced to death.

250 scale

| Step 03 | **1.** 4 **2.** 1 **3.** 3 **4.** 2 **5.** 4 **6.** 1 **7.** 2 **8.** 3 |

| Step 04 | **1.** She scraped the scales off the fish. |
2. The clerk weighed the parcel on the scales.
3. The girl practiced her scales on the piano.

---

4. They decided to reduce the scale of the business.

Review

A. 01. sentence **02.** critical **03.** correspond **04.** scale
05. desert **06.** scale **07.** desert **08.** correspond
09. sentence **10.** desert **11.** scale **12.** critical
13. scale **14.** correspond **15.** critical

B. 01. desert **02.** scales **03.** sentence **04.** corresponds
05. desert **06.** critical **07.** scale **08.** sentence
09. corresponds **10.** critical **11.** scales
12. correspond **13.** critical **14.** scales **15.** desert

수능기출예문 점검

01. 아마 당신이 그 두 집단에서 다른 정도의 비판적인 면밀한 검토를 기대했기 때문일 것이다.

02. 많은 사람들은 그들이 관계를 맺고 있는 사람과 똑같지는 않더라도, 비슷한 신념과 가치관을 공유하는 것이 매우 중요하다고 생각한다.

03. 그러다가 예술가들의 초상을 완비한 1568년에 발행된 개정판 〈생애〉에서 그는 전기적인 일화들을 비판적인 언급과 결합시켰다.

04. 당신이 사막을 가로질러 운전을 하고 있다고 가정해 보자.

05. 나는 마을을 유심히 본다. 움직임의 모습은 없다. 마을 전체가 황량해 보인다.

06. 따라서 유럽의 good이라는 등급은 미국 체계의 20에 일치하며, fine은 30에, very fine은 40에, extremely fine은 50에, 그리고 almost perfect는 60에 일치한다.

07. 나는 당신이 우리들의 서신 왕래의 결과로 어떤 식으로든 더 이상 감정이 상하시거나 불편함을 느끼지 않으시기를 바랍니다.

08. 당신은 이 두 문장을 이해하기 위해 경찰관과 슈퍼맨에 대한 배경 지식을 사용하기 때문에 그것을[해답을] 알게 되는 것이다.

09. 지구의 크기는 변하지 않았지만, 인간의 활동규모는 상당히 증가해 왔다.

10. M: 이 소포를 LA에 보내고 싶습니다. W: 알겠습니다. 저울 위에 올려놓으세요. 무게가 10파운드입니다. 어떻게 보내실 건가요?

11. 이것들은 실물 크기의 모델이다. 그것들은 인간과 동일한 무게가 나가고 팔과 다리는 인간과 동일한 동작을 한다.

>>> DAY 26

Group-51

251 converse

| Step 03 | **1.** 2 **2.** 1 **3.** 2 **4.** 1 |

| Step 04 | **1.** He sat next to Judy and conversed with her on the subject. |
2. I think the converse of what she just said is true.

252 vice

| Step 03 | **1.** 3 **2.** 2 **3.** 1 **4.** 3 **5.** 2 **6.** 1 |

| Step 04 | **1.** He has the vice of continual lying. |
2. He used the vice to hold that object firmly.

3. Mike was elected as the vice-captain of our
   team.

253 organ
Step 03 **1.** 1 **2.** 2 **3.** 1 **4.** 3 **5.** 2 **6.** 3
Step 04 **1.** Pipe organs is more expensive than electric
   organs.
2. The heart is one of the most important organs.
3. He didn't believe the news he read in the
   organ of the ruling party.

254 page
Step 03 **1.** 3 **2.** 1 **3.** 2 **4.** 1 **5.** 3 **6.** 2
Step 04 **1.** Write your name on the top of the first page.
2. Tony has worked as a page at that hotel since
   last month.
3. She couldn't see Mr. Smith at the airport, so
   she had him paged.

255 school
Step 03 **1.** 2 **2.** 4 **3.** 1 **4.** 4 **5.** 3 **6.** 2 **7.** 1 **8.** 3
Step 04 **1.** My school is between the library and the
   museum.
2. School begins at 8:30 every morning.
3. It is a wonderful thing to see a school of
   dolphins.
4. Zeno, the Greek philosopher, founded the
   Stoic school.

Review

A. **01.** organ **02.** school **03.** page **04.** school
05. converse **06.** vice **07.** organ **08.** vice **09.** page
10. school **11.** organ **12.** vice **13.** page **14.** school
15. converse
B. **01.** vice **02.** organ **03.** page **04.** school **05.** converse
06. organ **07.** school **08.** page **09.** vice **10.** school
11. page **12.** converse **13.** school **14.** organ **15.** vice

수능기출예문 점검

01. 그녀는 오르간을 연주하고 시 쓰는 것을 즐겼습니다.
02. 사람들이 파피루스처럼 펼쳐지는 것보다 넘겨질 수 있는 페이지를 가진
책을 제본하기 시작했을 때, 정보를 찾는 과정이 변했다.
03. 그 결과 그들은 학교의 개선과 학생들의 배움에 더 많이 기여하게 될 것
이다.
04. 호수에서는 작은 입 배스가 종종 수면 가까이에 떼 지어 몰려드는데, 그
것은 한 마리를 잡으면 한 무리를 잡을 수 있다는 것을 의미한다.
   * school up (물고기 따위가) 수면 가까이 몰려들다
05. 재학 기간은 학생들이 자신들의 강점을 발전시킬 기간이어야 하는데, 그
이유는 오늘날의 세계가 만능인이 아닌 전문인을 요구하기 때문이다.

Group-52

256 certain
Step 03 **1.** 2 **2.** 1 **3.** 2 **4.** 1

Step 04 **1.** Chris is certain to join us.
   (=It is certain that Chris will join us.)
2. Certain plants will not grow in this region.

257 cell
Step 03 **1.** 1 **2.** 3 **3.** 2 **4.** 2 **5.** 3 **6.** 1
Step 04 **1.** The cell will split up many pieces.
2. The criminal was imprisoned in a cell
   immediately.
3. Sollar cells will generate electricity directly
   when struck by sun light.

258 channel
Step 03 **1.** 2 **2.** 1 **3.** 2 **4.** 3 **5.** 1 **6.** 3
Step 04 **1.** An interesting documentary is about to start
   on Channel 7.
2. We had to fly or sail to cross the English
   Channel to France.
3. He got the information through official channels.

259 beam
Step 03 **1.** 2 **2.** 3 **3.** 2 **4.** 1 **5.** 3 **6.** 1
Step 04 **1.** These steel beams will be used for building a
   ship.
2. He saw a single beam of light radiated from
   the lighthouse.
3. This new transmitter will beam radio waves all
   over the country.

260 cover
Step 03 **1.** 3 **2.** 1 **3.** 2 **4.** 4 **5.** 1 **6.** 2 **7.** 4 **8.** 3
Step 04 **1.** She will cover the table with a white cloth.
2. When the shooting began, the soldiers ran for
   cover quickly.
3. Professor A's lectures did not cover the
   subject thoroughly.
4. Our company will cover all the expenses.

Review

A. **01.** cell **02.** channel **03.** cover **04.** beam **05.** cover
06. certain **07.** cell **08.** channel **09.** cover **10.** beam
11. certain **12.** cover **13.** beam **14.** channel **15.** cell
B. **01.** channels **02.** cell **03.** cover **04.** cell **05.** beams
06. cover **07.** channel **08.** certain **09.** cover
10. beam **11.** channel **12.** cover **13.** certain **14.** cell
15. beam

수능기출예문 점검

01. 왜 먹거나 번식하는 것과 같은 일부 활동들은 모든 유기체에 공통되지만,
둥지를 짓는 것과 같은 다른 활동들은 어떤 특정한 종들에만 제한될까?
02. 가장 중요한 것은 회사의 기밀이 안전하게 지켜지는지를 확인할 수 있는
[확실히 할 수 있는] 방법을 가지고 있어야 한다는 것이다.
03. 인간의 경우, 인체 내부의 세포들이 계속적으로 대체되는 것에 반해 인
체의 모양과 크기는 상대적으로 항상성을 유지한다.
04. 이와 유사하게, 연료전지가 자동차 엔진으로 선택 가능할 때, 내연기관의

효율성을 높이는 데 초점을 맞추는 자동차 회사들은 자신들이 뒤쳐져 있다는 것을 알게 될 수도 있다.

05. 오늘 밤에 그의 건너편에 있는 소녀가 밝게 미소를 지으며 그것을 끼고 있었다.

06. 7대의 위성이 100여 개 나라에 그 행사를 중계했다.

07. 무수한 다양한 품종의 야생화 수십 그루가 길 양편으로 땅을 덮고 있다.

08. M: 손님, 도와드릴까요?
W: 매트리스 덮개[커버]와 어울리는 담요를 찾고 있어요.

09. 출발하기 전에, 당신은 당신의 관광 담당자에게 여행기간을 포함하는 보험증권의 사본을 제출하도록 요구받을 것이다.

10. 음악은 감정의 전 범위를 아우른다[다룬다]. 그것은 우리를 기쁘게 혹은 슬프게, 무기력하게 혹은 기운 넘치게 만들 수 있으며 어떤 음악은 그 밖의 모든 것을 잊을 때까지 마음을 압도할 수 있다.

11. 만약 그렇지 않다면 당신은 식사, 교통비, 숙박비 같은 기본 경비를 충당하기 위해 비상금을 사용해야만 할 것이고, 갑작스러운 계획 변경에 따른 예기치 않은 상황에서 지출하게 될 돈이 줄어들 것이다.

12. 귀하는 소개서에서 문학을 직업으로 삼고 싶다는 점을 언급하고 있습니다.

>>> DAY 27 

Group-53

261 drill

Step 03 **1.** 1 **2.** 2 **3.** 2 **4.** 1

Step 04 **1.** He drilled holes for screws with an electric drill.
2. The teacher drilled us on pronunciation everyday.

262 service

Step 03 **1.** 1 **2.** 2 **3.** 3 **4.** 1 **5.** 3 **6.** 2

Step 04 **1.** Fast-food restaurants are popular because the service is fast.
2. There was a funeral service at this church this morning.
3. The ferry is not in service during winter season.

263 staff

Step 03 **1.** 1 **2.** 2 **3.** 1 **4.** 2

Step 04 **1.** The man rolled the flag round its staff.
2. The hotel staff are very friendly and courteous.

264 regard

Step 03 **1.** 3 **2.** 4 **3.** 1 **4.** 4 **5.** 2 **6.** 3 **7.** 2 **8.** 1

Step 04 **1.** We must regard the safety regulations.
2. This bill regards the payment for your new mobile phone.
3. He is highly regarded as a statesman.
4. Please give my regards to your parents.

265 run

Step 03 **1.** 2 **2.** 4 **3.** 1 **4.** 3 **5.** 4 **6.** 1 **7.** 2 **8.** 3

Step 04 **1.** She runs around the school track every morning.
2. The ferry runs between Mokpo and Jeju.

3. Tears ran down from Jane's eyes.
4. The restaurant is run by a Japanese-American.

Review

A. 01. regard **02.** run **03.** drill **04.** service **05.** run
06. regard **07.** staff **08.** run **09.** regard **10.** service
11. staff **12.** regard **13.** run **14.** drill **15.** service

B. 01. service **02.** run **03.** regard **04.** service **05.** drill
06. run **07.** staff **08.** regard **09.** regards **10.** run
11. staff **12.** runs **13.** regard **14.** drill **15.** service

수능기출예문 점검

01. 그것들의 사용 범위는 치과의 드릴부터 바위 절단용 톱과 유리 절단기까지 이른다.

02. 이러한 변화 때문에 상점 주인들은 쇼핑과 고객 서비스가 용이하게 매장 구조를 바꾸고 있다.

03. 교통, 의료, 교육 서비스와 같은 농촌의 편의 시설이 농촌 생활에 대한 더 긍정적인 태도를 촉진하도록 향상되어야 한다.

04. 새 병원 혹은 개조된 병원과 요양소들은 점차 환자들과 직원들이 황폐한 실내 환경으로부터 벗어날 수 있는 치유의 정원을 갖추어 나가고 있다

05. 예를 들어, 건설하는 데 4년이 걸린 Erie 운하는 당대에 최고의 효율성을 가지고 있다고 여겨졌다.

06. 이 점에 관해서 문화는 때때로 아주 다양하다.

07. Min-ho: 안됐구나. 건강하고 부모님께 안부 전해주렴.
Susan: 고마워. 그렇게 할게.

08. 꿈은 적절하게 해석되면 미래를 예언할 수 있게 해주는 예언적인 소통으로 간주되었다.

09. 천식이 있는 여자 아이들에 관해서는, 도시 지역에서의 가장 낮은 비율이 시골 지역에서의 가장 높은 비율보다도 더 높았다.

10. 스포츠 캠프를 운영하는 사람들은 아이들을 가장 우선적으로 고려한다.

11. 아래로 흐르는 것이 물의 본성이다.

12. 그가 현관에 도착하기도 전에 어머니와 나는 소리를 지르면서 밖으로 뛰어갔다.

13. 실망스럽게도, 상대팀이 3점을 얻었다.

14. 너무나 많은 생각이 내 머리를 스쳐 지나가고 있었다.

15. 그러나 Arthur는 Jack을 위해 값비싼 생일선물을 사서 돈이 바닥나 있었다.

Group-54

266 refrain

Step 03 **1.** 1 **2.** 2 **3.** 1 **4.** 2

Step 04 **1.** Jane refrained from saying what she thought.
2. The refrain from the old song can never be boring.

267 stalk

Step 03 **1.** 3 **2.** 1 **3.** 3 **4.** 2 **5.** 1 **6.** 2

Step 04 **1.** The stalk of this plant is very tough.
2. The soldiers stalked along the street yesterday.
3. The actress was stalked by a fan for two years.

268 code

Step 03   **1.** 2   **2.** 1   **3.** 3   **4.** 2   **5.** 3   **6.** 1

Step 04   **1.** Refer to Clause 1, Article 3 of the Criminal Code.
    2. The school has a strict dress code.
    3. Could you write down your street name and zip code?

269 resort

Step 03   **1.** 3   **2.** 1   **3.** 3   **4.** 2   **5.** 1   **6.** 2

Step 04   **1.** Sokcho is a place to which many tourists resort in summer.
    2. Nuclear weapons should be used only as a last resort.
    3. This is an optimal place for a winter resort.

270 due

Step 03   **1.** 2   **2.** 3   **3.** 1   **4.** 4   **5.** 1   **6.** 4   **7.** 3   **8.** 2

Step 04   **1.** These are the bills due next week.
    2. The flight from Sydney is due (to arrive) at 4:00.
    3. Severe punishment is due to him this time.
    4. Her failure was not due to lack of ability.

Review

A. **01.** code   **02.** resort   **03.** due   **04.** refrain   **05.** due
    06. code   **07.** stalk   **08.** due   **09.** code   **10.** resort
    11. due   **12.** resort   **13.** stalk   **14.** refrain   **15.** stalk

B. **01.** resort   **02.** due   **03.** resort   **04.** code   **05.** stalked
    06. code   **07.** due   **08.** stalked   **09.** refrain   **10.** due
    11. resort   **12.** due   **13.** refrain   **14.** stalk   **15.** code

수능기출예문 점검

01. 그는 계속되는 안내 방송을 듣고 안심이 되었다. "제 아이들은 저기 왼쪽으로 보이는 언덕 위에 있는 집에 있는데, 아이들이 모스 부호로 '좋은 저녁 되세요, 아빠.'라는 메시지를 보내왔습니다."

02. 최근에 새로운 건축법이 우리 시에서 시행되었다.

03. 세 번째 그룹은 다채로운 야간 생활이 보장된 휴양지에 매료되어 있다.

04. 모호한 '두뇌의 개념'으로 불만족을 느낄 때마다 Poe는 "나는 펜의 도움으로, 필요한 형식, 결과 그리고 정확성을 얻을 목적으로 즉시 펜에 의존한다."라고 말했다.

05. 그는 월요일이 제출 기한인 화학 보고서를 작성하는 것을 미루어 오고 있었다.

06. 커피를 보관하기에 좀 더 나은 곳은 냉동실인데, 그것은 아주 낮은 온도 때문에 훨씬 더 건조한 환경을 가지고 있다.

07. 그러나 불행히도 이러한 안락함은, 이러한 욕구에 알맞은[상응하는] 주의를 기울이지 않은 채 발전이 지속된다면 곧 향유할 수 없게 될 것이다.

08. W: 알았습니다. 언제 이 책을 반납해야 하나요? 반납일 말입니다.
    M: 오늘부터 2주일입니다.

>>> DAY 28

Group-55

271 coach

Step 03   **1.** 1   **2.** 2   **3.** 1   **4.** 2

Step 04   **1.** He coaches a bowling team in his spare time.
    2. We went to France on a coach tour.

272 compact

Step 03   **1.** 2   **2.** 1   **3.** 3   **4.** 2   **5.** 3   **6.** 1

Step 04   **1.** I will buy a compact car to save money on gas.
    2. Julie took out her compact and fixed her makeup.
    3. A compact was reached between Korea and France.

273 room

Step 03   **1.** 2   **2.** 3   **3.** 2   **4.** 1   **5.** 3   **6.** 1

Step 04   **1.** The living room looks neat and cozy.
    2. There is room in the car for another person. (=There is room for one more in the car.)
    3. There is some room for improvement in his work.

274 hail

Step 03   **1.** 3   **2.** 1   **3.** 2   **4.** 3   **5.** 2   **6.** 1

Step 04   **1.** It was hailing as he drove home.
    2. The crowd hailed her as Figure Queen.
    3. Standing on the sidewalk, she hailed a passing taxi.

275 sense

Step 03   **1.** 3   **2.** 1   **3.** 3   **4.** 2   **5.** 4   **6.** 1   **7.** 2   **8.** 4

Step 04   **1.** The horse sensed danger and stopped suddenly.
    2. I have never doubted my own senses.
    3. What is the sense of speaking to me like that?
    4. If you had any sense, you wouldn't behave like that.

Review

A. **01.** compact   **02.** room   **03.** sense   **04.** hail
    05. compact   **06.** room   **07.** sense   **08.** hail
    09. compact   **10.** coach   **11.** sense   **12.** room
    13. hail   **14.** sense   **15.** coach

B. **01.** compact   **02.** coach   **03.** sense   **04.** room
    05. compact   **06.** room   **07.** sense   **08.** hail   **09.** room
    10. sense   **11.** hail   **12.** sense   **13.** coach   **14.** compact
    15. hail

수능기출예문 점검

01. 불행히도, 캠프의 일부 운동 코치들은 아이들이 탁월한 실력을 갖추는 것을 돕기 위해 때로는 지나치게 열성적이게 된다.

02. 서유럽에서는 엄청난 유류세, 미개발 초지보다 건물이 들어찬 지역을 선호하는 투자 정책, 대중교통에 대한 계속적인 투자, 그리고 다른 정책들이 상대적으로 조밀한[빽빽한] 도시를 만들었다.

03. 하지만 고립 상태는 출구가 없는 방 안에 있는 것과 같다.

04. 일직선상으로 만들어져야 하기 때문에 밧줄을 만드는 데는 공간이 필요했다.

05. M: 어서! 타라. 네가 탈 자리가 있다. W: 안 돼, 승강기가 이미 만원이야.

06. 아마도 열정적인 오페라 관객이 되는 것에 있어서 가장 좋은 점은 성장을 위한 많은 여지[가능성]가 있다는 것이다.

07. 상식을 제외하고 사업에서 가장 중요한 자산은 자신이나 어떤 상황에 대해 웃을 수 있는 능력, 즉 유머 감각이다.

08. 너무 거대해서 납득할 수 없는 것들에 직면할 때, 우리는 경험에다 지식을 덧붙여 그것들을 이해한다.

09. 시간 그 자체는 수백만 년 동안 그래 왔던 것처럼 똑같은 방식으로 지나간다는 점에서 변치 않고 유지된다.

10. 우리에게 옳고 그름에 대한 분별력과, 사랑에 대한 이해, 그리고 우리가 누구인지에 대한 인식을 주신 분은 우리의 부모님이시다.

11. 무술에서, 어떤 것을 새롭게 바라보는 이런 의식 상태는 '초보자의 마음'이라고 알려져 있다.

Group-56

276 might

Step 03 1. 2 2. 1 3. 2 4. 1

Step 04 1. She said that she might come tomorrow.
2. He swung the bat with all his might.

277 digest

Step 03 1. 3 2. 1 3. 2 4. 3 5. 1 6. 2

Step 04 1. She has a weak stomach, so she doesn't digest food very well.
2. This book is too difficult for an elementary school student to digest.
3. He gave me a digest of the week's news.

278 apt

Step 03 1. 2 2. 1 3. 3 4. 2 5. 1 6. 3

Step 04 1. Her dress appears to be apt for the party.
2. He is apt at foreign languages.
3. Foods are apt to go bad quickly in summer.

279 withdraw

Step 03 1. 3 2. 1 3. 2 4. 1 5. 2 6. 3

Step 04 1. The boy quickly withdrew his hand from the hot stove.
2. She might withdraw her support for our campaign.
3. How much may I withdraw from the ATM?

280 spot

Step 03 1. 3 2. 1 3. 2 4. 3 5. 4 6. 2 7. 1 8. 4

Step 04 1. She was wearing a dark blue skirt with white spots.
2. These plants grow best in a sunny spot.
3. The girl student spotted her fingers with ink.

4. She finally spotted him in the crowd.

Review

A. 01. apt **02.** digest **03.** spot **04.** might **05.** digest
06. withdraw **07.** apt **08.** spot **09.** withdraw **10.** apt
11. might **12.** spot **13.** withdraw **14.** spot **15.** digest

B. 01. apt **02.** digest **03.** spot **04.** apt **05.** digest
06. might **07.** spot **08.** withdraw **09.** spot
10. withdraw **11.** apt **12.** spot **13.** might **14.** digest
15. withdraw

수능기출예문 점검

01. 만일 당신이 이곳에 걸어 들어온다면, 당신은 아마도 쉽게 어느 개인의 집에 있다고 생각할 것입니다.

02. 이 모든 것들을 고려해 봤을 때, 이삿짐센터에 맡기는 것이 더 좋을 수 있습니다.

03. 과일을 먹기 전에 껍질을 제거해야 하는 또 다른 이유는 사과, 배, 포도와 같은 일부 과일들이 껍질이 질겨서 씹고 소화시키기가 더 어려울 수 있다는 것이다.

04. 식사 때 스트레스의 원인이 되는 것은 어떤 것이든 음식물의 소화에 방해가 될 수 있다.

05. W: 현금을 인출하고 싶습니다. M: 문제없습니다. 얼마를 원하시나요?

06. 점이란 인간의 피부에 있는 검은 반점이다.

07. 호주에서 온 Amy는 처음으로 서울을 방문하고 있다. 그녀는 이번 주에 경복궁과 남대문 시장과 같은 많은 관광 명소로 여행을 했다.

08. 그러나 망원경에 나타난 것은 커다란 검은 점에 가까워 보였다.

09. 그것들은 작은 정육면체로 각각의 면에 1개부터 6개에 해당하는 점을 가지고 있다.

>>> DAY 29

Group-57

281 traffic

Step 03 1. 1 2. 2 3. 1 4. 2

Step 04 1. She was late because of a traffic congestion.
2. That gang traffics in drugs.

282 relate

Step 03 1. 1 2. 3 3. 2 4. 2 5. 1 6. 3

Step 04 1. She related all that had happened to her.
2. I think that this law does not relate to your case.
3. They are related to each other.

283 sterile

Step 03 1. 3 2. 1 3. 2 4. 3 5. 2 6. 1

Step 04 1. The trees grew well even in sterile land.
2. Surgical knives must be always kept sterile.
3. The room always feels cold and sterile.

284 degree

Step 03 1. 3 2. 1 3. 2 4. 3 5. 2 6. 1

Step 04 **1.** His job demands a high degree of skill.

2. Water freezes at 32 degrees Fahrenheit or zero degrees Celsius.

3. She finally took a doctor's degree from Harvard.

285 act

Step 03 **1.** 4 **2.** 1 **3.** 3 **4.** 1 **5.** 2 **6.** 4 **7.** 3 **8.** 2

Step 04 **1.** She acted as if she'd never seen me before.

2. This law is called the Environmental Pollution Prevention Act.

3. The third act of the play has just begun.

4. This medicine acts on the heart.

Review

A. 01. sterile **02.** relate **03.** traffic **04.** act **05.** degree
06. act **07.** relate **08.** degree **09.** act **10.** sterile
11. degree **12.** relate **13.** traffic **14.** act **15.** sterile

B. 01. sterile **02.** degree **03.** act **04.** sterile **05.** related
06. traffics **07.** act **08.** degree **09.** related **10.** traffic
11. act **12.** sterile **13.** relate **14.** act **15.** degree

수능기출예문 점검

01. 결론적으로, 우리는 교통 신호 없이는 운전할 수 없다.

02. 당신은 쇼핑몰이 어디에 있는지를 안다. 그리고 당신은 그곳까지의 거리와 신호등의 수, 교통량에 관하여 당신이 알고 있는 것을 토대로 최고의 경로를 선택한다.

03. 음, 웃음이 단지 감정 표현하고만 연관이 있는 것은 아닙니다.

04. 무엇보다도 먼저 전통적인 교실들은 학생들이 얼굴을 맞대고 이야기할 수 있는 장소이다.

05. 젖은 잉크와 관련된 문제들이 이제는 해결될 수 있었고, 더 나은 어떤 것에 대한 필요성이 마침내 해결되었다.

06. 확산의 범위와 비율은 사회적인 접촉의 정도에 달려 있다.

07. 그는 공학 석사 학위를 가지고 있다. 그는 언젠가는 자기의 사업체를 갖고 싶어 한다.

08. 어느 정도라도 음악에 반응하지 않는 사람은 거의 없다.

09. M: 하지만 오늘 끝마쳐야만 했어요. 시간이 따로 없거든요.
W: 하지만 바깥은 거의 30도가 넘을 거예요.
M: 덥긴 했지만 어쨌든 이젠 다 끝마쳤잖아요.

10. 예를 들어, 30대의 남자는 자신의 나이답게 행동해야 하며 청년이나 노인처럼 행동해서는 안 된다고 느낀다.

11. "오, 난 그를 알아,"라고 당신의 친구가 대답한다. "그는 처음에는 멋진 것처럼 보이지만, 그것은 전부 꾸민 것이야."

12. 당신은 이 단순한 행동의 직접적인 결과로 당신 삶에서 사람들과의 상호작용이 얼마나 많이 향상될 것인지를 즉시 알아챌 수 있을 것이다.

13. 하지만 지금은 디지털 시대의 도구들이 우리에게 손쉽게 정보를 모으고, 공유하고, 실행시키는 새로운 방법을 제공한다.

Group-58

286 condemn

Step 03 **1.** 2 **2.** 3 **3.** 1 **4.** 3 **5.** 1 **6.** 2

Step 04 **1.** He was condemned as a traitor.

2. The man was condemned for stealing a car.

3. He was condemned to a life of suffering.

287 stake

Step 03 **1.** 1 **2.** 2 **3.** 1 **4.** 2

Step 04 **1.** He will stake rose vines in his garden.

2. Mr. Smith staked all his fortune on that business.

288 appropriate

Step 03 **1.** 1 **2.** 2 **3.** 1 **4.** 2

Step 04 **1.** This exercise is not appropriate for beginners.

2. Nick has been accused of appropriating club funds.

289 spare

Step 03 **1.** 4 **2.** 2 **3.** 1 **4.** 3 **5.** 4 **6.** 1 **7.** 3 **8.** 2

Step 04 **1.** How do you spend your spare time?

2. She spared no pains to please her son.

3. He begged that his family (should) be spared.

4. Could you spare one room for us?

290 project

Step 03 **1.** 4 **2.** 1 **3.** 2 **4.** 3 **5.** 1 **6.** 4 **7.** 3 **8.** 2

Step 04 **1.** A visit by President Obama is projected for November.

2. The missile was projected into space.

3. The clouds projected their shadows on the grass in the afternoon.

4. His house has a balcony that projects over the street.

Review

A. 01. sentence **02.** critical **03.** correspond **04.** scale
05. desert **06.** scale **07.** desert **08.** correspond
09. sentence **10.** desert **11.** scale **12.** critical
13. scale **14.** correspond **15.** critical

B. 01. desert **02.** scales **03.** sentence **04.** corresponds
05. desert **06.** critical **07.** scale **08.** sentence
09. corresponds **10.** critical **11.** scales
12. correspond **13.** critical **14.** scales **15.** desert

수능기출예문 점검

01. 세계 어디서든, 어떻게 도시 성장을 이룩할 것이냐의 문제는 공공 영역에서의 높은 위험 부담과 복잡한 정책 결정, 그리고 맹렬하게 가열되는 갈등을 불러일으킨다.

02. 우리들은 끊임없이 옳은 것과 잘못된 것을 구별하고 적절한 행동을 본보기로 제시할 필요가 있다.

03. 당신 자신이나 가족을 위해 충분한 음식을 확보하려는 결심은 당신으로 하여금 땅을 갈고 가축을 돌보는 데 지치는 날들을 보내게 한다. 그러나 자연이 식탁에 차려질 음식과 고기를 충분히 제공한다면, 당신은 많은 노동이 덜어지게 된 것에 대해 자연에게 감사해하고, 스스로 훨씬 더 낫다고 여길 것이다.

04. W: 틀림없이 하실 수 있을 것입니다. 마지막 질문입니다. 여가시간에는 무엇을 하십니까? M: 팬들의 편지에 답장하느라 바쁩니다.

05. 지난 10년간에 걸쳐서, Chattanooga는 믿을 수 없을 도시로 복구되었

는데, 전기 버스와 유기농 시장이 생겼고 일억 이천만 달러의 강변지역 복구사업이 지난해에 끝났다.

06. 저속 필름이 초당 24장의 정상 속도로 투영[영사]되면 땅에서 콩의 싹이 자라는 것을 볼 수 있다.

07. W: 당신 학생들의 연구과제는 어떻게 되어 갑니까? 모든 학생이 다 했나요? M: 음, 한 조는 다 되었고, 다른 네 조는 아직 진행 중입니다.

>>> DAY 30

Group-59

291 liable

| Step 03 | **1.** 2 **2.** 1 **3.** 2 **4.** 1 |

Step 04　**1.** Babies are more liable to catch cold.
　　　　2. He will be liable to pay his wife's debts.

292 speculate

Step 03　**1.** 1 **2.** 2 **3.** 1 **4.** 2

Step 04　**1.** We can only speculate about why she did it.
　　　　2. He had speculated in gold and made a large profit.

293 row

Step 03　**1.** 3 **2.** 1 **3.** 2 **4.** 3 **5.** 2 **6.** 1

Step 04　**1.** There is a row of trees along the road.
　　　　　(=A row of trees lines the road.)
　　　　2. He rowed across the river this morning.
　　　　3. She's always rowing with her neighbors.

294 vision

Step 03　**1.** 4 **2.** 3 **3.** 1 **4.** 2 **5.** 4 **6.** 2 **7.** 1 **8.** 3

Step 04　**1.** He can lose vision from surgery.
　　　　2. The beautiful vision of the sunrise is beyond description.
　　　　3. He was a statesman without vision.
　　　　4. He had a vision of a world without wars.

295 stress

Step 03　**1.** 4 **2.** 1 **3.** 2 **4.** 4 **5.** 3 **6.** 1 **7.** 3 **8.** 2

Step 04　**1.** It is essential for bridge-designers to know about stress.
　　　　2. Stress is an indirect cause of cancer.
　　　　3. Our school stressed the study of foreign languages. (=Our school laid stress on the study of foreign languages.)
　　　　4. The word "hotel" is stressed on the second syllable. (=The stress is on the second syllable in the word "hotel.")

Review

A. 01. stress **02.** vision **03.** speculate **04.** vision
　05. liable **6.** stress **07.** vision **08.** row **09.** stress
　10. speculate **11.** row **12.** liable **13.** vision **14.** row
　15. stress

B. 01. stress **02.** speculate **03.** stress **04.** vision
　05. speculate **06.** stress **07.** row **08.** vision **09.** liable
　10. stress **11.** row **12.** vision **13.** row **14.** vision
　15. liable

수능기출예문 점검

01. 미루기 쉬운 자아 성찰적 반성은 풍경의 흐름에 따라 촉진된다.

02. 양쪽에 세 줄의 벤치와 선생님들 앞쪽 여섯 줄에는 마을의 존경받는 분들과 학부형들이 앉아 있었다.

03. 정기검진을 하는 동안에 의사는 체중, 시력과 청력 문제, 혈압 등을 점검한다.

04. 세계 지도자들은 우리의 환경을 보호할 비전을 가져야 한다.

05. 그때 나는 차갑고 죽음의 기운이 느껴지는 듯한 손을 가진 미이라가 우리 쪽으로 다가오는 환영을 보았다.

06. 저는 여러분께 미래에 대한 저의 비전을 말씀드리고 여러분에게 대단히 새로운 제품에 투자할 기회를 드리고자 이 자리에 있습니다.

07. 오늘날 많은 어려움과 스트레스는 우리가 시간이 충분하지 않다고 생각하는 데서 온다.

08. 혼잡함은 우리에게 스트레스를 준다. 혼잡하다고 느끼면 느낄수록 더 스트레스를 받는다. 일도 우리에게 스트레스를 준다.

Group-60

296 remark

Step 03　**1.** 2 **2.** 1 **3.** 1 **4.** 2

Step 04　**1.** She took his remark as an insult.
　　　　2. There was nothing worthy of remark at the Motor Show.

297 submit

Step 03　**1.** 2 **2.** 1 **3.** 2 **4.** 1

Step 04　**1.** He decided to submit to all criticism.
　　　　2. I submit that there is no absolute proof of his being guilty.

298 dispense

Step 03　**1.** 3 **2.** 2 **3.** 1 **4.** 4 **5.** 2 **6.** 3 **7.** 4 **8.** 1

Step 04　**1.** The officials dispensed food and clothing to the poor.
　　　　2. Our government dispenses the law justly.
　　　　3. The drugs were dispensed in a lawful manner.
　　　　4. The new office machine dispensed with the need for a secretary.

299 nut

Step 03　**1.** 3 **2.** 4 **3.** 1 **4.** 2 **5.** 4 **6.** 3 **7.** 1 **8.** 2

Step 04　**1.** She needs to buy a can of nuts.
　　　　2. He's trying to unscrew the nut with the pliers.
　　　　3. What are you doing? Are you nuts?
　　　　4. That is a hard nut for me to crack.

300 section

Step 03　**1.** 3 **2.** 1 **3.** 2 **4.** 3 **5.** 1 **6.** 2

Step 04　**1.** A fishing rod is made up of three sections.

2. Mike was promoted to a section chief this
    time.

3. He read the financial section of the newspaper.

Review

A. 01. dispense **02.** nut **03.** remark **04.** dispense
  05. nut **06.** section **07.** submit **08.** nut **09.** section
  10. dispense **11.** submit **12.** remark **13.** nut
  14. dispense **15.** section
B. 01. submit **02.** dispense **03.** nut **04.** section
  05. dispense **06.** remarks **07.** nut **08.** dispense
  09. remark **10.** nut **11.** section **12.** nut **13.** submit
  14. dispense **15.** section

수능기출예문 점검

01. Albert Einstein은 "핵에너지를 얻을 가능성은 전혀 없다."라고 말했다.

02. 다시 말하면, 아이들과 어른들 모두 긍정적인 말을 듣기 원한다.

03. 내일 새 신청서를 제출하고 싶습니다.

04. 이제 독자는 본문에서 쉽게 뒤로 가서 예전에 읽은 구절을 찾거나 동일
  한 작품의 멀리 떨어져 있는 부분 사이에서 이것저것 찾아볼 수도 있다.

05. 그 연구에 따르면, 폭력과 재산 범죄는 식물들이 많이 있는 구역과 비교
  해, 식물이 적게 있는 구역에서 거의 두 배나 더 많았다.

06. W: Matthew, 유리 뒤의 저 오래된 항아리들을 봐.
  M: 저기 고대 도기류 섹션을 말하는 거니?

heart	280	mine	175	pop	105	season	46
hide	173	minute	312	post	168	second	144
hold	266	miss	98	present	112	section	427
horn	12	model	150	press	181	sense	392
hot	54	move	319	pretty	34	sentence	356
industry	248	nail	67	project	413	service	375
interest	179	nature	285	punch	31	set	133
iron	237	needle	167	race	194	shade	227
issue	292	note	222	raise	298	share	276
jack	26	notice	214	range	333	shop	45
kid	10	novel	115	rare	269	sight	49
kind	38	nut	426	rear	314	sign	229
land	96	object	306	reason	124	since	279
last	110	observe	341	record	203	sound	257
lay	180	odd	308	refrain	381	space	25
lead	243	operation	277	regard	377	spare	412
lean	278	order	256	relate	403	speculate	417
leave	111	organ	362	remark	423	spell	339
left	69	own	236	resort	384	spot	399
letter	208	pack	223	rest	145	spring	152
liable	416	page	363	right	166	square	63
lie	189	paper	89	ring	21	stable	143
light	14	part	35	roll	228	staff	376
like	48	party	104	room	390	stake	410
long	74	patient	213	row	418	stalk	382
lose	140	pen	73	ruler	136	stamp	76
lot	207	period	185	run	378	stand	42
major	273	pet	55	safe	153	state	305
march	40	physical	293	save	123	step	131
master	147	pick	88	saw	159	sterile	404
match	244	plant	61	scale	357	stick	188
mean	322	please	80	school	364	still	251
might	395	point	252	score	187	story	27
mind	265	pole	215	seal	87	stress	420

Book List 반석 도서목록

TOEFL

iBT 토플 초급자를 위한 TOEFL START Reading
Steven Oh 저 / 4×6배판 / 332쪽 / 20,000원 (mp3 파일 무료 제공)
신경향 TOEFL 출제유형 기초다지기
- 토플 입문자를 위한 자세한 해설과 내용 설명
- 학습자 중심의 문제 유형과 테마별 지문 수록
- 어휘 관련 전 지문 원어민 녹음
- 토플의 중요 어휘와 어구 문제 별도 수록
- MP3 파일 무료 제공 (www.bansok.co.kr)

iBT 토플 초급자를 위한 TOEFL START Writing
Jack Betts, Naomi Kim 공저 / 4×6배판 / 332쪽 / 15,000원
(mp3 파일 무료 제공)
본서는 iBT 토플 Writing 섹션의 출제경향을 철저히 분석하고 고득점을 얻을 수 있는 최적의 전략과 학습 방법을 제시하고 있다. 다양한 출제 예상문제와 대화 상황, 강의 주제를 다루고 있으며, 시험을 단계적으로 공략할 수 있도록 난이도를 조정하였다. 자신의 생각을 명확하게 표현할 수 있도록 문제의 이해와 답변 제시 등의 과정을 실제 시험 상황과 동일하게 훈련할 수 있도록 체계적으로 구성하였고, 권말에는 Actual Test를 수록하여 최종 점검이 가능하도록 하였다.

iBT 토플 초급자를 위한 TOEFL START Listening
Rebecca Hardy, Naomi Kim 저 / 4×6배판 / 368쪽 / 19,000원
(mp3 파일 무료 제공)
iBT 토플 Listening 출제경향을 분석하고 고득점을 얻을 수 있는 최적의 전략과 학습 방법을 제시하고 있다. 실질적인 청취력 향상을 위하여 Dictation 훈련에 중점을 두고 있다. 긴 지문 중 군데군데에 밑줄로 듣기 능력을 테스트해 나아가 보면 점점 자신감이 높아지는 걸 느낄 수 있다.
다양한 출제 예상문제와 대화 상황, 강의 주제를 다루고 있으며, 시험을 단계적으로 공략할 수 있도록 난이도를 조정하였다. 지문들의 상황은 거의 대학 캠퍼스에서 일어날 수 있는 강의, 학생간의 대화, 교수님과의 상담 등으로 엮었다. 권말에는 Actual Test를 수록하여 최종 점검이 가능하도록 하였다.

iBT 토플 초급자를 위한 TOEFL START Speaking
Rebecca Hardy, Naomi Kim 저 / 4×6배판 / 379쪽 / 15,000원
(mp3 파일 무료 제공)
본서는 iBT Speaking 섹션에 대한 길잡이로서의 역할을 하도록 구성되었다. Speaking 섹션의 출제경향을 철저히 분석한 후 고득점을 얻을 수 있는 최적의 전략과 학습 방법을 제시하고 있다. 다양한 출제 예상문제와 대화 상황, 강의 주제를 다루고 있으며, 문제의 이해와 답변 제시 등의 과정을 실제 시험 상황과 동일하게 훈련할 수 있도록 체계적으로 구성되었다. 4주 또는 6주간의 계획에 맞춰 학습하도록 하였고 권말에는 Actual Test를 수록하여 최종 점검이 가능하도록 하였다.

iBT 토플 초급자를 위한 TOEFL START Vocabulary 1, 2
Steven Oh 저 / 4×6배판 / 〈1권〉 419쪽 〈2권〉 427쪽 / 각 권 15,000원
(mp3 파일 무료 제공)
iBT TOEFL의 어휘, 청취, 독해를 한 권으로 마스터하려는 학습자를 위한 교재. 영역별로 실전에 가장 빈번히 등장하는 중요 어휘와 5천여 개의 어구를 모두 영영한 사전 방식으로 해설하였고 어휘학습 후 청취 문제를 접함으로써 청취 실력을 향상시킬 수 있다. 한 테마에 어휘와 그에 해당하는 다양한 독해를 수록하였으며 독해 지문을 청취와 병행하여 청취 실력을 동시에 올리는 학습 효과를 누릴 수 있다. native speaker에 의해 녹음된 mp3 파일을 반석출판사 홈페이지의 자료실에서 무료로 다운받을 수 있으며 흥미로운 테마로 이루어진 지문 내용을 반복 청취하다보면 몰라보게 향상된 자신의 영어실력을 발견하게 될 것이다.

ALL ABOUT JUNIOR iBT TOEFL Listening 시리즈
L1 Pre-intermediate
Naomi Kim, Alan Hahn / 4×6배판 / 208쪽
(Answer Keys 포함) / 12,000원 (mp3용 CD 포함)
L2 Intermediate
Naomi Kim, Alan Hahn / 4×6배판 / 240쪽
(Answer Keys 포함) / 12,000원 (mp3용 CD 포함)
L3 Advanced
Naomi Kim, Alan Hahn / 4×6배판 / 260쪽
(Answer Keys 포함) / 12,000원 (mp3용 CD 포함)
본 교재는 크게 영어 발음과 영어 리듬 원리를 공부하는 Part I과 유형별로 토플 문제를 공략하는 Part II로 구성되어 있다. Part I에서는 혼동하기 쉬운 영어 발음을 구분하고 영어의 리듬에 적응하여 청취력을 향상시키는 훈련을 한다. Part II에서는 리스닝 섹션의 출제경향을 철저히 분석하여 각 문제 유형별로 최적의 전략과 학습방법을 제시하고 있다. 또한 시험에 실제로 자주 출제되는 대화 상황과 강의 주제를 중심으로 지문을 제작하여 실전 시험과의 유사성을 높였으며, 학습 효과를 극대화 하기위해 난이도가 높은 문제들을 뒤쪽에 배치하였다.

ALL ABOUT JUNIOR iBT TOEFL Reading 시리즈
R1 Pre-intermediate
Naomi Kim, Alan Hahn / 4×6배판 / 216쪽 / 12,000원
R2 Intermediate
Naomi Kim, Alan Hahn / 4×6배판 / 232쪽 / 12,000원
R3 Advanced
Naomi Kim, Alan Hahn / 4×6배판 / 268쪽 / 12,000원
All About Junior TOEFL 시리즈는 토플을 전반적으로 다루고 섹션마다 모든 문제형식을 훈련시킨다. 최신 출제경향을 반영한 본 시리즈는 학습자들을 토플 학습에 자신감을 갖게 하고 고득점에 필요한 모든 것을 제공한다. Reading, Listening, Speaking, Writing 섹션은 수준별로 각 초급, 중급, 고급이 있다.

TEPS

텝스급상승 이정로의 논리독해
이정로 저 / 국배변형판 / 243쪽(해설집포함) / 15,000원
텝스의 실제적인 문제들을 바탕으로 엄선된 본 교재의 각종 독해 문제들은 기존의 출제 경향을 정확히 반영하면서도 저자의 강점이자 특징인 〈논리적인 독해〉 능력을 키울 수 있도록 하였다. 논리적인 독해로 그 논리성만 파악한다면 보다 쉽게 주제문을 찾을 수 있게 되고 근거를 통한 답 찾기로 텝스 독해는 보다 쉽게 해결이 될 것이다.

텝스급상승 이정로의 논리청해
이정로 저 / 국배변형판 / 304쪽(해설집포함) / 15,000원
형식적인 문법사항의 나열 대신 텝스의 출제 경향에 따른 맞춤 해설과 설명을 통해 영어의 기본기는 물론 실전감각도 함께 기를 수 있도록 구성한 교재이다. 각 문제유형별로 효과적인 해결 전략을 파악한 후 다양한 실전문제를 풀면서 실제 시험에 대비한 학습을 할 수 있다. 또한 본문에서 배운 내용을 실제 시험과 동일한 상황에서 연습할 수 있는 Actual Test 2회분을 제공한다. mp3 파일 무료제공 | www.bansok.co.kr

텝스급상승 이정로의 논리문법
이정로 저 / 국배변형판 / 340쪽(해설집포함) / 15,000원

텝스 출제 경향에 따른 맞춤 해설과 설명으로 탄탄한 영어의 기본기를 다질
수 있도록 한 교재이다. 텝스 기출문제들과 유사한 유형의 문제를 통해 실전
감각을 익히고, 짜임새 있는 해설로 논리적인 문법 능력을 키울 수 있게 하였
다. 단원별로 제공된 문제들을 실전처럼 풀어볼 수 있도록 한 실전문제, 핵심
내용들과 출제 포인트를 정리했다.

텝스급상승 이정로의 논리어휘
이정로 저 / 국배변형판 / 508쪽 / 15,000원

전타임 최단기 마감강사의 텝스 어휘 결정판!! 어휘 한 권으로 텝스 독해, 청해
까지 한번에!! 본 교재는 모두 두 파트로 이루어져 있으며, 파트 1은 주제별 구
성으로 텝스 어휘에서 가장 빈번히 출제되는 표제어들을 담고 있다. 총 30과
구성으로 30일 동안 텝스 어휘의 기본기를 다지고, 파트 2에서 텝스 어휘 시
험의 맛보기로 미니실전문제를 풀고 마무리한다. 텝스 시험의 어휘영역만 국한
되는 것이 아니라 나머지 영역(청해, 독해 등)을 모두 아우르는 교재임을 확신
한다.

독해·어휘·문법·작문

지성인을 위한 영문독해 컬처북 1~9
이원준 저 / 150×220 / 각 권 7,000원(mp3 무료제공)

지성인을 위한 영문독해 컬처북 시리즈에는 TOEFL, SAT, 텝스, 대학편입시
험, 대학원, 국가고시 등에 고정적으로 인용되는 주옥같은 텍스트들을 인문,
사회, 자연과학 분야별로 엄선, 체계적으로 엮어 놓았다.

중고등학생을 위한 My Self Grammar Basic 1, 2
Thomas Bang 저 / 국배변형판 / (Basic1) 204쪽 (Basic2) 208쪽 /
각 권 10,000원

중학교 교과과정부터 고등학교 전 과정의 모든 영문법
본 책은 기본 중학 영어는 중학교 2학년 영어 교과서를 종합·분석하여 해당
학년 수준의 기본 문형을 모두 다루었으며, 더 나아가 중학 문법의 기본을 전
부 수록하였다.

중학생을 위한 My Self Grammar Start 1, 2
Thomas Bang 저 / 국배변형판 / (Start1) 128쪽 (Start2) 128쪽 /
각 권 8,000원

중학교 수준의 영문법은 물론 독해력 향상에 초점
본 책은 기본 중학 영어의 중학교 2학년 영어 교과서를 종합·분석하여 해당
학년 수준의 기본 문형을 모두 다루었으며, 더 나아가 중학 문법의 기본을 전
부 수록하였다.

반석 영문 독해 핵심전략
이원준 / 4×6배판 / 710쪽 / 17,000원

국내 최다 영문 독해지문(647개) 수록!
– 독해구문 완벽 정리를 위한 핵심구문 110
– 수준별(단문, 중문, 장문) 지문 배치
– 다양한 분야에 걸친 방대한 양의 Reading Text를 제공한다.